DATE DUE

NOV 2 '05			

DEMCO 38-296

CRITICAL SURVEY
OF
SHORT FICTION

CRITICAL SURVEY
OF
SHORT FICTION

REVISED EDITION
Sil-Wol

6

Edited by
FRANK N. MAGILL

SALEM PRESS
Pasadena, California   Englewood Cliffs, New Jersey

Library of Congress Cataloging-in-Publication Data
Critical survey of short fiction/edited by Frank N.
    Magill. — Rev. ed.
        p.   cm.
    Includes bibliographical references and index.
    1. Short story. 2. Short stories—Dictionaries.
3. Short stories—Bio-bibliography. 4. Novelists—
Biography—Dictionaries.
I. Magill, Frank Northen, 1907-
PN3321.C7   1993
809.3'1'03—dc20   92-41950
ISBN 0-89356-843-0 (set)   CIP
ISBN 0-89356-849-x (volume 6)

Second Printing

PRINTED IN THE UNITED STATES OF AMERICA

LIST OF AUTHORS IN VOLUME 6

CRITICAL SURVEY
OF
SHORT FICTION

LESLIE MARMON SILKO

Born: Albuquerque, New Mexico; March 5, 1948

Principal short fiction
Storyteller, 1981.

Other literary forms
Leslie Marmon Silko is known most widely for the novel *Ceremony* (1977). An early collection of poetry, *Laguna Woman* (1974), established her as an important young Native American writer, and most of the lyric and narrative poems in that book are integrated with the autobiographical writings and short stories that make up *Storyteller*. Silko has also adapted, with Frank Chin, one of her short stories into a one-act play of the same title, *Lullaby*, which was first performed in 1976. Silko has also written film scripts; in one, she adapted a Laguna Pueblo myth, "Estoyeh-muut and the Kunideeyah" (arrowboy and the destroyers), for television production in 1978. Earlier, she wrote a film script for Jack Beck and Marlon Brando that depicted, from a Native American viewpoint, the Francisco Vásquez de Coronado expedition of 1540 (the script was sent to Hollywood in 1977 but was not used).

Several of Silko's critical essays and interviews provide useful insights into her short fiction, as does her correspondence with the poet James Wright, which is collected in *The Delicacy and Strength of Lace* (1986). Two particularly useful essays are "An Old-Time Indian Attack Conducted in Two Parts," published in *The Remembered Earth: An Anthology of Contemporary Native American Literature* (1981), and "Language and Literature from a Pueblo Indian Perspective," published in *English Literature: Opening Up the Canon* (1979). Silko's interviews often supply autobiographical and cultural contexts that enhance the understanding of her work; among the most insightful are "Leslie Silko: Storyteller," in *Persona* (1980), "Two Interviews with Leslie Marmon Silko," in *American Studies in Scandinavia* (1981), and the videotape *Running on the Edge of the Rainbow: Laguna Stories and Poems* (1979), which offers Silko reading from her work and is interspersed with her commentary on Laguna culture. A collection of Silko's work and related material is housed at the University of Arizona library in Tucson.

Achievements
Silko, along with Louise Erdrich, N. Scott Momaday, Simon Ortiz, and James Welch, is regarded by critics as among the best of the more than fifty Native American writers with significant publications to have emerged between the mid-1960's and the mid-1980's. While she is well read in the canonical tradition of Anglo-American writing, having delighted particularly, at an early age, in Edgar Allan Poe, John Steinbeck, William Faulkner, Flannery O'Connor, and, later in college, Wil-

liam Shakespeare and John Milton, she brings to her own work the sensibility and many of the structures inherent in the Laguna oral tradition, creating, for example, a subtext of revisioned Laguna mythology to the more conventional aspects of her novel *Ceremony*. Although, in a manner similar to that of other American writers drawing upon an ethnic heritage, Silko chooses to place her work in the context of Laguna culture, her work appeals to diverse readers for its insights not only into the marginal status of many nonwhite Americans but also into the universal celebration of the reciprocity between land and culture.

Formal recognition of Silko's fiction came quite early in her career. Her story "Lullaby" was included in *The Best American Short Stories, 1975*, and "Yellow Woman" was included in *Two Hundred Years of Great American Short Stories* (1975), published to commemorate the American bicentennial. In 1974, she won the *Chicago Review* Poetry Award, and in 1977 she won the Pushcart Prize for Poetry. She has also been awarded major grants from the National Endowment for the Humanities and the National Endowment for the Arts for her work in film and in fiction. In 1981, Silko received a five-year fellowship from the MacArthur Foundation, permitting her the freedom to pursue whatever interests she wished to develop. In addition, Silko has held writing residencies in fiction at several universities and has been invited for lectures and readings at schools from New York to California.

Biography

Leslie Marmon Silko was born in Albuquerque, New Mexico, on March 5, 1948, the descendant of Laguna, Mexican, and Anglo peoples. Silko's mixed ancestry is documented in *Storyteller*, in which she recounts the stories of the white Protestant brothers Walter Gunn Marmon and Robert G. Marmon, her great-grandfather, who, with his older brother, settled in New Mexico at Laguna as a trader, having migrated west from Ohio in 1872. Her great-grandmother Marie, or A'mooh, married Robert Marmon, and her grandmother Lillie was a Model A automobile mechanic. Both were well educated and well informed about both Anglo and Laguna life-styles. Growing up in one of the Marmon family houses at Old Laguna, in western New Mexico, Silko inherited from these women and from her grandfather Hank Marmon's sister-in-law Susie Marmon a treasury of Laguna stories, both mythological and historical. Indeed, "Aunt Susie" is created in *Storyteller* as Silko's source for many of the traditional stories that shaped her childhood.

Silko's early years were spent in activities that neither completely included her in nor fully excluded her from the Laguna community. She participated in clan activities but not to the same extent as the full-bloods; she helped prepare for ceremonial dances, but she did not dance herself. Attending the local day school of the Bureau of Indian Affairs, she was prohibited from using the Keresan language which her great-grandmother had begun teaching her. She had her own horse at eight, and she helped herd cattle on the family ranch; at thirteen, she had her own rifle and joined in the annual deer hunts. From the fifth grade on, Silko commuted to schools in Albuquerque. After high school, she entered the University of New Mexico, also in Albuquerque, and, in 1969, she was graduated summa cum laude from the English department's honors program. After three semesters in the American Indian Law Program at the same university, Silko decided to pursue a career in writing and teaching. For the next two years, she taught English at Navajo Community College in Tsaile, Arizona. She spent the following two years in Ketchikan, Alaska, where she wrote *Ceremony.* She returned to teach in the University of New Mexico's English department for another two years before she moved, in 1980, to Tucson, where she became a professor of English at the University of Arizona for a few years.

Analysis

Leslie Marmon Silko's short fiction is "told" in the context of her personal experience as a Laguna Pueblo and serves as a written extension, continuation, and revitalization of Laguna oral tradition. Blurring the genre of the short story with historical anecdotes, family history, letters, cultural legacies, photographs, and lyric and narrative poems, *Storyteller* includes most of Silko's published short stories and poems. While the stories certainly stand on their own, and, indeed, many of them are included in various anthologies, Silko's matrix of thick description, conveying the mood of events as well as describing them, testifies to the essential role of storytelling in Pueblo identity, giving the people access to the mythic and historic past and relating a continuing wisdom—about the land, its animals, its plants, and the human condition—as an integral part of the natural process. About her collection, Silko has said, "I see *Storyteller* as a statement about storytelling and the relationship of the people, my family and my background to the storytelling—a personal statement done in the style of the storytelling tradition, i.e., using stories themselves to explain the dimensions of the process."

In unifying the past and the present to illuminate the kinship of land and people, Silko's story "Lullaby" evokes both beauty and loss. Set north of the Laguna Reservation, the story traces the life of an old Navajo couple, Chato and Ayah, from whose point of view the story is told by an omniscient narrator. While Ayah sits in the snow, presiding over her husband's death, she recalls various episodes in her own life just as if she were sharing in Chato's last memories. She is wrapped in an old army blanket that was sent to her by her son Jimmie, who was killed while serving in the army. She recalls, however, her own mother's beautifully woven rugs, themselves symbolic of stories, on the hand loom outside her childhood hogan. Again contrasting the past with the present, Ayah gazes at her black rubber overshoes and remembers the high buckskin leggings of her childhood as they hung, drying, from the ceiling beams of the family hogan.

What Ayah remembers seems better than what she has at present—and it was, but she does not escape into nostalgia for the old ways. Ayah remembers events and things as they were, for they have brought her to the present moment of her husband's death. She remembers Jimmie's birth and the day the army officials came to tell Chato of his death. She remembers how doctors from the Bureau of Indian Affairs came to take her children Danny and Ella to Colorado for the treatment of tuberculosis, which had killed her other children. Despite their good intentions, the white doctors frightened Ayah and her children into the hills after she had unknowingly signed over her custody of the children to them. When the doctors returned with reservation policemen, Chato let them take the children, leaving Ayah powerless in her protest that she wanted first to try the medicine men. Chato had taught her to sign her name, but he had not taught her English. She remembers the months of refuge in her hatred of Chato for teaching her to sign her name (and thus to sign away her children) and how she fled to the same hill where she had earlier fled with her children. She remembers, too, Chato's pride during his years as a cattlehand and how, after he broke his leg in a fall from a horse, the white rancher fired him and evicted them from the gray boxcar shack that he had provided for the couple.

As Ayah recalls these losses, she also recalls the peacefulness of her own mother, as if she were rejoining her mother in contrast to the alienation of her own children from her after they had been away from home and learned to speak English, forgetting their native Navajo and regarding their mother as strangely backward in her ways. Now, with Chato reduced to alcoholism, senility, and incontinence, the old couple lives in the hogan of Ayah's childhood, and her routine is interrupted only by her treks to Azzie's bar to retrieve her husband. Ayah now sleeps with Chato, as she had not since the loss of Danny and Ella, because only her body will keep him warm. Fused with the heat of her body is the heat of her memory, as Ayah recalls how the elders warned against learning English: it would endanger them.

Ayah's recollection is presumably in Navajo (though Silko writes in English): the language is the story of her life and her relationship with the land on which she lived it. Place dominates her values; an arroyo and a cowpath evoke precise memories, yet the evocation of her life culminates in her decision to allow Chato to freeze to death rather than see him suffer through the last days of his degradation. She wraps him in Jimmie's blanket and sings a lullaby to him which her grandmother and her mother had sung before her: "The earth is your mother,/ she holds you./ The sky is your father,/ he protects you./ Sleep. . . . / We are together always/ There never was a time/ when this/ was not so." Ayah's closing song in the story joins birth with death, land with life, and past with present. Through her story, Ayah creates an event that supersedes the oppression of the white rancher, the stares at the Mexican bar, the rejection of her acculturated children, and the apparent diminution of traditional ways: the story continues the timeless necessity of the people to join their land with the sacredness of their language.

In a later story set in Alaska, Silko focuses even more emphatically on the power of the story to create and to sustain the life of a people. By shifting from Laguna characters to Navajo characters and, finally, by using an Eskimo context, Silko stresses the universality of storytelling among peoples who codify the world through an oral tradition. Further, her contrast of orality with literacy is also a contrast in consciousness and values: in orality, meaning resides in the context of the linguistic event, be it in Keresan or Yupik, and that context implies an identification yet a diversity of nature and culture; in literacy, meaning resides in the coding of the script or print itself, be it the sign in English or in Chinese, and that coding implies a compartmentalization that permits abstract categories in both nature and culture. In short, orality encourages a holistic perspective while literacy seeks to preserve duality. The title story of the collection seeks to explore the ramifications of just such divergent ways of seeing the world (or hearing it), and, at the same time, the story models the process of the oral tradition: it is not a Yupik story so much as it is one that is written as if it were a Yupik story.

"Storyteller," like "Lullaby," begins *in medias res*, as do many stories in any oral tradition. It, too, is told from the point of view of a woman, but the Eskimo protagonist is a young girl, anonymous though universal as the storyteller. She is in jail for killing a "Gussuck" (a derogatory term for a white person) storekeeper. According to Anglo law and logic, however, the girl is innocent. Through juxtaposed flashbacks, Silko's omniscient narrator reconstructs the events that have led to her imprisonment. Moving away from the familiarity of a Pueblo context, Silko sets the story in Inuit country on the Kuskokwim River near Bethel, where she spent two months while she was in Alaska; she brings, then, her own attentiveness to the land to her fashioning of the story about attentiveness to storytelling. The imprisoned girl grew up with an old couple who lived in a shack outside the village, and she was nurtured by the stories of her grandmother. Although the girl had attended a "Gussuck school," she was sent home for refusing to assimilate, having been whipped for her resistance to speaking English. Sexually abused by the old man, the girl takes the place of her grandmother in the old man's bed after her death. Before the grandmother's death, however, the girl had learned about the death of her parents, who had been poisoned with bad liquor by a trader who was never taken to court for the crime. Her grandmother had not told her the complete story, leaving much of it ambiguous and unfinished. While the girl witnesses the destruction of village life by oil-drillers and listens to her "grandfather" ramble on and on with a story of a polar bear stalking a hunter, she recalls her grandmother's last words: "It will take a long time, but the story must be told. There must not be any lies." The girl believes that the "story" refers to the old man's bear story, but, in fact, it is the story which the girl herself will act out after the grandmother's death.

Bored by sex with the old man, the girl begins sleeping with oil-drillers, discovering that they are as bestial as the old man, who sleeps in a urine-soaked bed with dried fish while he adds to his story throughout the winter. When she is about to have sex with a red-haired oil-driller, he tapes a pornographic picture of a woman mounted by a dog to the wall above the bed, and then in turn mounts the girl. When she tells the old man about it, he expresses no surprise, claiming that the Gussucks have "behaved like desperate people" in their efforts to develop the frozen tundra. Using her sexuality to comprehend the strange ways of the Gussucks, the girl stalks her parents' killer as the old man's bear stalks the hunter. The Gussucks, seemingly incapable of grasping the old man's story, fail in their attention to the frozen landscape; they do not see or hear the place, the people, or the cold, blue bear of the story.

That failure to grasp the analogy of the bear story to the impending freeze of winter is what finally permits the girl to avenge the death of her parents. She lures the "storeman" from his store, which doubles as a bar, to the partially frozen river. Knowing how to breathe through her mitten in order to protect her lungs and wrapped in her grandmother's wolf-hide parka, the girl testifies mutely to the wisdom of her grandmother's stories. She knows where it is safe to tread on the ice and where it is not—she hears the river beneath her and can interpret the creaking of the ice. The storekeeper, taunted by her body, which is symbolic itself of her repository of knowledge for survival, chases her out onto the ice, trying to catch her by taking a single line to where she stands on the ice in the middle of the river. Without mittens and parka and oblivious to the warning sounds from below the ice, the storeman ignores the girl's tracks that mark a path of safety and crashes through the thin ice, drowning in the freezing river. He has had many possessions, but he lacked a story that would have saved him.

When the state police question her, the girl confesses: "He lied to them. He told them it was safe to drink. But I will not lie. . . . I killed him, . . . but I don't lie." When her court-appointed attorney urges her to recant, saying, "It was an accident. He was running after you and he fell through the ice. That's all you have to say in court," the girl, disregarding the testimony of children who witnessed the man's death, insists: "I will not change the story, not even to escape this place and go home. I intended that he die. The story must be told as it is." Later, at home under a woman trooper's guard, the girl watches as the old man dies, still telling his story even as it evokes the death of the hunter; his spirit passes into the girl, who will now continue the story of the bear's conquest of the man.

Now the storyteller herself, the girl has become her story: the story has taken revenge on both the storeman and the old man, her first seducer, through her actions, namely the telling of the stories. The story, then, does not end, but returns to itself, the bear turning to face the hunter on the ice just as the myth of natural revenge turns the story against the storeman and the seductive power of the story turns against the storyteller, the old man. Even, however, with a new storyteller, the girl, the story has no beginning and no end: it continues as long as the people and the land continue. Indeed, the story's survival is the survival of the people; ironically, the girl's story will provide the lawyer with a plea of insanity, ensuring the survival of the story and the storyteller despite the degradation involved in charging her with madness.

While Silko's stories are about the characterization of individuals, of a culture, of the land's significance to a people and their values, and of discrimination against a people, they are most fundamentally about the oral tradition that constitutes the peoples' means of achieving identity. Storytelling for Silko is not merely an entertaining activity reminiscent of past glories but an essential activity that informs and sustains the vitality of present cultures, shaping them toward survival and bestowing meaning for the future. The people, simply put, are their stories: if the stories are lost, the people are lost.

Other major works

NOVEL: *Ceremony*, 1977.
PLAY: *Lullaby*, 1976 (with Frank Chin).
POETRY: *Laguna Woman*, 1974.
NONFICTION: *The Delicacy and Strength of Lace: Letters Between Leslie Marmon Silko and James A. Wright*, 1986 (edited by Anne Wright).

Bibliography

Allen, Paula Gunn. "The Feminine Landscape of Leslie Marmon Silko's *Ceremony*." In *Studies in American Indian Literature: Critical Essays and Course Design*. New York: Modern Language Association of America, 1983. Interprets Silko's novel from a feminist perspective and sees it as divided into two kinds of female and male characters: earth spirits in harmony with the earth and spirit destroyers. Allen says that this is a novel of feminine life forces and the mechanistic death force of witchery. The women are equatable with the land, the life force, a thesis that is central to Native American culture. Analyzes the main characters and the causes for Tayo's illness from a Jungian perspective. Gives a brief and helpful bibliography of Silko's work and of criticism about her fiction. Also discusses her poetry and the storyteller tradition that underpins her fiction.

Brumble, H. David. *American Indian Autobiography*. Berkeley: University of California Press, 1988. Gives brief biographical data. Compares Silko's work to N. Scott Momaday's *The Way to Rainy Mountain* (1969) and *The Names* (1976). Silko uses the traditional as well as the personal in her stories. Her fiction reflects the Native American oral culture and the traditional sense of a lifetime of stories. Says that Silko wants to convey a sense of herself as a storyteller, just as Momaday does in his fiction, and that she adopts his form and methods, which give Silko a sense of tribal identity.

Larson, Charles R. *American Indian Fiction*. Albuquerque: University of New Mexico Press, 1978. Views Silko as an author who is very aware of her cultural and ethnic identity and as a writer of "authentic" Native American novels. Provides an in-depth analysis of *Ceremony*, summarizes the plot, and discusses the experimental structure of the novel. Relates the story in *Ceremony* to the Grandmother Spider motif and myth. Discusses the poems included in *Ceremony*, asserting that they act as a second persona in the novel, as a medicine man. Relates Silko to N. Scott Momaday, Hyemeyohsts Storm, and James Welch.

McAllister, Mick. "Homeward Bound: Wilderness and Frontier in American Indian Literature." In *The Frontier Experience and the American Dream: Essays on American Literature*, edited by David Mogen, Mark Busby, and Paul Bryant. College Station: Texas A&M Press, 1989. Considers the nature of the frontier in Silko's works. Compares Silko's treatment of the frontier to that of Frank Waters' *The Man Who Killed the Deer* (1942). Says that *Ceremony* and N. Scott Momaday's *House Made of Dawn* (1968) are two important American novels. All three of these books treat individuals as being spiritually dissociated from their homes.

Says that *Ceremony* is more positive in affirming the survival of Native American values than Momaday's novel.

Ronnow, Gretchen. "Tayo, Death, and Desire: A Lacanian Reading of *Ceremony.*" In *Narrative Chance: Postmodern Discourse in Native American Indian Literatures*, edited by Gerald Vizenor. Albuquerque: University of New Mexico Press, 1989. Provides a detailed reading of *Ceremony*, applying the perspectives of Lacanian psychology and poststructuralist literary criticism.

Wiget, Andrew. *Native American Literature*. Boston: Twayne, 1985. Offers an overview analysis of *Ceremony* and compares the novel to N. Scott Momaday's *House Made of Dawn* (1968). Says the book explores the death of, or threats to, traditional Native American values and ways. *Ceremony* sets the human struggle against mythic Native American legends. Examines *Storyteller*. Says that Silko successfully uses the possibilities afforded her by Native American myths and the persona of the storyteller figure to do more than provide local color: instead Silko uses these references to develop her characters and plot. Provides a useful but brief bibliography.

Michael Loudon
(Revised by *Melissa E. Barth*)

ALAN SILLITOE

Born: Nottingham, England; March 4, 1928

Principal short fiction

The Loneliness of the Long-Distance Runner, 1959; *The Ragman's Daughter*, 1963; *A Sillitoe Selection*, 1968; *Guzman Go Home and Other Stories*, 1968; *Men, Women, and Children*, 1973; *The Second Chance and Other Stories*, 1981.

Other literary forms

Alan Sillitoe's more than three dozen published books include novels, collections of poetry, books for children, as well as travel literature, essays, and plays. Four of his books, including *The Loneliness of the Long-Distance Runner* and *The Ragman's Daughter* have been made into films. His first novel, *Saturday Night and Sunday Morning* (1958), was also produced in a stage adaptation, and his second, *The General* (1960), carried the film title *Counterpoint*.

Achievements

Sillitoe's early novels and stories fall within the tradition of British working-class fiction established by Charles Dickens and Mrs. Elizabeth Gaskell in the 1840's and carried on by George Gissing, Arthur Morrison, and Walter Greenwood. *Saturday Night and Sunday Morning* won the Author's Club Prize as the best English novel in 1958, and Sillitoe's best-known story, "The Loneliness of the Long-Distance Runner," won the Hawthornden Prize in 1959 and is widely accepted as a modern classic on proletarian life. *The General*, which began as a short story in 1950, won the Nottingham Writers' Club competition in 1960. Believing the concept of class is a degradation, Sillitoe is not so political in his later work, which shows a willingness to experiment in form and style. His stories have been frequently anthologized and have been translated into more than twenty languages.

Biography

Born into a working-class family in the English industrial city of Nottingham, Alan Sillitoe was educated to the age of fourteen at Radford Boulevard School for Boys and worked in local factories until he joined the Royal Air Force in 1946. He served in Malaya for two years, followed by sixteen months spent in an English sanatorium recuperating from tuberculosis. During this period he read voraciously and began to write. From 1952 to 1958, he lived in France and Spain, where he became friends with Robert Graves. On the publication of *Saturday Night and Sunday Morning*, he returned to England, and he settled in Kent. He has traveled frequently and widely and has made extended visits to North Africa, Israel, and the U.S.S.R. He married the poet Ruth Fainlight in 1959 and has one son, David. His avocations are wireless telegraphy and collecting maps.

Analysis

"The Loneliness of the Long-Distance Runner," the title story of Alan Sillitoe's first collection of short fiction, quickly became one of the most widely read stories of modern times. Its basic theme, that one must be true to one's own instincts and beliefs despite intense social pressure to go against them, is echoed in many of his best-known stories, including "On Saturday Afternoon," "The Ragman's Daughter," "The Good Women," and "Pit Strike." Such an attitude strikes a responsive chord in modern readers who feel hemmed in by the dictates of "official" bureaucracies and by government interference in their personal lives. It is important for Sillitoe's characters to establish their independence in a conformist world, yet at the same time they often subscribe to a class-oriented code of values which pits the disadvantaged working class against the rest of society.

Many of Sillitoe's stories are located in urban working-class ghettos and reflect the slum environment he knew himself as a child and young adult. In story after story these ghetto-dwellers are seen as society's underdogs, as victims of a series of injustices, real or imagined, which undermine their sense of personal dignity and self-esteem. Ernest Brown, for example, the protagonist in "Uncle Ernest," is a lonely, aging upholsterer who befriends Alma and Joan, two young schoolgirls he meets at a local café. In a series of encounters, always at the café and in public view, he buys them food and small gifts and takes pleasure in learning something of their lives. He asks nothing of the girls in return, and they come to think of him affectionately as "Uncle Ernest." After a few weeks, however, he is accosted by two detectives who accuse him of leading the girls "the wrong way" and forbid him to see them again. Unable to cope with this "official" harassment, Ernest Brown retreats into alcohol and despair.

In one sense "Uncle Ernest" is an anomaly in Sillitoe's short fiction, for although it illustrates the victimization his characters often face, it chronicles a too-ready acceptance of the larger society's interference and power. For the most part his characters remain defiant in the face of directives from those in positions of authority. "On Saturday Afternoon," the story of an unnamed working-class man's attempt to commit suicide, offers a sardonic example of this defiance. The man first tries to hang himself from a light fixture, but before he can succeed the police arrive and arrest him. In response to his bitter comment, "It's a fine thing if a bloke can't tek his own life," the police tell him "it ain't your life." They take him to a psychiatric hospital and unwittingly put him in a sixth floor room and fail to restrain him. That night he jumps from the window and succeeds in killing himself.

"On Saturday Afternoon" is typical of Sillitoe's stories in its assumed attitude to social authority: although "they" interfere and place controls on an individual's right to act as he pleases, they can usually be outwitted. Here and in other stories Sillitoe's workers place great stress on "cunning," the ability to preserve individual freedom of action in a restrictive or oppressive social environment. Such an attitude is well illustrated in his best-known story, "The Loneliness of the Long-Distance Runner." The protagonist in this story is simply called Smith, the modern equivalent of Everyman. He is a seventeen-year-old boy who has been put in a Borstal, a reform school, for theft from a baker's shop. He is also an accomplished long-distance runner and has been chosen by the Governor, or warden, to represent the Borstal in a competition for the All-England Championship. As the reader meets Smith, he is running alone over the early-morning countryside, and as he runs he considers his situation. It soon becomes apparent that he has rejected the warden's platitudes ("if you play ball with us, we'll play ball with you") and has seen through the hypocrisy of his promises as well. He recognizes the difference between his own brand of honesty, which allows him to be true to his own instincts, and the warden's, which rejects the needs of the individual in favor of social expediency. Smith's only counter to the warden's attempt to use him for his own ends is cunning. As he sees it, the warden is "dead from the toenails up," living as he does in fear of social disapproval and manipulating the inmates of his Borstal to gain social prestige. Smith, on the other hand, resolves to fight against becoming swallowed up in social convention, to be true to his own concept of honesty. Adopting such a stance means recognizing "that it's war between me and them," and leads to his decision to lose the upcoming race.

In the second part of his three-part story the reader shares Smith's reminiscences about his boyhood in a Nottingham slum. He first engages sympathy by telling how he impulsively took part in the theft for which he was sent to Borstal, and then moves quickly to describe the confrontations with police who investigated the robbery. In this section Sillitoe manages a difficult feat by maintaining support for his protagonist even though readers know the boy is guilty of theft. He does this by turning the investigation into a series of skirmishes between Smith and the authorities which allow the reader to be caught up in admiration of the boy's ability to outwit for a time a vindictive, slow-thinking policeman. Not unexpectedly, persistence pays off for the investigators, and in a highly original and amusing climax the stolen money is found and Smith is taken into custody. The facts are less important here, however, than Sillitoe's narrative skill in sustaining the reader's sympathetic involvement with his protagonist. Having manipulated the reader into becoming Smith's ally by allowing conventional notions of right and wrong to be suspended, he also paves the way for the acceptance of Smith's dramatic gesture in the final section of the story.

The third part brings the reader back to time present and the day of the race. The warden, anticipating Smith's win and the reflected glory it will bring to him, has invited numbers of influential friends to witness the competition. Ironically, none of the boys' parents is present, their invitations having been worded so that they would be likely to mistrust or misunderstand them. Details such as this add to the impression of the callousness of the Borstal authorities and help to confirm Smith's conviction that they are using the boys as pawns in a selfish social game. The purity of Smith's intentions, on the other hand, is underscored during the race by his sense of communication with the natural surroundings through which he runs and his Edenic perception of himself as "the first man ever to be dropped into this world." As he runs, his thoughts alternate between lyrical commentary on the physical satisfaction of running well and consideration of his decision to lose the race and the punitive consequences this will bring him. Nevertheless he remains firm in his decision, committed to showing the warden "what honesty means if it's the last thing I do." In the end he does lose the race and makes his point, but in much more dramatic manner than he had foreseen. Arriving at the finish line well in advance of the other runners, he is virtually forced to mark time in front of the grandstand until one of his competitors passes him and crosses the line. Smith has made his point: like so many other of Sillitoe's protagonists, he refuses to be manipulated.

The fierce independence espoused by Sillitoe's working-class characters, and the rejection of what they see as unwarranted interference by society's authority figures in their personal affairs, is also evident in "The Good Women." The heroine of this story is Liza Atkin, a vital and earthy woman whom one critic called "a Nottingham Mother Courage." Liza's life, like that of Bertolt Brecht's protagonist, is plagued by economic hardship and marked by injustice and the stupidity of war. Although the story has no real plot—readers are shown a series of disconnected events which take place over a period of years—they are caught up in the problems of Liza's life and come to applaud her feisty, tough-minded manner of coping with them.

Dogged by poverty, she ekes out a precarious existence supporting her out-of-work husband and two young boys by filling a decrepit baby carriage with old rags and bits of metal from local dumps and selling them to scrap dealers, and by taking in washing from troops stationed nearby. When the means-test man attempts to deny her welfare payments because of her "business," she shouts him down so the whole street can hear. She makes her gesture of protest against war by harboring a deserter; and standing up for workers' rights in the factory where she eventually finds work, she quickly becomes known to management as "the apostle of industrial unrest." Later, when her son dies because Allied planes bombed his unit by mistake, she is devastated. She recovers, however, to become a passionate advocate of violent revolution at a time in life when most women would be settling into comfortable grandmother roles.

"The Good Women," like many of Sillitoe's stories, has strong didactic overtones. Liza Atkin, along with Smith, Ernest Brown, and the unnamed protagonist in "On Saturday Afternoon," finds herself in a world in which the dictates of society at large often contradict her personal convictions. Yet she is able to resist the pressure to conform, partly because of her strong belief in what is right (harboring the deserter to protest against war, for example), partly because she shares the habitual working-class mistrust of "them" (the authority figures who come from outside and above her own social station) and their motives. From her perspective, and from Sillitoe's, society is badly flawed, and it is up to the individual to strive for a new order in which the unjust exercise of power and the suffering it can cause are eliminated. Memorable characters such as Liza Atkin are meant to show the reader how to begin.

In "Pit Strike," which was filmed for British Broadcasting Corporation Television, Sillitoe offers yet another working-class hero, a champion of fairness and integrity.

Joshua, a fifty-year-old Nottingham miner, journeys to the South of England with a number of his friends to support a strike by fellow colliers. In a well-organized program of action, the men race from one coal-powered generating station to another to form picket lines and halt deliveries of coal. In a number of cases they are confronted by police whose job it is to see that deliveries are uninterrupted. Clashes between the workers, who feel they are being treated unjustly, and the police, representing the power of society as a whole, are inevitable in such circumstances. Although Joshua acts to restrain his more belligerent companions in these confrontations, he makes his own mark in a dramatic and courageous manner. When a fully loaded coal truck is seen crawling up an incline away from a picketed power station to make its delivery at another, Joshua daringly and at great personal risk runs after it and forces open the rear gate safety catches, allowing tons of coal to fall on the highway. Although he narrowly escapes death, the gesture seems worth making, and soon after this the strike is settled in the miners' favor.

Like Joshua, the characters in Sillitoe's other stories are usually agitators, passionately and defiantly reaffirming the value of the individual spirit in a world which too often encourages unthinking conformity to social norms. Sillitoe's audience may not always concur with the views his characters express, nor wish to accept the methods they use to further their aims, but their stories nevertheless touch the reader and stay tenaciously with him, disturbing, provoking, and making him more aware of the imperfect world and of himself.

Other major works

NOVELS: *Saturday Night and Sunday Morning*, 1958; *The General*, 1960; *Key to the Door*, 1961; *The Death of William Posters*, 1965; *A Tree on Fire*, 1967; *A Start in Life*, 1970; *Travels in Nihilon*, 1971; *The Flame of Life*, 1974; *The Widower's Son*, 1976; *The Storyteller*, 1979; *Her Victory*, 1982; *The Lost Flying Boat*, 1983; *Down from the Hill*, 1984; *Life Goes On*, 1985; *Out of the Whirlpool*, 1987; *The Open Door*, 1989.

PLAYS: *All Citizens Are Soldiers*, 1967 (with Ruth Fainlight; adaptation of a play by Lope de Vega); *Three Plays*, 1978.

SCREENPLAYS: *Saturday Night and Sunday Morning*, 1960; *The Loneliness of the Long-Distance Runner*, 1961; *Che Guevara*, 1968; *The Ragman's Daughter*, 1974.

POETRY: *Without Beer or Bread*, 1957; *The Rats and Other Poems*, 1960; *A Falling Out of Love and Other Poems*, 1964; *Shaman and Other Poems*, 1968; *Love in the Environs of Voronezh and Other Poems*, 1968; *Poems*, 1971 (with Ted Hughes and Ruth Fainlight); *Barbarians and Other Poems*, 1974; *Storm: New Poems*, 1974; *Snow on the North Side of Lucifer*, 1979; *More Lucifer*, 1980; *Sun Before Departure*, 1984; *Tides and Stone Walls*, 1986.

NONFICTION: *The Road to Volgograd*, 1964; *Raw Material*, 1972; *Mountains and Caverns: Selected Essays*, 1975; *The Saxon Shore Way: From Gravesend to Rye*, 1983 (with Fay Weldon); *Nottinghamshire*, 1986 (with David Sillitoe); *Every Day of the Week*, 1987.

CHILDREN'S LITERATURE: *The City Adventures of Marmalade Jim*, 1967; *Big John and the Stars*, 1977; *The Incredible Fencing Fleas*, 1978; *Marmalade Jim at the Farm*, 1980; *Marmalade Jim and the Fox*, 1984.

Bibliography

Atherton, Stanley S. *Alan Sillitoe: A Critical Assessment*. London: W. H. Allen, 1979. This study primarily emphasizes the revolutionary spirit of Sillitoe's first novels, but it deals with short fiction and lesser works as well.

Hurrell, John Dennis. "Alan Sillitoe and the Serious Novel." *Critique: Studies in Modern Fiction* 4 (Fall/Winter, 1960-1961): 3-16. Hurrell asserts that Sillitoe is better when striving not to be serious. Therefore, he concludes, *Saturday Night and Sunday Morning* is better than *The Loneliness of the Long-Distance Runner* and *The General*.

Nardella, Anna R. "The Existential Dilemmas of Alan Sillitoe's Working-Class Heroes." *Studies in the Novel* 5 (Winter, 1973): 469-482. Nardella focuses on the blue-collar protagonists in Sillitoe's early fiction. Important to the discussion are Frank Dawley of *The Death of William Posters* and Arthur Seaton of *Saturday Night and Sunday Morning*.

Penner, Allen Richard. *Alan Sillitoe*. Boston: Twayne, 1972. A useful midcareer overview of Sillitoe's work. Penner offers a short biography and a helpful bibliography. The discussion covers Sillitoe's poetry and fiction.

Rothschild, Joyce. "The Growth of a Writer: An Interview with Alan Sillitoe." *Southern Humanities Review* 20 (Spring, 1986): 127-140. This interview sheds light on Sillitoe's career and the irrelevance of class on his artistic sensibility. Sillitoe stresses the importance of character in his fiction.

Skovmand, Michael, and Steffen Skovmand, eds. *The Angry Young Men*. Aarhus, Denmark: Akademisk Forlag, 1975. Hans Hauge's essay on Sillitoe considers *Saturday Night and Sunday Morning* as a representative novel from an angry generation of young writers that included John Osborne, John Wain, John Braine, and Kingsley Amis.

Stanley S. Atherton
(Revised by *Jerry Bradley*)

WILLIAM GILMORE SIMMS

Born: Charleston, South Carolina; April 17, 1806
Died: Charleston, South Carolina; June 11, 1870

Principal short fiction

The Book of My Lady, 1833; *Carl Werner: An Imaginative Story*, 1838; *The Wigwam and the Cabin*, 1845; *Southward Ho!*, 1854.

Other literary forms

William Gilmore Simms was one of the most versatile and prolific writers of his day; his eighty-two volumes include novels, short stories, poetry, plays, literary criticism, essays, biographies, and histories. Simms was also highly respected in his time as a magazine and newspaper editor.

Achievements

The enormous literary output of Simms places him among the foremost writers of the early nineteenth century in the United States; indeed, he was the most important writer in the South at the time. His many novels are mostly historical romances in the tradition of Sir Walter Scott and James Fenimore Cooper, but they use Southern settings, dialects, and heroes as their subject. His best-known novel, *The Yemassee* (1835), deals with the issue of Indian dispossession, a theme also common to Cooper. Simms's short stories are often told in the tall-tale mode, which was later popularized by the Southwest humorists. In addition to his fiction, Simms wrote a number of volumes of poetry and several plays, which, like the novels, have patriotic settings and subjects. His nonfiction works include histories, biographies, and several important essays of literary criticism, one of which details the difference between romance and novel. Though often noted for the quantity rather than the quality of his work, Simms occupies an important position in American letters.

Biography

William Gilmore Simms was the son of an Irish immigrant tradesman. His mother died when he was two, and Simms was left in the care of his maternal grandmother when his father moved to Tennessee and later to Mississippi. Simms's formal schooling amounted to less than six years, and he was largely self-educated. At the age of twelve, he was apprenticed to a druggist but later left that trade to study law. In 1827, he was admitted to the bar in Charleston. His marriage to Anna Malcolm Giles in 1826 ended with her death in 1832. Simms's literary talents became manifest very early in his life. At nineteen, he edited the literary journal, *The Album* (1825), and two years later published his first two volumes of verse. In 1828, he cofounded and edited *The Southern Literary Gazette*. He ventured into journalism as the editor of the daily newspaper, the Charleston *City Gazette*, from 1830 until its bankruptcy in 1832. Between 1833 and 1835, he published four novels, *Martin Faber* (1833), *Guy*

Rivers (1834), *The Yemassee*, and *The Partisan* (1835), and established his reputation as a significant voice in American fiction. In 1836, he married Chevilette Roach and moved to her father's seven-thousand-acre plantation, "Woodlands." His newly acquired wealth freed him to pursue his literary career more fully and to venture into new avenues, such as serving, from 1844 to 1846, as a representative to the South Carolina legislature. His marriage to Roach lasted until her death in 1863 and produced fourteen children. During the period from 1836 to 1860, in addition to his many literary productions, Simms was active in the editing of several magazines, including *The Southern and Western Monthly Magazine* (1845), *The Southern Quarterly Review* (1849-1855), and *Russell's Magazine* (1857-1860), which he helped Paul Hamilton Hayne to edit. Simms's fortunes were ruined by the Civil War; in 1865, "Woodlands" was burned by stragglers from William Tecumseh Sherman's army. Reduced to poverty, Simms spent the final years of his life editing newspapers and writing desperately to support himself and his children. He died in Charleston on June 11, 1870.

Analysis

William Gilmore Simms is often viewed as the successor to Sir Walter Scott in the fostering of Romanticism. Simms was fond of asserting that his works should be viewed as romances, filled with sweeps of the imagination, bold characterization, and clearly defined moral stances. His literary works, considered as a whole, can be viewed as an epic of the South; in the epic, there are realistic elements to be sure, but Simms was interested in realism only when it served his more consuming passion for creating works of originality and vitality that portrayed the South as it was and as it aspired to be ideally. Simms's writings, too, can be associated with regionalism and the local-color movement in American letters, for he borrowed richly from the traditions and mores of his region to capture a sense of a spirit and a time.

"How Sharp Snaffles Got His Capital and His Wife," published posthumously in *Harper's New Monthly Magazine* in October, 1870, is a short story which demonstrates at a high level of quality Simms's particular and fanciful interest in local color and Southern tall-tale humor. In early winter, a group of seven hunters, four professionals and three amateurs, gather around the campfire on a Saturday night after a week of hunting in the "Balsam Range" of mountains in North Carolina. Saturday night is dedicated among the professional hunters to what is called "The Lying Camp," in which mountaineers engaged in a camp hunt, which sometimes lasts for weeks at a time, are encouraged to tell "long yarns" about their adventures and the wild experiences of their professional lives. The hunter who actually inclines to exaggeration in such a situation is allowed to deal in "all the extravagances of invention; nay, he is *required* to do so." To be literal or to confine oneself to details of fact is a finable offense. The hunter is, however, required to exhibit a certain degree of art in his invented tales, "and thus he frequently rises into a certain realm of fiction, the ingenuities of which are made to compensate for the exaggerations, as they do in the 'Arabian Nights' and other Oriental romances."

The tale for the evening is told, in dialect fashion, by Sharp Snaffles to the "Jedge," the narrator of the story. Sharp tells the tale of how fourteen years ago he was in love with Merry Ann Hopson and sought to marry her. When Sharp appears at Squire Hopson's house and announces his intentions, the squire tells Sharp that he does not have the types of possessions, or capital, that would attract a woman or that would enable her to live in style. Sharp knows he must get himself some capital, but he cannot figure out how, although he spends half the night thinking and figuring.

The next day, Sharp sees a flock of wild geese landing on a lake. Sharp calculates that there must be forty thousand geese on the lake and considers that he could get fifty cents a head for them if he could get them to the markets in Spartanburg and Greenville. His plan is to spread a huge net across the lake, and, after the geese have landed, at a key moment pull both ends of the net in quickly and catch all the geese. The plan works perfectly, except for the fact that after reeling all the geese in, Sharp wraps the rope around his left arm and his right thigh rather than tying it to the tree in front of him. As if of one mind and body, the geese lift from the lake and carry Sharp for several miles until they hit a tree and land in its branches. Suddenly the branch on which Sharp is sitting gives way and throws him backwards into the tree trunk, which is hollow and filled with honey. In the midst of his prayers for deliverance, a huge bear begins to lower himself down, bottom end first, to get to the honey. Sharp sees his chance and grabs hold of the bear's ankle; the bear is so frightened he claws his way out of the tree, taking Sharp with him. When they get to the top, Sharp pushes the bear out of the tree; the bear falls and breaks his neck.

Safely out of the tree, Sharp realizes the potential capital available to him in the bear, the geese, and the honey. When all of his dealings are done, he has sold 2,700 geese for $1,350, the bear's hide, meat, grease, and marrow for $100, and 2,000 gallons of honey for $1,400. His wealth accumulated, Sharp then sets about the business of establishing himself as a man of capital by buying a 160-acre farm with a good house on it, furniture, and a mule for working his land. The rest of his money he has converted to gold and silver coins and loads up his pockets and his saddlebags.

As he prepares to go to Squire Hopson's, Sharp tells his friend, Columbus Mills, of the squire's talk about capital. Columbus tells Sharp that the squire has no room to talk; the squire owes Columbus a 350-dollar-note on which he has not paid a cent in three years and on which Columbus is holding the mortgage to the squire's farm as security. Sharp asks Columbus if he will sell him the squire's mortgage for the face value of the note, and Columbus agrees. Dressed in his best new outfit, Sharp then goes to Squire Hopson's house; on the way, he meets Merry Ann and tells her that they are going to be married that evening. Merry Ann thinks that he has gone slightly crazy but agrees to follow along after him and see what happens.

The squire receives Sharp coldly, but he is impressed by Sharp's rich clothing and his fancy new appearance. Sharp states that he has come on business and brings up the issue of the debt to Columbus Mills. The squire tells Sharp to tell Columbus he will pay him soon, and Sharp says that the squire misunderstands Sharp's mission.

The note, and consequently the mortgage, now belong to him, and, since he plans to be married this evening, he wants the squire to move out so that Sharp and his new bride can move in in the morning. The only way the squire can acquire any capital now and save his farm is to allow Sharp to marry Merry Ann. At first the squire protests, but when Sharp shows him the gold and silver coins in his saddlebags and his pockets he finally gives in and agrees to the wedding. Sharp fetches Parson Stovall, and the wedding is performed that evening, exactly as Sharp had promised Merry Ann. Thirteen years later, Sharp tells the Judge at the conclusion of his tale that he and Merry Ann have a happy marriage, nine beautiful children, and more capital than Sharp ever imagined.

Simms's passion for the wonderful and the mysterious is exemplified by "Grayling," a story which Edgar Allan Poe admired and which begins with the lamentation that the world has become so matter-of-fact lately that "we can no longer get a ghost story, either for love or money." To break the hold which "that cold-blooded demon called Science" has upon "all that concerns the romantic," the narrator proposes to tell a story that he heard as a boy from his grandmother and that involves ghosts and many things wondrous.

Set in the Carolinas in the period immediately following the Revolutionary War, the tale is of the murder of Major Lionel Spencer by Sandy Macnab. Macnab has learned that Spencer is to sail from Charleston to England to claim a large inheritance. All the Major need do to secure the estate is prove that he is Lionel Spencer. With the intention of impersonating Spencer in England, Macnab follows the Major, murders him, and throws his body in the bay.

James Grayling, a close friend of Major Spencer and an army comrade with whom Spencer camped the night before he was murdered, learns that Spencer has neither reached the tavern in the next town on his journey nor has he been seen on the road. While searching for Spencer, Grayling sees the ghost of Major Spencer, which tells Grayling that Macnab has murdered him and hidden his body in the bay. The murderer, Spencer is sure, is on his way to Charleston to sail for England. Spencer pleads with Grayling to have Macnab brought to justice, and Grayling hurriedly sets out to avenge his friend's murder.

In Charleston, Grayling's search eventually uncovers Macnab, hiding under the alias of Macleod. Macleod protests his innocence, but his guilty behavior leads the sheriff to arrest Macleod as the murderer.

Macleod secures a lawyer who files a writ of *habeas corpus*, and the judge states the case against Macleod would be stronger if the body were discovered and the murder actually proven. Grayling sets out to search the bay area, and he eventually finds Spencer's body. Macnab, alias Macleod, is found guilty and hanged.

Here ends the grandmother's tale; the narrator's father, however, suspicious of such irrationalities, tells his son the ghost was an invention of Grayling's mind and that all the supposed mysterious happenings of the tale can be accounted for by natural laws. Grayling was a bold, imaginative man. When he learned his friend had not made it to the tavern, he thought of Macnab traveling along the same road and became suspicious of foul play. He also was aware that Macnab knew Spencer was on his way to England to prove his identity and claim a large fortune. The spot where the "ghost" appeared was simply one which had already struck Grayling's keen intelligence as a perfect place for an ambush; these thoughts were in his mind as he sat down to rest by the tree. Falling asleep—or so the father contends—Grayling sees a "ghost"; you will note, however, the father states, that, although Spencer told Grayling he had been murdered by Macnab, he did not tell him how or by what weapons. Neither does he reveal what wounds he has suffered. To ride to Charleston and discover the murderer onboard the very ship Major Spencer would have sailed upon for England required no great or superior logical deduction from Grayling. "The whole story," the father tells the son, "is one of strong probabilities which happened to be verified." The son hears his father "with great patience to the end," noting that the father "had taken a great deal of pains to destroy one of my greatest sources of pleasure." The son, however, chooses to believe in ghosts and to reject his father's philosophy, saying that "it was more easy to believe the one than to comprehend the other."

Both "How Sharp Snaffles Got His Capital and His Wife" and "Grayling" demonstrate Simms's penchant for stories which unmask villains, reward the just and virtuous, and show the eventual triumph of good over evil. A similar pattern can be seen in the story "The Snake of the Cabin," which focuses upon the mysterious death of Ellen Ramsay, a young maiden of health and vigor who faded rapidly into sickness and death barely a year after her marriage to Edward Stanton. At her funeral, her spurned lover, Robert Anderson, appears and accuses Stanton of using slander and witchcraft to steal Ellen away from him. Stanton is enraged, and the men have to be separated before a fight ensues. Anderson keeps up a steady vigil at Ellen's grave for several months, until he himself dies, presumably of a broken heart. Upon his death, it is discovered that he has carved matching headstones for his grave and Ellen's. Stanton, however, is adamant that the headstone is not to be erected over his wife's grave.

The tale is narrated by Mr. Atkins to a stranger who has appeared upon the scene and made inquiries about Edward Stanton. Hearing the details of the story, he tells Atkins that he has proof against Stanton which will end his claim to Ellen's estate and thus save her father, John Ramsay, the pain of having to sell several of his slaves to pay Stanton his share. The stranger is taken to Mr. Ramsay's house, where Stanton is engaged in an argument with Ramsay over how he is to receive his share of his wife's estate. The stranger listens for a while, then asks Stanton to which wife he is referring. Stanton, obviously flustered, responds that he is talking about Ellen Ramsay, of course. The stranger responds that he thinks not, since Stanton has recently married three women in different parts of the country and claimed shares of their estates. Stanton shouts that the stranger can prove none of these charges, and the stranger reveals papers he has carried with him that substantiate his claims. Stanton is confused and shaken, and those present conclude that his behavior and the legal papers at hand reveal his guilt. The stranger unmasks himself as Henry Lamar of Georgia, the cousin and once the betrothed of a girl Stanton married and later wronged. Lamar tells Stanton he has no claim against Ellen Ramsay's estate and warns him to be out of town within forty-eight hours or Lamar will have him prosecuted.

Later that evening, Abraham, one of the slaves Stanton wanted Ramsay to sell, comes up to Ellen's brother, Jack Ramsay, and shows him a twenty-dollar bill, asking him if it is genuine. Ramsay tells him it is not and asks him where he got it. Abraham responds that he got it from Mr. Stanton, who gave Abraham twenty dollars to convince the slaves to run away with him and achieve their freedom in the North. Ramsay decides that they will hatch a plot to seize Stanton at once, and he tells Abraham to round up Lamar, Atkins, and several others to disguise themselves as the Negro slaves and meet Stanton later that night at the designated spot. The men wait for Stanton in the woods, and when he appears, they move to capture him. He escapes and runs down the path, only to be tripped up by Abraham. In trying to escape once more, Stanton shoots at Abraham and wounds him in the arm. Abraham falls, however, and lands upon Stanton's knife, driving the blade deep into Stanton's side and killing him. For his virtuous conduct in revealing Stanton's plot to Jack Ramsay and in aiding in Stanton's capture, Abraham is provided for by the Ramsay family and becomes the official recounter of the tale of Stanton's efforts to attain gain by evil and devious means. The moral of the story is presented by Lamar, who states that evil is not an exclusive possession of the wealthy or the powerful; "the same snake, or one very much like it, winds his way into the wigwam and the cabin—and the poor silly country girl is as frequently the victim, as the dashing lady of the city and city fashions."

Simms's writings are often regarded as frivolous and criticized for their heavy Romanticism and simplistic conceptions of morality. Those who find Simms's works to be insubstantial often charge him with being a dated historical writer, one whose works must fade in significance and interest as quickly as the era they depicted passes into history and into memory. While there is some obvious merit to these charges against Simms, it cannot be denied that Simms never aspired to be anything more than a recorder of his era and its particular charms and peculiarities. More than any other writer of the Old South he achieved that aim, and his collected works remain the most sensitive, insightful, and imaginative record of the formative years of Southern culture.

Other major works

NOVELS: *Martin Faber: The Story of a Criminal*, 1833; *Guy Rivers: A Tale of Georgia*, 1834; *The Yemassee: A Romance of Carolina*, 1835; *The Partisan: A Tale of the Revolution*, 1835; *Mellichampe: A Legend of the Santee*, 1836; *Richard Hurdis: Or, The Avenger of Blood, a Tale of Alabama*, 1838; *Pelayo: A Story of the Goth*, 1838; *The Damsel of Darien*, 1839; *Border Beagles: A Tale of Mississippi*, 1840; *The Kinsmen: Or, The Black Riders of the Congaree*, 1841 (revised as *The Scout*, 1854); *Confession: Or, The Blind Heart*, 1841; *Beauchampe: Or, The Kentucky Tragedy, a Tale of*

Passion, 1842; *Helen Halsey: Or, The Swamp State of Conelachita, a Tale of the Borders*, 1845; *Count Julian: Or, The Last Days of the Goth, a Historical Romance*, 1845; *Katharine Walton: Or, The Rebel of Dorchester*, 1851; *The Sword and the Distaff: Or, "Fair, Fat and Forty,"* 1852 (revised as *Woodcraft*, 1854); *Vasconselos: A Romance of the New World*, 1853; *The Forayers: Or, The Raid of the Dog-Days*, 1855; *Eutaw: A Sequel to the Forayers*, 1856; *Charlemont: Or, The Pride of the Village*, 1856; *The Cassique of Kiawah: A Colonial Romance*, 1859.

PLAY: *Michael Bonham: A Tale of Texas*, 1852.

POETRY: *Monody on the Death of Gen. Charles Cotesworth Pinckney*, 1825; *Early Lays*, 1827; *Lyrical and Other Poems*, 1827; *The Vision of Cortes*, 1829; *The Tri-Color*, 1830; *Atalantis: A Story of the Sea*, 1832; *Areytos: Or, Songs of the South*, 1846; *Poems Descriptive, Dramatic, Legendary and Contemplative*, 1853.

NONFICTION: *The History of South Carolina*, 1840; *The Geography of South Carolina*, 1843; *The Life of Francis Marion*, 1844; *Views and Reviews in American Literature, History and Fiction*, 1845; *The Life of Captain John Smith*, 1846; *The Life of the Chevalier Bayard*, 1847; *The Life of Nathanael Greene*, 1849; *The Lily and the Totem: Or, The Huguenots in Florida*, 1850; *South-Carolina in the Revolutionary War*, 1853; *Sack and Destruction of the City of Columbia, S. C.*, 1865; *The Letters of William Gilmore Simms*, 1952-1956 (Mary C. Simms Oliphant, editor, 5 volumes).

MISCELLANEOUS: *The Centennial Edition of the Writings of William Gilmore Simms*, 1969-1975 (John C. Guilds and James B. Meriwether, editors, 16 volumes).

Bibliography

Butterworth, Keen, and James E. Kibler, Jr. *William Gilmore Simms: A Reference Guide.* Boston: G. K. Hall, 1980. This very thorough bibliography lists all writings about Simms in chronological order, from 1825 to 1979. The lengthy introduction gives general background information, and the index provides an efficient means of locating books and articles on specific topics relating to Simms.

Current-Garcia, Eugene. *The American Short Story Before 1850: A Critical History.* Boston: Twayne, 1985. Current-Garcia gives a useful overview of early nineteenth century American short fiction, including a chapter on "Simms and the Southern Frontier Humorists." Several bibliographies are also included.

Guilds, John Caldwell, ed. *"Long Years of Neglect": The Work and Reputation of William Gilmore Simms.* Fayetteville: University of Arkansas Press, 1988. The twelve essays in this collection address Simms as novelist, poet, historical philosopher, humorist, lecturer, and literary critic. Mary Ann Wimsatt's essay on "The Evolution of Simms' Backwoods Humor" deals particularly with Simms's short fiction.

Ridgely, J. V. *William Gilmore Simms.* New York: Twayne, 1962. Ridgely discusses the life and work of Simms in an easily accessible format. He focuses on Simms as a Southern writer, providing much historical and cultural background on the literature of the South in Simms's time.

Trent, William P. *William Gilmore Simms.* New York: Greenwood Press, 1969. This reprinting of Trent's 1892 biography of Simms is still the only available book-length study of Simms's life. Relying mostly on information from letters to and from Simms, Trent discusses the writer's early life as well as his literary career and political involvement. Readers should note, however, that Trent is largely unfavorably biased against Simms.

Wimsatt, Mary Ann. *The Major Fiction of William Gilmore Simms: Cultural Traditions and Literary Forms.* Baton Rouge: Louisana State University Press, 1989. Although Wimsatt focuses primarily on Simms's novels, this study is one of the most useful discussions of Simms's work as it reevaluates many of the misconceptions and dismissive attitudes about his fiction. Wimsatt makes use of biographical as well as historical information, and she discusses Simms's novels within the context of twentieth century critical formulations about the romance genre.

Christina Murphy
(Revised by *Ann A. Merrill*)

ISAAC BASHEVIS SINGER

Born: Leoncin, Poland; July 14, 1904
Died: Surfside, Florida; July 24, 1991

Principal short fiction

Gimpel the Fool and Other Stories, 1957; *The Spinoza of Market Street*, 1961; *Short Friday and Other Stories*, 1964; *The Séance and Other Stories*, 1968; *A Friend of Kafka and Other Stories*, 1970; *A Crown of Feathers and Other Stories*, 1973; *Passions and Other Stories*, 1975; *Old Love*, 1979; *The Collected Stories*, 1982; *The Image and Other Stories*, 1985; *The Death of Methuselah and Other Stories*, 1988.

Other literary forms

Among Isaac Bashevis Singer's prodigious output are several translations; numerous novels, including *Sotan in Goray* (1935; *Satan in Goray*, 1955), *Der Knekht* (1961; *The Slave*, 1962), and *Sonim, de Geshichte fun a Liebe* (1966; *Enemies: A Love Story*, 1972); several volumes of memoirs and autobiographical stories; more than a dozen collections of children's stories; and a variety of adaptations of his stories or novels for other media, including opera, stage, and film.

Achievements

Singer, more than any other writer in the twentieth century, kept alive the rich traditions of a vanishing language and culture. Born into Eastern European Orthodox Judaism, Singer witnessed both the gradual assimilation of his generation into gentile culture and the tragic Nazi Holocaust that decimated Eastern Europe's Jewish populations.

Yiddish, a language written in Hebrew characters and derived from German, with borrowings from Polish, Lithuanian, and other languages, was spoken by millions of Jews. Inextricably connected to it are centuries of traditional beliefs and customs, as well as fascinating folklore, demonology, and mysticism that evolved from religious teaching. Writing exclusively in Yiddish (though translating much of his work into English himself) and mining both the language and the culture, Singer nourished a population stricken with tragedy and dispersed by exile.

His greatest achievement, however, lay in expressing the universality of that very particular milieu. Never did Singer cater to audiences unfamiliar with Yiddish culture, yet, by finding the truly human aspects of the people and conflicts in his stories, he earned impressive popularity among a wide and varied audience. It is no doubt the profound universality of his vision that earned for Singer election to the National Institute of Arts and Letters in 1964, as the only member writing in a language other than English, and the Nobel Prize in Literature in 1978.

Biography

Isaac Bashevis Singer was born in Leoncin, Poland, on July 14, 1904. His grandfathers had been rabbis, and his father was a Hasidic scholar, whom Singer's mother chose over other suitors for his scholarly excellence. The Singers moved to Warsaw in 1908, and the young Bashevis (a name adapted from his mother's name Bathsheba) grew up with his sister and two brothers in a ghetto tenement at 10 Krochmalna Street, which was his father's rabbinical court.

Rabbi Pinchos-Mendel Singer was a warm, mystical, and deeply spiritual man who was loved and revered by the entire community. Bathsheba Singer was a cool, sharp, practical, and rational woman who in many ways held the family together. The young Singer grew up among parental balances and contrasts that inform much of his writing. Singer read widely, including Fyodor Dostoevski's *Prestupleniye i nakazaniye* (1866; *Crime and Punishment*, 1886) in Yiddish at age nine, and studied languages. In addition, his older brother Israel Joshua, eleven years his senior, was an intelligent and rebellious spirit who very early began to influence Singer's intellectual development.

In 1917, Singer accompanied his mother to her native Bilgoray, where they lived for four years. There, he taught Hebrew—considered an affront to tradition, as the language of the Scriptures was not to be used for mundane purposes. In 1921, Singer's father took a rabbinical post in a small town in Galicia; Singer, then seventeen, refused to follow, and instead stayed in Warsaw to study at the Tachkemoni Rabbinical Seminary. He later characterized his stay in Warsaw as the worst year of his life: undernourished and ill fit to follow in his forefathers' footsteps, Singer left the seminary after a year to rejoin his family, only to return to Warsaw in 1923. He would never see his parents and younger brother Moishe again.

His father wrote religious tracts, and Israel Joshua wrote secular pieces: it was inevitable that Singer too would write. During his year at the seminary, he had translated Knut Hamsun's novel *Sult* (1890; *Hunger*, 1899). In 1923 he became a proofreader for six dollars a week at the *Literarische Bletter*, a Yiddish literary magazine. He translated popular novels into Yiddish for newspaper serialization and experimented with writing in both Hebrew and Yiddish. In the late 1920's, the *Literarische Bletter* and *Warshaver Shriften* began accepting his Yiddish stories, such as "Women," "Grandchildren," and "The Village Gravedigger" for publication; meanwhile, his brother Israel Joshua's first novel, *Blood Harvest*, appeared in 1927.

Singer became involved with a young Communist woman, Runia; they lived in common-law marriage, and in 1929 they had a son, Israel. They became estranged, however, and Runia and the child left for Russia, then Turkey and Palestine. Singer would not meet his son again for decades.

During the 1930's, the Singer brothers' lives and careers became interwoven. In 1932, Isaac Bashevis became the editor of *Globus*, another literary magazine, and Israel Joshua published *Yoshe Kalb*, the popularity of which led to serial publication in the *Jewish Daily Forward* in New York. Isaac Bashevis' first novel, *Satan in Goray*, was serialized in *Globus* in 1933; in 1934, the older brother left for New York to escape the rise of European Nazism and to find success in the thriving Yiddish-American community; and in 1935 the younger brother followed.

Singer moved into the Williamsburgh section of Brooklyn. The poverty and hunger that he met there were not new to him, but exile brought on an unprecedented spiritual collapse. He felt isolated from his family in Poland, his wife and child in Palestine, and his beloved culture devastated by war and genocide across Europe. He could not write, virtually forgot Yiddish, despaired for the future of Yiddish literature, and even at times became suicidal.

In 1937, Singer met Alma, a married German Jew with a son and daughter, who captured his mind and heart. She was divorced from her husband in 1939, and the following year they married. He was free-lancing for the *Forward*, which continually encouraged him to resume his writing, in Yiddish. In 1943, he became an American citizen, and in 1944, with World War II raging, Singer was struck by a personal tragedy: his brother Israel Joshua, to whom he was devoted personally and artistically, died suddenly at the age of fifty-one.

The following year, the war ended and Singer began work on a novel, *Di Familie Muskat* (1950; *The Family Moskat*, 1950), which was serialized in the *Forward* over the next three years, broadcast on a Jewish radio station, chosen by publisher Alfred A. Knopf for translation into English, and awarded the Louis Lamed Prize in 1950. He began to write steadily, and in the early 1950's, nearing the age of fifty himself, Singer came to the attention of the American literary community. Editor Cecil Hemley and his wife Elaine Gottlieb helped Singer in several ways: they translated his stories, got them placed in major periodicals such as *Commentary* and *Partisan Review*, and published his novels through their Noonday Press, which in 1960 became part of Farrar, Straus & Giroux.

In the 1960's and 1970's, Singer produced a steady stream of stories and novels. His stories were published in numerous magazines as well as collections; some collections included reissues of much older pieces; translations appeared under his own hand or those of his nephew Joseph, Hemley, Gottlieb, writer Saul Bellow, or others. In the late 1960's, well past his sixtieth birthday, Singer took the suggestion of a friend and began writing stories for children as well. He also taught widely, serving as writer-in-residence at such institutions as Oberlin College and the University of Wisconsin.

Ironically, though well known in Yiddish and literary circles, Singer did not enjoy mass popularity and recognition until the 1983 release of the film *Yentl*, featuring Barbra Streisand, based on Singer's 1952 story "Yentl der Yeshive Bucher" ("Yentl the Yeshiva Boy"). A similar success was enjoyed by the 1989 film *Enemies: A Love Story*, based on Singer's 1972 novel.

For much of his later life, Singer lived with his wife Alma on West Eighty-sixth Street in New York; he later divided his time between New York and Miami Beach, where he ultimately retired. He died of a stroke on July 24, 1991, ten days after his eighty-seventh birthday.

Analysis

Isaac Bashevis Singer relished the short story; he believed that it offered, much more than the novel, the possibility of perfection. His stories, however, seldom reveal signs of a painstaking artisan conscious of form; rather, they flow naturally, even mindlessly, without any sense of manipulation. Indeed, Singer's art grows out of a thriving tradition of oral storytelling that had been fermenting through Eastern Europe for centuries.

Like many authors, Singer writes about the places and lives he knows. He sets most of his stories in pre-World War II Poland, in the small villages (Shtetlach) or the urban ghettoes of his childhood and youth. In his stories, these places are the Polish cities of Warsaw and Kraków, or semifictional towns such as Goray and Frampol; they appear over and over again with recurring motifs and character types, until most of Singer's tales seem to happen in the same prototypical settings.

Given the specificity of Singer's cultural milieu, the individual's relationship to his or her community becomes important, whether that relationship focuses on the collective attitude toward unusual characters and behavior or the individual's dislocation from family, community, and nation. Singer spent most of his life with such dislocation; it is not surprising that many of his characters are in some sort of exile. That exile can involve a new country, a new language, a new culture, or a new identity. Later in his career, Singer set stories among the expatriate Yiddish communities of New York or Israel and dealt explicitly with issues faced by an aging writer in exile.

As de facto chronicler of twentieth century Jewish experience, Singer chooses to leave untouched its central event: the Holocaust and the slaughter of six million European Jews under Adolf Hitler's Third Reich. Believing that a simple storyteller could never tell such an incomprehensible and horrific story, he rather evokes it through the richness with which he portrays the culture that it eradicated and the scattered pathos that it left in its wake. Like the Jewish people as a whole, Singer's characters struggle with identity in a changing world, they confront incomprehensible horrors and either surrender or survive. The individual in his community and his world is ultimately the individual in his universe, often alone with the supernatural powers that govern it.

Singer borrows from and embellishes on the wide array of Jewish mysticism and demonology to personify such powers and their involvement in the human condition. Sometimes the result is explicitly mythological; sometimes it explores the depths of possibility in very real circumstances. Whatever the form, Singer never hesitates to explore life and death, sin and redemption, good and evil, and heaven and hell in broad, literal terms. For him, imagination is paramount, and there are never any limits to what is possible. Much of the charm in his stories comes from the striking juxtaposition of the astoundingly cosmic with the laughably trivial, the apocalyptic with the quotidian, the macabre with the sentimental.

Nowhere is this approach more successful than in Singer's treatment of human sexuality. He never takes for granted the difficulties that sex engenders or the social rules and taboos that it confronts; at the same time, however, he consistently attributes to it its role as a driving force, and a truly beautiful one, in human affairs.

His characters—be they rabbis, devils, simpletons, maidens, or whores—are all of flesh and blood, and they act accordingly. Singer portrays violence, rape, and hatred as unflinchingly as he portrays the deepest romantic love or most spiritual piety, never with judgment or disapproval, always striving to plumb the depths of the human heart.

One of Singer's early stories shows the playfulness with which he treats death, demons, and infidelity. "Two Corpses Go Dancing," first published in *The Jewish Daily Forward* in 1943, is told from the point of view of the so-called "Evil One," a device Singer also employs in such stories as "The Destruction of Kreshev" and "The Unseen." In "Two Corpses Go Dancing," the Evil One amuses himself by reinvigorating the corpse of a forgotten pauper named Itche-Godl, who "had been a corpse even when alive." Itche-Godl returns to his home, only to find his widow remarried to a more substantial man. His two appearances at her door inspire terror, but, believing himself to be alive, Itche-Godl cannot understand her behavior.

He soon encounters Finkle Rappaport, a widow who had gone to Vienna with a serious illness a year before and had long been believed dead but had recently reappeared in Warsaw. Finkle and Itche-Godl soon become betrothed; the couple's mysterious romance and macabre appearance astonish those around them. After the wedding, they retire to their wedding chamber only to find themselves transformed into corpses again and to realize that their return to life was only an illusion.

In "Two Corpses Go Dancing," Singer avoids all pretense of realism and rather depicts a surreal universe where no assumptions are valid. The physical and spiritual worlds are interwoven: corpses are visible to the outside world but lack self-knowledge; they possess desire but are ultimately incapable of consummating it; they have superhuman powers but are essentially powerless.

A story that similarly plays on the border between the real and spiritual realms but does not in the end sacrifice literal plausibility is "Taibele and Her Demon." Taibele is an abandoned wife in the shtetl of Frampol. Forbidden to remarry until her husband is proven dead, she is sentenced to a life of solitude. The village prankster Alchonon one day overhears Taibele's fascination with a story of a woman seduced by a demon, and he devises a scheme to take advantage of her credulity. One night he appears naked in her bedroom claiming to be the demon Hurmizah. He testifies that her husband is dead, charms her with tales of the demon world, and is welcomed into her bed. Though at first fearful and ashamed, Taibele gradually becomes dependent on Hurmizah's biweekly visits.

Winter comes, however, and with it the inescapable truth of Alchonon's humanity. His naked body cannot tolerate the cold during his nocturnal visits; he is taken ill and stops coming to see Taibele. She despairs at Hurmizah's absence and takes it as a pronouncement on her. Then one day, she sees a modest funeral procession on the snowy village street. When she realizes that it is the idler Alchonon, whom she often mocked at the well, she feels a deep sympathy and accompanies him to the grave. She lives the rest of her life alone and carries her secret to the grave.

The power of this story lies in the irony of Taibele's passion for the demon Hurmizah. Here, the surreal world exists only in the minds of the characters: so long as people believe in demons, their existence is real enough. Singer is suggesting the unseen and unknown connections that can be forged between individuals when the imagination is free. At the same time, the love that results is not without its price. For Alchonon, that price is untimely death; for Taibele, it is the burden of sin, mystery, and desertion.

One of Singer's most celebrated stories, "Gimpel the Fool," also locates the individual's happiness in his or her power to believe. This, however, is a lighthearted tale where the willingness to let go of belief, to distrust one's senses and logic, defines the shape of the story. Gimpel the baker is known throughout Frampol for his gullibility. He recounts the nicknames that people have given him and the tricks that they have played on him but does not regret his simpleness, for he feels that he must always be open to all possibilities.

As such, he allows himself to be prodded into marrying an unprincipled woman named Elka. He accepts her bastard son as her little brother and believes her explanation of a premature birth when she bears another son seventeen weeks after their wedding night. She is repeatedly unfaithful to him; he accuses and even catches her but always eventually accepts her explanations and returns to his natural state of contentment. They live in this way for twenty years. Finally, on her deathbed, Elka confesses that she has lived sinfully and deceived him constantly. Soon after her death, Gimpel is tempted by the Evil Angel to have revenge on the scornful townsfolk by baking urine into their bread, but a vision of Elka returns and stops him. With his innocence restored, he leaves Frampol and travels the world, witnessing falsehood and truth in people. At the story's end, he is old, wise, accepting, prepared for death, free of regret, and full of love.

Throughout the story, Gimpel knows that the true factuality of events is less important than their effect on people's minds and hearts. He knows that he is incapable of skepticism but that his innocence and belief are his strength. Though Singer makes it clear that Gimpel is indeed a gullible fool, the simple joy with which he approaches life ultimately reveals itself to be a subversive wisdom. "Whatever doesn't really happen is dreamed at night," he says. "It happens to one if it doesn't happen to another, tomorrow if not today, or a century hence if not next year. What difference can it make?" Gimpel's doctrine is essentially Singer's affirmation of the power and validity of creating and telling stories.

"The Spinoza of Market Street" is another of Singer's most popular and most often reprinted tales. It is the story of Dr. Nahum Fischelson, a librarian, teacher, and revered philosopher who has devoted his life to studying the ideas of the seventeenth century Dutch Jewish philosopher Baruch Spinoza. Spinoza's *Ethics* dictates a rigid rational philosophy that Fischelson strives to embody. He contemplates the heavens and the mysteries of astronomy and contrasts them with the world below, in which the mindless rabble represents the antithesis of reason.

Then, as World War I descends on Warsaw, Fischelson's bitterness and stomach problems worsen, and he takes to a sickbed, where he has a stunning apocalyptic dream that he immediately dismisses as irrational. He seems to be on the verge of death, but a grotesque old spinster neighbor named Black Dobbe comes to take care of him. She nurses him back to health with simple attention and conversation, and soon Fischelson's study of Spinoza begins to seem less relevant. Before long, Black Dobbe announces to the rabbi that she and Fischelson will wed, and the story ends with their wedding night. When Black Dobbe comes to the so-called Spinoza of Market Street, he drops the *Ethics* to which he has devoted his life, and in his new wife's arms miraculously regains his health, his youth, and his passion for living.

In "Zeitl and Rickel," Singer again focuses on an unpredictable relationship and the depth of human love and obsession, this time setting it more firmly in a context of social attitudes. The narrator says that the incredible tale she is about to relate demonstrates that anything is possible. She tells of two women, Zeitl and Rickel, one the daughter of a follower of the false Messiah, and the other an abandoned wife and the daughter of the town's ritual slaughterer. Rickel comes to attend on Zeitl's dying father, and the two women become absorbed in each other. Their relationship becomes steady and secretive, as seen from outside by the women of the community. They are overheard one day in a seeming catechism regarding hell and their shared future and eventually commit suicide in succession by throwing themselves into the well.

On one level, this is a story about an obsessive love shared by two women (with the suggestion, though never explicit, of lesbianism) and the mystical and eventually self-destructive form it assumes. On another level, it is about community perception: as told by one of Rickel's former students, the tale is an accumulation of gossip ennobled into spiritual mystery. Implicit in the story is a view of the place of women as daughters and wives in shtetl society, and the unorthodoxy of two women forging a spiritual connection and devoting their lives to each other. While Singer has never been accused of feminism, he is sometimes keenly aware, and even in awe, of the shape and power of the female psyche.

"Grandfather and Grandson" powerfully reflects the tension between the old insularity of Yiddish culture and the new worldliness that comes with greater exposure and assimilation. Reb Mordecai Meir is a widowed Hasid who devotes his life to his study of Judaism. He abhors everything worldly, including newspapers, theater, atheism, religious reform, and even the integration of the sexes. Having disowned his liberal-minded daughter, he is surprised when his long-forgotten grandson Fulie shows up on his Warsaw doorstep. Fulie, dressed like a Gentile, is a Communist sought by the authorities for political subversion. Though his presence and beliefs threaten Reb Mordecai Meir, blood flows deep and the grandfather welcomes the fugitive into his home. Their shared life is precarious: each wants to convert the other, each has guarded distrust, and ultimately they find a silent and respectful balance.

When Fulie announces that he must leave, possibly never to return, and asks his grandfather to keep an envelope to be passed on to a contact from the movement, Reb Mordecai Meir is put to a test of faith and conscience. He begrudgingly complies, and even when he later sees his grandson's revolver, accepts with silence the world's intrusion into his life. Finally, Fulie's dead body is returned to his bewildered grandfather, who utters prayers over the slain youth as best he can, finding reaffirmation of his faith and identity in their tragic blood connection.

"Grandfather and Grandson" reflects a larger awareness of the political events that shook European Jewry through the twentieth century. Though still set in prewar Poland, it is a story that reaches beyond to a universal experience of the painful changes that mark the passage of generations.

"The Manuscript" also reflects larger historical realities and creates a sense of political urgency. Set at the outbreak of World War II, it is a story, retold much later in a café in Tel Aviv, of a woman's sacrifice for the man she loves and her response to his betrayal.

Shibtah is an actress married to a writer and womanizer named Menasha. When war comes to Warsaw, they flee to Białystok, leaving behind all Menasha's writing except a promising novel called *Rungs*. When a Białystok publisher expresses interest in the piece, they discover that they have someone else's manuscript; *Rungs* was left in Warsaw. Seeing no other option, and against Menasha's wishes, Shibtah undertakes a perilous ten-day journey back to Warsaw to retrieve it. On her return to Białystok, however, she finds Menasha in bed with another woman. She impulsively tosses the manuscript in the stove and leaves Białystok alone the following day.

Shibtah was never obsessively jealous; it is the particular infidelity, set against her journey and the backdrop of war, that constitutes a deception she cannot tolerate. Singer is not telling a simple story of broken vows; rather, he portrays the response of the human heart to a unique and complex set of circumstances, where love, sex, art, politics, and history find dramatic junction in a particular moment of time. As in much of his later work, the world of all possibility becomes a world where the individual can depend on nobody and nothing but his or her own heart and will to act.

Many of Singer's stories are loosely biographical, drawn from specific people and events from his own experience. "Schloimele," written during the period that the adaptation was being done for the film *Yentl*, is about a virtually unknown Yiddish writer in New York and a fast-talking aspiring stage producer whose perennial promise of a lucrative deal for the narrator dissolves into a humorous and pathetic refrain. In a series of vignettes tracing the two men's encounters over the course of several years, the pretentious Schloimele becomes a symbol first for the artifice of "showbiz" and ultimately for the narrator's own idleness, professional failure, mediocre love life, and general discontent. At the story's end, the two men escape the city on a bus to bucolic Monticello, but their departure is more like a funeral than a vacation.

"Schloimele" no doubt draws on both the despair that Singer felt at times in his career and the type of ambitious businessman that he knew well. While free of the tortures of demons or melodrama of lost worlds, straightforward, unsensational narratives such as "Schloimele" evoke, in their understated realism, an amazingly strong and personal sense of tragedy and longing.

There are certainly links from Taibele to Rickel to Shibtah, from Dr. Fischelson to

Reb Mordecai Meir, or from Alchonon to Gimpel to Schloimele, and while no story can be said to sum up Singer's vision, some come strikingly close to a clear articulation of deep existential belief. An example is "The Smuggler," published three years before the author's death. It is a simple tale, most certainly based in truth (if only loosely), about a stranger's visit to the narrator (an author himself, living in a small New York apartment), seeking autographs for a cartload of his books. The man is a gentle old bum who met the narrator years before at a speech in Philadelphia; he does not want to intrude, only to get his books signed and leave.

During his short visit, however, he offers samples of the wisdom by which he has lived. Born to a family of Polish Jews, he learned to smuggle for a living, until he eventually realized that he survived by smuggling himself. He has come to recognize the intrinsic corruptibility of human beings, that power breeds wickedness, and that victims who overcome tyrants become tyrants themselves. He knows that evil and good are not mutually exclusive opposites, that there is nothing strange or inhuman about a Nazi leaving a concentration camp, where humans are systematically killed, and returning home to write heartfelt poetry. Finding security in this knowledge, the smuggler is at peace.

While the message is harsh, it is for Singer, as for the smuggler of the story, only a starting point. Beyond it is a world of possibilities—for goodness and evil, love and violence, sex and piety—in which the human heart and mind rule. In his clever and paradoxical way, Singer affirms, "We must believe in free will. We have no choice."

Other major works

NOVELS: *Sotan in Goray*, 1935 (*Satan in Goray*, 1955); *Di Familie Muskat*, 1950 (*The Family Moskat*, 1950); *Der Hoyf*, 1953-1955 (*The Manor*, 1967, and *The Estate*, 1969); *Der Kunstnmakher fun Lublin*, 1959 (*The Magician of Lublin*, 1960); *Der Knekht*, 1961 (*The Slave*, 1962); *Sonim, de Geshichte fun a Liebe*, 1966 (*Enemies: A Love Story*, 1972); *Neshome Ekspeditsyes*, 1974 (*Shosha*, 1978); *Der Bal-Tshuve*, 1974 (*The Penitent*, 1983); *Der Kenig vun di Felder*, 1988 (*The King of the Fields*, 1988); *Scum*, 1991.

PLAYS: *The Mirror*, 1973; *Yentl, the Yeshiva Boy*, 1974 (with Leah Napolin); *Shlemiel the First*, 1974; *Teibele and Her Demon*, 1978 (with Eve Friedman); *Schlemiel the First*, 1984 (with Sarah Blacker Cohen).

NONFICTION: *Mayn Tatn's Bes-din Shtub*, 1956 (*In My Father's Court*, 1966); *A Little Boy in Search of God: Mysticism in a Personal Light*, 1976; *A Young Man in Search of Love*, 1978; *Isaac Bashevis Singer on Literature and Life*, 1979 (with Paul Rosenblatt and Gene Koppel); *Lost in America*, 1980; *Reaches of Heaven: A Story of the Baal Shem Tov*, 1980; *Love and Exile*, 1984; *Conversations with Isaac Bashevis Singer*, 1985 (with Richard Burgin).

CHILDREN'S LITERATURE: *Zlateh the Goat and Other Stories*, 1966; *The Fearsome Inn*, 1967; *Mazel and Shlimazel: Or, The Milk of a Lioness*, 1967; *When Shlemiel Went to Warsaw and Other Stories*, 1968; *A Day of Pleasure: Stories of a Boy Growing Up in Warsaw*, 1969; *Elijah the Slave*, 1970; *Joseph and Koza: Or, The Sacrifice to the Vistula*, 1970; *Alone in the Wild Forest*, 1971; *The Topsy-Turvy Emperor of China*, 1971; *The Wicked City*, 1972; *The Fools of Chelm and Their History*, 1973; *Why Noah Chose the Dove*, 1974; *A Tale of Three Wishes*, 1975; *Naftali the Storyteller and His Horse, Sus, and Other Stories*, 1976; *The Power of Light: Eight Stories*, 1980; *The Golem*, 1982; *Stories for Children*, 1984.

TRANSLATIONS: *Romain Rolland*, 1927 (by Stefan Zweig); *Die Vogler*, 1928 (by Knut Hamsun); *Victoria*, 1929 (by Knut Hamsun); *All Quiet on the Western Front*, 1930 (by Erich Remarque); *Pan*, 1931 (by Knut Hamsun); *The Way Back*, 1931 (by Erich Remarque); *The Magic Mountain*, 1932 (by Thomas Mann); *From Moscow to Jerusalem*, 1938 (with Leon Glaser).

Bibliography

Allentuck, Marcia, ed. *The Achievement of Isaac Bashevis Singer.* Carbondale: Southern Illinois University Press, 1969. A collection of eleven essays devoted to various aspects of Singer's work. While most articles focus on themes in individual novels, the collection does include pieces on Singer's memoirs and children's stories, and examinations of "The Spinoza of Market Street" and "Gimpel the Fool." Though inevitably uneven, the volume is generally straightforward and easy to read.

Buchen, Irving H. *Isaac Bashevis Singer and the Eternal Past.* New York: New York University Press, 1968. Buchen provides an interesting though not painstakingly detailed look at Singer's early career. While his efforts to relate the author to other contemporary writers and the overall tradition of English and American literature are excessive, he explores and understands the balances of Singer's writing. Includes a chapter on selected early stories and a good bibliography.

Kresh, Paul. *Isaac Bashevis Singer: The Magician of West Eighty-sixth Street.* New York: Dial Press, 1979. A lively account of Singer's first seventy-five years, told in an often seemingly day-by-day account that creates a delightful sense of intimacy for the reader. Kresh incorporates refreshing quotes and anecdotes and includes thirty-two photographs. His careful attention to facts clarifies the often ambiguous details of Singer's works in terms of creation, translation, publication, and reissue. More than four hundred pages, with a good index and a bibliography.

Milbauer, Asher Z. *Transcending Exile.* Miami: Florida International University Press, 1985. A thoughtful contemplation of exile in the works of three writers: Joseph Conrad, Vladimir Nabokov, and Singer. The fifty-page chapter on Singer focuses on three novels—*Shosha, The Slave,* and *Enemies: A Love Story*—but is mindful of thematic parallels to the short stories.

Sinclair, Clive. *The Brothers Singer.* London: Allison & Busby, 1983. A fascinating examination of Singer and his work in the context of one of the most important personal and literary relationships of the author's life. Sinclair effectively interweaves biography and literary analysis, conveying a deep understanding of the lives and works of Isaac and Joshua Singer.

Barry Mann

ANDREI SINYAVSKY

Born: Moscow, Soviet Union; October 8, 1925

Principal short fiction

Fantasticheskie povesti, 1961 (*Fantastic Stories*, 1963); *Kroshka Tsores*, 1980 (novella).

Other literary forms

Prior to his arrest in 1965, Andrei Sinyavsky was a senior research associate at the Gorky Institute of World Literature in Moscow and had become a well-known literary critic, focusing primarily on modern Russian literature. After emigrating to Paris in 1973, he published more criticism as well as book-length literary essays. The works that led to his arrest, however, were, except for the literary essay *Chto takoe sotsialisticheskii realizm* (1959; *On Socialist Realism*, 1960), fiction: two novels and some half-dozen stories. All appeared in the West under the pseudonym Abram Tertz. He also wrote a book of aphorisms, *Mysli vrasplokh* (1966; *Unguarded Thoughts*, 1972).

Achievements

Sinyavsky's literary efforts served as a daring challenge to the tenets of Socialist Realism, the doctrine that was supposed to guide Soviet authors in their choice of subject matter as well as in their treatment of it. His essay *On Socialist Realism*, written in 1956, at the height of the post-Stalinist thaw, contained an attack on the very conjunction of the words "socialist" and "realism," as well as a historical analysis of the manner in which the doctrine had harmed Soviet literature. His own underground fiction was both antisocialist, in his effort to include a religious dimension antithetical to Marxism, and antirealistic, with a strong inclination toward the fantastic and the grotesque. The consequences of writing in isolation as well as of determinedly breaking with the dominant tradition sometimes show—he occasionally seems to be trying too hard for effect or to make a point—but Sinyavsky nevertheless stands as a writer who helped undermine the influence of Socialist Realism.

Along with his fellow writer Yuli Daniel he also helped popularize the very notions of *samizdat* (self-publishing) and *tamizdat* (publishing "there," or abroad). Despite the government's persecution of these two authors, many others throughout the 1960's and 1970's came to write outside the permissible norms—sometimes circulating their work privately, sometimes attempting to publish outside the Soviet Union, and sometimes simply writing "for the drawer." His example did much to help a clandestine Soviet literature flourish during a trying period.

Biography

By the time he was in his early forties, Andrei Donatovich Sinyavsky had achieved a large measure of success within Soviet society. Born and reared in Moscow, he attended Moscow University, from which he received the Soviet equivalent of a doctorate in 1952. His thesis was on Maxim Gorky, often considered the "father" of Socialist Realism. He then received a position at the Gorky Institute of World Literature, a branch of the Soviet Academy of Sciences; during the next dozen years, he published several studies on Gorky and also wrote about twentieth century poetry. At the end of the 1950's, he began to publish reviews in the prestigious literary journal *Novy mir*, aligning himself with those struggling for greater artistic freedom through his attacks on some of the more conservative writers. Still, his name was not widely known until he published the introductory essay to a major 1965 collection of Boris Leonidovich Pasternak's poetry (translated in *For Freedom of Imagination*, 1971).

Later that same year, much to the surprise of nearly everyone, he and a close friend, Yuli Daniel, were arrested; employing the pseudonyms Abram Tertz (the rogue hero of a thieves' song once popular in Odessa) and Nikolai Arzhak respectively, each had smuggled out stories to the West that were seen by the authorities as examples of "anti-Soviet propaganda." Their trial, in February of 1966, was significant in that it was the first time that Soviet writers were actually convicted of a crime on the basis of their literary works. It also marked the end of the fitful liberalizing tendencies that had characterized the years since the death of Joseph Stalin in 1953 and the imposition of a harsher regime that was to force many writers into exile.

As it turned out, Sinyavsky's life prior to his arrest was more complex than it might have appeared on the surface. Although he grew up as a believer in the ideals of the revolution that brought the Communists to power in the Soviet Union, his faith was shaken by the arrest of his father in 1951 for political activities that predated the Revolution of 1917, and by efforts of the secret police, beginning in 1948, to involve him in a plot that would somehow compromise a friend, Hélène Peltier-Zamoyska, daughter of the French naval attaché in Moscow. He managed to resist, but the machinations continued for several years; later, she served as the courier for bringing the manuscripts of "Abram Tertz" out of the Soviet Union. In 1955, Sinyavsky wrote the first of his underground works, the story "V tsirke" ("At the Circus"). Then in 1956, the year that is generally regarded as marking the height of the post-Stalinist "thaw," he composed both his essay *On Socialist Realism* and his first novel, *Sud idyot* (1960; *The Trial Begins*, 1960) which can be seen as a literary illustration of the writing that Sinyavsky advocates in the essay. Over the next several years, he continued to compose the works that made Abram Tertz a well-known figure in the West and a wanted man in the Soviet Union.

Sinyavsky ended up serving five and one-half years of a seven-year term (and Daniel four of the five years to which he had been sentenced). While in prison, Sinyavsky continued to write, sending out his works in letters to his wife: *Golos iz khora* (1973; *A Voice from the Chorus*, 1976), *Progulki s Pushkinym* (1975; strolls with Pushkin), and *V teni Gogolya* (1975; in Gogol's shadow). He was allowed to emigrate in 1973 and became a professor of Russian literature at the Sorbonne. Re-maining active in the literary world, Sinyavsky began his own journal (*Sintaksis*) and wrote the autobiographical novel *Spokoynoy nochi* (1984; *Goodnight!*, 1989). His works remained sufficiently controversial in the Soviet Union that he could be pub-lished there only well into the period of *glasnost*; in 1989, he was allowed to visit the country to pay respects upon the death of Yuli Daniel.

Analysis

Andrei Sinyavsky's short fiction resembles his longer work in both its themes and its manner. While for the most part less overt in their political message than the novels, the stories contain heroes who are equally alienated—from society, from themselves, or both—and who seem trapped in an existence from which they would like to escape. Elements of fantasy abound; in some cases the stories verge on sci-ence fiction, while in others the emphasis is more on extreme psychological states. The plots, to the extent that they can be discerned at all, are usually fairly straightfor-ward. Interpretation, however, can be difficult; sometimes a given scene may be viewed as fantastic, as reflecting a character's mental aberration, or as purposefully ambiguous. The first-person narrators are often not helpful in this regard, and situa-tions may appear to be allegorical or metaphorical representations of themes that are not mentioned directly within the works. In short, Sinyavsky is demanding of his readers.

"At the Circus" stands out from the other stories: it predates them by several years and is also the most conventional in form. The narrator has a distinctive voice, but for once he is not a chief figure within the story itself. Still, the tale offers an early glimpse into some of Sinyavsky's concerns. The hero, Kostia, is a ne'er-do-well who dreams of achieving the skill of those he admires at the circus. During a botched burglary, he kills the very magician he has admired, is sentenced to twenty years of hard labor, and then is himself killed during an attempt to escape. Kostia is the first of Sinyavsky's many outsiders, those who feel in some way oppressed and want to escape into new lives; indeed, dreams of, or efforts at, getting away from ordinary life lie behind all the major events. Despite the third-person narration, Sinyavsky often limits the perspective to that of Kostia; the narrow focus and the frequent absence of conventional transitions pull the reader deep into the protago-nist's psyche, so that his distorted outlook becomes the norm for the world of the story. The narrative, as well as the settings and the subject matter, thus emphasizes the sense of oppression and enclosure; nearly all Sinyavsky's stories seem, in this way, to be claustrophobic.

Sinyavsky's next stories, "Kvartiranty" ("Tenants") and "Ty i ya" ("You and I"), both composed in 1959, are perhaps his most obscure. The setting of "Tenants," a Russian communal apartment, is sufficiently realistic, but the narrator turns out to be a house sprite. His addressee—not interlocutor, since he does not say a word—is Sergei Sergeevich, a drunkard and writer who now lives within the apartment. The story is open to a variety of interpretations: it can be seen as a genuine fantasy or, less likely, as the drunken hallucinations of Sergei Sergeevich. The tales related by the house sprite are themselves fantastic, filled with references to literature or writers, and at first seem to be of little purpose. Eventually, though, certain themes emerge. The house sprite points to the prevalence of evil; not only do the names often contain hidden references to the devil or to various spirits, but also relatively mundane occurrences, such as a spat in the communal kitchen, lead to dire consequences. Many of the figures in the story have been driven out of one existence into another; even water nymphs and wood sprites have been forced from the country to the city. Ultimately, though, "Tenants" concerns the writer: the threats to his well-being, his position as an outsider, his (perhaps unfulfilled) obligation to deal with the evil around him.

"You and I" is arguably even more resistant to any single interpretation. Much of the work employs a "second-person" narrative, with the "You" of the title addressed directly. This individual is named Nikolai Vasilyevich (the first name and patronymic of Nikolai Gogol, who, along with Fyodor Dostoevski, clearly influenced this and other works by Sinyavsky) and apparently suffers from a persecution mania. After an opening scene at a party, he hides out in his apartment, refusing to have contact with others until he eventually slashes his throat. The true mystery of the story, though, is the identity of "I," who plays a direct role in the fate of "You." Some critics have seen "You and I" as describing a single individual who suffers from schizophrenia as well as paranoia; others believe that the relationship is more that between the author and his character or between a godlike figure and the individual (there is sufficient evidence to support all these views).

Despite the purposeful complexity of the narrative—which includes disjointed descriptions of wildly different events taking place simultaneously throughout the city—it is possible to discern several of Sinyavsky's major concerns in "You and I." Part of Nikolai Vasilyevich's paranoia is based on a fear of women; the erotic scenes that are sprinkled throughout the stories, beginning with "At the Circus," not only serve to violate one of the restrictions of Socialist Realism but also portray sex in a less than flattering manner. The perception of the outside world recalls that of the house sprite in "Tenants": evil forces threaten "You" and promise to drive him out of his refuge. Most crucially, though, Sinyavsky again raises the question of the responsibility of the creator, the "I," and of his relationship to the world around him.

"Gololeditsa" ("The Icicle"), written in 1961, is both the longest of Sinyavsky's early stories and one of the richest. The narrator abruptly achieves the power to see into the future and the past. He finds out that the woman he loves, Natasha, will be killed by a falling icicle in a specific place in Moscow at a certain time. He attempts to flee the city with her, but on the way he is arrested by the authorities and questioned about his magical powers. Natasha returns to Moscow and is killed by the icicle, at which point the narrator loses his special gift.

The topic allows Sinyavsky to display fully his talents as a writer and to probe his most deeply felt ideas. The narrative is fast-paced and almost jaunty; while some old-fashioned suspense makes the work gripping, Sinyavsky imparts a special air by interspersing the sad and at times tragic events with comic interludes. Particularly effective is his portrayal of Colonel Tarasov, the interrogator, whose naïve efforts to obtain politically useful predictions allow Sinyavsky to satirize the mentality of those in power under Stalin (the story is subtly but clearly dated at the very end of Stalin's reign). Most striking, though, are the meditations that arise from considering the effects of being able to see endlessly into the past and the future; besides the more obvious question of how a knowledge of the future would affect an individual's actions in the present, Sinyavksy considers the meaning of death, experiments with converting time into space (so that the present "self" represents a simultaneous amalgam of past and future selves), and suggests that an individual with special knowledge or powers has some degree of moral responsibility for others.

"Pkhentz" appeared in the West later than the other "fantastic stories," in 1966, and has been widely seen as an allegory for the situation of the writer in Soviet Russia. Only little by little does it become clear that the narrator of the story is an alien creature, stranded on earth, who has wrapped his body and put on a disguise to hide his true identity. In some ways, his dilemma resembles that of Sinyavsky before his arrest: the creature's pseudonym resembles Sinyavsky's real name, and he too has a fear of discovery. More broadly, though, "Pkhentz" is concerned with the threat of persecution and mockery directed by society toward the one who is different and also with the alienation of the outsider—which here is presented through the revulsion that the alien feels toward such basic human activities as sex and eating. It is one of Sinyavsky's simplest, most direct, and yet most powerful stories.

Kroshka Tsores (little Tsores) was written after Sinyavsky's emigration and is generally referred to as a novella, though it is no longer than "The Icicle." The story is dedicated to E. T. A. Hoffmann and inspired by his *Klein Zaches, genannt Zinnober* (1819; *Little Zaches, Surnamed Zinnober*, 1971). Sinyavsky replaces Hoffmann's good fairy with a pediatrician, Dora Alexandrovna, who cures the stuttering that afflicts the narrator Tsores (Yiddish for grief; he is also sometimes called Sinyavsky). Tsores achieves a gift with words, but he also unintentionally causes the deaths of each of his five half-brothers. Here, it becomes possible to discern a clear direction in Sinyavsky's short fiction; even more clearly than in "Pkhentz," he is writing simultaneously about himself (this story was originally intended to serve as an episode in his autobiographical *Goodnight!*) and more broadly about the condition of the writer, particularly in a totalitarian society. Thus, the story is both about isolation on the one hand and about moral responsibility and guilt on the other; like so many of the earlier other heroes, Tsores/Sinyavsky finds that the role of creator becomes an obligation and incurs inescapable burdens—such is the dilemma with which Tertz/Sinyavsky has had to cope as well.

Other major works

NOVELS: *Sad idzie*, 1959 (in Polish; *Sud idyot*, 1960, as Abram Tertz; *The Trial Begins*, 1960); *Lubimow*, 1963 (in Polish; *Lyubimov*, 1964, as Abram Tertz; *The Makepeace Experiment*, 1965); *Spokoynoy nochi* (1984; *Goodnight!*, 1989).

NONFICTION: *Chto takoe sotsialisticheskii realizm*, 1959 (as Abram Tertz; *On Socialist Realism*, 1960); *Pikasso*, 1960 (with I. N. Golomshtok); *Poeziya pervykh let revolyutsii, 1971-1920*, 1964 (with A. Menshutin); *Mysli vrasplokh*, 1966 (as Abram Tertz; *Unguarded Thoughts*, 1972); *For Freedom of Imagination*, 1971 (essays); *Golos iz khora*, 1973 (*A Voice from the Chorus*, 1976); *Progulki s Pushkinym*, 1975; *V teni Gogolya*, 1975; *"Opavshie list'ya" V. V. Rozanova*, 1982; *Soviet Civilization: A Cultural History*, 1990.

Bibliography

Dalton, Margaret. *Andrei Siniavskii and Julii Daniel': Two Soviet "Heretical" Writers.* Würzburg: Jal-verlag, 1973. Along with a discussion of the other works that Sinyavsky wrote prior to his arrest, this study contains a detailed story-by-story analysis of the six stories from that period. Throughout, Dalton pays special attention to the unusual literary devices that often make the works difficult to interpret. Contains notes and a bibliography.

Durkin, Andrew R. "Narrator, Metaphor, and Theme in Sinjavskij's *Fantastic Tales.*" *Slavic and East European Journal* 24 (1980); 133-144. Durkin divides the six early stories into three pairs for the purposes of analysis, but his goal is to discern the thematic concerns and formal devices that link all the stories. He emphasizes the role of art and of the artist, as well as the theme of escape, or liberation.

Kolonosky, Walter F. "Inherent and Ulterior Design in Sinyavsky's 'Pxenc.' " *Slavic and East European Journal* 26 (1982): 329-337. Accepting the notion that "Pkhentz" is, on one level, a work of scientific fiction, Kolonosky claims that it is primarily an allegory about faith, and he traces examples of Christian symbolism within the story.

Lourie, Richard. *Letters to the Future: An Approach to Sinyavsky-Tertz.* Ithaca, N.Y.: Cornell University Press, 1975. Lourie devotes a separate chapter to the *Fantastic Stories*; his analyses are distinctive both for his critiques of certain stories (he believes that only "The Icicle" and "Pkhentz" are totally successful) and for his efforts to show their relationship to other works in Russian literature. Includes notes, bibliography, and an index.

Pevear, Richard. "Sinyavsky in Two Worlds: Two Brothers Named Chénier." *The Hudson Review* 25 (1972): 375-402. Pevear contrasts Sinyavsky and Yevgeny Yevtushenko in an effort to elucidate Sinyavsky's views about the tasks of the writer. Contains a thoughtful analysis of "The Icicle."

Theimer Nepomnyashchy, Catherine. "Andrei Sinyavsky's 'You and I': A Modern Day Fantastic Tale." *Ulbandus Review* 2, no. 2 (1982): 209-230. Notes Sinyavsky's flaunting of his literary antecedents (Hoffmann, Gogol, Dostoevski). Prefers to view the story not so much as a study in mental disorder as "a realized metaphor—a literal working out of the vision of the artist as God" and thus as a tale combining both the biblical and the fantastic.

_____. "Sinyavsky/Tertz: The Evolution of the Writer in Exile." *Humanities in Society* 7, no. 314 (1984): 123-142. After providing a brief overview of

Sinyavsky's career during his first decade in the West, the author goes on to detail Sinyavsky's concerns with the role of the writer in relationship to reality and society at large. Concludes with a discussion of *Kroshka Tsores.*

Barry Scherr

JANE SMILEY

Born: Los Angeles, California; September 26, 1949

Principal short fiction
The Age of Grief, 1987; *Ordinary Love and Good Will,* 1989.

Other literary forms
Jane Smiley has published several novels as well as collections of short fiction. In addition to studies of family life, she has experimented with several novelistic sub-genres, including a murder thriller (*Duplicate Keys,* 1984) and a historical epic (*The Greenlanders,* 1988).

Achievements
Smiley's short fiction has drawn consistent praise for its linguistic economy and incisive detail in the service of the complex mysteries of American family life. Critic David Leavitt has called her "the contemporary American master of the novella form," and she herself regards the novella's "more meditative" thematic concentration and streamlined plotting as particularly congenial to her artistic ends. Having begun her career as what she calls a "devoted modernist" preoccupied with the nihilistic anomie dramatized in the great literature of the early twentieth century, Smiley found herself losing that alienated edge when she first became pregnant. In trying to resolve the ensuing creative challenge plaguing her—"Can mothers think and write?"—she discovered her true subject: the continually shifting dynamics of familial relationship. Her best work captures the intricate dance of need, love, retribution, and loss that entwines competing subjectivities within every family. *The Age of Grief,* which signaled a new gathering of creative force in Smiley's writing, was nominated for the National Book Critics Circle Award.

Smiley has proven especially adept at writing the maternal experience into literature, challenging the familiar cultural idealizations and caricatures of "mother love" produced by writers invariably engaging their subject from the position of the child; she regards her version of parenting as "a critique and correction" of both the child's and the father's stories. Yet Smiley's investigations are not limited to female protagonists; she regularly assumes male personas and argues that doing so is a less arduous imaginative feat for her than writing as a mother, since few viable models exist for the latter. Smiley's versatile experiments in character, voice, and plot line are well suited to short fictional forms. The psychological immediacy she achieves bespeaks a compassionate interest in decent people caught at dramatic crossroads, where they must assess the compromises and delusions that have shaped their lives.

Biography
Born to James La Verne Smiley and Frances Graves Nuelle in 1949, Jane Graves

Smiley began life during her father's military tour of duty in California. She was transplanted early to the Midwest and grew up in St. Louis, Missouri. The daughter of a writer mother, she attended Vassar College and received her B.A. in English in 1971; she composed her first novel for her senior thesis and discovered that "this was for me, this creation of worlds." Smiley completed a master of fine arts at the University of Iowa in 1976, and in 1978 she received an M.A. and a Ph.D. in medieval literature from the same institution. In 1981, she began teaching literature and creative writing as a member of the faculty at Iowa State University and became a full professor in 1989. In 1981 and 1987, she also served as a visiting professor at the University of Iowa. A Fulbright Fellowship in 1976-1977 allowed her to spend time in Iceland, where she continued a study of the Norse sagas that would later provide the framework for her novel *The Greenlanders.* Grants from the National Endowment for the Arts supported her writing in 1978 and 1987.

Smiley has commented that a childhood shadowed by the existence of the atomic bomb and an adolescence informed by the invention of "the Pill" have attuned her imagination to two major subjects: "sex and apocalypse." Her personal history reflects an intimate engagement with the tensions of family life that have inspired her best fiction. A first marriage to John Whiston in 1970 took place before her graduation from college and lasted until 1975. Her second marriage, to editor William Silag in 1978, produced two daughters, Phoebe and Lucy; it was with Phoebe's birth that she says her imagination was first "fully engaged." A third marriage, to Stephen Mark Mortensen, began in 1987. She lists her "avocations" as "cooking, swimming, playing piano, quilting."

Analysis

Taken together, Jane Smiley's short-fiction collections delineate the steady course of her imagination toward its true subject: the crisis of the adult who must confront not only the flawed and destructive nature of individual desire but also the unfathomable enormity of that individual's emotional power within the familial network both to create and to annihilate. In the first volume, Smiley offers a series of glimpses at the potent appeal of the family idyll, her tone at times bordering on the satiric. Yet the hunger of the family romance is not, finally, a laughing matter but the very engine of bourgeois tragedy as Smiley portrays it. In her works, she examines the myth of familial ideality from various positions—that of insider and outsider, homebuilder and home-wrecker—proving the seductiveness of the dream of family and the anguish of its heartbreakingly predictable insufficiency.

The Age of Grief is a loosely constructed volume. Consisting of five short stories and a novella, it presents a seemingly wide array of characters who range from active aggressors to passive victims in the contemporary battles for and against emotional commitment raging among adults who are still not quite willing to see themselves in their parents' roles. While the stories do not provide the depth of insight offered in the volume's closing novella, they establish the cultural ambiance of fragmentation and insubstantiality through which the longed-for idyll of family life demolished in "The Age of Grief" achieves its tragic incandescence.

Thus *The Age of Grief* breaks essentially into two parts: the first section, composed of the short stories, allows Smiley to examine family life through a series of characters peripheral to its most immediate and intimate dynamics. In "Lily" and "The Pleasure of Her Company," the female protagonists are admiring outsiders to the marital relationships they observe, and both find themselves unprepared for the destruction they witness. Their limited notions about the violence of human emotions possible and all too probable within conventional frames result in part from the absence of such entanglements in their own lives. In Lily's case, her preference for an emotional "virginity" that permits the freedom needed for her work as a poet has led her to meddle unwittingly in the heart of marital darkness, whose capacity for long-borne compromise and truce she has failed to comprehend and for which she stands profoundly humbled at the end. Florence, the narrative consciousness of the other tale, is allowed a more graceful if ironically inflected exit; faced with the dissolution of a marriage that she had regarded as ideal, she rejects the cynic's conclusion that love is delusion and pursues her own blossoming relationship with the realist's admonition "that it's worth finding out for yourself." Florence differs from Lily in this willingness to attempt the risk of emotional involvement in the very face of its failures.

Smiley is most harshly disposed toward those who attempt to orchestrate their emotional destinies with the same kind of professional calculation that they apply to their stock portfolios, as in the case of the female letter-writer of "Jeffrey, Believe Me." Smiley wittily satirizes the narcissism and determined self-gratification of 1980's urbanites by presenting a protagonist so intent on satisfying her biological clock that she devises the seduction of a gay male friend to achieve pregnancy. Perhaps the most scathing element of this sketch is its absence of any glimmer of personal responsibility within the narrator for the emotional network of obligations and yearnings that she has brought into being with her fetus. Her opposite number in the collection is the male protagonist of "Long Distance," whose literal odyssey to join his brothers for the Christmas holidays necessitates a reassessment of the callous disregard he has shown a young Japanese woman with whom he has had an affair. Never having taken a good look at the continual negotiations that make possible the sustained family relationships he has traditionally scorned, he now recognizes that he has been more than eager to jettison all such complications in his own life and, as a result, has proven morally bankrupt when confronted with the cost to others of his self-serving actions.

Stock-taking of this kind is at the heart of Smiley's most deeply felt writing, and hence her narratives are most effective when they enter the unmediated psychological terrain of the first person. Her characteristic tone, a laconic meditative stillness, emerges for the first time in *The Age of Grief* in "Dynamite," a piece in which the outsiders of the earlier stories give way to the hybrid insider-outsider Sandy, a woman in her early middle age caught between lifelong conflicting impulses to connect and to disrupt. Oscillating between past and present, as well as the discrete

identities into which Sandy's life has split as a result of a radical political commitment that has kept her underground for twenty years, the fiction traces her inescapable desire to recover ties with a mother whom she feels she has never truly known,
alongside a still evident restlessness "to do the most unthought-of thing, the itch to
destroy what is made—the firm shape of my life, whether unhappy, as it was, or
happy, as it is now." The twin complications of memory and fantasy make the present an elaborate web of past and future longings that motivate her wild swings of
behavior and shake them loose from the bourgeois stability they seem superficially
to relish. Smiley offers, however, a glimpse inside the paradox of Sandy's character
to illuminate the logic of its contradictions—mysteries of the human heart that defy
taming and that make Sandy emblematic of the struggle with self typical of Smiley's
protagonists.

With "The Age of Grief," Smiley moves full force into that theme, shifting the
angle of vision from the aggressor to the victim of a family crisis but in reality
exposing the insufficiency of such categories to describe the emotional upheavals
that beset "normality" from within its own preserve. The novella unfolds as the first
person narration of David Hurst, a dentist whose wife, Dana, his partner in a busy
dentistry practice and the mother of their three daughters, falls suddenly in love with
another man. At the real center of the drama, however, is David's struggle with his
knowledge of the affair and his choice to remain silent about it. Smiley is familiar
not only with the routines of parenting small children but also with the social changes
that have necessitated that fathers become full participants in all the nuances of
that routine. Thus she creates a poignant exactness around David's intimate involvement in the daily lives—including illnesses—of his young children, ages seven,
five, and two. The emotional tyranny of Leah, a toddler who insistently demands all
of her father's attention, mimics the jealous ownership of a lover that becomes all
the more bittersweet in the face of the waning love between her parents. Neither
spouse can speak to the other of the schism between them, and in his anguish David
concludes:

> I am thirty-five years old, and it seems to me that I have arrived at the age of grief. . . . It is not
> only that we know that love ends, children are stolen, parents die feeling that their lives have been
> meaningless. . . . It is more that the barriers between the circumstances of oneself and of the rest
> of the world have broken down, after all—after all that schooling, all that care . . . it is the same
> cup of pain that every mortal drinks from.

The narrative moves right up to the edge of dissolution as Dana's obsession finally
disrupts even her carefully orchestrated daily schedule and keeps her away from
home for twenty-four hours. When she reappears, they agree not to discuss what has
led her to relinquish her affair and resume her marriage. David—with a generosity
of spirit, or failure of will, that is utterly convincing because of its profound sadness—offers by way of explanation his dearly bought insight that "marriage is a
small container, after all. . . . Two inner lives, two lifelong meditations of whatever
complexity, burst out of it and out of it, cracking it, deforming it." The tragic center

of Smiley's fictions rests upon her illumination of the impossible burden placed on the emotional bonds of family and marriage, and the challenge of learning to live with the diminishment of faith in the future.

Each of the novellas composing *Ordinary Love and Good Will* offers another sustained examination into the disruption of a once idyllic homelife. While strikingly dissimilar in story line, atmospherics, and point of view, the two works together provide variations on a common theme: the loss of parental illusions about the real scope of one's protective power within the family circle and the potential compensatory wisdom of recognizing the mysterious otherness and inevitable falling from innocence—and into humanity—of one's children.

The first person narrator of *Ordinary Love*, a fifty-two-year-old divorced Iowan mother of five adult children, typifies Smiley's clear-eyed rejection of sentimental pieties about the heartland matriarch. Rachel Kinsella does indeed attend to the baking of cakes and spoiling of grandchildren as she awaits the homecoming of a long-absent son. Rachel's story, however, matter of factly told in a voice that is both accepting and unrepentant, includes the jarring paradox of having proudly borne five children in five years with a doting, ambitious doctor husband, yet also having initiated a love affair that caused an ugly divorce, prolonged separation from her still young children, and eventual separation of the children in custody arrangements that divided even their twin sons. Rachel realizes that in yielding to the destructive power of desire, she acted on an unspoken but profoundly felt need to escape the suffocating control of her husband, Pat, a man aggressively committed to the bourgeois family fantasy in which all other subjectivities were subsumed with his own powerful optimism.

Rachel's perspective, however, is not self-serving. She admits the contradictions driving her emotional life: the allure of creating a timeless domestic haven free from the typical ravages of family life; her relief upon being freed from the marriage that lay as the cornerstone to that haven; her "terror" upon entering the void left when her family collapsed and her children disappeared for a time from her life. Smiley plots Rachel's history as an arc of emotional loss and recovery, and in late middle age she is self-possessed and steady, a mature woman who, because she has consciously made herself anew out of wildness, grief, and perseverance, now possesses the strength to confront the ongoing costs of the past within the present.

Rachel's more immediate story, while inseparable from the rupture of twenty years earlier, involves her effort to mediate the return of her son Michael from a two-year stint as a teacher in poverty-stricken areas of India. In a family where each separation recollects the primal rifts of mother from child and sibling from sibling, Michael's transformation overseas exposes once again the discontinuities afflicting even the most fundamental human ties. Within this atmosphere, a series of confidences delivers a powerful lesson about the tantalizing impenetrability of each family member's private reality. Rachel tells her children for the first time of the love affair that upended their lives; her elder daughter, Ellen, retaliates with a description of their neglect by a vengeful father who transplanted them to London; Michael reveals his destructive relationship with a married woman that produced an abortion and the loss of the woman he really loved. The shock created by each of these "secrets" is multiple, and Rachel registers them all. Unlike her ex-husband, she struggles to subordinate the possessive assumptions of a parent and instead tries "to accept the mystery of my children, of the inexplicable ways they diverge from parental expectations, of how, however much you know or remember of them, they don't quite add up." She muses on the disruptive irrationality of human desire and realizes that Michael's new maturity reflects his own discovery of that fact. The real fruit of knowledge, she concedes, lies not simply in one's own suffering but in learning one's potential to inflict suffering on others, especially those one holds most dear. With a fatalism balanced against faith in the human capacity for renewal, Rachel squarely confronts the fact that she cannot spare her children life's bitterest lesson—the perverse and unrelenting hunger of the heart for what it cannot have, and that given the destructive pressure of the inner life, a parent may unforgivably offer her children "the experience of perfect family happiness, and the certain knowledge that it could not last."

Good Will offers a starker dramatic enactment of an adult's costly getting of wisdom but within a matrix of unnerving suspense about what is coming rather than through the retrospective melancholy about what has been, which colors *Ordinary Love*. Smiley deliberately places a mother's story beside a father's story, acknowledging the former as "more feminine, in which things are hidden and then revealed," and the latter as "more masculine" and "essentially linear." *Good Will* also shows Smiley's talent for constructing suspense out of the daily struggles for psychological control that underlie even the smoothest surfaces of family life. Here, the first-person narrator is Bob Miller, a Vietnam veteran who has systematically created a world for his nuclear family of three that exists parallel to, not within, mainstream American society. The novella opens eighteen years into his countercultural experiment, when the rearing of the child he and his wife Liz thought had completed their idyll begins instead to erode the illusory self-sufficiency to which he had devoted himself.

Smiley rises to the challenge of constructing a deeply flawed character from within his own point of view. Bob's remarkable talents as a craftsman correspond to his principled determination to live by a moral code purged of the empty materialism of his time. Slowly, however, he reveals the contours of a personality whose virtues slip over into dogmatism, and whose ingenuity is actually trained on keeping his loved ones within the range of his imagination and authority. The evidence of discord within Bob's self-willed paradise comes from the very people whom he believes to be his allies: Liz becomes a member of a fundamentalist religious community whose pull on her suggests the spiritual hunger she cannot feed through her married life; more sinister and ultimately more devastating is the seemingly racist hostility conceived by their seven-year-old son for the African-American newcomer whose affluent homelife becomes the target of the boy's rage at his own marginality to American material culture. Tommy's innocence offers him no defense against a corrosive envy of Annabelle's playthings and clothing, and his cool destruction of them forces his parents to consider, first, the folly of their assumption that they could maintain an uncompromised decency in their son simply by keeping him away from the establishment, and second, that they themselves were not imparting judgmental attitudes in him.

Finally, even Bob finds that he has not renounced the world as effectively as he has assumed: Lydia Harris, the mother of Tom's victim, a new professor of mathematics whose speciality is the suggestive realm of probabilities, offers her own fascination for him. To compensate for Tom's vandalism, he does various odd jobs for her and becomes increasingly preoccupied with her home, her personality, her assessment of his life. To the degree that he feels drawn to the mother, he finds himself inexplicably hostile to the daughter on whom she lavishes such affectionate concern. Bob in essence repeats his son's definition of Annabelle as a privileged being whose existence exposes the limitations of his own circumstances and choices.

Bob's willful refusal to accept his family's dissatisfaction with their paradise contributes to a steadily escalating tension within the text, which augers a catastrophe that unfolds with the surreal pacing of a dream. The drowning of Tom's beloved pony, Sparkle, is closely followed by an arson fire that destroys the Harris home, and Tom's complicity becomes increasingly undeniable. His real target, of course, is the father who has isolated him from the world of his peers and who has refused him his own choices in regard to that world.

The spotlight Tommy casts on his parents puts in motion a grim social services machinery that has all the inexorability of a Dreiserian tragedy. Insurance demands for reparations force the sale of the Millers' homestead and the conversion of both parents to wage-earners struggling simply to keep up with the expenses of apartment living. All three family members enter therapy and face threat of further legal action for the "recklessness" that led them to live without the amenities that could have enabled interception of, and intervention in, the unfolding crisis. Bob's anguish takes the form of a metaphysical stoicism that his wife regards as more stubborn unwillingness to yield to processes beyond his control, but his thoughts reveal that he has conceded to the incoherence of modern life that his farm was an attempt to keep at bay: "Let us have fragments, I say. . . . if no wholes are made, then it seems to me that I can live in town well enough . . . and remember the vast, inhuman peace of the stars pouring across the night sky above the valley. . . ." He rejects efforts to buffer the grinding truth of Eden's evanescence or of his own role as the worm at the very heart of that dream.

In her fictional preoccupation with the family, then, Smiley has decidedly not abandoned her early artistic attraction to the condition of modernist anomie that inspired her to become a writer. Rather, she has concentrated upon the innumerable ways in which the family, that bedrock of middle-class faith challenging nihilistic despair, dramatizes the unbridgeable chasm between the capacity for selflessness and self-love within the same individual, and the terrible grief to be had in experiencing that gap within oneself.

Other major works

NOVELS: *Barn Blind*, 1980; *At Paradise Gate*, 1981; *Duplicate Keys*, 1984; *The Greenlanders*, 1988; *A Thousand Acres*, 1991.

Bibliography

Bernays, Anne. "Toward More Perfect Unions." Review of *The Age of Grief. The New York Times Book Review*, September 6, 1987, 12. Bernays praises Smiley's powerful use of short-fictional forms to examine the contours of troubled personal relationships. Most of the commentary is devoted to the "splendid" title novella, which offers "a poignant and rich meditation on the nature of love and change."

Carlson, Ron. "King Lear in Zebulon County." Review of *A Thousand Acres. The New York Times Book Review*, November 3, 1991, 12. Carlson examines the ways in which Smiley adopts the terrain of William Shakespeare's *King Lear* (c. 1605-1606) to explore contemporary family dynamics in rural Iowa. He praises the novel's skill in conveying the interplay of factors—nature, business, community—that shape the farmer's life. He also cites the powerful impact of telling the tale through the eyes of the eldest daughter of the tyrant-father at the center of the tale.

Humphreys, Josephine. "Perfect Family Self-Destructs." Review of *Ordinary Love and Good Will. The New York Times Book Review*, November 5, 1989, 1, 45. Calling the novella a fictional form "most closely resembling a troubled dream," Humphreys discusses Smiley's artistry in *Ordinary Love and Good Will* and praises her provocative investigations into the role of power, imagination, and desire in family life. The first piece in the collection explores the consequences of desire, while the second involves "imagination as an act of power," the two together elaborating "the myth of the family, told by two principals: an Eve and an Adam," both of whom achieve a "realized ignorance" as "one ancient form of wisdom."

Kakutani, Michiko. Review of *The Age of Grief. The New York Times*, August 26, 1987, C21. This strong review examines each of the pieces in the collection and pays particular attention to the novella "The Age of Grief," wherein Smiley proves her "talent for delineating the subtle ebb and flow of familial emotions" and her attunement for the multiple levels on which everyday communication operates in such close quarters—so much so that "we are left with a sense of having participated in her characters' lives."

Klinkenborg, Verlyn. "News from the Norse." Review of *The Greenlanders. The New Republic* 198 (May 16, 1988): 36-39. Cites Smiley's ability to bring to life the experience of a culture remote both in time and worldview. Noting Smiley's debt to the Old Norse sagas on which the novel is based, Klinkenborg notes the complex narrative structuring of the text, its skillful narrative voice, and its powerful fusion of grim story line and philosophical "grace" in the midst of inevitable disaster.

Leavitt, David. "Of Harm's Way and Farm Ways." *Mother Jones* 14 (December, 1989): 44-45. Leavitt praises the probing power of *Ordinary Love and Good Will*, calling Smiley "one of our wisest writers" for her insight into the tragic center of her characters' most admirable dreams. He also cites her knowledgeable evocation of the real-world activities that fill their lives and her sensitivity to the physical landscape through which they move.

Barbara Kitt Seidman

LEE SMITH

Born: Grundy, Virginia; November 1, 1944

Principal short fiction

Cakewalk, 1981; *Me and My Baby View the Eclipse: Stories by Lee Smith,* 1990.

Other literary forms

Lee Smith's first published work was a novel, *The Last Day the Dogbushes Bloomed* (1968). It was followed by two more novels, *Something in the Wind* (1971) and *Fancy Strut* (1973). After a seven-year hiatus, Smith brought out what has been called the first work of her second career, *Black Mountain Breakdown* (1980), which was followed by additional novels, including *Family Linen* (1985) and *Fair and Tender Ladies* (1988).

Achievements

With the publication of *Black Mountain Breakdown*, Smith was recognized as one of the outstanding Southern writers of her generation; the novels and short stories that appeared after *Black Mountain Breakdown* have only strengthened this estimate. Like earlier Southern writers, Smith has an eye for interesting characters and an ear for colorful speech, as well as both a sense of place and a sense of humor. Except when she reaches back into history, Smith's settings are the New South, and her characters are ordinary people, most of them trying to escape from their ordinary lives. Perhaps the quality for which Smith is most admired is her compassion; although she dramatizes her characters' ignorance and satirizes their pretensions, she respects them as human beings, coping as best they can with the human condition.

Biography

Lee Smith was born on November 1, 1944, in Grundy, Virginia, a mining town in the southwestern part of the state. Her father, Ernest Lee Smith, was in business, running the local Ben Franklin store; her mother, Virginia Marshall Smith, was a teacher. An only child who was born to her parents late in their lives, Lee had a quiet childhood, spending much of her time reading and writing.

Smith was educated at St. Catherine's School in Richmond, Virginia, and then at Hollins College, where she studied creative writing with Richard Dillard and Louis Rubin. Her first novel, *The Last Day the Dogbushes Bloomed*, developed out of a senior writing project. It was published after bringing Smith a Book-of-the-Month Club fellowship. In 1967, Smith was graduated from Hollins College and married the poet James E. Seay, the father of her two children. The marriage later ended in divorce.

From 1968 to 1969, Smith was in Tuscaloosa, Alabama, working as a writer for the *Tuscaloosa News* and gathering the material that would appear in her third novel,

Fancy Strut. Finding it almost impossible to combine a career in journalism with fiction writing, Smith turned to teaching. In 1971, the year her second novel appeared, she began teaching seventh grade in Nashville, Tennessee; in 1974, after the publication of *Fancy Strut*, she moved to Durham, North Carolina, to teach language arts and continue writing.

By 1977, Smith was teaching creative writing on the college level at the University of North Carolina at Chapel Hill. After three of her books had lost money for her publishers, however, her fourth novel was rejected, and other publishers followed suit. As years went by, Smith began to believe that her career as a writer was ending. She credits a new agent and a new editor, one who wished to work actively with her, for enabling her to begin writing again. The critics were impressed with *Black Mountain Breakdown*, the first book from Smith's second period.

In 1981, Smith joined the faculty of North Carolina State University at Raleigh. In 1985, she married Hal Crowther. Meanwhile, the quality of her fiction was indicated by the awards she won—for example, Doubleday's O. Henry Award in 1979 for "Mrs. Darcy Meets the Blue-Eyed Stranger at the Beach" and in 1981 for "Between the Lines," as well as the Sir Walter Raleigh Award in 1984 and the North Carolina Award for Literature in 1985. Smith's growing importance can be seen in the increasing number of interviews with her, the articles about her work published each year, her inclusion in the lists of theses and dissertations, and the full-length studies on her; such as the one by Dorothy Combs Hill, published as part of the Twayne series on established authors.

Analysis

Lee Smith's short stories are set in the contemporary South of shopping malls and convenience stores, where dreams and hopes are defined not by tradition or faith but by the images on the television screen. Her protagonists are ordinary people, who are dissatisfied with their ordinary lives but have small chance of changing them because they have neither the talent nor the intelligence that would enable them to move up in the world. Furthermore, because most of Smith's protagonists are women, many of whom have been betrayed and abandoned by men, they are especially vulnerable, both emotionally and socially. It is clear that Smith is pessimistic about the future of such characters, and perhaps, by extension, about life in general. One cannot, however, simply define her tone as pessimistic. There is too much comedy and gentle satire in Smith's works for that kind of assessment; furthermore, she emphasizes the courage of her characters, who despite defeat upon defeat refuse to give up on life.

It is interesting that of the fourteen stories in *Cakewalk*, thirteen are told through the eyes of women. This focus is typical of Smith's fiction. The point of view varies; sometimes the writer uses first person, sometimes third person with limited omniscience, which concentrates on the thoughts and activities of a single character and thus has much the same effect as first person. No matter which technique she chooses, Smith does not interfere with her characters but lets them reveal themselves in the words and rhythms of everyday speech.

For example, Mrs. Jolene B. Newhouse, the first-person narrator in "Between the Lines," seems to be speaking to the reader rather than writing her own story. She begins by explaining why her gossip column is called "Between the Lines," but it is soon clear that what Jolene really wants to do is to point out how superior both she and her newspaper column are. There are dozens of lines in the story that enable Smith to satirize Jolene's character, for example, all the smug self-evaluations: she has a sunny nature, she is naturally good, she is highly intelligent, she has always been a remarkable writer. There is also comedy of situation, such as the real story of Alma Goodnight, who has been hospitalized because her husband hit her with a rake and who now is getting her revenge, lying in luxury in a hospital bed while he suffers the torments of guilt. Clearly, Jolene is not so self-centered that she cannot see a situation as it really is. Her admirable grasp of reality is later illustrated when she describes her youngest daughter as an indecisive whiner. The realist Jolene, however, has a surprising depth to her character. She responds to the beauties of nature, which she describes in her column. Furthermore, she cherishes the memory of an almost mystical sexual encounter in the woods with a visiting evangelist. Perhaps because of her own experience, she has accepted her husband's frailty, along with all the mysterious human actions that are written "between the lines" of her column.

Another of Smith's first-person stories in *Cakewalk*, "Dear Phil Donohue," is told by a woman who, like Jolene, has broken the rules, but who, unlike Jolene, has not been able to control her own situation. Having married her high school sweetheart, twenty-eight-year-old Martha Rasnick is living the life she always expected to live. However, isolated with her babies, uncertain who she is and uncertain who her husband really is, she cracks. When a mentally disturbed boy hides in her garage, she feeds him as if he were a stray cat and even comforts him. As a result, she is abandoned by both her husband and their supposed friends, and she has to tell her story to her only human contact, a television personality.

Many of Smith's characters are as isolated as Martha, but because of what might be interpreted either as an unwillingness to face reality or as a triumph of the human spirit, they refuse to give up hope. For example, the protagonist in "All the Days of Our Lives" is a mother of three, who has been divorced by her husband because she ran off to Daytona Beach with an insurance claims adjuster, long since departed, and who now alternates between disappearing into the world of television and imagining her lost husband to be some ideal creature, instead of the perfectionist who actually drove her away. At the end of the story, however, she snaps out of her depression and makes some decisions, including a resolution to take another look at the neighbor who obviously adores her and who might give her a new love or at least a new interest. Similarly, in "Gulfport," a young girl who has been used, betrayed, and abandoned by a lover, who she had convinced herself was going to marry her, clings to some possibilities for the future. Her lover might come back to her, she thinks, or she might go for a walk with the young Mormon missionary, after all, or she might take a job in a lounge. As long as there is life, there are possibilities; as long as there are possibilities, there is hope.

Like "All the Days of Our Lives" and "Gulfport," the title story of the collection, "Cakewalk," is told in the third person. The character whose thoughts are related, however, Stella Lambeth, is not really the protagonist. When she emphasizes her own superiority in the community, her elegance at the department store cosmetic counter, and points out the deficiencies of her disorganized, cake-baking sister, it becomes clear which of the two is more capable of loving and of being loved. At the end of the story, a brief excursion into the thoughts of Stella's husband suggests that Stella's own world is not as secure as she believes it to be. Again, Smith ends with possibilities, leaving the future up to her characters.

Indeed, one of the major themes in Lee Smith's stories is the fragility not only of life itself but also of a seemingly fixed pattern. Actually, it takes very little to change a life: a chance encounter, an impulse, a vivid memory, a sudden glimpse of happiness. The protagonist of "Heat Lightning," Geneva, comments on this fact, when, in the midst of cooking and mothering, she senses that a change is coming. In the past, this feeling foretold a major event in her life—the death of her father, the first glimpse of the man she was to marry, and the death of a baby she was carrying. As it turns out, the fourth prediction is as insignificant as heat lightning. Geneva takes the children to a carnival, grins at a carnival worker, and returns cheerfully to her husband.

An event so slight, however, might have had tragic results. In "Saint Paul," it is unclear whether Paul Honeycutt was destroyed by the fact that in his childhood he could not bring himself to declare his love for his young playmate or by the fact that she shattered his image of himself and of her by offering herself to him many years later. At any rate, at the end of the story, although the narrator has proceeded with her life, she realizes that Paul has become almost as important to her as she has always been to him. This suggestion that the world is ruled not by Providence but by chance is basic to Smith's pessimism. It is consistent with the fact that her characters do not ordinarily make real choices. They do not act in accordance with some master plan; instead, they look at the limited possibilities for their lives, and then drift in one direction or another, governed by impulse or by whim.

The first story in Smith's second collection of short stories, *Me and My Baby View the Eclipse*, illustrates this kind of aimlessness. Again, the central character in this story, which is entitled "Bob, A Dog," is a wife deserted by her husband, who at thirty-nine has decided that he needs to make his life simpler and has left his family for a singles apartment complex and a young woman. His wife, Cheryl, a good-natured woman who has spent her life being agreeable to everyone, especially to men, cannot even bring herself to be angry with him. Meanwhile, she drifts. She sleeps with one man, then drops him; she refuses to sleep with another. The central problem in the story illustrates both Cheryl's kindness and her purposelessness. She has adopted a dog, who, not unlike her husband, is determined to run free. Despite all the trouble that Bob, the dog, causes her, Cheryl continues to love him and to forgive him. At the end of the story, she considers the possibility that her husband will return to her; ironically, just at that point, Bob runs away again.

Sometimes a Smith story will move not merely toward possibilities but toward love. "Life on the Moon" is the story of two cousins, the narrator, June, who stayed at home, lived by the rules, took care of her family, and has just been abandoned for a younger woman, and Lucie, who went away to college and made her own decisions. Even though June has not approved of Lucie, it is Lucie who persuades her to load the children in the car for a trip to Washington, and it is Lucie who enables June to see her marriage and her husband as they really were. The story ends with a scene of reconciliation between the cousins. Similarly, at the end of the title story, "Me and My Baby View the Eclipse," even though Sharon Shaw knows that she cannot continue her affair with her imaginative lover, Raymond Stewart, she also knows that she will never forget the magic he has brought into her life. While they will part and she will once again be faithful to her dull husband, Sharon will always be grateful to Raymond and, in her way, she will always love him.

Because in each of her stories Lee Smith concentrates on a single point of view, and because she so carefully imitates the rhythms of speech, reading her work is similar to interviewing various individuals on the meaning of life. Although Smith's comedy is delightful and her satire effective, her most memorable stories are those such as "Between the Lines," "Cakewalk," "Life on the Moon," and "Me and My Baby View the Eclipse," which prove that ordinary people can sometimes break free of life's prisons through the power of love. Even though life is ruled by chance and people are ruled by impulse, Smith suggests that there can be relationships that make life bearable, and there can be memories that cast their spell over the years that follow. That is probably the most that human beings can expect out of life, but it is much better than nothing.

Other major works

NOVELS: *The Last Day the Dogbushes Bloomed*, 1968; *Something in the Wind*, 1971; *Fancy Strut*, 1973; *Black Mountain Breakdown*, 1980; *Oral History*, 1983; *Family Linen*, 1985; *Fair and Tender Ladies*, 1988.

Bibliography

Buchanan, Harriette C. "Lee Smith: The Storyteller's Voice." In *Southern Women Writers: The New Generation*, edited by Tonette Bond Inge. Tuscaloosa: University of Alabama Press, 1990. A thoughtful critique of Smith's fiction, organized chronologically and culminating in *Family Linen*. While quoting Smith on her avowed intention of simply telling stories, Buchanan points out the profound thematic implications of her works, noting in particular the ironic difference between Smith's own tolerant understanding of her characters and their lack of tolerance toward one another. A number of the short stories in *Cakewalk* are discussed as evidence of Smith's humanistic viewpoint.

Canin, Ethan. "The Courage of Their Foolishness." Review of *Me and My Baby View the Eclipse*. *The New York Times Book Review*, February 11, 1990, 11. A brief but perceptive summary of Smith's themes, her strengths, and her weaknesses. Although it deals specifically with the short-story collection cited, this essay is an excellent introduction to Smith's fiction as a whole.

Jones, Anne Goodwyn. "The World of Lee Smith." In *Women Writers of the Contemporary South*, edited by Peggy Whitman Prenshaw. Jackson: University Press of Mississippi, 1984. An incisive exploration of the relation between the spoken and written word in Smith's fiction, which makes classification of her work according to the tenets of contemporary criticism extremely difficult, while richly rewarding her readers. The stories in *Cakewalk* are analyzed separately and in relation to the novels.

MacKethan, Lucinda H. "Artists and Beauticians: Balance in Lee Smith's Fiction." *The Southern Literary Journal* 15 (Fall, 1982): 3-14. This important article discusses the problem of attaining a balance in life, which is involved in every choice Smith's characters make. Also looks at Smith's own attempts to achieve artistic balance, primarily through alterations in tone and variations in point of view.

Smith, Virginia A. "Luminous Halos and Lawn Chairs: Lee Smith's *Me and My Baby View the Eclipse*." *The Southern Review* 27 (Spring, 1991): 479-485. Argues that the stories in this collection have a repeated pattern, which takes the characters from darkness to moments of illumination, occurring primarily through the power of love. Stresses Smith's sensitivity to the experiences of women.

Walsh, William J. "Lee Smith." In *Speak So I Shall Know Thee: Interviews with Southern Writers*. Jefferson, N.C.: McFarland, 1990. In this interview, conducted in November, 1987, Smith comments on her development as a writer, her experience with editors and publishers, her methods of research, and her evaluation of her own work, as well as on various opinions and personal details.

Rosemary M. Canfield Reisman

ALEKSANDR SOLZHENITSYN

Born: Kislovodsk, North Caucasus, U.S.S.R.; December 11, 1918

Principal short fiction

Stories and Prose Poems, 1971 (includes poetry); *Rasskazy*, 1990.

Other literary forms

Although Aleksandr Solzhenitsyn is best known for his novels and his multi-volume historical-artistic investigation of the Soviet prison system, *Arkhipelag GU-Lag* (1973-1976; *The Gulag Archipelago*, 1974-1978), in which inset tales figure notably, he has also written independent short fiction, prose poems, narrative poetry, a film scenario, essays, biography and autobiography, and drama. His short novel *Odin den Ivana Denisovicha* (1962; *One Day in the Life of Ivan Denisovich*, 1963) was adapted for American television. Solzhenitsyn was awarded the Nobel Prize in Literature in 1970, but Soviet authorities blocked a reception ceremony. His *Nobelevskara lektsira po literature* (the nobel lecture) was published in 1972.

Achievements

Seldom has a writer emerged from total obscurity and risen so meteorically in such a short time as has Solzhenitsyn, achieving in little more than a decade world fame and winning the Nobel Prize. He has accomplished all this by adhering to the nineteenth century realistic tradition and also by bringing new elements into Russian literature. His greatest successes lie in the field of the novel, but he has been as forceful in his nonfiction writings, especially in his *Gulag Archipelago* trilogy. Even his prose poems or miniature stories are comparable to the best in their genre. Through his artistic achievements, resistance to tyranny, and personal courage, he has become the conscience not only of Russian people but also of all humankind and one of the greatest writers in Russian literature.

Biography

Aleksandr Isayevich Solzhenitsyn grew up fatherless and poor in Rostov-on-Don, where he took his university degree in mathematics in 1941, having also studied literature by correspondence from Moscow University. After four years of unbroken service as a frontline artillery officer, he was sentenced in 1945 to eight years of hard labor in gulag, the Soviet prison system, for criticizing Joseph Stalin in a private letter. Inexplicably exiled to Kazakhstan from 1953 to 1956, Solzhenitsyn recovered from a near-fatal cancer, taught mathematics and physics in a high school, and began to set his prison experiences down as fiction. Rehabilitated in 1956, he moved to Ryazan, near Moscow, where he continued to write. The publication of his camp novel *One Day in the Life of Ivan Denisovich* marked a brief thaw in Soviet literary restrictions under Nikita S. Khrushchev in 1962. Upon the retightening of censorship, Solzhenitsyn's work was banned from publication in the Soviet Union. After being expelled from the Soviet Writers' Union in 1969 and barred from formal acceptance of the Nobel Prize in Literature he had won in 1970, Solzhenitsyn was ejected from the Soviet Union in 1973. He settled in Vermont with his second wife and children. In his later years, Solzhenitsyn has experienced some misgivings in the West on account of his uncompromising stand against the regime in his country and "conservative" views on the future of Russia. He has retired from public life, spending all his time writing the *Red Wheel* novels.

Analysis

Aleksandr Solzhenitsyn initially responded to his prison and labor camp experiences in easy-to-memorize poetry and later in tiny self-contained prose poems, written down in the 1950's and assembled as a rough set around 1962, although not published at that time in the Soviet Union. Shortly after his initial success in the journal *Novy Mir* with the short novel *One Day in the Life of Ivan Denisovich*, Solzhenitsyn also published there his short stories "Incident at Krechetovka Station," "Matryona's House," and "For the Good of the Cause" in 1963. Like "The Easter Procession," "The Right Hand" never appeared in the Soviet Union until the end of *glasnost* in the late 1980's, although "Zakhar the Pouch" was published in *Novy Mir* in 1966, the last of Solzhenitsyn's works printed publicly in the Soviet Union. Each of these short pieces contains the germ of a larger work to come, just as each of the individuals or groups named in the titles of the stories reflects one facet of Solzhenitsyn's overriding theme of his country's agony under Communism.

The essence of Solzhenitsyn's message lies in his peculiarly Russian view of shared suffering as vital, even necessary, to human spiritual survival. To this end, he announced in his Nobel lecture that only art, only literature, can bridge the immense gulfs of time and space between human beings, bringing experiences of those faraway others close enough so that their lessons may help overcome evil. Although Solzhenitsyn has not completed large-scale treatments of all the themes presented in his short fiction, the individualization of experience he began with Ivan Denisovich, the lowly camp inmate whose shining humanity enables him to survive, clearly emerges from the prose poems and the short stories, its successive stages mirroring Solzhenitsyn's own existence in Stalin's prison system.

"Incident at Krechetovka Station" draws heavily upon Solzhenitsyn's wartime experience. Set in the critical autumn of 1941, this story defies all the conventions of Soviet war literature, in which the cliché of patriotic self-sacrifice predominates. Its protagonist, Lieutenant Zotov, an assistant transit officer, is sympathetically portrayed in sharp contrast to the self-serving functionaries around him, who collectively form the story's antagonist, the "system" to blame for categorically condemning both the guilty and the innocent.

"Incident at Krechetovka Station" opens in cold pouring rain with one of Solzhenitsyn's typically abrupt laconic dialogues which achieve a forceful immediacy. Zotov, a youngish man isolated by the war from his family, has gentle features that toughen as he self-consciously straightens his glasses. He observes the misery of the wretched civilians who clutter the station, but he submerges his sympathy for them in his devotion to Marxism. Soon Zotov is miserable himself, however, distressed by a growing suspicion that the war is not proceeding in tune with Party propaganda.

For more than half of the story, Solzhenitsyn shuttles between the chilly "present" and events in Zotov's past, gradually hinting at the shattering perception Solzhenitsyn himself had grasped as a youth: the vast gap between Communism's promises and reality. Zotov haltingly approaches the truth through chance encounters with other actors in the drama, first in a few poems from line officers critical of their leadership, then in the hunger and cold of the old people and the children in the town. Solzhenitsyn characteristically allows Zotov to linger over the predicament of starving Russian soldiers being repatriated, like Ivan Denisovich, to Stalin's labor camps, their only crime being their surrender to the German army. Lonely and often despairing, Zotov tries to take refuge in his cheap volume of *Das Kapital*, but somehow he cannot finish it. Distracted by the pain of the war's victims, which his heart sees, and by his revulsion at those who prey on them, which his Communist glasses cannot quite shut out, Zotov is disturbed time and again, finally by an "incident" in the bedraggled person of Tveritinov, a former actor trying to find the military detachment from which he had somehow become separated.

Tveritinov strikes up an acquaintance with Zotov, and as they reminisce about prewar times, the actor's rich voice and winning manner create a mood that for the first time warms the dreary little station with the ceaseless rain beating down on its roof. Solzhenitsyn characteristically insinuates a darker undercurrent when they speak of 1937. Zotov associates that year only with the Soviet involvement in the Spanish Civil War, but Tveritinov, older, recalls an entirely different side to it, the height of Stalin's terrifying purges; his moment of silence, eyes downcast, reveals far more than any speech.

The rapport is suddenly shattered when Tveritinov mistakenly uses the pre-Communist name for Stalingrad. Zotov, struck by the horrifying possibility that he may be harboring an enemy of the state, deceitfully leads the actor into the arms of the security police. Not long after, when Zotov inquires about Tveritinov, he is ominously warned not to look into the matter further. This "incident" at apparently insignificant Krechetovka Station is Solzhenitsyn's metaphor for his country's wartime tragedy. So caught up in Communist zeal that they are able to see the world as Zotov at first did, only through a point of view that obliterates their vital connection to the rest of humanity, Solzhenitsyn's countrymen were being forced to share a perverted brotherhood of opportunism and betrayal, brutality, and inhumanity. As a measure of Solzhenitsyn's burningly ironic message in this story, the "incident" at Krechetovka Station remains Zotov's torment forever.

In "The Right Hand," a miniature forerunner of *Rakovy korpus* (1968; *Cancer Ward*, 1968), Solzhenitsyn ruthlessly depicts what Zotov might have become if he had not experienced·that cruel enlightenment. The story not only excoriates a state-run hospital system that dehumanizes the very patients it purports to serve, but it also unveils the devastating fate of those whose Party blinders are not removed until it is too late. Having served Communism faithfully, a new patient, clearly terminal, is hypocritically refused admittance to a cancer clinic on a technicality, and this denial of every Party ideal he has slavishly followed snaps his last thread-thin hold on life.

Like the narrator of "The Right Hand," himself a sufferer, the man who tells the story of "Matryona's House" recently emerged from the crucible of the prison system. All he wants at the outset is to lose himself in the heart of Russia, yearning for the peace of its countryside to restore his soul. Like Solzhenitsyn himself, he takes a position as a mathematics teacher in a shabby ancient village, living in a large old ramshackle house with a sick and aged peasant woman named Matryona. Matryona owns few things, and what she does have is as decrepit as her cockroach-ridden kitchen: a lame cat, a marginal garden, a dirty white goat, and some stunted house plants. Although she had worked on the collective farm for twenty-five years, bureaucratic entanglements have choked off her dead husband's pension—she herself is entitled to nothing—and she is almost destitute. Meager as her life is, however, Matryona's goodness sustains both herself and her lodger, who comes to prize her smile even more than the bit of daily bread they share.

In a strange though altogether convincing way, Matryona's very generosity is responsible for her death. She had loved one of the villagers deeply and waited three years for him to return from World War I. Thinking him dead then, she married his brother, and when the first man returned, he cursed them both. After Matryona's six children died in infancy, she reared one of the daughters of her former sweetheart as her own, and now, feeling she has not long to live, Matryona allows the girl and her friends to dismantle the top part of her house for its lumber. In struggling to help pull the heavy timber sledge over a railroad crossing, Matryona is killed by a speeding train.

For Solzhenitsyn, generosity, purity of heart, goodness, and love, the best qualities of the Russian folk, are as endangered under Communism as they had been under the czars. Now it may even be worse; Matryona's village has become wretchedly poor, with women instead of horses plowing the kitchen gardens, and the system that promised so much offers only corruption, lackadaisical confusion, and mistrust, racing carelessly over people like Matryona on its way to some future too obscure to believe. And yet (one of the hallmarks of Solzhenitsyn's fiction is the simple "and yet" that illuminates an otherwise hopeless life), he says, Matryona, poor in all but spirit, is the one righteous person without whom not a village or a city or the world can stand. Matryona is the personification of the mystical regeneration held inviolate in the Russian people that Solzhenitsyn instinctively sought upon his release and found intuitively in her. Like the old caretaker of a tatterdemalion monument to a forgotten battle in "Zakhar the Pouch," Matryona's stubborn, patient self-sacrifice restored Solzhenitsyn's faith in humanity at a time when he had learned its opposite all too well.

In his political polemic of the early 1960's, "For the Good of the Cause," Solzhenitsyn again pits genuine human affection against villainous bureaucracy. Students of a provincial technical college have helped build themselves a badly needed building, but Party officials usurp it, with the resulting disillusion wrenching the consciences of director and teachers and breaking the will of many of the students. Their helpless, bitter frustration at official hypocrisy underlies the actions of the vicious hoodlums, inhuman products of a system he feels they eventually will indiscriminately trample down, who aimlessly harass "The Easter Procession" in Solzhenitsyn's last short story.

Solzhenitsyn's short fiction resembles an Easter procession of his own, advancing from the Good Friday of the repatriated Soviet prisoner of war through loving recognition of the healing goodness in the peasants Matryona and Zakhar and a clear-eyed estimate of perversion of an honest teacher's responsibility to his students, finally arriving at the realization that the Soviet system and its creatures contain the seeds of universal destruction. The only hope Solzhenitsyn can see lies in the willing acknowledgment of the bond between human beings that springs from the Christian consciousness that all people share their fellows' suffering. In Solzhenitsyn's short fiction, his overture to a powerful literary and spiritual mission, we recognize that however separated we are in time and space, his is the voice of our brother.

Other major works

NOVELS: *Odin den Ivana Denisovicha*, 1962 (novella; *One Day in the Life of Ivan Denisovich*, 1963); *Rakovy korpus*, 1968 (*Cancer Ward*, 1968); *V kruge pervom*, 1968 (*The First Circle*, 1968); *Lenin v Tsyurikhe*, 1975 (*Lenin in Zurich*, 1976); *krasnoe koleso: Povestvovane v otmerennykh strokakh*, 1983-1986 (includes *Avgust chetyrnadtsatogo*, 1971, rev. ed. 1983 [*August 1914*, 1972, rev. ed. 1989]; *Oktiabr shestnadsatogo*, 1984; *Mart semnadsatogo*, 1986).

PLAYS: *Olen' i shalashovka*, 1968 (*Love Girl and the Innocent*, 1969; also as *Respublika truda*, 1981); *Svecha na vetru*, 1968 (*Candle in the Wind*, 1973); *Dramaticheskaya trilogiya-1945: Pir Pobediteley*, 1981 (*Victory Celebrations*, 1983); *Plenniki*, 1981 (*Prisoners*, 1983).

SCREENPLAYS: *Znayut istinu tanki*, 1981; *Tuneyadets*, 1981.

POETRY: *Etudy i krokhotnye rasskazy*, 1964 (translated in *Stories and Prose Poems*); *Prusskie nochi*, 1974 (*Prussian Nights*, 1977).

NONFICTION: *Arkhipelag GULag*, 1973-1975 (*The Gulag Archipelago*, 1974-1978); *Iz-pod glyb*, 1974 (*From Under the Rubble*, 1975); *Bodalsya telyenok s dubom*, 1975 (*The Oak and the Calf*, 1980); *The Mortal Danger*, 1980; *Rebuilding Russia: Reflections and Tentative Proposals*, 1991.

MISCELLANEOUS: *Sobranie sochinenii*, 1978-1983 (10 volumes).

Bibliography

Dunlop, John B., Richard Haugh, and Alexis Klimoff, eds. *Aleksandr Solzhenitsyn: Critical Essays and Documentary Materials.* 2d ed. New York: Collier Books, 1975. A thick volume of more than fifty critical and documentary materials and bibliographical surveys. Contains some of the most significant articles about Solzhenitsyn, of general nature and as treatments of individual works, primarily novels. Also contains an article on short stories by John Dunlop.

Feifer, Georg, and David Burg. *Solzhenitsyn*. New York: Stein & Day, 1972. A solid biography of Solzhenitsyn, covering his beginnings, his emergence as a writer, his problems with authorities, the concentration camps, his literary achievements, and his activities in exile through autumn, 1972. A lively and readable biography.

Feuer, Kathryn, ed. *Solzhenitsyn*. Englewood Cliffs, N.J.: Prentice-Hall, 1976. A collection of thirteen essays. The articles illuminate Solzhenitsyn as a writer, which, in turn, inform readers' understanding of his works, including short fiction. In this connection, Robert Louis Jackson's " 'Matryona's Home': The Making of a Russian Icon" offers some keen interpretations of the story.

Labedz, Leopold, ed. *Solzhenitsyn: A Documentary Record*. New York: Harper & Row, 1971. A collection of documents about Solzhenitsyn's life and works, through which his development from his literary debut to the Nobel Prize is followed. Valuable for Solzhenitsyn's biography.

Lottridge, Stephen S. "Solzhenitsyn and Leskov." *Russian Literature Triquarterly* 6 (1973): 478-489. In this comparative essay, Lottridge examines Solzhenitsyn's debt to Russia's greatest storyteller, Nikolai Leskov. He sees the connection in Solzhenitsyn's creation of "Christian" and righteous characters, especially in "Matryona's Home" and in the use of *skaz* technique.

Scammel, Michael. *Solzhenitsyn*. New York: W. W. Norton, 1989. This exhaustive but lively biography deals with practically all important aspects of Solzhenitsyn's life. Unfortunately, his works, especially the short fiction, are not discussed at great length.

Zekulin, Gleb. "Solzhenitsyn's Four Stories." *Soviet Studies* 16, no. 1 (1964): 45-62. In this compact and authoritative essay, Zekulin discusses "Matryona's House," "Incident at Krechetovka Station," "We Never Make Mistakes," and "One Day in the Life of Ivan Denisovich," which Zekulin treats as a short story rather than as a novel.

Mitzi M. Brunsdale
(Revised by *Vasa D. Mihailovich*)

MURIEL SPARK

Born: Edinburgh, Scotland; February 1, 1918

Principal short fiction

The Go-Away Bird and Other Stories, 1958; *Voices at Play*, 1961 (short stories and radio plays); *Collected Stories I*, 1967; *Bang-Bang You're Dead and Other Stories*, 1983; *The Stories of Muriel Spark*, 1985.

Other literary forms

Muriel Spark is known primarily for her novels and short fiction, but her writing career also includes works of nonfiction, children's literature, poetry, film adaptations, and radio plays. She began her career writing news articles as a press agent. Later she expanded her range to include works of poetry and literary criticism, contributing poems, articles, and reviews to magazines and newspapers, occasionally using the pseudonym Evelyn Cavallo. Spark published her first short story in 1951. In 1954, she began writing novels, her best known being *The Prime of Miss Jean Brodie* (1961).

Achievements

Spark's literary associations are as numerous as her works. She founded a short-lived literary magazine, *The Forum*, in 1949. Her memberships include the Poetry Society, the Royal Society of Literature, and the International Association of Poets, Playwrights, Editors, Essayists, and Novelists (PEN Club). She is also an honorary member of the American Academy and Institute of Arts and Letters. Spark's first short story, "The Seraph and the Zambesi," won *The Observer* short-story prize in 1951. Her other awards include: Prix Italia (1962) for her radio play adaptation of *The Ballad of Peckham Rye* (1960); Yorkshire Post Book of the Year Award (1965) and the James Tait Black Memorial Prize (1966), both for *The Mandelbaum Gate* (1965); Commander, Order of the British Empire (1967); LL.D., University of Strathclyde (1971); and the Booker McConnell Prize nomination (1981) for *Loitering with Intent* (1981).

Biography

Muriel Sarah (Camberg) Spark was born and educated in Edinburgh, Scotland. In 1937, she went to Rhodesia. During her stay in Africa, she married S. O. Spark but was divorced a short time later. She has one child, her son Robin. Spark's parents, Bernard and Sarah Elizabeth Camberg, held diverse religious faiths; her father was Jewish, while her mother was Presbyterian. Spark practiced the Anglican faith until her interest in the writings of John Henry Newman, a nineteenth century Catholic theologian, convinced Spark to convert to Catholicism. She entered the Roman Catholic church in 1954. Her personal search for spiritual belief and theological truth is reflected in many of the themes and elements of her fiction.

Spark spent several years living in British colonies in Central Africa. In 1944, she returned to England. During the war years, she wrote news articles for the political intelligence department of the British government. After the war, she held various posts in the publishing field, including a position as founder of the short-lived literary magazine *Forum*. In the early 1950's, Spark began to produce serious work in literary criticism and poetry. Hand and Flower Press published her first volume of poetry in 1952. At the same time, she was involved in editing and researching critical and biographical work on several nineteenth century literary figures, including William Wordsworth, Mary Wollstonecraft Shelley, and Emily Brontë.

Spark's initial attempt at fiction writing received considerable attention when her short story "The Seraph and the Zambesi" won top honors in a writing contest in 1951. She was encouraged to expand her fiction-writing horizons in 1954, when Macmillan, Spark's publisher, persuaded her to write a full-length novel. At the same time that Spark began to develop a strategy or technique for composing a novel, she was also struggling with her religious beliefs and her decision to convert to Catholicism. Consequently, her first novel, *The Comforters*, completed in 1957, examines theological issues, reflecting Spark's own private search for a belief that was consistent with her personal need for an adequate faith during the time that she was writing the novel. The link between her conception of the world, both physically and spiritually, and the subjects of her fiction is evident in her later novels as well.

Muriel Spark is a prolific writer, competent in many genres and unafraid of diversity and experimentation in her forms, plots, characters, and use of narrative voice.

Analysis

Muriel Spark is an adept storyteller. Her narrative voice is often distant or aloof. Her tales are psychologically interesting because Spark is an author who is reluctant to reveal all that her characters think and feel. Readers are forced to evaluate the stories, think about issues from a different perspective, and try to fill in the gaps. Critics regard Spark's novels as her strongest genre, but her short stories are also well constructed and intriguing. Her volumes of short stories, published over a period of thirty years, contain many of the same stories reprinted, with new stories added to each new edition.

Spark's tales are often set in England, a British colony in Africa, or European locations. Her works reflect a sense of moral truth, which some critics view as the influence of her conversion to Catholicism in 1954. Her descriptive narrative is rarely wordy. The story line relies on the impressions and dialogue of the characters or narrator to convey the plot. She makes frequent use of first-person narrative, but none of her voices "tells all." One of the distinguishing elements in Spark's style is her penchant for leaving gaps that her readers must fill for themselves.

Spark's first short story, "The Seraph and the Zambesi," won an award in a Christmas contest sponsored by *The Observer* in 1951. In characteristic Spark style, this story does not mince words but focuses on action and sparse dialogue. Set in Africa at Christmastime, the story portrays the events surrounding preparations for a Christmas pageant. Besides sweltering temperatures, curious natives, and preoccupied performers, the presentation is "hindered" by the presence of a heavenly Seraph, complete with six wings and a heat-producing glow. Though Spark refuses to offer a moral at the close of "The Seraph and the Zambesi," the story resembles a parable, illustrating the egocentrism of human beings, especially "artists." The narrative also serves as a metaphor for the definition of genuine "art."

A related story dealing with art and creativity is entitled "The Playhouse Called Remarkable." This story, published several years after "The Seraph and the Zambesi," features a character named Moon Biglow. Moon confesses to the narrator that he is really a native of the Moon who migrated to Earth on the "Downfall of [the] Uprise" some time in the distant past. His primary mission was to save earth's residents from suffocating aesthetic boredom. It seems human beings had no form of recreation other than that of gathering in groups to chant "Tum tum ya" each evening. The moon migrants organize the "playhouse called Remarkable" to offer alternative entertainment and also to give earthlings a creative outlet for their imaginations. Two additional stories "The Dragon" and "The Fortune Teller," both published in 1988, are also parable-like tales about art and creativity.

Often Spark's short fiction depicts varied types of female personalities. "The Pawnbroker's Wife" and a later story "The Curtain Blown by the Breeze" deal with African colonials. These stories, narrated in first person, tell little about the narrators themselves but focus on the manipulative power of two central female characters. The pawnbroker's wife, Mrs. Jan Cloote, is never identified by her first name. Her pawnbroker husband has disappeared, and Mrs. Cloote carries on the business as the pawnbroker herself but denies the slightly sordid reputation of her vocation by claiming that she is only the pawnbroker's wife. Thus, in her name and her speech, she employs the use of distance to separate her actions from her image. Such "distancing" allows Mrs. Cloote freedom in refusing to accept responsibility for her conduct, no matter how cruel or petty, as she performs the duties of a pawnbroker (and ironically she is far more successful in business than her husband had been). She uses a show of politeness to remain corrupt without having to admit fault or make concessions. Mrs. Cloote's poor taste, grasping manipulation, and innocent pretense give her character an insidious cast. Yet the narrator who reveals these facts refuses to pass judgment regarding Mrs. Cloote's morality. That matter is left to the reader.

In a similar manner, Sonia Van der Merwe, the female protagonist in "The Curtain Blown by the Breeze," also gains power over her domain in the absence of her husband. Mr. Van der Merwe, who lives in the remote territory of Fort Beit, is imprisoned for fatally shooting a young native boy who was a "peeping Tom." While her husband's conviction and imprisonment might have prompted a feeling of tragedy, the opposite occurs. Sonia finds that she has considerable financial resources at her disposal with her husband gone. Like Mrs. Cloote, Sonia takes charge, egged on by the British medical women serving in the colony. She soon learns to use her feminine wiles to access power and control in Fort Beit. The male British medical workers seek her attention, captivated by her "eccentric grandeur." Much to the chagrin of the British women who helped to create the "new Sonia," Sonia gains influence even over government officials. Just as the English nurse, however, who narrates the story can never truly decide what she wants, the same applies to Sonia. Once Mr. Van der Merwe returns from prison, Sonia and her image are quickly eliminated. In these two stories, Spark explores the roles of greedily ambitious females, the irony of their plight, and their cloak of politeness.

Often Spark deals with themes of childhood or adolescent memories in her short fiction. She may contrast the innocent but terrifyingly real fears of children with the more serious cruelty of adults or reverse the irony and explore the cruelty of "devilish" children, who are shielded by a guise of adult politeness. For example, "The Twins" is a story about two seemingly polite children who exercise some invisible but insidious control over their parents and other adults who enter their household. In "Alice Long's Dachshunds," a young girl faces the fearful plight of making a childish mistake with serious consequences. Mamie's innocent neglect of the five dachshunds left in her charge is contrasted with the more dastardly, conscious cruelty of the adults in her world. While Mamie's mistake does no serious harm to the dogs, the animals are brutally treated by an adult in the story.

"The Portobello Road" and "Bang-Bang You're Dead" juxtapose the childhood memories of two young girls with their lives as "grown-ups." These stories explore the serious ramifications of situations in which childish conceptions or antagonisms are transferred into adulthood. Both stories are excellent examples of Muriel Spark's ability to create unique narrative forms. "The Portobello Road" is narrated by Needle, a childhood nickname given to a young girl who found a needle in a haystack. When the story opens, Needle is dead and her ghostly voice chronicles the events that led to her murder—when she becomes the "Needle" who is murdered and buried in a haystack by a childhood friend. (The use of ghosts and the supernatural are also present in two later stories by Spark, "Another Pair of Hands" and "The Executor."

"Bang-Bang You're Dead" connects the present and the past in a related but more complex manner than "The Portobello Road." In the present, represented in the story's opening scene, a group of Sybil's friends gather to view four reels of eighteen-year-old films from Sybil's past years spent in Africa. As the group views the "silent movies," the third-person narrative reveals Sybil's memories—not those seen by the spectators of the film but as Sybil remembers them. As each reel ends, Sybil's mental narrative is interrupted by the surface chatter of her friends, who are impressed by the appearance of the people and exotic scenes revealed in the film. When the final reel ends, the reader finds, through Sybil's mental recollections, that two murders were committed shortly after the scenes were recorded on film. As the acquaintances agree to view the last reel again because it is their "favorite," Sybil remains stoically unmoved by the memories of the tragedy. Her indifference and objectivity regarding the memories of her deceased friends reveal a chilling aspect of her personality. Coldly intellectual and detached, Sybil remains indifferent and unmoved by the recorded memories even though she was largely responsible for the murders. "The Portobello Road" and "Bang-Bang You're Dead" are excellent examples of Spark's ability to manipulate narrative voice while communicating chilling aspects of human nature.

"The Go-Away Bird" is one of the longest of Spark's stories. It is also about a woman and murder. Daphne, the central female figure, is reared in a British colony in Africa. Caught between two cultures, that of the Dutch Afrikaners and the English colonists, Daphne searches for her identity—for a world in which she can not only belong but also find safety. Set in Africa and England during World War II, "The Go-Away Bird" presents characters who reflect diverse backgrounds, personalities, motivations, and societies. Daphne's struggles and her relationship with the African Go-Away Bird illustrate an individual's difficulty in trying to fulfill one's need for love and identity within diverse cultural and social structures.

At the opposite end of the spectrum, "The First Year of My Life" does not struggle with maturing in society but presents the first-person commentary of an infant, born during World War I. The adults who care for the baby treat the child as an "innocent infant," unaware of the newborn's ability to grasp the tragedy of war. Such diversity in narrative voice, subject, and style is a trademark of Muriel Spark. As a writer, she avoids classification and is unafraid of experimentation.

Spark's stories wittily expose human foibles. Her tone can be ironic, mysterious, or satiric. She often introduces elements of the supernatural in her plots. She is adept at illustrating the slightly macabre, evil, or sometimes hypocritical nature of human beings. Her characters may be subtilely malevolent or sinisterly civilized. While her characters might never be thoroughly explained from a psychological view, they are unsettlingly believable in their milieu.

Other major works

NOVELS: *The Comforters*, 1957; *Robinson*, 1958; *Memento Mori*, 1958; *The Ballad of Peckham Rye*, 1960; *The Bachelors*, 1960; *The Prime of Miss Jean Brodie*, 1961; *A Muriel Spark Trio*, 1962 (contains *The Comforters, Memento Mori,* and *The Ballad of Peckham Rye*); *The Girls of Slender Means*, 1963; *The Mandelbaum Gate*, 1965; *The Public Image*, 1968; *The Driver's Seat*, 1970; *Not to Disturb*, 1971; *The Hothouse by the East River*, 1973; *The Abbess of Crewe: A Modern Morality Tale*, 1974; *The Takeover*, 1976; *Territorial Rights*, 1979; *Loitering with Intent*, 1981; *The Only Problem*, 1984; *A Far Cry From Kensington*, 1988; *Symposium*, 1990.

PLAY: *Doctors of Philosophy*, 1962.

POETRY: *The Fanfarlo and Other Verse*, 1952; *Collected Poems I*, 1967 (published as *Going Up to Sotheby's and Other Poems*, 1982).

NONFICTION: *Child of Light: A Reassessment of Mary Wollstonecraft Shelley*, 1951, 1987; *Emily Brontë: Her Life and Work*, 1953 (with Derek Stanford); *John Masefield*, 1953; *Mary Shelley: A Biography*, 1989.

CHILDREN'S LITERATURE: *The Very Fine Clock*, 1968.

EDITED TEXT: *Tribute to Wordsworth*, 1950 (with Derek Stanford); *A Selection of Poems by Emily Brontë*, 1952; *My Best Mary: The Letters of Mary Shelley*, 1953 (with Derek Stanford); *The Letters of the Brontës: A Selection*, 1954; *Letters of John Henry Newman*, 1957 (with Derek Stanford).

Bibliography

Bold, Alan. *Muriel Spark*. London: Methuen, 1986. Bold is concerned with the relationship between Spark's personal background and the development of her characters, particularly links between Spark's religious experience and the religious facets of her fiction. He includes biographical information, then discusses Spark's works in chronological order, specifically the novels. An extensive bibliography is included, listing criticism, articles, essays, interviews, and books related to Spark and her work.

_____, ed. *Muriel Spark: An Odd Capacity for Vision*. Totowa, N.J.: Barnes & Noble Books, 1984. Bold has compiled a collection of nine essays from different contributors, regarding various aspects of Spark's fiction. The volume is organized into two sections. The first four essays explore Spark's background and the content of her work. The remaining chapters contain critical articles centered on the diverse forms of Spark's writings, including discussions of her use of satire, her poetry, and an essay by Tom Hubbard that deals exclusively with her short stories.

Richmond, Velma B. *Muriel Spark*. New York: Frederick Ungar, 1984. Richmond explores Spark's writing in terms of content and emphasis. Spark's novels, poetry, and short stories are discussed in relation to their themes rather than their chronology. The closing chapter includes a discussion of Spark's "comic vision." Richmond includes biographical material along with a detailed chronology, a bibliography, and an extensive index.

Stubbs, Patricia. *Muriel Spark*. Essex: Longman, 1973. Stubbs's essay deals with theme in Spark's novels, from *The Comforters* through *Not to Disturb*. She traces the chronological development of Spark's work, range, and attempts at experimentation. She criticizes Spark's sense of distance and failure to solve problems but praises her efforts to force readers to view the world in a new way.

Whittaker, Ruth. *The Faith and Fiction of Muriel Spark*. New York: St. Martin's Press, 1982. Whittaker's work elaborates on the diversity of Spark's themes, meanings, and purpose. The chapter divisions are organized according to topics—religion, style, structure, and form. The book is limited primarily to a discussion of Spark's novels. Whittaker includes a biographical section as well as an extensive bibliography, notes, and an index.

Paula M. Miller

ELIZABETH SPENCER

Born: Carrollton, Mississippi; July 19, 1921

Principal short fiction
Ship Island and Other Stories, 1968; *Marilee: Three Stories*, 1981; *The Stories of Elizabeth Spencer*, 1981; *Jack of Diamonds and Other Stories*, 1988; *On the Gulf*, 1991.

Other literary forms
In addition to the numerous short stories published in periodicals as well as in book-length collections, Elizabeth Spencer has produced several novels and novellas during the first three and a half decades of her literary career. These include her best-known work, the novella *The Light in the Piazza* (1960), which was made into a film.

Achievements
Spencer has established herself as one of the major fiction writers of the Southern Renaissance, a writer whose subjects and preoccupations have kept pace with the times through which she has lived, while her style has remained unique. Her themes are those frequently found in works by Southern writers. Throughout her career, Spencer has been particularly interested in the influence of memory, the sense of place, and the power of tradition in the life of the individual. Although in theme and complexity she reminds critics of her fellow Southerner William Faulkner and in subtlety of Henry James, no comparisons do justice to Spencer's art, for, as her readers inevitably realize, the voice in Spencer's fiction is unmistakably her own.

In terms of tone, Spencer's fiction might be described as a combination of disciplined detachment from her subject matter and passionate attachment to her Southern roots, to lush, semitropical natural settings, to the rich language of born storytellers, and to the conviction that the past dwells in the present. Spencer is much admired for her craftsmanship, which enables her to handle complexities of time, memory, and imagination so deftly that the shifts of focus are almost imperceptible. It is this combination of intellectual power and disciplined skill that ensure Spencer permanent recognition as one of the important writers of her generation.

Biography
Elizabeth Spencer was born on July 19, 1921, in Carrollton, Mississippi, the daughter of Mary J. McCain Spencer and James L. Spencer, a businessman. Both her mother's family and that of her father had lived in northern Mississippi for almost a century. Spencer's childhood was almost an ideal one for a writer. Her mother and her mother's family gave her a passion for books, and her father, who took her on hunting trips, gave her a love of nature. During long summer visits to the McCain

plantation, she developed an appreciation of the land. Meanwhile, like the character in her short stories who she says most resembles her, the intensely curious Marilee Summerall, Spencer was storing local legends and gossip. She would never lack material for her fiction, and even as a child, she had begun to write.

After graduating from her local high school, Spencer attended Belhaven College, a Presbyterian girls' school in Jackson, Mississippi. There, she edited a newspaper, won awards for fiction and poetry, and became a friend of Eudora Welty, who lived across the street from the college. Welty comments in her foreword to *The Stories of Elizabeth Spencer* that although Spencer could giggle as much as any other Southern girl, there was a seriousness and determination about her that convinced Welty that she would indeed become a writer. After receiving her B.A., Spencer went to Vanderbilt University in Nashville, carrying with her a partially completed novel. While there, she encountered the Fugitive scholar and writer Donald Davidson, who later helped her to get a book contract for the novel by submitting several chapters to an editor at the publishing firm Dodd, Mead. In 1948, the book was published under the title *Fire in the Morning.* Meanwhile, after receiving her M.A. from Vanderbilt University in 1943, Spencer taught English at Northwest Mississippi Junior College in Senatobia and at Ward-Belmont College in Nashville, Tennessee. She also worked for a year as a reporter for the Nashville *Tennessean.* In 1948, she went to the University of Mississippi to teach creative writing while she worked on *This Crooked Way* (1952). After this second novel was published, Spencer was given an award by the National Institute of Arts and Letters, which enabled her to spend a summer in New York. In 1953, she went to Italy on a Guggenheim Fellowship. There, Spencer met and married an Englishman from Cornwall, John Arthur Blackwood Rusher, a language school director.

After five years in Italy, Spencer and Rusher moved to Montreal, Canada, where he had been offered a position. That city was to be their home for twenty-eight years. For most of that time, Spencer worked full-time at her writing, publishing novels, novellas, and short stories at regular intervals. In 1976, however, she began to teach creative writing courses and conduct workshops at Concordia University in Montreal. In 1986, Spencer and her husband moved to Chapel Hill, North Carolina. There, she continued to write, while also teaching courses in creative writing at the University of North Carolina.

Analysis

For the subject matter of her novels and novellas, Elizabeth Spencer often chooses issues tied to a particular place and time; for example, *The Voice at the Back Door* (1956) deals with changing attitudes toward race after World War II; *The Salt Line* (1984), set on the Mississippi Gulf Coast, describes the transformation of that area after Hurricane Camille; and *The Night Travellers* (1991) examines the ongoing plight of the Vietnam War period activists. In most of Spencer's short stories, however, the narrative is less clearly dependent on a particular time in history. Instead, in the tradition of her medium, Spencer concentrates on a brief period in an individual's life, when that person comes to recognize some need or some truth.

The themes of Spencer's short stories remain constant from her earliest works to her later ones. One of these themes pits the demands for social conformity, often expressed in the family, against an individual's need for freedom; similarly, the conflict may be internalized, with the individual torn between two desires, one for security, the other for independence. A related theme is the search for identity, particularly by women, whose enslavement to conformity has been especially evident in the conservative South. In addition, there is always a moral element in a Spencer story; to her, evil is very real, and her characters make difficult choices between good and evil. Spencer also recognizes, however, the fact that fate, or chance, can restrict those choices. Finally, as a writer, she is conscious of the importance of imagination and memory as part of life; these human faculties can torment or liberate her characters.

It is the imagination that dominates the earliest story in *The Stories of Elizabeth Spencer*, "The Little Brown Girl." The story is told in the third person, but the point of view is limited to that of the seven-year-old white girl, Maybeth, who is charmed by a black man, Jim Williams, who works for her father. Maybeth loves Jim's stories, some of which she knows he invented. She chooses, however, to believe one of them, that he has a little girl who is going to come and play with her. Even though her parents tell her that Jim is not telling the truth, and even though she half knows it, Maybeth lets herself think about the little girl and even gives Jim her own birthday money, supposedly to buy the little girl a dress. Prompted by Jim, she even sees a glimpse of her playmate in the yellow dress. At this point, frightened, Maybeth runs home to her mother's arms. What Spencer leaves unstated is the source of Maybeth's fear. Is it the fact that she can be so deceived by a friend, or is it the fact that her imagination can be prompted to see the unseen? Obviously, Maybeth is too young to analyze her own reactions. Even with adult protagonists, Spencer frequently ends her short stories with this kind of uncertainty, which leaves room for the reader's interpretation.

"First Dark" and "A Southern Landscape" illustrate the conflict between conformity and independence, the security to be found in family and home and the freedom to be experienced when one escapes. In "First Dark," Frances Harvey is surprised to find her elderly mother urging her marriage to Tommy Beavers, whose family background is distinctly inferior to that of the Harveys. In fact, Mrs. Harvey evidently commits suicide in order to make sure that she will not stand in the way of the marriage. What both Frances and Tommy know, however, is that the house in which Mrs. Harvey has expected them to live would possess them and stifle them. At the end of the story, Tommy insists that Frances leave with him, and she chooses to do so.

In "A Southern Landscape," however, the earliest of the Marilee Summerall stories, Spencer reveals her very real appreciation of those things that never change, symbolized by Windsor, an antebellum mansion that is in ruins, and by Foster Hamilton, whom Marilee is dating. Like the mansion, Foster has grace. He so admires

Marilee's mother, his ideal of Southern womanhood, that simply the suggestion of her presence can shock him into instant sobriety. Foster, too, is already in ruins, joyfully addicted to drink. Years later, when she tells the story, Marilee rejoices that some things have not changed, among them, the mansion Windsor, the heaven-pointing hand on the Presbyterian church, and Foster Hamilton's addiction. Obviously, Spencer is not arguing for alcoholism; her point, instead, has to do with permanence: "I feel the need of a land, of a sure terrain, of a sort of permanent landscape of the heart."

Spencer does realize that this sense of a sure terrain may be one of the fringe benefits that comes with an assured place in society, such as that which is given at birth to a Harvey or a Summerall. Tommy Beavers knows that if he stays in the Harvey house, it will possess and govern him; he will become less than nothing. Similarly, in "Ship Island," one of the stories to which Spencer frequently refers, Nancy Lewis is painfully aware that she is, and always will be, an outsider in Mississippi Gulf Coast society. Her family has no money, no background, and no taste. Nancy is accepted by the young aristocrats only because one of them has chosen to sponsor her, and even then, she must watch every word she says, every move she makes. Perhaps she could have moved into that society, but as the story progresses, Nancy rebels against her own denial of her self. The subtitle, "The Story of a Mermaid," suggests that Nancy will die if she attempts to live out of her own natural element, where she can be free. In order to save herself, she runs off to New Orleans with a couple of men she has picked up. The action is heroic; certainly it could have caused Nancy's death. When she returns home, however, she knows that she can never become a part of Gulf Coast society. That society will no longer accept her. Therefore she need not worry about being tempted to do something that she knows is wrong: to deny her own self in order to become socially and financially secure.

In an essay on Spencer, Elsa Nettels points out that after the mid-1950's, the theme of women's search for their identity took on major importance in Spencer's fiction. Certainly the long short story "Knights and Dragons," which was expanded into a novella and published separately, is concerned with this issue. The title is significant: trained from childhood to look for knights to rescue them from dragons, women often mistake selfish, destructive men for good, protective ones. Thus Martha Ingram knows that her divorced husband is determined to play psychological games with her, but she cannot resist reacting when he decides to pull her strings, either with a letter from his lawyer or with carefully chosen clippings sent in the mail. Clearly, Gordon Ingram is her dragon. Fortunately, two other men help Martha to break free from her husband's tyranny. Naturally, she sees them as her chivalric knights, providentially appearing to protect their lady. Martha comes to understand, however, that life is not so simple. In their own benevolent way, these knights are as oppressive as her dragon husband. Like him, they demand the surrender of her identity; each of them has invented a role that she must play. That is the price of a knight's protection. At the end of the story, Martha realizes that she has freed herself from all roles. In a kind of death of the old self, she has become truly free.

Although Spencer never resorts to simplistic delineations of good and evil, it is obvious that she does believe in those opposing forces. Even though Gordon Ingram's friends find him delightful, it is obvious that he is motivated by malice in his attempt to destroy Martha. Clearly, there is a difference between malice such as his and simple nonconformity, which seeks to harm no one. "The Bufords," for example, is the story of an unequal battle between a young schoolteacher and a large family of people who seem to live life simply for the joy of it. The teacher is determined to discipline the Buford children. Unable to make headway at school, she goes to see their parents. There, she discovers that the behavior that she has found outrageous is simply a source of pride to the rest of the family. The adults all find it wonderful that their offspring are the most irrepressible in school. The fact that there is no ill-will in the Buford temperament, however, is shown by the warm hospitality that they offer the teacher. Although they do not understand her, they forgive her for lashing out at their children. Actually, they consider her, and her way of thinking, simply a bit exotic, as if she were a member of another species or of another society. At the end of the story, the well-meaning teacher realizes not only that she has been defeated by the family at whose table she has just been entertained but also that she has been adopted by them, as an interesting if peculiar pet, like their possum in a cage.

The sense of family, which is treated so comically in "The Bufords," is at the center of a very different narrative, set not in the Deep South but in Montreal. "Jean-Pierre" is a love story, in which a Protestant, English-speaking woman and a Catholic, French-speaking man marry and then begin to understand each other. After the couple have been married almost a year, Jean-Pierre Courtois disappears without any explanation to his young wife. Courageously, she gets a job, endures her loneliness, and waits until he returns. In the meantime, she picks up bits and pieces of knowledge about him and his people, enough to know that, for some reason, he had to go to his home. When Jean-Pierre returns, his wife is waiting. Despite being tempted to leave him, she has remained faithful. At that point, then, he is ready to change his emotional address and to establish a new home with her.

Like "Jean-Pierre," most of Spencer's short stories are essentially optimistic. Her characters have proven their courage by being willing to seek understanding, both of themselves and of their relationship to their families and their societies. After the concluding revelation, it is implied that Spencer's protagonists, armed with that understanding and that courage, are ready to seek their destinies.

Other major works

LONG FICTION: *Fire in the Morning*, 1948; *This Crooked Way*, 1952; *The Voice at the Back Door*, 1956; *The Light in the Piazza*, 1960; *Knights and Dragons*, 1965; *No Place for an Angel*, 1967; *The Snare*, 1972; *The Salt Line*, 1984; *The Night Travellers*, 1991.

Bibliography

Nettels, Elsa. "Elizabeth Spencer." In *Southern Women Writers: The New Generation*, edited by Tonette Bond Inge. Tuscaloosa: University of Alabama Press, 1990.

This insightful essay draws on biographical details, as well as on comments in a number of published interviews with Spencer, in order to trace the development of her art and thought. The extensive annotations and the list of interviews in the bibliography are particularly helpful.

Phillips, Robert. "The Art of Fiction CX: Elizabeth Spencer." *The Paris Review* 31 (Summer, 1989): 184-213. A lengthy series of questions and answers assembled from Phillips' three interviews with Spencer, as well as from some questions submitted in written form. Focuses on her theories about writing and her personal approach to the practice of her craft. The essay contains some interesting comments about literary influences on her work. A one-page typed draft, with handwritten corrections, from a short story is printed opposite the initial page of the article.

Prenshaw, Peggy Whitman. *Elizabeth Spencer.* Boston: Twayne, 1985. An authoritative book-length study based on numerous interviews with the author and checked by her for factual accuracy. The novella *Knights and Dragons* and "Ship Island" are treated together; other short stories are discussed in another chapter. Contains a chronology and a helpful select bibliography.

_____. "Mermaids, Angels, and Free Women: The Heroines of Elizabeth Spencer's Fiction." In *Women Writers of the Contemporary South*, edited by Peggy Whitman Prenshaw. Jackson: University Press of Mississippi, 1984. Argues that in Spencer's later fiction, strong female heroines characteristically move from confusion through pain and dislocation to assertion of the self, courageously accepting the alienation which that implies.

Spencer, Elizabeth. "Elizabeth Spencer: The Southern Writer Optimistically Explores the Almost Impenetrable Mysteries of the Human Heart." Interview by Amanda Smith. *Publishers Weekly* 234 (September 9, 1988): 111-112. This interview took place after Spencer's return to the South, where she established a permanent residence. Focuses on Spencer's assessment of her own relationship with the South. Includes perceptive comments by the author about the stories in the collection *Jack of Diamonds and Other Stories.*

Welty, Eudora. Foreword to *The Stories of Elizabeth Spencer.* Garden City, N.Y.: Doubleday, 1981. Welty offers a brief but significant description of her first meeting with Spencer and the friendship that developed between the two writers. Welty's succinct evaluation of Spencer as a writer who is both part of the Southern tradition and uniquely herself is essential reading for students.

Winchell, Mark Royden. "A Golden Ball of Thread: The Achievement of Elizabeth Spencer." *The Sewanee Review* 97 (Fall, 1989): 581-586. In this overview of Spencer's fiction, Winchell argues that its excellence can be explained, at least in part, by two facts: that moral issues and moral decisions are inherently complex, and that real independence can be attained only by someone who recognizes and accepts every human being's need for a memory of home.

Rosemary M. Canfield Reisman

JEAN STAFFORD

Born: Covina, California; July 1, 1915
Died: White Plains, New York; March 26, 1979

Principal short fiction
Children Are Bored on Sunday, 1953; *Bad Characters*, 1964; *The Collected Stories of Jean Stafford*, 1969.

Other literary forms
Jean Stafford's first three books were novels, *Boston Adventure* (1944), *The Mountain Lion* (1947), and *The Catherine Wheel* (1952). She also published juvenile fiction and a short, book-length interview with the mother of Lee Harvey Oswald, *A Mother in History* (1966).

Achievements
Although critics suggest that her insightful, carefully crafted fiction deserves more attention, Stafford is generally considered to be a minor writer. Best known for her more than forty short stories, which—like her novels—are largely autobiographical, Stafford investigates the complexities of human nature and explores the powerlessness of women in society as a major theme. Her treatment of women has generally been viewed as a metaphor for universal human alienation in modern society.

Stafford's reputation as a fiction writer was established with the publication of *Boston Adventure* in 1944, the same year she was awarded a prize by *Mademoiselle*. Over the years, she received numerous other awards, including grants from the National Institute of Arts and Letters, the Guggenheim and Rockefeller foundations, and the National Press Club. She also received an O. Henry Memorial Award for her story "In the Zoo" in 1955 and the Pulitzer Prize for *The Collected Stories* in 1970.

Biography
Although born in California, where she spent part of her childhood, Jean Stafford grew up in Colorado, attended the University of Colorado (A.M., 1936), and did postgraduate work at the University of Heidelberg. Her father, at one time a reporter, had written a number of Western stories. After a year teaching at Stephens College in Missouri and then briefly at the Writer's Workshop in Iowa, Stafford decided to focus on her own writing and moved to Boston. There she married poet Robert Lowell in 1940; they were divorced in 1948. After a short marriage to Oliver Jensen in 1950, Stafford married again in 1959—to A. J. Liebling, critic and columnist for *The New Yorker*. After Liebling's death in 1963, Stafford withdrew from the New York literary world and made her home in Springs, Long Island. There she lived, becoming more and more reclusive, until her death in 1979.

Analysis

It is clear from a brief preface she wrote for *The Collected Stories* that Jean Stafford did not wish to be considered a regional writer. Her father and her mother's cousin had both written books about the West, but she had read neither before she began writing. Moreover, as soon as she could, she "hotfooted it across the Rocky Mountains and across the Atlantic Ocean" and came back to the West only for short periods. Her roots might therefore remain in Colorado but the rest of her abided "in the South or the Midwest or New England or New York." The short stories in this collection, which span twenty-five years of her productive life, she grouped under headings that both insisted on the national and international character of her art and echoed universally known writers with whom she clearly wished to associate herself: Henry James, Mark Twain, Thomas Mann.

It is true, as one discovers from the stories themselves, Stafford's fiction is not limited geographically but is set in such widely separated places as Colorado, Heidelberg, France, New York, and Boston; if, therefore, one thinks of these stories as the result of social observation they do indeed have the broad national and international scope their author claimed for them. Her stories, however—and this may have been as apparent to Stafford as it has been to some of her critics—are not so much the result of observation and intellectual response as they are expressions of Stafford's personal view of life, a reflection of her own feeling of having been betrayed by family and friends. Her protagonists are often girls or young women, pitted against persons who feel themselves superior but are revealed to be morally, emotionally, or even physically corrupt. Although Stafford's fiction was all but forgotten at the time of her death, it has been rediscovered by a new generation of readers, mainly through the work of feminist scholars. This is ironic because Stafford herself did not embrace feminist views and, in fact, spoke harshly about aspects of the feminist movement.

The thirty stories in Stafford's *The Collected Stories* are unified by one pervasive theme, illness—physical, mental, and emotional—and the snobbery which she finds an accompaniment, the snobbery of aberrant behavior. Fascinated, repelled, and at times outraged by the way illness can be used to purchase power over vulnerable individuals, Stafford describes the various forms of this currency, the number of places where it can be spent, and the way it can be used by those of any age or sex willing to employ it. The emotional and physical invalids in these stories clearly think themselves superior to ordinary folk, and the tensions built up in these stories are often the result of conflicts between a protagonist (who usually appears to speak for the author) and neurotic individuals who think themselves justified in exploiting others. Sometimes there is an actual physical sickness—disease, old age—but the illness or psychological aberration frequently becomes a metaphor for moral corruption.

In "Maggie Meriwether's Rich Experience" the protagonist is a naïve young American woman from Tennessee visiting in France, where she has been invited to spend the weekend at a fashionable country house. There she discovers a crowd of titled

Europeans, rich, overdressed, and eccentric, who look down their collective nose at the simple girl from the American South. The reader, who sees through the eyes of the young American, sees how stupid and arrogant these aristocrats are and understands Maggie's relief at escaping to Paris where she telephones the older brother of her roommate at Sweet Briar and spends the evening delighting in the wholesome provincialism of her Southern American friends, regaling them with stories about her recent experience.

In "The Echo and the Nemesis" the combination of neurosis and snobbery becomes more convincingly sinister. The story is also set in Europe, in Heidelberg, but the two main characters are Americans. The protagonist, Sue, appears to be a rather unexceptional young woman from a family of ordinary means; the "invalid," Ramona, is an enormously fat girl from a very rich family (so she says), living permanently in Italy. Sue is at first impressed by Ramona's learning and by the stories she tells of her family's wealth, and the two girls become constant companions. At first the relationship, with frequent meetings in cafés, becomes routine, like another philosophy lecture or seminar in Schiller, but then Ramona begins a series of revelations about herself and her family that embarrass, mystify, and then entrance Sue. Ramona reveals that she had a twin sister who died at an early age, a beautiful girl of whom there are many drawings and paintings, and whose room had been turned into a shrine. Ramona next reveals that she has come to Heidelberg not to study but to lose weight, and she enlists Sue's aid. Captivated by Ramona's stories about her loose-living family, Sue readily accepts an invitation to visit Ramona's brothers at a ski resort in Switzerland.

Thereafter Ramona begins to change. She misses lunches, fails to show up for appointments, and wildly indulges herself in food. When Sue makes inquiries about the coming trip and questions her about her doctor, Ramona snaps at her and, once, even slaps her face. Ramona tells Sue that she (Sue) resembles her dead sister Martha and implies that the trip to Switzerland must therefore be called off, since Ramona's family would be too upset by the resemblance. Ramona's mysterious behavior is partially explained by Sue's discovery in Ramona's room of a photograph of a younger, thinner, and beautiful Ramona. In a final scene prior to Ramona's departure from Heidelberg, the revelation about her is made complete: Sue promises to remain her friend, and Ramona replies " 'Oh, no, no, there would be nothing in it for you. Thank you just the same. I am exceptionally ill.' She spoke with pride, as if she were really saying, I am exceptionally talented' or 'I am exceptionally attractive.' " When Sue responds, "I'm sorry," Ramona snaps back, "I'm not sorry. It is for yourself that you should be sorry. You have such a trivial little life, poor girl. It's not your fault. Most people do."

The neurotics in Stafford's stories are not always so aggressive and unappealing. In "The Bleeding Heart" an elderly dandy who is browbeaten by his invalid mother attempts to establish a "fatherly" relationship with a young Mexican girl who has come East and works as a secretary in a "discreet girl's boarding school." The girl is at first impressed with the old gentleman's aristocratic bearing and imagines she would like him for a stepfather, but when she visits his mother with a plant, a gift from the school, she is appalled by the odors, the repellent condition of the mother, and the disgusting behavior of a parrot. When the old man attempts to force his attentions on her, she turns on him and tells him to leave her alone. "Rose," he tells her, "All I am asking is a little pity."

A briefer summary of several other stories will show how pervasive is this theme in Stafford's stories, both in the way characters are conceived and relationships established, and in the way the main action is resolved. The point of the story "The Liberation" has to do with the way an old couple, pathetic in their loneliness, try to prevent their young niece from marrying. At her announcement of her forthcoming marriage in Boston to a teacher at Harvard (the story takes place in Colorado), the aunt (who "suffers" from chronic asthma) wrings her hands and her uncle glares at her and both are outraged at the idea of her marrying and going off to live somewhere else. The story takes a curious turn as word comes that the girl's fiancé has died of a heart attack. The girl is at first stunned and about to resign herself to remaining in Colorado, but her uncle and aunt try to "appropriate" her grief and bind her even faster to themselves. In a panic, without luggage, the girl flees for Boston and her emotional freedom from the "niggling hypochondriacs she had left behind."

"The Healthiest Girl in Town" also takes place in Colorado, where a girl, whose mother is a practical nurse in a town inhabited mainly by tuberculous patients and their families, is forced to become friends with two sisters because her mother nurses the girls' grandmother. At first the girl is impressed with the sisters (they also have illnesses) and their Eastern pretentiousness and ashamed of her own good health, but then, after a quarrel with them, she proudly declares herself to be the healthiest girl in town.

Two other Easterners also proud of their abnormalities are a Boston spinster in "The Hope Chest" who delights in humiliating her maid and in tricking a boy who comes to her door selling Christmas wreaths into kissing her, and an elderly woman in "Life Is No Abyss" from a rich and socially prominent Boston family whom she punishes by going to the poorhouse and allowing them to come and observe her in her impoverishment. "A Country Love Story" also deals with an invalid, in this instance a writer who neglects his wife and then accuses her of being unfaithful to him and so drives her to the brink of insanity. Other characters include a woman (in "The End of a Career") who devotes her life to looking beautiful and dies when her hands betray her age and a woman ("Beatrice Trublood's Story") who marries three times and each time selects the same brutal kind of husband.

"Bad Characters," which is perhaps Stafford's most amusing story, treats her usual theme comically. Here the neurotic invalid is cast as a vagabond girl with an appealing swagger, a female Huck Finn but without Huck's decency. She charms the daughter of a respectable family into shoplifting and, when the two are caught, feigns deaf-and-dumbness and allows the respectable girl (the protagonist) to bear the responsibility alone.

F. Scott Fitzgerald said that a writer has but one story to tell. Stafford tells hers in many different places, about people from rather different social levels, ages, education, and backgrounds: there is almost always an innocent charmed or somehow trapped by neurotic individuals from whom she finally escapes. Sometimes Stafford gives the stage to this neurotic individual and gradually peels away the mystery that always shrouds those who think themselves superior to others. The story holds up well in the retelling, for it is a universal and timeless theme.

Other major works

NOVELS: *Boston Adventure*, 1944; *The Mountain Lion*, 1947; *The Catherine Wheel*, 1952; *A Winter's Tale*, 1954.

NONFICTION: *A Mother in History*, 1966.

CHILDREN'S LITERATURE: *Arabian Nights: The Lion and the Carpenter and Other Tales from the Arabian Nights, Retold*, 1959; *Elephi: The Cat with the High I.Q.*, 1962.

Bibliography

Avila, Wanda. *Jean Stafford: A Comprehensive Bibliography.* New York: Garland, 1983. This reference contains short summaries of 220 publications by Stafford (books, stories, articles, essays, book and movie reviews) and 428 critical works about her.

Goodman, Charlotte. *Jean Stafford: The Savage Heart.* Austin: University of Texas Press, 1990. This 390-page literary biography emphasizes the connections between Stafford's life and art, with their often contradictory demands. Drawing heavily from Jean Stafford's letters, it is well researched and makes interesting reading.

Oates, Joyce Carol. "The Interior Castle: The Art of Jean Stafford's Short Fiction." *Shenandoah* 30 (Spring, 1979): 61-64. Part of a memorial issue for Jean Stafford, this article looks closely at characters in some of Stafford's short stories. The issue also includes Stafford's last story, "Woden's Day," which was extracted from her unfinished novel *The Parliament of Women*; parts of Stafford's letters to friends; and essays and reminiscences by Peter Taylor, Nancy Flagg, Howard Moss, Dorothea Straus, and Wilfrid Sheed.

Roberts, David. *Jean Stafford: A Biography.* Boston: Little, Brown, 1988. This comprehensive, 494-page biography includes photographs and a select bibliography of primary and secondary sources.

Ryan, Maureen. *Innocence and Estrangement in the Fiction of Jean Stafford.* Baton Rouge: Louisiana State University Press, 1987. This detailed study of Stafford's themes and technique includes two chapters that focus on the feminine situations Stafford creates in her short fiction. Supplemented by a bibliography.

Walsh, Mary Ellen Williams. *Jean Stafford.* Boston: Twayne, 1985. This extended critique examines Stafford's fiction from the perspective of the stages in women's lives: childhood, adolescence, young womanhood, maturity, and old age. It gives considerable attention to her stories, both collected and uncollected, and includes a chronology and select bibliography.

W. J. Stuckey
(Revised by *Jean C. Fulton*)

RICHARD STEELE

Born: Dublin, Ireland; March, 1672
Died: Carmarthen, Wales; September 1, 1729

Principal short fiction

The Tatler, 1709-1711 (with Joseph Addison; periodical essays); *The Spectator*, 1711-1712, 1714 (with Addison; periodical essays); *The Englishman*, 1713-1714, 1715 (periodical essays); *The Guardian*, 1713 (with Addison; periodical essays); *The Lover*, 1714 (periodical essays).

Other literary forms

Richard Steele is well known for his four plays, his prose work, *The Christian Hero* (1701), and his later periodicals. His plays are strongly didactic in purpose and tone, and this intention carries over to his short fiction in his periodicals. Perceived as a reformer of the stage, Steele was named Governor of the Drury Lane Theatre in order to improve the moral tone of the playhouse. His last play, *The Conscious Lovers* (1722), is often identified as "sentimental" drama whose influence changed the course of the English theater.

Achievements

Steele enjoyed a well-rounded and successful writing career. He was well known as "Mr. Spectator" and enjoyed a tremendous success with his daily. Nearly all fashionable London knew about *The Spectator*, and its influence on the taste, fashion, and opinions of the well-to-do is hard to discount. Steele was also widely influential when he began his dramatic career. His play *The Conscious Lovers* was touted as a new genre, the domestic comedy. It was controversial because it broke the dramatic rules of the day, but the controversy merely improved its popularity. Steele increased his influence on Londoners yet again when he became stage manager of Drury Lane, one of the leading theaters. He became responsible for deciding the very plays they would see in an era when the theater was the major source of entertainment. In 1714, Steele was knighted, having served the government's cause through his writing.

Biography

Educated at the Charterhouse and the University of Oxford, Richard Steele lived in England and made his living first as a soldier and later as a writer and a politician. Although his plays and periodicals earned him some money, he always seemed to be in debt. He married Margaret Ford Stretch in 1705, but, unfortunately, she died the following year. In 1707, he married Mary Scurlock, owner of a small estate in Wales where he ultimately retired. He became the major propagandist for the Whigs from 1710 to 1714, when they were the opposition, and after the Whigs regained power under King George I in 1714, he was knighted as a reward for his industriousness in the Whig cause. His later life was filled with financial difficulties, family problems, and political discouragement; after a stroke, he retired to Wales in 1724, where he died in 1729.

Analysis

Richard Steele's short fiction appears in *The Tatler, The Spectator,* and *The Guardian,* as well as in some shorter periodicals. There is a double level of fiction in all three of these periodicals: the first is the fictional creation of the narrator and his family or club, with all the telling details that make Steele's narrators interesting; the second is the storytelling of the narrator himself. The narrator of *The Tatler* is Isaac Bickerstaff, a name made popular by Jonathan Swift in his attack on the astrologer John Partridge. Bickerstaff is an elderly, benevolent astrologer who enjoys relating humorous stories about his family and friends while good-naturedly poking fun at himself. In contrast, *The Spectator* has as its narrator Mr. Spectator, the most taciturn member of The Spectator Club and the undisputed master observer of human nature and human foibles. Because of his careful observation of those around him, Mr. Spectator is an excellent storyteller as well. Finally, the narrator of *The Guardian* is Nestor Ironside, the feisty protector of the Lizard family and adviser to the British nation. To a large degree, *The Tatler* and *The Spectator* are the mutual creation of Steele and his friend and schoolfellow Joseph Addison, although Steele alone signed his name to the final issue of both periodicals; in contrast, *The Guardian* is largely Steele's and is generally recognized as inferior to the two earlier works. Steele's contribution to these works is a lively imagination and a facile wit; he promotes benevolence as the proper response to the sorrows and sufferings of one's fellow humans, and he satirizes slavish adherence to fashion. Plain-dealing honesty and kindly benevolence are Steele's major moral themes in both *The Tatler* and *The Spectator*; Steele's didactic purpose is always foremost, in both his fiction and his plays.

In *The Tatler,* Isaac Bickerstaff enjoys teaching the correct way to treat one's spouse by describing his sister's marital problems. Poor Jenny Distaff has more than her share of difficulties to overcome with her spouse, Tranquillus; Isaac's bachelor wisdom helps them both to achieve happiness. The essential problem is Jenny's desire for domination over her husband, and Isaac teaches her to accept her husband's superior position in marriage. At first glance, it appears that Steele is preaching a very reactionary attitude toward marriage; however, this is not quite the case. Steele believes that women are people, not objects, and that they must be treated as thinking human beings by their husbands. Such an attitude was not universally held by men in the early eighteenth century, and, although Steele's attitude may seem conservative by today's standards, he deserves to be credited with some advancement of women's situations in his own century. For example, he decries the double standard of sexual morality and the marriage contract based solely on financial considerations. Women were losers in both situations, and Steele saw and spoke against what he considered serious social evils. In *The Tatler*, Steele is master of the dramatic scene, nowhere better exemplified than in the reconciliation between Jenny and Tranquillus through the efforts of Isaac Bickerstaff.

It is reasonable to assert that Steele was fascinated by all the various pleasures and problems in domestic relationships. Primary, of course, are courtship, marriage, and married life, but the parent-child relationship was also very important to Steele. Mr. Spectator enjoys almost nothing more than a didactic story about the improvement of marital relations, parent-child relations, or a study of the potential for happiness in an impending marriage. *The Spectator* proves the ideal vehicle for these short, succinct stories, providing a different story daily and a need for constant reinforcement of central themes. One of Steele's often reinforced themes is the difficulty caused by parents who insist on choosing a spouse for their child. In *The Spectator* 533, in a letter appealing to Mr. Spectator's sense of justice, a male correspondent describes his unhappy situation as his elderly family insist that they choose their son's wife. This twenty-two-year-old is pleading for assistance: "You have often given us very excellent Discourses against that unnatural Custom of Parents, in forcing their Children to marry contrary to their Inclinations." The same theme in a different setting appears in *The Spectator* 220, in a letter from a twenty-one-year-old woman to an elderly suitor who is appealing to her father and not to her. She complains stridently of the injustice foisted upon her by a father and a suitor who believe that she must accept the suitor because her father does. Steele lets the letter communicate its message without additional comment, but it is clear that he wholly supports the unjustly treated young woman.

Steele enjoyed using the letter device as a mode of developing his short fictions; he used letters, for example, much more often than did Addison. Letters helped him to develop various perspectives, which are more effectively presented through various points of view than through Steele's voice alone. A parallel example might be the epistolary format in Samuel Richardson's *Clarissa* (1747-1748), where four perspectives are well developed through letters. Steele is interested in brevity as well as perspective, and yet his need as an author to create perspectives other than his own is similar to Richardson's. Steele presents another of his favorite themes in a letter to Mr. Spectator from an admirer in *The Spectator* 268, wherein the correspondent laments the tragedy of so many people marrying for the wrong reasons. What are these wrong reasons? They are: money, position, power. What then are proposed as the right reasons to marry? They are: virtue, wisdom, a person's good qualities, good humor, similar manners and attitudes. In this letter—and throughout Steele's writings—marriage is spoken of reverently, as the state which may "give us the compleatest Happiness this Life is capable of." For this to happen, however, Steele warns repeatedly through precept and example, men and women must be free to choose their spouses on the basis of lasting and endearing qualities.

One of the most famous stories in *The Spectator*, "Inkle and Yarico," depicts the suffering and misery of a less than circumspect love. In *The Spectator* 11, Steele describes the selfish and mean treatment by Mr. Thomas Inkle of an Indian maiden who trusted him completely. Inkle, having landed with a group of Englishmen in America, was attacked by Indians and retreated into the woods, where he was found and protected by Yarico, the Indian maid. They fell in love, he made great promises of wealth and comfort, and, when the ship came, Yarico left her people to go with Inkle. Shortly thereafter and safe once again with his own people, Inkle sold Yarico to a Barbadian merchant as a slave. The story is a warning to both sexes, but especially to women, to be circumspect in choosing a mate. Although the potential for great happiness does exist in marriage, numerous traps for the unwary, Steele warns, may make marriage a source of great unhappiness as well.

On another narrative level, two members of Mr. Spectator's club, Sir Roger de Coverley and Sir Andrew Freeport, provide a continuing story line and numerous little anecdotes. Sir Roger is an old-fashioned country squire, while Sir Andrew is a vigorous, intelligent merchant. Whereas loveable Sir Roger's ideas are as out of date as his clothing, Sir Andrew's clear concepts on the role of trade in England's future are of the utmost importance. Usually these two club members get along well, but when an argument develops on the relative value of merchants to the British nation, Sir Andrew proves his superiority. Many of these little stories subtly identify the Tories with Sir Roger and the Whigs with Sir Andrew. Both Steele and Addison were wholeheartedly committed Whigs, and, despite their assurances that *The Spectator* was nonpolitical, their political beliefs inevitably surfaced. Their propaganda is delightfully subtle, as it slowly proves Sir Roger's ineffectiveness and Sir Andrew's undeniable capability.

As one might suppose, Steele remained consistent in his attitudes on marriage, parent-child relationships, and politics as he discontinued writing for *The Spectator* in order to begin *The Guardian*. Although in some places the tone does become more stern and foreboding, there are still delightful stories in *The Guardian* that promote the values of charity, benevolence, and love rather than authority, and unselfishness rather than self-centeredness. For example, Nestor Ironside himself, although he would like to appear stern and crusty, exemplifies in his own story an overriding concern with the joys and sufferings of those about him. Nestor accepts the responsibility of guiding the Lizard family upon the death of his good friend, Sir Marmaduke Lizard. The lessons he inculcates in the family are based on love of neighbor rather than of self; he leads the daughters away from vanity and pride, while he admonishes the eldest son against keeping a mistress.

Steele's approach to moral issues remained essentially fixed from 1701, the date of his lengthy explication of moral values in his prose tract, *The Christian Hero*. Steele argued there that reason is incapable of guiding the passions to virtue, that only religion is capable of aiding reason sufficiently to guide the passions effectively, and that once so directed the passions may become an additional impetus to virtue. Steele posits in *The Christian Hero* a fundamentally irrational view of human nature. For this reason, perhaps, he teaches morality in his periodicals not by precept and argument but by example and story.

The influence of *The Tatler* and *The Spectator*, and to a lesser degree *The Guard-*

ian, was extraordinary. When one realizes that each periodical lasted less than two years, the fact of such widespread influence is all the more remarkable. In both England and America, *The Spectator* was revered in many families as a repository of moral teaching as well as an entertaining book, and one may imagine that there were many, such as Benjamin Franklin, who developed a polished writing style through imitation of *The Spectator*. Although some topics contemporary to the eighteenth century may appear of little interest today, many of the stories still prove enjoyable for twentieth century readers.

Other major works

PLAYS: *The Funeral: Or, Grief à-la-mode*, 1701; *The Lying Lover: Or, The Ladies' Friendship*, 1703, (based on Pierre Corneille's play *Le Menteur*); *The Tender Husband: Or, The Accomplished Fools*, 1705 (based on Molière's play *Le Sicilien*); *The Conscious Lovers*, 1722, (based on Terence's play *Andria*); *The Plays of Richard Steele*, 1971 (Shirley Strum Kenny, editor).

POETRY: *The Procession*, 1695; *Prologue to the University of Oxford*, 1706; *Epilogue to the Town*, 1721; *The Occasional Verse of Richard Steele*, 1952 (Rae Blanchard, editor).

NONFICTION: *The Christian Hero*, 1701; *The Importance of Dunkirk Considered*, 1713; *The Theatre*, 1720 (later published as *Richard Steele's "The Theatre,"* 1920, 1962; John Loftis, editor); *Tracts and Pamphlets by Richard Steele*, 1944 (Blanchard, editor); *The Correspondence of Richard Steele*, 1968 (Blanchard, editor).

Bibliography

Calhoun, Wineton. *Captain Steele: The Early Career*. Baltimore: The Johns Hopkins University Press, 1964. Primarily a biographical study, this book discusses *The Tatler* and *The Spectator*, but focuses mostly on the circumstances surrounding them rather than on actual analysis.

Connely, Willard. *Sir Richard Steele*. New York: Charles Scribner's Sons, 1934. This volume is the standard biography on Steele. While it is old, it is relatively useful. The chapters on *The Tatler* and *The Spectator* are helpful, including information on the business aspects of producing the two papers.

Dammers, Richard H. *Richard Steele*. Boston: Twayne, 1982. A good overview of Steele's work. This study discusses Steele's essays, dramas, and includes two excellent chapters on his short fiction in *The Tatler* and *The Spectator*. Contains a chronology and a select bibliography.

Ketcham, Michael G. *Transparent Designs: Reading, Performance, and Form in the Spectator Papers*. Athens: University of Georgia Press, 1985. This study takes apart *The Spectator* by examining its readers, its treatment of time, family, and language, and the social and historical context. A good, closely detailed examination of *The Spectator*.

Loftis, John. *Steele at Drury Lane*. Berkeley: University of California Press, 1952. The book details Steele's theatrical career and provides a good understanding of the eighteenth century stage and business management. Includes a useful appendix.

Richard H. Dammers
(Revised by *Kimberley L. Jacobs*)

WALLACE STEGNER

Born: Lake Mills, Iowa; February 18, 1909
Died: Santa Fe, New Mexico; April 13, 1993

Principal short fiction

The Women on the Wall, 1950; *The City of the Living and Other Stories*, 1956; *Collected Stories of Wallace Stegner*, 1990.

Other literary forms

Primarily a novelist and historian, Wallace Stegner is the author of many novels, from *Remembering Laughter* (1937) to *The Spectator Bird* (1976); his best-known and perhaps his best novel, *The Big Rock Candy Mountain*, was published in 1943, and *Angle of Repose* (1971) was awarded the Pulitzer Prize. *Mormon Country*, his first book of nonfiction, was published in 1942; it was followed by approximately a dozen others, including *Beyond the Hundredth Meridian: John Wesley Powell and the Second Opening of the West* (1954), *The Sound of Mountain Water* (essays, 1969), and *The Uneasy Chair: A Biography of Bernard DeVoto* (1974). In addition, he has edited many books, including *Great American Short Stories* (with Mary Stegner, 1957), numerous annual volumes of *Stanford Short Stories* (with Richard Scowcroft), and *The Letters of Bernard DeVoto* (1975).

In 1987, Stegner published the novel *Crossing to Safety*, which he has said is "a sort of memoir . . . for Mary [his wife] and myself." A gentle and affectionate portrait of two very different academic couples, *Crossing to Safety* met with great critical and popular acclaim. In an offshoot to his long teaching career, Stegner published *On the Teaching of Creative Writing: Responses to a Series of Questions* in 1988.

Achievements

Stegner's talent lay in his evocation of the West, which otherwise has been poorly documented in so-called Westerns, whether they be films or novels. As writer Richard Etulain has noted, what gives Stegner's work "its essential character is a deep familiarity with American historical, cultural, and political terrain." Stegner's work reveals the many aspects that make up American culture, or Americana. In addition, it provides a basis for understanding modern life in the United States. His literary efforts in this pursuit to portray fast-disappearing cultural and geographic sections of the United States were recognized with the Western History Association Prize in 1990.

Stegner received many awards and honors, including a Guggenheim Fellowship, a Rockefeller Fellowship, the Pulitzer Prize, a National Endowment for the Humanities Senior Fellowship, and an American Academy in Rome fellowship. In the spring of 1990, Stegner was given a lifetime achievement award by PEN USA

Center West. In September of the same year, he was awarded a senior fellowship by the National Endowment for the Arts.

Biography

Born in Iowa on his grandfather's farm, Wallace Earle Stegner moved with his family to East End, Saskatchewan at the age of five. He was educated in Utah, where he received an A.B. from the University of Utah, in 1930; and in his native state, where he earned an M.A., in 1932, and a Ph.D., in 1935, from the University of Iowa. Although he was briefly enrolled at the University of California at Los Angeles, he never actually attended any classes—he did not like California and returned to Utah as soon as he could.

Stegner once commented that his subjects and themes, both in fiction and in nonfiction, "are mainly out of the American West, in which I grew up." He taught at various colleges and universities, primarily at Stanford University, where he was director of its creative writing program. Stegner coauthored books with both his wife, Mary, and his son, Page, but he stopped publishing short stories after 1960. He said that everything he wanted to write "somehow wanted to be long." His attention continued to remain focused on the environment, a concern that began after World War II but that probably dated back to his childhood, when, as he said, he was "imprinted by the prairies."

Analysis

Of the eighteen stories in *The Women on the Wall*, almost half are concerned with incidents in the life of Brucie, a young boy growing up in Saskatchewan in the later years of the second decade of the twentieth century. In these semirelated stories, strongly rooted in time and place, Wallace Stegner is in complete control of his material and writes with insight and understanding which never lapse into sentimentality. The Brucie stories revolve around relatively commonplace subjects: the trapping of a gopher, the slaughtering of a sow, a family picnic. "Two Rivers," an O. Henry second-prize winner in 1942, is characteristic. The action is simple. Following an unhappy Fourth of July (the failure of the family's dilapidated Ford and the subsequent missed ball game in Chinook, the missed parade and fireworks, climaxed by the cuff on the ear from his father), the family set off for a picnic. Very little actually happens in this effective account of family relations, but at the story's end the reader shares Brucie's quiet pleasure:

> The boy looked up at his father, his laughter bubbling up, everything wonderful, the day a swell day, his mother clapping hands in time to his father's fool singing (an impromptu song about "a kid and his name was Brucie").
> "Aw, for gosh sakes," he said, and ducked when his father pretended he was going to swat him one.

In his stories about adults, Stegner's vision is considerably darker. Life was essentially good for a boy in 1917, he suggests; for an adult in the 1940's, it is likely to be just the opposite. "Beyond the Glass Mountain" (like "Two Rivers," the recipient of an O. Henry Award, second-prize, 1948) is characteristic. The narrative is structurally simple, uncluttered, and admirably economical: an account of a few moments during the reunion of two men who had been close friends during their college days. The narrator, "prepared . . . for nostalgia," finds his friend to be a pathetic alcoholic, irreparably damaged by the passing of time and a destructive marriage (For the "love of God," he thinks, "Get rid of her . . . She'll cheat on you. . . . She'll suck you dry like an old orange skin").

"Beyond the Glass Mountain," "The View from the Balcony," "The Women on the Wall," and others similarly depict the encroachment of the always present scourges of man upon lives that might or should be "ordinary" or "happy": the itch for domination, the dark shadow of emotional instability or insanity, the tyranny of sex, and the insecurity of the unloved.

The seven stories and one novella of *The City of the Living and Other Stories* share in common with *The Women on the Wall* Stegner's thoroughly disciplined narrative skill and his unblinking understanding of his characters. These later stories are more varied than their predecessors, ranging as they do from a fleabag of a California pool hall during the American Depression ("The Blue-Winged Teal," the O. Henry Memorial Award first-prize winner in 1950); to Egypt ("The City of the Living"); to Salt Lake City ("Maiden in a Tower"); to the French Riviera ("Impasse"); to an unspecified snowswept rural landscape-with-figures piece ("The Traveler"); to life among the wealthy and not-so-beautiful people in Southern California ("Field Guide to the Western Birds").

Stegner is again at his best in his shorter, less complicated, pieces. "Maiden in a Tower," for example, is virtually without incident: the drama of the story is the evocation of the past. The narrator has driven from San Francisco to a funeral home in Salt Lake City where his aunt lies awaiting burial. By coincidence, the funeral home was, a quarter of a century ago, the setting of the narrator's first love, and evokes in him memories of life in the Jazz Age and his infatuation with the girl who epitomized all the glamour, the folly, the joy of youth and love and aspiration of the past, a past as dead as the narrator's aunt and the corpse of another woman whom he contemplates in her coffin in what had been the enchanted tower of his youth. Thoroughly controlled, moving, and full of emotion which never degenerates into sentimentality, "Maiden in a Tower" is a masterly piece. So too is the title story "The City of the Living," a glimpse of a father and son during a few hours of almost unbearable crisis (the son is desperately ill in a hotel in Egypt); here Stegner presents a brilliant picture of father-son relations; and the setting, with its contrast of luxury and poverty, sickness and health, is unforgettable. Stegner is equally effective in his other stories of parent-child relations which furnish subject and theme for "The Blue-Winged Teal," "Impasse," and "The Volunteer."

The novella, "Field Guide to the Western Birds," on the other hand, in spite of some memorable moments, seems rather too long for what it accomplishes, too predictable in its denouement. As social history, however, Stegner's creation of well-heeled intellectuals and pseudo-intellectuals, frauds, hangers-on and circuit riders of the "good and opulent life," narrated by a self-congratulatory retired literary agent, has about it the ring of permanence. As John Galsworthy said of his Forsytes, here are characters miraculously preserved, pickled in their own juices.

Other major works

NOVELS: *Remembering Laughter,* 1937; *The Potter's House,* 1938; *On a Darkling Plain,* 1940; *Fire and Ice,* 1941; *The Big Rock Candy Mountain,* 1943; *Second Growth,* 1947; *The Preacher and the Slave,* 1950; *A Shooting Star,* 1961; *All the Little Live Things,* 1967; *Angle of Repose,* 1971; *The Spectator Bird,* 1976; *Recapitulation,* 1979; *Joe Hill,* 1980; *Crossing to Safety,* 1987.

NONFICTION: *An Exposition Workshop,* 1939 (edited); *Readings for Citizens at War,* 1941 (edited); *Mormon Country,* 1942; *One Nation,* 1945 (with the editors of *Look*); *Look at America: The Central Northwest,* 1947; *The Writer in America,* 1951; *Beyond the Hundredth Meridian: John Wesley Powell and the Second Opening of the West,* 1954; *This Is Dinosaur: The Echo Park and Its Magic Rivers,* 1955 (edited); *The Exploration of the Colorado River of the West,* 1957 (edited); *Report on the Lands of the Arid Region of the United States,* 1962 (edited); *Wolf Willow: A History, a Story, and a Memory of the Last Plains Frontier,* 1962; *The Gathering of Zion: The Story of the Mormon Trail,* 1964; *Modern Composition,* 1964 (edited, 4 volumes); *The American Novel: From Cooper to Faulkner,* 1965 (edited); *The Sound of Mountain Water,* 1969; *The Uneasy Chair: A Biography of Bernard DeVoto,* 1974; *Ansel Adams: Images 1923-1974,* 1974; *The Letters of Bernard DeVoto,* 1975 (edited); *One Way to Spell Man,* 1982; *American Places,* 1983; *Conversations with Wallace Stegner on Western History and Literature,* 1983; *The American West as Living Space,* 1987; *On the Teaching of Creative Writing: Responses to a Series of Questions,* 1988 (edited by Edward Connery Lathem).

ANTHOLOGIES: *Stanford Short Stories, 1946,* 1947 (with Richard Scowcroft); *Great American Short Stories,* 1957 (with Mary Stegner); *Selected American Prose: The Realistic Movement,* 1958; *Twenty Years of Stanford Short Stories,* 1966.

Bibliography

Arthur, Anthony, ed. *Critical Essays on Wallace Stegner.* Boston: G. K. Hall, 1982. Although not an exhaustive discussion of Stegner's works, these essays cover much of his most important writing, including his short fiction. Notes for further reference are included, as are primary and secondary bibliographical information and an index.

Burrows, Russell. "Wallace Stegner's Version of Pastoral: The Topic of Ecology in His Work." *Western American Literature* 25 (May, 1990): 15-25. Stegner's environmentalist stance has had a definite effect on his work, and this article discusses Stegner's use of the pastoral setting in much of his fiction, both long and short. Includes bibliographical information and notes for further reference on points within the article.

Colberg, Nancy. *Wallace Stegner: A Descriptive Bibliography*. Lewiston, Idaho: Confluence Press, 1990. This text contains detailed descriptions of Stegner's works, from his very early writing to *The American West as Living Space*. Colberg also provides sections for other Stegner material, such as contributions to books and edited works. A short appendix that also serves as a secondary bibliography is a good resource for the original publication information for Stegner's individual short stories.

Robinson, Forrest G. *Wallace Stegner*. Boston: Twayne, 1977. This text is a combination of biographical information on Stegner and interpretation and literary criticism of his work up to the mid-1970's. Robinson provides a chronology of Stegner's life and writings as well as detailed bibliographical information, both primary and secondary. Supplemented by notes and an index.

Stegner, Wallace. "The Art of Fiction: An Interview with Wallace Stegner." Interview by James R. Hepworth. *The Paris Review* 115 (Summer, 1990): 58-90. In this interview, Stegner talks about how he became a writer, as well as about writing in general. Although no references are included, this article is useful for the firsthand information it provides about Stegner through the interview process.

Stegner, Wallace, and Richard Etulain. *Conversations with Wallace Stegner*. Rev. ed. Salt Lake City: University of Utah Press, 1990. This edition is an expanded version of a book that first came out in 1983—a later interview section has been added to the first part of the book. In it, Stegner talks about all of his work up to *Crossing to Safety*. Includes biographical information in the form of answers to interview questions and also covers Stegner's view of the American literary West as well as the West—such as Western history and the wilderness areas of the West—in general. References to individual short stories (as well as to the collections) can be found in the index.

Willrich, Patricia Rowe. "A Perspective on Wallace Stegner." *The Virginia Quarterly Review* 67 (Spring, 1991): 240-258. This article covers the high points of Stegner's long career as a writer and scholar, giving both biographical details and information about his work. Good for an overview of, as well as for specifics on, Stegner's literary output.

William Peden
(Revised by *Jo-Ellen Lipman Boon*)

GERTRUDE STEIN

Born: Allegheny, Pennsylvania; February 3, 1874
Died: Paris, France; July 27, 1946

Principal short fiction

Three Lives, 1909; *Tender Buttons*, 1914; *Portraits and Prayers*, 1934; *Mrs. Reynolds and Five Earlier Novelettes, 1931-1942*, 1952; *As Fine as Melanctha*, 1954; *Painted Lace and Other Pieces, 1914-1937*, 1955; *Alphabets and Birthdays*, 1957.

Other literary forms

It is difficult to classify Gertrude Stein's writings, because she radically upset the conventions of literary genres and because she worked in many different forms. Traditional generic labels simply do not describe individual works. Even when Stein names the genre in a work's title (*Ida, a Novel*, 1941, for example), the conventional form only marks how far Stein has digressed from the norm. Works such as *Ida, a Novel* and *Mrs. Reynolds and Five Earlier Novelettes* are Stein's version of the novel, while *The Autobiography of Alice B. Toklas* (1933) and *Operas and Plays* (1932), among other works, encourage comparison with other genres. Stein became famous in the United States with *The Autobiography of Alice B. Toklas*, and her success encouraged her to experiment further with the genre (*Everybody's Autobiography*, 1937). Even when writing "autobiography," however, Stein did not adhere to conventional restrictions, using multiple viewpoints in the composite work. Similarly, although Stein wrote many plays, some of which have been performed, they do not follow dramatic conventions, for frequently they lack plot and character. Stein also wrote meditations and other quasi-philosophical and theoretical musings, and in numerous essays she attempted to explain her theories of composition and her notions of art. In addition, she experimented in verse and developed a special genre which she called portraits. Regardless of the form, however, the style is unmistakably Stein's and serves as a signature to all of her works.

Achievements

Stein's greatest achievement was her wily and strong independence, which revealed itself as much in her life-style as in her work. She was a creative person with a strong personality, a gift for conversation, and a good ear, and her home became a center for the avant-garde circle of artists in Paris during the early 1900's. Perhaps this salon would not be so famous were it not for the fact that those associated with it were later accepted as the outstanding figures of the modern art world. In time, artists as different as Ernest Hemingway, Sherwood Anderson, Virgil Thomson, Guillaume Apollinaire, Henri Matisse, and Pablo Picasso became associated with Stein and were drawn into the discussions and activities that took place in her home. Among contemporaries she was recognized as a fascinating individual, a woman of strong opinions and definite views, a lively intelligence and vibrant mind; among the cultural historians who came later, she was acknowledged to be a person of enormous creative influence and empowering force.

Stein's achievements were not limited to her role as a cultural catalyst, however, for she was a pioneering writer in her own right. Working from a sense that the present moment of consciousness is supreme, Stein increasingly radicalized her writing to focus on the here and now, on the mystery of consciousness, and ultimately on the enigma of language and words. This drive led Stein increasingly away from the conventions of language as commonly understood and practiced through the structures and preoccupations of genre, through the patterns and assumptions of syntax, and finally even through the basic referential quality of words. Repetition—of sounds and words themselves—became the hallmark of Stein's writing. Some contemporaries thought her experimental language to be foolish and childlike, but others hailed her efforts as truly pioneering literary breakthroughs. Most of the key terms in the criticism of modern literature have been applied to Stein at one time or another—abstractionist, cubist, minimalist, and so on. Indeed, most historians of the period agree that her work and her personality must be acknowledged before any serious discussion of any of these movements can proceed. However her work is defined, regardless of whether one likes or dislikes it, it has made a significant impact on the development of modern literature.

In addition to its variety and inventiveness, the sheer bulk of Stein's canon should not be overlooked as an accomplishment. Richard Bridgman's *Gertrude Stein in Pieces* (1970) lists nearly six hundred titles in the Stein bibliography, some very short pieces but others significantly longer. She was prolific, flexible, and varied—at her best in the unclassifiable writings that mingle verse, prose, and drama into a unique species of art that bears the imprint of Gertrude Stein alone.

Stein had the misfortune of living through two world wars. During the first she obtained a Ford van, which she drove for the American Fund for French Wounded. In 1922, she was awarded the Médaille de la Reconnaissance Française for wartime activities.

Biography

When Daniel Stein and Amelia Keyser were married in 1864, the seeds of Gertrude Stein's future independence were sown, for the couple had some unusual ideas about child rearing and family life. Perhaps most psychologically damaging to the children was the parents' firm decision to have five children—no more and no fewer. Consequently, Gertrude's beloved older brother Leo and she were conceived only after the deaths of two other Stein children. In *Everybody's Autobiography* Stein says that the situation made her and her brother feel "funny." Knowing that one's very existence depends on the deaths of others surely would have some psychological effect, and some biographers attribute Stein's lifelong interest in identity to her knowledge of her parents' decision about family size.

Daniel Stein was apparently as quarrelsome and independent as his daughter was to become. Having operated a successful cloth and clothing business in Baltimore with his brothers, Daniel and another brother broke up the partnership by moving out to Pittsburgh to open a new business. When Daniel had earned enough money, he moved the family across the Ohio to Allegheny, and it was there that Gertrude Stein was born in 1874. She was the last child the Steins were to have, completing the unit of five children. Michael Stein was the oldest child (born in 1865); Simon was next (1867); then came Bertha (1870) and Leo (1872). When Allegheny was hit with fire and flood, Daniel once again moved the family, this time to Austria, having decided that the older children needed the benefits of a European education.

The family went first to Gemünden and then to Vienna. Although not wealthy, they lived well and were able to afford a nurse, a tutor, a governess, and a full domestic staff. The children were exposed to music and dancing lessons, and they enjoyed all the sights and activities of the upper middle class in Europe at the time. In his concern for the education of his children, Daniel resembled Henry James, whose educational theories also featured the advantages of the European experience to a developing mind. During this period, letters from Amelia and her sister Rachel Keyser, who accompanied the Steins, reveal that the baby was speaking German and experiencing an apparently contented, pampered, and protected infancy.

The roaming continued. In 1878, the family moved to Paris, and Stein got her first view of the city she would later make her home. When the Steins returned to the United States in 1879, they lived at first with the Keyser family in Baltimore, but Daniel was set on living in California. By 1880, the family had relocated to Oakland, where they stayed for some time (until 1891), long enough for the artist to develop an attachment to the place. It was Oakland that Stein always thought of as home.

The unsettled life of the Steins continued with the death of Amelia when the artist was fourteen. Three years later (in 1891), Daniel died, leaving Michael head of the family. He moved the family to San Francisco that year, but by the following year the family was dispersed—Michael and Simon remaining in San Francisco, Gertrude and her sister Bertha going back to Baltimore to live with their mother's sister, and Leo transferring from the University of California at Berkeley to Harvard. In the fall of 1893, Gertrude Stein herself entered Harvard Annex (later renamed Radcliffe College), thus rejoining the brother to whom she had grown so attached. Their strong bond was to survive into adulthood, being broken only by Gertrude's lifelong commitment to Alice B. Toklas and her ascendancy in Parisian art circles.

Stein was at Harvard during a wonderful period in that institution's history. She had the good fortune to study under William James, whose theories of psychology intrigued the young woman and initiated a lifelong interest in questions of personality, identity, and consciousness. Stein's later attempts to present in her writing awareness of a continuing flux in the present, the immediacy of present existence, and the inclusiveness and randomness of consciousness can be traced in part to James's influence. Stein's first publication came out during this Harvard period. "Normal Motor Automatism," co-authored with Leon M. Solomons, was published in *Psychological Review* in September, 1896. Although this essay was primarily Solomons',

Stein published her own work on the subject in the *Psychological Review* of May, 1898—"Cultivated Motor Automatism: A Study of Character in Its Relation to Attention." Stein's early interest in automatic writing has led some readers to believe that the method directed her own subsequent writing, but that claim has been generally discredited. Harvard did more to focus her attention on the consciousness behind the work than on the techniques and strategies of the writing process.

The Harvard experience was not, however, completely successful. In the spring of 1897, Stein failed the Radcliffe Latin entrance examination and consequently was not awarded her bachelor's degree. Undaunted, in the fall of 1897 she entered The Johns Hopkins School of Medicine, and she received the Harvard degree in 1898, having been privately tutored in Latin so that she could pass the examination. It was William James who encouraged her to take the Harvard degree and to continue her education; Johns Hopkins seemed a likely choice both because it was funded to accept women into the program on a basis equal to men and because her brother Leo was studying there. The first two years of medical study went well, but after that, Stein complained of boredom and began to dislike her classes. In the end, she did not pass her final examinations and never took the degree. She had learned what she wanted to learn and had no interest in practicing medicine.

For some time, Stein had been spending her summers in Europe with Leo, so it seemed natural that they would settle in London in September, 1902. In February of the following year, Stein sailed back to the United States, this time staying in New York until rejoining Leo once again for summer travel. In the fall of 1903, they occupied the house at 27 rue de Fleurus, the address which was to become famous as an artistic mecca. *Quod Erat Demonstrandum* (1950; also known as *Things As They Are*) was written there, although Stein then overlooked the work for some thirty years.

In 1904, Gertrude and Leo began purchasing paintings by men destined to become the leading figures of modern art. Having studied the great masters throughout the museums of Europe, the Steins were not automatically impressed with the world of modern art, yet something about Paul Cézanne's work struck Leo, and he took his sister to a gallery of his works. After the purchase of their first Cézanne, they were soon given freer rein to look among the canvases of the Paris art dealers. They purchased works by Honoré Daumier, Édouard Manet, Pierre-Auguste Renoir, Henri Toulouse-Lautrec, Paul Gauguin, and others. Thus Leo and Gertrude Stein laid out a new direction in their own cultural life and established a new model for American art collectors. People began to go to the rue de Fleurus address to see the paintings and then to talk about art and to socialize. The cultural center of modern art was born.

During this time, Stein was also writing. *The Making of Americans* (1925) and *Three Lives* date to this period, *Three Lives* being published in 1909 as Stein's first book. Another important event of the period was Stein's meeting Alice Toklas in September, 1907; Toklas moved into the Stein household on rue de Fleurus early in 1909. Her presence hastened the deterioration of the relationship between Stein and her brother (he finally left in 1913) and facilitated Stein's writing, because Toklas learned to type and transcribed Stein's work. She was Stein's companion for the remainder of the artist's life.

In June, 1914, *Tender Buttons* was published. The work marks a significant movement on Stein's part toward abstractionism, as she focuses more on things than on people and blurs the distinction between poetry and prose. When war broke out, Stein and Toklas were houseguests of the Alfred North Whiteheads in Lockridge, and they did not return to Paris until October of that year. In 1915, they left Paris for Spain, returning in 1916. In 1917, Stein obtained a Ford van from the United States, which she drove for the American Fund for French Wounded as a supply truck, and Stein's preoccupation with automobiles, especially Fords, began. She contributed to the war effort in France in various ways and in various areas of France, not returning to Paris "permanently" until May of 1919.

After the war, writing and socializing could once again begin in earnest. In 1922, she met Hemingway and became godmother to his son born the following year. Stein continued to write and began also to lecture during this period; she continued also to cultivate her interest in cars (she was now on her third) and in pet dogs. In 1930, *Lucy Church Amiably* was published, and in 1932, *The Autobiography of Alice B. Toklas* was written at Bilignin. It became a literary sensation in 1933, and it continues to be the most widely read and appreciated of all Stein's writings. Early in 1934, the first public performance of *Four Saints in Three Acts* (1932) took place in Hartford, Connecticut. Performances in other cities soon followed, and Stein began a lecture tour in the United States that established her reputation.

When Paris was occupied in 1940, Stein was advised to leave, which she did, not returning until December of 1944. In the following year, she toured United States Army bases in occupied Germany and lectured in Belgium and elsewhere. In July of 1946, en route to a friend's summer house, Stein fell ill and was admitted to the American hospital at Neuilly-sur-Seine. On July 27, she died following an operation for cancer. Her brother Leo died a year later, almost to the day, and Toklas, Gertrude Stein's dearest companion, survived another twenty-two years. A chapter in the history of modern art had come to an end.

Analysis

Gertrude Stein's work has never been easily accessible to the reader. During her lifetime, her work was both ridiculed and celebrated, and indeed these two attitudes continue to prevail among Stein's readers. Now that historical distance has provided a supportive context for Stein's work, however, and now that readers can see Stein in a milieu of highly creative artists devoted to wrenching art from the restrictions of realism and verisimilitude, her work is more easily appreciated for the inroads it makes against conventions, although perhaps not more easily understood. Stein was a powerful initiator, a ruthless experimenter, and a bold and forthright manipulator of words.

Having already written *Things As They Are*, *Three Lives*, and *The Making of Amer-*

icans, Stein was in full command when she made the surprising innovations of *Tender Buttons*. The author herself always rated the work highly, considering it to be one of her most significant writings despite the ridicule and scorn it received from those who did not agree that it added a new dimension to literature. Prior to *Tender Buttons*, Stein had grown increasingly abstract in her writing. *Tender Buttons* marks something of a culmination in this progressing abstractionism, for here she produces a set of "still lifes," each of which sustains abstraction. The subject matter, too, has changed from earlier writing. In *Tender Buttons*, Stein moves from people to things. The book is divided into three sections: "Objects," "Food," and "Rooms." While the divisions classify, the effect is still that of eclecticism, for no perceptible principles of order determine either the arrangement within each section or the sequencing of the sections themselves.

The title of *Tender Buttons* indicates some of the ironies of the collection. A button is something hard, concrete, and functional, while the word "tender" as an adjective suggests the opposite—something soft. "Tender" can also be a verb, and in this sense, the collection is Stein's offering of discrete bits of prose. "Tender" may suggest an emotional state, but, if so, the emotion must emanate from the reader, for the hard little buttons of prose in *Tender Buttons* do not themselves develop an emotional state. In the title, as in the name of each passage within the work, Stein seems to be offering the reader something tangible, something realistic, but she does so only to challenge the reader's notions of reality and to tease the mind.

The verbal fragments in *Tender Buttons* reveal a variety of strategies, and it is the flexibility of language and idea that keeps one reading. Each entry is titled; "A Red Stamp," "A Plate," "Roastbeef," "Sugar," and "Oranges" are typical examples. Entries range in length from a single short line to the approximately twelve pages of the undivided section "Rooms." In some of the entries, the title shapes the suggestions and hints, while in others, the title seems to bear little or no relationship to what follows. Stein's prose does not describe the objects realistically, but rather, opens the mind to the flow of thoughts that the title evokes. In these verbal fragments there is no logic, no sequence; sometimes an entry shows accretion, but no line of thought is developed. Indeed, even the logic of syntax is refused in favor of phrases and, ultimately, in favor of single words.

The work is abstract not only because it collects seemingly discrete verbal fragments but also because it seems to follow one of Stein's axioms about abstract painting: that a painting has its own existence, its own life. Aesthetic value does not derive from a work's referential quality but rather from itself. In modern painting, the focus is on the colors of the paint, the shapes, the textures, the forms. In *Tender Buttons*, the focus is on the words themselves, their sounds, juxtapositions, and the life that emanates from their unconventional arrangement. Stein recognized that words bring with them a whole series of associations that are different for each reader and uncontrollable by the artist, so she deliberately aimed to remove words from their usual contexts to reduce their associational qualities and to cause new associations to arise from novel juxtapositions. A reader of Stein's work must surrender selfhood to the text and accept the linguistic experience offered.

In naming volume 4 of the Yale edition of Stein's writings *As Fine As Melanctha*, the editors draw attention to one of Stein's short pieces of prose that takes the appearance of a short story but turns out to defy the conventions of that genre, just as Stein defies other literary conventions. "As Fine as Melanctha" was Stein's answer when requested to write something "as fine as 'Melanctha,'" one of the three pieces that constitute *Three Lives*. Yet "As Fine as Melanctha" is radically different from the earlier work. The 1922 piece has no characters, no setting, no plot, and no chronology. The opening line announces that it is "a history of a moment," but a moment has no history. "As Fine as Melanctha" is a moment out of time, or rather many moments out of time, moments so common as to be timeless and timely simultaneously.

"As Fine as Melanctha" is a good example of Stein's perfected verbal strategies throughout the decade of the 1920's as she attempted to make immediate and alive the verbal moment. She ignores, for example, the rules of syntax, mingling phrases and clauses and sentences indiscriminately. The only punctuation mark in the piece is the period, and it closes sentence fragments and sentences alike. Even questions end in a period rather than the expected question mark. The effect is that syntax no longer aids communication; consequently, readers must release their fierce hold on sentence structure as a way to capture meaning. Where, however, can they turn in their desperate drive to understand? The logical next step is the word itself. Yet the reader is so accustomed to thinking of words as they relate to one another that when Stein violates expected word order as well as the rules of syntax, the reader confronts the stunning reality that words themselves are empty. Since everything one knows is understood through context, the removal of context both in the larger areas of character development and plot and in the smaller areas of language renders the reading of "As Fine as Melanctha" something of an existential experience.

Reading Stein's work puts the reader in tension with the text—that is, when the sparks fly for those willing to accept the challenge. Repeatedly, and in a variety of ways, Stein makes language meaningless. One of the hallmarks of Stein's work is repetition. Yet repetition does not contribute to communication by stressing meaning; instead, it reduces meaning. The following sentence from "As Fine as Melanctha" uses internal repetition: "I mean that it has been noticed again and again that abundance that in abundance that the need of abundance that there is therein a need of abundance and in this need it is a necessity that there is stock taking." A reader is grateful to emerge from the tangled web in the inner core of the sentence—repetition of "abundance," "need," and "need of abundance." The sentence seems to accumulate words that lose meaning in the process of being accumulated. Even the apparent meaning at the end (the necessity of stocktaking) vanishes in the light of "abundance." The repetition so confuses the reader that the end of the sentence seems to have meaning because it apparently follows normal English syntax, yet even that meaning reduces itself to the redundancy of "stock taking" and "abundance." The reader is left with a single, uncontextualized word, systematically emptied of meaning and association.

There are other kinds of repetition in "As Fine as Melanctha." Repetitions of sounds as well as words prevail in a passage such as the following: "How dearly clearly merely is she me, how dearly clearly merely am I she. How dearly is she me how dearly is she me how dearly how very dearly am I she." The words "dearly," "clearly," "merely," "she," and "me" are repeated in varied arrangements that challenge syntax. The sounds of the words tend to flatten them, to make them anonymous. Repetition of the sound "erely" eventually is reduced to repetition of the "e" sound, as in "me." The sentence shows Stein's progressive reductionism: the meanings of different words are reduced to sounds; the repetition of multiple sounds is reduced to a single sound. Not only do the words become meaningless when repeated in such close proximity, but also characters (the difference between "she" and "me") become such close approximations of one another that identity is destroyed. Language here is subversive and destructive.

In another example, repetition is used to change syntax: "The difference between humming to-day yesterday and to-morrow is this, it always means more. The difference between humming to-day yesterday and to-morrow is this. It always means more." The reader yearns to believe that this variation of syntax is meaningful, because that is the way readers have been taught to read. Yet once again, the repetition is used to destroy meaning. When Stein's reader puts mind against text, the mind returns as a wet noodle, aware only of its own limpness. Such awareness, however, is knowledge of one's fleeting consciousness, and Stein's objective is achieved.

"Brim Beauvais" represents Stein's work during the decade of the 1930's, when she became increasingly minimalist. In this work, her paragraphs are shorter, most being only a single line, and formal sections come from division into chapters, although such divisions are useless. Many chapters have the same identifying label: for example, three sections are identified as "Chapter X"; two are "Chapter Ten." Furthermore, the numbers are not always sequential. More confusion in the structure occurs through embedding. Several pages into "Brim Beauvais" appears the heading "Beauvais and His Wife: A Novel." There are labeled episodes within sections, although neither the chapter headings nor other labels contribute to communication. The work has a "Part II," but no Part I. All these devices are merely added to the verbal disruptions seen in earlier work. Even the opening of "Brim Beauvais" suggests how much further Stein has gone in her developing abstractionism. The work begins with the single word "once." It functions elliptically to suggest the "once upon a time" opening of fairy tales. Yet the second line truncates that suggestion. "Always excited to say twice" forces readers to understand "once" in a numerical framework and thus to count something they do not know; similarly, the adjective "excited" describes a person not yet introduced. Stein is a master at invoking emptiness. Like the cubists, she presented a part without feeling it necessary to fill in or even suggest the surrounding whole. She believed that the mind partakes of the world through fragments, not through complete systems, and that her writing was an open window on this process.

By the winter of 1940, another war had begun in Europe, and Stein was finding it difficult to carry on any sustained writing project. "To Do: A Book of Alphabets and Birthdays" (published in 1957 as *Alphabets and Birthdays*) provided a structure while allowing for the intermittent composition that met Stein's needs during this period. The structure was provided by the alphabet, which Stein marched progressively through, assigning four names to each letter and creating episodes, events, and nonsense rhymes around each. The work has the fantastic actions and situations that children love, and Stein had children in mind when she wrote it. On the other hand, some publishers have insisted that the work is really more appropriate for adults than for children. If so, it must be adults who are young at heart, for the work has a delightful lightness, a happy flippancy, and a joy of language that emerges from repetition of sounds and words. The alphabet book shows Stein's skill at duplicating the rhythms and sounds of conversation and thoughts as people silently talk to themselves. Stein's ear for speech has often been noted, and here the speech of conversation conveys a swiftness and easy familiarity that make the work especially pleasant to read. At the same time, it remains true to the developing minimalism throughout Stein's career, for the letter is a reduction of the word.

Stein adhered to her principles throughout her life, always finding new ways to bring the meaning of her craft to the reader's awareness—even if this meant shocking the reader out of the lethargy of language. When she began to attract more people than her brother, Leo's support deteriorated and he claimed to find her work silly. His evaluation is shared by many. Stein is not a woman for all readers. Indeed, she tends to attract only coterie groups. Because her work is amenable to literary critics practicing deconstruction, however, and because the feminist movement has brought lesbian relationships into the open and searches out the quiet subversions such a lifestyle encouraged, both the work of Gertrude Stein and the artist herself have been looked at anew. The new reader and the returning reader alike will find Stein's work ever fresh, ever varying, ever innovative, and ever shocking, and for that reason alone it will always have enthusiastic readers somewhere, someplace.

Other major works

NOVELS: *Three Lives,* 1909; *The Making of Americans,* 1925; *Lucy Church Amiably,* 1930; *A Long Gay Book,* 1932; *Ida, a Novel,* 1941; *Brewsie and Willie,* 1946; *Blood on the Dining-Room Floor,* 1948; *Quod Erat Demonstrandum,* 1950 (also known as *Things As They Are*); *Mrs. Reynolds and Five Earlier Novelettes, 1931-1942,* 1952; *As Fine as Melanctha,* 1954; *A Novel of Thank You,* 1958.

PLAYS: *What Happened: A Five Act Play,* 1922; *White Wines,* 1922; *Do Let Us Go Away,* 1922; *For the Country Entirely: A Play in Letters,* 1922; *Counting Her Dresses,* 1922; *Geography and Plays,* 1922; *Capital Capitals,* pr. 1929 (libretto; music by Virgil Thomson); *Operas and Plays,* 1932; *Four Saints in Three Acts,* 1932 (libretto; music by Thomson); *Lucretia Borgia,* 1939; *In Savoy: Or, Yes Is for a Very Young Man (A play of the Resistance in France),* 1946; *The Mother of Us All,* 1947 (opera);

Doctor Faustus Lights the Lights, 1949; *Last Operas and Plays*, 1949; *In a Garden: An Opera in One Act*, 1951; *Selected Operas and Plays*, 1970.

POETRY: *Tender Buttons: Objects, Food, Rooms*, 1914; *Geography and Plays*, 1922; *Before the Flowers of Friendship Faded Friendship Faded*, 1931; *Two (Hitherto Unpublished) Poems*, 1948; *Bee Time Vine and Other Pieces: 1913-1927*, 1953; *Stanzas in Meditation and Other Poems: 1929-1933*, 1956.

NONFICTION: "Composition as Explanation," 1926; *How to Write*, 1931; *The Autobiography of Alice B. Toklas*, 1933; *Matisse, Picasso, and Gertrude Stein, with Two Shorter Stories*, 1933; *Portraits and Prayers*, 1934; *Lectures in America*, 1935; *Narration*, 1935; *The Geographical History of America*, 1936; *Everybody's Autobiography*, 1937; *Picasso*, 1938; *Paris France*, 1940; *What Are Masterpieces?*, 1940; *Wars I Have Seen*, 1945; *Four in America*, 1947; *Reflections on the Atomic Bomb*, 1973; *How Writing Is Written*, 1974.

CHILDREN'S LITERATURE: *The World Is Round*, 1939.

MISCELLANEOUS: *The Gertrude Stein First Reader and Three Plays*, 1946; *The Yale Edition of the Unpublished Writings of Gertrude Stein*, 1951-1958 (eight volumes, edited by Carl Van Vechten); *Selected Writings of Gertrude Stein*, 1962; *The Yale Gertrude Stein*, 1980.

Bibliography

Bridgman, Richard. *Gertrude Stein in Pieces*. New York: Oxford University Press, 1970. The first detailed, chronological study of all Stein's work. Bridgman's approach is primarily psychobiological; he locates Stein's experimentalism in pathology rather than intention, seeing guilty evasiveness about lesbian sexuality as the crucial impetus for her avant-garde writing.

Brinnin, John Malcom. *The Third Rose: Gertrude Stein and Her World*. Boston: Little, Brown, 1959. Aside from its significant biographical value, this study contains provocative comments on Stein's writing, twentieth century painting, and modern intellectual and artistic movements. Includes a useful bibliography.

DeKoven, Marianne. *A Different Language: Gertrude Stein's Experimental Writing*. Madison: University of Wisconsin Press, 1983. DeKoven's feminist study focuses on Stein's experimental work published after *Three Lives* and before *The Autobiography of Alice B. Toklas*. She argues that this period of Stein's writing is important not so much because of its influence on other writers but because of its attempt to redefine patriarchal language and provide alternatives to conventional modes of signification.

Hoffman, Michael J. *Critical Essays on Gertrude Stein*. Boston: G. K. Hall, 1986. A collection of reviews and essays, most of which appeared during and immediately after Stein's long career in letters. Diverse literary criticisms, such as new criticism, structuralism, feminism, and deconstruction are represented. Among the contributors are Lisa Ruddick, Marianne DeKoven, Wendy Steiner, Catharine R. Stimpson, Donald Sutherland, and Allegra Stewart. Also included are Sherwood Anderson, Marianne Moore, William Carlos Williams, B.F. Skinner, Katherine

Anne Porter, Edmund Wilson, and W.H. Auden.

_____. *The Development of Abstractionism in the Writings of Gertrude Stein*. Philadelphia: University of Pennsylvania Press, 1965. Hoffman traces the progressive development of abstractionism in Stein's early writing (1903-1913), focusing on the varieties of abstractionism manifesting themselves in each work. In his subsequent study, published more than a decade later, Hoffman again focuses on the abstract, refining his earlier definition of Stein's abstractionism as a "leaving-out" of stylistic and thematic elements normally appearing in the major works of American and European literature. This second study, covering the period from 1902-1946, stresses the ways in which Stein progressively abstracted from her writing most of the traditional elements of fictional prose narrative.

Ruddick, Lisa. *Reading Gertrude Stein: Body, Text, Gnosis*. Ithaca, N.Y.: Cornell University Press, 1990. Examines the cultural and psychosocial contexts of "Melanctha," *The Making of Americans, G.M.P.* (Stein's abbreviated title for the work she also called *Matisse, Picasso, and Gertrude Stein*), and *Tender Buttons*—works that Ruddick argues have a creative momentum rarely achieved in Stein's later experimental works because all four are serial acts of self-definition. Ruddick's study combines poststructuralism with a humanist understanding of the artistic process; she sees *Tender Buttons* as Stein's work of genius because it orients the reader ethically rather than disorienting the reader in the play of language.

Sutherland, Donald. *Gertrude Stein: A Biography of Her Work*. Westport, Conn.: Greenwood Press, 1951. The first substantial critical book on Stein's writing, this work treats Stein's radical writings as an illustration of her own modernist philosophy and aesthetics. The book also justifies the modern movement in writing and painting. Includes a useful appendix, which catalogs Stein's writing according to stylistic periods.

Paula Kopacz
(Revised by *Cassandra Kircher*)

JOHN STEINBECK

Born: Salinas, California; February 27, 1902
Died: New York, New York; December 20, 1968

Principal short fiction

The Pastures of Heaven, 1932; *Saint Katy the Virgin*, 1936; *The Long Valley*, 1938.

Other literary forms

Besides two volumes of short fiction, John Steinbeck produced numerous novels, among which is his masterpiece, *The Grapes of Wrath* (1939). He also authored several screenplays and three dramas, two of which were based on his novels, *Of Mice and Men* (1937) and *The Moon Is Down* (1942). Among his nonfiction are several travel books and a collection of war sketches. His last work was a translation of Sir Thomas Malory's Arthurian stories. A volume of letters was published posthumously.

Achievement

Steinbeck assumes an important place in American literature chiefly for his powerful and deft portrayal of the common people—the migrant worker, the ranch hand, and the laborer—whose capacity for survival surpassed the attempts of economic and corporate forces to defeat them. His novels, especially, render the human condition with sensitivity and lyrical grace. His work often shows a versatility unrivaled among his contemporaries. The comic, the tragic, the whimsical, and the naturalistic all merge in such a way as to make Steinbeck one of the United States' most popular writers, one whose art form is particularly suited to the cinema. Many of his books have been turned into successful films. Though much of Steinbeck's best work was written in the 1930's, he is not only a propagandist of the Great Depression era but also a writer who is deeply concerned with the dignity of human beings. A human being as an individual may pass away, but the human being as a group, humankind as a species, is immortal. As Ma Joad remarked in the final pages of *The Grapes of Wrath*: "We're the people. We go on."

Biography

The Salinas valley, where John Steinbeck was born, lies about a hundred miles south of San Francisco. It is a fertile, temperate trough between two mountain ranges and encompasses some of central California's most picturesque areas, notably Pacific Grove and the serenity of Monterey Bay. Such a landscape was at the heart of Steinbeck's boyhood experience and forms a crucial link with the characteristics of the writer's work. The son of a mill owner and a schoolteacher, Steinbeck grew up in the small railroad town just entering the twentieth century, a town not quite pastoral yet not quite industrial, whose people were farmers and ranchers and shopkeepers but whose location and natural resources were quickly making it an agricultural and mercantile hub. This unique duality of the Salinas valley—the long valley of Steinbeck's fiction—became a formative agent in the quality of Steinbeck's work, stories at once gently romantic and mythic as they were also realistic and proletarian. His early reading was evidence of his growing dualism. The realistic novels of Gustave Flaubert and Thomas Hardy were supplemented by his readings in Greek and Roman mythology, the Bible, and especially Sir Thomas Malory's *Le Morte d'Arthur* (c. 1469, printed 1485), the first book given to him as a child and the last to serve as a source for his fiction. (A retelling of the King Arthur stories was published posthumously in 1976.)

By the time Steinbeck entered Salinas High School in 1915, he was a widely read young man, tall, with rugged good looks and a desire to write. At seventeen, he entered Stanford University, already convinced that he was going to be a writer. Like many creative artists before and since, Steinbeck found the discipline of the college curriculum too irksome. Though he enjoyed reading contemporary European and American writers such as Theodore Dreiser and Sinclair Lewis, he was uninterested in much else and took a leave of absence after two years. For the next few years, he worked in the San Francisco area as a clerk and a field hand on a ranch, gaining invaluable experience of ranch life and ranch hands that was to figure in such works as *Of Mice and Men* and *The Long Valley*.

He returned to Stanford University briefly as an English major but finally left in 1925 without a degree. He had written two stories for the *Stanford Spectator*, one a satire on college life and the other a bizarre tale about a strangely inarticulate woman and her marriage to a migrant worker who kept horses' heads in a rain barrel. The story is insignificant but interesting for its odd mixture of the real and the whimsical, a characteristic typical of much of Steinbeck's mature work.

Steinbeck was in New York during the late 1920's, working as a construction worker on the original Madison Square Garden by day and writing stories by night. Unsuccessful, he returned to California, married, and settled in his family's cottage in Pacific Grove. He wrote constantly, and in 1929, his first novel, *Cup of Gold*, was published. This thinly fictionalized account of the pirate Henry Morgan was both an artistic and a financial failure. *The Pastures of Heaven* (1932), Steinbeck's second book, was a collection of short stories about the people of an almost mythically beautiful valley. Influenced by Sherwood Anderson's *Winesburg, Ohio* (1919), published a decade earlier, neither it nor his next novel, *To a God Unknown* (1933), brought Steinbeck much critical or popular success.

His apprenticeship, however, was over. Beginning in 1935 with the publication of *Tortilla Flat*, Steinbeck was to produce half a dozen books over the next ten years, works that were to establish his reputation as a writer of power and versatility. *Tortilla Flat* was followed by *In Dubious Battle* (1936), regarded by some as one of the best strike novels ever written. *Of Mice and Men* was followed by *The Long Valley*, containing his best short stories. His masterpiece, upon which he had been working for three years, was published as *The Grapes of Wrath* in 1939.

During World War II, Steinbeck wrote propaganda scripts for the U.S. Army and published *The Moon Is Down*, a short novel set in Nazi-occupied Norway. His postwar work showed a marked decline. Aside from the massive *East of Eden* (1952), the works of this period are marked by a bland whimsy. *Cannery Row* (1945) is generally recognized as the novel that signaled the beginning of Steinbeck's decline. Throughout the 1950's and 1960's, Steinbeck, now a national celebrity, continued to produce a variety of fiction, novels such as *Sweet Thursday* (1954), *The Short Reign of Pippen IV* (1957), and *The Winter of Our Discontent* (1961). They are works of minor importance and show little of the narrative strength that won for Steinbeck the Nobel Prize in Literature in 1962.

His last years were spent quietly in New York City and on Long Island. By then he had become an honored American writer. In 1963, he was selected as honorary consultant in American literature for the Library of Congress. He was elected to the National Arts Council in 1966. Steinbeck died peacefully in his sleep on December 20, 1968.

Analysis

The qualities that most characterize the work of John Steinbeck are a supple narrative style, a versatility of subject matter, and an almost mystical sympathy for the common human being. His fiction is peopled with men and women somehow shoaled from society's mainstream yet possessed of a vision that is itself a source of strength. His characteristic narrative method is to portray these people with an unerring mixture of realism and romance.

Though the Great Depression is the central social focus of his best work, his characters respond to those social forces not only in terms of realistic confrontation but also in the form of a romantic, intuitive escape. His characters become not so much victims of social or economic failure but celebrants of a life-force beyond society and economics. The best of Steinbeck's work maintains this tension—developed by a narrative tone—between the world of harsh reality and the world of animal-like freedom. Even in a late novel such as *East of Eden*, his best books behind him, Steinbeck symbolically construed this duality in the reference to the two mountain ranges that defined the territory of his narrator's childhood, the "sunny" flowered slopes of the Gabilans to the east and the dark, brooding peaks of the Santa Lucias to the west.

Nowhere is this duality—the tension between realism and romance—more evident than in Steinbeck's earliest short stories, those forming his first major work, *The Pastures of Heaven*. Structurally the book shows the influence of Anderson's *Winesburg, Ohio*, a series of short stories, each independent but each connected by the locale and the theme of psychic isolation.

Using the frame narrative of Winesburg as a model, *The Pastures of Heaven* deals with the lives of a number of characters living in the peaceful, idyllic valley in the hills beyond Monterey. Secluded like some medieval bower or enchanted castle, the place evokes images of romance and peace. Yet for all the outward tranquillity, the valley cannot remain isolated from the real world of economic hardship and violence.

The Munroe farm, for example, is cursed, and the curse executes itself on all the characters who come into contact with the Munroes. The theme of this collection of short stories is the conflict inherent in the tension between the characters' desire to live in the peaceful valley and their own human weaknesses, which prevent them from fulfilling their desires. Put in another way, the stories form a latter-day Garden of Eden myth. The land is beautiful, fruitful, prosperous; but the people of the land are thwarted by the serpent of human frailty.

Though some of the characters are spiritual kin to the "grotesques of Anderson's famous collection," they are markedly different in their attempts to reconcile their romantic intuition with the reality of social convention. Tularecito, for example, is all instinct. Though an idiot, he possesses great strength and an intuitive ability to draw. The title of the story, "The Legend of Tularecito," suggests that, like a legend, Tularecito is a child of romance. In his contradictory nature, he is the archetype of all the characters in the collection. Foreshadowing the half-witted giant, Lenny, in *Of Mice and Men*, Tularecito brings destruction on himself when he attacks Bert Munroe and is sent to a state asylum outside the valley. His punishment is not physical death, as in Lenny's case, but banishment from the valley, from Eden. Tularecito has come into contact with the reality of social convention and is defeated. Intuition is thwarted in the interest of social stability.

The conflict between an idyllic life, communing with nature, and the demands of middle-class respectability is the focus of another story, "Junius Maltby." Like prelapsarian man, Junius lives innocently off the land. Reminiscent of the *paisanos*, such as Danny and Mac in later novels such as *Tortilla Flat* and *Cannery Row*, Junius is shiftless and, by society's standards, an irresponsible dreamer. Like Tularecito, Junius is intuitive, instinctual, indifferent to the economic imperatives of being a farmer, and casually indecorous in his personal appearance. To Mrs. Munroe, Junius' life of the imagination is a threat. Junius is forced to abandon his farm and to leave the valley. There is no place for the poor and the romantic in Eden.

The garden as instinct, as the life of the spirit, is a prominent image in two stories in a later collection. Published in 1938, *The Long Valley* contains some of Steinbeck's most brilliant work in the genre of short fiction. In "The Chrysanthemums," Steinbeck presents the figure of Eliza Allen, a woman whose romantic gentleness conflicts with the brusque matter-of-factness of her husband and the deceitful cunning of a tinker. The story reveals a skillful meshing of character and setting, of symbol and theme. The garden is at once the chief setting and abiding symbol that define Eliza's character and her predicament as a woman.

Dressed in a man's clothing, Eliza is working in her garden when the story opens. Already the contrast is clear between Eliza's sensitive nature and the manlike indifference of her dress, her husband and life on the ranch, bathed in "the cold grey-flannel fog of winter." Eliza's only emotional outlet, her only contact with a deeper life-pulse, is her growing of chrysanthemums, symbolic of both her sexual need and her recognition of the dominance in her nature of the life of the instinct. Like the virgin queen Elizabeth, Eliza has no children and her mannish ways merely disguise her sensitivity, a sensitivity that her husband Henry does not understand.

When a tinker stops his wagon at the ranch, looking for pots to repair, Eliza at first has no work for him, but when he praises her chrysanthemums, implying an understanding of her nature, Eliza gives him the flowers in a pot. That night, on their way to town for dinner and—the husband teases—to the prizefights, Eliza sees the discarded flowers on the road and realizes that the tinker had deceived her. Like her husband, the tinker did not really understand her; he had merely used her to his own advantage. At the end of the story, Eliza cries quietly, "like an old woman."

Still another story in the collection presents the image of the garden as both physical and psychic landscape. The garden that Mary Tiller tends in "The White Quail," however, is symbolic not of a healthy life of the spirit but of self-love and egotism. Mary's happiness with her garden, complete when she sees a white quail in it one night, is at the expense of her love for her husband. Harry is shut out of her love, often forced to sleep alone, though he virtually idolizes her. Mary's garden is her dream of an ordered, nonthreatening and nonsexual existence. In a sense, Mary "quails" before a life of passion or the body. When a cat one day wanders into the garden, Mary is fearful of its potential as a predator and demands that Harry shoot it. Inexplicably, he shoots the quail; in destroying Mary's dream, he has brought his wife back to the real world, to a sexuality that she had refused to admit.

A story of maturity and death is the much-praised "Flight." Opening amid the rocky crags of the Torres farm, the story centers on Pepe, the oldest son of the widow Torres. A tall, lazy youth, Pepe has inherited his father's knife and yearns for the day when he will become, like his father, a man. Sent into Monterey on an errand, Pepe is insulted by a townsman and kills the man with his knife. Returning, he bids his mother good-bye and, armed with his father's rifle and horse, leaves his home to flee into the mountains. Gradually, he loses his rifle, then his horse. Now alone, he faces the threat of natural forces and the human pursuers. In the end, he is shot by one of the unseen "dark watchers."

Significantly, Pepe relies more on his own strength and courage as he flees deeper into the wild mountain passes; as he leaves his childhood behind, however, he also approaches his own death. Pepe's journey has become not only a physical escape from society's retribution but also a symbolic pilgrimage toward manhood and a redemptive death.

Other major works

NOVELS: *Cup of Gold*, 1929; *To a God Unknown*, 1933; *Tortilla Flat*, 1935; *In Dubious Battle*, 1936; *Of Mice and Men*, 1937; *The Red Pony*, 1937, 1945; *The Grapes of Wrath*, 1939; *Cannery Row*, 1945; *The Pearl*, 1947; *The Wayward Bus*, 1947; *Burning Bright*, 1950; *East of Eden*, 1952; *Sweet Thursday*, 1954; *The Short Reign of Pippen IV*, 1957; *The Winter of Our Discontent*, 1961; *Acts of King Arthur and His Noble Knight*, 1976.

PLAYS: *Of Mice and Men: A Play in Three Acts*, 1937; *The Moon Is Down: A Play in Two Parts*, 1942; *Burning Bright*, 1951.

SCREENPLAYS: *The Forgotten Village*, 1941; *Lifeboat*, 1944; *A Medal for Benny*, 1945; *The Pearl*, 1945; *The Red Pony*, 1949; *Viva Zapata!*, 1952.

NONFICTION: *Their Blood Is Strong*, 1938; *The Forgotten Village*, 1941; *Sea of Cortez*, 1941 (with Edward F. Ricketts); *Bombs Away*, 1942; *A Russian Journal*, 1948 (with Robert Capa); *Once There Was a War*, 1958; *Travels with Charley*, 1962; *Letters to Alicia*, 1965; *America and Americans*, 1966; *Journal of a Novel*, 1969; *Steinbeck: A Life in Letters*, 1975 (Elaine Steinbeck and Robert Wallsten, editors).

Bibliography

Astro, Richard, and Tetsumaro Hayashi, eds. *Steinbeck: The Man and His Work.* Corvallis: Oregon State University Press, 1971. One of the first full-length works published after Steinbeck's death, this superb collection of essays presents opinions which regard Steinbeck as everything from a mere proletarian novelist to an artist with a deep vision of humans' essential dignity.

Benson, Jackson D. *The True Adventures of John Steinbeck, Writer.* New York: Viking Press, 1984. This biography emphasizes Steinbeck's rebellion against critical conventions and his attempts to keep his private life separate from his role as public figure. Benson sees Steinbeck as a critical anomaly, embarrassed and frustrated by his growing critical and popular success.

Fontenrose, Joseph. *John Steinbeck: An Introduction and Interpretation.* New York: Holt, Rinehart and Winston, 1963. A good introduction, this book discusses some of the symbolism inherent in much of Steinbeck's fiction and contains some insightful observations on Steinbeck's concept of the "group-man"—that is, the individual as a unit in the larger sociobiological organism.

McCarthy, Paul. *John Steinbeck.* New York: Frederick Ungar, 1980. Though much of this study is a recapitulation of earlier critical views, the book has the virtues of clarity and brevity and contains a fairly thorough bibliography.

Steinbeck, Elaine, and Robert Wallsten. *Steinbeck: A Life in Letters.* New York: Viking Press, 1975. An indispensable source for the Steinbeck scholar, this collection of letters written by Steinbeck between 1929 and his death forty years later shows a writer both well read and well disciplined. Those letters to his friend and publisher, Pascal Covici, shed light on the writer's working methods and are particularly revealing.

Edward Fiorelli

RICHARD G. STERN

Born: New York, New York; February 25, 1928

Principal short fiction

Teeth, Dying, and Other Matters, 1964; *1968: A Short Novel, an Urban Idyll, Five Stories, and Two Trade Notes*, 1970; *Packages*, 1980; *Noble Rot: Stories, 1949-1988*, 1989.

Other literary forms

Richard Stern is best known as a novelist. He has written literary criticism, both of his work and of that of others. He has also written autobiographical sketches and several poems.

Achievements

Stern has written numerous volumes of prose. His novels have received wide critical acclaim from reviewers, including Saul Bellow, Joan Didion, and Bernard Malamud, yet none has been widely read, and few have received attention from professional literary critics. His first novel, *Golk* (1960), was hailed as one of the best fictive accounts of the early days of television and the ways in which it intrudes into the lives of people who work in the medium and those who watch it. He has received numerous awards for his work, including a Longwood Award (1960), a Friends of Literature Award (1963), a Rockefeller grant (1965), an American Academy and Institute of Arts and Letters grant (1968), a National Endowment for the Arts grant (1969), a Guggenheim Fellowship (1973-1974), a Carl Sandburg Award from the Friends of the Chicago Public Library for his 1978 novel *Natural Shocks* (1979), and an American Academy and Institute of Arts and Letters Award of Merit for the Novel (1986). In 1965, his novel *Stitch* was selected as an American Library Association book of the year.

Biography

Richard Gustave Stern was born in New York City on February 25, 1928, the son of German-Jewish immigrants. He married Gay Clark in 1950 and was divorced in 1972. He married Alane Rollings in 1985. He has four children.

Stern received his B.A. degree from the University of North Carolina at Chapel Hill in 1947, where he became a member of Phi Beta Kappa. After graduating, he worked in a department store in Indiana, in a Florida radio station, and at Paramount International Films in New York. He earned his M.A. degree from Harvard University in 1949, writing the Bowdoin Prize essay on the poet John Crowe Ransom. He was a lecturer at Collège Jules Ferry in Versailles, France, from 1949 to 1950; a lecturer at the University of Heidelberg in Germany from 1950 to 1951; and an educational adviser for the U.S. Army from 1951 to 1952. While teaching at the

University of Heidelberg, he worked nights as a cable clerk with the American occupation army. He received his Ph.D. from the University of Iowa in 1954. From 1954 to 1955, he was an instructor at Connecticut College in New London, Connecticut.

In 1956, Stern became an assistant professor of English at the University of Chicago, where he continued to teach. He became an associate professor in 1962 and a full professor in 1965. He has been a visiting lecturer at the University of Venice (1962-1963); the University of California, Santa Barbara (1964, 1968); the State University of New York at Buffalo (1966); Harvard University (1969); the University of Nice (1970); and the University of Urbino (1977).

In one of his autobiographical sketches, he describes his elation at having his first important story accepted in 1952 for *The Kenyon Review* by Ransom, who was the subject of Stern's essay that won the Bowdoin Prize. This acceptance occurred in the same year that he went to Iowa to begin work on his Ph.D. Following this first publication, he contributed numerous stories and essays to literary magazines, including *The Kenyon Review*, *The Antioch Review*, *Commentary*, *The Atlantic*, *Harper's*, *The Hudson Review*, *Partisan Review*, *The Paris Review*, *Encounter*, *Transatlantic Review*, *TriQuarterly*, and *Western Review*.

In 1957, he met Bellow, who became his friend and who greatly influenced his ideas about writing and about the writer's life. Bellow, Stern has said, showed him that one could be a Jew and still be a great American novelist. Stern would continue to live in the Chicago area, to write, and to teach at the University of Chicago.

Analysis

Saul Bellow, Richard Stern's friend and colleague at the University of Chicago, has been known to wonder aloud why Stern's work is not more popular. Like many other discerning reviewers, Bellow notes the excellence of Stern's novels and short stories and their lack of readers. The answer to Bellow's question probably lies in the kinds of demands that Stern makes on his readers.

According to Stern, his early writing was done under the influence of *Understanding Fiction*, a highly influential textbook-anthology edited by Robert Penn Warren and Cleanth Brooks. Under the influence of Brooks and Warren, Stern tried to achieve what he calls a polished style, to integrate the materials in his stories, and "to suspend the meaning of the story in action as 'naturally' as orange bits in jello." Between 1952 and 1954, he said, he wrote about ten stories following these principles, but he became dissatisfied with what he was producing and, in 1957, stopped working on short stories, interrupted work on what became his second published novel, *Europe: Or, Up and Down with Schreiber and Baggish* (1961), and started working on what became his first published novel, *Golk*.

Like Bellow's writing, Stern's tends to be highly erudite and allusive. In fact, it tends to be even more erudite and allusive than Bellow's. To understand Stern's stories fully, readers must be familiar with a large body of Western literature. They must also be at least slightly familiar with several languages, including French, German, and Italian. In some stories, he demands that his readers be familiar with such topics as Eastern and Western European history, anatomy, and the history of philosophy. Stern is at his best as a humorist. He is sometimes classified as a black humorist and even a satirist, but his works tend to reflect more love for humankind than those of most black humorists and satirists.

Even in many of his short works of humorous fiction, he makes inordinate demands on his readers. Most of his best short works are collected in *Noble Rot*, a book that can serve as an extremely good introduction to Stern's techniques as a story writer. His extremely short story "Good Morrow, Swine," for example, is included in the collection. This early work is hilarious, yet to comprehend the jokes in it one must recognize the allusions in the title and be able to understand at least a bit of French, since most of the jokes within the story depend on recognizing French mistranslations of English phrases. In the story, Mr. Perkins misinforms his young male students constantly about the meanings of English words, quotations, and everyday expressions.

Similarly, in "Veni, Vidi . . . Wendt," a long short story that Stern calls a short novel, which appeared in *1968*, he writes a comic study of Jeffrey Charles Wendt, a composer of operas to which no one listens and who desires to have his operas listened to by no one. This story, not collected in *Noble Rot*, is set in the same year as the assassinations of Martin Luther King, Jr., and Robert F. Kennedy and the Democratic Convention in Chicago that nominated Hubert H. Humphrey while young people rioted in the streets. Yet Wendt, who has been called a modern Nero, although aware of these events, largely ignores them, concentrating instead on writing an opera based on the life of Horace Walpole and trying to satisfy his own sexual lust and desire to show his superiority to his colleagues. Wendt and his wife and children are spending the summer in Santa Barbara, California. In the course of the story, he rediscovers his love for his wife and children.

Still, to understand the humor in "Veni, Vidi . . . Wendt," the reader must bring something to the story. The title itself alludes to Julius Caesar's famous words "Veni, Vidi, Vici" ("I came, I saw, I conquered"), which he used to report to the Roman Senate about his Pontic victory. Wendt, on the other hand, does not conquer. He came, he saw, and through a terrible pun, he left (Wendt-went). Even the Latin pronunciation of the letter *v* as *w* and the German pronunciation of the letter *w* as *v* seems part of the joke involved in the story's title.

The irony of comparing Wendt to Caesar becomes greater when one compares Caesar's amorous conquests to Wendt's. In his Egyptian conquest, achieved shortly before his Pontic one, Caesar also won Cleopatra. Comparing Caesar's conquest to Wendt's one amorous conquest in "Veni, Vidi . . . Wendt" produces more humor. Unlike Caesar, Wendt finds that he can ultimately take no pride in his dalliance, even though the woman with whom he has an affair is Patricia Davidov, the beautiful wife of a musicologist whom Wendt abhors. In the course of his first assignation with Patricia, he wonders whether there is no mouthwash in the Davidov household. Shortly thereafter, he finds himself exhausted by his extramarital affair and extremely anxious for it to end. No Caesar, Wendt runs from the affair back to his home in Chicago, feeling only relief that he has escaped from the demanding Patricia. The writing throughout the story is similarly allusive and erudite.

For one able or willing to make his way through Stern's short stories, the rewards are great. At his best, he is wildly comic, illustrating the absurdity of the human situation in humorous scene after humorous scene in stories such as "Good Morrow, Swine," "Veni, Vidi . . . Wendt," "Packages," "Milius and Melanie," and "A Recital for the Pope."

In fact, Stern is often classified as a writer of the absurd. He can write good, slightly sentimental fiction in works such as "Arrangements at the Gulf." In it, Mr. Lomax, an old man, wants to die away from his family in Lake Forest, Illinois, but with his bachelor friend Granville, whom he sees every other summer on the Florida Gulf Coast. On the summers in between, Granville goes to California. The arrangements of the title involve seeing to it that Granville will go to the Gulf Coast every summer so that he can be present when Mr. Lomax dies.

Many of Stern's stories involve the kinds of reversals found in "Arrangements at the Gulf." In one, "Double Charley," Charley Rangel discovers that his girlfriend slept with his partner in songwriting, Charley Schmitter, when he asks Olive, Schmitter's wife, to allow Agnes, Schmitter's girlfriend, to visit Schmitter's grave. In another, "A Counterfactual Proposal" (collected only in *Teeth, Dying, and Other Matters*), after years of longing for a beautiful woman, Patchell finally is able to get Twyla K. Diggs into bed with him. Diggs is a student at the college where Patchell teaches. Shortly after they go to bed, they are discovered by Diggs's roommate and landlady. Immediately after the discovery, Patchell confronts the college president, Miss Emory, and succeeds in persuading her to grant him a year's research grant, which he will use to go to France to study at the Bibliothèque Nationale. He also enlists Miss Emory's aid in getting Diggs's father to agree to send her to the Sorbonne for the year.

In "Wissler Remembers," a fairly sentimental story, an aging teacher recalls the students he has taught over the years and the love that he has felt for all of them. In this work, too, Stern shows the absurdity of the human situation. "Wissler Remembers" also has its humorous moments, especially when Wissler recalls that while teaching at the Collège Jules Ferry in Versailles, France, where Stern himself taught, Wissler assigned his students the task of translating back into English a poem for which he supplied the French translation. Anyone who could come within twelve words of the original would, Wissler announced, get a present. The poem itself is a French version of Robert Frost's "Stopping by Woods on a Snowy Evening," and the student translation that Wissler recalls is hilarious. Yet the reader must understand enough French to recognize the original poem in order to see how hilarious the student version is.

Critics have recognized in Stern's novels a unique mixture of what they call the language of the street and of the library. This same mixture of colloquialisms and book language pervades his tales. Story after story in *Noble Rot* exemplifies this mixture. At the same time, the actions in the stories often echo this mixture by placing grotesque characters in extremely formal situations. "A Recital for the Pope," for example, begins like a history textbook, describing magnificent old buildings in Rome but quickly places in that setting a violinist, Yerva Grbisz, who tortures horrible tunes out of the violin and refuses to use deodorant or practice other elements of hygiene. Yerva has a brief audience with the pope, after which she, along with some others, and the pope pose for a picture together. As they pose, she tells the pope that she wants to play her violin for him. He says that he would love for her to do so. She then plays execrable music, which he claims to enjoy very much.

Similarly, "La Pourriture Noble" (meaning "noble rot," from which the collection gets its title) shows Dennis Sellinbon climbing up some very expensive curtains in a very elegant apartment at which he is attending a party. Readers never discover any reasonable explanation for Dennis' actions but cannot help laughing when they hear the excuse that Dennis makes up to get himself released from the mental ward to which he has had himself committed.

Another story in the collection that deserves special attention is "Dying," in which F. Dorfman Dreben, through repeated entreaties, gets Professor Bly, a plant physiologist who has published a volume of poetry, to write a poem to be entered into a competition, the winner of which will receive $250, with the winning poem to be inscribed on Dreben's mother's tombstone. Dreben's persistence leads Bly to understand that his poem will be the only one in the contest. At first, Bly is uninterested. Then, however, he decides to use the money for a trip, so he quickly conceives of, writes, and sends what he considers a good poem to Dreben, requesting that Dreben send the prize by return mail. After not hearing from Dreben, Bly, while in bed with his girlfriend, calls Dreben to find out why he has not received his check. As it turns out, there were two other contestants, a yearbook editor and a friend of Dreben's sister. The yearbook editor won first prize, the sister's friend won second, and Bly, Dreben says, won honorable mention.

In one of his uncollected tales, "Aurelia Frequenzia Reveals the Heart and Mind of the Man of Destiny" (*The Paris Review*, 1976), Frequenzia writes the transcript of several interviews presented as though they are one interview with Tao Thinh, once ruler of Annam, which the reader quickly recognizes as a thinly disguised version of Vietnam. In the story, Stern shows the basic similarity between Frequenzia and Thinh, even though she claims to hate him and all for which he stands. She especially hates his having worked beside colonial powers—the French and Americans—while claiming to be a patriot, and his having enriched himself at the expense of his country. Yet the reader quickly discovers that Frequenzia and Thinh lust for each other. Actually, the transcript reveals far more about Frequenzia than it does about either the heart or mind of Thinh.

Stern's short stories then provide a mirror of the absurdity of the human situation at the same time that they display not only a toleration for human foibles but also a love for humankind. At his best, Stern is extremely humorous at the same time that he makes extreme demands on his readers. A consummate craftsman, he admits to polishing his works by revising them again and again. The resulting stories are worth the time and effort he puts into them, and they are certainly worth the time and effort the reader must expend to appreciate them.

Other major works

NOVELS: *Golk*, 1960; *Europe: Or, Up and Down with Schreiber and Baggish*, 1961; *In Any Case*, 1962 (reissued as *The Chaleur Network*, 1981); *Stitch*, 1965; *Other Men's Daughters*, 1973; *Natural Shocks*, 1978; *A Father's Words*, 1986.

PLAYS: *Reparations*, 1958; *The Gamesman's Island*, 1964; *Dossier: Earth. Twenty-four Blackouts from the Middle Electric Age*, 1966.

ANTHOLOGIES: *Honey and Wax: The Powers and Pleasures of Narrative*, 1966; *American Poetry of the Fifties*, 1967.

MISCELLANEOUS: *The Books in Fred Hampton's Apartment*, 1973; *The Invention of the Real*, 1982; *The Position of the Body*, 1986.

Bibliography

Cavell, Marsha. "Visions of Battlement." *Partisan Review* 38, no. 1 (1971): 117-121. Cavell reviews four books in this article, including *1968*, by Stern. She discusses "Veni, Vidi . . . Wendt" and "East, West . . . Midwest" from Stern's collection, seeing him as a satirist whose writing is "at once gentle and biting."

Harris, Mark. *Saul Bellow: Drumlin Woodchuck*. Athens: University of Georgia Press, 1980. This book is primarily a study of Stern's friend, Saul Bellow. It is dedicated to Stern and repeatedly treats him, especially in connection with his friendships with Harris and Bellow. Also discusses his friendship with Philip Roth and recognizes the difficulty most readers have with Stern's work. Although Harris treats Stern throughout the book, the treatment is especially intensive in chapters 2 and 3.

Rogers, Bernard. Foreword to *Golk*. Chicago: University of Chicago Press, 1987. This introduction to the Phoenix reprint of Stern's first novel treats his fiction in general, especially his novels. It traces through Stern's novels four of his major themes: adapting to change, handling moral responsibility, dealing with problems of fatherhood and domestic life, and handling power. It also discusses his distinctive narrative voice.

Stern, Richard G. "Conversation with Richard Stern." Interview by Milton Rosenberg and Elliot Anderson. *Chicago Review* 31 (Winter, 1980): 98-108. This article is an edited transcript of an interview that took place on WGN radio. In it, Stern traces what he calls the change in his writing from creating stories drawn from the external world to creating ones drawn from inside himself. He also briefly discusses the works of several other contemporary American writers, including John Barth, Donald Barthelme, John Gardner, Truman Capote, and Irving Wallace.

_____. "PW Interviews Richard Stern." Interview by Molly McQuade. *Publishers Weekly* 235 (January 20, 1989): 126-128. This interview appeared after the publication of Stern's collection of short stories *Noble Rot*. It briefly traces his life, literary career, and career as a university professor. Includes a photograph of Stern.

Richard Tuerk

ROBERT LOUIS STEVENSON

Born: Edinburgh, Scotland; November 13, 1850
Died: Apia, Upolu, Samoa; December 3, 1894

Principal short fiction

The New Arabian Nights, 1882; *More New Arabian Nights*, 1885; *The Merry Men and Other Tales and Fables*, 1887; *Island Nights' Entertainments*, 1893.

Other literary forms

Despite poor health, Robert Louis Stevenson was a prolific writer, not only of juvenile fiction but also of poetry, plays, and essays. He is best known for adventure romances such as *Treasure Island* (1883), *Kidnapped* (1886), and the horror-suspense novel *The Strange Case of Dr. Jekyll and Mr. Hyde* (1886), works that appeal principally to youthful readers. A habitual voyager, Stevenson also wrote travelogues and sketches recounting his personal experiences. His children's poems, published in *A Child's Garden of Verses* (1885), remain perennial favorites, as do several of his beautiful family prayers.

Achievements

For clarity and suspense, Stevenson is a rarely equaled raconteur. He reveals his mastery of narrative in his economical presentation of incident and atmosphere. Yet, despite his sparse, concise style, many of his tales are notable for dealing with complex moral ambiguities and their diagnoses. Although influenced by a host of romantic writers, including Charles Lamb, William Hazlitt, William Wordsworth, and Nathaniel Hawthorne, Stevenson's theories of prose fiction were most directly provoked by Henry James's *The Art of Fiction* (1884). Stevenson placed himself in literary opposition to James and the "statics of character," favoring instead an action-fiction whose clear antecedents are allegory, fable, and romance. His tales of adventure and intrigue, outdoor life and old-time romance, avidly read by children and young adults, have had a continuous and incalculable influence since their first publication in the 1880's.

Biography

The only child of a prosperous civil engineer and his wife, Robert Louis Stevenson was a sickly youth, causing his formal education to be haphazard. He reacted early against his parents' orthodox Presbyterianism, donning the mask of a liberated Bohemian who abhorred the hypocrisies of bourgeois respectability. As a compromise with his father, Stevenson did study law at Edinburgh University in lieu of the traditional family vocation of lighthouse engineer. In 1873, however, he suffered a severe respiratory illness, and although he completed his studies and was admitted to the Scottish bar in July, 1875, he never practiced. In May, 1880, Stevenson married

Fanny Van de Grift Osbourne, a divorcée from San Francisco and ten years his senior. The new couple spent most of the next decade in health resorts for Stevenson's tuberculosis: Davos in the Swiss Alps, Hyères on the French Riviera, and Bournemouth in England. After his father's death, Stevenson felt able to go farther from Scotland and so went to Saranac Lake in the Adirondack Mountains of New York, where treatment arrested his disease. In June, 1888, Stevenson, his wife, mother, and stepson sailed for the South Seas. During the next eighteen months they saw the Marquesas, Tahiti, Australia, the Gilberts, Hawaii, and Samoa. In late 1889, Stevenson decided to settle and bought "Vailima," three miles from the town of Apia, Upolu, Samoa, and his home until his death. His vigorous crusading there against the white exploitation of native Samoans almost led to expulsion by both German and English authorities. Stevenson's tuberculosis remained quiescent, but he suddenly died of a cerebral hemorrhage on December 3, 1894, while working on the novel *Weir of Hermiston* (1896), a fragment which many now think to be his best writing. Known to the natives as "Tusitala," the Storyteller, Stevenson was buried on the summit of Mount Vaea.

Analysis

Robert Louis Stevenson has long been relegated to either the nursery or the juvenile section in most libraries, and his mixture of romance, horror, and allegory now seems jejune. In a century where narrative and well-ordered structure have become the facile tools of Harlequin paperbacks and irrelevant to high-quality "literature," Stevenson's achievement goes quietly unnoticed. To confine this technique of "Tusitala" solely to nursery and supermarket, however, is to confuse Stevenson's talents with his present audience.

Stevenson's crucial problem is the basic one of joining form to idea, made more difficult because he was not only an excellent romancer but also a persuasive essayist. In Stevenson, however, these two talents seem to be of different roots, and their combination was for him a lifelong work. The aim of his narratives becomes not only to tell a good story, constructing something of interest, but also to ensure that all the materials of that story (such as structure, atmosphere, and character motivation) contribute to a clear thematic concern. Often Stevenson's fictional talents alone cannot accomplish this for him, and this accounts—depending in each instance on whether he drops his theme or attempts to push it through—for both the "pulp" feel of some stories and the "directed" feel of others.

Appearing in the *Cornhill Magazine* for May, 1874, an essay on Victor Hugo was Stevenson's very first publication. The short stories he began writing soon after demonstrate a strong tendency to lapse into the more familiar expository techniques either as a solution to fictional problems or merely in order to bolster a sagging theme. A blatant example of this stylistic ambiguity is the early story "A Lodging for the Night."

The atmosphere of the first part of the story is deftly handled. It is winter and its buffets upon the poor are reemphasized in every descriptive detail. Paris is "sheeted up" like a body ready for burial. The only light is from a tiny shack "backed up against the cemetery wall." Inside, "dark, little, and lean, with hollow cheeks and thin black locks," the medieval poet François Villon composes "The Ballade of Roast Fish" while Guy Tabard, one of his cronies, sputters admiringly over his shoulder. Straddling before the fire is a portly, purple-veined Picardy monk, Dom Nicolas. Also in the small room are two more villains, Montigny and Thevenin Pensete, playing "a game of chance." Villon cracks a few pleasantries, quite literally gallow's humor, and begins to read aloud his new poem. Suddenly, between the two gamesters:

> The round was complete, and Thevenin was just opening his mouth to claim another victory, when Montigny leaped up, swift as an adder, and stabbed him to the heart. The blow took effect before he had time to utter a cry, before he had time to move. A tremor or two convulsed his frame; his hands opened and shut, his heels rattled on the floor; then his head rolled backward over one shoulder with the eyes wide open; and Thevenin Pensete's spirit had returned to Him who made it.

Tabard begins praying in Latin, Villon breaks into hysterics, Montigny recovers "his composure first" and picks the dead man's pockets. Naturally, they must all leave the scene of the murder to escape implication, and Villon departs first.

Outside, in the bitter cold, two things preoccupy the poet as he walks: the gallows and "the look of the dead man with his bald head and garland of red curls," as neat a symbol as could be for the fiery pit of hell where Villon eventually expects to find himself. Theme has been handled well, Stevenson's fiction giving us the feeling of a single man thrown by existence into infernal and unfavorable circumstances, being pursued by elements beyond his control, the gallows and Death, survival itself weaving a noose for him with his own trail in the snow, irrevocably connecting him to "the house by the cemetery of St. John." The plot is clear and the situation has our interest. On this cold and windy night, after many rebuffs, Villon finally finds food and shelter with a "refined," "muscular and spare," "resonant, courteous," "honorable rather than intelligent, strong, simple, and righteous" old knight.

Here, the structure of "A Lodging for the Night" abruptly breaks down from fiction, from atmospheric detail, plot development, and character enlargement, to debate. What Stevenson implied in the first part of his story, he reasserts here in expository dialogue, apparently losing faith in his fictional abilities as he resorts back to the directness of the essay.

Villon takes the side of duty to one's own survival; he is the first modern skeptic, the prophet of expediency. On the other hand, the knight stands for honor, *bonne noblesse*, with allegiance always to something greater than himself. The moral code of the criminal is pitted against the hypocrisy of the bourgeoisie. One's chances in life are determined by birth and social standing, says Villon. There is always the chance for change, implores the knight. In comparison to Stevenson's carefully built atmosphere and plot, this expository "solution" to his story is extremely crude.

"Markheim," a ghost story that deals with a disturbing problem of conscience, also contains a dialogue in its latter half. This dialogue, however, is a just continuation of the previous action. Different from "crawlers" such as "The Body-Snatcher," "Markheim" reinforces horror with moral investigation. Initial atmospherics contribute directly to Stevenson's pursuit of his thematic concern, and the later debate with the "visitant" becomes an entirely fitting expression for Markheim's own madness.

An allegory of the awakening conscience, "Markheim" also has the limits of allegory, one of which is meaning. In order for readers to understand, or find meaning in, an allegory, characters (or actors) must be clearly identified. In "Markheim" this presents major difficulties. Not only is an exact identity (or role) for the visitant finally in doubt, but also the identity of the dealer is unclear. It can be said that he usually buys from Markheim, not sells to him, but exactly what the dealer buys or sells is a good question. Whatever, on this particular occasion (Christmas Day), Markheim will have to pay the dealer extra "for a kind of manner that I remark in you today very strongly."

Amid the "ticking of many clocks among the curious lumber" of the dealer's shop, a strange pantomime ensues. Markheim says he needs a present for a lady and the dealer shows him a hand mirror. Markheim grows angry:

> "A glass," he said hoarsely, and then paused, and repeated it more clearly. "A glass? For Christmas? Surely not!"
>
> "And why not?" cried the dealer. "Why not a glass?"
>
> Markheim was looking upon him with an indefinable expression. "You ask me why not?" he said. "Why, look here—look at it—look at yourself! Do you like to see it? No! nor I—nor any man."

After damning the mirror as the "reminder of years, and sins, and follies—this hand-conscience," Markheim asks the dealer to tell something of himself, his secret life. The dealer puts Markheim off with a chuckle, but as he turns around for something more to show, Markheim lunges at him, stabbing him with a "long, skewer-like dagger." The dealer struggles "like a hen" and then dies. The murder seems completely gratuitous until Markheim remembers that he had come to rob the shop: "To have done the deed and yet not to reap the profit would be too abhorrent a failure."

Time, "which had closed for the victim," now becomes "instant and momentous for the slayer." Like Villon, Markheim feels pursued by Death, haunted by "the dock, the prison, the gallows, and the black coffin." The blood at his feet begins "to find eloquent voices." The dead dealer extracts his extra payment, becoming the enemy who would "lift up a cry that would ring over England, and fill the world with the echoes of pursuit." Talking to himself, Markheim denies that this evil murder indicates an equally evil nature, but his guilt troubles him. Not only pursued by Death, Markheim is pursued by Life as well. He sees his own face "repeated and repeated, as it were an army of spies"; his own eyes meet and detect him. Although alone, he feels the inexplicable consciousness of another presence:

Ay, surely; to every room and corner of the house his imagination followed it; and now it was a
faceless thing, and yet had eyes to see with; and again it was a shadow of himself; and yet again
beheld the image of the dead dealer, reinspired with cunning and hatred.

Eventually, Markheim must project an imaginary double, a *Doppelgänger* or exteriorized voice with which to debate his troubles. Here, action passes from the styl-
ized antique shop of the murdered to the frenzied mind of the murderer. The visitant, or double, is a product of this mind. Mad and guilty as Markheim appears to
be, his double emerges as a calm sounding sanity who will reason with him to commit further evil. Thus, the mysterious personification of drives buried deep within
Markheim's psyche exteriorizes evil as an alter ego and allows Markheim the chance
to act against it, against the evil in his own nature. Stevenson's sane, expository
technique of debate erects a perfect foil for Markheim's true madness.

In the end, although Markheim thinks himself victorious over what seems the
devil, it is actually this exteriorized aspect of Markheim's unknown self that conquers, tricking him into willing surrender and then revealing itself as a kind of
redemptive angel:

The features of the visitor began to undergo a wonderful and lovely change; they brightened and
softened with a tender triumph; and, even as they brightened, faded and dislimned. But Markheim
did not pause to watch or understand the transformation.

Material and intention are artistically intertwined in "Markheim," but the moral
ambiguities of Stevenson's theme remain complex, prompting various questions: is
Markheim's martyrdom a victory over evil or merely a personal cessation from action? Set on Christmas Day, with its obvious reversal of that setting's usual significance, is "Markheim" a portrayal of Christian resignation as a purely negative force,
a justification for suicide, or as the only modern solution against evil? What is the
true nature and identity of the visitant? Finally, can the visitant have an identity
apart from Markheim's own? Even answers to these questions, like Markheim's final
surrender, offer only partial consolation to the reader of this strange and complex
story of psychological sickness.

With Stevenson's improved health and his move to the South Seas, a new type of
story began to emerge, a kind of exotic realism to which the author brought his
mature talents. "The Bottle Imp," for example, juxtaposes the occult of an old German fairy tale (interestingly enough, acquired by Stevenson through Sir Percy Shelley, the poet's son) with factual details about San Francisco, Honolulu, and Papeete.
These settings, however, seem used more for convenience than out of necessity.

The long story "The Beach of Falesá" fulfills Stevenson's promise and gives evidence of his whole talents as a writer of short fiction. Similar to Joseph Conrad's
Heart of Darkness (1902), Stevenson's story deals with a person's ability or inability
to remain decent and law-abiding when the external restraints of civilization have
been removed. Action follows simply and naturally a line laid down by atmosphere.
Stevenson himself called it "the first realistic South Sea story," while Henry James

wrote in a letter the year before Stevenson's death, "The art of 'The Beach of Falesá' seems to me an art brought to a perfection and I delight in the observed truth, the modesty of nature, of the narrator."

In this adventure of wills between two traders on a tiny island, Stevenson is able to unify fitting exposition with restrained description through the voice of first-person narrator John Wiltshire. Three decades later, using Stevenson as one of his models, W. Somerset Maugham would further perfect this technique using the same exotic South Sea setting.

Stevenson's "The Beach of Falesá," along with the incomplete *Weir of Hermiston* and perhaps the first part of *The Master of Ballantrae* (1888), rests as his best work, the final integration of the divergent roots of his talents. If he had lived longer than forty-four years, "Tusitala" might have become one of the great English prose writers. As history now stands, however, Stevenson's small achievement of clear narrative, his victory of joining form to idea, remains of unforgettable importance to students and practitioners of the short-story genre.

Other major works

NOVELS: *Treasure Island*, 1883; *Prince Otto*, 1885; *The Strange Case of Dr. Jekyll and Mr. Hyde*, 1886; *Kidnapped*, 1886; *The Black Arrow*, 1888; *The Master of Ballantrae*, 1888; *The Wrong Box*, 1889; *The Wrecker*, 1892 (with Lloyd Osbourne); *Catriona*, 1893; *The Ebb-Tide*, 1894 (with Lloyd Osbourne); *Weir of Hermiston*, 1896 (unfinished); *St. Ives*, 1897 (completed by Arthur Quiller-Couch).

PLAYS: *Deacon Brodie*, 1880; *Admiral Guinea*, 1884; *Beau Austin*, 1884; *Macaire*, 1885 (with William Ernest Henley); *The Hanging Judge*, 1914 (with Fanny Van de Grift Stevenson).

POETRY: *Moral Emblems*, 1882; *A Child's Garden of Verses*, 1885; *Underwoods*, 1887; *Ballads*, 1890; *Songs of Travel and Other Verses*, 1896.

NONFICTION: *An Inland Voyage*, 1878; *Edinburgh: Picturesque Notes*, 1879; *Travels with a Donkey in the Cévennes*, 1879; *Virginibus Puerisque*, 1881; *Familiar Studies of Men and Books*, 1882; *The Silverado Squatters, Sketches from a Californian Mountain*, 1883; *Memories and Portraits*, 1887; *Across the Plains*, 1892; *A Footnote to History*, 1892; *Amateur Emigrant*, 1895; *Vailima Letters*, 1895; *In the South Seas*, 1896; *The Letters of Robert Louis Stevenson to His Family and Friends*, 1899 (2 volumes), 1911 (4 volumes); *The Lantern-Bearers and Other Essays*, 1988.

Bibliography

Calder, Jenni. *Robert Louis Stevenson: A Life Study*. New York: Oxford University Press, 1980. This excellent study, by the daughter of literary historian David Daiches, is richly documented with Stevenson's letters. Less a biography than a study of the writer's mind, it focuses on the personal values and attitudes informing Stevenson's work.

Chesterton, G. K. *Robert Louis Stevenson*. London: Hodder & Stoughton, 1927. An older but distinguished critical study of Stevenson that is still highly regarded for its insights as well as for its wit and lucidity.

Daiches, David. *Robert Louis Stevenson.* Norwalk, Conn.: New Directions, 1947. Along with J. C. Furnas, Daiches is credited with pioneering a positive reappraisal of Stevenson. His study is urbane and penetrating in the tradition of G. K. Chesterton.

Furnas, J. C. *Voyage to Windward.* New York: William Sloane, 1951. Furnas, who briefly lived in Stevenson's home in Samoa, traced the author's steps backward to his native Scotland. The work is a popular and sympathetic biography documented with unpublished letters. It contains an elaborate works-consulted bibliography.

Hennessy, James Pope. *Robert Louis Stevenson.* New York: Simon & Schuster, 1974. Designed for the general reader, this biography is a straightforward account written by a renowned writer and editor. It does not, however, document its sources and is therefore limited in value as a source for further study.

Kiely, Robert. *Robert Louis Stevenson and the Fiction of Adventure.* Cambridge, Mass.: Harvard University Press, 1964. Kiely offers solid interpretations of Stevenson's fiction from a pronounced Freudian point of view and offers comparisons between Stevenson and Joseph Conrad.

Saposnik, Irving S. *Robert Louis Stevenson.* New York: Twayne, 1974. A useful critical survey of Stevenson's major works. Saposnik's volume is the best starting point for serious study of Stevenson's fiction. Supplemented by a helpful annotated bibliography.

Kenneth Funsten
(Revised by *John W. Fiero*)

FRANK R. STOCKTON

Born: Philadelphia, Pennsylvania; April 5, 1834
Died: Washington, D.C.; April 20, 1902

Principal short fiction

The Floating Prince and Other Fairy Tales, 1881; *Ting-a-Ling Tales,* 1882; *The Lady: Or, The Tiger?, and Other Stories,* 1884; *A Christmas Wreck and Other Stories,* 1886; *Amos Kilbright: His Adscititious Experiences, with Other Stories,* 1888; *The Stories of the Three Burglars,* 1889; *The Rudder Grangers Abroad and Other Stories,* 1891; *The Clock of Rondaine and Other Stories,* 1892; *The Watchmaker's Wife and Other Stories,* 1893; *Fanciful Tales,* 1894; *A Chosen Few,* 1895; *New Jersey: From the Discovery of the Scheyichbi to Recent Times,* 1896; *Stories of New Jersey,* 1896 (also known as *New Jersey*); *A Story-Teller's Pack,* 1897; *Afield and Afloat,* 1900; *John Gayther's Garden and the Stories Told Therein,* 1902; *The Magic Egg and Other Stories,* 1907; *Stories of the Spanish Main,* 1913; *Best Short Stories,* 1957.

Other literary forms

Frank R. Stockton wrote many articles for periodicals and was on the staffs of *Hearth and Home, The Century Illustrated Monthly Magazine,* and assistant editor of *St. Nicholas* from the time he was thirty-nine until he was forty-seven. He began as a juvenile writer, and some of his children's stories are still popular, particularly "The Bee Man of Orn," illustrated by Maurice Sendak. Of his many adult novels, the best loved was *Rudder Grange* (1879), for which the public demanded two sequels, *The Rudder Grangers Abroad and Other Stories* and *Pomona's Travels* (1894).

Achievements

A prolific writer, Stockton is to be classed with Mark Twain and Joel Chandler Harris as one of the finest humorists of the last quarter of the nineteenth century. He was widely admired during his lifetime, especially for his short stories, and was perhaps the first American science-fiction novelist. Yet Stockton's name is all but unknown to the modern reader. The choice presented in his most popular story "The Lady: Or, The Tiger?" may be familiar to some today, but the story itself—which has been cited as a predecessor of modern recreative fiction—has been essentially forgotten.

It has been suggested that Stockton led the way for other more well-known authors. His novel *What Might Have Been Expected* (1874) was a forerunner of Twain's *The Adventures of Tom Sawyer* (1876) and *The Adventures of Huckleberry Finn* (1884); his portrayal of ordinary middle-class life in the 1880's preceded James Thurber's stories of the 1940's. Stockton's experiments with narrative technique inspired Gertrude Stein's approach in her *The Autobiography of Alice B. Toklas* (1933), and his political satire "The Governor-General" (1898) is remarkably similar to Leonard Patrick O'Connor Wibberley's 1950's bestseller *The Mouse That Roared* (1955).

Biography

Frank R. (Francis Richard) Stockton was a descendant of American pioneers, one of whom, Richard Stockton, had been one of the signers of the Declaration of Independence. The third son of nine children, he was expected to become a doctor. Instead, upon graduating from high school he studied wood engraving, at which he was proficient enough to support himself until he was thirty-two, when he decided to become a journalist. Until 1880 he specialized in children's stories; then he began writing for adults, although the tone and the situations were not much different from his earlier works. He completed more than a dozen novels, comedies, satires, scientific speculations, and whimsies.

Analysis

In "The Magic Egg," Frank R. Stockton successfully employed a narrative device as old as *The Arabian Nights' Entertainments:* the frame story. The enclosed tale is about a magic show put on by Herbert Loring for a few carefully invited friends. The first part of the exhibition is a slide show projected on the screen of what Loring calls "fireworks," a kind of kaleidoscope arrangement of pieces of colored glass which form, by means of mirrors and lights, into fascinating patterns. After half an hour of this, the host brings out a table upon which he places a box containing an egg. When he touches the egg with a wand, it hatches into a downy chick that continues to grow until it is an enormous cock. Flapping his wings, the cock ascends to a chair placed upon the table for that purpose, his weight nearly tipping it over. The audience stands, cheers, and becomes extremely excited. Then the magician reverses the growth process and the bird grows smaller and smaller until it enters the egg again, is put back into the box, and the host leaves the stage.

The frame narrative tells how the audience assembled at the Unicorn Club by invitation at three o'clock on a January afternoon has to wait fifteen minutes, because Loring sees that two reserved seats in the front row have not yet been filled. Because the audience is becoming restless, Loring decides to begin even though someone important has not yet arrived. A few minutes after the fireworks part of the show, Edith Starr, who had been betrothed to Herbert Loring a month before, enters unobtrusively; not wishing to disturb the proceedings to find her front-row reserved seat, she sits in the back behind two large gentlemen who completely conceal her person. Her mother had had a headache so she stayed with her until she fell asleep and then came alone to "see what she could."

At this point the narration changes from omniscient to first person, as the magician describes what is happening in a long monologue of six and a half pages which concludes the frame story. Elated with his success, Loring uses a metaphor in which he becomes the rooster that he produced. He feels as if he "could fly to the top of that steeple, and flap and crow until all the world heard me." Since the crowing cock who lords it over the hen yard is soon to be deflated, the emblem of masculine power is thus used as ironic foreshadowing, as well as summing up what preceded.

Herbert and Edith meet in her library. He has been in the habit of calling on her every night, so this is part of the acknowledged routine of the engaged lover. The remainder of the action is unfolded in dialogue. She says that she saw the audience wild with excitement. She, however, saw no chick, nor any full-grown fowl, no box, no wand, and no embroidered cloth. Nothing was what he said it was. "Everything was a sham and a delusion; every word you spoke was untrue. And yet everybody in the theatre, excepting you and me, saw all the things that you said were on the stage." Loring explains that he had hypnotized the audience with the revolving pieces of colored glass by which he had forced them to strain their eyes upward for half an hour in order to induce hypnotic sleep. He had been careful to invite only "impressionable subjects." When he was absolutely sure that they were under his influence, he proceeded to test his hypnotic powers with the illusion which they believed they saw.

"Did you intend that I should also be put under that spell?" she asks, indignant that he would have considered taking away her reason and judgment and making her "a mere tool of his will." She now understands that "nothing was real, not even the little pine table—not even the man!" She says a final good-bye to him, never to see him again, because she wants nothing further to do with a man who would cloud her perceptions, subject her intellect to his own, and force her to believe a lie. As the rejected suitor leaves, he says "And this is what came out of the magic egg!"

This is an inverted fairy tale. The normal formulaic plot would have ended in a marriage whose happy ending was achieved by the use of magical objects. Instead, the magic object here leads to the dissolution of the happy ending because the "princess" has a mind of her own; she is a strong-willed woman who refuses to submit to male domination. The second important aspect of the story is that it is a metaphor for the art of storytelling. The speaker, with his words alone, hypnotizes his audience into suspending their disbelief. His power over them is very like that of a magician, and Stockton, whose enthusiastic public followed his legerdemain through more than a dozen novels, must have at times confronted the ambiguities of his position. The blank page must have seemed the white shell of a magic egg which he alone could "crack" to release wonders that lasted only as long as he was relating them, and then, when the cover was closed, went back to being only an object.

"His Wife's Deceased Sister" is a charming tale built on the interrelations between life and literature and on the paradox that failure results from too-great success. A newly married author in the elation of his honeymoon writes a moving story. He has supported himself quite adequately up to that time with his fictions, but this story is a masterpiece. The problem is that everything he writes afterward is rejected because it would disappoint the public for not being on the same level which they have come to expect from him. The author then meets a pauper who earlier had the same paradoxical experience of having been ruined by the success of one story. Depressed by his visit to the pauper's room, where the pauper sleeps on newspapers and lives by grinding heads on pins, the author consults his editor, saying he faces similar ruin. They hit on the device of an assumed name.

Once more the author is making a good, steady income when a son is born. In his first joy of fatherhood, he composes a story which is even superior to "His Wife's Deceased Sister." He buries it in a tin box with the edges soldered together, which he hides in the attic with instructions to throw away the key to the solid lock he has purchased for it. The underlying assumption is that great fiction is inspired by happy events in life, which contradicts the Freudian notion that art sublimates suffering. The problem with the plot is that readers may think they have a better solution to the author's problem. Why not publish the story under his real name? The spark for "His Wife's Deceased Sister" is clearly Stockton's own experience with "The Lady: Or, The Tiger?"—which made him a cult figure—and subsequent publication problems that ensued. Although Stockton's work generally expressed admiration for the middle class, with all of its weaknesses, he could also be satirical and interpreted on many levels. In this story, the main character chooses to relegate his masterpiece to oblivion rather than again subject himself to the upheaval of public adulation. Because the masses read Stockton mainly for escape, it was easy for them to miss the underlying thought and sophistication in much of his work. Simply because he was so popular with the general public, Stockton has tended to be ignored by scholars and critics.

Other major works

NOVELS: *What Might Have Been Expected*, 1874; *Rudder Grange*, 1879; *A Jolly Fellowship*, 1880; *The Story of Viteau*, 1884; *The Transferred Ghost*, 1884; *The Late Mrs. Null*, 1886; *The Casting Away of Mrs. Lecks and Mrs. Aleshine*, 1886; *The Hundredth Man*, 1887; *The Dusantes: A Sequel to "The Casting Away of Mrs. Lecks and Mrs. Aleshine,"* 1888; *The Great War Syndicate*, 1889; *Personally Conducted*, 1889; *Ardis Claverden*, 1890; *The Squirrel Inn*, 1891; *The House of Martha*, 1891; *Pomona's Travels*, 1894; *The Adventures of Captain Horn*, 1895; *Mrs. Cliff's Yacht*, 1896; *Captain Chap: Or, The Rolling Stones*, 1896; *The Great Stone of Sardis: A Novel*, 1898; *The Girl at Cobhurst*, 1898; *The Buccaneers and Pirates of Our Coasts*, 1898; *The Associate Hermits*, 1899; *The Vizier of the Two-Horned Alexander*, 1899; *The Young Master of Hyson Hall*, 1899; *A Bicycle of Cathay: A Novel*, 1900; *Kate Bonnet: The Romance of a Pirate's Daughter*, 1902; *The Captain's Toll-Gate*, 1903; *The Lost Dryad*, 1912; *The Poor Count's Christmas*, 1927.

NONFICTION: *A Northern Voice Calling for the Dissolution of the Union of the United States of America*, 1860; *The Home: Where It Should Be and What to Put In It*, 1872.

CHILDREN'S LITERATURE: *Ting-a-Ling*, 1870; *Roundabout Rambles in Lands of Fact and Fancy*, 1872; *Tales Out of School*, 1875; *The Bee-Man of Orn and Other Fanciful Tales*, 1887; *The Queen's Museum*, 1887.

MISCELLANEOUS: *The Novels and Stories of Frank R. Stockton*, 1899-1904 (23 volumes).

Bibliography

Golemba, Henry L. *Frank R. Stockton.* Boston: Twayne, 1981. Part of Twayne's United

States Authors series, this extended examination of Stockton and his art includes an introductory bibliography and chronological investigation of Stockton's works. Golemba also suggests reasons for Stockton's neglect, not only in relation to the works themselves but also to the history of publishing and literary criticism over the last hundred years. The 182-page volume contains a select bibliography of primary and secondary sources.

Griffin, Martin I. J. *Frank R. Stockton.* Philadelphia: University of Pennsylvania Press, 1939. This biography gathers together details of Stockton's life—many taken from original sources—and shows the relationship between his life and his works. In the discussion of Stockton's work, however, plot summary dominates over critical interpretation. Includes a bibliography.

Howells, William Dean. "Stockton's Stories." *The Atlantic Monthly* 59 (January, 1887): 130-132. Citing particular Stockton stories, Howells discusses Stockton's influence on the short-story form, analyzing characteristics of both the author and the form that make them such a good match. This article, along with three others Howells wrote during Stockton's lifetime, provides some of the best criticism of Stockton's art.

Johnson, Robert U. *Remembered Yesterdays.* Boston: Little, Brown, 1923. This memoir by a former editor in chief of *The Century Illustrated Monthly Magazine* includes information about many men and women memorable in the fields of letters and publishing. His short chapter on Stockton, entitled "A Joyful Humorist," gives a feeling for the man through personal recollections and anecdotes.

Vedder, Henry C. *American Writers of Today.* Boston: Silver Burdett, 1894. This analysis of American writers includes a twelve-page chapter on Stockton and his work. Although obviously dated and considering works only to the early 1890's, the chapter offers interesting insights and a flavor of the times in which Stockton wrote. Vedder gives considerable attention to Stockton's originality and droll humor.

Ruth Rosenberg
(Revised by *Jean C. Fulton*)

JESSE STUART

Born: W-Hollow, Riverton, Kentucky; August 8, 1907
Died: Ironton, Ohio; February 17, 1984

Principal short fiction

Head o' W-Hollow, 1936; *Men of the Mountains*, 1941; *Tales from the Plum Grove Hills*, 1946; *Clearing in the Sky and Other Stories*, 1950; *Plowshare in Heaven: Tales True and Tall from the Kentucky Hills*, 1958; *Save Every Lamb*, 1964; *My Land Has a Voice*, 1966; *Come Gentle Spring*, 1969; *Come Back to the Farm*, 1971; *Votes Before Breakfast*, 1974; *The Best-Loved Short Stories of Jesse Stuart*, 1982.

Other literary forms

Although Jesse Stuart probably found the best outlet for his artistic expression in the short story, he published more than two thousand poems, a number of autobiographical works, nine novels—the latter including the best-selling *Taps for Private Tussie* (1943), and six children's books.

Achievements

Through the vivid pictures that he presents in his stories of life in the Kentucky hill country, Stuart opened up significant veins of material for other writers who follow him. While not adding new dimensions to the short story, he did nevertheless produce many excellent examples in that genre.

Virtually all Stuart's stories deal with the hill country of eastern Kentucky, where generations ago people dropped off from the movement West to settle in the hills and hollows of what has come to be a part of Appalachia. The life depicted in these stories is hard, and the people who live it are fundamentally religious and close to the earth. A natural storyteller, Stuart captured not only the idiom of his characters but also the very essence of their relationship to one another and to the natural world around them. He does not take solely the realist's approach but blends in a strain of romantic optimism.

Although cast in what appears to be a realist mode, Stuart's stories often blend a romantic optimism with an exuberance for life that is sometimes expressed in comic juxtapositions that verge on the grotesque. A popular as well as prolific author, Stuart was named poet laureate of Kentucky in 1954, won an award for *Taps For Private Tussie* in 1943, and was nominated for a Pulitzer Prize in 1975 for *The World of Jesse Stuart: Selected Poems* (1975).

Biography

A native of Kentucky, Jesse Hilton Stuart was educated at Lincoln Memorial University. Following his graduation, he began a career as a writer and teacher, starting what was, for him, a lifetime concern for educational reform and a lifelong struggle with the educational establishment. During his long career, he served as both teacher and administrator, and, after retiring from teaching to turn to full-time farming, writing, and lecturing, he never lost his passionate belief in the power of knowledge.

In 1939, after a courtship of seventeen years, Stuart married Naomi Deane Norris. They had one child, a daughter, Jessica Jane, born in 1942. During World War II, he served in the U.S. Navy, accepting disability in 1945. During subsequent years, though he traveled extensively, Stuart continued to live on the working farm in W-Hollow, the area where he was born and that he made famous through his poems, novels, and stories, many of which were published in *Esquire*.

He suffered the first of several heart attacks in 1954 but was able to return to normal activity. After a second stroke in 1982, however, he was unable to recover and remained more or less bedridden until his death two years later.

Analysis

America's southern highlands have long been viewed as an area removed from the influences of the "civilized" world; indeed, for more than a century they were. Rich in folklore and tradition, these highlands have provided stimulus to a vast number of writers as far back as William Gilmore Simms. The majority produced mostly second-rate novels and stories that relied on melodrama, sentimentality, and effusive description of natural setting to carry their plots. A few of the more recent writers, however, have risen above that level to present the southern highlanders and their land in a more graphic and realistic light. Jesse Stuart was one such writer.

Once commenting that as a child he "read the landscape, the streams, the air, and the skies," Stuart had "plenty of time to grow up in a world that I loved more and more as I grew older." With his abiding love and respect for the people and the land of this picturesque region, Stuart, in a fashion matched by few American regional writers, brought the southern highlands into sharp focus for his readers. His short stories—the fictional form in which he was at his best—are a journey of exploration into the many aspects of life in the region. Using his home place of W-Hollow as a vantage point and springboard, Stuart treated various themes and motifs in his stories: religion, death, politics, folklore, sense of place, nature, and the code of the hills. While these themes are treated from a realistic stance, through all of them runs the romantic idea of the ever-renewing power of the earth, and through many of them an exuberant sense of humor, where the comic juxtaposition is the primary structural pattern.

A story that clearly illustrates a blending of realism and Romanticism is "Dawn of Remembered Spring." Like so many of Stuart's stories, this one has an autobiographical ring to it. The main character is Shan, a young boy who appears in a number of Stuart's stories. In this particular instance, Shan is being cautioned by his mother not to wade the creek because of the danger of water moccasins. Just a few days prior, Roy Deer, another youngster, was bitten by a water moccasin and is now near death. To Shan's comment that all water moccasins ought to be killed, his mother agrees but adds, "They're in all these creeks around here. There's so many of them we can't kill 'em all." As idyllic as one side of life in W-Hollow may be, there is the ever-present factor of death, in this case symbolized by water moccasins.

Shan, however, is not to be deterred by his mother's warning, and, armed with a wild-plum club, he sets out wading the creek to kill as many water moccasins as he can. It is a suspenseful journey as Shan, frightened but determined, kills snake after snake. "This is what I like to do," he thinks. "I love to kill snakes." He wades up the creek all day, and when he steps out on the bank at four o'clock, he has killed fifty-three water moccasins. As he leaves the creek, he is afraid of the snakes he has killed and grips his club until his hands hurt, but he feels good that he has paid the snakes back for biting Roy Deer—"who wasn't bothering the water moccasins that bit him. He was just crossing the creek at the foot-log and it jumped from the grass and bit him."

As he goes near home, Shan sees two copperhead snakes in a patch of sunlight. "Snakes," he cries, "snakes a-fightin' and they're not water moccasins! They're copperheads!" The snakes are wrapped around each other, looking into each other's eyes and touching each other's lips. Shan's Uncle Alf comes upon the scene and tells Shan that the snakes are not fighting but making love. A group of onlookers soon gathers, including Shan's mother who asks him where he has been. "Killin' snakes," is his reply. To her statement that Roy Deer is dead, Shan says that he has paid the snakes back by killing fifty-three of them. At this point his mother, along with the rest who have gathered at the scene, is spellbound by the loving copperheads. She sends Shan to the house to get his father. As the boy goes, he notices that the snakes have done something to the people watching: "The wrinkled faces were as bright as the spring sunlight on the bluff; their eyes were shiny as the creek was in the noon-day sunlight."

In "Dawn of Remembered Spring" Stuart has juxtaposed images of death and life; Shan has killed fifty-three snakes, and Roy Deer has died from his snake bite. The two copperheads making love reminds the reader and the people watching that, cruel though nature may be at times, there is always the urge for life. The hate that demands revenge is somehow redeemed in the laughter that Shan hears from the group—a laughter "louder than the wild honeybees I had heard swarming over the shoemake, alderberry, and wild flox blossoms along the creek."

In "Sylvania Is Dead" Stuart uses the death motif to bring out the prevalent stoicism of the highlanders as well as their ability to see humor in a grotesque situation. The story opens as Bert Pratt and Lonnie Pennix are on their way to the funeral of the story's namesake. It is September, and nature is presented through images of death: "The backbone of the mountain was gray and hard as the bleached bone of a carcass. The buzzards floated in high circles and craned their necks." When the men reach Sylvania's cabin at the top of the mountain, they see a large crowd already gathered and buzzards circling low overhead. Lonnie pulls his pistol and shoots into the buzzards, scaring them away. When Skinny, Sylvania's husband, runs from the cabin scolding them for firing guns at such a sorrowful time, they respond that they were only trying to shoo away buzzards. Skinny says it is all right, for buzzards are a "perfect nuisance in a time like this."

The black humor in the story derives from Sylvania's size and her occupation. She weighs six hundred and fifty pounds; her husband, only about one hundred. Her occupation has been moonshining, and as one of the men digging her grave says, "I say we'll never miss Sylvania until she's gone. She's been a mother to all of us." Sylvania is so big that when she was caught "red handed" by the revenuers on one occasion, she simply laughed and said that even "if they could get her out of the house, they couldn't get her down the mountain."

Getting Sylvania out of the house is the big problem now. Building a coffin that takes six men to carry, they finally get Sylvania in it, but it will not go through the door. The only answer is to tear down the chimney. Before carrying the coffin out, however, the men stop for a drink from Sylvania's last barrel. "I patronized Sylvania in life and I'll patronize her in death," Bert says. The drinks from Sylvania's last barrel, combined with the sorrow at her death, make the crowd noisy. As the coffin is carried to the grave, there is laughing, talking, and crying, accompanied by another pistol shot at circling buzzards. Finally Sylvania is lowered to her rest, and, as Skinny is led back to his cabin, there are "words of condolence in the lazy wind's molesting the dry flaming leaves on the mountain."

The human drama played out at this mountaintop funeral is marked not predominantly by sorrow but by acceptance and humor. Sylvania was mother to them all in life, and it is only fitting that her "children" should see her to her grave. The humor in the story is not strained or out of place; on the contrary, the comedy underlines the grotesque element of human behavior as juxtaposed with the natural order. Humor is part of the hard life lived close to nature that is common to the people of Stuart's fictional world—as much a part as are Sylvania's moonshine and the buzzards circling overhead.

In "Sunday Afternoon Hanging" Stuart again blends the comedy with grim realism, as an old man describes to his grandson what old-time hangings in Blakesburg, Kentucky, were like. Viewing the electric chair as a poor substitute for a hanging, he points out that at a hanging "everybody got to see it and laugh and faint, cuss or cry." Indeed, they would come from as far as forty miles for such an opportunity. As the old man relates one particular incident to his grandson, the reader is made aware of a combination of characteristics in the people Stuart writes about—violence, vengeance, fatalism, and a desire to escape the tedium of their daily lives.

The Sunday afternoon hanging that the old man describes is the result of the brutal murder of an elderly couple by five men—Tim and Jake Sixeymore, Freed Winslow, Dudley Toms, and Work Grubb. They are all sentenced to be hanged on the same day, and hundreds of people congregate to witness the affair. In contrast to the grisly vengeance to be exacted, the day is bright, with a June wind blowing and roses in bloom. Providing music for the event is a seven-piece band dressed in gaudy yellow pants with red sashes and green jackets. "It was the biggest thing we'd had in many a day," recalls the old man. "Horses broke loose without riders on them and took out through the crowd among the barking dogs, running over them and the children. People didn't pay any attention to that. It was a hanging and people wanted to see every bit of it."

The procedure for the hanging is to have each man brought to the hanging on a horse-drawn wagon standing on his coffin. After a rousing number by the band and a confession from the condemned, the wagon is pulled away, leaving him "struggling for breath and glomming at the wind with his hands." When he is pronounced dead, the procedure begins for the next man. As each man is hanged, the gruesome scene becomes even more grotesque. The last to be hanged is Tim Sixeymore, and he is so large that he breaks six ropes before the execution is finally carried out. His confession, reminiscent of the ballad "Sam Hall," begins, "Gentlemen bastards and sonofabitches. Women wenches and hussies and goddam you all." As the hanging is completed and the parents of the Sixeymores carry off their dead sons, the band plays softer music. The crowd breaks up, "getting acquainted and talking about the hanging, talking about their crops and the cattle and the doings of the Lord to the wicked people for their sins"; and so life goes on. The blending of the comic and the tragic in "Sunday Afternoon Hanging" is so subtle that one is not sure whether to be horrified at the terrible vengeance exacted amid frivolity and hatred or to laugh at the black humor apparent in the contradiction.

Whatever his feelings of admiration for the people about whom he wrote, Stuart was not blind to the aspect of their character that encourages a kind of macho violence. A number of his stories, for example, deal with feuding and moonshining, which, although they are usually thought of now in a more or less humorous vein, were in reality serious and often deadly activities. Fiercely proud, Stuart's characters consider such activities their own business and go about them in their own way, as shown in the story "The Moonshine War."

Combining moonshine and feuding, this story is narrated by Chris Candell, whose father in earlier days was one of four moonshiners in Greenwood County, Kentucky. With the help of his three sons, Charlie, Zeke, and Chris, he moonshined for twenty years before his wife prevailed upon him to lay his sins on the mourner's bench in the Methodist Church and give up "the business." Shortly after, the federal agents close in on the other three families that are still moonshining—the Whaleys, the Fortners, and the Luttrells—sending members from each to prison for varying terms.

When Willie Fortner is released because of his youth, he returns to Greenwood County, vowing revenge on the other families because he thinks that they helped the federal agents to discover his father's still. Two weeks later Jarwin Whaley is found stabbed to death. In quick succession, two more deaths by stabbing occur, of Lucretia Luttrell and Charlie Candell, Chris's brother. There is no real evidence to connect these crimes to Willie Fortner, and, although he is arrested, he is acquitted, moving Zeke Candell to say, "Damn this circumstantial evidence stuff! We've got to take the law into our own hands." Before the Candells can do anything, however, Willie Fortner is killed in an auto wreck, the only one of five in the car who dies in the crash. Chris's father, obviously attributing Willie's death to the Lord, says that "we'll have peace. The knife killings are over."

Stuart does not condemn any of the actions in "The Moonshine War," but, as in all of his stories, he accepts the characteristics of his highland ancestors. Indeed, in another story, "My Father Is an Educated Man," he says of the fiercely independent men of his family now sleeping in the Virginia, West Virginia, and Kentucky mountains, "Though I belong to them, they would not claim me since I have had my chance and unlike them I have not killed one of my enemies." The code of conduct that arises from such a life view may be a combination of savagery, civility, and moral contradiction, but it attests to the belief of the highlander that he is master of his own destiny.

For those wishing to see another side of Stuart's writing, there is the volume of stories entitled *Save Every Lamb*. Virtually all the stories in this volume are autobiographical in background and have nature themes. In them Stuart harks back to another era—a time "when everybody in the country lived by digging his livelihood from the ground." It was a time when humans were in tune with the natural world about them and were better for it. "My once wonderful world has changed into a world that gives me great unhappiness," Stuart says in the Introduction to *Save Every Lamb*. For the moment, at least, Stuart in these stories takes the reader back with him to that wonderful world of his youth.

In all of his stories Stuart writes with an easy, almost folksy, style. Avoiding experimentation and deep symbolism, he holds his readers by paying close attention to detail and by painting starkly graphic scenes as he brings to life the characters and settings of W-Hollow. As a regionalist, Stuart draws constantly on his background in his stories, with the result that his style is underlined by an autobiographical bias, which contributes strongly to the sense of immediacy that marks all his work. Just as William Faulkner has his microcosm of the universe in Yoknapatawpha County, so too does Stuart in W-Hollow, and the American literary chronicle is the richer for it.

Other major works

NOVELS: *Trees of Heaven*, 1940; *Taps for Private Tussie*, 1943; *Foretaste of Glory*, 1946; *Hie to the Hunters*, 1950; *The Good Spirit of Laurel Ridge*, 1953; *Daughter of the Legend*, 1965; *Mr. Gallion's School*, 1967; *The Land Beyond the River*, 1973; *Cradle of the Copperheads*, 1988.

POETRY: *Harvest of Youth*, 1930; *Man with a Bull-Tongue Plow*, 1934; *Album of Destiny*, 1944; *Kentucky Is My Land*, 1952; *Hold April*, 1962; *The World of Jesse Stuart: Selected Poems*, 1975.

NONFICTION: *Beyond Dark Hills*, 1938; *The Thread That Runs So True*, 1949; *The Year of My Rebirth*, 1956; *God's Oddling*, 1960; *To Teach, To Love*, 1970; *My World*, 1975; *The Kingdom Within: A Spiritual Autobiography*, 1979; *Lost Sandstones and Lonely Skies and Other Essays*, 1979; *If I Were Seventeen Again and Other Essays*, 1980.

CHILDREN'S LITERATURE: *Mongrel Mettle: The Autobiography of a Dog*, 1944; *The Beatinest Boy*, 1953; *A Penny's Worth of Character*, 1954; *Red Mule*, 1955; *The Rightful Owner*, 1960; *Andy Finds a Way*, 1961.

Bibliography

Blair, Everetta Love. *Jesse Stuart: His Life and Works.* Columbia: University of South Carolina Press, 1967. Blair opens with a brief account of Stuart's life and background. Subsequent chapters survey his poetry, short stories, novels, and other accomplishments. General discussions provide insight into particular works and overall trends.

Foster, Ruel E. *Jesse Stuart.* New York: Twayne, 1968. One of the earliest, and with a few exceptions, one of the best of the critical studies. Contains biographical information as well as extensive critiques on Stuart's work up to the date of publication.

Le Master, J. R. ed. *Jesse Stuart: Selected Criticism.* St. Petersburg, Fla.: Valkyrie Press, 1978. A good start to Stuart criticism, this volume includes previously published articles by different scholars. Excellent introduction to Stuart's work.

Le Master, J. R. and Mary Washington Clark, eds. *Jesse Stuart: Essays on His Work.* Lexington: University Press of Kentucky, 1977. These essays (written specifically for this volume) provide critical perspectives on different facets and forms of Stuart's work, including poetry, short fiction, and novels, as well as his humor and use of folklore. The editors indicate that a primary purpose here is to bring into sharper focus Stuart's use of multiple perspectives.

Pennington, Lee. *The Dark Hills of Jesse Stuart.* Cincinnati: Harvest Press, 1967. Pennington discusses Stuart's system of symbolism as it emerges in his early poetry and later through his novels. Argues that Stuart is far more than a regionalist; rather, he is an important creative writer and spokesman not only for a region but for all humankind.

Richardson, H. Edward. *Jesse: The Biography of an American Writer—Jesse Hilton Stuart.* New York: McGraw-Hill, 1984. This inclusive study, printed in the year of Stuart's death, contains some photographs. Sensitively written, it offers invaluable reading for anyone with more than a passing interest in Stuart's life and work.

Wilton Eckley
(Revised by *Mary Rohrberger*)

THEODORE STURGEON
Edward Hamilton Waldo

Born: Staten Island, New York; February 26, 1918
Died: Eugene, Oregon; May 8, 1985

Principal short fiction

Without Sorcery, 1948; *E Pluribus Unicorn*, 1953; *Caviar*, 1955; *A Way Home*, 1955; *A Touch of Strange*, 1958; *Aliens 4*, 1959; *Beyond*, 1960; *Sturgeon in Orbit*, 1964; . . . *And My Fear Is Great/Baby Is Three*, 1965; *The Joyous Invasions*, 1965; *Starshine*, 1966; *Sturgeon Is Alive and Well*, 1971; *The Worlds of Theodore Sturgeon*, 1972; *To Here and the Easel*, 1973; *Sturgeon's West*, 1973 (with Don Ward); *Case and the Dreamer*, 1974; *Visions and Venturers*, 1978; *The Stars Are the Styx*, 1979; *The Golden Helix*, 1980.

Other literary forms

It seems as though no literary form was wrong for Theodore Sturgeon. He wrote newspaper stories in the late 1930's, book and film reviews in the 1950's, and for twenty years after that, radio and television scripts, and a wide variety of fiction. He also published a coauthored Western novel, a (pseudonymous) historical romance, a psychological vampire novel, a film novelization, and five highly acclaimed science-fiction novels.

Achievements

Sturgeon's name is one of those most cited in lists of the writers of science-fiction's golden age. Many consider him the best golden age author, mainly because he concentrated less on scientific hardware and more on character interaction than did his contemporaries. A moralistic and romantic writer, his major themes are tolerance for otherness of all kinds and concern for the environment before these became fashionable opinions. He was among the first American science-fiction writers to write plausibly about sex, homosexuality, race, and religion. He has sometimes been accused of writing pornography by those who prefer their science fiction in the standard starched-collar puritan mode. In reality, Sturgeon is among the first to turn American science fiction into a fiction for mature, thinking adults, as his influence on writers such as Ray Bradbury and Samuel R. Delany attests. He received several awards nominations and won three awards: the International Fantasy Award in 1954, for *More than Human* (1953), and the science-fiction Hugo and Nebula awards in 1970, for "Slow Sculpture." The University of Kansas offers an annual science-fiction short-story award in his name.

Biography

Born Edward Hamilton Waldo, Theodore Sturgeon led one of those archetypal writer's lives, roaming the world and holding many different kinds of jobs. In 1929, his name was officially changed to Theodore Sturgeon. As a child, he wanted to be a circus performer, even gaining an athletic scholarship to Temple University, but his career in gymnastics was stopped by rheumatic fever. As an adult, he sold newspapers; collected garbage; sailed the seas as an engine-room wiper; worked as a musician, a ghostwriter, and a literary agent; operated a bulldozer and a gas station; and held several door-to-door sales positions. During World War II, he worked building airstrips and later writing technical manuals. Married five times, usually to younger women, he fathered six children. Sturgeon died in Eugene, Oregon, on May 8, 1985.

Analysis

In a commercial literature devoted to galaxy-spanning concepts of paper-thin consistency, mechanical characters of whatever origin (human, alien, metal, or chemical), and wooden verbal expression, Theodore Sturgeon was an anomaly as early as 1939, when his stories began appearing in science-fiction magazines. A writer more of fantasy than of science fiction, whose predilection for words over machines was immediately apparent, Sturgeon was concerned with specific fantasies less for themselves than as means to the end of writing about human beings and human problems. Unlike those of so many of his colleagues, his tales usually take place in small, circumscribed locations, where love and healing can overshadow lesser, more conventional marvels and wonders.

Although style has always been somewhat suspect in science fiction, Sturgeon (along with Alfred Bester and Ray Bradbury) fought a rear-guard action throughout his career. His example speaks louder than theory about the importance of words, especially in terms of the planned resonance of images and the conscious manipulation of symbols to invite emotional responses to his romantic, even utopian view of the relationship between human beings and their technologies. Viewing "science" as "wisdom," he wrote of the search for wholeness, often without the aid of conventional means of attaining knowledge. He was antimachine in a way but more opposed to people's self-enslavement to mechanical procedures, be they metal or mental. Illustration of these themes calls forth as often as not a kind of fantasy that bears a close relationship to magic, events being caused by words and gestures. His is not a "science" that tediously accumulates and interprets observations of the world as it can be measured with instruments fashioned by and limited to the rational capacities of human beings.

There is no typical Sturgeon story, so varied is his surface subject matter, which includes many traditional science-fiction "inventions" and "discoveries," space travel, planetary exploration, matter transmission, cloning, alien contact, and paranormal powers among them. Sturgeon's stories usually speculate on love and sex in terms often considered radical for their market. Like D. H. Lawrence, he showed concern for the roots of human behavior in publicly repressed areas of behavior and thought; like Lawrence, too, he may have exaggerated the usefulness for everyone of his own particular cures. More sentimental than Lawrence, he was also more experimental, obviously with respect to subject matter but also in terms of literary forms, playing with chronology, point of view, and other elements of storytelling in a way highly unusual for science fiction prior to the mid-1960's.

Sturgeon sold some remarkable "horror" stories in his early years of writing, such as "It," told from the point of view of a putrescent monster as dead as it is alive, and "Bianca's Hands," about a man in love with, and eventually strangled by, the hands of a girl who has the mind of an idiot. In "Killdozer," he created a masterpiece of contemporary terror in which two members of an eight-man construction crew on a deserted Pacific island barely withstand and defeat a malevolent alien consciousness which has taken possession of one of their bulldozers. The television motion picture made from this story did not do it justice. The most anthologized of Sturgeon's early pieces, however, is "Microcosmic God," whose popularity he resented because its relatively clumsy handling and apparently ruthless attitude toward certain life-forms are uncharacteristic of his best work and his own self-image.

Primarily narrative, what dialogue there is being rather stiff and self-conscious, "Microcosmic God" is somewhat of a self-parody, with its protagonist a "Mister Kidder" and his antagonist a stereotyped grasping banker named Conant who would exploit Kidder's discoveries to take over the world. Almost lost in the reader's obvious antipathy to Conant's manipulation of human beings is its direct parallel to Kidder's even more ruthless manipulation of the tiny conscious beings whose evolution he has accelerated purely to satisfy his own curiosity.

Explicitly science fictional, the story is not rooted in practical experience with the details of construction machinery which makes "Killdozer" so dramatically convincing. Kidder's literal creation of an entire race for experimental purposes is couched, rather, in more theoretical and conceptual detail. The story's headlong pace races past problems in verisimilitude, in keeping with the simplistic morality of good (Kidder) versus evil (Conant), but intrusive commentary by the narrator reminds the reader sporadically that this is a fable, even if it does not specifically single out Kidder for censure.

Characterizing Kidder only minimally—both men are comic-book figures—the story shows his impatience with other people, with orthodox science (he claims no academic degrees), and with practical applications for his findings. In Conant, his alter ego, the reader sees explicitly the potential for abuse in his work, which reflects back on Kidder's own amorality. A god to his creatures, Kidder is a stand-in, not for the "mad scientist" whose image Sturgeon specifically disavows, but for the short-sighted tinkerer, representing all those who endeavor by mechanical means to improve the lot of human beings. The danger within the story is that, when Kidder dies, the creatures will conquer the world; the real danger to which the story points is that the misapplication of science to means or ends in the real world will do the same.

Irresponsibility is also the theme of "Mewhu's Jet," in which an alien visitor with fabulous technological powers turns out to be a young child; of "The Sky Was Full of Ships," in which a naïve meddler unwittingly calls to Earth a menacing alien fleet; and of "Maturity," in which that quality is disavowed as the ripeness immediately preceding death. Sturgeon, however, was also concerned with the other side of the coin. In "Thunder and Roses," the beautiful Starr Anthim tries, in a nuclear-devastated America, to prevent late retaliation that might wipe out all human civilization. In "Saucer of Loneliness," another girl preserves the message given her by a miniature flying saucer, which assuages her despair with the knowledge that loneliness is shared. In "The Skills of Xanadu," an entire planet's people have overcome dependence on ugly machine technology and achieved a utopian state which is both dynamic and transferable.

Communication is central to these stories, as it is to "Bulkhead," in which the "partner" assigned to a space pilot with whom he has an intense love-hate relationship turns out to be another part of himself, part of a schizophrenic condition deliberately induced by his employers for his own good. In the classic novella, "Baby Is Three," centerpiece of the award-winning novel *More than Human*, a "gestalt" being, composed of adolescent parapsychological misfits, fights to define its identity, which the last section of the novel will provide with maturity, responsibility, even community. Although this is arguably Sturgeon's best story ever, the novel to which it is converted is too well known to require analysis here of one of its parts.

The many ways that love and sex connect fascinated Sturgeon as early as "Bianca's Hands," but several provocative variations on this theme occupied him in the 1950's. *Venus Plus X* (1960) hypothesized physiological bisexuality in a "utopian" community on Earth. *Some of Your Blood* (1961) is a psychological case study of physiological vampirism. In "Affair with a Green Monkey," a psychologist obsessed with adjustment confuses gentleness with homosexuality, completely misjudging a humanoid alien whose sexual equipment would put to shame the best-endowed pornographic film star. His best treatment of "aberrant" sexuality is probably "The World Well Lost."

Again attacking the obsession with normalcy of America in the 1950's, Sturgeon describes a future world enchanted by the love for each other and for things earthly of a couple of unexpected alien visitors, before their home world requests the return of the "loverbirds." Having once sent an ambassador to Earth and found it wanting, the planet Dirbanu has stonewalled further contact attempts until this time, when humans' intolerance at being kept out prompts them to sacrifice the fugitives in quest of anticipated interplanetary relations. The "prison ship," however, is crewed by two men whose perfect record results from a complementariness unrecognized by Rootes and unspoken by Grunty. Discovery of the aliens' telepathic powers threatens the tongue-tied Grunty, whose threat to kill them is countered by two things: the fact that Dirbanu wants them dead, and the reason why.

Dirbanu females are so different in appearance from males that all human beings look to them to be of the same sex and just as repulsive as the two fugitive "loverbirds." Acknowledging their homosexuality, the alien prisoners recognize the same propensity in their captors. Rootes's tales of heterosexual exploits are repetitive and hollow-sounding, while Grunty suffers consciously from an involuntary attraction to his partner which he can never voice, for all the poetry that swirls within his mind. Grunty lets the prisoners escape in a lifeboat which will isolate them for years before, if ever, they reach planet-fall. Although Rootes berates Grunty, Dirbanu is grateful for the presumed deaths; they still will have nothing to do with Earth, however, and their bigotry strikes a sympathetic chord in Rootes, as presumably it would back home. For all the "space opera" trappings, the tenuous coincidences, and the dated attitude toward homosexuality—even contextually, it seems inconsistent with an Earth that pursues, the reader is told, many other euphoric and aphrodisiac thrills—the story evokes with minimal sentimentality a love that literally "cannot speak its name" and the pathetic intolerance that will not let it.

In contrast to such a plot-laden construct, "The Man Who Lost the Sea" is as near to stream-of-consciousness style as market considerations would allow. Exploring the senses, hallucinatory experiences, and memories of the first astronaut to reach Mars alive, the story weaves past and present, childhood and adulthood, mechanical and psychological drives into a haunting impression of a time which might prove as traumatic and epoch-making as the emergence of the first air-breathers out of the sea of life's origin on Earth. As shifting point of view and chronology represent the man's dazed mental and emotional state, Sturgeon only gradually reveals the nature of the man's predicament (his ship has crashed and there is no way back), until the emotional shock of simultaneous gain and loss has prepared the way for the triumphant irony of the protagonist's dying exultation: "We made it!"

Sturgeon's rather few stories of the 1960's and 1970's continued to deal with love and responsibility, especially healing, but often in a talky mode. His greatest success in that period is "Slow Sculpture," named best of the year by science-fiction fans and readers alike. This novella is a loving exploration of how an unnamed "man" and a "girl" come tentatively to know each other, although the specific means are entwined with science-fiction and fantasy motifs as the two people are with each other and with the fifteen-foot bonsai tree that grows in this garden. Like other Sturgeon protagonists, the man is a polymath, credentialed in law and in two kinds of engineering, who in this instance practices medicine without a license.

That his cure for her cancer works the reader is asked to take on faith as she does, since establishment means and methods are deliberately eschewed, and the "technology" that he uses is more obscured than revealed by the metaphorical language with which he describes it. There are some appropriate "special effects," suggesting the interrelatedness of house and garden, house and mountain, man and tree, matter and energy, mind and body. The medium and the message, however, are primarily communication, in conversation which may be more expressive than it is true to life, but which is far from stilted. The speeches, moreover, are contextually true, since the man, whatever his healing powers for others, fends off the girl's involvement with him, her own halting attempts to connect with the anger, fear, and frustration in him at the world's resistance to all he has offered to better it.

Throughout the story, the dominant symbol is the bonsai, which resists "instruction" because it knows how it should grow, and achieves its form by compromising between its essential nature and the manipulation to which it is subjected, not by its "owner" but by its "companion." As in many of Sturgeon's works, but never more appropriately than here, the prose itself is "sculptured," reminding the reader that the magic of fantasy resides less in the act than in the telling of it.

Sturgeon's stories are in some ways "hopelessly romantic," conjuring impossible cures and utopian solutions, even when they are not projected long ahead and far away. Like the best science fiction, they lead the reader back to the present, not to external realities, but rather to emotional confrontations with human problems, situations, characters. Although readers may detach themselves from the ostensible subjects, removed from the here and now, the situation of the writer, often as a stand-in for the reader-as-dreamer, is frequently apparent, sometimes intensely personal. For all of their variety, Sturgeon's stories betray an almost obsessive concern for wholeness and healing, for communication and tolerance of the misfit, and often for "September-June" relationships between "men" and "girls." That his work maintained, even increased its popularity as he wrote less and less suggests that he mined a vein of ore rich in its appeal, to women as well as men, to the adolescent in everyone. Almost despite their paraphernalia of science fiction and fantasy, Sturgeon's modern-day fairy tales communicate what his characters continually try to communicate: the truth of emotion and the magic of words.

Other major works

NOVELS: *The Dreaming Jewels*, 1950 (also known as *The Synthetic Man*, 1957); *More Than Human*, 1953; *I, Libertine*, 1956 (as Frederick R. Ewing); *The Cosmic Rape*, 1958; *Venus Plus X*, 1960; *Some of Your Blood*, 1961; *Voyage to the Bottom of the Sea*, 1961; *Alien Cargo*, 1984; *Godbody*, 1986.

Bibliography

Delany, Samuel. "Sturgeon." In *Starboard Wine: More Notes on the Language of Science Fiction*. Pleasantville, N.Y.: Dragon Press, 1984. Delany is not only one of science fiction's best authors, but also he is one of its best critics, particularly in analysis of style. Here Delany explores some of the nuances of Sturgeon's language and the "realism" of Sturgeon's stories.

Diskin, Lahna. *Theodore Sturgeon*. Mercer Island, Wash.: Starmont House, 1981. The only book-length study of Sturgeon's fiction, this volume focuses primarily on his most famous science fiction.

Malzberg, Barry N. "Grandson of the True and the Terrible." In *The Engines of the Night*. Garden City, N.Y.: Doubleday, 1982. A brief but poignant evaluation of Sturgeon's importance in the history of science fiction.

Moskowitz, Sam. "Theodore Sturgeon." In *Seekers of Tomorrow: Masters of Modern Science Fiction*. Westport, Conn.: Hyperion Press, 1966. This essay is a good general introduction to Sturgeon in terms of his place in science-fiction history and in what makes him "unique."

Sackmary, Regina. "An Ideal of Three: The Art of Theodore Sturgeon." In *Critical Encounters*, edited by Dick Riley. New York: Frederick Ungar, 1978. Sackmary discusses the motif of threes in Sturgeon's fiction as his symbol for unity.

David N. Samuelson
(Revised by *David Layton*)

JUN'ICHIRŌ TANIZAKI

Born: Tokyo, Japan; July 24, 1886
Died: Yugawara, Japan; July 30, 1965

Principal short fiction

"Kirin," 1910; "Shisei," 1910 ("The Tattooer," 1963); "Shōnen," 1910; "Hōkan," 1911; "Akuma," 1912; "Kyōfu," 1913 ("Terror," 1963); "Otsuya goroshi," 1913; "Watakushi," 1921 ("The Thief," 1963); "Aoi Hano," 1922 ("Aguri," 1963); *Tade Kuu mushi*, 1928-1929 (*Some Prefer Nettles*, 1955); "Mōmoku monogatari," 1931 ("A Blind Man's Tale," 1963); "Ashikari," 1932 (English translation, 1936); "Shunkinshō," 1933 ("A Portrait of Shunkin," 1936); *Hyofu*, 1950 (collection); *Kagi*, 1956 (*The Key*, 1961); "Yume no ukihashi," 1959 ("The Bridge of Dreams," 1963); *Yume no ukihashi*, 1960 (collection); *Fūten rojin nikki*, 1961-1962 (*Diary of a Mad Old Man*, 1965); *Kokumin no bungaku*, 1964 (collection); *Tanizaki Jun'ichirō shu*, 1970 (collection); *Seven Japanese Tales*, 1981.

Other literary forms

For Western readers, Jun'ichirō Tanizaki is best known for his short stories and short novels. Throughout his career, however, he was a prolific writer of plays, essays, and translations as well. Many English readers favor his long novel *Sasameyuki* (1943-1948, 1949; *The Makioka Sisters*, 1957) as his best work. It is the story of a family's efforts to arrange a marriage for Yukiko, the third of four daughters in a respectable Osaka family. Tanizaki has written a number of plays, and also noteworthy are his two translations into modern Japanese of Murasaki Shikibu's *Genji monogatari* (c. 1004; first English translation, *The Tale of Genji*, 1925-1933). The earlier translation was restricted by the severe censorship during the time of the war with China; the later one was in more liberal and colloquial language.

Achievements

The modern Japanese writers most commonly suggested as comparable to Tanizaki for the quality of their fiction are the 1968 Nobel Prize winner Yasunari Kawabata, and Yukio Mishima. It is widely believed that Tanizaki was Kawabata's chief rival for the Nobel Prize that year. Mishima's easier fiction gains more readers but cannot match Tanizaki's more innovative complexity. From his earliest years, however, Tanizaki has had his detractors, as many found his youthful "demoniac" works offensive. Throughout his career, for that matter, his frank portrayal of unconventional, even bizarre sexual and marital relationships among his characters caused consternation. In spite of such reservations, Tanizaki was elected to the Japanese Academy of Arts in 1937. He was awarded the Mainichi Prize for Publication and Culture for *The Makioka Sisters* and the Asaki Culture Prize and the Imperial Cultural Medal, both in 1949. These are the most important awards the Japanese can give a writer.

Biography

Jun'ichirō Tanizaki, whose father owned a printing establishment, was born in Tokyo on July 24, 1886. He attended the Tokyo Imperial University, studying classical Japanese literature, but had little interest in attending lectures and did not earn a degree. Even at the university, however, he wrote stories and plays for small magazines, some of them serialized; indeed, he continued to be productive throughout his life. In his early years, he was noted for dissolute habits, and some readers blamed him for what they believed was worship of women. His three marriages were unconventional, the experiences of which some will say are hinted at in his short fiction. The suggestion is made occasionally that Tanizaki's moving from Tokyo to the Kansai after the earthquake of 1923 contributed to changes in his writing, but changes in phrasing, characterization, or dialogue in these different years are not easy to see in English translations. As one reviews the publications of his life, one finds no time when he was unproductive. In fact, he continued writing to the time of his death, on July 30, 1965, in Yugawara.

Analysis

The dominant theme in Jun'ichirō Tanizaki's best work is love, but few writers so successfully explore this universally preferred topic with such unconventional revelations. Commentators often identified his earliest writings as "demoniac"; his later work they might have characterized as "sardonic." As labels prove to be insufficient for most good writers, however, one must struggle to understand Tanizaki's probing style as he uncovers complicated motives for lovers, spouses, family members, and friends, who continually surprise one another. In addition, as one finishes reading Tanizaki's works of fiction, most characteristically, one finds oneself more than a little uncertain as to how things really work out. The dispute, the rivalries, or the resentments always seem resolved or brought to a close; most commonly, though, the reader finds himself needing to fill in indeterminate gaps using his own imagination. This challenge, in fact, contributes to much of the pleasure in reading Tanizaki's fiction.

In his early sensational tale, "The Tattooer," the exceptional tattooer, Seikichi, behaves much like a sadist in his attitudes toward some of his customers, as he revels in the excruciating pain they endure for the honor of having such an artist adorn their bodies. He outdoes himself in embellishing the back of a beautiful young woman with a huge black widow spider. Readers are told that "at every thrust of his needle Seikichi . . . felt as if he had stabbed his own heart." After he assures the woman that he has poured his soul into this tattoo and that now all men will be her victims, she accepts this prophecy, turns her resplendently tattooed back to him, and promptly claims the tattooer himself as her first conquest.

With similar emphasis upon intimate revelation of pain, and with similarly ambivalent implications for the suffering endured, in "Terror," a young man describes his peculiar phobia for riding in a train or any other vehicle. For the occasion in the story, he must travel by train to take a physical examination for military duty. His nervous trembling almost drives him mad and certainly drives him to excessive alcoholic consumption. With the combination of neurotic fearfulness and drunkenness, he seems unlikely to pass his physical; the reader, however, hears a doctor reassuring the young man: "Oh, you'll pass all right. A fine husky fellow like you." Such open-endedness in Tanizaki's short fiction seems practically his trademark.

The probing into the psychology of nonconforming personalities reveals itself also in "The Thief." In this story, a young man shares the discomfort and embarrassment with his university dormitory roommates as one by one they admit their shame at having suspected the narrator as the perpetrator of recent thefts. Readers can hardly avoid sympathizing with the young man as he reveals his private thoughts about the unfortunate, painful admissions by others who suspect and distrust him. Then one suddenly discovers that this sensitive young man, in fact, truly is the thief. In fact, the thief boasts that, with an outward show of innocence, he can deceive not only roommates and readers but even himself.

In the story "Aguri," Tanizaki goes further, with his presentation of a self-conscious narrator brooding over his fears and inadequacies. The middle-aged Okada, accompanied by his slim, shapely mistress on a shopping trip, describes in extravagant detail how he is wasting away physically while the young woman, Aguri, craves the most expensive luxuries. As in "The Thief," the narrator of this story carries the reader along with him in his imagination, momentarily at least, with a painful scene of ruinously expensive purchases for Aguri, followed by Okada's fainting embarrassingly in public from weakness. Almost before one realizes the change, however, the reader learns that these disasters were merely an imagined vision. The man and woman end up making modest purchases and with no physical collapse.

In what is probably Tanizaki's most widely read work, *Some Prefer Nettles*, readers are shown a husband and wife, Kaname and Misako, who seem to torture each other with continuing irritations, discomfort, and worry for lack of ability to speak candidly to each other about their heartfelt desires; neither is capable of a forthright decision. Both incline partially toward Western culture and convention-free social values. Kaname prides himself on tolerant generosity when he learns of his wife's interest in another man and encourages her to experiment with this affair until such a time when the two of them can rationally decide whether to dissolve their own marriage or to renew it again with no hard feelings. Readers are limited, however, to the thoughts of Kaname for speculation about what causes the current division. Both these young people look on at contrasts in social relationships as Misako's father, accompanied by a complacent, obedient mistress, indulges himself as a connoisseur of puppet shows. As the story continues, one receives hints that Misako's extramarital romance offers no future hopes for her; Tanizaki intrigues readers more obviously, however, in showing that Kaname desires to follow the older man's conservative style of life. He, too, wants to be waited on with the flattering attentions of an old-fashioned, obedient woman. At the conclusion, readers are told that Kaname is joined at night by a woman whom the narrator does not name, bearing old-style Japanese books; most commentators assume that the old man has sent his mistress to Kaname as a generous gift, but the woman could just as plausibly be Misako adapting to the old-fashioned role to recover their marriage.

In "A Blind Man's Tale," Tanizaki offers what might be his boldest experiment in narrative point of view. A blind masseur, while massaging a nobleman, recalls the insight he gained thirty years before into a complicated series of events in sixteenth century Japanese history. What he knows he learned largely through the experience of serving as masseur for a beautiful noblewoman. The blind man depends upon his own intuition, overheard conversations, and confidential hints. His story not only opens up multiple perspectives on historical events, interesting for their own sake, but it also leaves readers pondering choices in judging these acts as honorable, cowardly, or opportunistic.

In "Ashikari" the author appeals to easy emotionalism by beginning with a sentimental narrator taking a walk, visiting the Shrine of Minase and then, in the evening, enjoying the moonlight on the river. His detailed observations of ancient scenes and nostalgic thoughts about the past are accompanied by recitation of favorite verses, Chinese and Japanese. He also composes verses of his own, reciting them aloud while admiring the moonlight. Soon, however, this simple sentimentalism gives way.

The brash visitor, Serizawa, who appears suddenly, dominates the scene from this point. Serizawa tells the story of his father's love for the elegant widow Oyu, a woman surrounded by symbols of refinement. This leads to the self-sacrificing of both the father and Oyu's younger sister Oshizu, who marry but remain chaste in respect for the love between Oyu and the father. The three of them remain close companions in this setting for two or three years. In retrospect, though, one is left intrigued with the mystery of what kind of satisfaction either the father or the son gained from their limited sharing in the Lady Oyu's aristocratic way of life.

"A Portrait of Shunkin" invites attention for another narrative technique favored by Tanizaki, the use of abundant circumstantial detail to lend an initial air of credence to the unusual love story that follows. At the beginning, the narrator gives precise descriptions of a pair of tombstones in a temple graveyard and then of a privately printed biography, and the only known photograph of the beautiful, blind woman Shunkin, famous for her samisen lessons. With this narrator, however, one discovers Tanizaki's characteristic ambivalence as the storyteller regularly admits uncertainty about how to interpret the evidence he has found. One suspects that Shunkin gained pleasure from tormenting Sasuka, her disciple, who may have been, in effect, her slave, but quite possibly he also was her lover. The most startling event, Sasuka's blinding of himself following the cruel, disfiguring scalding of Shunkin by an assailant, invites a great range of speculation about Sasuka's motives: to preserve the memory of her beauty, to gain a measure of acceptance from her, or to distract her from demanding so much of him because of her own handicaps.

Tanizaki varies the formula for an epistolary novel in fine comic style in *The Key*, by representing two supposed diarists, husband and wife, emphatically directing their intimate confessions to each other while insisting that they never will read each other's secret thoughts. Yet the diaries for each are readily accessible, as is the conspicuously placed "key" to which the title refers.

The love relationships, as each character defines them, are challenges to imaginative reader response. The husband's poor health and troublesome combination of great sexual desire with limited ability contrasts with the wife Ikuko's apparent lack of interest in sex compensated by her considerable talent and durability. With each sexual act, which she presumably tries to avoid, she exposes her husband's gullibility and endangers his life because it causes his blood pressure to rise. The young gentleman, Kimura, kept on the scene as a marriage prospect for the daughter Toshiko, actually interests the mother and functions both as a substitute for the deficient husband and to provoke his high blood pressure further with jealousy. At the conclusion, Ikuko confesses her motives more explicitly than is usual in Tanizaki, but the continuing family relationship—with the plan that Kimura will marry Toshiko so that the three can live together—invites the usual, wide range of speculation.

Certainly one of Tanizaki's most difficult tales is "The Bridge of Dreams," the story of a boy's affectionate memories of his mother and stepmother with resulting family complications. The most striking images in Tadasu's few recollections of his mother are of her sitting by the pool soaking her pretty feet in the water and of her permitting him to suckle her breasts at night when they were in bed together. This was when he was nearly five years old. The new mother, who had been a geisha, was chosen for her striking resemblance to Tadasu's real mother. She even took the same name and adopted similar habits as a full replacement. In time, as the boy grew old enough to marry, he had difficulty distinguishing the two mothers in his memory. When the second mother has a son, too, the new baby is sent off for adoption. The narrator even relates that Tadasu sucked the milk from his stepmother's swollen breasts after she had given up the child. Following the deaths of his father and second mother, Tadasu adopted his stepbrother with a vow to protect him from loneliness. In this story, with the powerful emphasis on family protectiveness, readers can hardly avoid pondering the relative gains and losses from the characters' exceptional watchfulness over their loved ones.

Another excellent comic representation of obsessive love reveals itself in Tanizaki's novella *Diary of a Mad Old Man*. In this story, Utsuki, a sickly old man, age seventy-seven, fits into the traditional family pattern as the unchallengeable head of the family, whose word is law. The narrative comes across mostly through the old man's notes in his diary. Tanizaki leaves indeterminate the private thoughts of Utsuki's wife and grown children, but they know of his squandering wealth and affection on his daughter-in-law, the scheming Satsuko. The family had been suspicious of her as a bride for the son, Jokichi, right from the start, because of her background as a lowly cabaret dancer. In fact, as the story begins, Jokichi has already lost interest in her anyway, and Satsuko is visited frequently by another young man, Utsuki's nephew, Haruhisa. Nevertheless, the old man's dotage reveals itself in expensive gifts for her, including a cat's-eye ring costing three million yen, the plan to enshrine her footprints on his gravestone, and niggardliness toward his own children. One's disgust for the old man grows with the combination of abundant references to Utsuki's medicines, drugs, and treatments, and Satsuko's obvious contempt for him. After Utsuki boldly kisses her on the neck one time, she tells him that she felt as if she had "been licked by a garden slug." Near the end, the narrative trails off with a long series of notes attesting the failing health of an apparently dying man. Then, in the final entry, one reads that Utsuki recovered enough to supervise excavation of the garden to construct a swimming pool for his darling Satsuko. Even in his last years, Tanizaki never lost his ability to catch his readers off guard.

Other major works

NOVELS: *Chijin no ai*, 1924 (*Naomi*, 1985); *Kōjin*, 1926; *Manji*, 1928-1930; *Yoshinokuzu*, 1931 (*Arrowroot*, 1982); *Bushuko hiwa*, 1931-1932, 1935 (*The Secret History of the Lord of Musashi*, 1982); *Sasameyuki*, 1943-1948, 1949 (*The Makioka Sisters*, 1957); *Shōshō Shigemoto no haha*, 1950 (*The Mother of Captain Shigemoto*, 1956).

PLAYS: *Aisureba koso*, 1921; *Okumi to Gohei*, 1922; *Shirogitsune no yu*, 1923 (*The White Fox*, 1930); *Mumyō to Aizen*, 1924; *Shinzei*, 1949.

NONFICTION: *Bunsho no dukohon*, 1934; "*In'ei raisan*," 1934 ("In Praise of Shadows," 1955); *Kyō no yume, Ōsaka no yume*, 1950.

TRANSLATION: *Genji monogatari*, 1936-1941, 1951-1954 (of Murasaki Shikibu's medieval *Genji monogatari*).

MISCELLANEOUS: *Tanizaki Jun'ichirō zenshu*, 1930 (twelve volumes); *Tanizaki Jun'ichirō zenshu*, 1966-1970 (twenty-eight volumes).

Bibliography

Keene, Donald. "Tanizaki Jun'ichiro." In *Dawn to the West: Japanese Literature in the Modern Era*. Vol. 1. New York: Holt, Rinehart and Winston, 1984. This two-volume work, indispensable in the study of modern Japanese literature, has an extensive chapter on Tanizaki's life and works, including his short fiction. Extensive notes and a bibliography.

Lippit, Noriko Miuta. *Reality and Fiction in Modern Japanese Literature*. White Plains, N.Y.: M. E. Sharpe, 1980. Considers the struggle of several Japanese writers to define the function of art and literature both socially and personally. Sections on Tanizaki deal with his aesthetic preference for fantasy and complex structure, with a comparison to Edgar Allan Poe. Notes.

Rubin, Jay. *Injurious to Public Morals: Writers and the Meiji State*. Seattle: University of Washington Press, 1984. In this unusual approach, the author tackles censorship in Japan and analyzes the relationship between writers and the government. The sections on Tanizaki, an apolitical period writer, suggest ways censorship affected his early career. Contains interesting discussions of the bans on his short stories. Chronology, notes, a bibliography, and an index.

Ueda, Makoto. "Tanizaki Jun'ichirō." In *Modern Japanese Writers and the Nature of Literature*. Stanford, Calif.: Stanford University Press, 1976. Discusses Tanizaki as one of the eight major writers who make up the bulk of modern Japanese fiction familiar to Western readers. Provides an introduction to major literary theories underlying Japanese novels and stories. Supplemented by source notes, a bibliography, and an index.

Yamanouchi, Hisaaki. *The Search for Authenticity in Modern Japanese Literature.* Cambridge, England: Cambridge University Press, 1978. Discusses twelve modern Japanese writers, analyzing the ways each dealt with the difficult personal, social, and intellectual questions in art. The sections on Tanizaki focus on the concept of eternal womanhood in his works. Includes notes, a bibliography, and an index.

David V. Harrington
(Revised by *Shakuntala Jayaswal*)

PETER TAYLOR

Born: Trenton, Tennessee; January 8, 1917

Principal short fiction

A Long Fourth and Other Stories, 1948; *The Widows of Thornton,* 1954; *Happy Families Are All Alike,* 1959; *Miss Leonora When Last Seen and Fifteen Other Stories,* 1963; *The Collected Stories of Peter Taylor,* 1968; *In the Miro District and Other Stories,* 1977; *The Old Forest and Other Stories,* 1985.

Other literary forms

In addition to his short fiction, Peter Taylor has published novels (*A Woman of Means,* 1950, and *A Summons to Memphis,* 1986) and plays. Several of his plays were performed at Kenyon College, and three of them have been published separately; a collection of seven dramas was also published in 1973. Taylor was one of three editors of a memorial volume, *Randall Jarrell, 1914-1965* (1967).

Achievements

The publication of *The Collected Stories of Peter Taylor* brought general acknowledgment that he has been one of the most skillful practitioners of the modern short story in the United States. While his reputation prior to that volume had for the most part been limited to a fairly small circle of enthusiastic readers, the list of his awards indicates the respect in which he has always been held by his peers. Taylor has been honored twelve different times by inclusion in the annual volume of *Best American Short Stories* and has been included six times in the *O. Henry Award Stories.* He has been awarded the Pulitzer Prize, the PEN/Faulkner Award, and the Gold Medal of the National Academy of Arts and Letters.

While acknowledging his admiration for the work of Anton Chekhov, Ivan Turgenev, and Henry James, Taylor has put his own unique mark on the short story. Much of his fiction is set in the South, recalling the work of William Faulkner and Flannery O'Connor, but he is less concerned with violence and moral themes than either of those writers, concentrating instead on social relationships and the inevitability of betrayal in the interactions of men and women.

Biography

Peter Taylor grew up in middle-class circumstances in border states. His family moved to Nashville when he was seven, spent several years in St. Louis, and settled in Memphis when he was fifteen. Expected to follow his father and older brother into the practice of law, Taylor chose early to try to make his career as a writer. He studied with the poet Allen Tate. After a brief enrollment at Vanderbilt University, he preferred to follow the poet, editor, and teacher John Crowe Ransom to Kenyon

College in Ohio. At Kenyon College, he was befriended by the poet and critic Randall Jarrell and shared a room with the poet Robert Lowell.

After service in the United States Army during World War II, Taylor took up teaching as a profession. Between 1945 and 1963, he held faculty appointments at Indiana State University and Ohio State University, and on three different occasions he was appointed to teaching positions at the University of North Carolina at Greensboro. In 1967, he accepted a professorship at the University of Virginia, where he remained until his retirement in 1984.

Success as a short-story writer came fairly early in his career. Prestigious magazines such as *The Southern Review* and *The New Republic* published some of his stories written while he was still in college, and his first recognition in *Best American Short Stories* came in 1941, just after his graduation from Kenyon College. By 1948, his work was appearing in *The New Yorker*, which over the next three decades would publish more than two dozen of his works. Popular success, however, waited until the publication of *A Summons to Memphis* in 1986. The novel was a best-seller and won for Taylor the Pulitzer Prize for fiction.

Analysis

The art of Peter Taylor is ironic and subtle. In a typical story, the narrator or point-of-view character is an observer, perhaps a member of a community who remembers someone or something in the town's past that is puzzling or strange, or a character whose understanding of his or her life falls short of reality. In tone, the stories are deceptively simple and straightforward, masking their complex ironies in seemingly ordinary actions. Taylor does not experiment with form or structure in the manner of a Jorge Luis Borges or a Robert Coover, but his stories are not always about commonplace experience; the grotesque plays a major role in such stories as "The Fancy Woman" and "Venus, Cupid, Folly, and Time."

Low-keyed and rarely involving violent action, the stories are more complex in their effect than at first appears, often revealing more about the narrator or the society than about the character being described. Their settings are often in small towns or minor cities in the upper South, Tennessee or Missouri, places such as those where Taylor lived as a boy and young man. Familial relationships, including those between husband and wife, are often central. Racial and economic matters enter into many of the stories, but such major social issues are generally depicted in the context of the social interactions of ordinary people. Nevertheless, Taylor provides considerable insight into the effects of the radical changes that affected the South in the 1960's and 1970's.

Betrayal is a recurrent theme in Taylor's short fiction, and it is no accident that the story he chose to place first in *The Collected Stories of Peter Taylor* is the relatively late "Dean of Men," a recital of the history of the men in a family. The narrator, an older man and a successful academic, tries in the story to explain to his son the background of his career and his divorce from his first wife, the son's mother. The story unfolds by an examination of the past, in which the narrator's grandfather was a successful politician, governor of his state, and then United States senator. Younger men in his party convinced him to give up his Senate seat and run for governor again to save the party from a man he despised, and he agreed. It turned out that the plan was intended to get him out of his Senate seat. He would give up politics in disgust and live out his live as an embittered man.

The narrator's father was similarly betrayed by a man he had known all of his life, who had installed the father on the board of a bank. During the Great Depression of the 1930's, the friend promised to come from New York to explain doubtful investments he had made, but he never arrived, and the father was left holding the bag. In his turn, the narrator, as a young instructor in a small college, was used by other faculty members to block an appointment they all feared, but when the move was avenged by its target, the young man was left to suffer the consequences alone. In the aftermath, he left to take another job, but his wife did not go with him; both later remarried. The story is the narrator's attempt to explain his life to the son who grew up without him. What the narrator is unaware of is the decline in the importance and stature of his family through the generations; his achievements and his place in life, of which he is unduly proud, are notably less important than those of his father, which were in turn significantly less than those of the grandfather. The entire family's history is flawed by the men's lack of initiative, their acceptance of what others do to them. This lack of self-knowledge on the part of a narrator will characterize Taylor's first-person fictions as late as "The Captain's Son."

The narrator's or central figure's ignorance of her or his own attitudes is present from the beginning of Taylor's career, in his first published story, "A Spinster's Tale," a study of sexual repression. Taylor's only explicit investigation of sexual deviance would come much later, in "The Instruction of a Mistress," although "Venus, Cupid, Folly, and Time" contains strong overtones of incest. In "A Spinster's Tale," the narrator, the spinster of the title, is a woman whose youth was blighted by her fear of an old drunk who often passed the house in which she lived with her father and brother. As she tells the story, it is clear that her fear of "Mr. Speed" is a transference of her inadmissible attraction to her older brother, who also drinks, often and to excess. She is unaware that her irrational fear is really fear of any kind of departure from the most repressed kinds of behavior. In the old man, drunkenness is revolting; in her brother, she fears it only because her dead mother had told the young man that he would go to hell if he continued, but her brother's antic behavior when drunk exercises an attraction on her that she struggles to deny. In her old age, she still has revealing dreams laden with sexual implications. The betrayal in this story, of which she is only dimly aware, is the narrator's calling the police to haul away Mr. Speed when he stumbles onto their lawn during a driving rainstorm. She acknowledges late in life that she had acted "with courage, but without wisdom."

Betrayal of one kind or another seems to be inevitable in the relations between races, especially as those relations undergo the changes brought about by the Civil Rights movement and the push for integration. Since most of Taylor's stories are set in the South of the 1930's and 1940's, those relations are often between masters and servants, but that will change in the later tales. "What You Hear from 'Em?" is written from the point of view of an old black servant, Aunt Munsie, who lives in retirement, raising pigs and dogs and a few chickens. Her only real interest is in the lives of the two white men she reared when their mother died, and the question she addresses to people she meets in her daily rounds asks when they will return to the small town where she still lives. Their visits to her, bringing wives and children and eventually grandchildren, do not matter to Aunt Munsie; things will not be right until they again live in Thornton, a Nashville suburb. The betrayal is by the two men. Worried by her refusal to acknowledge automobiles or traffic rules as she goes through town collecting slop for her pigs, they arrange for an ordinance to be enacted that will forbid pig farming within the town limits. Aunt Munsie knows what they have done; she sells her pigs and loses her individuality, becoming a kind of parody of an old former servant.

A different kind of betrayal and a different kind of response occur in another early story, "A Wife of Nashville." On the surface, this is a story about a marriage between John R. and Helen Ruth Lovell, in some ways a typical Southern couple. He has succeeded in the insurance business, but he has spent much of his time over the years with other businessmen, hunting and traveling. Helen Ruth, as a result, has been occupied with rearing her children, and her chief companions over the years have been the black women who have cooked and cleaned for her: Jane Blakemore, when they were first married; Carrie, during the time their two younger boys were born; Sarah, who at the age of sixty-eight left for Chicago and a new marriage; and Jess, hired during the Depression and the most durable and helpful of them all.

"A Wife of Nashville," however, is only partly about the marriage and the rearing of a family. It becomes clear as the story develops that Helen Ruth's genuine emotional life has increasingly been centered on her relationships with her servants and that they have been an integral part of the family. Jess, who does not drive a car herself, is essential to the boys' learning to drive, a symbol of their adulthood. In the end, she concocts a scene to explain her leaving the family; Helen Ruth knows that the explanation is false and that Jess and a friend are leaving Nashville for what they think is a more glamorous life in California. The husband and sons are shocked and resentful at the way they think Helen Ruth has been treated by Jess; Helen Ruth herself, however, rejects their sympathy and refuses to share their anger. It is clear that she wishes she had a means of escape, even one as improbable as that taken by Jess and her friend. On another level, it is clear also that she, unlike the men in the family, recognizes the social changes that are under way, changes that will alter the ways in which the races will survive. Other stories having to do with difficult marital relations were written throughout Taylor's career and include the early "Cookie," "Reservations," and "The Elect."

Perhaps the story most typical of Taylor's work, and one of the most powerful, is the one he chose to conclude *The Collected Stories of Peter Taylor*, "Miss Leonora When Last Seen." Narrated by one of the middling-successful men who populate this fiction, a small-town druggist, the story operates on several levels. It encompasses the narrator's sadness at having to carry bad news to the woman who was his teacher and who had encouraged him to aspire to greater things than he was able to achieve. At the same time, it is a story about a town's revenge on Miss Leonora's family, the wealthiest and most powerful residents of the town; over the years, they had prevented every "improvement" that might have brought business and "progress" to Thomasville, using their influence to keep out the railroad, the asylum, and other projects that would have changed the town. Most of them moved away, but they retained the home place, and they continued to exercise their influence. Now the town has decided to condemn the old manor house in which Miss Leonora lives in order to build a new high school. The irony that Miss Leonora had been a superb teacher in the old school is not lost on the narrator.

More important, "Miss Leonora When Last Seen" shows the mixed blessings and curses of the old ways and of the changes that are coming to the "New South." The old ways were autocratic and sometimes unfair, and they depended upon a servant class descended from slaves, such as the blacks who still live on Miss Leonora's place. Modernity, however, may not be much of an improvement; the new high school is being pushed as a final attempt to avoid the horrors of racial integration. The narrator is caught between these times and has nothing to look to for support.

While these elements are at work, and the narrator is showing his own lack of understanding of Miss Leonora, the story is presenting a picture of an eccentric but fascinating individual who has lived in Thomasville all of her life, teaching, trying to inspire the young men who were her favorites to achievement, and living close to the blacks who still reside on the family property, which she has inherited. In her retirement, she has taken to traveling by car, driving always at night in an open convertible, wearing one of two strange costumes, and stopping at "tourist homes," which were the motels of the time. Informed of the town's decision, she has taken to the road. Postcards come from surrounding states, but "She seems to be orbiting her native state of Tennessee." There is no sign that she will ever return; the old ways are indeed dead, and those who lived in the old way are anachronisms.

Other major works

NOVELS: *A Woman of Means*, 1950; *A Summons to Memphis*, 1986.

PLAYS: *The Death of a Kinswoman*, 1949; *Tennessee Day in Saint Louis: A Comedy*, 1957; *A Sound in the Mountains*, 1968; *Presences: Seven Dramatic Pieces*, 1973.

EDITED TEXT: *Randall Jarrell, 1914-1965*, 1967 (with Robert Lowell and Robert Penn Warren).

Bibliography

Baumbach, Jonathan. *Modern and Contemporaries: New Masters of the Short Story.* New York: Random House, 1968. Includes a brief analysis of Taylor's place in the development of the post-World War II short story.

Kramer, Victor A., Patricia A. Bailey, Carol G. Dana, and Carl H. Griffin. *Andrew Lytle, Walker Percy, Peter Taylor: A Reference Guide.* Boston: G. K. Hall, 1983.

One of the later and most complete bibliographies of Taylor's work and the reviews and criticism.

Oates, Joyce Carol. "Realism of Distance, Realism of Immediacy." *The Southern Review* 7 (Winter, 1971): 295-313. A novelist's sensitive appreciation of other writers, including Taylor.

Robinson, Clayton. "Peter Taylor." In *Literature of Tennessee*, edited by Ray Willbanks. Rome, Ga.: Mercer University Press, 1984. This article relates Taylor's fiction to his early years and explains his mother's influence on his techniques and subject matter.

Robison, James C. *Peter Taylor: A Study of the Short Fiction.* Boston: Twayne, 1987. This volume not only is the only extended study of Taylor's short stories but also contains two interviews with the author as well as essays by a number of critics. Robison's comments are occasionally wide of the mark, but he is an earnest and generally intelligent reader of Taylor's work. Essential reading.

Taylor, Peter. "Interview with Peter Taylor." Interview by J. H. E. Paine. *Journal of the Short Story in English* 9 (Fall, 1987): 14-35. The most extended interview with Taylor, dealing with his techniques and influences.

John M. Muste

WILLIAM MAKEPEACE THACKERAY

Born: Calcutta, India; July 18, 1811
Died: London, England; December 24, 1863

Principal short fiction

The Yellowplush Papers, 1837-1838; *Some Passages in the Life of Major Gahagan*, 1838-1839; *Stubb's Calendar: Or, The Fatal Boots*, 1839; *Barber Cox and the Cutting of His Comb*, 1840; *The Bedford-Row Conspiracy*, 1840; *Comic Tales and Sketches*, 1841 (2 volumes); *The Confessions of George Fitz-Boodle, and Some Passages in the Life of Major Gahagan*, 1841-1842; *Men's Wives*, 1843 (as George Savage Fitz-Boodle); *A Legend of the Rhine*, 1845 (as M. A. Titmarsh); *Jeame's Diary: Or, Sudden Wealth*, 1846; *The Snobs of England, by One of Themselves*, 1846-1847 (later as *The Book of Snobs*, 1848, 1852); *Mrs. Perkin's Ball*, 1847 (as M. A. Titmarsh); *'Our Street,'* 1848 (as M. A. Titmarsh); *A Little Dinner at Timmins's*, 1848; *Doctor Birch and His Young Friends*, 1849 (as M. A. Titmarsh); *The Kickleburys on the Rhine*, 1850 (as M. A. Titmarsh); *A Shabby Genteel Story and Other Tales*, 1852; *The Rose and the Ring: Or, The History of Prince Giglio and Prince Bulbo*, 1855 (as M. A. Titmarsh); *Memoirs of Mr. Charles J. Yellowplush [with] The Diary of C. Jeames De La Pluche, Esqr.*, 1856.

Other literary forms

William Makepeace Thackeray published seven novels during his lifetime, and the unfinished *Denis Duval* was printed posthumously in 1864. *Vanity Fair* (1847-1848) and *The Luck of Barry Lyndon* (1844), which was filmed, are considered his masterpieces, both of them featuring memorable protagonists who exhibit both heroic and venal qualities. Thackeray was a prolific contributor to periodicals of parodies, satires, humorous sketches, essays, reviews, and articles. He was a correspondent for many newspapers and an editor of several magazines. He also issued popular Christmas annuals for many years.

Achievements

In the last decade of his life, Thackeray was considered one of Great Britain's most powerful novelists. His novels, taken together, form an appraisal of English social history and morals between 1690 and 1863. The lasting value of both the novels and his shorter works, however, rests in their huge cast of vivid characters, ranging from despicable, amoral scoundrels through attractive rascals to truly noble heroes, male and female, from every class. What brings these characters to energetic life is Thackeray's command of style and narrative technique and his gift for satire. Thackeray experimented with every sort of first-person narration. By manipulating his various personae, he created subtle distinctions in tone. Even when Thackeray employed an omniscient narrator, he was always a mask, distinct from the author.

For his Victorian audience, this mediating voice was one of the pleasures of reading Thackeray, who built on the oral nature of storytelling. To moderns, however, the tendency to tell rather than to dramatize can seem an intrusive disruption of illusion, and thus, they sometimes do not appreciate the very commentary that made him so popular in his own time.

Almost as valuable is the impression that remains of Thackeray's personality. He was a man of good will and a loving father, financially improvident but generous and kindly. Even the difficult times in his own life he reshaped in his works into positive experiences. As a writer and talented caricaturist, he deftly skewered pretension and folly where he found them; as a man, he seemed to view human nature with charity and tolerance, above all affirming what he saw as its inherent good sense.

Biography

Born in India, William Makepeace Thackeray was the only son of Richmond and Ann Becher Thackeray. His grandfathers on both sides of the family had been with the Indian civil service, and after his father died in September, 1815, he was sent to school in England. He attended schools in Southampton, Chiswick, and Charterhouse; the bullying he received there was later fictionalized. One of his first pen names was Michael Angelo Titmarsh, adopted because his nose was broken by a classmate, as Michelangelo's had been three centuries earlier. He called his school "Slaughterhouse" for the brutality he endured there. His mother remarried, and he spent 1828 in Devon with her and Major-General Henry Carmichael-Smythe. From February, 1829, to July, 1830, he attended Trinity College, Cambridge. He traveled in Germany until May, 1831, and met Johann Wolfgang von Goethe in Weimar. He briefly studied law in England. In 1832, he spent four months in Paris, and from 1834 he began training as a professional artist since he had always had a talent for drawing. On August 20, 1836, he married Isabel Shawe, whose neurotic, domineering mother became the model for all the terrible mothers-in-law in Thackeray's fiction. Their daughter Anne was born in June, 1837; she later became a novelist and the editor of her father's letters to Edward Fitzgerald, and of his complete works. She married Sir Richmond Ritchie of the India office. Jane was born in July, 1838, and died eight months later. Harriet, born in May, 1840, was to marry Sir Leslie Stephen in 1867. In 1840, Isabel became so depressed that she attempted suicide and in 1846 she was declared incurably insane. The fortune Thackeray had inherited was dissipated by 1833, and the professional gamblers who swindled him out of his money figure in several of his stories. His stepfather invested in a paper so that Thackeray could write for it, but it failed, leaving them financially ruined. He wrote for twenty-four different periodicals between 1830 and 1844 trying to support his family, even applying to Charles Dickens for the job of illustrating the *Pickwick Papers* (1836-1837). Finally, the publication of *Vanity Fair* in 1848 made him a public figure. He began a series of public lectures which took him twice to the United States, from 1852 to 1853 and from 1855 to 1856. He died at the age of fifty-two on Christmas Eve, 1863.

Analysis

William Makepeace Thackeray's "Yellowplush" was first introduced in *Fraser's* in November, 1837, and was republished in the United States and translated into German. In 1845, the footman was revived in *Punch*, having been promoted to Charles James De La Pluche, Esq., through successful speculation in railway shares. On his first appearance in "Miss Shum's Husband," Yellowplush tells how he got his name. His mother, who always introduced him as her nephew, named him for the livery of a famous coachman, Yellowplush. Although he was illegitimate, he has gentlemanly tastes, and his cockney speech is spiced with affectations. His employer, Frederic Altamont, takes rooms in a crowded house in John Street. The footman reports that they breakfast from his master's tea leaves and dine on slices of meat cut from his joints, but Frederic endures this to be near his loved one Mary. In the next episode and with his next employer, Yellowplush has descended to petty thievery (which he calls his "perquisites") himself. During his courtship, Altamont refuses to reveal where he works, but assures Mary that he is honest and urges her never to question him about what it would cause her misery to learn.

After their marriage, Frederic and Mary move to an elegantly furnished house in Islington, from which he mysteriously disappears each day. After their baby is born, Mrs. Shum becomes a daily visitor. This mother of twelve daughters who spent her time reading novels on the drawing room sofa, scolding, screaming, and having hysterics is the first of the terrible mothers-in-law so prominent in Thackeray's fiction, including Mrs. Gam, Mrs. Gashleigh, Mrs. Cuff, Mrs. Crum, Lady Kicklebury, and Mrs. Baynes. They are always snobbish, interfering, and domineering. Mrs. Shum undermines the mutual affection in her daughter's household by implanting suspicions. "Where does his money come from? What if he is a murderer, or a housebreaker, or a forger?" When Mary answers that he is too kind to be any of those things, Mrs. Shum suggests that he must be a bigamist. At this moment, as Mary faints, Mrs. Shum has hysterics, the baby squalls, the servants run upstairs with hot water, and Frederic returns. He expels Mrs. Shum, double-locks the door, and tries to appease his wife without exposing his secret. His in-laws set up a spy network and finally discover that he is a crossing sweeper. Frederic sells his house and starts his new life abroad. His footman renders his snobbish judgment of the whole affair:

> Of cors, I left his servis. I met him, a few years after, at Badden-Badden, where he and Mrs. A. were much respectid, and pass for pipple of propaty.

The satire depends for its effect on the dissonance between the social pretensions and the misspellings in which they are conveyed. In Victorian England, a gentleman did not work for a living, and a footman conscious of his position could not work for a laborer. He could "pass" abroad, because foreigners were unable to tell the difference between inherited and earned money. Obviously, only income from property qualified one to enter society.

"Dimond Cut Dimond" is about Yellowplush's next master, who is penniless but titled. He is the Honorable Algernon Percy Deuceace, fifth son of the Earl of Crabs.

If he had been a common man, he would have been recognized as a swindler, but since he is a gentleman, with his family tree prominently displayed in his sitting room, his gambling is considered acceptable. Dawkins, just out of Oxford, moves in with his entire fortune of six thousand pounds to establish himself as a barrister. Deuceace manipulates an introduction by tripping the servant carrying Dawkins' breakfast tray. He substitutes a pastry he has purchased for this purpose with an elaborate letter, claiming it had been sent to him by an aristocratic friend. Once they are acquainted, he suggests a game of cards, which he deliberately loses as a setup.

The scheme is complicated by a second con man, Richard Blewitt, who tells Deuceace that Dawkins is his pigeon to pluck, and that he means to strip this one alone since he already has him securely in his claws. Deuceace makes a deal to split the gains; after he wins, however, he coldly announces to Blewitt, who has come for his share, that he never had any intention of keeping his promise. Blewitt "stormed, groaned, bellowed, swore" but gets nothing, and the villain escapes to Paris, telling Yellowplush that he can come too if he likes.

Thackeray, as a student, had actually lost large sums to such gamblers. The insolent criminality with which Deuceace robs both Dawkins and Blewitt is not condemned by his footman, who is engaged in robberies of his own. "There wasn't a bottle of wine that we didn't get a glass out of . . . we'd the best pickens out of the dinners, the livvers of the fowls, the forcemit balls out of the soup, the egs from the sallit . . . you may call this robbery—nonsince—it's only our rights—a suvvant's purquizzits." In the eyes of the footman, the cold-blooded malice of his master is superior to the blustering passion of Blewitt.

The next episode, "Foring Parts," tells how Deuceace has posted a sign on his door, "Back at seven," and departed, owing the laundress. The footman learns that to gain respect in France, one must be rude. His master had abused the waiters, abused the food, and abused the wine, and the more abusive he was, the better service he got; on his example, the footman also practices insolence because people liked being insulted by a lord's footman. Deuceace writes to Lord Crabs for his allowance; but the answer comes back that since all of London knows of Deuceace's winnings, could he instead lend Lord Crabs some money. He encloses clippings from the newspapers about the transaction. Shortly afterward, a retraction appears in the paper for which Deuceace had sent a ten-pound note, with his compliments. The narrator comments that he had already sent a tenner before it came out, although he cannot think why.

"Dorothea" appeared in 1843 along with "Miss Loewe" and "Ottilia" as part of "Confessions of Fitz-Boodle." Since their narrator is a leisured gentleman, these stories differ in pace and tone from the Yellowplush series; Fitz-Boodle's aristocratic birth and classical education enable him to make social commentary of a different sort. The story turns on his failure to have learned dancing at Slaughterhouse school, where he learned little that was useful. He adds ruefully, however, that such is the force of habit that he would probably send his sons there, were he to have any. In a series of semiscenes typical of Thackeray's style, Fitz-Boodle describes the many dancing lessons he has taken from various instructors in London, in Paris, and finally in Germany, from Springbock, the leader of the Kalbsbraten ballet.

The continual shifting of temporal perspectives is also typical of Thackeray. He interrupts chronology for an amiable digression which meanders back to the starting point, and also digresses into the future consequences of an action, or presents retrospective memories of an event from years later. For example, the discursive soliloquy on dancing is suddenly interrupted by "The reader, perhaps, remembers the brief appearance of his Highness, the Duke." This is followed by an elaborate description of the Duke's pump, the whole point of which is that Speck, who designed it, is Dorothea's father. He ingratiates himself into the family by sketching the pump and is consequently introduced to the beauty, whose charms inspire him to classical allusions. Then the narrative redoubles again:

> In thus introducing this lovely creature in her ball-costume, I have been somewhat premature, and had best go back to the beginning of the history of my acquaintance with her.

Next follows a history of the Speck family leading up to the narrator's first glimpse of her, and the narrative resumes.

The next semiscene, midway between summary and dramatization, is characteristic of Thackeray's refusal to disguise his fictions, to mount them dramatically. His narrators set the stage but do not retire from it; they remain to pose alternatives, suggest possibilities, speculate, and muse expatiatingly. Thackeray constructs a model which the reader must then fill in; by concealing as much as he discloses, he forces the reader's participation in completing his paradigm, using a pronoun shift to the second person which asks "you" to participate. Thackeray appeals to universality (an eighteenth century device probably derived from his study of Henry Fielding, whom he had both imitated and parodied), and the interjected "I have often said" is a strategy found throughout his work. *Vanity Fair* contains countless "Captain Rawdon often said" interspersings, a technique that allows the author to interpolate commentary and to leave the rest to the reader's imagination. The story concludes with the ball at which Fitz-Boodle has managed to sign up Dorothea for a waltz, and his subsequent fall on the dance floor.

"Mr. and Mrs. Frank Berry" is part of the story sequence called *Men's Wives* which first appeared in *Fraser's* in March, 1843. In two parts, it shows Frank as a boy bravely battling the school bully and being hero-worshiped by the narrator; then, in a later encounter, he is seen as a uxorious husband who has shaved off his mustache and grown fat and pale. Part 1 is called "The Fight at Slaughter House." After the preliminaries, as the air resounds with cries of "To it, Berry!" there is a typical Thackerayan footnote, "As it is very probable that many fair readers may not approve of the extremely forcible language in which the combat is depicted, I beg them to skip it and pass on to the next chapter."

This chapter is entitled "The Combat at Versailles," and this time the heroic Frank is not the victor. Mrs. Berry has "a rigid and classical look" and wears a miniature of her father, Sir George Catacomb, around her thin neck. Her genteel coldness is aptly caught in her maiden name, Miss Angelica Catacomb. She spends her time making notes in the Baronetage on her pedigree, and she entertains her guest with an icy silence. After several pages about the other guests, Thackeray provides the apostrophe that if there had been anything interesting, "I should have come out with it a couple of pages since, nor have kept the public looking for so long a time at the dishcovers and ornaments of the table. But the simple fact must now be told, that there was nothing of the slightest importance at this repast."

The narrator then tells how Angelica controlled her husband's smoking, drinking, and conversation. The narrator decides to rescue Frank from his captivity and orders claret, which, after sufficient quantity has been consumed, leads to riotous singing. He feels free enough to complain, when he is inebriated, about having to spend his evenings reading poetry or missionary tracts out loud, about having to take physics whenever she insists, about never being allowed to dine out, and about not daring even to smoke a cigar. In a moment of daring, the narrator accepts an invitation for the next night, but he is not permitted to keep the appointment, and the next time he meets Frank, the latter sheepishly crosses over to the other side of the street; he is wearing galoshes. The boy who was courageous enough to beat the school bully has turned into a henpecked husband.

Other major works

NOVELS: *Catherine: A Story*, 1839-1840 (as Ikey Solomons, Jr.); *The History of Samuel Titmarsh and the Great Hoggarty Diamond*, 1841 (later as *The Great Hoggarty Diamond*, 1848); *The Luck of Barry Lyndon: A Romance of the Last Century*, 1844; *Vanity Fair: A Novel Without a Hero*, 1847-1848; *The History of Pendennis: His Fortunes and Misfortunes, His Friends and His Greatest Enemy*, 1848-1850; *Rebecca and Rowena: A Romance upon Romance*, 1850 (as M. A. Titmarsh); *The History of Henry Esmond, Esquire, a Colonel in the Service of Her Majesty Q. Anne*, 1852 (3 volumes); *The Newcomes: Memoirs of a Most Respectable Family*, 1853-1855; *The Virginians: A Tale of the Last Century*, 1857-1859; *Lovel the Widower*, 1860; *The Adventures of Philip on His Way Through the World, Shewing Who Robbed Him, Who Helped Him, and Who Passed Him By*, 1861-1862; *Denis Duval*, 1864.

PLAYS: *The Wolves and the Lamb*, 1854; *The Rose and the Ring*, 1854.

POETRY: *The Chronicle of the Drum*, 1841.

NONFICTION: *The Paris Sketch Book*, 1840 (as M. A. Titmarsh, 2 volumes); *The Irish Sketch Book*, 1843 (as M. A. Titmarsh, 2 volumes); *Notes of a Journey from Cornhill to Grand Cairo, by Way of Lisbon, Athens, Constantinople and Jerusalem, Performed in the Steamers of the Penninsular and Oriental Company*, 1846 (as M. A. Titmarsh); *The English Humourists of the Eighteenth Century*, 1853; *Sketches and Travels in London*, 1856; *The Four Georges: Sketches of Manners, Morals, Court and Town Life*, 1860.

Bibliography

Carey, John. *Thackeray: Prodigal Genius.* London: Faber & Faber, 1977. Carey's appreciation of Thackeray's "imaginative vitality," particularly as it is expressed in his earlier, shorter, largely satirical literary and journalistic work, provides the focus for this absorbing study. Many of Thackeray's major short works are discussed and analyzed in their chronological context.

Dodds, John Wendell. *Thackeray: A Critical Portrait.* New York: Oxford University Press, 1941. This scholarly, twelve-chapter study of Thackeray's genius and the art of his fiction includes, particularly in chapter 3, "The Early Humorist and Story-Teller: 1838-1840," an assessment of his short satirical sketches and stories. A thorough index is useful. An important book in the canon of Thackeray criticism.

Mudge, Isadore Gilbert, and M. Earl Sears. *A Thackeray Dictionary: The Characters and Short Stories Alphabetically Arranged.* 1910. Reprint. New York: Humanities Press, 1962. As the title indicates, this volume is an essential reference book for students of Thackeray's works. The "Chronological List of Novels and Stories" clarifies and lists the individual and collected works titles under which many of Thackeray's short sketches and stories were published and republished; "Synopses" provides invaluable annotations on the contents of all Thackeray's works, short and long. The main "Dictionary" section is an alphabetical reference book for Thackeray's characters.

Peters, Catherine. *Thackeray's Universe: Shifting Worlds of Imagination and Reality.* New York: Oxford University Press, 1987. The purpose of this thorough, fresh, intelligent, and readable twelve-chapter study is, in the author's words, "to identify the raw materials, but to be aware that the finished work is a work of art, and not a covert autobiography." In defining what Thackeray's writings owed both to his life and to his particular genius, Peters provides invaluable insights. Short works such as *Men's Wives* and *The Yellowplush Papers* are analyzed, and individual short pieces are discussed in context. A thorough index helps readers to search out discussion of individual works.

Welsh, Alexander, ed. *Thackeray: A Collection of Critical Essays.* Englewood Cliffs, N.J.: Prentice-Hall, 1968. Thirteen essays by a selection of the foremost Thackeray scholars can always be a useful introduction to the student of Thackeray's works, though discussion of the short works is included only in the analyses of Thackeray's narrative techniques and style.

Wheatley, James H. *Patterns in Thackeray's Fiction.* Cambridge, Mass.: MIT Press, 1969. This volume is a lucid, readable study of the development of Thackeray's techniques and concerns as a fiction writer. Follows his literary career from chapter 1, "Early Parody," through chapter 6, "Later Fiction: The Sentiment of Reality." Two works of short fiction, *The Yellowplush Papers* and *A Shabby Genteel Story and Other Tales*, are discussed at some length in chapter 2, "Developments from Parody." The "Works Cited" guides the reader to other relevant critical sources.

Ruth Rosenberg
(Revised by *Jill Rollins*)

DYLAN THOMAS

Born: Swansea, Wales; October 27, 1914
Died: New York, New York; November 9, 1953

Principal short fiction

Portrait of the Artist as a Young Dog, 1940; *Selected Writings of Dylan Thomas*, 1946; *A Child's Christmas in Wales*, 1954; *Quite Early One Morning*, 1954; *Adventures in the Skin Trade and Other Stories*, 1955; *A Prospect of the Sea and Other Stories*, 1955; *Early Prose Writings*, 1971; *The Followers*, 1976; *The Collected Stories*, 1984.

Other literary forms

In addition to his short fiction, Dylan Thomas published several collections of poetry, including *18 Poems* (1934), *Twenty-five Poems* (1936), *New Poems* (1943), and *Collected Poems: 1934-1952* (1952). *Under Milk Wood* (1954) is a verse drama that affectionately portrays a day in the life of the inhabitants of a tiny Welsh fishing village. Thomas also wrote many film scripts, most notably *The Doctor and the Devils* (1953) and a comic detective novel *The Death of the King's Canary* (1976).

Achievements

The lyricism of Thomas' poetry probably constitutes his most powerful contribution to twentieth century verse and is also a notable characteristic of his prose. One source of that lyric quality is surely Thomas' Welsh origins and his awareness of the depth and richness of Welsh poetic traditions. He also paid homage to Wales in his short fiction, lovingly (if sometimes satirically) describing it in works such as *A Child's Christmas in Wales* and in the stories that make up *Portrait of the Artist as a Young Dog* and *Adventures in the Skin Trade*. In those works appear characters and events from his childhood in Swansea and his early work as a news reporter.

His poetry won the "Poet's Corner" Prize of the *Sunday Referee* in 1934, the Blumenthal Poetry Prize in 1938, the Levinson Poetry Prize in 1945, and Foyle's Poetry Prize (for *Collected Poems: 1934-1952*) in 1952. Thomas also received a grant from The Authors' Society Traveling Scholarship Fund in 1947.

Biography

Dylan Marlais Thomas' father, John David Thomas, was an embittered schoolmaster, emotionally remote from his son, but he possessed a fine library of contemporary fiction and poetry in which his son was free to read. His father's distance and unhappiness may have made Thomas more susceptible to the indulgences of his mother, Florence Williams Thomas. It is her family who appears in Thomas' work as the chapel-going farmers, and it is her oldest sister whose husband owned the farm near Llangain where the young Thomas often spent summer vacations. Thomas also had a sister, Nancy, nine years older than he. The family home at 5 Cwmdonkin

Drive, Swansea, was across the street from the park which sometimes appears in his poems ("The Hunchback in the Park," for example). Likewise the beautiful Gower peninsula and his aunt's farm appeared in his adult work as subjects for his poetry and memoirs (most notably in "Fern Hill"). Thomas' early life in Wales furnished him with material that surfaced in his work for the rest of his life.

Thomas was a lackadaisical student at Swansea Grammar School. Talented in English, he edited the school magazine while he was there, and he began to keep the notebooks that reveal his early attempts to form his style, but he gave little attention to subjects that did not interest him. It was at school that he began his friendship with Dan Jones with whom he composed poems and played elaborate word games. In adulthood, Jones became Dr. Daniel Jones, musical composer and editor of Thomas' work.

Thomas left school in 1931 to work—not very successfully—as a reporter for the *South Wales Evening Post*, a job which gave him material for many of his stories. During the next three years, he also experienced a period of exciting poetic growth, learning about Welsh poets of the past and producing much work of his own. Late in 1934, he moved to London where he cultivated a conscious bohemianism and began to gain a reputation as drinker, brilliant conversationalist, and poet of merit. Through the rest of his life, the two parts of his personality—the serious poet who cared about his craft and the hard-drinking bohemian—were at odds in dominating his behavior.

In 1937, he married Caitlin Macnamara, a strong-willed, passionate dancer with whom he was intensely in love. They had three children—Llewelyn, Aeron, and Colm. During the war, Thomas, a conscientious objector, wrote mostly prose. Afterward, his life alternated between London and the Welsh fishing village of Laugharne, where he lived with his family and did his most profitable work. In London, when he was in need of money (as he usually was), he often worked for the British Broadcasting Corporation, but there too, his drinking began to cause him more and more troubles.

In 1950, he made the first of four tours to the United States, reading his work at colleges and universities. It was an enormous success, but it documented his reputation as an "outlaw" poet—a hard drinker and womanizer who spent the proceeds of his readings on women and whiskey while his family went without necessities. The subsequent tours intensified that legend. He died of alcohol poisoning in St. Vincent's Hospital in New York City in 1953.

Analysis

Dylan Thomas' ten stories in *Portrait of the Artist as a Young Dog* are charming reminiscences of his relatives, school friends, and neighbors in the town where he grew up. Their wit and accessibility made them immediately popular, in contrast to the dark, subjective stories he had written prior to 1938, for which he had difficulty finding a publisher. In March, 1938, he wrote to Vernon Watkins that "A Visit to Grandpa's" was "the first of a series of short, straightforward stories about Swansea." Published on March 10, 1939, in the *New English Weekly*, it told of a boy's waking up on a mild summer night to the sounds of "gee-up and whoa" in the next room where his grandfather, wearing his red waistcoat with its brass buttons, is reining invisible horses. On their morning walks, the grandfather has expressed his wish not to be buried in the nearby churchyard. When he is missing a few days later, the entire village is summoned to go in search of him, and they find him on Carmarthen Bridge in his Sunday trousers and dusty tall hat on his way to Llangadock to be buried. They try to persuade him to come home to tea instead.

In "The Peaches," first published in the October, 1938, issue of *Life and Letters Today*, the naïve narrator tells of his spring holiday on a farm in Gorsehill. His uncle Jim drives him there in a green cart late one April evening, stopping for a drink at a public house. The squeal coming from the wicker basket he takes inside with him prepares the reader for the fact that cousin Gwilym will note that one of the pigs is missing the next day. The terror of being abandoned in a dark alley is assuaged by Aunt Annie's warm welcome of him later that night at the farmhouse. He enters, small, cold, and scared, as the clock strikes midnight, and is made to feel "among the shining and striking like a prince taking off his disguise." Next morning, Gwilym takes him to see the sow, who has only four pigs left. "He sold it to go on the drink," whispers Gwilym rebukingly. The boy imagines Jim transformed into a hungry fox: "I could see uncle, tall and sly and red, holding the writhing pig in his two hairy hands, sinking his teeth in its thigh, crunching its trotters up; I could see him leaning over the wall of the sty with the pig's legs sticking out of his mouth." Gwilym, who is studying to be a minister, takes him to the barn which he pretends is his chapel and preaches a thunderous sermon at him, after which he takes up a collection.

Next, the complication begins. Gwilym and Jim are told to dress up for Jack Williams, whose rich mother will bring him in an automobile from Swansea for a fortnight's visit. A tin of peaches has been saved from Christmas; "Mother's been keeping it for a day like this." Mrs. Williams, "with a jutting bosom and thick legs, her ankles swollen over her pointed shoes," sways into the parlor like a ship. Annie precedes her, anxiously tidying her hair, "clucking, fidgeting, excusing." (The string of participles is typical of Thomas' prose style; one sentence [in "Return Journey"] contains fifteen.) The rich guest declines refreshments. "I don't mind pears or chunks, but I can't bear peaches." The boys run out to frolic, climb trees, and play Indians in the bushes. After supper, in the barn, Gwilym demands confessions from them, and Jack begins to cry that he wants to go home. That night in bed, they hear Uncle Jim come in drunk, and Annie quietly relating the events of the day, at which he explodes into thunderous anger: "Aren't peaches good enough for her!" At this, Jack sobs into his pillow. The next day Mrs. Williams arrives, sends the chauffeur for Jack's luggage, and drives off with him, as the departing car scatters the hens and the narrator waves good-bye.

Two aspects of the point of view are significant. The first, its tone, is what made all the stories so immediately beloved. The genial Chaucerian stance, which perceives and accepts eccentricities, which notes and blesses all the peculiarities of humanity, is endearing without being sentimental, because the acuteness of the observations stays in significant tension with the nonjudgmental way in which they are recorded. This combination of acuity and benevolence, of sharpness and radiance, is the special quality of Thomas' humor. The second aspect of the author's style is its expansion and contraction, which indicates the view of a visionary poet. The narrator is both a homesick, cold, tired little boy, and "a royal nephew in smart town clothes, embraced and welcomed." The uncle is both a predatory fox and an impoverished farmer, as he sits in "the broken throne of a bankrupt bard." The splendid paradise where the narrator romps is simultaneously a poor, dirty "square of mud and rubbish and bad wood and falling stone, where a bucketful of old and bedraggled hens scratched and laid small eggs." The "pulpit" where Gwilym's inspired sermon is "cried to the heavens" in his deepest voice is a dusty, broken cart in an abandoned barn overrun with mice; but this decrepit building on a mucky hill becomes "a chapel shafted with sunlight," awesome with reverence as the "preacher's" voice becomes "Welsh and singing." The alternate aggrandizement and diminution of the perceptions energize the style as the lyric impulse wars with the satiric impulse in the narrator's voice.

The naïve narrator of the third of the *Portrait of the Artist as a Young Dog* stories entitled "Patricia, Edith and Arnold" is totally engrossed in his imaginary engine, whose brake is "a hammer in his pocket" and whose fuel is replenished by invisible engineers. As he drives it about the garden, however, he is aware of his maid, Patricia, plotting with the neighbor's servant, Edith, to confront Arnold with the identical letters he wrote to both of them. The girls take the child to the park as it begins to snow; Arnold has been meeting Edith there on Fridays, and Patricia on Wednesdays. As the girls wait for Arnold in the shelter, the boy, disowning them, pretends he is a baker, molding loaves of bread out of snow.

Arnold Matthews, his hands blue with cold, wearing a checked cap but no overcoat, appears and tries to bluff it out. Loudly he says, "Fancy you two knowing each other." The boy rolls a snowman "with a lop-sided dirty head" smoking a pencil, as the situation grows more tense. When Arnold claims that he loves them both, Edith shakes her purse at him, the letters fall out all over the snow, and the snowman collapses. As the boy searches for his pencil, the girls insist that Arnold choose between them. Patricia turns her back, indignantly. Arnold gestures and whispers to Edith behind Patricia's back, and then, out loud, chooses Patricia. The boy, bending over his snowman, finds his pencil driven through its head.

Later, during a discussion of lying, the boy tells Patricia that he saw Arnold lying to both of them, and the momentary truce, during which Patricia and Arnold have been walking arm in arm, is over. She smacks and pummels him as he staggers backward and falls. The boy says he has to retrieve the cap that he left near his snowman. He finds Arnold there, rereading the letters that Edith dropped, but does not tell Patricia this. Later, as his frozen hands tingle and his face feels on fire, she comforts him until "the hurting is gone." She acknowledges his pain and her own by saying, "Now we've all had a good cry today." The story achieves its effects through the child's detachment. Totally absorbed in his play, he registers the behavior of the adults, participating in their sorrows without fully comprehending them. In spite of his age-appropriate egocentricity and his critical remarks about her girth (her footprints as large as a horse's), he expresses deep affection for her and such concern as he is capable of, given the puzzling circumstances.

The narrator of "The Fight" is an exuberant adolescent. Although he is fourteen, he deliberately adds a year to his age, lying for the thrill of having to be on guard to avoid detection. The self-conscious teenager is continually inventing scenarios in which he assumes various heroic postures. The story tells of his finding an alter ego, as gifted as he, through whom he can confirm his existence, with whom he can share his anxieties, collaborate imaginatively, and play duets. The opening incident illustrates Dylan's testing himself against the adults about him. He is engaged in a staring contest with a cranky old man who lives beside the schoolyard when a strange boy pushes him down. They fight. Dylan gives Dan a bloody nose, and gets a black eye in return. Admiring each other's injuries as evidence of their own manliness, they become fast friends.

Dylan postures, first as a prizefighter, then as a pirate. When a boy ridicules him at school the next day, he has a revenge fantasy of breaking his leg, then of being a famous surgeon who sets it with "a rapid manipulation, the click of a bone," while the grateful mother, on her knees, tearfully thanks him. Assigned a vase to draw in art class, the boys sketch inaccurate versions of naked girls instead. "I drew a wild guess below the waist." This boyish sexual curiosity leads him mentally to undress even Mrs. Bevan, the minister's wife, whom he meets later at supper at Dan's house, but he gets frightened when he gets as far as the petticoats.

Dan shows Dylan the seven historical novels he wrote before he was twelve, plays the piano for him, and lets him make a cat's noise on his violin; Dylan reads Dan his poems out of his exercise book. They share feelings, such as their ambivalences toward their mothers, a love tinged with embarrassment. They decide to edit a paper. Back upstairs, after supper, they imitate the self-important Mr. Bevan and discuss the time Mrs. Bevan tried to fling herself out the window. When she joins them later, they try to induce her to repeat this by pointedly opening the window and inviting her to admire the view. When he has to leave at 9:30, Dan announces that he "must finish a string trio tonight," and Dylan counters that he is "working on a long poem about the princes of Wales." On these bravura promises, the story closes.

Thomas called these luminous remembrances of his youth "portions of a provincial autobiography." The stories he wrote earlier, drafts of which exist in "The Red Notebook" which he kept from December, 1933, to October, 1934, were not published until later. Considered obscure, violent, and surrealistic, the stories are difficult because of the use of narrative devices borrowed from lyric poetry. In "A Prospect of the Sea," for example, the scenery seems to contract and expand. A boy lying in a cornfield on a summer day sees a country girl with berry-stained mouth, scratched legs, and dirty fingernails jump down from a tree, startling the birds. The landscape shrinks, the trees dwindle, the river is compressed into a drop, and the yellow field diminishes into a square "he could cover with his hand." As he masters his fear and sees she is only "a girl in a torn cotton frock" sitting cross-legged on the grass, things assume their proper size. As she makes erotic advances, his terror rises again, and everything becomes magnified. Each leaf becomes as large as a man, every trough in the bark of the tree seems as vast as a channel, every blade of grass looks as high as a house. This apparent contraction and expansion of the external world is dependent upon the protagonist's internal state.

Thomas uses another device commonly employed in lyric poetry, the literalized metaphor. Because a thing seems like another, it is depicted as having been transformed into that other thing. For example, the "sunburned country girl" frightens the lonely boy as if she were a witch; thus, in his eyes, she becomes one. "The stain on her lips was blood, not berries; and her nails were not broken but sharpened sideways, ten black scissorblades ready to snip off his tongue." Finally, not only space and character are subject to transformations, but also time. As the narrator fantasizes union with this girl, he attains a mystical vision of history unrolling back to Eden. The story ends as it began; she disappears into the sea. He had imagined, at the beginning, as he dabbled his fingers in the water, that a drowned storybook princess would emerge from the waves. The apparent obscurities are resolved by seeing the plot of this story as simply the daydreams of a lonely boy on a summer's day.

"The Orchards" is another prose-poem about a man's attempt to record a vision in words. Marlais has a repetitive dream about blazing apple trees guarded by two female figures who change from scarecrows to women. He tries and fails to shape this into a story, and finally sets out on a quest. Striding through eleven valleys, he reaches the scene he has dreamed of, where he reenacts the kissing of the maiden as the orchard catches fire, the fruit falls as cinders, and she and her sister change to scarecrows. These smoldering trees may be related to the sacrificial fires of the Welsh druids on Midsummer Day. The woman figure might be connected with Olwedd, the Welsh Venus, associated with the wild apple. Marlais' adventure, however, is a mental journey undertaken by the creative writer through the landscape of his mind, and the temporal and spatial fluctuations are the projections of that mind, mythicized.

"The Tree" illustrates this same process. A gardener tells a boy the story of Jesus, reading the Bible in his shed by candlelight. While he is mending a rake with wire, he relates the twelve stages of the cross. The boy wants to know the secrets inside the locked tower to which the bearded gardener has the key. On Christmas Eve, the gardener unlocks the room through whose windows the boy can see the Jarvis Hills to the east. The gardener says of this "Christmas present" in a tone which seems prophetic: "It is enough that I have given you the key."

On Christmas morning, an idiot with ragged shoes wanders into the garden, "bearing the torture of the weather with a divine patience." Enduring the rain and the wind, he sits down under the elder tree. The boy, concluding that the gardener had not lied, and that the secret of the tower was true, runs to get the wire to reenact the crucifixion. The old man's obsessive religiosity has been transmitted to the boy, who takes it literally: "a tree" has become "The Tree," "a key" has become "The Key," and a passive beggar stumbling from the east has become Christ inviting his martyrdom.

"The Visitor" is the story of a dying poet, Peter, tended lovingly by Rhiannon, who brings him warm milk, reads to him from William Blake, and at the end pulls the sheet over his face. Death is personified as Callaghan, whose visit he anticipates as his limbs grow numb and his heart slows. Callaghan blows out the candles with his gray mouth, and lifting Peter in his arms, flies with him to the Jarvis Valley where they watch worms and death-beetles undoing "brightly and minutely" the animal tissues on the shining bones through whose sockets flowers sprout, the blood seeping through the earth to fountain forth in springs of water. "Peter, in his ghost, cried with joy." This is the same assurance found in Thomas' great elegies: death is but the reentry of the body into the processes of nature. Matter is not extinguished, but transformed into other shapes whose joyous energies flourish forever.

Other major works

NOVEL: *The Death of the King's Canary*, 1976 (with John Davenport).

PLAY: *Under Milk Wood*, 1954.

SCREENPLAYS: *Three Weird Sisters*, 1948 (with Louise Birt and David Evans); *No Room at the Inn*, 1948 (with Ivan Foxwell); *The Doctor and the Devils*, 1953; *The Beach at the Falesá*, 1963; *Twenty Years A'Growing*, 1964; *Rebecca's Daughters*, 1965; *Me and My Bike*, 1965.

RADIO PLAYS: *Quite Early One Morning*, 1944; *The Londoner*, 1946; *Return Journey*, 1947; *Quite Early One Morning*, 1954 (twenty-two radio plays).

POETRY: *18 Poems*, 1934; *Twenty-five Poems*, 1936; *The Map of Love*, 1939; *New Poems*, 1943; *Deaths and Entrances*, 1946; *Twenty-six Poems*, 1950; *In Country Sleep*, 1952; *Collected Poems, 1934-1952*, 1952; *The Poems of Dylan Thomas*, 1971 (Daniel Jones, editor).

NONFICTION: *Letters to Vernon Watkins*, 1957 (Vernon Watkins, editor); *Selected Letters of Dylan Thomas*, 1966 (Constantine FitzGibbon, editor); *Poet in the Making: The Notebooks of Dylan Thomas*, 1968 (Ralph Maud, editor); *Twelve More Letters by Dylan Thomas*, 1969 (Constantine FitzGibbon, editor).

MISCELLANEOUS: *"The Doctor and the Devils" and Other Scripts*, 1966 (two screenplays and one radio play).

Bibliography

Cox, C. B., ed. *Dylan Thomas: A Collection of Critical Essays*. Englewood Cliffs, N.J.: Prentice-Hall, 1966. Of the thirteen essays in this collection, only Annis Pratt's deals specifically with Thomas' prose; three others analyze *Under Milk Wood*.

Emery, Clark M. *The World of Dylan Thomas*. Coral Gables, Fla.: University of

Miami Press, 1962. This volume contains explications of ninety of Thomas' poems with some brief commentary on the short fiction.

FitzGibbon, Constantine. *The Life of Dylan Thomas.* London: J. M. Dent & Sons, 1965. The standard biography, this work includes a list of Thomas' film scripts, itineraries of his reading tours, and a detailed index that gives the reader access to references to individual works.

Kidder, Rushworth M. *Dylan Thomas: The Country of the Spirit.* Princeton, N.J.: Princeton University Press, 1973. This volume analyzes three types of religious imagery found in Thomas' poetry.

Korg, Jacob. *Dylan Thomas.* Boston: Twayne, 1965. Korg includes a long chapter on Thomas' prose and analyzes several stories. Supplemented by a bibliography.

Tindall, William York. *A Reader's Guide to Dylan Thomas.* New York: Farrar, Straus and Cudahy, 1962. Although primarily offering analyses of the poems, Tindall includes some biography as well as some discussion of themes and interests in the introduction.

Ruth Rosenberg
(Revised by *Ann Davison Garbett*)

JAMES THURBER

Born: Columbus, Ohio; December 8, 1894
Died: New York, New York; November 2, 1961

Principal short fiction

Is Sex Necessary?, 1929 (with E. B. White); *The Owl in the Attic and Other Perplexities*, 1931; *The Seal in the Bedroom and Other Predicaments*, 1932; *My Life and Hard Times*, 1933; *The Middle-Aged Man on the Flying Trapeze*, 1935; *Let Your Mind Alone! And Other More or Less Inspirational Pieces*, 1937; *Fables for Our Time and Famous Poems Illustrated*, 1940; *My World—And Welcome to It!*, 1942; *The Great Quillow*, 1944; *The White Deer*, 1945; *The Thurber Carnival*, 1945; *The Beast in Me and Other Animals: A New Collection of Pieces and Drawings about Human Beings and Less Alarming Creatures*, 1948; *The 13 Clocks*, 1950; *Thurber Country: A New Collection of Pieces About Males and Females, Mainly of Our Own Species*, 1953; *Further Fables for Our Time*, 1956; *The Wonderful O*, 1957; *Alarms and Diversions*, 1957; *Lanterns and Lances*, 1961; *Credos and Curios*, 1962.

Other literary forms

James Thurber's more than twenty published volumes include plays, stories, sketches, essays, verse, fables, fairy tales for adults, reminiscences, biography, drawings, and cartoons.

Achievements

Thurber's writings are widely known and admired in English-speaking countries and his drawings have a world following. He has been compared with James Joyce in his command of and playfulness with English, and he invites comparison with most of his contemporaries, many of whom he parodies at least once in his works. He greatly admired Henry James, referring to him often in his works and parodying him masterfully several times, for example, in "Something to Say." While Thurber is best known as a humorist (often with the implication that he need not be taken seriously as an artist), his literary reputation has grown steadily. His short story "The Secret Life of Walter Mitty" became an instant classic after it appeared in 1939 and was subsequently reprinted in *Reader's Digest.* After his death in 1961, several major studies and a volume in the Twentieth Century Views series have appeared, all arguing that Thurber should rank with the best American artists in several fields including the short story. In 1980, "The Greatest Man in the World" was chosen for dramatization in the American Short Story series of the Public Broadcasting Service. Thurber received numerous awards for his work, including honorary degrees from Kenyon College (1950), Williams College (1957), and Yale University (1953), as well as the Antoinette Perry Award for the revue, *A Thurber Carnival* (1962). His drawings were included in art shows worldwide. He was the first American after Mark Twain to be invited to *Punch*'s Wednesday Luncheon (1958).

Biography

On December 8, 1894, James Grover Thurber was born in Columbus, Ohio, where he spent his childhood except for a two-year stay in Washington, D.C. In Columbus, he absorbed the midwestern regional values that remained important to him all of his life: a liberal idealism, a conservative respect for the family, a belief in the agrarian virtues of industry and independence, and a healthy skepticism about the human potential for perfecting anything. He lost his left eye in a childhood accident that eventually led to almost complete blindness forty years later. He attended but did not graduate from Ohio State University, where he met Elliott Nugent, who was crucial in helping and encouraging Thurber to write. Thurber began his writing career as a journalist, earning his living primarily as a reporter in Ohio and France before he joined *The New Yorker* in 1927. There his friendship with E. B. White provided opportunities for him to perfect and publish the stories he had been working on since college. Within five years of beginning at *The New Yorker*, he became one of the best-known humorists in America. He married Althea Adams on May 20, 1922, and they had one daughter before their divorce in 1935. He married Helen Wismer on June 25, 1935. Despite increasing blindness that seriously interfered with his work, beginning in the early 1940's, Thurber nevertheless continued writing, though he gave up drawing in 1951. He published more than twenty volumes in his lifetime and left many works uncollected at his death. He died of pneumonia on November 2, 1961, a month after suffering a stroke.

Analysis

Thurber is best known as the author of humorous sketches, stories, and reminiscences dealing with urban bourgeois American life. To discuss Thurber as an artist in the short-story form is difficult, however, because of the variety of things he did that might legitimately be labeled short stories. His essays frequently employ stories and are "fictional" in recognizable ways. His "memoirs" in *My Life and Hard Times* are clearly fictionalized. Many of his first-person autobiographical sketches are known to be "fact" rather than fiction only through careful biographical research. As a result, most of his writings can be treated as short fiction. Thurber seemed to prefer to work on the borderlines between conventional forms.

There is disagreement among critics as to the drift of the attitudes and themes reflected in James Thurber's work. The poles are well represented by Richard C. Tobias on the one hand and the team of Walter Blair and Hamlin Hill on the other. Tobias argues that Thurber comically celebrates the life of the mind: "Thurber's victory is a freedom within law that delights and surprises." Blair and Hill, in *America's Humor* (1978), see Thurber as a sort of black humorist laughing at his own destruction, "a humorist bedeviled by neuroses, cowed before the insignificant things in his world, and indifferent to the cosmic ones. He loses and loses and loses his combats with machines, women, and animals until defeat becomes permanent." While Tobias sees women as vital forces in Thurber's work, Hill and Blair see Thurber as essentially a misogynist bewailing the end of the ideal of male freedom best portrayed in 1950's Western film and pathetically reflected in the fantasies of Walter Mitty. In fact, it seems that critics' opinions regarding Thurber's attitudes about most subjects vary from one text to the next, but certain themes seem to remain consistent. His weak male characters do hate strong women, but the males are often weak because they accept the world in which their secret fantasies are necessary and, therefore, leave their women no choice but to try to hold things together. When a woman's strength becomes arrogance as in "The Catbird Seat" and "The Unicorn in the Garden," the man often defeats her with the active power of his imagination. Characterizing Thurber as a Romantic, Robert Morsberger lists some themes he sees pervading Thurber's writing: a perception of the oppression of technocracy and of the arrogance of popular scientism especially in their hostility to imagination; an antirational but not anti-intellectual approach to modern life; a belief in the power of the imagination to preserve human value in the face of contemporary forms of alienation; and a frequent use of fear and fantasy to overcome the dullness of his characters' (and readers') lives.

Because "The Secret Life of Walter Mitty" is so well known, it will receive a little less attention here than it deserves in order to give more attention to the variety of forms Thurber practiced. Mitty lives in a reverie consisting of situations in which he is a hero: commander of a navy hydroplane, surgeon, trial witness, bomber pilot, and condemned martyr. The dream is clearly an escape from the external life which humiliatingly interrupts it: his wife's mothering, the arrogant competence of a parking attendant and policeman, the humiliating errands of removing tire chains, buying overshoes, and asking for puppy biscuits. In his dreams, he is Lord Jim, the misunderstood hero, "inscrutable to the last"; in his daily life he is a middle-aged husband enmeshed in a web of the humdrum. Tobias sees Mitty as ultimately triumphant over dreary reality. Blair and Hill see him as gradually losing grip of the real world and slipping into psychosis. Whether liberated or defeated by his imagination, Mitty is clearly incompetent and needs the mothering his wife gives him. Often described as an immoral and malicious woman, she is actually just the wife he needs and deserves; she seems to exist as a replacement ego to keep him from catching his death of cold as he somnambulates. The story's artfulness is readily apparent in the precise choice and arrangement of details such as sounds, objects, and images that connect fantasy and reality. The technical devices are virtually the same as those used by William Faulkner and Joyce to indicate shifts in levels of awareness in their "free-association internal monologues." Mitty has become a representative figure in modern culture like T. S. Eliot's Prufrock and Faulkner's Quentin Compson, although perhaps more widely known. While many of Thurber's stories are similar to this one in theme and form, they are astonishingly diverse in subject, situation, and range of technique.

Another large group of Thurber stories might be characterized as fictionalized autobiography. One of the best of these sketches is "The Black Magic of Barney Haller" in *The Middle-Aged Man on the Flying Trapeze*. In this story, "Thurber" exorcises his hired man, a Teuton whom lightning and thunder always follow and who mutters imprecations such as "Bime by I go hunt grotches in de voods," and "We go to the garrick now and become warbs." The narrator becomes convinced that despite his stable and solid appearance, Barney is a necromancer who will transform reality with his incantations. At any moment, Barney will reveal his true devilish form and change "Thurber" into a warb or conjure up a grotch. It does not comfort him to learn the probable prosaic meanings of Haller's spells, even to see the crotches placed under the heavy peach tree branches. At the end of the story, he feels regret that the only man he knows who could remove the wasps from his garret has departed. The humor of these incidents is clear, and a humorous meaning emerges from them. The narrator would rather hide in *Swann's Way*, reading of a man who makes himself in his book, but he feels threatened by the external supernatural power of another's language to re-create the world. He first attempts exorcism with Robert Frost, well-known for having successfully disposed of a hired man. He quotes "The Pasture" in an attempt to make the obscure clear, but only succeeds in throwing a fear that mirrors his own into Barney. This gives "Thurber" his clue; in the next attempt he borrows from Lewis Carroll and the American braggart tradition, asserting his own superior power as a magician of words, "Did you happen to know that the mome rath never lived that could outgrabe me?" The man with the superior control of language, the man of superior imagination, really is in control; he *can* become a playing card at will to frighten off black magicians. This story is typical of Thurber in its revelation of the fantastic in the commonplace, its flights of language play, and its concern for the relations among reality, self, imagination, and language. *My Life and Hard Times* is the best-known collection of fictional/autobiographical sketches.

Also an author of fables, Thurber published two collections of fables. "The Moth and the Star" is a typical and often anthologized example. A moth spends a long life trying to reach a star, defying his disappointed parents' wish that he aspire normally to get himself scorched on a street lamp. Having outlived his family, he gains in old age "a deep and lasting pleasure" from the illusion that he has actually reached the distant star: "Moral: Who flies afar from the sphere of our sorrow is here today and here tomorrow." The moth and the star suggest images in F. Scott Fitzgerald's *The Great Gatsby* (1925), one of Thurber's favorite books, but in partial contrast to that book, this story echoes the import of the great artist of the "Conclusion" of Henry David Thoreau's *Walden* (1854). The aspiring idealist who rejects the suicidal life of material accumulation and devotes himself to some perfect work ultimately conquers time and enriches life whether or not he produces any valuable object. Because the moth, like the artist of Kouroo, succeeds and is happy, this story seems more optimistic than *The Great Gatsby*. Many of the fables are more cynical or more whimsical, but all are rich in meaning and pleasure like "The Moth and the Star."

Critics and scholars have noted ways in which Thurber's career and writings parallel Mark Twain's. For example, both, as they grew older, grew more interested in fables and fairy tales. In the latter, Thurber was perhaps the more successful, publishing four fantasy stories for adults in the last twenty years of his life. Completed while blindness was descending upon him, these stories are characterized by heightened poetic language, highly original variations on the fairy formulae, sparkling humor, and a common theme: in the words of Prince Jorn, hero of *The White Deer*, "Love's miracle enough." Love is the key that frees imagination by giving it strength to do, and strength of imagination makes the wasteland fertile. The fairy tales may be seen as intentional responses to Eliot's vision of the wasteland in his famous poem of 1922, perhaps from a point of view similar to that of Percy Bysshe Shelley's *A Defence of Poetry* (1840). While "The Secret Life of Walter Mitty" and *Further Fables for Our Time* may be seen as affirming the view of modern life as a wasteland, the fairy tales suggest that the ash heap of modern culture is escapable. It seems especially significant that the mode of escape is represented in tales of magic in remote settings.

The White Deer opens in the third period in King Clode's memory of waiting for the depleted game of his hunting grounds to replenish itself. The story develops in triads, the central one being the three perilous tasks set for the three sons of King Clode to determine which shall claim the hand of the fair princess who materializes when the king and his sons corner the fleet white deer in the enchanted forest. The sons complete their tasks simultaneously, but in the meantime, King Clode determines that the nameless Princess is not a disenchanted woman but an enchanted deer. When the returned sons are told of this, Thag and Gallow refuse her. If denied love three times, she would be a deer forever, but Jorn accepts her: "What you have been, you are not, and what you are, you will forever be. I place this trophy in the hands of love. . . . You hold my heart." This acceptance transforms her into a new and lovelier princess, Rosanore of the Northland, and the April fragrance of lilacs fills the air suggesting direct opposition to the opening of Eliot's *The Waste Land*: "April is the cruellest month, breeding/Lilacs out of the dead land." As King Clode later sees the full wisdom and beauty of Rosanore, he repeats, "I blow my horn in waste land." Echoes of Eliot show up repeatedly in the fairy tales, but the greater emphasis falls on the powers of love and imagination, which in this fairy world inevitably blossom in beauty and happiness.

The cast of secondary characters and the perilous labors provide opportunities to characterize wittily the world in need of magic. There are an incompetent palace wizard as opposed to the true wizards of the forest, an astronomer-turned-clockmaker who envisions encroaching darkness ("It's darker than you think"), and a royal recorder who descends into mad legalese when the Princess' spell proves to be without precedent. Gallow's labor is especially interesting because he must make his way through a vanity fair bureaucracy in order to conquer a sham dragon, a task that tests his purse and persistence more than his love. This task allows a satire of the commercial values of modern culture. Each of the fairy tales contains similar delights as well as bizarre and beautiful flights of language: the Sphinz asks Jorn, "What is whirly?/ What is curly?/ Tell me, what is pearly early?" and in a trice, Jorn replies, "Gigs are whirly,/ Cues are curly/ and the dew is pearly early."

Other major works

PLAYS: *The Male Animal*, 1940 (with Elliott Nugent); *Many Moons*, 1943; *A Thurber Carnival*, 1962 (revue).

NONFICTION: *The Thurber Album*, 1952; *The Years with Ross*, 1959; *Selected Letters of James Thurber*, 1982.

Bibliography

Bernstein, Burton. *Thurber: A Biography.* New York: Dodd, Mead, 1975. This official biography, written with the cooperation of Thurber's widow, provides a thorough survey of Thurber's life and career.

Bowden, Edwin T. *James Thurber: A Bibliography.* Columbus: Ohio State University Press, 1968. This book provides a complete listing of Thurber's published writings and drawings.

Holmes, Charles S. *The Clocks of Columbus: The Literary Career of James Thurber.* New York: Atheneum, 1972. This literary biography devotes special attention to the relations between Thurber's Ohio background and his works. Supplemented by drawings, photographs, and a bibliography.

_____, ed. *Thurber: A Collection of Critical Essays.* Englewood Cliffs, N.J.: Prentice-Hall, 1974. This useful collection includes twenty-five critical and biographical essays, as well as a chronology and a brief annotated bibliography.

Long, Robert Emmet. *James Thurber.* New York: Continuum, 1988. This biographical and critical study divides Thurber's works into drawings, fiction, autobiography, fables, fairy tales, and occasional pieces, giving each a chapter. Complemented by a bibliography.

Morsberger, Robert E. *James Thurber.* New York: Twayne, 1964. Morsberger sketches Thurber's life and then analyzes his works, looking at his contributions to various art forms and his characteristic themes. Contains a chronology of Thurber's life and a brief annotated bibliography.

Tobias, Richard Clark. *The Art of James Thurber.* Athens: Ohio University Press, 1970. Tobias studies Thurber's themes and worldview, with special attention to his methods and techniques in creating humor.

Terry Heller

LEO TOLSTOY

Born: Yasnaya Polyana, Russia; September 9, 1828
Died: Astapovo, Russia; November 20, 1910

Principal short fiction

Sevastopolskiye rasskazy, 1855-1856 (*Sebastopol*, 1887); *Semeynoye schastye*, 1859 (novella; *Family Happiness*, 1888); *Smert Ivana Ilicha*, 1886 (novella; *The Death of Ivan Ilyich*, 1887); *Kreytserova sonata*, 1891 (novella; *The Kreutzer Sonata*, 1890); *The Kreutzer Sonata, The Devil, and Other Tales*, 1940; *Notes of a Madman and Other Stories*, 1943; *Tolstoy Tales*, 1947.

Other literary forms

Leo Tolstoy is most famous as the author of two superb novels, *Voyna i mir* (1865-1869; *War and Peace*, 1886) and *Anna Karenina* (1875-1878; English translation, 1886). He wrote one other full-length novel, *Voskreseniye* (1899; *Resurrection*, 1899), and a number of novellas, such as *Destvo* (1852; *Childhood*, 1862), *Otrochestvo* (1854; *Boyhood*, 1886), *Yunost* (1857; *Youth*, 1886), *Kazaki* (1863; *The Cossacks*, 1872), and *Khadzi-Murat* (1911; *Hadji Murad*, 1911). His fiction tends to overshadow his achievement as a dramatist; his plays include *Vlast tmy* (1887; *The Power of Darkness*, 1888) and *Plody prosveshcheniya* (1889; *The Fruits of Enlightenment*, 1891).

Achievements

Tolstoy is one of the undisputed titans of fiction, recognized by friend and foe alike as a great artist and man. He is Homeric in the epic sweep of *War and Peace* and *Anna Karenina*; in his stress on the primacy of human beings' senses and physical acts; in the clarity, freshness, and gusto with which he presents his world; in his celebration of nature's processes, from brute matter to the stars; in his union of an omniscient perspective with a detached vision. Unlike Homer, however, he often shows war as wanton carnage resulting from the vainglory and stupidity of a nation's leaders.

While most critical evaluations of Tolstoy's writings are highly laudatory, he has been reproached by some interpreters for his disparagement of science, technology, and formal education, his hostility to aesthetics and the life of the mind, and most of all for his insistence, in his later works, on dictating programs of moral and religious belief to his readers. As a writer, his greatest achievement is to convey an insight into the living moment that renders with unequaled verisimilitude the course of human passions and the pattern of ordinary actions, enabling him to present a comprehensive, coherent, and usually convincing sense of life. His influence, while not as pervasive as that of his rival Fyodor Dostoevski, is evident in the works of Maxim Gorky, D. H Lawrence, Ernest Hemingway, Giuseppe Tomasi di Lampedusa, Ignazio Silone, Isaac Babel, Mikhail Sholokhov, Aleksandr Solzhenitsyn, and Boris Pasternak when he composed his novel, *Doktor Zhivago* (1957; *Doctor Zhivago*, 1958).

Biography

Leo Nikolayevich Tolstoy was born on September 9, 1828, to a retired army officer, Count Nikolay Ilyich Tolstoy, and a wealthy princess, Maria Nikolaevna Bolkonskaya, who was descended from Russia's first ruling dynasty. His birthplace was a magnificent estate 130 miles south of Moscow, Yasnaya Polyana (serene meadow). Throughout his life, particularly from the late 1850's, when he settled there, this beautiful manorial land, featuring an avenue of lime trees and several lakes, was a romance he kept reinventing, lodged at the center of his self. He disliked urban civilization and industrialization, instead preferring with increasing fidelity the rural simplicities and patriarchal order that had governed the lives of his ancestors and that gave him commanding knowledge of the ways of the landowners and peasants who dominate his writings.

Tolstoy's mother died when he was two, his father when he was nine. He was lovingly brought up by an aunt, Tatyana, who became the model for Sonya in *War and Peace*, just as his parents sat for the portraits of Nicholas Rostov and Princess Maria in that novel. Aunt Tatyana both built the boy's confidence and indulged all of his wishes, inclining him to extremes beginning in childhood. He largely wasted several years at the University of Kazan in drinking, gambling, and wenching, then joined an artillery unit in the Caucasus in 1851. That same year, he began working on his first, short novel, *Childhood*, to be followed by *Boyhood* and *Youth*. These works are thinly disguised autobiographical novellas, which unfold a highly complicated moral consciousness.

As a writer, Tolstoy is an inspired solipsist, identifying all other humans in examining his flesh and spirit. His art is essentially confessional, representing the strenuous attempt of a complex and exacting man to reconcile himself with himself. His diary, which he began in 1845, reveals what was to be an inveterate thirst for rational and moral justification of his life. It includes a list of puritanical Rules of Life, which he would update during the tormented periods of guilt that followed his lapses. The biographer Henri Troyat called him "a billy-goat pining for purity." The demands of his senses, mind, and spirit were to contest one another in his character as long as he lived.

Tolstoy served bravely in the Crimean War until 1856, also writing his *Sebastopol* stories as well as a number of other military tales. When he returned to European Russia, he found himself lionized as his country's most promising young author. He passed the years 1856-1861 shuttling between St. Petersburg, Moscow, Yasnaya Polyana, and foreign countries. His two trips abroad disgusted him with what he considered the selfishness and materialism of European bourgeois civilization. In 1859, he founded a school for peasant children at Yasnaya Polyana; in 1862, he launched a pedagogical periodical there; both followed a Rousseauistic model that glorified children's instincts, ignored their discipline, and insisted that intellectuals should learn from the common people, instead of vice versa.

In 1862, the thirty-four-year-old Tolstoy married the eighteen-year-old Sophia Andreyevna Behrs. Family life became his religion, and the union was happy for its first fifteen years, producing thirteen children. He dramatized the stability of marriage and family life in *War and Peace* (written 1863-1869), which his wife was to copy out seven times. Sophia efficiently managed Yasnaya Polyana, often served as his secretary, and nursed him through illnesses. She never recovered from the shock she received, however, a week before their wedding, when he insisted she read every entry of his diary, which recorded not only his moral struggles but also seventeen years of libidinous conduct.

Unhappy times followed the composition of *War and Peace*: the deaths of Aunt Tatyana, a favorite son, and several other relatives; quarrels with Sophia; illness; and depression. *Anna Karenina* (written 1873-1877), is a more somber and moralizing book, with the certainty of death hovering over it, and with sexual passion both given its due and dramatized as destructive to happiness. The male protagonist Levin's search for faith is a pale outline of Tolstoy's own spiritual journey, which next led him to write, between 1879 and 1882, an account of his emotional and ethical pilgrimage entitled *Ispoved* (1884; *A Confession*, 1885).

Shortly after finishing *Anna Karenina*, Tolstoy suffered a shattering midlife crisis that brought him close to suicide. Even though he had much to value—good health, a loving wife, family, fame, wealth, genius—life nevertheless seemed to him a cruel lie, purposeless, fraudulent, empty. For answers, he turned to philosophers, to educated people, and finally to the uneducated but religious peasants whose faith made their lives possible, and he decided to become a religious believer, although rejecting most ecclesiastical dogma.

A Confession is the best introduction to the spiritual struggle that Tolstoy was to wage for his remaining thirty years, which he spent in a glaringly public retirement. Trying to live up to his principles of purity and simplicity, he stripped his personal demands to the barest necessities, dressed and often worked as a peasant, published doctrines of moral improvement in both tracts and tales, signed over to his wife the right to manage his copyrights as well as his property, and renounced (not always successfully) almost all institutions, his title, concert and theatergoing, meat, alcohol, tobacco, hunting, and even sex. He became the high priest of a cult of Christian anarchy, professing the moral teachings of the Gospel and Sermon on the Mount while rejecting the divinity of Christ and the authority of the Church, which excommunicated him for blasphemy in 1901.

Some typical titles of Tolstoy's didactic last years are *V chom moya vera* (1884; *What I Believe*, 1885), "Gde lyubov', tam i Bog" ("Where Love Is, God Is") and "Mnogo li cheloveku zemli nuzhno?" ("How Much Land Does A Man Need?"). His best-known narrative was the tendentious three-part novel *Resurrection*, which is as long as, but far inferior to, *Anna Karenina*. Its protagonist, Nekhlyudov, experiences remorse after having seduced a peasant woman and expiates his transgression by adopting a moral life. Of greatest interest to literary critics is the book-length essay, *Chto takoye iskusstvo?* (1898; *What Is Art?*, 1898), in which Tolstoy rejects all art based on other than gospel ethics and concludes that only the Old Testament's story of Joseph and primitive popular art will satisfy his standards.

Even in his doctrinaire phase, however, Tolstoy managed to produce great stories and novellas, particularly *The Death of Ivan Ilyich*, "Khozyain i rabotnik" ("Master and Man"), *The Kreutzer Sonata*, and *Hadji Murad*. He also wrote a powerful naturalistic tragedy, *The Power of Darkness*, which featured adultery and infanticide in a somber peasant setting. By contrast, *The Fruits of Enlightenment* is a satiric, farcical comedy revolving around the foibles of the gentry and the land hunger of the peasantry.

Tolstoy's last years were often mired in squabbles with his wife and some of his children, intrigues concerning his legacy, and bitter enmity between Sophia Tolstoy and his chief disciple, Vladimir Chertkov, who became Tolstoy's close confidant. By 1909, the marriage had become extremely stressful, with Countess Tolstoy repeatedly threatening suicide. On November 9, 1910, Leo Tolstoy, driven to distraction, fled his wife and family; on November 13, he was taken ill with what became pneumonia, at the rail junction of nearby Astapovo, and died in the station master's bed there on November 20. His death was mourned as a loss in every Russian family.

Analysis

Leo Tolstoy's ego embraces the world, so that he is always at the center of his fictive creation, filling his books with his struggles, personae, problems, questions, and quests for answers, and above all with his notion of life as an ethical search as strenuous as the pursuit of the Holy Grail. He does not try to puzzle or dazzle; his work is not a clever riddle to be solved or a game to be played but a rich realm to be explored. He disdains the kind of exterior purism practiced by Gustave Flaubert and Henry James among others, which concentrates on the inner lives of individuals—although he is superbly skilled at psychological perception. His aim, rather, is to discover, as far as he can, the essential truth of life's meaning, the revelation to be gained at the core of the vast mesh of human relations. What energizes his work is his conviction that this truth is good, and that, once discovered, it will resolve the discords and conflicts that plague humanity.

In Tolstoy's art, the natural, simple, and true is always pitted against the artificial, elaborate, and false, the particular against the general, knowledge gained from observation against assertions of borrowed faiths. His is the gift of direct vision, of fundamental questions and of magical simplicity—perhaps too simple, as a distinguished historian of ideas has indicated. Isaiah Berlin, in a famous essay titled "The Hedgehog and the Fox," sees Tolstoy as torn between his pluralism (the fox, perceiving reality as varied, complex, and multiple) and monism (the hedgehog, reducing life's fullness to one single truth, the infinity of sensory data to the finite limits of a single mind). Tolstoy, Berlin concludes, was a pluralist in his practice but a monist in his theory, who found himself unable to reconcile the foxiness of his multifarious awareness with his hedgehoglike need to discover one all-embracing answer to its myriad problems.

Tolstoy's first stories are set in the Caucasus, where he spent the years 1851 to 1854, with many of the officers and soldiers whom he met serving as thinly disguised models. In "Nabeg: Razskaz volontera" ("The Raid: A Volunteer's Story"), he poses several problems: What is the nature of courage? By what tests does one determine bravery or cowardice? What feelings cause a man to kill his fellow? The first-person narrator discusses these questions with a Captain Khlopov (derived from a Captain Khilkovsky in Tolstoy's diary) and illustrates different types of courage among the military characters. Tolstoy deflates warfare, emphasizing ordinary details and casual, matter-of-fact fortitude rather than dashingly proud heroism. His descriptions of nature are simple, concrete, and expert. The story's most powerful scene has a dying young ensign pass from carefree bravado to dignified resignation as he encounters his end.

The element of eyewitness reportage is carried over from the Caucasian tales to the three *Sebastopol* sketches, which are fiction passing as war dispatches. Tolstoy took part in the Crimean War (1854-1856) as a sublieutenant, with Russia fighting a complex series of actions against a multiple enemy composed of not only Turkish but also some British, French, and Sardinian troops. While aggressively patriotic, he was appalled by the disorganization of his country's military forces, with the average Russian peasant soldier poorly armed, trained, and led, while many company commanders nearly starved their men by pocketing much of the money allocated for their food.

"Sevastopol v dekabre" ("Sebastopol in December") has no characters and no particular topography. The first-person narrator constructs a guidebook homily out of lived experience, familiarly addressing readers, inviting them to listen to his frontline experiences as he wanders from Sebastopol's bay and dockside to a military hospital filled with shrieking, often mutilated soldiers. Says the speaker,

> . . . you will see war not as a beautiful, orderly, and gleaming formation, with music and beaten drums, streaming banners and generals on prancing horses, but war in its authentic expression—as blood, suffering and death.

Tolstoy concludes this sketch with a stirring salute to the epic heroism of Sebastopol's residents and Russian defenders. Yet a somber awareness of death's imminence, as the surgeon's sharp knife slices into his patients' flesh, pervades the sketch.

In "Sevastopol v mae" ("Sebastopol in May"), Tolstoy sharply denounces the vainglory of militarism, stressing the futility of the fighting and the madness of celebrating war as a glorious adventure. The passage describing the death by shellfire of an officer is a superb tour de force, with the author using interior monologue to have the lieutenant crowd his many hopes, fears, memories, and fantasies into a few seconds. The speaker comes to consider war as senseless, horrifying, but also—given human nature—inevitable. He concludes that the only hero he can find is the truth. This is perhaps the finest of Tolstoy's military tales, anticipating the battle and death scenes of *War and Peace*.

In the third narrative, "Sebastopol in August," Tolstoy uses well-developed characters to unify an episodic plot. He focuses on two brothers whose personalities contrast, but who are both killed in action. He also strikes a note of shame and anger at Russia's abandonment of the city and the consequent waste of many thousands of lives. He celebrates, however, the quiet heroism of countless common soldiers who risked and often met death with calm nobility.

Before Tolstoy began *War and Peace* in 1863, he wrote a number of long stories or novellas, which he called *povesti*, defined as "A literary narrative of lesser size than a novel." Their compass is usually too small to accommodate the didacticism that his longer works absorb painlessly. One successful story that avoids moralizing is "Dva gusara" ("Two Hussars"). Its first half is devoted to the officer-father, the second to his son. Twenty years apart, they enact the same sequence of card playing, drinking, and philandering, in the same small town, meeting the same people. Their characters, however, differ drastically. The father is gallant, generous, honorable, charming. The son is mean, cold, calculating, cowardly. The father's temperament is natural and open. The son's is contrived and devious, corrupted by decadent society. As always with Tolstoy, he gives his allegiance to the authentic and intuitive, while sardonically scorning the artificial and scheming.

In *Family Happiness*, Tolstoy treats a problem to which he was to return throughout his career: the place of women, both at home and in society. He had courted a much younger and very pretty girl, Valerya Arseneva, but had become irritated by her fondness for high society and had broken off the relationship. He transforms the experience into a narrative by the young woman, Masha, in the fashion of Charlotte Brontë's novel *Jane Eyre* (1847), which he had read and admired. Now married and a mother, Masha recalls, in the story's first half, her courtship by a man who knew her dead father, considered himself her guardian as she grew up, and was thirty-five to her seventeen when they married. Tolstoy magnificently captures the rapturous chemistry of first love as the girl awakens to womanhood. By the story's second half, however, he undermines her dreams of romantic happiness as she becomes addicted to the whirl of urban high society, driving her husband into rural retreat and seclusion. Toward the end, at home in the country after disillusionments in the city, she and he agree to a different sort of marriage than they envisioned at its start, basing it not on passion but on companionship and parenthood. Tolstoy has here sounded some of his most pervasive notes: sophistication is evil, simplicity is good; the city is decadent, the country is healthy; and romance is dangerous, often a "charming nonsense," while marriage, though a necessary institution, should never be sentimentalized.

The story now called "Kholstomer" ("Strider") was originally translated into English as "Kholstomer: The Story of a Horse," because Tolstoy modeled his equine, first-person narrator on a horse by that name celebrated for his enormous stride and speed. The author humanizes his outcast animal, which is consistently stigmatized as a piebald and a gelding, in a keenly compassionate manner, with Strider's sorrowful life made a parable of protest against unjust punishment of those who are somehow different. "He was old, they were young. He was lean, they were sleek; he was miserable, they were gay; and so he was quite alien to them, an outsider, an utterly different creature whom it was impossible for them to pity." Strider's victimization by greedy, selfish owners enables Tolstoy to lash the evils of private property, using an equine perspective to expose its immorality.

The second phase of Tolstoy's production of short fiction follows his two great novels and the tremendous spiritual crisis chronicled in *A Confession*. No other author has ever undergone so profound a change. The sublime artist comes to repudiate almost all art; the nobleman now lives like a peasant; the wealthy, titled country gentleman seeks to abandon his property, preaching humility and asceticism; the marvelous novelist and story writer prefers the roles of educational reformer, religious leader, social sage, cultural prophet. Yet Tolstoy's artistic instincts refuse to atrophy, and he manages to create different yet also masterful works, less happy and conventional, uncompromising, sometimes perverse, always powerful, preoccupied with purity, corruption, sin, sex, and death. His late stories express his Rousseauistic hostility to such institutions as the state, which forces citizens to pay taxes and serve in the military; the church, which coerces its communicants by fear and superstition; private property, whereby one person owns another; and modern art, which is elitist. The creative gold nevertheless continues to flow from Tolstoy's pen, despite his moralistic resistance to aesthetics, in such novellas as *The Death of Ivan Ilyich*, *The Kreutzer Sonata*, and the story "Master and Man."

The Death of Ivan Ilyich, perhaps his finest story, was Tolstoy's first published work after his conversion. It is more schematic and deliberate than the earlier tales, more selective and condensed in the choice of descriptive and analytic detail. It is a parable of a life badly lived, with Tolstoy here allying his highest art with an exigent passion for establishing the most profound and encompassing truths.

Ivan Ilyich is a cautious, correct, typical representative of his social class. He has achieved success in his profession of judge, in love, in marriage, in his family, and in his friendships, or so appearances indicate. Yet when, confronted with the inescapability of a cancer-ridden death, he reviews his past, he slowly arrives at the realization that he has led a life of selfishness, shallowness, smugness, and hypocrisy. Significantly, his surname, Golovin, is derived from the Russian word for "head." He has excluded any deep feelings, as he has lived according to principles of pleasantness and propriety, conforming to the values of his upper-middle-class social sphere in his striving for status, materialism, bureaucratic impersonality and power, decorous appearance, and pleasure.

In part 1, which begins with the announcement of Ivan Ilyich's death, Tolstoy's tone is caustically satiric. Ivan's wife/widow, Praskovya Fedorovna, defines the nature of his loveless home life, grieving formally for her loss and accepting colleagues' condolences while really concerned with the cost of the grave site and the possibility of increasing her widow's pension. Ivan Ilyich, however, deserves no better. He is shown as a prisoner of his cherished possessions who wanted Praskovya primarily for her property, secondarily for her correct social position and good looks. The density of things dominates Ivan Ilyich's feelings and conduct, pain and pleasure, happiness and misery. His highest moment comes with the furnishing of a new house; and his fall comes from reaching to hang a drape when he is on a ladder.

Symbolically, his fall is one from pride and vanity.

The physicians enter to examine Ivan Ilyich's bruised side. They pursue their profession much as he does, from behind well-mannered, ritualistic masks. Ivan Ilyich soon discovers that not only his doctors but also his wife, daughter, colleagues, and friends all refuse him the empathy and compassion that he increasingly needs; they act on the same principle of self-interested pleasure that he has followed. As his physical suffering grows, he experiences the emotional stages that modern psychology accepts as characteristic of responses to lingering terminal illness: denial, loneliness, anger, despondency, and, finally, acceptance. He begins to drop his protective disguises and to realize that his existence has consisted of evasions of self-knowledge, of love, of awareness of the deepest needs of others. His fall into the abyss of death thus brings him to spiritual birth.

At the nadir of Ivan Ilyich's suffering, partial grace comes to him through the care of his servant, Gerasim. He is, like Platon Karataev in *War and Peace*, one of those simple, spontaneous, kindly souls whom Tolstoy venerates. In contrast to the sterile pretensions of Ivan Ilyich's social circle, Gerasim, modest and strong, personifies the Tolstoyan principle of living for others. He is in every sense a "breath of fresh air," showing his master unstinting compassion as he exemplifies the health of youth and naturally loving behavior.

Inspired by Gerasim's devotion, Ivan Ilyich becomes capable of extending compassion to his wife and son. When his condition takes a final, fatal turn, as he feels himself slowly sucked into the bottom of death's sack, he comes to the realization that his life has been trivial, empty, worthless. Two hours before his death, he stops trying to justify it and instead takes pity on his wife, son, and himself. He dies loving rather than hating, forgiving rather than whining, at last surrendering his egoism. Both the story and Ivan Ilyich's life thus end on a note of serenity and joyous illumination. Tolstoy shows that profound consciousness of death can bring one to the communion of true brotherhood. Through his relentless pain, Ivan Ilyich discovers the truth about himself, akin to Prince Andrey in *War and Peace*.

The Kreutzer Sonata, like *The Death of Ivan Ilyich*, is a condensed masterpiece of harrowing intensity, a poem of the poignant pains of the flesh. Tolstoy presents the nature of marriage more directly and comprehensively than any other writer. In *Family Happiness*, he tries to define its benefits and banes; in *War and Peace*, he celebrates it; in *Anna Karenina*, he upholds yet also questions it; in *The Kreutzer Sonata*, he denounces it vehemently. Though he previously advocated marriage as the morally and socially legitimate release for sexual needs, by the late 1880's, his new views on morality, as well as his own increasingly burdensome marriage, caused him to equate sexuality with hostility and sinfulness and to regard sexual passion as degrading, undermining human beings' spiritual self.

The novella's protagonist, Pozdnyshev, confesses on a train journey that he murdered his wife on suspicion—groundless, as circumstances indicate—of her adultery with an amateur violinist with whom she, a pianist, enjoyed playing duets—such as Ludwig van Beethoven's "Kreutzer Sonata." In the spring of 1888, a performance of this work did take place in Tolstoy's Moscow residence. He proposed to the great realistic painter also present, Ilya Repin, that the artist should paint a canvas, while he would write a story, on the theme of marital jealousy. While Tolstoy fulfilled the bargain, Repin did not. The tale was submitted to the state censor in 1888; Czar Alexander III, who read a copy, issued an imperial banning order. Sophia Tolstoya thereupon removed some of the story's sexual explicitness, and the czar permitted its publication, in bowdlerized form, in 1891. Not until the 1933 Jubilee Edition of Tolstoy's works was the text issued in its original form. Yet even in its toned-down version, it aroused a storm of controversy among readers.

Pozdnyshev relates his conduct to a lightly sketched narrator. His dramatic monologue is powerful and polemical, although his arguments are often exaggerated and inconsistent. The point of his narrative is that sex is sinful, that those who submit to its drives often become vicious and, in Pozdnyshev's case, murderous. Even in marriage, the protagonist insists, sex is ugly, repulsive, and destructive. Despite the deranged character of Pozdnyshev and the manifest injustice of many of his views, the story is disturbing, forceful, and gripping, as he shows how his sexual lust degraded his character and ruined his marriage. Some critics have interpreted the structure of the tale as equivalent to the sonata form, falling into three movements with a slow introduction and the final chapter as a coda. Tolstoy was himself an accomplished pianist.

In a long, uncompromising afterword to the story, Tolstoy addresses the controversy it caused and clearly links Pozdnyshev's views—but not his pathological personality—to his. He argues that carnal love lowers human beings to animalistic conduct, advocates chastity within as well as outside marriage, denounces society for featuring erotic allure, and dismisses marriage itself as a trap for humanity's finest energies. Men and women should replace conjugal relations "with the pure relations that exist between a brother and a sister." Only thus would they behave as true Christians. Tolstoy thus dismisses sex as relevant—let alone fundamental—to human behavior. Rather, he regards it as a diabolic temptation sent to divert human beings' purpose from seeking the kingdom of God on earth.

In his moralistic monograph, *What Is Art?*, Tolstoy asks for writing that is easily understandable, whose subject matter is religious, situations universal, style simple, and technique accessible. None of his successful works embodies these criteria more faithfully than "Master and Man," which is essentially a morality play based on the New Testament. The master is Vasíli Andréevich Brekhunov: selfish, overbearing, coarse, rich, rapacious, the biblical gatherer of wealth who neglects his soul. The servant is Nikíta, a reformed drunkard, who is humane, sensitive, skilled in his work, strong, meek, kindly, rich in spirit though poor in pocket. The contrast between them is stark, with Tolstoy stressing the unambiguous and heavily symbolic nature of the novella: two opposed sorts of men, two opposed sets of moral values, and the conversion of the master to the ethics of his man. The man of flesh and the man of spirit join in the journey of life and the confrontation with death.

Brekhunov, a merchant proud of his ability to drive a hard bargain, sets off with

Nikíta on a business trip to make a down payment on a grove. He can consider nothing but his possessions and how to increase them; his relationships to others are governed by materialistic calculations. On their trip, the pair find themselves immersed in a raging snowstorm, which obliterates all landmarks and turns the landscape into a perilous Wood of Error, a moral Wasteland, through which they must make life's passage. Tolstoy masterfully uses the storm for its emblematic qualities. It "buries" the travelers in snowdrifts, is cold like death, turns the substantial into the spectral and vice versa. They lose their way as Brekhunov insists on movements to the left, since men find their reward only on the right hand of God. As Brekhunov urges his horse away from the sled, after having (temporarily) deserted Nikíta, he can only come around in a circle to the same spot, marked by wormwood stalks— wormwood being identified with sin and punishment in Revelation. He is ritualistically confronted with himself in the person of a horse-thief, for Brekhunov has been cheating Nikíta of his wages and has stolen a large sum of money from his church to buy the grove.

Nikíta accepts his master's wrong turns without anger or reproof, resigns himself to the snowstorm, and patiently prepares to wait it out when they are forced to settle down for the night in their sled. Around midnight, ill-clad and half-frozen, meekly awaiting likely death before morning, Nikíta asks his master to give the wages owed him to his family and to "Forgive me for Christ's sake!" Finally, moved to pity by Nikíta's words, Brekhunov opens his heavy fur coat and lies down on top of his servant, covering Nikíta with both his coat and body as he sobs.

Just before dawn Brekhunov has a visionary dream, in which "it seemed to him that he was Nikíta and Nikíta was he, and that his life was not in himself but in Nikíta." He wonders why he used to trouble himself so greatly to accumulate money and possessions. At noon the next day, peasants drag both men out of the snow. Brekhunov is frozen to death; Nikíta, though chilled, is alive.

Some critics have faulted the story's ending because Tolstoy has inadequately prepared the reader for Brekhunov's sudden adoption of Christian humility, brotherhood, and self-sacrifice, since he has previously shown not the slightest inclination toward moral regeneration. Be that as it may, most of the tale is enormously impressive in the power of its sensuous description as the snowstorm isolates the couple from ordinary existence, strips them of external comforts, exposes them to the presence of death, forces them to encounter their inmost selves.

Tolstoy's celebration of Brekhunov's redemption through fellowship is his answer to a universe that he has feared all of his life as he confronts the horror of nonexistence conveyed by death. Master and man—or man and man, or man and woman— should cling to each other, love each other, forgive each other. Will such conduct vault their souls into immortality? Tolstoy desperately hopes so.

Other major works

NOVELS: *Detstvo*, 1852 (*Childhood*, 1862); *Otrochestvo*, 1854 (*Boyhood*, 1886); *Yunost*, 1857 (*Youth*, 1886); *Kazaki*, 1863 (*The Cossacks*, 1872); *Voyna i mir*, 1865-1869

(*War and Peace*, 1886); *Anna Karenina*, 1875-1878 (English translation, 1886); *Voskreseniye*, 1899 (*Resurrection*, 1899); *Khadzi-Murat*, 1911 (wr. 1904; *Hadji Murad*, 1911).

PLAYS: *Vlast tmy*, 1887 (*The Power of Darkness*, 1888); *Plody prosveshcheniya*, 1889 (*The Fruits of Enlightenment*, 1891); *Zivoj trup*, 1911 (*The Live Corpse*, 1919); *I svet vo tme svetit*, 1911 (*The Light Shines in Darkness*, 1923); *The Dramatic Works*, 1923.

NONFICTION: *Ispoved*, 1884 (*A Confession*, 1885); *V chom moya vera*, 1884 (*What I Believe*, 1885); *O zhizni*, 1888 (*Life*, 1888); *Kritika dogmaticheskogo bogosloviya*, 1891 (*A Critique of Dogmatic Theology*, 1904); *Soedinenie i perevod chetyrekh evangeliy*, 1892-1894 (*The Four Gospels Harmonized and Translated*, 1895-1896); *Tarstvo Bozhie vnutri vas*, 1894 (*The Kingdom of God Is Within You*, 1894); *Chto takoye iskusstvo?*, 1898 (*What Is Art?*, 1898); *Tak chto zhe nam delat?*, 1902 (*What to Do?*, 1887); *The Diaries of Leo Tolstoy, 1847-1852*, 1917; *The Journal of Leo Tolstoy, 1895-1899*, 1917; *Tolstoi's Love Letters*, 1923; *The Private Diary of Leo Tolstoy, 1853-1857*, 1927; *"What Is Art?" and Essays on Art*, 1929; *L. N. Tolstoy o literature: Stati, pisma, dnevniki*, 1955; *Lev Tolstoy ob iskusstve i literature*, 1958; *Leo Tolstoy: Last Diaries*, 1960.

CHILDREN'S LITERATURE: *Azbuka*, 1872; *Novaya azbuka*, 1875; *Russkie knigi dlya chteniya*, 1875.

MISCELLANEOUS: *The Complete Works of Count Tolstoy*, 1904-1905 (24 volumes); *Tolstoy Centenary Edition*, 1928-1937 (21 volumes); *Polnoye sobraniye sochinenii*, 1928-1958 (90 volumes).

Bibliography

Bayley, John, ed. Introduction to *The Portable Tolstoy*. New York: Viking, 1978. Bayley has written a discerning introduction as well as compiled a comprehensive chronology and select bibliography. This anthology of course omits the long novels but does excerpt *Childhood*, *Boyhood*, and *Youth*. The fiction choices are fine. Also included are *A Confession* and *The Power of Darkness*.

——————. *Tolstoy and the Novel*. London: Chatto & Windus, 1966. Influenced by Henry James's organic conception of the novel, Bayley concentrates on trenchant analyses of *War and Peace* and *Anna Karenina*. He also perceptively examines *Family Happiness*, *The Kreutzer Sonata*, and *The Devil*.

Berlin, Isaiah. "The Hedgehog and the Fox" and "Tolstoy and Enlightenment." In *Russian Thinkers*. New York: Viking, 1978. The first essay is a famous analysis of Tolstoy's philosophy of history; the second focuses on his indebtedness to Jean-Jacques Rousseau. Both are eloquently written by a distinguished historian and philosopher.

Christian, R. F. *Tolstoy: A Critical Introduction*. Cambridge, England: Cambridge University Press, 1969. Christian is a leading Tolstoyan who is knowledgeable about his subject's sources and influences, writes clearly, and provides particularly helpful interpretations of *Family Happiness* and *The Kreutzer Sonata*.

Simmons, Ernest T. *Introduction to Tolstoy's Writings.* Chicago: University of Chicago Press, 1968. Simmons is the dean of Russian literature studies in the United States and has also written a two-volume biography of Tolstoy. This book is compact, well organized, comprehensive, and reliable. Its style, unfortunately, is pedestrian.

Wasiolek, Edward. *Tolstoy's Major Fiction.* Chicago: University of Chicago Press, 1978. Having written a superb study of Fyodor Dostoevski's fiction, Wasiolek has composed an equally first-rate critique of Tolstoy's. He concentrates on thorough analyses of ten Tolstoyan works, including *Family Happiness, The Death of Ivan Ilyich,* and "Master and Man." His is a close and acute reading, influenced by Russian Formalists and by Roland Barthes. A twenty-page chronicle of Tolstoy's life and work is illuminating.

Gerhard Brand

TATYANA TOLSTAYA

Born: Leningrad, Soviet Union; May 3, 1951

Principal short fiction

Na zolotom kryl'tse sideli, 1989 (*On the Golden Porch*, 1989); *Sleepwalker in a Fog*, 1992.

Other literary forms

Tatyana Tolstaya is known primarily for her short fiction.

Achievements

When her first collection of short stories was published in the United States in 1989 as *On the Golden Porch*, Tatyana Tolstaya was acclaimed by critics as an original and important new voice in Soviet literature. Her second book, also a group of stories, published in 1992 as *Sleepwalker in a Fog*, was generally conceded to be a worthy successor to her well-received first collection. Among those who paid enthusiastic tribute to Tolstaya were the American poet laureate Joseph Brodsky and Helena Goscilo, editor of *Balancing Acts: Contemporary Stories by Russian Women Writers* and *Heritage and Heresy: Recent Fiction by Russian Women*.

Biography

Tatyana Tolstaya was born in Leningrad, the Soviet Union, on May 3, 1951, the daughter of Nikita Tolstoy, a professor of physics, and Natalia Lozinskaya. Her great-granduncle was the writer Leo Tolstoy, and her grandfather, also a writer, was Alexei Tolstoy. Tolstaya was graduated from Leningrad State University in 1974 with a degree in languages and literatures. She worked as a junior editor in the Oriental literature department of a publishing house in Moscow and later held the following positions in American universities: writer-in-residence at the University of Richmond, senior lecturer in Russian literature at the University of Texas at Austin, and writer-in-residence at Texas Tech University, Lubbock. In May, 1974, she married Andrei Lebedev, a professor of philology; with their two sons, they settled in Moscow. Her short stories were published in several Soviet journals as well as in *The New Yorker*.

Analysis

The title of Tatyana Tolstaya's story "Na zolotom kryl'tse sideli" ("On the Golden Porch") comes from an old Russian counting song that names several different unrelated persons—a czar, a king, a cobbler, and so forth. This is an appropriate allusion because the collection comprises stories about all sorts of people—a five-year-old girl and her nanny, a little boy in love with a beautiful neighbor, an old woman who still dreams of joining her first lover, a desperate young woman who traps a coarse and insensitive man into marriage, a shy fat man who dreams his life away—to mention only a few of the disparate and varied characters. The stories have some elements in common. Similar settings, themes, and style give the stories more unity and connection with one another than the nursery-rhyme title might suggest. A similar kind of variety as well as unifying elements characterizes the stories in *Sleepwalker in a Fog* as well.

The stories are all set in Moscow or Leningrad, with an only slightly less frequent setting being the dacha, or country summer home so often found in Russian literature. More particularly, the stories repeatedly contrast the cramped, drab, and dismal environments of late twentieth century Soviet citizens with the idyllic life in rural surroundings. There are exceptions to the idyllic quality of the dacha settings, but the connotation is always consistent with relaxation, plenitude, and natural beauty.

Tolstaya seems to have particular favorites among the kinds of characters she portrays: innocent though sometimes mischievous children; hardworking and loving elderly people, especially women; and a distinctive group of weak, deluded, and disillusioned persons of less determinate age but all suffering from vulnerability, deprivation of one sort or another, and a strong tendency to mix dreams and fantasy with harsh reality.

While there is not a totally cheerful story in the two collections, there is much that is joyful, merry, tender, and humorous. The stories are not tightly plotted. Incidents and events are used to reveal characters' interactions, situations, and conditions. Tolstaya seems to be more concerned with evoking moods and portraying unforgettable characters, whether they be a child dreaming of running away with a beautiful woman who betrays him, an old nanny who spends her life living for others, a weak and ineffectual librarian who longs for love, or a no-longer-young woman who traps a man into a loveless marriage. In fact, every principal character in her collections has a story that lifts each of them out of the ordinary, into the realms of brilliant, rich imagination.

Tolstaya has been lauded again and again as one of the most original and impressive writers of the late twentieth century in the Soviet Union. Her use of multivoiced narrators has been cited, as has her ability to combine sadness with humor, tenderness with cruelty. Her tendency to use objects in anthropomorphic ways has also been praised: gardens wave handkerchiefs, cabbage soup talks to itself, dresses tuck up their knees inside dark trunks, and a lamp shade is young and skittish.

The metaphor of dream is one of Tolstaya's most distinctive devices. It appears in almost all of her stories; some of them consist almost entirely of dreams. The overall effect is evocative, evanescent, wry, and sometimes bizarre. Her stories have a natural, conversational style, whether in the narrator's voice, in the talk among characters, or even in a character's monologue. Tolstaya's themes reveal her special concerns: the dreadful contrasts between the disappointments and failures of everyday life and the joyful life of the imagination, between reality and fantasy, and between dream and nightmare.

Three stories in Tolstaya's first collection exemplify both the similarities and contrasts in her writing. One is set in Leningrad, the other two in a dacha. All three stories are told from the point of view of a child, one of Tolstaya's favorite narrative forms. This method allows her to use a fluid, rambling conversational style, laden with images and strong feeling. In all three stories, the nature of childhood, which is not entirely innocent, is contrasted with cruel betrayals by adults, indeed, by life. The differences, however, are what make each story distinctive and memorable in its own way.

The title story of the first collection alludes to a Russian counting rhyme in its title. Beginning with a brief poetic description of childhood as a garden, it shifts to the less idyllic aspects of childhood and uses several images of blood to convey the cruel and frightening side of that period. For example, a beautiful neighbor sells strawberries, her fingers red with berry blood. The narrator recalls how the same beautiful neighbor once smiled about her red hands after she had just killed a calf, and thus the contrast is established. The child narrator's fears are expressed in fantasies about her mother crawling over broken glass to steal a strawberry runner. Uncle Pasha, the scary neighbor's elderly, meek, henpecked husband, an accountant, runs every day to catch the commuter train to Leningrad. With his black cuff protectors, his scurrying to and from his job in a smoky basement, Uncle Pasha inevitably reminds one of Nikolai Gogol's Akaky Akakyevich. Uncle Pasha's house, however, is an Aladdin's cave of treasures, which are described in fantastic terms. With abrupt speed, the accountant grows old, and his treasure-filled room is now seen with the adult eyes of the narrator as filled with trash and rubbish, tacky, worn, cheap, fake. Uncle Pasha freezes to death on the porch. Juxtaposed against the picture of him face down in the snow are white snow daisies growing between his still fingers.

"Liubish'—ne liubish'" ("Loves Me, Loves Me Not"), the first story in the collection, is also told by a child, a five-year-old who resents having to be taken to the park by Maryvanna, an old servant, whom the child hates because of her ugliness, her poverty, her endless boring reminiscences. The old woman appears to be harmless, but the poems that she recites to the child are filled with frightening images that express night fears of monsters and other threatening creatures that never appear in the daytime. The child's occasional bouts of flu give rise to a different kind of fantasy, fever dreams of banging red drums, a round loaf of bread running along an airfield with a nasty smile, tiny planes like bugs with claws. A flea market provides another setting for fantastic people and objects. In contrast to Maryvanna, who personifies the self-absorption and silly, scary kind of adult, there is Nanny Grusha, who is too old and feeble to go out but who understands the child's anxieties and suffering and weeps compassionate tears with wordless love.

"Svidanie s ptitsei" ("Date with a Bird") is another story set in the country, told by a detached and omniscient narrator who observes the boyish play and infatuation with a beautiful, fantasizing woman named Tamila. Petya is completely captivated by her stories and her possessions—a ring in the form of a snake, a squashed silver toad, a black robe with a red dragon on the back. Petya vows to himself that he will marry Tamila and lock up Uncle Borya in a tower because he teases and torments the boy with ridicule and nagging. The contrast between the two male figures, the boy and the man, is sharply drawn. Between them is the seductive enchantress. Frightened by a nightmare, Petya wakes up and goes to the room where his grandfather has lain ill for a long time; he is dead. Petya runs to Tamila's dacha and there encounters the final betrayal and disillusionment.

Another group of stories illustrates the capacity to dream and apprehend fantasy on a somewhat more adult level. Among these stories, that of "Peters" serves as an outstanding example. Abandoned by his parents, Peters is brought up by his grandmother, is never allowed to play with other children, and imagines his scoundrel father living on a tropical island. He attends a library school and goes to work in a library after his grandmother dies. Fat and clumsy, Peters lives in fantasies about beautiful ladies and love. When Faina begins her employment in the library, Peters' dreamworld becomes connected to the real world, a trick that Tolstaya often plays on her characters. Then Peters happens to overhear Faina call him "a wimp . . . an endocrinological sissy," and he realizes that his youth is over. Nevertheless, when spring comes, he falls in love with Valentina, a young woman whom he happens to see buying postcards. He imagines that he might be able to astonish and impress her if he knew German; then, in a restaurant, he is picked up by a "flying flower" named Peri, who steals his money. Peters continues to live as in a dream, sleeps through several years of marriage to a stern, unfeeling woman who eventually abandons him. Now old, Peters feels stirring within him a renewed sense of life. Now he neither desires nor regrets but is simply grateful for life, though it is slipping past him indifferently, treacherously, mysteriously. Still, he sees it as "marvelous, marvelous, marvelous," and with these significant words, the book ends.

In the title story of *Sleepwalker in a Fog*, Tolstaya blends several of her characteristic devices and portraits. Denisov is one of her favorite types: middle aged, pensive, fearful of dying and being forgotten. His fiancée, Lora, is thoughtless, talkative, affectionate. With her in a cramped communal apartment lives her gentle widower father, a retired zoologist who is a bit strange but harmless. In her incessant, mindless chatter, Lora provides a considerable amount of humor in the story, while Papa, laboring over scientific articles for children, is the source of an anxious kind of pathos, wandering every night in his sleep.

Denisov, tormented by doubts and despair, lives in a constant round of visions, nightmares, and dreams. Thus he too, like the old somnambulist, walks through his troubled life in confusion, his waking life a dream. The story takes a bizarre turn as Denisov, attempting to do a favor for a young couple, looks up his comrade Bakhtiyarov, who is relaxing at the Woodland Fairy restaurant. There, events turn nightmarish, as Denisov envisions his friend Makov frozen to death on a mountaintop, while Bakhtiyarov teases and taunts Denisov, who slips into a state resembling the kind of rational illogic that one experiences in dreams. When he wakes up, he finds that everyone has gone. He calls Lora, who thinks that he has gone out of his mind when he tells her that he was locked in a fairy tale. She herself is in the middle of her own nightmare; having taken Papa to a healer in the country, she left him there, and he ran off in his sleep. The story ends in a poetic passage in which Denisov imagines the old man running through the night, through the forest, up and down hills, in the moonlight, smiling, fast asleep.

One of the longer works in Tolstaya's second collection, "Samaia liubimaia" ("Most Beloved"), is set, like many of her stories, in Leningrad and at the "dacha" (summer house in the country). It is a vivid, poignant account of the narrator's recollections of Zhenechka, the woman who has worked for the family as nurse and governess for as long as the children can remember. She has always been there.

The narrator recalls especially the first summer morning at the dacha, when Zhenechka would walk through the house, distribute presents, clear the desk, and get organized for the daily lessons, much resented by the children. Zhenechka is implacable, having taught their mother, and before that, having been their grandmother's childhood friend. Zhenechka wears a hearing aid on her chest that chirrs like a nightingale. Walking with a limp, she wears an orthopedic shoe. She never takes off her amber necklace, because she believes that some sort of healthful electricity emanates from it. She is strict, loving, devoted. Once, Zhenechka gives one of the girls a box, on the cover of which she has written, "Don't wish to be the prettiest; wish to be the most beloved."

The motif of gift-giving is present throughout the story. Tolstaya uses this theme as a very effective way of characterizing Zhenechka. As the children grow up, she continues to bring presents when she comes to visit the family, which is all that she has left in the world. Aging, Zhenechka has become tiresome and boring, endlessly retelling her stories of bygone days. Interspersed with incidents from Zhenechka's last years are brief recollections of the first child she ever took care of, a little deaf boy, and of the only love in her life—"short, stunted, meager."

The story closes with a brief description of the deserted dacha, slowly deteriorating as the grasses take over the path, the mold blooms on the porch, and a spider spins the keyhole shut. The children have all grown up, Zhenechka has died. Although the narrator speaks of the old nurse's wish to be the most beloved as being naïve, the implication is clear that she really was just that. The greatest gift, of course, was herself, in her unthinking, simple, and total love.

"The Moon Came Out" is another story about an elderly figure, this time one named Natasha, born fifty years earlier. The story begins with childhood memories of a dacha near Leningrad, of games played to incantations such as "The moon came out behind the cloud." The parents, breaking all the rules, died but Grandmother hung on to life. Natasha's adolescence is described in Tolstayan fashion, with nightmarish images of filth and horror. There is a brief interlude when Konovalov is attracted to Natasha, but she feels unworthy and retreats into a world of dreams, which the author describes with images of flowers, wind, sleepy forests, bears, and friendly old women—images straight out of the Russian fairy tales on which Tolstaya draws so frequently and effectively.

Natasha becomes a teacher of geography and never mentions the world in her mind, Queen Maud Land. Natasha lives in a communal flat, crowded, dismal, full of daily humiliations. She goes to Moscow once and falls in love with bearded, joyful Pyotr Petrovich, who has come into the city to shop for his family. As he leaves on the train, quite unaware of Natasha's short-lived devotion, she feels old age gripping her firmly by the shoulder.

Stories in which cruelty and death are themes include "Sarafim," about a misanthrope who kicks a small dog to death, and "Heavenly Flame" about a pointless practical joke played on a man awaiting death in a sanatorium. These themes are also fully expressed in "Limpopo," again a combination of burlesque and fantasy, reality and ridicule, revolving around the narrator's friends, Judy, from Africa, and Lyonechka, a poet who fights for truth. The dismal lives of Soviet citizens under the rule of the Communist Party is described with all the bite and snap of satire, with macabre humor and bitter irony. The political undertones are clearly present but under the guise of weird and grotesque incidents, such as an inexplicable massacre of innocent people by soldiers of "their own side." This story is Tolstaya's richest in terms of wild fancy, a large group of precisely and concisely delineated characters, a plot of complex and enigmatic events, and numerous and widely ranging literary allusions (to Dante, the Old Testament, Russian fairy tales, Don Juan, Alexander Pushkin, Dr. Doolittle, Søren Kierkegaard, and Homer, to mention only a few).

While critics have, of course, disagreed over which of her stories is her best, "Limpopo" exemplifies most of the distinctive features of her work. Critics do agree that Tolstaya is indebted to such writers as Gogol, Pushkin, Mikhail Bulgakov, and even Franz Kafka. She seems, however, to have drawn on these writers without losing her own wild imagination, deep and intense sympathy, and wry, sardonic humor. Tolstaya is a writer very much in the Russian tradition yet consistently retaining her own brilliant and original vision.

Bibliography

Gifford, Henry. "The Real Thing." *The New York Review of Books* 36 (June 1, 1989): 3-5. This article contains a review of *On the Golden Porch* and of three books on contemporary Soviet fiction, including *Balancing Acts* by Helena Goscilo, cited below.

Goscilo, Helena, ed. *Balancing Acts: Contemporary Stories by Russian Women.* Bloomington: Indiana University Press, 1989. This 337-page anthology includes one story by Tolstaya, "Peters," and the short-story collection *On the Golden Porch.*

_____, ed. *Heritage and Heresy: Recent Fiction by Russian Women.* Bloomington: Indiana University Press, 1988. This volume includes three stories by Tolstaya, all published in *On the Golden Porch.*

_____. "Tatyana Tolstaia's 'Dome of Many-Colored Glass': The World Refracted Through Multiple Perspectives." *Slavic Review* 47 (Summer, 1988): 280-290. A detailed scholarly analysis of Tolstaya's stories. Includes explanatory and reference footnotes, several of them in Russian and untranslated.

Trosky, Susan M., ed. *Contemporary Authors.* Vol. 130. Detroit: Gale Research, 1990.

Includes a brief personal history of Tolstaya, a concise summary of her career, and a short general description of her characters.

Zalygin, Sergei, comp. *The New Soviet Fiction: Sixteen Short Stories.* New York: Abbeville Press, 1989. This 318-page anthology contains one story by Tolstaya, one of only three women represented. A critical introduction by the compiler analyzes the state of fiction in the Soviet Union during *perestroika* and *glasnost*.

Natalie Harper

JEAN TOOMER

Born: Washington, D.C.; December 26, 1894
Died: Doylestown, Pennsylvania; March 30, 1967

Principal short fiction

Cane, 1923 (prose and poetry); "Mr. Costyve Duditch," in *The Dial*, 1928; "York Beach," in *New American Caravan*, 1929; *The Wayward and the Seeking*, 1980 (Darwin T. Turner, editor; prose and poetry).

Other literary forms

All Jean Toomer's best fiction appears in *Cane*, which also includes fifteen poems. Toomer later wrote fragments of an autobiography and several essays, the most important of which are found in *Essentials: Definitions and Aphorisms* (1931).

Achievements

Toomer's *Cane*, published in 1923, is considered to be one of the masterpieces of experimental fiction and one of the most important and relevant evocations of African-American life in the twentieth century. Toomer's book was rediscovered in the late 1960's after it was reprinted in 1967. *Cane* is represented in most anthologies of American literature, guaranteeing the author a distinguished place in American literary history.

Biography

Born Nathan Eugene Toomer in Washington, D.C., on December 26, 1894, Jean Toomer stayed in the North for his education, attending the University of Wisconsin and the City College of New York. He began writing and was published in the little magazines of his time before moving South to become a schoolteacher in rural Georgia, an experience which he uses in "Kabnis," the final part of *Cane*. Married twice to whites, Toomer was often equivocal about his blackness, partially because of his involvement in Unitism, the philosophy of George Ivanovitch Gurdjieff. Toomer's later essays and stories expound his version of the philosophy and are often weakened by an excess of mystery and a deficiency of manners. In later life, he lived among the Quakers in Pennsylvania. Toomer died in 1967.

Analysis

Divided into three parts, Jean Toomer's *Cane* consists of short stories, sketches, poems, and a novella. The first section focuses on women; the second on relationships between men and women; and the third on one man. Although capable of being read discretely, these works achieve their full power when read together, coalescing to create a novel, unified by theme and symbol. Like all Toomer's work, *Cane* describes characters who have within a buried life, a dream that seeks expression and fulfillment; *Cane* is a record of the destruction of those dreams. Sometimes the dreams explode, the fire within manifesting itself violently; more often, however, the world implodes within the dreamer's mind. These failures have external causes—the inadequacy or refusal of the society to allow expression, the restrictions by what Toomer calls the herd—and internal ones—the fears and divisions within the dreamer himself, as he struggles unsuccessfully to unite will and mind, passion and intellect, what Toomer in the later story, "York Beach," calls the wish for brilliant experience and the wish for difficult experience.

The one limitation on the otherwise thoroughgoing romanticism of this vision is Toomer's rigorous separation of humankind into those who dream, who are worth bothering about, and those who do not. While the struggle of Toomer's characters is for unity, it is to unify themselves or to find union with one other dreamer, never to merge with man in general. Like Kabnis, many find their true identity in recognizing their differences, uniqueness, and superiority. At the end of "York Beach," the protagonist tells his listeners that the best government would be an empire ruled by one who recognized his own greatness.

Toomer's dreamers find themselves in the first and third sections of *Cane* in a Southern society which, although poor in compassion and understanding, is rich in supportive imagery. In the second part, set in the North, that imagery is also absent, so the return of the protagonist to the South in part 3 is logical, since the North has not provided a nurturing setting. Athough the return may be a plunge back into hell, it is also a journey to an underground where Kabnis attains the vision that sets him free.

The imagery is unified by a common theme: ascent. Kabnis says, "But its the soul of me that needs th risin," and all the imagery portrays the buried life smoldering within, fighting upward, seeking release. The dominant image of the book, the one that supplies the title, is the rising sap of the sugarcane. Cane whispers enigmatic messages to the characters, and it is to cane fields that people seeking escape and release flee. Sap rises, too, in pines, which also whisper and sing; and at the mill of part 1, wood burns, its smoke rising. The moon in "Blood-Burning Moon" is said to "sink upward," an oxymoronic yoking that implies the difficulty of the rising in this book.

A second pattern of imagery is that of flowing blood or water, although generally in the pessimistic *Cane*, water is not abundant. In "November Cotton Flower," dead birds are found in the wells, and when water is present, the characters, threatened by the life it represents, often fear it. Rhobert, in a sketch of that name, wears a diver's helmet to protect him from water, life which is being drawn off. Dreams denied, blood flows more freely than water.

"Esther," the most successful story in *Cane*, comes early and embodies many of the book's major themes. It opens with a series of four sentences describing Esther as a girl of nine. In each, the first clause compliments her beauty, the second takes the praise away; the first clauses of each are progressively less strong. Esther represents the destruction of potential by a combination of inner and outer forces. On the outside there is her father, "the richest colored man in town," who reduces Esther to a drab and obsequious life behind a counter in his dry goods store. "Her hair thins. It looks like the dull silk on puny corn ears." Then there is King Barlo, a black giant, who has a vision in the corner of town known as the Spittoon. There, while townspeople gather to watch (and black and white preachers find momentary unity in working out ways to rid themselves of one who threatens their power), Barlo sees a strong black man arise. While the man's head is in the clouds, however, "little white-ant biddies come and tie his feet to chains." The herd in Barlo's vision, as in Toomer's, may destroy the dreamer.

Many, however, are affected by what Barlo has seen, none more so than Esther, who decides that she loves him. The fire begins to burn within. As she stands dreaming in her store, the sun on the windows across the street reflect her inner fire, and, wanting to make it real, Esther calls the fire department. For the next eighteen years, Esther, the saddest of all Toomer's women, lives only on dreams, inventing a baby, conceived, she thinks, immaculately. Sometimes, like many of his characters, sensing that life may be too much for her, knowing that "emptiness is a thing that grows by being moved," she tries not to dream, sets her mind against dreaming, but the dreams continue.

At the end of the story, Esther, then twenty-seven, decides to visit Barlo, who has returned to town. She finds the object of her dream in a room full of prostitutes; what rises is only the fumes of liquor. "Conception with a drunken man must be a mighty sin," she thinks, and when she attempts to return to reality, she, like many Toomer characters, finds that the world has overwhelmed her. Crushed from without, she has neither life nor dreams. "There is no air, no street, and the town has completely disappeared."

So, too, in "Blood-Burning Moon," Toomer's most widely anthologized short story and also from the woman-centered first section, is the main character destroyed emotionally. Here, however, the destructive force is primarily internal. Among the most conventional of Toomer's stories, "Blood-Burning Moon" has both a carefully delineated plot and a familiar one at that: a love triangle. What is inventional is the way Toomer manages the reader's feelings about the woman whom two men love. Both men are stereotypes. Bob Stone is white and repulsively so. Himself divided and content to be, he makes his mind consciously white, and approaches Louisa "as a master should." The black, Tom Burwell, is a stereotype too: having dreams, he expresses his love sincerely, but inarticulately; denied or threatened, he expresses himself violently.

The first two sections open with rhythmic sentences beginning with the word "up"; Louisa sings songs against the omen the rising moon portends, seeking charms and spells, but refusing the simple act of choosing between the two men. Because Louisa does not choose, the story comes to its inevitable violent climax and the death of both men. There is more, however: when Louisa is last seen she too has been destroyed, mentally, if not physically. She sings again to the full moon as an omen, hoping that people will join her, hoping that Tom Burwell will come; but her choice is too late. Burwell is dead, and the lateness of her decision marks the end of her dreams. Like Esther, she is separated from even appropriate mental contact with the world that is.

Barlo's vision, then, is accurate but incomplete as a description of what happens to Toomer's protagonists. While it is true that the herd will often destroy the dreamer, it is just as likely that the dreamer, from inaction, fear, and division, will destroy himself. The four stories of section 2 all focus on pairs of dreamers who can isolate themselves from the rest of society but who cannot get their dreams to merge. In "Avey" it is the man who, focused on his own dreams, refuses to listen to and accept the value of Avey's. In "Bona and Paul," Paul, a black, takes Bona away from the dance, not, as everyone assumes, to make love to her, but to know her; but knowing a human is denied him because Bona assumes she already knows him, "a priori," as he has said. Knowing he is black, she "knows" that he will be passionate. When he is interested in knowledge before passion, she discovers that to know *a priori* is not to know at all and flees him, denying his dream of knowing her.

In "Theater" the divided main character, sitting half in light, half in shadow, watches another dreamer, the dancer on stage, Dorris. She is dreaming of him, but, although "mind pulls him upward into dream," suspicion is stronger than desire, and by the end of the story John has moved wholly into shadow. When Dorris looks at him, "She finds it a dead thing in the shadow which is his dream." Likewise, in "Box Seat" Muriel is torn between the dreamer Dan, who stands with one hand lying on the wall, feeling from below the house the deep underground rumbling of the subway, literal buried life, and Mrs. Pribby, the landlady, rattling her newspaper, its thin noise contrasting with the powerful below-ground sound. Muriel chooses respectability. At the theater, to which Dan has followed her, she is repelled by a dwarf who offers her a rose; Dan rises to his feet to proclaim that Jesus was once a leper. This last, insistent image, suggesting the maimed sources of beauty that Muriel is too timid to accept, also indicates the overexplicit inflation of claims that damages some of Toomer's fiction. Although in *Cane* most of the stories are under control, some seem rather too sketchy; "Box Seat," however, foreshadows the fault that mars all of Toomer's later fiction: the sacrifice of dramatic idea in favor of, often pallid, philosophical ones.

The last and longest story in *Cane* integrates the themes, making explicit the nature of the destructive forces. The story is "Kabnis," a novella, and the force is sin, a word contained backward in Kabnis' name. It is the story of a black man out of place in the rural South, threatened not so much by whites as by his own people, by his environment, and by his sense of himself.

As the story opens, Kabnis is trying to sleep, but he is not allowed this source of dream; instead, chickens and rats, nature itself, keep him awake. He wants to curse it, wants it to be consistent in its ugliness, but he senses too the beauty of nature, and as that prevents him from hating it entirely, he feels that even beauty is a curse. Intimidated by nature, Kabnis is also attacked by society, by the local black church, of which the shouting acclamations of faith torture Kabnis, and by the black school superintendent who fires him for drinking. As in "Box Seat," the protagonist is thus caught between expressions of life, which are yet too strong for him, and its repression, which traps him. So positioned, Kabnis, like Rhobert, is a man drowning, trying vainly to avoid the source of life. From this low point, for the only time in the book, Toomer describes the way up, and Kabnis gains enough strength to throw off his oppression.

He has three friends: Halsey, an educated black who has been playing Uncle Tom; Layman, a preacher, whose low voice suggests a canebrake; and Lewis, a *Doppelgänger* who suggests a version of what a stronger Kabnis might have become and who drops out of the story when Kabnis does indeed become stronger. Once fired, Kabnis takes up residence with Halsey, a Vulcan-like blacksmith who gives him work repairing implements, work for which Kabnis is ill-suited. In his basement, however, Halsey has his own buried life, an old man, Father John, and in the climactic scene, the three men descend into the underground for a dark night of the soul, for the *Walpurgisnacht* on which Kabnis confronts his own demons. Prefiguring the descents in such black fiction as Richard Wright's "Man Who Lived Underground" and Ralph Ellison's *Invisible Man* (1952), this is likewise a descent during which the values of the world above, met on unfamiliar terrain, are rethought. It is a night of debauchery, but also the night when the destructive illusions and fears of the men are exposed.

Father John represents those fears; when he speaks, his message is sin; but Kabnis knows, and for the first time can say, that because of sin the old man has never seen the beauty of the world. Kabnis has, and as he says, "No eyes that have seen beauty ever lose their sight." Kabnis then proclaims a new role for himself: if he is not a blacksmith, he may be, having known beauty, a wordsmith. "I've been shapin words after a design that branded here. Know whats here? M soul." If sin is what is done against the soul and if the soul of Kabnis is what needs the rising, then, as Kabnis says, the world has conspired against him. Now, however, Kabnis acknowledges and confronts that conspiracy, no longer fearing it or Father John. Exhausted by his effort, Kabnis sinks back, but Halsey's sister, Carrie K, does indeed carry K. She lifts him up, and together they ascend the stairs into the daylight, as the risen sun sings a "birth-song" down the streets of the town.

The end is not unequivocally optimistic: it is too small and too tentative a note in this large catalog of the defeated and destroyed. *Cane* does, however, suggest finally that as destructive as dreams may be, once one has seen beauty, if he can free himself from repression, from sin, he may re-create himself. "Kabnis is me," wrote Toomer to Waldo Frank, and he had more in mind than just his use of his experiences. For what Toomer has done in *Cane* is to chart the varieties of sin that society has done to people and, more important, since individuals are always more interesting than society to Toomer, that people have done to themselves. Wholeness is the aim, a wholeness that breaks down barriers between mind and will, man and woman, object and subject, and that allows the potential of dreams to be fulfilled. That the wholeness is so difficult to achieve is the substance of Toomer's short fiction; that Toomer achieves it, both for a character in "Kabnis" and more permanently in his only successful work, a book uniting fiction and poetry, songs and narration, images of fire and water, of descent and ascent, is his testimony that wholeness can be achieved by those who dream of it.

Other major works

PLAY: "Balo," in Alain Locke's *Plays of Negro Life*, 1927.

POETRY: "Banking Coal," in *Crisis*, 1922; *Cane*, 1923 (prose and poetry); "Blue Meridian," in *New American Caravan*, 1936; *The Wayward and the Seeking*, 1980 (Darwin T. Turner, editor; prose and poetry); *The Collected Poems of Jean Toomer*, 1988.

NONFICTION: "Winter on Earth," in *The Second American Caravan*, 1929; "Race Problems and Modern Society," 1929; *Essentials: Definitions and Aphorisms*, 1931; "The Flavor of Man," 1949.

Bibliography

Byrd, Rudolph. *Jean Toomer's Years with Gurdjieff: Portrait of an Artist, 1923-1936*. Athens: University of Georgia Press, 1990. A good introduction to Toomer's years of studying orientalism and the mystical philosophy of George Ivanovitch Gurdjieff. It indicates that although Toomer was an African-American writer, his concerns were primarily spiritual and philosophical rather than social and ethnic. It is a fascinating account of one part of Jean Toomer's life.

_____. "Was He There With Them?" In *The Harlem Renaissance: Reevaluations*. New York: Garland, 1989. This article examines Toomer's tenuous relationship with the writers of the Harlem Renaissance. It asserts that although Toomer identified with many of the issues and social concerns being addressed by African-American writers, his style, techniques, and philosophy made him something of an outsider and gave him a unique position among the major African-American writers of the 1920's.

Jones, Robert B. Introduction to *The Collected Poems of Jean Toomer*. Edited by Robert B. Jones and Margery Toomer Latimer. Chapel Hill: University of North Carolina Press, 1988. Although this book is not about Toomer's fiction, the introduction gives an excellent account of Toomer's life and work within the context of the various phases of his writing and philosophical studies. In addition, it discusses the authors and poets who influenced Toomer's life and writings.

Kerman, Cynthia. *The Lives of Jean Toomer: A Hunger for Wholeness*. Baton Rouge: Louisiana State University Press, 1988. This book gives an account of the various stages of Jean Toomer's life and his attempts to find spiritual guidance and revelation throughout his lifetime. An interesting account of a fascinating life.

Moore, Lewis D. "Kabnis and the Reality of Hope: Jean Toomer's *Cane*." *North Dakota Quarterly* 54 (Spring, 1986): 30-39. Moore's article discusses the elements of "hope" within the context of the characters in *Cane*. In particular, he indicates that despite the repressive aspects of the society in which they live, Toomer's characters are redeemed and indeed triumph over that society by virtue of the positive aspects of their humanity.

Howard Faulkner
(Revised by *Earl Paulus Murphy*)

WILLIAM TREVOR
William Trevor Cox

Born: Mitchelstown, County Cork, Ireland; May 24, 1928

Principal short fiction

The Day We Got Drunk on Cake and Other Stories, 1967; *The Ballroom of Romance and Other Stories*, 1972; *The Last Lunch of the Season*, 1973; *Angels at the Ritz and Other Stories*, 1975; *Lovers of Their Time and Other Stories*, 1978; *Beyond the Pale and Other Stories*, 1981; *The Stories of William Trevor*, 1983; *The News from Ireland and Other Stories*, 1986; *Family Sins and Other Stories*, 1990.

Other literary forms

Though probably best known as a writer of short stories, William Trevor has also written television and radio scripts, plays, and numerous novels. Among Trevor's novels, *The Old Boys* (1964), *Miss Gomez and the Brethren* (1971), *Elizabeth Alone* (1973), *The Children of Dynmouth* (1976), and *Fools of Fortune* (1983) have been particularly praised.

Achievements

Trevor is widely regarded as one of the finest storytellers and craftsmen writing in English. In Great Britain, his work has long been widely and favorably reviewed and has frequently been adapted for radio and television broadcast by the British Broadcasting Corporation (BBC). In 1964, Trevor's second novel, *The Old Boys*, was awarded the Hawthornden Prize; his fourth collection, *Angels at the Ritz and Other Stories*, was hailed by Graham Greene as "one of the finest collections, if not the best, since Joyce's *Dubliners*." In addition, Trevor has won the Royal Society of Literature Award, the Allied Irish Banks' Prize for Literature, and the Whitbread Prize for Fiction; he is also a member of the Irish Academy of Letters. In 1979, "in recognition for his valuable services to literature," Trevor was named an honorary Commander, Order of the British Empire. In the United States, knowledge of Trevor's work increased markedly when *The Stories of William Trevor*, an omnibus collection, was published in 1983 and received wide and highly enthusiastic reviews.

Biography

Born William Trevor Cox in Ireland's County Cork, William Trevor, the son of a bank manager, spent much of his childhood living in small Irish towns and attending a series of boarding and day schools that included St. Columba's in Dublin. After earning a B.A. in history from Dublin's Trinity College, Trevor, a Protestant, began work as a sculptor and schoolmaster, taking his first job as an instructor of history in Armagh, Northern Ireland. In 1952, Trevor married Jane Ryan and moved to England, where he spent the next eight years teaching art at two prestigious public schools—first at Rugby and then at Taunton. Between 1960 and 1965, Trevor worked as a copywriter at an advertising agency in London; he simultaneously began devoting an increasing portion of his free time to the writing of fiction. By the early 1970's, following the appearance of several novels and a steady stream of stories in such publications as *Encounter, The New Yorker,* and *London Magazine,* Trevor's reputation was secure. The father of two sons, Trevor settled in Devon and continued to write full-time.

Analysis

Like his novels, William Trevor's short stories generally take place in either England or the Republic of Ireland. For the most part, Trevor focuses on middle-class or lower-middle-class figures whose lives have been characterized by loneliness, disappointment, and pain. Many of Trevor's characters are trapped in jobs or familial circumstances that are dull or oppressive or both; many retreat frequently to fond memories or romantic fantasies. Trevor rarely mocks the men and women who inhabit his fiction, nor does he treat them as mere ciphers or automatons. In fact, like James Joyce, to whom he is often compared, Trevor assumes a detached authorial stance, but occasionally and subtly he makes it clear that he is highly sympathetic to the plight of underdogs, self-deluders, and the victims of abuse and deceit. Invariably, his principal characters are carefully and completely drawn—and so are the worlds they inhabit. Few contemporary writers of short fiction can render atmosphere and the subtleties of personality as precisely and as tellingly as William Trevor. Few can capture so accurately and wittily the rhythms and nuances of everyday speech. Though its themes can be somber and settings quite bleak, Trevor's brilliantly paced and carefully sculpted fiction consistently moves, amuses, and invigorates.

One of Trevor's earliest stories, "The General's Day," illustrates with particular clarity the darkest side of his artistic vision. Contained in *The Day We Got Drunk on Cake and Other Stories,* "The General's Day" centers on a decorated and now retired military man who, at seventy-eight, has never quite come to grips with his retirement and so spends his days wandering around the local village looking for something to do. On the day of the story, a sunny Saturday in June, General Suffolk greets the day with energy and resolution but ends by simply killing time in the local tea shop, where he musters what is left of his once-celebrated charm and manages to convince a woman—"a thin, middle-aged person with a face like a faded photograph"—to join him for drinks at the local hotel. There, fueled by gin, General Suffolk flirts so blatantly and clumsily with the woman that she flees, "her face like a beetroot." Fueled by more gin, the lonely man becomes increasingly obnoxious. After suffering a few more rejections and humiliations, he finally stumbles back home, where he is mocked further by his "unreliable servant," Mrs. Hinch, a crude woman who habitually cuts corners and treats herself to secretive swigs of the general's expensive South African sherry. In the story's final scene, General Suffolk, "the hero of Roeux and Monchy-le-Preux," is shown leaning and weeping on his cleaning woman's fat arm as she laughingly helps him back to his cottage. "My God Almighty," General Suffolk, deflated, mutters; "I could live for twenty years."

Trevor often portrays older men and women who make stoic adjustments to the present while living principally in the past. He also sometimes focuses on children and adolescents who use vividly constructed daydreams as a means of escaping dreary surroundings or obtuse parents who are themselves sunk in the deadness of their cramped and predictable lives. In "An Evening with John Joe Dempsey," from *The Ballroom of Romance and Other Stories*, Trevor's central figure is a boy of fifteen who lives in a small house in a small Irish town where, daily, he sits in a dull classroom in preparation for a deadend job at the nearby sawmills. John Joe lives with his widowed mother, a wiry, chronically worried woman whose principal interest in life is to hover protectively about her only son. John Joe escapes his mother's smothering solicitations by wandering about the town with one Quigley, a rather elderly dwarf reputed to be, as one local puts it, "away in the head." Quigley likes to fire John Joe's already active imagination by regaling the boy with detailed descriptions of the sexual vignettes he claims to have witnessed while peeping through area windows. In his own daydreams, John Joe dallies with many of the same sizable matrons whom Quigley likes to portray in compromising positions. One of them, Mrs. Taggart, "the wife of a postman," is a tall, "well-built" woman who in John Joe's fantasies requires repeated rescuing from a locked bathroom in which she stands unblushingly nude. Like many of Trevor's characters, John Joe is thus a convincing mix of the comic and the pathetic. If his incongruous sexual fantasies are humorous, the rest of his life looks decidedly grim. In the story's particularly effective closing scene, Trevor portrays John Joe in his bed, in the dark, thinking again of impossible erotic romps with wholly unobtainable women, feeling "more alive than ever he was at the Christian Brothers' School . . . or his mother's kitchen, more alive than ever he would be at the sawmills. In his bed he entered a paradise: it was grand being alone."

In "Nice Day at School," from the same collection, Trevor's principal character is a girl of fourteen, Eleanor, who lives on a housing estate with her cranky, chain-smoking mother and her father, a former professional wrestler who now works as a nightclub bouncer and likes to claim that his work has made him the trusted friend of many celebrities, including Rex Harrison, Mia Farrow, Princess Margaret, and Anthony Armstrong-Jones. Though Eleanor is embarrassed by her father's obviously exaggerated accounts of his encounters with the rich and famous, she is much given to vivid imaginings of her own. Bombarded daily by saccharine pop songs and the more blatantly sexual chatter of her friends, Eleanor thinks obsessively of her ideal lover:

> a man whose fingers were long and thin and gentle, who'd hold her hand in the aeroplane. Air France to Biarritz. And afterwards she'd come back to a flat where the curtains were the colour of lavender, the same as the walls, where gas fires glowed and there were rugs on natural-wood floors, and the telephone was pale blue.

Subtly, however, Trevor indicates that Eleanor is not likely to find a lover so wealthy and suave. Like her friends and most girls of the same social class, this daughter of a

bloated bouncer and a bored, gin-sipping housewife will instead wind up with someone like Denny Price, the young butcher's apprentice with "blubbery" lips, who
once moved his rough hand up and down her body "like an animal, a rat gnawing at
her, prodding her and poking."

Trevor often focuses on women who find themselves pursued by or entangled with
insensitive or calculating males. In "Office Romances," from *Angels at the Ritz and
Other Stories,* Trevor's central character is Angela Hosford, a typist who works quite
anonymously in a large London office appointed with "steel-framed reproductions"
and "ersatz leather" sofas and chairs. At twenty-six, Angela is pleasant but plain
and myopic: she wears contact lenses that give her eyes a slightly "bulgy look." Her
pursuer, Gordon Spelle, is, at thirty-eight, tall and "sleek," but his left eyelid droops
a bit, and the eye it covers is badly glazed. While watching old films on television
when she was fourteen, Angela had developed a crush on the American actor Don
Ameche and had imagined "a life with him in a cliff-top home she'd invented, in
California." Now, she finds herself drawn to the deliberately "old fashioned" Spelle,
and at one point imagines herself "stroking his face and comforting him because of
his bad eye." One day, after his flatteries succeed in rendering Angela both "generous and euphoric," Spelle manages to lure her into a dark and empty office, where—
muttering "I love you" repeatedly—he makes love to her, inelegantly, on the floor.
Angela finds this experience "not even momentarily pleasurable, not once," but afterward, she basks in the memory of Spelle's heated professions of love. Angela
eventually takes a job elsewhere, convinced that Spelle's passion for her "put him
under a strain, he being married to a wife who was ill." Like many of Trevor's
characters, she understandably decides not to look past her comforting delusions;
she refuses to accept the well-known fact that Spelle was "notorious" and "chose
girls who were unattractive because he believed such girls, deprived of sex for long
periods of time, were an easier bet."

The vast gulf that often separates romantic fantasy from unsavory fact is similarly
revealed in the title story of *Lovers of Their Time and Other Stories.* In this piece, set
in the 1960's, Trevor's lovers are Norman Britt, a mild-mannered travel agent with
"a David Niven moustache," and a young woman, Marie, who tends the counter
at Green's the Chemist's. Norman and Marie meet regularly in one of Trevor's favorite fictional locations—a dark pub filled with a wide array of drinkers, talkers, and
dreamers. In that same place, in "The Drummer Boy," the two listen to Beatles
songs and talk of running away with each other to some romantic foreign country—
an event they realize is not likely to materialize. Marie is single, but Norman is
married to the loud and bawdy Hilda, who spends the better part of her life sipping
cheap wine and watching police dramas on the television and who has previously
hinted that she is quite content in the odd marital arrangement that Norman loathes.
Thus, at Norman's instigation, the two lovers begin to rendezvous more intimately at
the nearby hotel, the Great Western Royal. More specifically, they begin to sneak
into a large, infrequently used bathroom, "done up in marble," on the hotel's second
floor. Here, luxuriating in an enormous tub, they talk hopefully of happier days that,

unfortunately, never arrive. Hilda dismisses her husband's request for a divorce by telling him, "You've gone barmy, Norman"; Marie, tired of waiting, weds "a man in a brewery." Thus, as the years pass, Norman is left with a nostalgic longing not only for Marie but also for that brief period in the 1960's when playful risk-taking was much in the air. Often, while riding "the tube" to work, Norman

> would close his eyes and with the greatest pleasure that remained to him he would recall the delicately veined marble and the great brass taps, and the bath that was big enough for two. And now and again he heard what happened to be the sound of distant music, and the voices of the Beatles celebrating a bathroom love, as they had celebrated Eleanor Rigby and other people of that time.

This allusion to a popular and bittersweet Beatles song is especially appropriate in yet another Trevor story about two thoroughly average and lonely people whose lives have not often been marked by episodes of great passion.

In "Flights of Fancy," also from *Lovers of Their Time and Other Stories*, Trevor's principal character, Sarah Machaen, is yet another Eleanor Rigby-like character destined, one assumes, to spend the rest of her life uneasily alone. Sarah, a clergyman's daughter, is an executive secretary in a large London firm that manufactures lamps; she visits museums, sings in a Bach choir, and is "a popular choice as a godmother." Well into middle age, Sarah is quite content with the externals of her life and gradually has become "reconciled to the fact that her plainness wasn't going to go away." Sometimes, however, she gets lonely enough to daydream of marriage—perhaps to an elderly widower or a blind man. Ironically, the one person who does express a romantic interest in Sarah is another woman, a young and pretty but unschooled factory worker called Sandra Pond. Sarah is shocked at the very idea of lesbianism, yet she cannot stop her mind from "throwing up flights of fancy" in which she pictures herself sharing her flat with Sandra and introducing her to London's many cultural delights. Though her shyness and acute sense of propriety prompt her to reject Sandra's clumsy but clearly genuine professions of love, Sarah is haunted by the sense that she has perhaps passed up her last chance for passion and romance.

"Broken Homes," also from *Lovers of Their Time and Other Stories*, is one of Trevor's most powerful stories. Its principal character, Mrs. Malby, lives with her two budgerigars in a little flat that is scrupulously neat and prettily painted. Mrs. Malby, a widow, lost both of her sons thirty years earlier during World War II; now, at eighty-seven, she has come to terms with her own impending death and wants nothing more than to spend her remaining days in familiar surroundings, her faculties intact. Unfortunately, Mrs. Malby's flat is destroyed and her serenity threatened by a squad of loud and insensitive teenagers from a nearby comprehensive school—"an ugly sprawl of glass and concrete buildings," Mrs. Malby recalls, full of "children swinging along the pavements, shouting obscenities." As part of a community relations scheme, the teenagers have been equipped with mops and sponges and brushes and sent out into the neighborhood in search of good deeds to perform. Mrs. Malby politely asks these obnoxious adolescents to do nothing more than wash her walls, but they treat her with condescension and contempt, and while she is out, they proceed to make a complete mess of her apartment, splattering its walls and floors with bright yellow paint. The students' "teacher," an obtuse and "untidily dressed" bureaucrat, patronizingly assures Mrs. Malby that the damage is slight. He reminds her that, in any event, one must make allowances for the children of "broken homes."

Perhaps more than any of his other stories, "Broken Homes" reveals Trevor's sympathy for the plight of the elderly and his acute awareness of the infirmities and insecurities that accompany old age. The story certainly reveals a strong suspicion that, by the mid-1970's, the British welfare state had become both inefficient and rudely intrusive. Indeed, "Broken Homes" is informed by the subtly expressed sense—not uncommon in Trevor's later fiction—that contemporary Great Britain and Ireland have grown increasingly crass and tacky and that the old social fabric is rapidly and perhaps deleteriously unraveling.

Arguably, "The Paradise Lounge," from *Beyond the Pale and Other Stories*, is Trevor's most representative story. Set principally in the small bar of Keegan's Railway hotel, in "a hilly provincial town" in the Republic of Ireland, "The Paradise Lounge" shifts its focus between two recognizably Trevoresque figures. One of them, Beatrice, is thirty-two; the other, Miss Doheny, is in her eighties. Beatrice—who wanted to be an actress, once—drives often to Keegan's and its adjoining Paradise Lounge to rendezvous with her lover, a middle-aged businessman already married. Miss Doheny, one of the locals, goes regularly to the lounge for a bit of company and several good, stiff drinks. The two have never formally met. Yet Beatrice—observing Miss Doheny from across the room—is convinced that the old woman is an intriguing figure with a fascinating and no doubt satisfyingly romantic past; she does not realize that Miss Doheny is not only lonely but also full of anger and regret. Miss Doheny, in turn, envies Beatrice's freedom—her ability, in a more liberated and enlightened age, to enter into a friendly sexual affair without running the risk of paralyzing guilt and ostracism. She does not realize that the younger woman's affair has grown stale and mechanical and that by her own estimation Beatrice is about to engage in nothing more than a "mess of deception and lies."

Like all of Trevor's stories, "The Paradise Lounge" features tight organization and lean but detailed prose. Its very "average" characters are made interesting by Trevor's careful attention to the traits and quirks that make them individuals, to the memories and regrets they have of the past. Trevor, often wry and always detached, refuses to sentimentalize Miss Doheny and Beatrice; he does not, however, subject them to ridicule. "The Paradise Lounge" reveals once again that Trevor understands that for most people expectation and reality infrequently coincide and that among men and women a periodic yearning for adventure and escape is surely universal.

Other major works

NOVELS: *A Standard of Behaviour*, 1958; *The Old Boys*, 1964; *The Love Department*, 1966; *Miss Gomez and the Brethren*, 1971; *Elizabeth Alone*, 1973; *The Children of Dynmouth*, 1976; *Other People's Worlds*, 1980; *Fools of Fortune*, 1983; *Nights at the Alexandra*, 1987; *The Silence in the Garden*, 1988; *Two Lives*, 1991.

PLAYS: *The Elephant's Foot*, 1965; *The Girl*, 1967; *A Night Mrs. da Tanka*, 1968; *Going Home*, 1970; *The Old Boys*, 1971; *A Perfect Relationship*, 1973; *The 57th Saturday*, 1973; *Marriages*, 1973; *Scenes from an Album*, 1975; *Beyond the Pale*, 1980.

NONFICTION: *A Writer's Ireland*, 1984.

EDITED TEXTS: *The Oxford Book of Irish Short Stories*, 1989.

Bibliography

Firchow, Peter, ed. *The Writer's Place*. Minneapolis: University of Minnesota Press, 1974. In this volume, the editor has interviewed a number of contemporary authors from the British Isles, including Trevor, Kingsley Amis, Roald Dahl, Margaret Drabble, John Wain, and Angus Wilson. Trevor discusses such items as writing for radio, his interest in Ireland after living in England, and the then current British literary scene.

Gitzen, Julian. "The Truth-Tellers of William Trevor." *Critique: Studies in Modern Fiction* 21, no. 1 (1979): 59-72. Gitzen claims that most critics of Trevor's work have found it in the comedic tradition, sometimes dark and at other times more compassionate in its humor, but he argues that if it is comic, it is also melancholic in its journey from "psychological truth" to "metaphysical mystery."

Rhodes, Robert E. "William Trevor's Stories of the Troubles." In *Contemporary Irish Writing*, edited by James D. Brophy, and Raymond D. Porter. Boston: Twayne, 1983. Rhodes claims that although most of Trevor's fiction had until the 1980's revolved around English characters, his Anglo-Irish stories and protagonists, because of their environment and historical experience, are of greater significance in exploring the complexities of the human condition.

Schirmer, Gregory A. *William Trevor: A Study in His Fiction*. London: Routledge, 1990. One of the first full-length studies of Trevor's fictional writings. Schirmer notes the tension in Trevor's works between morality and the elements in contemporary society that make morality almost an impossibility, with lonely alienation the result. He also discusses Trevor as an outsider, both in Ireland and in England. An excellent study. Includes bibliographical references.

Trevor, William, ed. *The Oxford Book of Irish Short Stories*. Oxford, England: Oxford University Press, 1989. In this collection of Irish short stories from the earliest times through the second half of the twentieth century, Trevor in his introduction makes insightful comments about the significance and context of that literary form to Irish letters and, by implication, discusses his own work.

Brian Murray
(Revised by *Eugene S. Larson*)

FRANK TUOHY

Born: Uckfield, Sussex, England; May 2, 1925

Principal short fiction
The Admiral and the Nuns, with Other Stories, 1962; *Fingers in the Door and Other Stories*, 1970; *Live Bait and Other Stories*, 1978; *The Collected Stories*, 1984.

Other literary forms
Frank Tuohy has written several novels, a biography of William Butler Yeats, a travel book of Portugal, numerous articles for British newspapers, and television scripts for British public television.

Achievements
Tuohy has never had a wide general audience, nor has he found favor with academic critics. Still, his writing has received high praise from reviewers and from prominent fiction writers. C. P. Snow, Muriel Spark, and Graham Greene have all praised Tuohy's fiction. Snow, for example, in a long review of *Fingers in the Door and Other Stories*, wrote: "Mr. Frank Tuohy is a master of the short story, one of the best now writing in English." In the mid-1980's, when Tuohy's *The Collected Stories* appeared, Peter S. Prescott in *Newsweek* said that "Tuohy must be counted—with V. S. Pritchett and William Trevor—as one of the best living English practitioners of the short story."

This high praise from reviewers and fellow writers is reflected in the honors that have been bestowed on Tuohy. His first short-story collection, *The Admiral and the Nuns and Other Stories*, received the Katherine Mansfield-Menton prize, and *Live Bait and Other Stories* won the William Heinemann Memorial Award. Tuohy's third novel, *The Ice Saints* (1964), received both the James Tait Black Memorial Prize and the Geoffrey Faber Memorial Prize. In England, Tuohy was elected a Fellow of the Royal Society of Literature in 1965. In 1972, the American Institute of Arts and Letters bestowed on him the E. M. Forster Award.

Biography
Frank Tuohy's father was Irish, his mother Scottish. Tuohy was educated in Stowe School, King's College, Cambridge. He has traveled widely and lived for extended periods in Finland, Brazil, Poland, Japan, Portugal, and the United States. He has taught and lectured and has written reviews and articles for newspapers and journals. His travels and his interest in journalism have had a decisive influence on his fiction, for he thinks of himself as an observer of the world, not as a writer expressing his inner self. The contrast and conflict of manners and cultures has become the chief subject of his fiction.

Tuohy was ineligible for military service during World War II because of a defective heart valve, a condition later corrected by surgery. After the war, he divided his time between his home in southern England and residencies abroad. He served for a year as a lecturer at Turku University in Finland, spent six years in Brazil as a professor of English language and literature at the University of Sao Paulo, and two years as a visiting professor in Poland at the Jagiellonian University. In the United States he has been visiting writer at various universities, including Purdue University and Texas State University. He has also been a lecturer at Japanese universities, principally at Waseda University in Tokyo.

Analysis

An initial impression of Frank Tuohy's short stories is likely to be that they are the observations of a sharp-eyed and widely traveled reporter who is filling us in on life in such diverse places as Japan, Poland, South America, London, rural England, New England, and New York. Tuohy does have a remarkable talent for direct observation, for bringing before our eyes the look and feel, the sound and even the smell of actual places. The gestures of his characters, their speech, and their actions all ring true. He convinces the reader that, for example, this is the way it must be in the grim Communist world of Warsaw or the formal, alien world of Tokyo or the rumbling platform of a commuter train outside London. Tuohy's accuracy of observation and precision of language, although doubtless a reflection of his own interest in being literally truthful to the physical realities of the places he writes about, are all part of his strategy for supporting and making real his underlying view of life.

For despite the variety of locales, of character types, and even of subjects, Tuohy's three short-story collections are bound together by an overriding vision of the world as a place of moral confusion. Here and there one finds in unlikely places remnants of an older, more civilized way of life, but generally one finds, also in unsuspected places, moral baseness of the sort that would have made a decent man in former times put his hand firmly on his sword. These are modern times, however, and the decent men are either themselves victims or confused individuals who cannot in these confusing days sort out the proper from the improper way of acting.

The best people in Tuohy's stories are usually women. In the title story of his first collection, *The Admiral and the Nuns, with Other Stories*, an English woman, the daughter of an English admiral, is living in the interior of a South American country with her Polish husband. The place is a company town; the husband is employed as an engineer at a nearby factory; the neighbors, who are nationals of the country, have developed a deep dislike for the English woman and her husband and have, in effect, instituted a community-wide boycott. The grounds of dislike are these: the English woman is a dreadful housekeeper and cannot discipline her children; her husband drinks too much and pursues women. Tuohy's point is made clear by his narrator, also English, who sees that the woman is charming and valiant, having been formed by her father (the admiral) and trained by the nuns in her convent school. She remains loyal to her husband and, throughout her ordeal (which concludes with their deciding to return to Poland), keeps her chin firmly up.

There is a dreariness, however, in this kind of life and more dreariness ahead, and the narrator's admiration is tempered by what he regards as the woman's limitations: "she was one of those people whom experience leaves untouched. But she was durable. After all, she was an Admiral's daughter." As for the nuns, the narrator "cannot decide whether they had given her the worst, or the best education in the world."

A more clearly admirable character is the young mulatto woman in "A Survivor in Salvador," the last story in the first collection. The protagonist of this story is an exiled Polish prince who has arrived in San Salvador without money but with a packet of cocaine which he is attempting to sell. Without friends, liable to deportation if caught with the drug, without food or shelter, he is befriended by the girl who herself has been a victim of various kinds of exploitation, including sexual abuse by the chief of police. The girl, Antonieta, befriends the prince, becomes his mistress, keeps him from starving, and when he is seriously ill from exposure nurses him. Christophe, the prince, in return does what he can to show his love for Antonieta.

It frequently happens in Tuohy's stories that the main character or characters are exiled Europeans living in a simpler or more integrated culture in which even the poor are bound together by some mutually shared consciousness. The prince in Salvador perceives that even the most despised are not alone as he is. The prince is not usual in Tuohy's fiction, however, for most of Tuohy's exiles are unaware of their loneliness and alienation and are likely to regard those from simpler, more integrated cultures as inferiors to be exploited.

Exploitation of the weak or innocent—one of Tuohy's themes, and related to it, the snobbery that appears to be one of its causes—is treated in the title story of his second volume of short stories, *Fingers in the Door and Other Stories*. The story takes place on a train traveling to London; the occupants of a first-class carriage are Andrew Ringsett, a successful real estate agent who has moved up in the world, his overdressed wife, their spoiled, teenage daughter, Caroline, and for a time, an elderly woman in an ancient fur whom the agent's wife Merle recognizes as someone from a higher social class who (she believes) will always snub her (although, as Tuohy remarks, the snobbery is all in Merle's head). The train stops at a station, the husband alights for a few moments, and when he reenters the carriage through an outside door the train lurches suddenly and the steel door slams shut on his fingers. The husband is in terrific pain, but his wife, embarrassed before someone whom she regards as her social better, apologizes for him to the old woman. The daughter merely stares out the window, outraged that her trip to London has been ruined by her father's accident. The old woman rises from her place in the carriage and addresses the wife, telling her to look after her husband; to the man, she offers her sympathy and the advice to seek immediate medical assistance. It is the husband, however, who exhibits the most admirable behavior. He sees immediately that his wife is embarrassed and humiliated and puts his arm around her and tries to make light of his injury. He has something in common with other Tuohy characters who have not lost the power to feel affection.

In Tuohy's third collection, *Live Bait and Other Stories*, the theme of exploitation becomes predominant and as his camera eye moves closer to home, to New England and New York and then to England itself, the sense of moral confusion becomes more acute, the remoteness from human feeling even more profound.

In "Evening in Connecticut" an English visitor is attending a dinner party in the home of a very rich old man, an important benefactor of Barford College, and finds himself in a world which seems detached from reality, a kind of battered Eden in which things are plentiful but life abstract. What the visitor discovers, at last, under the banter and expensive food and drink, is the kind of exploitation Tuohy has found in other times and places but not in so odious a form: the elderly white-haired host informs his English guest that he regularly makes trips to England where an English doctor who shares his tastes has found him a suitable girl of the lower classes whose parents do not object. The English visitor is outraged but paralyzed by the social conventions and his own timidity. Later he believes that he was on the point of rising to his feet and attacking, but that, "surely, was self-delusion." In this kind of society, the sexual exploitation of children appears to be indistinguishable from any other kind of gratification.

Two other stories, both set in England, develop the same theme. In "A Summer Pilgrim" an elderly white-haired poet who once taught in Japan and now is retired and living in southern England is visited by a Japanese woman who is making a kind of literary pilgrimage, armed with camera to photograph her dear poet and a stack of his books to be autographed. The girl, who has been reared to behave dutifully, is timid and self-effacing and is used by her host in a shocking way.

The assault on innocence is also the subject of the title story of *Live Bait and Other Stories*. Here, a twelve-year-old boy, a scholarship pupil in a school attended mainly by the rich, accompanies a school acquaintance on a fishing expedition to a lake on the property of an elderly rich aunt and her eccentric son, Major Peverill. The boy is asked about his father's profession and is treated insultingly by both the old woman and by her son, who advises the boy, Andrew, to be grateful for being invited into the society of his betters and then, when the boy admits that he is a scholarship student, laughs in his face. Andrew's interest, however, is in the fishing; what in particular excites him is the gardener's account of a twenty-pound pike that inhabits the lake. He contrives to haul off his father's fishing gear and a boat that is usually kept locked away at the lake. His upper-class friend quarrels with him and makes insulting remarks about Andrew's mother; Andrew then fishes for the pike by himself. He hooks the big fish but it breaks his line, and while he is rolling about on the ground in anger, he is being watched by Major Peverill, who then attempts to molest him. Andrew escapes but is drawn back to the lake by the hope of catching the pike; this time he is visited by the Peverill's granddaughter, a strange girl who tries to be friendly until she discovers that Andrew is using a live frog for bait; she then runs off to denounce him to her family. Andrew lands the pike but is borne down on by Major Peverill and his laborers, and, from the other side of the lake, by his mother. Andrew is obliged to surrender.

It is impossible to indicate in so sketchy a summary the important effect of this story, for what Tuohy does is to catch, without sentimentalizing, the way a twelve-year-old boy at this particular time and place is himself "live bait" to those about him, using him to get some strange pleasure, social superiority, adventure, or sensual indulgence. One is made to feel, rather than merely to understand, the meaning of what has happened.

It is also impossible to indicate in summary the kind of pleasure afforded by Tuohy's fiction. Each of his stories is like a miniature novel of manners, in which persons of different classes, nationalities, races, religions, political persuasions, and ages are brought into a conflict that reveals an underlying moral conflict as well. There is nothing depressingly cynical nor fashionably despairing about Tuohy's stories. Life should be better than this—that is the assumption behind his fiction—and Tuohy is simply an observer-commentator, a truth-teller whose scalpel-like cutting away of pretense reveals the rottenness underneath. His stories say, in effect, that this is the way life is: awful, incredible, confusing, painful, but, at the same time, fascinating when seen for what it is. The act of experiencing the "bite down on the rotten tooth of fact," is what gives Tuohy's stories their characteristic pleasure. That is the kind of pleasure the best fiction has always given.

Other major works

NOVELS: *The Animal Game*, 1957; *The Warm Nights of January*, 1960; *The Ice Saints*, 1964.

NONFICTION: *Portugal*, 1970; *Yeats*, 1976.

Bibliography

Enright, D. J. "Among the Connoisseurs of Suffering." Review of *The Collected Stories*. *The Times Literary Supplement*, December 21, 1984: 1465. Enright finds that most of Tuohy's stories deal in various ways with those who suffer social embarrassments and finds that the best stories are the ones set in Poland.

Hazzard, Shirley. Review of *Fingers in the Door*. *The New York Times Book Review*, September, 1970: 5. Hazzard asserts that Tuohy writes with Chekhovian simplicity about "the violence we do to others and ourselves" and discusses several of the stories in the light of this assertion.

Prescott, Peter S. "The Whiplash Effect." Review of *The Collected Stories*. *Newsweek*, February 4, 1985, 78. Prescott argues that Tuohy's stories are "extremely pessimistic" but powerful in their portrayal of human pain. Particularly effective, he says, is the "whiplash effect" by means of which Tuohy, having caused the reader to sympathize with a character, suddenly reverses direction and shows the character in an unfavorable light.

Snow, C. P. "Snapshot Album." Review of *Fingers in the Door*. *Financial Times*, London, May 14, 1970. Snow remarks that Tuohy's "great gifts" are concentration, "intensive exactness," and a language that is "as firm and limpid as English can be." He discusses the "sociology" of Tuohy's stories and demonstrates how in three of these Tuohy's characteristic theme of pain and loneliness is effectively presented.

W. J. Stuckey

IVAN TURGENEV

Born: Orel, Russia; November 9, 1818
Died: Bougival, France; September 3, 1883

Principal short fiction

Zapiski okhotnika, 1852 (*Russian Life in the Interior,* 1855; better known as *A Sportsman's Sketches,* 1932); *Povesti i rasskazy,* 1856.

Other literary forms

In addition to *A Sportsman's Sketches,* Ivan Turgenev published several other short stories and novellas individually. His main contribution, however, were six novels, some of which are among the best written in Russian, especially *Ottsy i deti* (1862; *Fathers and Sons,* 1867). He also wrote poems, poems in prose, and plays, one of which, *Mesyats v derevne* (1855; *A Month in the Country,* 1924), is still staged regularly in Russian theaters.

Achievements

Turgenev's opus is not particularly large, yet with about four dozen stories and novellas and his brief novels, he became one of the best writers not only in Russian but in world literature as well. Turgenev was a leading force in the Russian realistic movement of the second half of the nineteenth century. Together with Nikolai Gogol, Fyodor Dostoevski, Leo Tolstoy, and Anton Chekhov, he built the reputation that Russian literature enjoys in the world. Perhaps more than other writers, he was responsible for acquainting foreign readers with Russian literature, and because he spent most of his adult life abroad, he was an esteemed figure in the international literary life.

Turgenev was also instrumental in arousing the sensitivity and consciousness of his compatriots, as he dealt with such burning social issues as the plight of Russian peasantry, in *A Sportsman's Sketches*; the "superfluous man" in Russian society, in "The Diary of a Superfluous Man"; the fixation of Russians with revolution, in *Rudin* (1856; English translation, 1947); the decaying nobility in *Dvoryanskoye gnezdo* (1859; *Liza,* 1869; better known as *A House of Gentlefolk,* 1894); and the age-old conflict between generations, in *Fathers and Sons.*

Turgenev also excelled in his style, especially in the use of the language. Albert Jay Nock called him "incomparably the greatest of artists in fiction," and Virginia Woolf termed his works as being "curiously of our own time, undecayed and complete in themselves." His reputation, despite some fluctuations, endures.

Biography

Ivan Sergeyevich Turgenev was born on November 9, 1818, in the central Russian town of Orel, into a small gentry family. His father was a loving, easygoing country squire, while his mother was an overbearing woman of whom Turgenev had many unpleasant memories. He spent his childhood at the family estate Spasskoe, which he visited every summer even after the family moved to Moscow. He received tutoring at home and later was graduated from the University of St. Petersburg in 1837. He continued his studies in Berlin, acquiring a master's degree in philosophy. His stay in Berlin marks the beginning of a lifelong shuffle between his homeland and the European countries, especially France, Germany, England, and Italy. On one visit to France, he met a French woman, Pauline Viardot, with whom he had a close relationship the rest of his life despite her being married. After serving briefly in the Ministry of Interior, he lived the remainder of his life off his estate income following his parents' death.

Turgenev started to write early, and in 1843, at the age of twenty-five, he published a long narrative poem, *Parasha*, written in imitation of Alexander Pushkin. He soon abandoned poetry for prose, although his reverence for Pushkin and the poetic slant remained constant in his writings. His stories about the dismal life of Russian peasants were much more successful, attracting the attention of readers and critics alike. When the collection of those stories, *A Sportsman's Sketches*, was published in 1852, his reputation as a promising young writer was firmly established. A successful play, *A Month in the Country*, added to his reputation. As his reputation grew, he became friends with many leading writers and critics—Vissarion Belinsky, Nikolai Nekrasov, Tolstoy, Aleksandr Herzen, Dostoevski, and others—but these friendships were often interspersed with heated arguments and enmity. Because of his connections in Europe and a pronounced liberal outlook, he was summoned on several occasions before the investigation committees back in Russia. He was always exonerated, however, and he continued to travel between Russia and Europe.

Turgenev never married, but he had several affairs, while Viardot remained the love of his life, and he was thought to have been the father of a son born to her. The steady stream of successful novels and stories enhanced the esteem in which he was held both at home and abroad. At the same time, he carried on a spirited debate with Russian intellectuals, advocating liberal reforms in Russian society, especially those concerning the plight of peasants, many of whom were still kept as serfs. When they were liberated in 1861, it was believed that not a small merit belonged to Turgenev and his efforts toward their emancipation.

Toward the end of his life, Turgenev kept writing and publishing, though at a slower pace. He also worked on the preparation of his collected works and continued to live in a *ménage à trois* with Viardot and her husband. During his last visit to Russia in the summer of 1881, he visited Tolstoy at Yasnaya Polyana. His health began to deteriorate in 1882, and, after several months of a serious illness, he died at the Viardots' estate in Bougival, near Paris, on September 3, 1883. As his friend Henry James wrote, "his end was not serene and propitious, but dark and almost violent." Turgenev's body was taken to Russia, where he was buried with great honors in St. Petersburg.

Analysis

The reputation of Ivan Turgenev as a short-story writer is based in equal measure on his stories about Russian peasant life and on stories about other segments of society. Although differing greatly in subject matter and emphasis, they nevertheless share the same mastery of storytelling and style and language. Turgenev wrote stories about the peasants early in his career, revealing his familiarity with life in the countryside and his preoccupation with liberal causes. As he grew older and traveled to Europe, his horizons expanded, and he became more interested in topics transcending his provincial outlook. His acquired cosmopolitanism was also reflected in his turning toward personal concerns of love, alienation, and psychological illumination of his characters. The last story that he wrote, "Klara Milich" ("Clara Milich"), takes him to the realm of the fantastic and supernatural, to life after death, and even to the bizarre twists of the human mind.

Turgenev's stories about Russian peasants are contained primarily in his collection *A Sportsman's Sketches.* As the title implies (the accurate translation is "notes of a hunter"), the twenty-five tales are more like notes and sketches than full-blown stories with plot and characterization. It is one of the few examples in world literature where the entire collection of separate and independent stories has a thematic unity; another example of this unity is Isaac Babel's *Konormiia* (1926; *Red Cavalry*, 1929). The unifying theme is the hard life of Russian peasants—many generations of whom had lived as serfs for centuries—and the neglect of their well-being on the part of their owners. Despite its innocuous title, chosen to mislead the censors, the collection provoked admiration as well as heated debates. It is credited with speeding up the process of the serfs' emancipation.

The stories are set in the countryside around Turgenev's family estate at the middle of the nineteenth century. They are told by the same narrator, a landowner, in fact the thinly disguised author himself. During his tireless hunting trips, Turgenev met various characters, mostly peasants, many of whom told stories worth listening to. The authentic human quality of the settings and marvelous characterization, rather than the social message, make the stories enduring literature.

The author approaches his characters with an open mind. He observes their demeanor "with curiosity and sympathy" and listens to their concerns and complaints without much comment, with a few questions for his own clarification. He refrains from passing judgment and avoids social criticism or satire. Through such unobtrusiveness, he gains the characters' confidence and allows them to talk freely, making the stories more believable. More important, he does not idealize the peasants; instead, he attempts to penetrate the crust of everyday appearances.

The woman in the story "Ermolai i mel'nichikha" ("Ermolai and Miller's Wife"), whose freedom had been bought by her husband, talks nonchalantly about her hard lot and the lack of love in her life. Yet beneath her story, the reader senses deep melancholy and hopelessness, reinforced by the author's remark to his hunting companion, "It seems she is ailing," and by the companion's retort, "What else should she be?" The burly, taciturn forest warden in the story "Biriuk" ("The Wolf"), who lives alone, excels in protecting the forest from the poachers, and is feared and hated by the peasants who are not above stealing wood from the landowner. He cannot be bribed and plays no favorites, finding the only pleasure in doing his job. Yet when he catches a poor peasant trying to fell a tree, he lets him go because it is hunger that drove him to thievery. In one of Turgenev's best stories, "Zhivye Moshchi" ("A Living Relic"), a young woman, dying of a fatal illness, gives the impression of total helplessness, yet she is nourished until her untimely death by her naïve religion and love of life. In all these stories, appearances are deceiving and the observer-narrator is able to get to the core of his characters.

Not all characters have an adversary relationship with their fate. The two friends in "Khor'i Kalynich" ("Khor and Kalynich") epitomize the two halves of a Russian character. Khor is a practical, down-to-earth man who has found success in life. Kalynich is a sensitive soul living in unison with nature, a dreamer who revels in simple pleasures, without worrying about more complex aspects of life. The doctor in "Uezdnyi lekar" ("The Country Doctor"), called to the sickbed of a young girl, falls in love with her, and his love is returned, but he realizes that he cannot save the young girl. He finds solace in the discovery that the girl has satisfied her own craving for love in the last moments of her life. Thus, the results are not as important as are the efforts to avoid or alleviate the blows, no matter how unsuccessful the efforts may be.

Peasants are not the only characters drawing the author's attention. The land-owners, who wield the power of life and death over their serfs, also appear in sev-eral stories. For the most part, they are depicted with much less sympathy and un-derstanding, despite the author's own social origin. In "Dva pomeshchika" ("Two Landowners"), both characters show negative traits: one, a major-general, is a social clown; the other, an insensitive brute, who thinks that a peasant will always be a peasant and who uses a homespun "philosophy" that "if the father's a thief, the son's a thief too . . . it's blood that counts." The author seems to be saying that with such a negative attitude, no improvement of the peasants' lot is possible. "Gamlet Shchigrovskogo uezda" ("Prince Hamlet of Shchigrovo") offers an even stronger castigation of the serf-owning class. Here, an intelligent and sensitive landowner fails to find understanding among his peers for his attempts to improve the lot of everybody. In a Dostoevskian fashion, he is forced to act like a buffoon in hopes of gaining attention that way. Turgenev's position here sounds very much like a sharp satire against the existing state of affairs, but, as mentioned, he abstains from open and direct criticism, thus making his points even more effective.

Not all of the stories in *A Sportsman's Sketches* are bleak or hopeless. The two best stories of the collection are also the most positive. In "Bezhin lug" ("Bezhin Meadow"), Turgenev relates his evening encounter with five young boys taking care of the horses in the countryside. Sitting by the fire in the evening, they tell one another fantastic stories, to amuse and even frighten one another. The narrator is impressed by the boys' natural demeanor, straightforwardness, bravery, and, above all, rich imagination of which folktales are spun. The author seems to imply that the future of the country is secure if judged by the young who are to inherit it. The second story, "Pevtsy" ("The Singers"), is even more uplifting. In another chance encounter, the narrator stumbles across an inn in the barely accessible backwoods. He is treated with a singing competition among the inn patrons unlike any other he had experienced. Turgenev uses the diamond-in-the-rough theme to show where the real talent can be found. As the narrator leaves the inn, he hears the people's voices calling each other from one hill to another—a possible explanation of where the marvelous singers learn how to sing. These stories, along with a few others, strike a balance between the negative and the positive aspects of the life depicted in the book.

Surrounded and suffused by nature, Turgenev reacts to it by stating his position concerning human beings in nature. He expresses his admiration for nature by using strikingly detailed descriptions, emphasizing colors, sounds, and scents. His subtlety of observation is complemented by genuine lyricism and careful use of a melodic, rhythmical language. Despite these ornamental features, however, the reader is tempted to view the author's notion of nature as being rather unfeeling and indifferent toward humankind, in the best tradition of Georg Brandes' theory of *la grande indifférante*. A closer look, however, reveals that nature in Turgenev's works shows the difference in degree, not in kind, and that for him, humankind is a part of nature, not outside it. Only in unison with nature can human beings fulfill their potential, in which case nature is not indifferent but, on the contrary, very helpful, as seen in the example of the singers in the aforementioned story.

Other artistic merits of these stories (which Turgenev was able to maintain throughout his writing career) can be found in his careful and delicate choice of suggestive and descriptive words; in the sketchy but pithy psychological portraiture; in the uncomplicated plot structure, consisting usually of an anecdote or episode; in the natural, calm, matter-of-fact narration; and in the effective imagery that is not strained or artificial. Superior craftsmanship goes hand in hand with the "social message" here, preventing the stories from being dated or used for nonartistic purposes.

The second group of Turgenev's tales strikes an altogether different path, although a kinship with his earlier stories can be easily detected. Among many stories outside the cycle of *A Sportsman's Sketches*, eight deserve to be singled out, either for the significance of their contents or for their artistic merit, or both. An early story, "Dnevnik lishnega cheloveka" ("The Diary of a Superfluous Man"), despite its relative immaturity, has a significance that surpasses its artistic quality. It is here that Turgenev coined the phrase "a superfluous man," which would reverberate throughout Russian literature of the nineteenth and twentieth centuries. Even though the superfluous man theme had been used before Turgenev by Pushkin's Eugene Onegin in the novel in verse by the same name and by Mikhail Lermontov's Pechorin in *Geroy nashego vremeni* (1840; *A Hero of Our Times*, 1854), it was Turgenev who made the phrase a literary byword. The story presages Dostoevski's *Zapiski iz podpolya* (1864; *Letters from the Underworld*, 1913; better known as *Notes from the Underground*, 1918).

Turgenev's "superfluous man" is a young scion of erstwhile wealthy landowners, who writes a diary knowing that he will soon die of a disease. To compound his misery, he is rejected in his love for a beautiful neighbor. The excessive introspection of the "hero" and his inability to cope with reality make this story primarily a psychological character study and not a social statement, as some of Turgenev's works of the same kind would become later.

Perhaps the best known of Turgenev's stories, "Mumu" comes the closest in spirit to the collection *A Sportsman's Sketches*. A deaf-mute servant loses the girl he loves when he is forced into marrying another woman. Later, he is ordered to kill his beloved dog because its barking is disturbing his mistress' sleep. Drawing the character of the insensitive mistress after his mother, Turgenev castigates the insensitivity of the entire serf-owning class. The story does not sink into sentimental bathos primarily because of the remarkable characterization of the servant as an ultimate sufferer, underscoring the proverbial capacity for suffering of an entire nation. Moreover, by arousing overwhelming pity for the deaf-mute, Turgenev clearly places the blame for this human and social injustice at the door of the unfeeling gentry.

"Stepnoi Korol' Lir" ("King Lear of the Steppes") is another story that in its countryside setting shows kinship with *A Sportsman's Sketches*. Yet it is entirely different in the subject matter, spirit, and atmosphere. In a takeoff on William Shakespeare's tragedy, the story shows children behaving toward their father in a similar manner. The atmosphere here, however, is typically Russian. Harlov, a descendant of a Russianized Swedish family, suffers the same indignity and ingratitude at the hands of his daughters, and he takes similar revenge upon them, but the tragedy is not relieved or ennobled. Turgenev shows a fine sense for plot, and the dialogues—more excessive than usual for him—are in line with the dramatic nature of its model. Artistically, this story is almost a masterpiece, keeping the reader in suspense until the end.

Love is an overriding theme in Turgenev's later stories. "Asya" ("Asya") and "Pervaya lyubov" ("First Love") are the best representatives of Turgenev's love stories. Both are told in the first person, tempting one to attribute to them autobiographical character, which may not be totally unjustified. "Asya" is set in a German town where the narrator (perhaps Turgenev) comes across two compatriots, a brother and a sister. As the story unfolds, the narrator is increasingly attracted to the woman and develops genuine love feelings, yet he is unable to declare his love openly, vacillating constantly until every chance for consummation is lost. Turgenev was known to have been indecisive in his love affairs, as illustrated by his strange attachment to the Viardot couple. Seen from that angle, the autobiographical element becomes very plausible, but there is more to the story than simply Turgenev's indecisiveness. At this stage of his development, Turgenev had published only one book of short stories and one novel, and he was beset by doubts and indecision, not only in his love relationships but also in his literary aspirations, all too similar to those of the narrator in "Asya." As he himself said, "There are turning points in life, points when the past dies and something new is born; woe to the man who doesn't know how to sense these turning points and either holds on stubbornly to a dead past or seeks prematurely to summon to life what has not yet fully ripened." The story reflects the wrenching doubts and soul searching of the protagonist, which did not enable him to take a resolute stance toward the young woman, who herself was searching for a more assuring love. Thus, the love between Asya and the narrator was doomed to failure almost before it began. The two part, and the only thing left is a bittersweet memory of what might have been.

Perhaps Turgenev was not yet ready to give the story the adequate treatment that it deserves. This is evidenced in the fact that Asya, wistful and charming though she may be, is not developed fully as a character. Turgenev will return soon to a similar theme and develop it to the fullest in his novel *A House of Gentlefolk*. It is also worth mentioning that "Asya" is another example of the theme of the superfluous man, which started with "The Diary of a Superfluous Man."

"First Love" is a better love story because both the plot and the characters are more fully developed. It involves a rivalry between a young man and his father, vying for the affection of the same woman, Zinaida. In Turgenev's own admission, the story is autobiographical; as he wrote about it in a letter, "It is the only thing that still gives me pleasure, because it is life itself, it was not made up . . . 'First Love' is part of my experience." Aside from this candid admission, the story has a wide appeal to all, both young and old; to the young because the first love is always cherished the most (the only true love, according to Turgenev), and to the old because it offers a vicarious pleasure of a last triumph. It invariably evokes a bittersweet nostalgia in everyone. It also presents a plausible, even if not too common, situation. Turgenev controls with a sure hand the delicate relationships between the three partners in this emotional drama fraught with the awakening of manhood in an adolescent, with the amorous playfulness of a young woman who is both a temptress and a victim, and with the satisfaction of a conquest by a man entering the autumn of his life. Similarly, the author handles tactfully a potentially explosive situation between the loving father and adoring son, producing no rancor in aftermath. The story is a throwback to Romanticism, which had already passed in Russian literature and elsewhere at the time of the story's publication. The story ends in a Turgenevian fashion—unhappily for everyone concerned. All these attributes make "First Love" one of the best love stories in world literature.

Twenty years later, Turgenev would write another love story, "Pesn' torzhestvuiushchei liubvi" ("The Song of Triumphant Love"), which differs from "First Love" in many respects. It again deals with a love relationship in a *ménage à trois* (it seems that Turgenev was constantly reliving his own predicament with the Viardot couple), but the similarities stop there. The setting is in sixteenth century Ferrara, and the male players—members of ancient patrician families—are on equal footing, even if one is a husband and the other a suitor. The ending is much more than unhappy: it is downright tragic. What makes this story decisively different from other love stories by Turgenev is the introduction of a supernatural element manifesting itself in the woman's conceiving, not by intercourse, but by the platonic desire and the singing of a song by the unsuccessful suitor.

"The Song of Triumphant Love" marks the transition to a more esoteric subject matter in Turgenev's writing. He had written fantastic stories before ("Prizraki," or "Phantoms"), but in the last decade of his life, he employed the supernatural with increasing frequency. In "Stuk . . . stuk . . . stuk . . ." ("Knock . . . Knock . . . Knock . . ."), he deals with a suicidal urge that borders on the supernatural. In his last story, "Clara Milich," he tells of a man who has fallen in love with a woman after her death. Turgenev believed that there is a thin line dividing the real and the fantastic and that the fantastic stories people tell have happened in real life. As he said, "Wherever you look, there is the drama in life, and there are still writers who complain that all subjects have been exhausted." Had he lived longer, most likely he would have tried to reconcile real life with so-called fantasy and the supernatural.

Other major works

NOVELS: *Rudin*, 1856 (*Dimitri Roudine*, 1873; better known as *Rudin*, 1947); *Asya*, 1858 (English translation, 1877); *Dvoryanskoye gnezdo*, 1859 (*Liza*, 1869; also as *A Nobleman's Nest*, 1903; better known as *A House of Gentlefolk*, 1894); *Nakanune*, 1860 (*On the Eve*, 1871); *Pervaya lyubov*, 1860 (*First Love*, 1884); *Ottsy i deti*, 1862 (*Fathers and Sons*, 1867); *Dym*, 1867 (*Smoke*, 1868); *Veshniye vody*, 1872 (*Spring Floods*, 1874; better known as *The Torrents of Spring*, 1897); *Nov*, 1877 (*Virgin Soil*, 1877); *The Novels of Ivan Turgenev*, 1894-1899 (15 volumes).

PLAYS: *Neostorozhnost*, 1843 (*Carelessness*, 1924); *Bezdenezhe*, 1846 (*A Poor Gentleman*, 1924); *Kholostyak*, 1849 (*The Bachelor*, 1924); *Zavtrak u predvoditelya*, 1849; *Nakhlebnik*, 1857; *Razgovor na bolshoy doroge*, 1850 (*A Conversation on the Highway*, 1924); *Mesyats v derevne*, 1855 (*A Month in the Country*, 1924); *Provintsialka*, 1851 (*A Provincial Lady*, 1934); *Gde tonko, tam i rvyotsya*, 1912 (*Where It Is Thin, There it Breaks*, 1924); *Vecher v Sorrente*, 1884 (*An Evening in Sorrento*, 1924); *The Plays of Ivan Turgenev*, 1924; *Three Plays*, 1934.

POETRY: *Parasha*, 1843; *Stikhotvoreniya v proze*, 1882, 1930 (*Poems in Prose*, 1883, 1945).

NONFICTION: "Gamlet i Don Kihot," 1860 ("Hamlet and Don Quixote," 1930); *Literaturnya i zhiteyskiya vospominaniya*, 1880 (*Literary Reminiscences and Autobiographical Fragments*, 1958); *Turgenev: Letters*, 1983 (edited by David Lowe); *Turgenev's Letters*, 1983 (edited by David Knowles).

MISCELLANEOUS: *The Works of Iván Turgenieff*, 1903-1904 (7 volumes).

Bibliography

Brodianski, Nina. "Turgenev's Short Stories: A Revaluation." *Slavonic and East European Review* 32, no. 78 (1953): 70-91. In this brief but thorough and stimulating study, Brodianski examines Turgenev's short stories in general, their themes, structure, and psychological illumination of characters, as well as his philosophy (as much as there is of it) and his literary theories about the short story. Inasmuch as it re-evaluates some long-standing opinions about Turgenev, it serves a good purpose.

Kagan-Kans, Eva. "Fate and Fantasy: A Study of Turgenev's Fantastic Stories." *Slavic*

Review 18 (1969): 543-560. Kagan-Kans traces Turgenev's treatment of fantasy and supernatural elements in his stories, as well as the role of fate and dreams. She also examines Turgenev's relationship with other writers, especially the Romanticists, and their influence on him as evidenced in individual stories, especially those dealing with fantasy and the supernatural.

Lloyd, John Arthur Thomas. *Ivan Turgenev.* 1942. Reprint. Port Washington, N.Y.: Kennikat Press, 1973. A practical, compact biography, tastefully illustrated, treating systematically Turgenev's life and works in a lively, succinct manner. It tends to cling to traditional views about Turgenev, which is useful for comparative purposes.

Magarshack, David. *Turgenev: A Life.* London: Faber & Faber, 1954. An illustrated biography by Turgenev's translator, describing extensively his life. Concentrates on the events that shaped the author's life, his relationships with Russian and foreign writers, and the factual circumstances surrounding his works. A useful introduction to Turgenev and his opus.

Moser, Charles A. *Ivan Turgenev.* New York: Columbia University Press, 1972. A brief but succinct essay in the Columbia series on modern writers, useful for a quick overview of Turgenev's life and works, with some stimulating ideas.

Seeley, Frank Friedeberg. *Turgenev: A Reading of His Fiction.* New York: Cambridge University Press, 1991. Seeley prefaces his thorough study of Turgenev's fiction with an outline of Turgenev's life and a survey of his poetry and plays. This volume incorporates later findings and challenges some established views, especially the traditional notion of the "simplicity" of Turgenev's works. Seeley stresses the psychological treatment that Turgenev allotted to his characters.

Yarmolinsky, Avrahm. *Turgenev: The Man, His Art, and His Age.* New York: Orion Press, 1959. Reprint. New York: Collier, 1962. Another reliable shorter biography, useful as an introduction to Turgenev. As the title implies, it touches on all important stages in his life and discusses his works as to their geneses, their salient features, and their overall significance for Turgenev and for Russian and world literature. Concludes with a useful chronology and a good bibliography.

Vasa D. Mihailovich

MARK TWAIN
Samuel Langhorne Clemens

Born: Florida, Missouri; November 30, 1835
Died: Redding, Connecticut; April 21, 1910

Principal short fiction

The Celebrated Jumping Frog of Calaveras County, and Other Sketches, 1867; *Mark Twain's Sketches: New and Old*, 1875; *The Stolen White Elephant and Other Stories*, 1882; *The £1,000,000 Bank-Note and Other New Stories*, 1893; *The Man That Corrupted Hadleyburg and Other Stories and Essays*, 1900; *A Double Barrelled Detective Story*, 1902; *King Leopold's Soliloquy: A Defense of His Congo Rule*, 1905; *The $30,000 Bequest and Other Stories*, 1906; *A Horse's Tale*, 1907; *The Mysterious Stranger and Other Stories*, 1916; *The Curious Republic of Gondour and Other Whimsical Sketches*, 1919; *The Adventures of Thomas Jefferson Snodgrass*, 1926; *The Complete Short Stories of Mark Twain*, 1957 (Charles Neider, editor); *Selected Shorter Writings of Mark Twain*, 1962.

Other literary forms

As a professional writer who felt the need for a large income, Mark Twain published more than thirty books and left many uncollected pieces and manuscripts. He tried every genre, including drama, and even wrote some poetry that is seldom read. His royalties came mostly from books sold door to door, especially five travel volumes. For more than forty years, he occasionally sold material, usually humorous sketches, to magazines and newspapers. He also composed philosophical dialogues, moral fables, and maxims, as well as essays on a range of subjects which were weighted more toward the social and cultural than the belletristic but which were nevertheless often controversial. Posterity prefers his two famous novels about boyhood along the banks of the Mississippi, *The Adventures of Tom Sawyer* (1876) and *The Adventures of Huckleberry Finn* (1884), although Twain also tried historical fiction, the detective story, and quasi-scientific fantasy.

Achievements

Certainly one of the United States' most beloved and most frequently quoted writers, Twain earned that honor by creating an original and nearly inimitable style that is thoroughly American. Although Twain tried nearly every genre from historical fiction to poetry to quasi-scientific fantasy, his novels about boyhood on the Mississippi, *The Adventures of Tom Sawyer* and *The Adventures of Huckleberry Finn*, are the works that permanently wove Twain's celebrity status into the fabric of American culture. During his own lifetime, Twain received numerous honors including an M.A., soon followed by an LL.D., from Yale University. The University of Missouri granted him another doctorate in 1902. His proudest moment, however, was in 1907, when the University of Oxford awarded him an honorary LL.D. He was so proud of his scarlet doctor's gown that he wore it to his daughter's wedding.

Biography

After his education was cut short by the death of a stern father who had more ambition than success, at the age of eleven Mark Twain was apprenticed to a newspaper office, which, except for the money earned from four years of piloting on the Mississippi, supplied most of his income until 1868. Then, he quickly won eminence as a lecturer and author before his marriage to wealthy Olivia Langdon in 1870 led to a memorably comfortable and active family life which included three daughters. Although always looking to his writing for income, he increasingly devoted energy to business affairs and investments until his publishing house declared bankruptcy in 1894. After his world lecture tour of 1895-1896, he became one of the most admired figures of his time and continued to earn honors until his death in 1910.

Analysis

Many readers find Mark Twain most successful in briefer works, including his narratives, because they were not padded to fit some extraneous standard of length. His best stories are narrated by first-person speakers who are seemingly artless, often so convincingly that critics cannot agree concerning the extent to which their ingenuousness is the result of Twain's self-conscious craft. While deeply divided himself, Twain seldom created introspectively complex characters or narrators who are unreliable in the Conradian manner. Rather, just as Twain alternated between polarities of attitude, his characters tend to embody some extreme, unitary state either of villainy or (especially with young women) of unshakable virtue. Therefore, they too seldom interact effectively. Except when adapting a plot taken from oral tradition, Twain does better with patently artificial situations, which his genius for suggesting authentic speech make plausible enough. In spite of their faults, Twain's stories captivate the reader with their irresistible humor, their unique style, and their spirited characters who transfigure the humdrum with striking perceptions.

"The Celebrated Jumping Frog of Calaveras County" is generally regarded as Twain's most distinctive story, although some readers may prefer Jim Baker's bluejay yarn, which turns subtly on the psyche of its narrator, or Jim Blaine's digressions from his grandfather's old ram, which reach a more physical comedy while evolving into an absurdly tall tale. In "The Celebrated Jumping Frog of Calaveras County," Jim Smiley's eagerness to bet on anything in the mining camp may strain belief, but it is relatively plausible that another gambler could weigh down Smiley's frog, Daniel Webster, with quailshot and thus win forty dollars with an untrained frog. Most attempts to find profundity in this folk anecdote involve the few enveloping sentences attributed to an outsider, who may represent the literate Easterner being gulled by Simon Wheeler's seeming inability to stick to his point. The skill of the story can be more conclusively identified, from the deft humanizing of animals to the rising power and aptness of the imagery. Especially adroit is the deadpan manner of Wheeler, who never betrays whether he himself appreciates the humor and the symmetry of his maunderings. Twain's use of the oral style is nowhere better represented than in "The Celebrated Jumping Frog of Calaveras County," which exemplifies the principles of the author's essay "How to Tell a Story."

In 1874, Twain assured the sober *Atlantic Monthly* that his short story "A True Story" was not humorous, although in fact it has his characteristic sparkle and hearty tone. Having been encouraged by the contemporary appeal for local color, Twain quickly developed a narrator with a heavy dialect and a favorite folk-saying that allows a now-grown son to recognize his mother after a separation of thirteen years. While she, in turn, finds scars confirming their relationship on his wrist and head, this conventional plot gains resonance from Rachel's report of how her husband and seven children had once been separated at a slave auction in Richmond. Contemporaries praised "A True Story" for its naturalness, testimony that Twain was creating more lifelike blacks than any other author by allowing them greater dignity, and Rachel is quick to insist that slave families cared for one another just as deeply as any white families. Her stirringly recounted memories challenged the legend of the Old South even before that legend reached its widest vogue, and her spirit matched her "mighty" body so graphically that "A True Story" must get credit for much more craftsmanship than is admitted by its subtitle, "Repeated Word for Word as I Heard It."

In "The Facts Concerning the Recent Carnival of Crime in Connecticut," in which Twain again uses first-person narration with a flawless touch for emphasizing the right word or syllable, the main character closely resembles the author in age, experience, habits, and tastes. Of more significance is the fact that the story projects Twain's lifelong struggles with, and even against, his conscience. Here the conscience admits to being the "most pitiless enemy" of its host, whom it is supposed to "improve" but only tyrannizes with gusto while refusing to praise the host for anything. It makes the blunder, however, of materializing as a two-foot dwarf covered with "fuzzy greenish mold" who torments the narrator with intimate knowledge of and contemptuous judgments on his behavior. When beloved Aunty Mary arrives to scold him once more for his addiction to tobacco, his conscience grows so torpid that he can gleefully seize and destroy it beyond any chance of rebirth. Through vivid yet realistic detail, "The Facts Concerning the Recent Carnival of Crime in Connecticut" dramatizes common musings about shame and guilt along with the yearnings some persons feel for release from them. If it maintains too comic a tone to preach nihilism or amorality, it leaves readers inclined to view conscience less as a divine agent than as part of psychic dynamics.

The shopworn texture of "The £1,000,000 Bank-Note" reveals Twain's genius for using the vernacular at a low ebb. Narrated by the protagonist, this improbable tale is set in motion by two brothers who disagree over what would happen if some penniless individual were loaned a five-million-dollar bill for thirty days. To solve their argument, they engage in an experiment with a Yankee, Henry Adams, a stockbroker's clerk stranded in London. Coincidence thickens when, having managed by the tenth day of the experiment to get invited to dinner by an American minister, Adams unknowingly meets the stepdaughter of one of the brothers and woos and wins her that very night. Having just as nimbly gained a celebrity that makes every merchant eager to extend unlimited credit, he endorses a sale of Nevada stocks that enables him to show his future father-in-law that he has banked a million dollars of his own. The overall effect is cheerfully melodramatic and appeals to fantasies about windfalls of money; the reader can share Adams' pleasure in the surprise and awe he arouses by pulling his banknote out of a tattered pocket. It can be argued that the story indicts a society in which the mere show of wealth can so quickly raise one's standing, but Twain probably meant Adams to deserve respect for his enterprise and shrewdness when his chance came.

"The Man That Corrupted Hadleyburg" is one of the most penetrating of Twain's stories. It achieves unusual depth of character and, perhaps by giving up the first-person narrator, a firm objectivity that lets theme develop through dialogue and incident. It proceeds with such flair that only a third or fourth reading uncovers thin links in a supposedly inescapable chain of events planned for revenge by an outsider who had been insulted in Hadleyburg, a town smugly proud of its reputation for honesty. Stealthily he leaves a sack of counterfeit gold coins which are to be handed over to the fictitious resident who once gave a needy stranger twenty dollars and can prove it by recalling his words at the time. Next, the avenger sends nineteen leading citizens a letter which tells each of them how to claim the gold, supposedly amounting to forty thousand dollars. During an uproarious town meeting studded with vignettes of local characters, both starchy and plebeian, eighteen identical claims are read aloud; the nineteenth, however, from elderly Edward Richards, is suppressed by the chairman, who overestimates how Richards once saved him from the community's unjust anger. Rewarded by the stranger and made a hero, Richards is actually tormented to death, both by pangs of conscience and by fear of exposure. Hadleyburg, however, has learned a lesson in humility and moral realism and shortens its motto from the Lord's Prayer to run: "Lead Us into Temptation."

"The Man That Corrupted Hadleyburg" exhibits Twain's narrative and stylistic strengths and also dramatizes several of his persistent themes, such as skepticism about orthodox religion, ambivalence toward the conscience but contempt for rationalizing away deserved guilt, and attraction to mechanistic ideas. The story raises profound questions which can never be settled. The most useful criticism asks whether the story's determinism is kept consistent and uppermost—or, more specifically, whether the reform of Hadleyburg can follow within the patterns already laid out. The ethical values behind the story's action and ironical tone imply that people can in fact choose to behave more admirably. In printing the story, *Harper's Monthly* may well have seen a Christian meliorism, a lesson against self-righteous piety that abandons true charity. The revised motto may warn that the young, instead of being sheltered, should be educated to cope with fallible human nature. More broadly, the story seems to show that the conscience can be trained into a constructive force by honestly confronting the drives for pleasure and self-approval that sway everyone.

Many of these same themes reappear in quasi-supernatural sketches such as "Extract from Captain Stormfield's Visit to Heaven." Twain never tired of toying with biblical characters, particularly Adam and Eve, or with parodies of Sunday-school lessons. He likewise parodied most other genres, even those which he himself used seriously. In his most serious moods he preached openly against cruelty to animals in "A Dog's Tale" and "A Horse's Tale," supported social or political causes, and always came back to moral choices, as in "Was It Heaven or Hell?" or "The $30,000 Bequest." Notably weak in self-criticism, he had a tireless imagination capable of daringly unusual perspectives, a supreme gift of humor darkened by brooding over the enigmas of life, and an ethical habit of thought that expressed itself most tellingly through character and narrative.

Other major works

NOVELS: *The Gilded Age*, 1873 (with Charles Dudley Warner); *The Adventures of Tom Sawyer*, 1876; *The Prince and the Pauper*, 1881; *The Adventures of Huckleberry Finn*, 1884; *A Connecticut Yankee in King Arthur's Court*, 1889; *The American Claimant*, 1892; *Tom Sawyer Abroad*, 1894; *The Tragedy of Pudd'nhead Wilson*, 1894; *Personal Recollections of Joan of Arc*, 1896; *Tom Sawyer, Detective*, 1896; *The Mysterious Stranger*, 1916 (revised as *The Chronicle of Young Satan*, 1969, by Albert Bigelow Paine and Frederick A. Duneka); *Simon Wheeler, Detective*, 1963.

PLAYS: *Colonel Sellers*, 1874; *Ah Sin, the Heathen Chinee*, 1877 (with Bret Harte).

NONFICTION: *The Innocents Abroad*, 1869; *Roughing It*, 1872; *A Tramp Abroad*, 1880; *Life on the Mississippi*, 1883; *Following the Equator*, 1897 (also known as *More Tramp Abroad*); *How to Tell a Story and Other Essays*, 1897; *My Debut as a Literary Person*, 1903; *Extracts from Adam's Diary*, 1904; *Eve's Diary, Translated from the Original Ms*, 1906; *What Is Man?*, 1906; *Christian Science*, 1907; *Extract from Captain Stormfield's Visit to Heaven*, 1909; *Is Shakespeare Dead?*, 1909; *Mark Twain's Speeches*, 1910; *Mark Twain's Letters*, 1917 (2 volumes); *Europe and Elsewhere*, 1923 (Albert Bigelow Paine, editor); *Mark Twain's Autobiography*, 1924, 1959 (2 volumes); *Sketches of the Sixties*, 1926 (with Bret Harte); *Mark Twain's Notebook*, 1935 (Albert Bigelow Paine, editor); *Letters from the Sandwich Islands, Written for the Sacramento Union*, 1937; *Letters from Honolulu, Written for the Sacramento Union*, 1939; *Mark Twain in Eruption*, 1940; *Mark Twain's Travels with Mr. Brown*, 1940; *Washington in 1868*, 1943; *The Love Letters of Mark Twain*, 1949; *Mark Twain to Mrs. Fairbanks*, 1949; *Mark Twain of the Enterprise, 1862-1864*, 1957; *Mark Twain-Howells Letters*, 1960; *Mark Twain's Letters to Mary*, 1961; *Letters from the Earth*, 1962; *The Complete Essays of Mark Twain*, 1963; *The Forgotten Writings of Mark Twain*, 1963; *Mark Twain's Letters from Hawaii*, 1966; *Mark Twain's Letters to His Publishers, 1867-1894*, 1967; *Clemens of the Call: Mark Twain in San Francisco*, 1969; *Mark Twain's Correspondence with Henry Huttleston Rogers, 1893-1909*, 1969; *A Pen Warmed-Up in Hell: Mark Twain in Protest*, 1972; *Mark Twain's Notebooks and Journals*, 1975-1979; *Mark Twain Speaking*, 1976 (Paul Fatout, editor).

MISCELLANEOUS: *The Writings of Mark Twain*, 1968 (25 volumes).

Bibliography

Budd, Louis J. *Our Mark Twain: The Making of His Public Personality.* Philadelphia: University of Pennsylvania Press, 1983. A thorough analysis of the public Mark Twain's American career. Discusses the emergence of the carefully crafted celebrity persona, smartly outfitted in a white formal dress suit and silk braid or flamboyant crimson Oxford robe. Examines the ongoing process Twain used to establish himself as a culture-hero.

Kaplan, Justin. *Mr. Clemens and Mark Twain.* New York: Simon & Schuster, 1966. This biography documents the author's life during the era that Mark Twain labeled the Gilded Age, the three to four decades that followed the Civil War. Covers the author's life from his early thirties, when he created the Mark Twain persona and discovered how to transform his colorful past into the many varied literary works that he would spend the rest of his life writing. Includes photographs of the author, his family, and his peers.

Sanborn, Margaret. *Mark Twain: The Bachelor Years.* New York: Doubleday, 1990. This biography covers the adventure-filled years from the author's boyhood to marriage in 1870 at age thirty-four. Based on extensive research into letters written to Twain's mother, sister, brothers, and close friends. Includes many letters not referenced by Twain's official biographer, Albert Bigelow Paine. Also includes valuable insights gained from 184 letters written between 1868 and 1870, while courting Olivia Langdon, whom Twain eventually married.

Smith, Henry Nash. *Mark Twain: A Collection of Critical Essays.* Englewood Cliffs, N.J.: Prentice-Hall, 1963. A collection of essays with an introduction by Smith. Among the contributors is W. H. Auden. A chronology of important dates in the author's life is also included.

_____. *Mark Twain: The Development of a Writer.* Cambridge, Mass.: Harvard University Press, 1962. An excellent discussion of how Twain used vernacular values to their fullest, especially in *The Adventures of Huckleberry Finn*, to achieve his status as a writer of literary merit. Focuses on nine principal works in which Twain overcame the prevailing attitude during his lifetime that a humorist could not be considered a writer of profound literary merit.

Wagenknecht, Edward. *Mark Twain: The Man and His Work.* 3d ed. Norman: University of Oklahoma Press, 1967. A thorough revision of the 1935 work in which Wagenknecht considers the vast historical and critical study conducted between 1935 and 1960. He has modified many of his original ideas, most notably, that Mark Twain was "The Divine Amateur." The original chapter with that title has been rewritten and renamed "The Man of Letters."

Louis J. Budd
(Revised by *Leslie A. Pearl*)

JOHN UPDIKE

Born: Shillington, Pennsylvania; March 18, 1932

Principal short fiction

The Same Door, 1959; *Pigeon Feathers and Other Stories*, 1962; *Olinger Stories: A Selection*, 1964; *The Music School*, 1966; *Bech: A Book*, 1970; *Museums and Women and Other Stories*, 1972; *Too Far to Go: The Maples Stories*, 1979; *Problems and Other Stories*, 1979; *Bech Is Back*, 1982; *Trust Me*, 1987.

Other literary forms

It would be an understatement to describe John Updike as a prolific and versatile writer. In addition to his short fiction, Updike is an accomplished novelist, perhaps best known for his "Rabbit" tetralogy, but he is also the author of *The Coup* (1978), in which the narrator is writing, in memoirs, the history of an imaginary African nation; *The Centaur* (1963), which fuses myth and realism in middle America; *Couples* (1968), which examines the social and sexual mores of a modern American town; and *Roger's Version* (1986) and *S* (1988), which are a creative reworking of the situation of Nathaniel Hawthorne's *The Scarlet Letter* (1850). Updike has also published more than a dozen books of verse and a play (*Buchanan Dying*, 1974), and he has continued to write reviews and critical essays on literature, music, and painting for about four decades. Beyond this, his tribute to the legendary baseball player Ted Williams, "Hub Fans Bid Kid Adieu," satisfied its subject, who remarked in praise, "It has the mystique."

Achievements

From the beginning of his career as a writer, Updike has demonstrated that he is a brilliant stylist, a master of mood and tone whose linguistic facility is such that it has sometimes overshadowed the dimensions of his vision of existence in the twentieth century. Now that his short fiction has ranged over more than five decades, it is apparent that his treatment of some of the central themes of modern times—sexual and social politics, the nature of intimate relationships, the collapse of traditional values, the uncertainty of the human condition as the twentieth century draws to a close—is as revealing and compelling as that of any of his contemporaries. Although he is still better known as a novelist, the short story may well be his true métier, and his ability to use its compressed structure to generate intensity and to offer succinct insight has made his work a measure of success for writers of short fiction, an evolving example of the possibilities of innovation and invention in a traditional narrative form.

Biography

John Updike was born in 1932, the only child of Wesley Updike, a cable splicer who lost his job in the Depression and had to support his family on a meager teacher's salary ($1,740 per year), and Linda Grace Updike, an aspiring writer. The family moved to Plowville from Shillington, Pennsylvania, in 1945, to live on the farm of Updike's maternal grandparents. Updike recalls that a gift subscription to *The New Yorker*, a Christmas present from an aunt at that time, was a significant moment in his decision to become an artist. In high school, he drew for the school paper, wrote articles and poems, and demonstrated sufficient academic gifts to be awarded a full scholarship to Harvard University, which he entered in 1950.

At college, Updike majored in English, became editor of the prestigious Harvard *Lampoon*, and was graduated with honors in 1954. That same year, *The New Yorker* accepted a poem and a story, an event that Updike remembers as "the ecstatic breakthrough of my literary life." After graduation, Updike and his wife of one year, Mary Pennington, a fine arts major from Radcliffe, spent 1955 in Oxford, where Updike held a Knox Fellowship. When E. B. White offered him a job as a staff writer with *The New Yorker*, Updike accepted and spent the next two years contributing brief, witty pieces to the "Talk of the Town" section at the front of the magazine. During this time, he worked on the manuscript of a six-hundred-page book, which he decided not to publish because it had "too many of the traits of a first novel." When his second child was born, he believed that he needed a different setting in which to live and work (the literary world in New York seemed "unnutritious and interfering") and moved to Ipswich, Massachusetts, where he found "the space" to write "the Pennsylvania thing," which became the novel *The Poorhouse Fair* (1959), and his first collection of short stories, *The Same Door*.

Choosing to work in a rented office in downtown Ipswich, Updike began an extremely active literary career that has continued for several decades. The first book in the Rabbit series, *Rabbit, Run*, was published in 1960, the same year in which the last of Updike's four children was born. *Rabbit, Run* caught the attention of the reading public with its combination of sexual candor and social insight, but *The Centaur* was Updike's first real success with serious critics, winning the National Book Award in 1964. That same year, Updike was elected a member of the National Institute of Arts and Letters, the youngest man to receive the honor at that time. During 1964 and 1965, Updike traveled in Eastern Europe, the source for his first story about Henry Bech ("The Bulgarian Poetess," which won an O. Henry Award), who became a kind of slightly displaced version of himself in the guise of a Jewish writer from New York. Further travels to Africa led to other Bech stories as well as *The Coup*, but Updike generally remained in Ipswich, involved in local affairs, writing constantly, and using the beach to find the sun, which was the only cure at that time for a serious case of psoriasis. The second Rabbit book, *Rabbit Redux*, was published in 1971, and short-story collections appeared regularly. In the late 1960's, Updike sold the screen rights to his novel *Couples* for a half-million dollars (the film has never been produced).

After fifteen years, Updike and his wife ended their marriage, and in 1974 he moved to Boston, returning to the North Shore area in 1976, the year before he married Martha Bernhard. In 1977, Updike published his fourth volume of verse, *Tossing and Turning*, from a major press, and in 1979, two collections of short stories that he had written during the emotional turmoil of the last years of his marriage and its conclusion were issued as *Problems and Other Stories* and *Too Far to Go*. The latter volume included all the stories about a couple named Maples whose lives were a literary transmutation of aspects of Updike's first marriage. *Rabbit Is Rich* (1981) won an American Book Award and a Pulitzer Prize, while *Hugging the Shore* (1983), a nine-hundred-page volume of essays and reviews, won the National Book Critics Circle Award. Updike continued his energetic and inventive career through the 1980's, writing two novels imaginatively derived from Hawthorne's *The Scarlet Letter*, possibly completing the Rabbit series with *Rabbit at Rest* (1990) and collecting another nine hundred pages of essays in *Odd Jobs* (1991). Clearly at the peak of his powers, he remains one of the United States' leading writers.

Analysis

Always eloquent about his aspirations and intentions—as he is about almost everything he observes—John Updike remarked to Charles Thomas Samuels in an interview in 1968 that some of the themes of his work are "domestic fierceness within the middle class, sex and death as riddles for the thinking animal, social existence as sacrifice, unexpected pleasures and rewards, corruption as a kind of evolution," and that his work is "meditation, not pontification." In his short fiction, his meditations have followed an arc of human development from the exuberance of youth to the unsettling revelations of maturity and on toward the uncertainties of old age, a "curve of sad time" (as he ruefully described the years from 1971 to 1978 when his first marriage failed), which contains the range of experience of an extremely incisive, very well-educated, and stylistically brilliant man who has been able to reach beyond the limits of his own interesting life to capture the ethos of an era.

Updike's artistic inclinations were nurtured by his sensitive, supportive parents, who recognized his gifts and his needs, while the struggles of his neighbors in rural Pennsylvania during the Depression left him with a strong sense of the value of community and the basis for communal cohesion in a reliable, loving family. At Harvard, his intellectual capabilities were celebrated and encouraged, and in his first job with *The New Yorker*, his ability to earn a living through his writing endowed his entire existence with an exhilaration that demanded expression in a kind of linguistic rapture. The 1950's marked the steepest incline in time's curve, and his first two collections, *The Same Door* and *Pigeon Feathers and Other Stories*, while primarily covering his youth and adolescence in the town of Shillington (which he calls Olinger), are written from the perspective of the young man who overcame the limitations of an economically strained and culturally depleted milieu to marry happily, begin a family, and capitalize on his talents in the profession that he adored. There is no false sentimentality about Olinger or the narrowness of some its citizens. Updike always saw right through the fakery of the chamber of commerce manipulators who disguised their bigotry and anti-intellectualism with pitches to patriotism, but the young men in these stories often seem destined to overcome whatever obstacles they face to move toward the promise of some artistic or social reward.

In "Flight," a high school senior is forced to relinquish his interest in a classmate because of his mother's pressures and his social status, but the loss is balanced by his initial venture into individual freedom. "The Alligators" depicts a moment of embarrassed misperception, but in the context of the other stories, it is only a temporary setback, an example of awkwardness that might, upon reflection, contribute to the cultivation of a subtler sensibility. "The Happiest I've Been" epitomizes the author's attitude at a pivotal point in his life, poised between the familiar if mundane streets of his childhood and the infinite expanse of a world beyond, enjoying the lingering nostalgia he feels for home ground, which he can carry in memory as he moves on to a wider sphere of experience. These themes are rendered with a particular power in the often-anthologized "A&P" and in "Wife-Wooing," both from *Pigeon Feathers and Other Stories*.

As in many of his most effective stories, Updike has found a voice of singular appropriateness for his narrative consciousness—a boy of nineteen from a working-class background who is working as a checkout clerk at the local A&P grocery store. The store stands for the assembly-line numbness that is a part of the lockstep life that seems to be the likely destiny of all the young men in the town, and it serves as a means of supply for a nearby resort area. When three young women pass the boy's register, he is enchanted by "the queen," a girl who appears "more than pretty," and when she is ordered to dress properly by the store manager on her next visit ("Girls, this isn't the beach"), Sammy feels compelled to deliver a declaration of passionate defense of their innocence. Frustrated by the incipient stodginess and puritanical repression of the entire town and moved by his heart-driven need to make some kind of chivalrous gesture, he finds that his only recourse is to mumble "I quit" as the girls leave the store.

Lengel, the aptly named manager-curmudgeon, speaking for unreasoning minor authority, uses several power trips to maintain his petty tyranny, but Sammy refuses to back down, even when Lengel presents the ultimate guilt ploy, "You don't want to do this to your Mom and Dad." This is an appeal to conformist quiescence, and Sammy, like most of Updike's protagonists, is susceptible to the possibility of hurting or disgracing his family in a small, gossip-ridden community. When Lengel warns him, "You'll feel this for the rest of your life," Sammy recognizes the validity of his threat but realizes that if he backs down now, he will always back down in similar situations. Frightened and uncertain, he finds the resolve to maintain his integrity by carrying through his gesture of defiance. He knows that he will have to accept the consequences of his actions, but this is the true source of his real strength. Acknowledging that now "he felt how hard the world was going to be to me hereafter," his acceptance of the struggle is at the root of his ability to face challenges in the future. As if to ratify his decision, Lengel is described in the last paragraph reduced to Sammy's slot, "checking the sheep through," his visage "dark gray and his back stiff." If the reward for selling out is a life like Lengel's, then even an act that no one but its agent appreciates (the girls never notice their champion) is better than the defeat of submerging the self in the despair of denial.

"Wife-Wooing" is the real reward for acting according to principle. If the A&P is the symbol of enclosure and the girl a figure for the wonder of the cosmos beyond, then marriage to a woman who incarnates the spirit of wonder contains the possibilities for paradise. The mood of ecstasy is established immediately by the narrator's declaration of devotion, "OH MY LOVE. Yes. Here we sit, on warm broad floorboards, before a fire. . . ." He is a man whose marriage, in its initial stages, is informed by what seems like an exponential progression of promise. Thus, although he has "won" his mate, he is impelled to continue to woo her as a testament to his continuing condition of bliss, of his exultation in the sensuality of the body's familiar but still mysterious terrain—its "absolute geography." The evocative description of the couple together—framed in images of light and warmth—is sufficient to convey the delight they share, but what makes the story noteworthy is Updike's employment and investigation of the erotics of language as a register of feeling. The mood of arousal becomes a kind of celebration of the words that describe it, so that it is the "irrefutably magical life language leads with itself" that becomes the substance of erotic interest.

Updike, typically, recalls James Joyce, using Blazes Boylan's word "smackwarm" from "the legendary, imperfectly explored grottoes of *Ulysses*" to let loose a chain of linguistic associations beginning with a consideration of the root etymology of "woman"—the "wide w, the receptive o. Womb." Located in a characteristically masculine perspective (inevitable considering Updike's background and the historical context), the narrator envisions himself as a warrior/hunter in prehistoric times, and in a brilliantly imaginative, affectionate parody of Anglo-Saxon alliterative verse, Updike continues to express the husband's exultation through the kind of linguistic overdrive that makes his mastery of styles the focus of admiration (and envy) of many of his peers. Beneath the wordplay and the almost self-congratulatory cleverness, however, there is still another level of intent. Once the element of erotic power in language itself has been introduced, Updike is free to employ that language in an investigation of sensuality that strains at the bounds of what was acceptable in 1960. His purpose is to examine a marriage at the potentially dangerous seven-year point, to recall the sexual history of the couple, and to show how the lessons of mutual experience have enabled them to deepen their erotic understanding as the marriage progressed. Continuing to use language to chart the erogenous regions of the mind and body, Updike arranges a series of puns ("Oh cunning trick") so that the dual fascination of love—for wife, words—is expressed in intertwined images of passion. The story concludes with the husband leaving for work in the cold stone of a city of "heartless things," then returning to the eternal mystery of woman/wooing, where, as Robert Creeley's poem "The Wife" expresses it, he knows "two women/ and the one/ is tangible substance,/ flesh and bone," while "the other in my mind/ occurs."

Updike's energetic involvement with the dimensions of life—the domestic and the artistic—crested on a curve of satisfaction for him as the 1950's drew to a close. The chaotic explosion of countercultural diversity that took place in the 1960's fractured the comforting coordinates of a world with which Updike had grown very familiar, and he began to find himself in an adversary position both toward the confines of bourgeois social values and toward the sprawling uncertainty of a country in entropic transition. As a means of confronting this situation at a remove that would permit some aesthetic distance from his displeasure, Updike created Henry Bech, an urban, blocked Jewish writer seemingly the polar opposite of the now urbane Updike but actually only a slight transmutation of his own sensibility. Bech is much more successful in managing the perils of the age than Harry Angstrom, who represents Updike's peevish squareness in *Rabbit Redux*, and the "interview" "Bech Meets Me" (November, 1971) is a jovial display of Updike's witty assessment of his problems and goals.

The individual Bech stories, beginning with "The Bulgarian Poetess" (from *The Music School*), which covers Updike's experiences on a trip to Eastern Europe sponsored by the State Department, generally work as separate entities, but they are linked sufficiently that there is a clear progression in *Bech: A Book*, while *Bech Is Back* is closer to a novel than a collection of short fiction. Through the personae of Henry Bech and Rabbit Angstrom, among others, Updike maintained a distinct distance from the political and incipient personal turmoil that he was experiencing. In *The Music School*, the stories include fond recollections of a positive, recent past, as in "The Christian Roommates" (which "preserved" aspects of his Harvard experience), or tentative excursions into the malaise of the times, as in the fascinating dissection of psychoanalytic methods offered by "My Lover Has Dirty Fingernails" and in the unusual venture into the possibilities of renewal in a natural setting of "The Hermit." In this story, the prickly, idiosyncratic spirit of the New England individualist and environmentalist Henry David Thoreau is expressed as an urge to escape from the social realities of *success*—an essentially forlorn quest for a larger sense of life than "they" will permit and an attempt to explore the possibility of a mystical essence beyond the attainment of intellectual power.

While Updike spoke admiringly of the "splendid leafiness" of Pennsylvania and could evoke the mood of Scotland's highland moors (as in "Macbech") with typical facility, his central subject has always been the nature of relationships. In *Museums and Women and Other Stories*, he returned to the consequences of marked changes in the social climate and his personal life that could not be avoided by fictional explorations of subsidiary concerns. The story "When Everyone Was Pregnant" is a paean to an old order passing into history, a celebration of years of relative pleasure and satisfaction that he calls "the Fifties" but which actually encompass the first half of the century. "*My* Fifties," he labels them, positioning himself at the center of a benign cosmos, where tests were passed ("Entered them poor and left them comfortable. Entered them chaste and left them a father") and life was relatively uncomplicated. The paragraphs of the story are like a shorthand list of bounty ("Jobs, houses, spouses of our own"), and the entire era is cast in an aura of innocence, a prelude to a sudden shock of consciousness that utterly changed everything. The factors that caused the shift are never identified, leaving the narrator bewildered ("Now: our babies drive cars, push pot, shave, menstruate, riot for peace, eat macrobiotic"), but the alteration in perception is palpable and its ramifications ("Sarah looks away" after fifteen shared years) unavoidable.

The last section of *Museums and Women and Other Stories* contains five stories under the subhead "The Maples." Updike eventually published all seventeen of the stories about Richard and Joan Maples, a family with four children that might be said to approximate Updike's first marriage, in *Too Far to Go*, and the narrative thread that becomes apparent in the full collection is the transition from optimism and contentment to uncertainty and fracture. A story that registers the process of psychological displacement particularly well is the last one in *Museums and Women and Other Stories*, "Sublimating," in which the Maples have decided to give up sex, which they have mistakenly identified as the "only sore point" in their marriage. Since nearly all that Updike has written on the subject indicates that sex is at the heart of everything that matters in a relationship, the decision—as Updike assumed would be obvious to everyone but the parties involved—was a false solution that could only aggravate the problem. What becomes apparent as the story progresses is that everything in the relationship has become a pretext for disguising true feeling, but the desperation of the participants makes their methods of camouflage sympathetic and understandable.

Unable to accept that change in both parties has permanently altered their position, Richard and Joan repeat strategies that have previously revitalized their marriage, but nothing can be successful, since the actors no longer fit their roles. The procedures of the past cannot be recapitulated, and their efforts produce a series of empty rituals that leave the Maples exhausted and angry. Using external remedies for internal maladies (the purchase of an old farmhouse, impulsive acquisition of trivia), bantering about each other's lovers to reignite passion, turning their children into would-be allies, exchanging barbed, bitchy, and self-regarding comments, the Maples are more baffled than destructive, but both of them are aware that they will eventually have to confront the fact that they have no solution. Sublimation is ultimately suppression of truth, and Richard Maples' description of the people in a pornographic film house on Forty-second Street in Manhattan as perpetual spectators, who watch unseeing while meaningless acts of obscenity occur in the distance, stands as an emblem of stasis and nullity, a corollary to the paralysis that engulfs the couple. Joan Maples' final comment on their current state, a pathetic observation about the "cleansing" aspects of their nonsensual behavior, brings the story to a conclusion that is warped with tension, a situation that Richard Maples' comment, "we may be on to something," does nothing to relieve.

Updike's next collection, *Problems and Other Stories*, contains a prefatory note that begins, "Seven years since my last short story collection? There must have been problems." The central problem has been the end of Updike's first marriage and the removal of the core of certainty that the domestic structure of his family provided. The unraveling of the threads that were woven through a lifetime of intelligent analysis and instinctual response called everything into question and opened a void that had been lurking near the surface of Updike's work. Updike was far too perceptive ever to assume that a stable family was possible for everyone or that it would provide answers for everything. From the start of the Rabbit tetralogy, the strains inherent in an ongoing marital arrangement were examined closely, but the dissolution of his own primary household drew several specific responses that expanded the range and depth of his short fiction. First, the sad facts of the separation and divorce were handled in the last Maples stories.

"Separating" recounts the parents' attempts to explain the situation to their children. It is written in bursts of lacerating dialogue, a conversation wrought in pain and doubt that concludes with a child posing the tormenting, unanswerable query "*Why?*" to Richard Maples. "Here Come the Maples" presents the ceremony of the divorce as a reverse marriage, complete with programmed statements forcing the couple to agree by saying "I do." The jaunty tone of the proceedings does not totally mask the looming cloud of uncertainty that covers the future. Then, the artist turned toward his work for sustenance. In "From the Journal of a Leper," Updike projects his psychic condition into the life of a potter who is afflicted with a serious skin disease akin to his own. The fear of leprosy stands for all of his doubts before an unknown universe no longer relatively benign; his work provides some compensation but is intricately connected to his psychological stability; a woman with whom he is developing a relationship improves and complicates the situation. The story is open-ended, but in a forecast of the direction Updike has begun to chart for his protagonists, the artist recognizes the necessity of standing alone, dependent ultimately on his own strength. The final words may be more of a self-directed exhortation than a summary of actuality, but they represent a discernible goal: "I am free, as other men. I am whole."

The difficulties of freedom and the elusiveness of wholeness are explored in "Transaction," one of Updike's most powerful stories. In *The Paris Review* interview with Charles Thomas Samuels, Updike said:

> About sex in general, by all means let's have it in fiction, as detailed as needs be, but real, real in its social and psychological connections. Let's take coitus out of the closet and off the altar and put it on the continuum of human behavior.

The transaction of the title involves a man in his middle years, married but alone in a city labeled "N——," in December at a conference, who somewhat impulsively picks up a prostitute and takes her to his hotel room. What exactly he is seeking is not entirely clear, because the cold, mechanical city and the "raffish army of females" occupying the streets are as much threat as promise and his temporary liberty to act as he chooses is undercut by his feelings of isolation and loneliness. Regarding his actions as a version of an exploratory adventure in which he is curious about how he will react and tempted not only by lust but also by the desire to test his virility and validity in establishing a human connection with the girl, he is moving into unknown country, where his usual persuasive strategies have no relevance. The "odorless metal" of the room mocks his efforts to re-create the warmth of a home in an anonymous city, and the false bravado of other men around him reminds him of the insecurity that lies beneath the bluster. Even what he calls the "paid moral agent" of his imagination—that is, his mostly vestigial conscience—is summoned briefly only as a source of comforting certainty in the uncharted, shifting landscape he has entered.

His initial investment in the room and in purchasing some aspect of the girl's time does not permit him to exercise any influence on their transaction, a reminder that his generally successful life (marriage, money, status) counts for less than he had thought. The language of commerce that he has mastered does not contain a vocabulary for expressing his current feelings. Ruled by old habits, the preliminary stages of the transaction are a capsule courtship, but he finds that his solicitations are subject to scorn or rebuke. The girl wavers in his imagination between alluring innocence and forbidding authority, an amalgam of a dream lover who accepts him and an indifferent critic who reinforces the mechanical motif by calling his genitals "them" and prepares for their assignation "with the deliberateness of an insult or the routine of marriage." Although Updike uses his extensive abilities of description to render the physical attributes of the girl in vivid detail, she does not seem sexually attractive—an implicit comment on the failure of erotic potential when it is restricted to the external surface, as well as a subtle dig at the magazine *Oui* (a *Playboy* clone), where the story originally appeared. Without the spontaneity of mutual discovery, the transaction becomes clinical and antierotic, an unnatural or perverse use of human capability.

The man is aware of the inadequacy of his supplications. He has been using the strategies of commerce—a mix of supposedly ingratiating self-pity and cold calculation—and when these fail he tries false compliance, then bogus amiability. In desperation, because of a severe reduction in sexual potence, he begins to "make love" to her, and in a shift in tone that Updike handles with characteristic smoothness, the writing becomes lyrical as the man becomes fully involved, and the woman finally responds freely and openly. Old habits intrude, however, and the man's heightened virility causes a reversion to his familiar self. He stops producing pleasure and seeks it again as his due. His excitement has been transformed from authentic passion to calculation, the transaction back on its original terms. Both parties to the agreement have reached a level of satisfaction (he is a successful sexual athlete, and she has met the terms of the contract), and when she offers to alter the original bargain in a mixture of self-interest and genuine generosity, he is unable to make a further break away from a lifetime of monetary measure. He contents himself with small gestures of quasi gallantry that carry things back toward the original situation of customer and salesperson. Thus, the true cost of real freedom is gradually becoming apparent. He feels an urge to go beyond the transactional to the honestly emotional, but he is hindered by fear, and his instincts are frozen. The residue of the encounter is a dreadful shrinking of his sense of the universe. "She had made sex finite," he thinks, but in actuality, it is only his cramped view of his own possibilities that he sees.

"Transaction" is the beginning of a phase of maturity in Updike's work in which recollection of an earlier time of certitude, confidence, and optimism is still possible, but in which a search for new modes of meaning is gradually taking precedence. "Deaths of Distant Friends," from *Trust Me*, which appeared in an anthology of *Best American Short Stories*, is a finely wrought philosophical meditation—exactly the sort of story cautious anthologists often include, a minor-key minirequiem for a grand past with only a twist of rue at the conclusion to relieve the sentimental mood. "The Egg Race," from *Problems and Other Stories*, is somewhat more severe in its recollection of the past. Here, the origins of the problems of the present are traced with some tolerance of human need back to the narrator's father. The title story, "Trust Me," is closer to the mood of middle-life angst that informs many of the stories. Again, the narrator reconsiders the past in an effort to determine the cause of the emptiness of the present, but in his attempts to explain the failure of faith in his life, he reveals (to himself) that his parents did not trust each other, that his first wife did not trust the modern world, that his child did not trust him, that with his girlfriend he does not trust himself, and that with a psychotropic agent, he does not (or cannot) trust his senses so he ultimately cannot trust his perceptions. Logically, then, he cannot know, with surety, anything at all. His predicament is a part of a larger vision of loss that directs many stories in the volume, as Updike's characters attempt to cope with a deterioration of faith that revives some of the earlier questions of a religious nature that formed an important dimension of Updike's writing in books such as *The Poorhouse Fair* or *A Month of Sundays* (1975). The situation has changed somewhat, though, since the more traditional religious foundations that Updike seemed to trust earlier have become less specifically viable, even if the theological questions they posed still are important. The newfound or sensed freedom that is glimpsed carries a terrifying burden of singularity.

"Slippage" conveys this feeling through its metaphors of structural fragility. A "not quite slight earthquake" awakens a man who is "nauseated without knowing why." His wife, a much younger woman, is hidden under the covers, "like something dead on the road," an image of nullity. Blessed or cursed with a memory that "extended so much further back in time than hers," he feels she is preparing them prematurely for senility. At sixty, he sees his life as a series of not-quite-achieved plateaus. His work as a scholar was adequate but not all that it might have been, and his "late-capitalist liberal humanism" now seems passé. Even his delight in the sensual has been shaken, "though only thrice wed." Updike depicts him in his confusion as "a flake of consciousness lost within time's black shale" and extends the metaphor of infirmity to a loose molar and a feeling that his children are "a tiny, hard, slightly shrivelled core of disappointment." In the story's denouement, the man meets a woman at a party; she excites him, but it turns out that she is "quite mad," an ultimate betrayal of his instincts. At the close, he lies in bed again, anticipating another earth tremor and feeling its unsettling touch in his imagination.

The aura of discouragement that "Slippage" projects is balanced by another of Updike's most forceful stories, "The City" (also from *Trust Me*). Recalling both "Transaction" with its portrayal of a business traveler alone in an urban wasteland and several later stories in which illness or disease disarms a man, "The City" places Carson—a "victim of middle-aged restlessness—the children grown, the long descent begun"—in a hospital, where he must face a battery of tests to determine the cause of a vague stomach pain. Confronted by doctors, nurses, orderlies, other patients, and fellow sufferers, none of whom he knows, Carson is alone and helpless in an alien environment. The hospital works as a fitting figure for the absurdity and complexity of the postmodern world. The health professionals seem like another species, and Carson's physical pain is a symbol of his spiritual discomfort as he proceeds with the useless repetition of his life's requirements. From the nadir of a debilitating operation, Carson begins to overcome the indignity and unreality of his plight. He becomes fascinated with people who are unknown to him, like a beautiful black nurse whose unfathomable beauty expands the boundaries of his realm. He calls upon his lifelong training as a stoic WASP and determines not to make a fuss about his difficulties. He finds his "curiosity about the city revived" and develops a camaraderie with other patients, a community of the wounded. His removal from the flow of business life—he is a computer parts salesman fluent in techno-babble—helps him regain an ironic perspective that enables him to regard his estranged daughter's ignorance of his crisis as "considerate and loving" because it contributes to the "essential solitude" he now enjoys. In a poetic excursion into Carson's mind, Updike illustrates the tremendous satisfaction available to a person with an artistic imagination capable of finding meaning in any pattern of life's variety. Carson makes the necessary leap of faith required to "take again into himself the miracle of the world" and seizes his destiny from a mechanized, indifferent cosmos. In a reversal of the curve of decline that has been the trajectory of Updike's thought since the problems of the early 1970's, Carson is depicted at the end of "The City" as a version of existential man who can, even amid doubt and uncertainty, find a way to be "free" and "whole"—at least as much as the postmodern world permits.

Other major works

NOVELS: *The Poorhouse Fair*, 1959; *Rabbit, Run*, 1960; *The Centaur*, 1963; *Of the Farm*, 1965; *Couples*, 1968; *Rabbit Redux*, 1971; *A Month of Sundays*, 1975; *Marry Me: A Romance*, 1976; *The Coup*, 1978; *Rabbit Is Rich*, 1981; *The Witches of Eastwick*, 1984; *Roger's Version*, 1986; *S*, 1988; *Rabbit at Rest*, 1990.

PLAYS: *Three Texts from Early Ipswich: A Pageant*, 1968; *Buchanan Dying*, 1974.

POETRY: *The Carpented Hen, and Other Tame Creatures*, 1958; *Telephone Poles and Other Poems*, 1963; *Verse*, 1965; *Midpoint and Other Poems*, 1969; *Tossing and Turning*, 1977; *Facing Nature*, 1985.

NONFICTION: *Assorted Prose*, 1965; *Picked-Up Pieces*, 1975; *Hugging the Shore: Essays and Criticism*, 1983; *Self-Consciousness*, 1989; *Just Looking: Essays on Art*, 1989; *Odd Jobs: Essays and Criticism*, 1991.

Bibliography

Detweiler, Robert. *John Updike.* Boston: Twayne, 1984. Within the confines of the Twayne series format, Detweiler supplies sound, thorough analysis of all Updike's work through the mid-1980's and provides a brief biography and a useful, annotated bibliography.

Greiner, Donald J. *The Other John Updike: Poems, Short Stories, Prose, Play.* Athens: Ohio University Press, 1981. While devoting a considerable amount of space to other critics, Greiner, who has written three books about Updike, here traces Updike's artistic development in his writing that both parallels and extends the themes of the novels.

Hunt, George W. *John Updike and the Three Secret Things: Sex, Religion, and Art.* Grand Rapids, Mich.: Wm. B. Eerdmans, 1980. An accurate and perceptive (if a bit scholarly in style) examination of the evolution of Updike's thematic focus. Hunt combines psychoanalytical (Jungian), New Critical, and theological approaches in his thesis that Updike's primary concern has changed in emphasis through his career.

Macnaughton, William R., ed. *Critical Essays on John Updike.* Boston: G. K. Hall, 1982. A comprehensive, eclectic collection, including essays by writers such as Alfred Kazin, Anthony Burgess, and Joyce Carol Oates, who provide reviews, and various Updike experts who have written original essays. Contains a survey of bibliographies and an assessment of criticism and scholarship.

Newman, Judie. *John Updike.* New York: St. Martin's Press, 1988. A part of the Modern Novelists series, Newman covers the long fiction with facility and insight and offers a solid foundation for understanding Updike's primary concerns throughout his writing. Contains a good, comprehensive introduction and a judicious bibliography.

Tallent, Elizabeth. *Married Men and Magic Tricks: John Updike's Erotic Heroes.* Berkeley, Calif.: Creative Arts, 1982. Offers, in Judie Newman's words, "a groundbreaking exploration of the erotic dimensions of selected works." A long-needed analysis that includes a feminist perspective missing from much previous Updike criticism.

Leon Lewis

GIOVANNI VERGA

Born: Catania, Sicily; September 2, 1840
Died: Catania, Sicily; January 27, 1922

Principal short fiction

Primavera ed altri racconti, 1876; *Vita dei campi*, 1880 (*Under the Shadow of Etna*, 1896); *Novelle rusticane*, 1883 (*Little Novels of Sicily*, 1925); *Per le vie*, 1883; *Vagabondaggio*, 1887; *I ricordi del capitano D'Arce*, 1891; *Don Candeloro e Cia.*, 1894; *Del tuo al mio*, 1905 (adaptation of his play); *Cavalleria Rusticana and Other Stories*, 1926; *The She-Wolf and Other Stories*, 1958.

Other literary forms

The published works of Giovanni Verga are of only two kinds, fiction and drama. Since he considered his primary vocation to be that of novelist, all of his earliest publications are novels. His first play, written when he was twenty-nine, was never produced and remained unpublished until after his death. Eventually he wrote seven plays, all of them derived from his own works of fiction. He first turned to short fiction with a relatively lengthy story called *Nedda*. It was long enough, at any rate, to be accorded separate publication in a tiny volume in 1874 but was clearly not of standard novel length. This publication is generally regarded as the start of his interest in the short story as a literary form.

Two years later he published his first collection of short stories, and that volume also included the previously published *Nedda*. Thereafter, he practiced this new literary form assiduously enough to make his short stories as important a part of his total achievement as were his novels. Verga is a rarity among writers of fiction in that he published no poetry—not even in his youth—and no literary criticism or travel books. Aside from his novels, short stories, and plays, only selections from his personal letters have ever appeared in print.

Achievements

As a socially conscious writer, Verga is considered the most determined spokesman of the conditions in which the poor of his native Sicily lived. A master writer of novels and short stories and the leader of an innovative literary current known as *Verismo*, Verga in his works explored the struggle of humankind to survive in adverse circumstances. He emphasized the importance of family, work, and basic moral and religious values, and he focused on the fundamental role these values play in overcoming difficult times. To enrich his highly humanitarian themes, Verga developed an intense dramatic expression characterized by detailed descriptive features and original linguistic solutions. Along with being widely recognized as one of the best Italian writers, Verga was bestowed with several official honors by the Italian government, while his works continue to endure lasting success as modern classics.

Biography

The city of Catania, where Giovanni Verga spent the first twenty-five years of his life, was a cultural center for Sicily and even possessed a university; but it was geographically so remote from the mainstream of Italy's cultural life and so small a place, that its atmosphere was nevertheless provincial and in some ways even primitive. Verga's family were well-to-do landowners in a society that was agricultural at its base and still feudal in its organization. Verga was fortunate in his schooling to have come under the influence of a teacher who was a writer and who also encouraged his literary bent; at the age of seventeen, Verga completed his first novel. Although he embarked on the study of law a year later, he quickly found he had no taste for the subject and dropped out of the university to pursue a literary career. He tried founding a journal and published a novel at his own expense, but Catania proved an impossible base from which to launch a literary career. In 1865, he went to Florence, where he became part of a circle of young writers, and a few years later he moved to Milan, which was even more active as a center of the arts.

During the 1870's, Verga was living in Milan, publishing novels and short stories, winning a small reputation, and seeking a new literary voice for himself which would express his ideal of what fiction should be. Because of illness in his family, he made frequent trips back to Catania during that period. From these factors emerged the Verga who would be recognized as one of Europe's master storytellers. The decision to write about his native Sicily, and the development of a new, disciplined style, produced in quick succession the short-story collection *Under the Shadow of Etna* in 1880 and the novel *I Malavoglia* (1881; *The House by the Medlar Tree*, 1890). Both volumes won quick recognition as masterpieces and inaugurated the most productive decade of Verga's career, when he was at the height of his powers and acknowledged as the leader of the new literary aesthetic called *Verismo*, an Italian version of the realism and naturalism which dominated the writing of fiction everywhere in Europe during the second half of the nineteenth century.

Verga's success in the 1880's failed to make him happy. His basic view of life was pessimistic, he was always something of a loner, and while he pursued many love affairs, he always avoided marriage. He grew restless and discontent with life in a great literary center, found himself spending more and more time in his native region, and by 1894 had resettled permanently in Catania. His literary output slowed to a trickle thereafter, and he lived out his years in quiet isolation. His eightieth birthday was officially celebrated in 1920, and honors were bestowed upon him by the Italian government, but he disdained to participate in any of the public ceremonies. He died two years later of a cerebral hemorrhage.

Analysis

Giovanni Verga's first experiments with the short-story form in the 1870's were quite conventional in theme and offered no originality of form or technique. At best, critics have discerned in this work the struggles of a writer in a period of crisis seeking a new basis for his art. The publication of the group of stories about Sicily, under the title *Under the Shadow of Etna*, demonstrated that he had found that new basis. For these stories he developed a new literary language and a new style: description and rhetoric were reduced to the barest minimum possible, and characters and action were portrayed in terse, nervous prose which was more impressionistic notation than precise narrative, and which often reproduced, as direct or indirect discourse, the speech patterns of the characters themselves.

The most renowned of these stories, "Cavalleria rusticana" ("Rustic Chivalry"), exemplifies this new style fully. The opening paragraph informs the reader that the story's hero, Turiddu Macca, having completed his military service, is trying unsuccessfully to attract the attention of his former beloved, Lola, by peacocklike antics in the public square. When he learns that she has betrothed herself to another during his absence, Turiddu swears that he will destroy his rival, and Verga makes this known to the reader by switching in midsentence to implied indirect discourse, in which Turiddu's own characteristic language, including curses, is abruptly intruded into a normal third-person narrative sentence: "When Turiddu first got to hear of it, oh, the devil! he raved and swore!—he'd rip his guts out for him, he'd rip 'em out for him, that Licodia fellow!" (Although D. H. Lawrence's translation is less than accurate, it nevertheless conveys the effect of the mixed narrative mode well enough.) A few paragraphs later Verga reports a direct conversation between Turiddu and Lola, and their words include local proverbial expressions, coarse language, and rough, ungrammatical constructions—all designed to communicate impressionistically but with great economy of means the nature of the characters and of their world.

Brevity and suggestion are the keynotes of Verga's prose style. Much is left unsaid, and transitions are abrupt, unelaborated, and unexplained. Thus, after the early conversation between Turiddu and Lola, Verga quickly states that Lola married the man from Licodia, and Turiddu swore he would get even "right under her eyes, the dirty bitch" (in Giovanni Cecchetti's much more accurate translation). Without the least probing of psychological motives, Verga then recounts Turiddu's cruel courtship of a girl named Santa, who lives across the street from Lola's house, to arouse Lola's jealousy and the abrupt success of the maneuver when Lola invites Turiddu to become her lover. Swiftly and relentlessly, the action moves to its inevitable climax; there is always a minimum of explanation or analysis from the narrator and as much as possible through the vehicle of direct or reported speech by the four principal characters. The jilted Santa tells Lola's husband, Alfio, that he has been cuckolded by Turiddu. In accordance with the crude customs of local "chivalry," Alfio challenges Turiddu to a "duel" to the death, with clasp knives. The violent fight is rapidly and vividly recounted in half a page, much of it dialogue, at the end of which Alfio is seriously wounded, and Turiddu is dead, having lost the fight when Alfio suddenly threw dirt in his face, blinding him. The ironic intention in the title of the story becomes especially clear in this last circumstance: in a primitive Sicilian village, the savage, violent, animalistic resolution of an "affair of honor" provides a mocking parody of the aristocratic traditions of chivalry. The Sicilian behavior is not admirable, but it is instinctive and entirely natural, compared to the ritualistic and artificial modes of chivalry.

Verga's grasp of the essentially instinctive nature of Sicilian peasant behavior is even more starkly presented in "La Lupa" ("The She-Wolf"). The title figure in this narrative is a middle-aged peasant woman of imperious sexuality who makes a sexual slave of her own son-in-law, as though she has cast a spell over him that he is incapable of resisting, in spite of his revulsion and hatred of her. The role of primitive superstition in the relationship is emphasized by Verga's incantatory repetition of the proverbial phrase, *fra vespero e nona* ("between the hours of nones and vespers"), that time of the most intense heat in the late afternoon, when all work stops, and when Pina, the she-wolf, would come to the threshing-floor to make love with her son-in-law. The story concludes with the unforgettable vision of the son-in-law, desperate to be rid of her torment, advancing on his mother-in-law with an axe, while she unflinchingly strides toward her death, holding a bouquet of red poppies, and devouring him with her black eyes. Both are the victims of uncontrollable instinct, beyond the reach of reason, and in the story's final moment, both acquire a kind of grim, tragic heroism.

Superstition and the dark force of instinct dominate most of the stories in *Under the Shadow of Etna*. In "L'amante di Gramigna" ("Gramigna's Mistress"), for example, the story concerns a girl of good family who suddenly abandons her respectable life to follow the notorious bandit, Gramigna, because he seems to her to embody her ideal of manhood. In "Rosso Malpelo" (the title is the nickname of the hero and means "the redheaded evil-haired one"), a young boy's character and fate are inevitably shaped by the local superstition that people born with red hair are evil and must be ostracized. Perhaps the greatest accomplishment of Verga's new style of writing in *Under the Shadow of Etna* was the immediacy with which he was able to plunge his readers into the violent emotional atmosphere of the Sicilian social system. By Verga's technique, the reader experiences this unfamiliar but fascinating world as directly as possible and with almost unnoticed mediation from the narrator.

Similar themes and similar techniques marked the new collection of short stories which Verga published three years after *Under the Shadow of Etna* under the title *Little Novels of Sicily*. Again he dealt with the raw passions of the Sicilian peasants, although now with a diminished sense of their heroism and with a heightened sense of the bitterness of their lives. The best-known story in this collection, "La roba" ("Property"), analyzes an instance of obsessive behavior in a man who has, in an exaggerated form, the traditional and instinctive peasant attachment to the land. Mazzarò has devoted all of his energy and all of his means to the acquisition of land, denying himself any pleasure or indulgence in this single-minded pursuit which has dominated his whole life. The impressive opening paragraph outlines the astonishing expanse of property which had come under Mazzarò's ownership by his middle years, and the story goes on to explore, from within, the compulsions and obsessive drives which overwhelm Mazzarò's reason and his humanity, turning him into nothing more than an acquisitive machine. The story concludes, as it must, with the vision of desperation in Mazzarò when he finally realizes that his death is close and that he will have to give up his property which has been so painfully accumulated. He reels crazily about his own courtyard, killing his ducks and turkeys, and screaming: "Roba mia, vientene con me!" ("My property, come with me!").

Verga applied the same techniques to urban themes in a collection of stories about Milan, entitled *Per le vie*. Critics generally have considered these stories somewhat less intense and therefore less effective than the Sicilian stories, but such a tale as "L'Ultima giornata" ("The Last Day") is surely in no way artistically inferior to "Rustic Chivalry" or to "The She-Wolf." It tells the story of the last hours of a vagabond who, in desperation, ends his hopeless life by throwing himself under the wheels of a train. The technical brilliance of the story lies in its indirection: it begins with an account of some well-to-do train passengers whose enjoyment is disturbed by a bump just as the train is passing through the outskirts of Milan; the next day, the newspapers report that a dead body has been found on the tracks, and soon the police investigate, following the few clues and tracking down witnesses so that a proper report can be filed on whether or not a murder for money had been involved since the victim's pockets have been found empty. The gradual unfolding of the victim's desperate plight is accomplished by the perfunctory efforts of the police, ironically operating on the wrong assumption, and in this way the final day of the suicide's life is reconstructed, clue by pathetic clue, for the reader. The story concludes with glimpses of the way various people react to "the day's suicide," demonstrating how little their lives are really touched by the event and emphasizing the melancholy truth that life goes grimly and obliviously on.

In the decade after 1883, Verga wrote more short stories; although some of them are fine, most of them mark a decline in his creative powers. By 1894, when he returned to live in isolation in Catania, his work as a short-story writer was virtually complete. In about fifteen years of peak productivity, however, Verga had truly created the art of the modern short story in Italy and had left as his legacy nearly two dozen stories of the highest excellence, as well as another two dozen or more stories of lesser quality, as models for his successors. In doing so, Verga renewed and brought up to the artistic standards of modernity a literary tradition that had been dormant in Italy since its distinguished beginnings with Giovanni Boccaccio in the fourteenth century.

Other major works

NOVELS: *I carbonari della montagna*, 1861-1862; *Sulle lagune*, 1863 (serial), 1975 (book); *Una peccatrice*, 1866; *Storia di una capinera*, 1871; *Eva*, 1873; *Eros*, 1874; *Tigre reale*, 1875; *I Malavoglia*, 1881 (*The House by the Medlar Tree*, partial translation 1890, 1953, complete translation 1964); *Il marito di Elena*, 1882; *Mastro-don Gesualdo*, 1889 (English translation, 1893, 1923); *Dal tuo al mio*, 1906.

PLAYS: *Cavalleria rusticana*, 1884 (based on his short story; *Cavalleria Rusticana: Nine Scenes from the Life of the People*, 1893); *In portineria*, 1884 (based on his short story "Il canario del N. 15"); *La Lupa*, 1896 (based on his short story); *La caccia al lupo*, 1901 (based on his short story; *The Wolf Hunt*, 1921); *La caccia alla volpe*, 1901; *Dal tuo al mio*, 1903; *Teatro*, 1912; *Rose caduche*, 1928.

NONFICTION: *Lettere al suo traduttore*, 1954; *Lettere a Dina*, 1962, 1971; *Lettere a Luigi Capuana*, 1975.

Bibliography

Bergin, Thomas Goddard. *Giovanni Verga*. New Haven, Conn.: Yale University Press, 1931. A well-organized study that traces a definite line of development from Verga's first published work to his last. Includes a useful bibliography and an informative commentary on Verga's style.

Cecchetti, Giovanni. *Giovanni Verga*. Boston: Twayne, 1978. An extensive study on Giovanni Verga and his work. Provides an overview of the most complex characteristics of the author.

_____. Introduction to *The She-Wolf and Other Stories*, by Giovanni Verga. Berkeley: University of California Press, 1958. This volume contains the best of Verga's short fiction available in translation. The book is divided in two parts, with selections of stories from Verga's early and late period. Cechetti emphasizes that this translation was made "as literal as possible" in order to "render the spirit as well as the letter of the original." The translator has made every effort to "convey Verga's style and the rhythm of his sentences."

Lane, Eric. Introduction to *Short Sicilian Novels*, by Giovanni Verga, translated by D. H. Lawrence. London: Daedalus Books, 1984. Lane's introduction provides the reader with an accurate historical overview and with perspicacious critical observations. The three-page chronology proves to be useful and informative and one of the best ever compiled on Verga. Lawrence's translation is by far the best-known and can be considered a commendable attempt to render Verga into English.

Patruno, Nicholas. *Language in Giovanni Verga's Early Novels*. Chapel Hill: University of North Carolina Press, 1977. An excellent study that examines, analyzes, and determines the linguistic norm of the early works of Giovanni Verga, namely *Una peccatrice*, *Eva*, *Tigre reale*, and *Eros*. Particular attention is given to Verga's Florentine period, between 1866 and 1875. This work comprises a historical introduction and an explanation of phonology and lexicon used by Verga in his early novels.

Murray Sachs
(Revised by *Rosaria Pipia*)

VERGIL
Publius Vergilius Maro

Born: Andes, near Mantua, Italy; October 15, 70 B.C.
Died: Brundisium (now Brindisi), Italy; September 21, 19 B.C.

Principal short fiction

Eclogae, 43-37 B.C. (*Eclogues*, 1575); *Georgics*, c. 37-29 B.C. (English translation, 1589); *Aeneid*, c. 29-19 B.C. (English translation, 1553).

Other literary forms

There are several minor poems attributed with varying degrees of cogency to Vergil. Among these are the *Culex* (c. 50 B.C.; *The Gnat*, 1916), *Ciris* (c. 50 B.C.; the seabird), and *Aetna* (c. 50 B.C.).

Achievements

More than any other poet of his age, Vergil adopted traditional Greek forms of poetry and adapted them to the Roman spirit. His *Eclogues* were inspired by the *Idylls* of Theocritus (third century B.C.), although they included allusions to real persons and events that would have been familiar to Vergil's audience. The *Georgics* transformed the style of didactic poetry seen in the works of Hesiod and Aratus into an idealization of the Italian landscape and rustic way of life; unlike earlier didactic poetry, the *Georgics* provides less practical instruction and more celebration of agriculture and the Roman farmer. The *Aeneid* contains many scenes and images inspired by the *Iliad* and the *Odyssey* but focuses upon a hero who embodies the ideals of Augustan Rome.

In addition, Vergil's poetry imbued traditional literary forms with the author's own devotion to the Roman virtues of *humanitas* (compassion for humanity) and *pietas* (sense of duty). Because of the influence of Vergil's works, especially the *Aeneid*, upon later periods, these virtues have become part of the entire Western literary tradition.

Vergil also interpreted, in a fictional and symbolic form, the most important moment in the history of ancient Rome: the transformation, under Augustus, of the Republic into the Empire. Vergil's Aeneas is, in many ways, an idealized image of the emperor Augustus himself. The view that later ages would have of Rome's first emperor was thus largely determined by Vergil's depiction of Rome's founder. Moreover, the *Aeneid* is also a profoundly patriotic poem, illustrating the belief of Vergil and Augustus that the founding of Rome fulfilled the will of the gods.

Biography

Vergil (Publius Vergilius Maro) was born near Mantua in Northern Italy in what was then Cis-alpine Gaul on October 15, 70 B.C. His father's name is of Etruscan origin, a fact of some modest significance, perhaps, in one's understanding of the

Italian wars depicted in the *Aeneid*. His boyhood was spent in relatively simple surroundings, but when he reached fifteen (putting on the toga virilis on the day that his greatest Latin predecessor, Lucretius, is said to have died), he went to Milan and then Rome to study rhetoric (a journey passed in reverse direction by St. Augustine four centuries later). His public career was limited and unsuccessful, however, for philosophy and science were his true interests. He joined the cultural circle of the Epicurean philosopher, Siro, near Naples (it is important to note that the *Aeneid* in large measure supports the Stoic, not the Epicurean, view of life). The influence of other prominent Romans not only made amends for the confiscation of his family's land following the Battle of Philippi (43 B.C.) but also introduced the poet, already in the midst of the composition of the *Eclogues*, to Octavian, the heir of Caesar, eventually to be called Caesar Augustus. Following the advice of Maecenas, the eponymous archetype of enlightened patronage, Vergil began the *Georgics*, a work which took seven years to complete, chiefly because of the care with which he composed, producing some lines in the morning and reducing them to a small number of perfected verses by the end of the day. Having celebrated first pastoral and then agricultural life, Vergil turned with the active encouragement of Octavian to the active life of the hero. The *Aeneid* slowly developed (with books 2, 4, and 6 the first to be completed) but it was never finished as Vergil hoped; he died with the request that the partly imperfect epic should be burned, but his executors and Augustus himself overrode his last wish and a central text of the Western imagination was thus preserved.

Analysis

The *Aeneid* of Vergil is an epic poem combining historical and mythical elements in twelve books celebrating the origin and destiny of the Roman people. It owes much to Homer, something to Apollonius Rhodius, and even something to the first Latin epic writer, Ennius. At the heart of the poem is a success story made poignant by the careful delineation of the great price of that success. Indeed, it is precisely this sense of loss which hovers over the successful plot line which makes the *Aeneid* a more richly ambiguous poem than its predecessors and all of its successors save *Paradise Lost* (1667).

In outline, the *Aeneid* tells the story of a Trojan prince Aeneas, the son of the goddess Venus and the mortal Anchises, from the time he leaves the burning city of Troy to his conquest on the site of the new Troy in Italy. In between he has many adventures, endures several temptations, displays little variety in personality, but emerges with a character experienced in Stoic fashion and representative or emblematic of the ideal Roman leader—in fact, not unlike Augustus, putatively descended from Trojan ancestors, as he seemed to some.

Book 1 begins as epic poems should, *in medias res*, with the storm-tossed Trojans and their captain Aeneas driven onto the coast of North Africa not far from Carthage. The storm was prompted by Juno, ever hostile to the Trojans from the time Paris, the Trojan prince, had made his famous judgment in favor of Venus, not Juno or Minerva (to continue the Latin names); but Venus in disguise provides her son with helpful background information. He enters Carthage and sees in the newly constructed temple painted scenes of the now-famous struggles of Achilles, Priam, Hector, and even himself. He meets the Carthaginian Queen Dido, who is hospitable to the wandering Trojans, chiefly because she has known what it is to suffer as a refugee. Indeed, her statement which has moved countless readers, moved especially another sufferer and student of suffering, Sigmund Freud, who kept her lines on his desk ("My own acquaintance with misfortune has been teaching me to help others who are in distress"). Dido orders a celebratory banquet and, already smitten with love for Aeneas, asks him to tell the entire story of the fall of Troy.

Book 2 is Aeneas' narrative of the destruction of Troy in which ruin he lost his wife, Creusa, and with difficulty persuaded his father, Anchises, to flee along with Aeneas and his son, Ascanius (also called Iulus). This book has firmly imprinted itself in the Western imagination. Among the most vivid episodes are Sinon's treachery; the death of Laocoon and his sons; the murder of Priam by Pyrrhus (see William Shakespeare's *Hamlet*, 1600-1601); the appeal of Creusa and the flaming sign about the head of little Ascanius; and most especially, Aeneas carrying his aged father, a necessary link with the Trojan past, and holding in his right hand little Ascanius, the necessary link with the future, struggling to keep up with his short steps to the strides of his heroic father. Meanwhile the wife, Creusa, significantly follows behind this trio of males and finally is lost in the flames of Troy. It is Creusa whose death frees Aeneas to meet the temptation of Dido and the opportunity of Lavinia, and whose ghost assures Aeneas that all is for the best as the gods have ordered it and that happiness and a kingdom await him in the West.

Book 3 continues Aeneas' tale of his wanderings, and along with book 10 shows most the signs that Vergil would have revised or polished it if he had lived. Among the adventures are the meeting with Andromache, the widow of Hector, another of the grieving women in this masculine world; the advice of the seer Helenus to look for the huge white sow with its thirty young as a sign guaranteeing the proper place for the founding of the new Troy; the counsel to avoid Scylla and Charybdis; the description and appearance of Polyphemus; and finally, the death of Anchises in Sicily, the last landfall before the arrival in Carthage.

Book 4, the most humanly moving, the most romantic, the saddest, and the most Vergilian segment of the poem, involves the love and death of Dido. Vergil's presentation with sympathetic understanding of the defeated moved Augustine to tears, reduced Aeneas in the eyes of readers immemorial to a mere instrument of the gods rather than a feeling human being, and tempted Milton to repeat the story in the form of Adam and Eve with an antithetical resolution. Like John Milton after him, Vergil had some difficulty in succeeding with the tactic of criticizing by authorial statement the all-too-moving conduct he depicts. The image of Rumor is especially memorable, but even it pales in comparison to the final lamentation and suicide of Dido, betrayed by Aeneas and destiny.

Book 5 is a relaxation between the two most powerful books, 4 and 6; its funeral games are a more morally sophisticated version of the games in book 23 of the *Iliad* (c. 800 B.C.). Although there is a relaxation in narrative tension, symbolic significance remains high, for the book is framed by two deaths. It opens with Aeneas, as his fleet heads for Sicily, looking backward at the walls of Troy which reflect the flames from Dido's funeral pyre, and it ends with the sacrificial death by drowning of the Trojan helmsman Palinurus. Both Dido and to a lesser degree Palinurus represent the cost in human terms of political obligation. Of the several events in the funeral games themselves, the most memorable is the boxing match between the huge braggart Dares and the old champion Entellus, whose initial humiliation and ultimate regeneration reveal in small the fortunes of the Trojans in large. The psychological understanding and symbolic patterning show Vergil at his best. This book and this episode are important influences upon the imagery, structure, and theme of Milton's drama, *Samson Agonistes* (1671).

Book 6, with Aeneas' descent into the underworld guided by the Sibyl, is the greatest of the books of the poem in terms of vision and poignancy. The obstacles and dangers which Aeneas avoids in the underworld are another version of the hurdles he has had to clear throughout his career presented in the first five books. Among the memorable scenes are Palinurus with his appeal for a proper burial, and Dido, marble cold in her scorn of Aeneas' exculpatory explanation, an episode described by T. S. Eliot as the most "civilized" in Western literature. Aeneas finally reaches that part of the underworld called the Land of Joy, where his father Anchises provides a vision of the destiny of his descendants, that is, a vision of the Roman future, a future already history to Vergil's contemporary audience. Of all the Roman heroes, the young Marcellus, son to Octavia and nephew to Augustus, is the last, and his tragic, early death foretold in the poem and experienced only recently by his readers led to his mother's swooning when Vergil read aloud the passage to her.

The sixth book brings an end to the "Odyssean" part of the *Aeneid*; Aeneas' wanderings are at an end. The last six books comprise the "Iliadic" *Aeneid*, concerned primarily with battles and the preparation for battle. As Vergil's nature was not very martial, his success in the last part of the work seems less memorable, although his profound insight into human character and into the inescapably tragic nature of existence has allowed him to create two unforgettable characters only less memorable than Dido herself. These are Turnus, the young king of the Rutulians who plays the role of the vanquished Hector to that of the avenging Achilles of Aeneas, and Mezentius, the savage tyrant, grieving at the loss of his son, indomitable in defeat. That Vergil's three most memorable characters should all suffer loss and defeat is not without significance in any analysis of the poet's sensibility and humanity.

Book 7 tells of Aeneas' landing in Latium, of his dealings with King Latinus, who obeys an oracle and offers Aeneas the hand of his daughter Lavinia. By the intervention of the ever hostile Juno, however, war is created between the Trojans and the Latins. Latinus does not oppose Aeneas but Turnus does, claiming Lavinia for himself.

Book 8 has Aeneas acquire allies in the form of Evander and his son Pallas, their troops, and the Etruscan troops and their leader Tarchon. Most celebrated is the description of the shield which Vulcan forges for Aeneas. On it are depicted scenes from a Roman history, the very beginning of which Aeneas is fighting to create. At the center of the shield is depicted the Battle of Actium and the consequent triumph of Augustus.

Book 9 presents the siege of the Trojan camp nearly successful in the absence of Aeneas and costing the lives of the two young men Nisus and Euryalus, who perish through the rashness of Euryalus and the profound loyalty of Nisus. Vergil stops his narrative at their deaths to expostulate on their happy fate of dying together and to argue for their immorality through his poetry. The intensity of this celebration of male bonding should not obscure the artistry with which Vergil has prepared this episode, for during the funeral games of book 5, Nisus, who is an apparent winner in the footrace, unexpectedly slips and in that slip saves victory for Euryalus by interfering with his rival Salius. His apparent triumph in book 9 should be compared with his sacrificial return to help his less able friend.

In book 10 the Trojan siege is relived, and in a great battle Pallas is killed, as are Lausus and Mezentius, son and father. The death of Mezentius is described in a particularly powerful manner, and the despoiling of Pallas by Turnus proves, like that of the Rutulians by Euryalus, to be the cause of the death of the conqueror.

Book 11 provides a temporary truce and the suggestion of single combat between Aeneas and Turnus. Turnus wishes to continue the war, but in the fight loses his most valuable ally Camilla, a warrior-maiden slain by a javelin while watching another whose resplendent armor she fancies. Like Euryalus before her and Turnus after her, she dies partly through her desire for spoil.

Book 12 brings Turnus and Aeneas into single combat for the hand of Lavinia and the possession of the city of Latium. Aeneas defeats Turnus, who asks for mercy. Aeneas begins to grant Turnus his request but sees the spoils of Pallas worn by Turnus and in a fit of rage kills the Rutulian king. On this note the epic ends and in its oddly un-Vergilian close provides further argument that the poet had left his work in need of some revision or addition.

The traditional Homeric devices of epic construction appear throughout the poem: the invocation to the muse, the beginning of the poem *in medias res*, the use of flashbacks, repetition by epithets and formulas, the catalogues, and the epic similes. All these devices contribute to a written work which, while lacking the power of its Homeric, oral predecessors, surpasses them in its psychological insights and structural subtleties. Modern readers perhaps no longer share Vergil's conception of the Roman imperium, of the moral supremacy of Stoicism, or even of the nature of the hero, but the broad drama of personal desire and political obligation, of the tension between the individual and the state, remains current. Even if it were the case that apolitical readers should come to the poem, they would find there the essential sadness of things expressed in language as close to perfect as language can be.

Bibliography

Anderson, William S. *The Art of the "Aeneid."* Englewood Cliffs, N.J.: Prentice-Hall, 1969. An excellent, though very brief, general introduction to the *Aeneid*, including information on the author's life and historical background. Also contains a short commentary on the *Aeneid* itself. A good place for the general reader to begin.

Bernard, John D., ed. *Vergil at 2000: Commemorative Essays on the Poet and His Influence.* New York: AMS Press, 1986. Fifteen essays by noted scholars, concerning most aspects of Vergilian scholarship, including the author's life and style and his historical background and influence.

Frank, Tenney. *Vergil: A Biography.* New York: Henry Holt, 1922. Reconstructs what can be known or surmised about Vergil's life and period by means of a careful study of the extant sources, general knowledge of the author's age and society, and a reasonable amount of speculation.

Knight, W. F. Jackson. *Roman Vergil.* London: Faber & Faber, 1944. A useful and detailed account of Vergil's life and poetry. Combines brief discussions of Vergil's life and predecessors with more lengthy literary analysis of Vergil's poetry.

Otis, Brooks. *Vergil: A Study in Civilized Poetry.* Oxford, England: Clarendon Press, 1963. One of the best, and most influential, general studies of Vergil's poetry. Contains a discussion of the author's background and style, as well as a brief analysis of all of his works. Traces the influences of Hesiod, Aratus, and Theocritus as well as Homer upon Vergil and presents Aeneas as the ideal of the Augustan individual.

Pöschl, Viktor. *The Art of Vergil*, translated by Gerda Seligson. Ann Arbor: University of Michigan Press, 1962. A detailed study of metaphor and symbolism in the poetry of Vergil, with special attention paid to the influence of Homer on the *Aeneid.*

Wiltshire, Susan Ford. *Public and Private in Vergil's "Aeneid."* Amherst: University of Massachusetts Press, 1989. An influential study of the theme of duty and public destiny, as well as a consideration of the cost of duty upon the individual in the *Aeneid.* Examines the ways in which the lessons of the *Aeneid* are relevant to the modern world.

Rosemary Barton Tobin
(Revised by *Jeffrey L. Buller*)

VOLTAIRE
François-Marie Arouet

Born: Paris, France; November 21, 1694
Died: Paris, France; May 30, 1778

Principal short fiction

Le Monde comme il va, 1748, revised as *Babouc: Ou, Le Monde comme il va*, 1749 (*Babouc: Or, The World as It Goes*, 1754; also as *The World as It Is: Or, Babouc's Vision*, 1929); *Memnon: Ou, La Sagesse humaine*, 1749 (*Memnon: Or, Human Wisdom*, 1961); *La Lettre d'un Turc*, 1750; *Le Blanc et le noir*, 1764 (*The Two Genies*, 1895); *Jeannot et Colin*, 1764 (*Jeannot and Colin*, 1929); *L'Histoire de Jenni*, 1775; *Les Oreilles du Comte de Chesterfield*, 1775 (*The Ears of Lord Chesterfield and Parson Goodman*, 1826).

Other literary forms

Voltaire's writings are vast, spanning more than one hundred volumes of letters, literature, and scholarship. He wrote in both French and English, publishing his works in several countries, depending on the prevailing political climate.

Voltaire has been remembered most for his incisive short stories, which convey complex philosophical ideas. During his own age, however, he was noted as a political satirist, playwright, and poet. He was a master of the epic poem, and his *La Henriade* (1728; a revision of *La Ligue*; *Henriade*, 1732) revived the popularity of this genre. His plays were renowned throughout France, and *Œdipe* (1718; *Oedipus*, 1761), produced when Voltaire was only twenty-four, received critical acclaim. His major philosophical work, *Dictionnaire philosophique portatif* (1764; *A Philosophical Dictionary for the Pocket*, 1765; also as *Philosophical Dictionary*, 1945), was an ambitious compendium of philosophical ideas and terms. In addition, his historical writings, such as *Le Siècle de Louis XIV* (1751; *The Age of Louis XIV*, 1752), have earned for him a reputation as one of the first modern historians.

Achievements

During his lifetime, Voltaire was both revered and rejected. He was alternately honored by kings for his brilliance and exiled or imprisoned for his radical political views. He was welcomed into the courts of George I and Princess Caroline of England, Frederick II of Prussia, and Louis XV of France. Louis XV appointed him as Royal Historiographer and as Ordinary Gentleman of the King's Bedchamber in the 1740's. In 1746, Voltaire realized one of his greatest ambitions when he was elected to the prestigious Académie Française. In the 1750's, Frederick II gave him a medal of merit, made him a chamberlain, and considered Voltaire to be his personal tutor and court philosopher until a bitter disagreement caused Voltaire to leave Prussia.

Voltaire's scathing attacks on intolerance, injustice, and superstition scandalized many of the powerful in the government and the French Roman Catholic Church, but his humor, imagination, and daring in expressing his opinions won for him numerous followers as well. When he was living in Switzerland in his later years, people made pilgrimages to his home and stood outside it hoping to catch a glimpse of him. At the end of his life, Voltaire returned to Paris to the acclaim of crowds of admirers. Yet, even in death, he stirred controversy: his body had to be smuggled out of Paris to allow him the decent burial in consecrated ground that the French Catholic hierarchy denied him.

Voltaire was one of the foremost philosophes of the French Enlightenment, and his influence went far beyond his long and successful lifetime. His ideas on the freedom and dignity of the individual are credited with having had a strong influence on the French Revolution of 1789. His satirical and irreverent wit gradually eroded some of the religious and political intolerance of eighteenth century France. Many who have fought for toleration, justice, and equality have looked back to the spirit of Voltaire's writings. He summarized his own sense of satisfaction about the successes of his and other philosophes' writings in a letter to Jean Le Rond D'Alembert dated July 18, 1766, in which he rejoiced that

> the Church of Wisdom is beginning to develop in our neighborhood where, twelve years ago the most somber fanaticism ruled. The provinces are becoming enlightened, the young magistrates are thinking boldly. . . . One is astonished by the progress that human reason has made in so few years.

Biography

Voltaire was born François-Marie Arouet on November 21, 1694, the son of a *grand bourgeois* lawyer. From 1704 to 1711, he attended a Jesuit boarding school, after which he pursued the study of law until his political writings earned for him his first exile from Paris in 1716 and his first imprisonment in the Bastille in 1717. From that time on, he devoted himself to his writing, beginning with plays and poetry and expanding to literature, philosophy, and history. He was socially and intellectually precocious, associating with many aristocratic and libertine men in the Société du Temple (Society of the Temple) by the time he was twelve. Voltaire was brilliant, witty, a talented writer, and, in later years, a social activist. Yet he could also be impulsive and hotheaded, which resulted in his arrest on several further occasions. Voltaire lived in various parts of France, England, Holland, Prussia, and Switzerland, moving in and out of these countries as his political sentiments and personal temperament made it unwise or impossible for him to stay where he was. He spent the last years of his life near the Swiss border, between his French homeland and the freer intellectual environment of Geneva, allowing himself an escape route to either country.

Voltaire was as untraditional in his personal life as in his political and philosophical ideas. His freedom from the norms of society, however, seemed to sustain his creative energies. In 1734, Voltaire met Madame Émilie du Châtelet, who would be his mistress and intellectual partner for the next fifteen years. He moved in with her and her husband at their estate at Cirey, where he wrote and studied with the "divine

Émilie." Even after Voltaire's widowed niece, Madame Denis, had become his new mistress, he maintained an intellectual relationship with Madame du Châtelet which would inspire him until her death in 1749. Her death saddened and depressed Voltaire for many years, contributing to the growing skepticism about the goodness of the world that is evident in his later fictional works, such as *Candide: Ou, L'Optimisme* (1759; *Candide: Or, All for the Best,* 1759). Throughout his life, Voltaire had suffered from bouts with ill health and severe hypochondria. He lived to be eighty-three, however, and was one of the most energetic and prolific authors in history.

Analysis

Voltaire's wit and insight into the human condition found a memorable forum in his short stories. These stories were not merely entertaining fantasies but were works of philosophical and social reflection as well. By allowing his readers to see the world through his characters' eyes, Voltaire taught new ways of thinking about the attitudes and situation of humanity.

Voltaire's fiction ranges from extremely short pieces to the longer works *Zadig: Ou, La Destinée, Histoire orientale* (1748; originally as *Memnon: Histoire orientale,* 1747; *Zadig: Or, The Book of Fate,* 1749), *Le Micromégas* (1752; *Micromegas,* 1753), *Candide,* and *L'Ingénu* (1767; *The Pupil of Nature,* 1771; also as *Ingenuous,* 1961). While those longer works are the primary stories for which he is remembered, his shorter tales contain many of the same themes in a tightly crafted and inventive form.

Voltaire was fascinated throughout his life with the issues of good and evil, freedom and determinism, and the nature of Providence. A Deist to the end of his life, convinced that God had created the world and left it to run according to an original plan, Voltaire yet struggled with the concepts of fate and Providence from the human perspective. The view of Gottfried Wilhelm Leibniz and others that this is the best of all possible worlds fit with Voltaire's Deism but not with his experience of the world. Voltaire's stories show a continually deepening sense of the evil and folly in life, in which it is difficult to find the good. His protagonists often undertake long and bizarre journeys, on which they learn tolerance from the experience of the universality of human suffering. Human goodness does not seem to be rewarded in the long run, and no obviously overarching plan shows itself to his heroes. It appears that existence is a pointless interplay of events in which evil people seem to be quite happy and successful, and the good often suffer miserably. Yet Voltaire always allows for the possibility that some good may be present in the worst of situations, even if that good is well hidden.

Within Voltaire's longer stories, this theme is quite obvious. In *Zadig,* the protagonist encounters a continually changing cycle of fortunes and misfortunes until he finally decides in despair that goodness will never be rewarded. An angel in disguise teaches him that the ways of Providence are inscrutable and all that happens in life creates the best possible world as a whole. Once Zadig realizes that the evil in the world is part of the divine plan, and that the world would be imperfect without it, he is freed from his ignorance and becomes the happy man that he had always believed he would be. He ends up a king, ruling more justly and compassionately because of the wisdom gained from his misfortunes. In the later work, *Candide*, Voltaire's growing pessimism is evident. Candide is an innocent and optimistic young man who undergoes an incredible series of cruel and painful disasters. Considering the enormity of the ills which meet him from all sides—he is exiled, drafted, beaten, robbed, and continually loses the woman he loves—he is amazingly slow to question his optimistic view of the world. By the end of his life, however, Candide settles down on a small farm with the woman he sought all his life (now grown quite ugly and disagreeable), and he brushes aside his original belief that things are all ordered for the best. He recognizes that the attempt to try to ignore the inevitability of suffering and evil in life leads to a tragic failure: the failure to try to improve the world in whatever ways are possible. He is now more content with the attitude that "we must cultivate our garden," thus abandoning the question of the good of the whole universe for the task of alleviating the misery of existence in his small corner of the world.

In Voltaire's shorter tales *Babouc* and *Memnon*, the issue of the apparent dominance of evil over good receives an answer similar to that given by *Zadig* in 1747. As in the novel *Zadig*, the protagonists learn that this world is imperfect but that it plays its appointed role in a universe that is ordered by Providence.

In *Babouc*, the jinni Ithuriel descends to earth to send Babouc on a fact-finding journey to Persia. Babouc is to travel throughout Persepolis to see if the Persians are worthy of punishment or destruction because of their evil actions. Babouc sets off and soon finds himself in the midst of a war between Persia and India. This war, begun over a petty dispute, has been ravaging the country for twenty years. Babouc witnesses bloody battles, treachery, and cruelty on both sides. He also witnesses many amazing acts of kindness and humanity. His journey continues in this vein. For every set of abuses in religion, politics, sexual conduct, and education, he finds also some good and noble elements. His cry of surprise echoes throughout the piece: "Unintelligible mortals! . . . How is it that you can combine so much meanness with so much greatness, such virtues with such crimes?" By the end, he agrees with a wise man whom he meets that evil is prevalent and good people are rare, yet the best is hidden from a visitor and needs to be sought more diligently. As he examines the society, he finds that those who have obtained positions of power through corrupt means are capable of devotion to their work and often pursue their careers with devotion and justice. He gains compassion for the people and their leaders and devises a way in which to communicate what he has learned to the jinni. He has a metalsmith fashion a statue out of every kind of stone, earth, and metal and takes this figure back to Ithuriel, asking, "Will you break this pretty little image, because it is not all gold and diamonds?" Ithuriel immediately comprehends and pardons the Persians, deciding not to interfere with "the way the world goes." Even though the world is not fully good, it contains enough good to merit its continued existence.

In *Memnon: Or, Human Wisdom* (not to be confused with *Memnon: Histoire ori-*

entale, the original title of *Zadig*), Voltaire takes a different path to a similar moral. In this humorous tale, a young man named Memnon plans to become perfectly wise by ridding himself of all of his passions. He decides to renounce love, drinking, wasting money, and arguing. He is assured that this will lead him to financial and emotional security, remove all hindrances to the exercise of his reason, and thus make him happy. After he forms this plan, he looks out his window and sees a young woman in tears. He rushes to counsel her, sheerly out of compassion, and ends in her embrace. Her uncle enters, and only a large sum of money convinces him not to kill Memnon. Memnon then has dinner with his friends and consoles himself by getting drunk and gambling, which leads to an argument in which he loses an eye. "The wise Memnon is carried back home drunk, with no money, and minus an eye." He recovers a bit, only to find that his investors have bankrupted him. He ends up sleeping on a pile of straw outside of his house and dreams that a six-winged heavenly creature, his good jinni, comes to him. Memnon wonders where his good jinni was the night before and is told that he was with Memnon's brother, who was blinded and imprisoned. Memnon comments that it is worthwhile "to have a good genie in a family, so that one of two brothers may be one-eyed, the other blind, one lying on straw, the other in prison." The jinni helpfully points out that the situation will get better if Memnon abandons his ridiculous attempt to be perfectly wise. This world is only one of many others, all of which are ordered by degrees of perfection, and the earth is far down near the craziest end of the scale. All is well, the jinni assures him, when one considers the arrangement of the universe as a whole. Memnon says that he will believe that all is well when he can see that it is with both eyes.

Although Voltaire's fiction depicts a crazy world where fortunes are uncertain, evils abound, and goodness does not ensure happiness, there are two things which are valued in most of his stories—the search for knowledge and the companionship of trusted friends. In *Jeannot and Colin*, Voltaire examines the worth of friendship and learning over the illusory happiness to be gained from wealth and power. Jeannot and Colin are friends and roommates at school until Jeannot's father sends for him to come home and enjoy the new family wealth. Jeannot does so, scorning his old friend and turning with relish to his new life of leisure. His mother and father discuss his future with a tutor, but each area of study, whether philosophy, mathematics, or history, is judged of no use to a young man of society who now has servants to do as he wishes. They decide to teach him to dance and be attractive, so that he can shine in social graces. He becomes a vaudeville singer and charms all the ladies of breeding. This, however, does not last: his father is bankrupted, his mother forced to become a servant, and Jeannot himself is homeless. In a state of distress, he runs into his old friend, Colin, whom he had snubbed. Colin is overjoyed to see him and offers to take Jeannot into his home and his business and to help Jeannot's mother and father out of their difficulties. Colin's kindness and forgiveness change Jeannot's heart and allow Jeannot's natural goodness to grow, free from the ravages of society. Jeannot lives happily, assisting his parents and marrying Colin's equally sweet-tempered sister.

Philosophical reflections and social satire weigh down the plots of some later stories, such as *The Ears of Lord Chesterfield and Parson Goodman*, making them tedious. These stories show the drier side of Voltaire's satire. At his best, however, Voltaire offered his readers richly woven tales which critiqued society, satirized pretensions, expressed new philosophical ideas, and simply entertained. The stories include much humor and piercing insight into the common follies of humanity. These philosophical tales succeeded, as no straightforward philosophy could, in offering many people new perspectives on reason, experience, and humanity.

Other major works

NOVELS: *Zadig: Ou, La Destinée, Histoire orientale*, 1748 (originally as *Memnon: Histoire orientale*, 1747; *Zadig: Or, The Book of Fate*, 1749); *Le Micromégas*, 1752 (*Micromegas*, 1753); *Histoire des voyages de Scarmentado*, 1756 (*The History of the Voyages of Scarmentado*, 1757; also as *History of Scarmentado's Travels*, 1961); *Candide: Ou, L'Optimisme*, 1759 (*Candide: Or, All for the Best*, 1759); *L'Ingénu*, 1767 (*The Pupil of Nature*, 1779; also as *Ingenuous*, 1961); *L'Homme aux quarante écus*, 1768 (*The Man of Forty Crowns*, 1768); *La Princesse de Babylone*, 1768 (*The Princess of Babylon*, 1769).

PLAYS: *Œdipe*, 1718 (*Oedipus*, 1761); *Artémire*, 1720; *Mariamne*, 1724 (English translation, 1761); *L'Indiscret*, 1725 (verse); *Brutus*, 1730 (English translation, 1761), *Ériphyle*, 1732; *Zaïre*, 1732 (English translation, 1736); *La Mort de César*, 1733; *Adélaïade du Guesclin*, 1734; *L'Échange*, 1734; *Alzire*, 1736 (English translation, 1763); *L'Enfant prodigue*, 1736 (verse; *The Prodigal*, 1750? prose translation); *Zulime*, 1740; *Mahomet*, 1742 (*Mahomet the Prophet*, 1744); *Mérope*, 1743 (English translation, 1744, 1749); *La Princesse de Navarre*, 1745 (verse; music by Jean-Philippe Rameau); *La Prude: Ou, La Grandeuse de Cassette*, 1747 (verse; based on William Wycherley's play *The Plain-Dealer*); *Sémiramis*, 1748 (*Semiramis*, 1760); *Nanine*, 1749 (English translation, 1927); *Oreste*, 1750; *Rome sauvée*, 1752; *L'Orphelin de la Chine*, 1755 (*The Orphan of China*, 1756); *Socrate*, 1759 (*Socrates*, 1760); *L'Écossaise*, 1760 (*The Highland Girl*, 1760); *Tancrède*, 1760; *Olympie*, 1763; *Le Triumvirat*, 1764; *Les Scythes*, 1767; *Les Guèbres: Ou, La Tolérance*, 1769; *Sophonisbe*, 1770 (revision of Jean Mairet's play); *Les Pélopides: Ou, Atrée et Thyeste*, 1772; *Les Lois de Minos*, 1773; *Don Pédre*, 1775; *Irène*, 1778; *Agathocle*, 1779.

POETRY: *Poème sur la religion naturelle*, 1722; *La Ligue*, 1723; *La Henriade*, 1728 (revision of *La Ligue*; *Henriade*, 1732); *Le Temple du goût*, 1733 (*The Temple of Taste*, 1734); *Le Mondain*, 1736 (*The Man of the World*, 1764); *Discours en vers sur l'homme*, 1738-1752 (*Discourses in Verse on Man*, 1764); *Poème de Fontenoy*, 1745; *Poème sur les événements de l'année 1744*, 1745; *Poème de la loi naturelle*, 1752 (*On Natural Law*, 1764); *La Pucelle d'Orléans*, 1755, 1762 (*The Maid of Orleans*, 1758; also as *La Pucelle*, 1785-1786); *Poème sur le désastre de Lisbonne*, 1756 (*Poem on the Lisbon Earthquake*, 1764); *Poème sur la loi naturelle*, 1756; *Le Pauvre Diable*, 1758; *Épître à Horace*, 1772.

NONFICTION: *Histoire de Charles XII*, 1731 (*The History of Charles XII*, 1732); *Let-*

tres philosophiques, 1734 (originally published in English as *Letters Concerning the English Nation*, 1733; also as *Philosophical Letters*, 1961); *Discours de métaphysique*, 1736; *Éléments de la philosophie de Newton*, 1738 (*The Elements of Sir Isaac Newton's Philosophy*, 1738; *Vie de Molière*, 1739; *Le Siècle de Louis XIV*, 1751 (*The Age of Louis XIV*, 1752); *Essai sur les mœurs*, 1756, 1763 (*The General History and State of Europe*, 1754, 1759); *Traité sur la tolérance*, 1763 (*A Treatise on Religious Toleration*, 1764); *Dictionnaire philosophique portatif*, 1764 (*A Philosophical Dictionary for the Pocket*, 1765; also as *Philosophical Dictionary*, 1945); *Commentaires sur Corneille* 1764; *Avis au public sur les parracides imputés aux calas et aux Sirven*, 1775; *Correspondence*, 1953-1965 (102 volumes).

MISCELLANEOUS: *The Works of M. de Voltaire*, 1761-1765 (35 volumes), 1761-1781 (38 volumes); *Candide and Other Writings*, 1945; *The Portable Voltaire*, 1949; *Candide, Zadig, and Selected Stories*, 1961; *The Complete Works of Voltaire*, 1968-1977 (135 volumes; in French).

Bibliography

Aldridge, A. Owen. *Voltaire and the Century of Light*. Princeton, N.J.: Princeton University Press, 1975. A teacher and student of comparative literature, Aldridge reexamines the life and career of Voltaire within the context of European intellectual and political history, providing many useful insights in a pleasant style equally suited to the specialist as to the general reader. Also offered are stimulating readings of *Candide* and other selected works, together with a valuable bibliography.

Havens, George R. *The Age of Ideas*. New York: Henry Holt, 1955. Often reprinted and providing a model and inspiration for many writers, Havens' witty, informed overview of the Enlightenment and its precursors remains authoritative as a guide to trends and thinkers of the period. Contains groups of chapters devoted to Charles de Montesquieu, Voltaire, Denis Diderot, and Jean-Jacques Rousseau. The four chapters devoted to Voltaire provide an excellent introduction to the man and his work, with brief but perceptive readings of such texts as *Zadig* and *Candide*.

Hearsey, John E. N. *Voltaire*. New York: Barnes & Noble Books, 1976. Rich in anecdote and incident, Hearsey's biography sets out to bring Voltaire, his friends, and his enemies back to life for the benefit of the contemporary reader. On balance, Hearsey succeeds in his task, but the result often more closely resembles a novel than a serious study. The select bibliography is quite brief, of use only to the most general of readers.

Mason, Haydn Trevor. *Voltaire*. New York: St. Martin's Press, 1975. Not to be confused with the biography published six years later and cited below, Mason's comprehensive monograph, intended for the interested undergraduate or general reader, steers clear of the traditional chronological approach in order to present Voltaire's work by genre, treating first his drama and dramatic criticism, proceeding thereafter to deal with historiography, short fiction, poetry, and polemics. Mason's approach, however unorthodox, proves quite effective, especially when dealing with the short fiction. Supplemented by a useful if brief bibliography.

_____. *Voltaire: A Biography.* Baltimore: The Johns Hopkins University Press, 1981. Building on the strengths implicit in his earlier, genre-oriented study of Voltaire's works, Mason here presents a concise but lively survey of his subject's life, clearly relating the major works to their context, including inspiration and/or (as is especially pertinent in the case of Voltaire) provocation. Closely documented, useful both as biography and as criticism, this volume is recommended to the student and to the general reader alike; those in search of a bibliography are, however, advised to consult Mason's earlier study cited above.

Mary J. Sturm
(Revised by *David B. Parsell*)

KURT VONNEGUT, JR.

Born: Indianapolis, Indiana; November 11, 1922

Principal short fiction
Canary in a Cat House, 1961; *Welcome to the Monkey House*, 1968 (includes most of the stories in the earlier collection).

Other literary forms
Kurt Vonnegut, Jr., has published numerous volumes, including essays, short stories, the plays *Happy Birthday, Wanda June* (1970) and *Between Time and Timbuktu: Or, Prometheus-5, a Space Fantasy* (1972), and the novels on which his reputation is principally based. His best-known novels include *The Sirens of Titan* (1959), *Cat's Cradle* (1963), and *Slaughterhouse-Five* (1969).

Achievements
For many years, the popular success of Vonnegut's writing exceeded critical recognition of his work. With his earlier work labeled as science fiction and published in paperback editions and popular magazines such as *Ladies' Home Journal* and *The Saturday Evening Post*, critical attention was delayed. After the publication of his masterpiece, *Slaughterhouse-Five*, however, his work received increasing serious critical commentary. He has emerged as a consistent commentator on American culture through the second half of the twentieth century. His short stories range from satiric visions of grotesque future societies, which are extensions of modern societies, and portrayals of ordinary people, which reassert the stability of middle-class values. In the novels, the social satire predominates, and Vonnegut blends whimsical humor and something approaching despair as he exposes the foibles of American culture and a world verging on destruction through human thoughtlessness. As in the short stories, however, attention to an unheroic protagonist doing his or her best and to the value of "common human decency" persists.

Biography
Although not specifically an autobiographical writer, Kurt Vonnegut, Jr., has frequently drawn on facts and incidents of his own life in his writing. The youngest in a family of three children, Vonnegut was born and reared in Indianapolis, Indiana. While serving in the army as an infantry scout during World War II, he was taken prisoner of war by the Germans and interned in Dresden, Germany, at the time of the 1945 Allied fire-bombing of the city that cost 135,000 lives. He himself survived only through the ironic circumstance of being quartered in an underground meat locker. Although the destruction of Dresden became a recurring motif in Vonnegut's work, not until twenty-three years later could he bring himself to write the novel of his war experiences, *Slaughterhouse-Five*. After the war, Vonnegut worked in public

relations for General Electric in Schenectady, New York (called "Ilium" in his fiction), before leaving in 1950 to devote himself full-time to his writing. In 1945, he married Jane Marie Cox, settling on Cape Cod, where they reared their own three children and the three children of Vonnegut's deceased sister, Alice. In 1972, he moved to New York City and was divorced from Cox early in 1974. He was married to the photographer Jill Krementz in November, 1979, and they adopted a daughter, Lily. They were divorced in 1991.

Analysis

Best known for his novels, Kurt Vonnegut has acknowledged the ancillary interest of short stories for him. In the preface to his collection of short stories, *Welcome to the Monkey House*, he describes the stories as "work I sold in order to finance the writing of the novels. Here one finds the fruits of Free Enterprise." Vonnegut's blunt comment, however, does not imply that the stories can be dismissed out of hand. The themes of the stories are the themes and concerns of all his work. Again in the preface to *Welcome to the Monkey House*, Vonnegut describes those concerns in a characteristically tough style. He recalls a letter his brother sent him shortly after bringing his firstborn home from the hospital: "Here I am," that letter began, "cleaning the shit off of practically everything." Of his sister, Vonnegut tells us that she died of cancer: "her dying words were 'No pain.' Those are good dying words. . . . I realize now that the two main themes of my novels were stated by my siblings: 'Here I am cleaning the shit off of practically everything' and 'No pain.' " These terms apply equally well to the themes of Vonnegut's short stories. His muckraking is frequently social satire; his concern is with the alleviation of human suffering.

Vonnegut's short stories generally fall into two broad categories: those that are science fiction, and those that are not. The science fiction characteristically pictures a future society controlled by government and technology, whose norms have made human life grotesque. The protagonist is often an outlaw who has found such norms or conventions intolerable.

In contrast, Vonnegut's stories that are not science fiction regularly affirm social norms. Ordinary life in these stories is simply not threatened by large-scale social evil. Some of these stories indeed depict the victims of society—refugees, displaced persons, juvenile delinquents—but primarily they show such people's efforts to recover or establish conventional lives. It is within the context of conventional life that Vonnegut's protagonists can achieve those qualities that in his view give a person stability and a sense of worth. These are the qualities of modesty, considerateness (which he often calls common human decency), humor, order, and pride in one's work. They are values interfered with, in the science-fiction stories, by governmental and technological controls.

Vonnegut has resented any dismissal of his work merely because it is science fiction, a kind of writing he describes as incorporating "technology in the human equation." In the novel, *God Bless You, Mr. Rosewater* (1965), Eliot Rosewater speaks for Vonnegut when he delivers an impassioned, drunken, and impromptu defense of the genre before a convention of science-fiction writers:

> I love you sons of bitches. . . . You're all I read any more. . . . You're the only ones with guts enough to *really* care about the future, who *really* notice what machines do to us, what wars do to us, what cities do to us, what big, simple ideas do to us, what tremendous misunderstandings, mistakes, accidents and catastrophes do to us.

In Eliot Rosewater's opinion, society's "greatest prophet" is an obscure writer of science fiction named Kilgore Trout, a recurring character in Vonnegut's fiction. His masterpiece, the work for which he will be revered in the far future, is a book entitled *2BRO2B*, a rephrasing of Hamlet's famous question.

The story of *2BRO2B* in Vonnegut's précis corresponds closely to his own short story, "Welcome to the Monkey House." Vonnegut writes of his fictional character, "Trout's favorite formula was to describe a perfectly hideous society, not unlike his own, and then, toward the end, to suggest ways in which it could be improved." The approach describes Vonnegut's writing as well. *2BRO2B* predicates an America crippled by automation and overpopulation. Machines have taken over most jobs, leaving people idle and feeling "silly and pointless." The government's solution has been to encourage patriotic suicide. Ethical Suicide Parlors have been widely established, each identifiable by its purple roof and each located next to a Howard Johnson's restaurant (with its orange roof), where the prospective client is entitled to a free last meal.

This is also the world of "Welcome to the Monkey House." The story takes place on Cape Cod in an unspecified future time. Fourteen Kennedys, by now, have served as presidents of the United States or of the world. There is a world government; in fact, in this world, Vonnegut writes, "practically everything was the Government." Most people look twenty-two years old, thanks to the development of anti-aging shots. The population of the world numbers seventeen billion people. For Vonnegut, the world's dilemma is the result of advanced technology combined with backward human attitudes. Suicide is voluntary, but everyone, under law, must use "ethical" birth control pills that, in fact, control not birth but sexuality. Their effect is to make people numb below the waist, depriving them not of the ability to reproduce "which would have been unnatural and immoral," but merely of all pleasure in sex. "Thus did science and morals go hand in hand," Vonnegut ironically concludes.

The kind of morality that could produce these pills is exemplified in J. Edgar Nation, their inventor. Walking through the Grand Rapids Zoo with his eleven children one Easter, he had been so offended by the behavior of the animals that he promptly developed a pill "that would make monkeys in the springtime fit things for a Christian family to see." In the opinion of Billy, the Poet, a renegade in this society, throughout history those people most eager "to tell everybody exactly how God Almighty wants things here on Earth" have been unaccountably terrified of human sexuality.

Billy the Poet's special campaign is to deflower Hostesses in Ethical Suicide Parlors, who are all, as part of their qualifications for the job, "plump and rosy" virgins at least six feet tall. Their uniform is a purple body stocking "with nothing underneath" and black leather boots. In this world, only death is permitted to be seductive. Billy's modus operandi is to single out a Hostess and send her some bawdy doggerel, calculated to offend (and to excite) narrow sensibilities. Nancy McLuhan, his present target, is more intrigued than she will admit to herself. Billy kidnaps her and takes her to his current hideout, the old Kennedy compound at Hyannis Port, now "a museum of how life had been lived in more expansive times. The museum was closed." The original lawn is now green cement; the harbor is blue cement. The whole of the compound is covered by an enormous plastic geodesic dome through which light can filter. The only "light" in which an earlier graciousness can now be seen is colored by the world's pervasive vulgarity. The current world president, named "Ma" Kennedy, but not the "real thing," keeps a sign reading "Thimk!" on the wall of her office in the Taj Mahal.

Nancy's encounter with Billy is not the licentious orgy she expects, but an approximation of an old-fashioned wedding night. Billy explains to her that most people only gradually develop a full appreciation of their sexuality. Embarrassed and confused, she tries conscientiously to resist her comprehension of his motives. As he leaves, Billy offers Nancy another poem, this time the famous sonnet by Elizabeth Barrett Browning, beginning "How do I love thee? Let me count the ways." The implication is, of course, that sexuality is one dimension of human love sorely lacking in their world. Far from being obscene, that love pursues a larger "ideal Grace," in the words of the poem, wholly unavailable either to the vulgarity of "Ma" Kennedy or to the narrow-minded purity of J. Edgar Nation. Billy also leaves with Nancy a bottle of birth-control pills that will not hamper sexual enjoyment. On the label are printed the words, "WELCOME TO THE MONKEY HOUSE." If Browning's poem risks sentimentality, the story ends in a comic readjustment of the reader's sense of proportion. Sex need not be humorless; the reader need not view himself and the human condition with the chilling seriousness and inflated self-importance of J. Edgar Nation. The reader is left with the impression that Nancy McLuhan has begun her conversion. There is a measure of hope in this world where, as Billy assures her, the "movement is growing by leaps and bounds."

Governmental domination of private life is nearly total, however, in the world of "Harrison Bergeron," whose inhabitants are tortured and shackled as a matter of course, all in the name of equality. In the United States of 2081, equality of all persons has been mandated by the 211th, 212th, and 213th Amendments to the Constitution. People are not merely equal under the law, but "equal every which way." Those people of "abnormal" capacities must wear equalizing handicaps at all times. Hazel Bergeron is a person of average intelligence, which means that "she couldn't think about anything except in short bursts." Her husband, George, however, as a man of superior intelligence, has to wear a "mental handicap radio" in his ear which broadcasts at twenty-second intervals strident noises designed to break his concentration: burglar alarms, sirens, an automobile collision, or a twenty-gun salute. A strong man as well, George wears "forty-seven pounds of birdshot in a canvas bag" padlocked around his neck.

Neither George nor his wife is able to recall that their fourteen-year-old son, Harrison, has just been arrested. They are watching on television a performance by ballerinas also weighted down with birdshot and masked to disguise their beauty. As a law-abiding couple, George and Hazel have only fleeting suspicions that the system is a bad one. If not for such handicaps, George says, "pretty soon we'd be right back to the dark ages again, with everybody competing against everybody else." When the television announcer cannot deliver a news bulletin because he—"like all announcers"—has a serious speech impediment, Hazel's response is a well-meaning platitude, "he tried. That's the big thing." A ballerina, disguising her "unfair" voice, reads the announcement for him: Harrison Bergeron, "a genius and an athlete," has escaped from jail.

Suddenly Harrison bursts into the television studio. A "walking junkyard," he wears tremendous earphones, thick glasses, three hundred pounds of scrap metal, a rubber ball on his nose, and black caps on his teeth. In this reductio ad absurdum of the ideal of equality, the technology is pointedly silly. "I am the Emperor!" Harrison cries, and tears off his handicaps, revealing a man who "would have awed Thor, the god of thunder." Harrison is rival to the gods. A ballerina joins him as his empress. Freed of her restraints, she is "blindingly beautiful." Whatever the reader may perceive as ultimate human beauty, Harrison and the ballerina are that. Together the two of them dance in "an explosion of joy and grace" equally as fantastic as the shackles they have thrown off. They leap thirty feet to kiss the ceiling and hover midair to embrace each other, "neutralizing gravity with love and pure will." They have defied the laws of the land, the law of gravity, the laws of motion. They dance out the soaring aspiration of the human spirit, for a moment made triumphantly manifest.

The United States Handicapper General, ironically named Diana Moon Glampers, then breaks into the television studio and shoots them both. Her ruthless efficiency is in marked contrast to the bumbling capabilities of everyone else. The reader is suddenly aware that the idea of equality has been made an instrument of social control. Clearly some are allowed to be more equal than others. In their home, Harrison's parents are incapable of either grief or joy. They resume their passive, acquiescent lives, having forgotten the entire scene almost as soon as they have witnessed it.

If the conventional life depicted in Vonnegut's nonscience fiction has not been made this grotesque by technology and government, it is, nevertheless, also humdrum and unaspiring. These limitations, however, are more than compensated for by the fact that ordinary people feel useful, not superfluous, and they are capable of sustaining love.

In "Go Back to Your Precious Wife and Son" the narrator's occupation is selling and installing "aluminum combination storm windows and screens" and occasionally a bathtub enclosure. He marks as "the zenith of my career" an order for a glass door for a movie star's bathtub specially fixed with a life-sized picture of the movie star's face on it. He is comically intent on installing the enclosure and on doing the job well, even as the star's household disintegrates around him. Yet if it is funny, the narrator's pride in his mundane work is also a basis for the stability in his life, a stability visibly lacking in the apparently glamorous life of Gloria Hilton, the movie star. Also installing two windows for her, he says about them, "The Fleetwood Trip-L-Trak is our first-line window, so there isn't anything quick or dirty about the way we put them up. . . . You can actually fill up a room equipped with Fleetwoods with water, fill it clear up to the ceiling, and it won't leak—not through the windows, anyway."

While the narrator is at work in the bathroom, Gloria Hilton is engaged in dismissing her fifth husband. She speaks to him, as she always speaks, in a series of fatuous clichés. She tells him now, "you don't know the meaning of love," as she had earlier seduced him away from his family with the words, "Dare to be happy, my poor darling! Oh, darling, we were *made* for each other!" She had then promptly announced to the press that the two of them were moving to New Hampshire "to find ourselves." In the narrator's (and the reader's) only glimpse of Gloria Hilton, she is without makeup ("she hadn't even bothered to draw on eyebrows") and dressed in a bathrobe. He decides, "that woman wasn't any prettier than a used studio couch." Her actual commonplaceness and utter self-absorption are patent.

Her hapless fifth husband is a writer, George Murra, of whom she had expected no less than "the most beautiful scenario anybody in the history of literature has ever written for me." In the constant publicity and tempestuousness of their lives together, however, he has been unable to work at all. He had been lured by a hollow glamour, and she by the possibility of greater self-glorification. The superficiality of their marriage is revealed in his references to her as "Miss Hilton," and her contemptuous parting words, "Go on back to your precious wife and your precious son."

In a long drinking session together after Gloria Hilton leaves, Murra explains to the narrator his earlier dreams of breaking free from the petty, marital squabbles, the financial worries, the drab responsibility and sameness of conventional life. The narrator momentarily and drunkenly succumbs to the appeal of the glamorous life; when he staggers home he immediately offends his wife. Murra is now repentant and nearly desperate for the forgiveness of his son, living at a nearby prep school. When the boy arrives to visit his father, it is apparent that the hurt and bitterness of his father's desertion have made him rigid with intolerant rectitude. The situation looks hopeless until the narrator (back to finish his job) suggests to Murra that he topple the boy from his pedestal with a kick in the pants. The gambit works, the family is reconciled, and the narrator returns home, having agreed to exchange bathtub doors with Murra. He finds his own wife gone and his own son stuffily self-righteous; but his wife returns, her equanimity restored. The new bathtub enclosure with Gloria Hilton's face on it amuses her. She is exactly Gloria Hilton's height; when she showers, the movie star's face on the door forms a "mask" for her. Gloria Hilton's glamour, of course, is all mask and pose; but his wife's good humor is genuine. The ordinary lives of the narrator and his wife have provided them with exactly what Gloria Hilton lacks and what George Murra and his son need to recover: the saving grace of humor, tolerance, and a sense of proportion.

Despite the fact that most of Vonnegut's short stories are not science fiction and similarly applaud conventional life, the happy triumph of kindness and work in this story seems contrary to the thrust of his novels. What he values remains the same, but the prospect of realizing those values becomes more desperate as the vision of normalcy recedes. The crises of the planet are too extreme and the capabilities of technology too great for Vonnegut to imagine a benign society in the future that could foster those values.

Vonnegut's novels are often described as "black humor," wholly unlike the generous good humor of "Go Back to Your Precious Wife and Son." This is another label that annoys the author ("just a convenient tag for reviewers"), but his description of black humor recalls his own lonely rebels whose cause is seriously overmatched by the monolithic enemy: "Black humorists' holy wanderers find nothing but junk and lies and idiocy wherever they go." Vonnegut has said that the writer functions like the canaries coal miners took with them into the mines "to detect gas before men got sick." He must serve society as an early-warning system so that one can work to improve the human condition while one still may.

Other major works

NOVELS: *Player Piano*, 1952; *The Sirens of Titan*, 1959; *Mother Night*, 1961; *Cat's Cradle*, 1963; *God Bless You, Mr. Rosewater: Or, Pearls Before Swine*, 1965; *Slaughterhouse-Five: Or, The Children's Crusade, a Duty-Dance with Death*, 1969; *Breakfast of Champions: Or, Goodbye Blue Monday*, 1973; *Slapstick: Or, Lonesome No More!*, 1976; *Jailbird*, 1979; *Deadeye Dick*, 1982; *Galápagos*, 1985; *Bluebeard*, 1987; *Hocus Pocus*, 1990.

PLAYS: *Happy Birthday, Wanda June*, 1970; *Between Time and Timbuktu: Or, Prometheus-5, a Space Fantasy*, 1972 (teleplay).

NONFICTION: *Wampeters, Foma, and Granfalloons (Opinions)*, 1974; *Palm Sunday: An Autobiographical Collage*, 1981; *Conversations with Kurt Vonnegut*, 1988; *Fates Worse Than Death: An Autobiographical Collage of the 1980's*, 1991.

CHILDREN'S LITERATURE: *Sun Moon Star*, 1980 (with Ivan Chermayeff).

Bibliography

Broer, Lawrence R. *Sanity Plea: Schizophrenia in the Novels of Kurt Vonnegut.* Ann Arbor: UMI Research Press, 1988. This volume focuses on the theme of social neurosis, with emphasis on schizophrenic behavior in the main characters of the novels through *Bluebeard*. The thesis has relevance to a number of the short stories and gives insight into the evolution of Vonnegut's fiction.

Giannone, Richard. *Vonnegut: A Preface to His Novels.* Port Washington, N.Y.: Kennikat, 1977. Treats the novels up to *Slapstick* and the play *Happy Birthday, Wanda June*, in the context of Vonnegut's life and times. Emphasizes developing themes and techniques connecting the novels, with chapters devoted to individual novels.

Klinkowitz, Jerome, Julie Huffman-Klinkowitz, and Asa B. Pieratt, Jr. *Kurt Vonnegut, Jr.: A Comprehensive Bibliography.* Hamden, Conn.: Archon Books, 1987. The authoritative bibliography of works by and about Vonnegut. Lists Vonnegut's works in all their editions, including the short stories in their original places of publication, dramatic and cinematic adaptations, interviews, reviews, secondary sources, and dissertations.

Klinkowitz, Jerome, and David L. Lawler, eds. *Vonnegut in America: An Introduction to the Life and Work of Kurt Vonnegut.* New York: Delacorte Press, 1977. A collection of essays ranging from biography and an "album" of family photographs to Vonnegut as satirist, science-fiction writer, and short-story writer. Discusses his reputation in the Soviet Union and Europe. Contains an authoritative bibliography.

Klinkowitz, Jerome, and John Somer, eds. *The Vonnegut Statement.* New York: Delacorte Press, 1973. A collection of essays by various authors, which establishes the nature and sources of Vonnegut's reputation at this important juncture. Analyzes his career from his college writing to the short fiction, and through the novels to *Slaughterhouse-Five.* Includes an interview and a bibliography. The most important accounting of his career through its first two decades.

Merrill, Robert, ed. *Critical Essays on Kurt Vonnegut.* Boston: G. K. Hall, 1990. A comprehensive collection of essays on Vonnegut's works and career, which includes reviews, previously published essays, and articles commissioned for this work. The extensive introduction traces in detail Vonnegut's career and critical reception from the beginnings to 1990.

Schatt, Stanley. *Kurt Vonnegut, Jr.* Boston: Twayne, 1976. Discusses the first eight novels, with separate chapters on the short stories and on the plays. Includes a chronology, a biography, and a bibliography up to 1975.

Martha Meek
(Revised by *Peter J. Reed*)

JOHN WAIN

Born: Stoke-on-Trent, England; March 14, 1925

Principal short fiction

Nuncle and Other Stories, 1960; *Death of the Hind Legs and Other Stories*, 1966; *The Life Guard*, 1971; *King Caliban and Other Stories*, 1978.

Other literary forms

John Wain built his reputation as a novelist in the 1950's, his first novel being *Hurry on Down* (1953), which was published in the United States as *Born in Captivity* in 1954, and a later one being *Where the Rivers Meet*, 1988. His further efforts include several volumes of poetry, criticism, and literary biography. He has also written an autobiography and edited anthologies of essays, poetry and fiction. An influential essayist, editor, critic, and literary biographer, Wain believes his poetry to be his most important literary contribution.

Achievements

Though frequently categorized as one of the "Angry Young Men" of the 1950's, Wain claims that his work is not decidedly bitter; moreover, it has often been confused with that of John Braine. Still, his reputation as a debunker of rigid English society and an apologist for the alienated young man has persisted. While Wain's short stories are disciplined and energetic, he is at times an acerbic social critic and frequently writes with a strong moral cast. Wain won the Somerset Maugham Travel Award in 1958 for *Preliminary Essays* (1957), the James Tait Black Memorial Prize and Heinemann Bequest Award in 1975 for *Samuel Johnson* (1974) and the Whitbread Literary Award in 1984 for *Young Shoulders* (1982). In 1973, he was elected the twenty-seventh professor of poetry at the University of Oxford.

Biography

The son of a dentist, John Wain earned his bachelor of arts degree at Oxford in 1946 and remained for the next three years as a Fereday Fellow. He also took a position as lecturer in English literature at the University of Reading, England, from 1947 to 1955, quitting the classroom to become a full-time writer in 1955. In 1953, he served as host of the British Broadcasting Corporation's "First Reading" program, which became a springboard for the British movement poets, particularly his friends Kingsley Amis and Philip Larkin. Although he objected to being classified as one of the "Angry Young Men," the label stuck. Because Wain, Amis, and John Osborne, all near thirty years old, were writing social protest and caustic humor, they were inevitably—if artificially—grouped by critics. Despite their individual differences, they did have the collective effect of sharpening England's social sensibility and invigorating its literature. Twice married, Wain and his wife Eirian James are the parents of three sons.

Analysis

Typically, John Wain's stories concern the internal conflict of a first-person narrator. The narrator usually is not very perceptive, whether for lack of intelligence or maturity. A frequent effect of Wain's stories is that a conflict is well developed, human narrowness is scourged with satire, and a thematic irony is made unmistakably clear. Two stories from Wain's first collection, *Nuncle and Other Stories*, provide insight into his early short fiction. Both "Master Richard" and "A Message from the Pig-Man" are dominated by the perceptions of their child-protagonists. Richard, a five-year-old prodigy, is the narrator of his story. It develops by means of the diary convention, with Richard recording his observations secretly in a notebook. The boy gauges his maturity of mind at roughly thirty-five because the conversation of adults is easily comprehensible. Such a voice puts considerable strain on the narrative credibility of the story.

Richard reads, writes, and types with the facility of an adult. Wain makes a few concessions to the age of his narrator: he faces pain and cries like any other child and throws china cups to get attention. At the other extreme, the boy has a sense of perspective that belies that of the most precocious child. He carries out a long conditioning process to prepare his parents gradually for the realization that he has learned to read on his own. The very notion of patience over a long period of time is alien to the mind of even a very bright child. Further, Richard makes jokes and uses a vocabulary of slang that cannot be accounted for, since these abilities come almost entirely from experience. The greatest breach of credibility occurs when Richard speaks of the absurd and of insanity, constructs that only time and experience—not precocity—can bring to the consciousness. The problem is that no clear frame of reference is established for the reader. The narrator's situation, environment, and comments are based on the presumption of conventional reality as the norm of the story; Richard's unique perception, however, forces the reader to view the story as somewhat surrealistic. The narrative exhibits both realism and surrealism but is committed consistently to neither, and the ambivalence is disconcerting.

Richard's crisis comes with the birth of a younger brother, whom he hates jealously. As a result of his contempt for his own cruelty to his brother and for his parents, who cannot understand him, he coolly decides to commit suicide. This conclusion, which has not been prepared for in the development of the story, is more convenient than satisfying.

Unlike "Master Richard," "A Message from the Pig-Man" is thoroughly believable. Eric, the viewpoint character, is also five years old, but the narrative is third-person, giving Wain more room to maneuver in disclosing the story. The thematic function of the boy's sensibility in the story is to comment on the need to confront fear. Eric finally faces the Pig-man, whom he assumes to be a grotesque creature rather than an old man simply collecting scraps for his pigs. He goes out with some scraps at his mother's insistence and tells himself, "It was the same as getting into icy cold water. If it was the end, if the Pig-man seized him by the hand and dragged him off to his hut, well, so much the worse."

Although his fear has a comic effect, it teaches the central lesson of the story. Once he has faced the Pig-man and found him harmless, he returns home to be put off when he asks his mother and his new stepfather why his father cannot live with them. Lacking Eric's courage to face up to problems, they hedge instead of answering. The viewpoint of the child generates humor and provides insight into the deeper weaknesses of adults; still the concluding irony is too heavy.

The stories in *The Life Guard* are more sophisticated than the earlier ones. In the title story there is overdone irony in the death of Hopper, who actually drowns when he is supposed to be acting out the part to make Jimmy look necessary as lifeguard. Despite the unrestrained turn of plot, the story achieves substance and interest as the narrative lets the reader see Jimmy's desperation. As a dull boy, he is in his element when he gets the job of lifeguard at the beach. He fears the future and lacks ambition, but he has skill and confidence in the water. Eager to prove that he is useful on the calm shore, Jimmy decides to win attention by appearing to save Hopper's life. When he sees that Hopper really is in trouble, he is faced with exactly the kind of test he had been waiting for all summer; only he fails and Hopper dies. In Jimmy's moral and physical agony as he brings Hopper to land, there is considerable dramatic energy—almost enough to make the reader overlook the predictable conclusion.

Another story from the collection, "While the Sun Shines," shows considerable control and is one of Wain's best stories by far. The conflict here between the tractor driver, the unnamed first-person narrator, and Robert, the son of the absent farm owner, is well drawn. First-person narration is particularly appropriate because the external conflict of the story is secondary to what goes on in the narrator's mind. Another man was seriously injured when the tractor overturned as he tried to mow a dangerously steep hill. When Robert orders the narrator to try the same task, he refuses more out of spite than fear. Later, however, he takes on the challenge, not for Robert's sake, but for his own, and possibly to impress Robert's roving wife Yvonne. The appeal she holds for the narrator adds a subtle dimension to the story. Although he knows she is a woman who uses men, she appeals to him more than he will admit. Thus in retrospect there is a question as to whether the narrator mastered the hill entirely for himself, as he thinks, or for Yvonne as well. Because he professes contempt for her throughout the story, his yielding to her at the end is a surprise, but a very effective one. The man who tells the story is ironically unaware of his own motives. He concludes, "What could I do? Another time, I'd have gone straight back to Mary and the kids. But today I was the king, I'd won and it was a case of winner take all." He goes from the tractor to her bed, and there is some question as to who has really won the day. The strength of the piece lies in what Wain does not say outright.

There is no doubt that Wain's concern as a writer is well placed; the problems he chooses to present are significant. The weakness in his short stories is a lack of restraint. When he makes the necessary effort to say less explicitly and more implicitly, his stories gain the light touch and resonance that mark good writing.

Other major works

NOVELS: *Hurry on Down*, 1953 (also known as *Born in Captivity*); *Living in the Present*, 1955; *The Contenders*, 1958; *A Travelling Woman*, 1959; *Strike the Father Dead*, 1962; *The Young Visitors*, 1965; *The Smaller Sky*, 1967; *A Winter in the Hills*, 1970; *The Pardoner's Tale*, 1979; *Young Shoulders*, 1982 (also known as *The Free Zone Starts Here*); *Where the Rivers Meet*, 1988.

PLAY: *Harry in the Night: An Optimistic Comedy*, 1975.

TELEPLAY: *Young Shoulders*, 1984 (with Robert Smith).

RADIO PLAYS: *You Wouldn't Remember*, 1978; *A Winter in the Hills*, 1981; *Frank*, 1982.

POETRY: *Mixed Feelings*, 1951; *A Word Carved on a Sill*, 1956; *A Song About Major Eatherly*, 1961; *Weep Before God: Poems*, 1961; *Wildtrack: A Poem*, 1965; *Selected Shorter Poems of Thomas Hardy*, 1966 (edited); *Letters to Five Artists*, 1969; *The Shape of Feng*, 1972; *Feng: A Poem*, 1975; *Poems for the Zodiac*, 1980; *Thinking About Mr. Person*, 1980; *Poems, 1949-1979*, 1981; *Twofold*, 1981; *Open Country*, 1987.

NONFICTION: *Contemporary Reviews of Romantic Poetry*, 1953 (edited); *Interpretations: Essays on Twelve English Poems*, 1955 (edited); *Preliminary Essays*, 1957; *Gerard Manley Hopkins: An Idiom of Desperation*, 1959; *International Literary Annual*, 1959, 1960 (edited); *Fanny Burney's Diary*, 1960 (edited); *Sprightly Running: Part of an Autobiography*, 1962; *Essays on Literature and Ideas*, 1963; *The Living World of Shakespeare: A Playgoer's Guide*, 1964; *Arnold Bennett*, 1967; *Shakespeare: Macbeth, a Casebook*, 1968 (edited); *Shakespeare: Othello, a Casebook*, 1971 (edited); *A House for the Truth: Critical Essays*, 1972; *Johnson as Critic*, 1973 (edited); *Samuel Johnson*, 1974; *Professing Poetry*, 1977; *Samuel Johnson 1709-1784*, 1984 (with Kai Kin Yung); *Dear Shadows: Portraits from Memory*, 1986.

CHILDREN'S LITERATURE: *Lizzie's Floating Shop*, 1981.

ANTHOLOGY: *Anthology of Modern Poetry*, 1963.

MISCELLANEOUS: Thomas Hardy's *The Dynasts*, 1966 (edited).

Bibliography

Burgess, Anthony. *The Novel Now: A Guide to Contemporary Fiction.* New York: W. W. Norton, 1967. Expanded from an earlier study, Burgess' work groups Wain with other class-conscious British fiction writers.

Gerard, David E. *John Wain.* Westport, Conn.: Meckler, 1987. Contains a comprehensive annotated bibliography of Wain's work. Lists materials of critical and biographical interest, including radio, television, and sound recordings.

Gindin, James J. *Postwar British Fiction: New Accents and Attitudes.* Berkeley: University of California Press, 1962. Gindin's chapter "The Moral Center of John Wain's Fiction" discusses Wain's use of morality as a thematic and structural

Critical Survey of Short Fiction

device and claims that each novel contains a central statement of the moral worth of the individual.

Salwak, Dale. *John Wain.* Boston: Twayne, 1981. Part of Twayne's English Authors series, this work is the first book-length study of Wain and is a useful introduction to Wain's career.

Skovmand, Michael, and Steffen Skovmand, eds. *The Angry Young Men.* Aarhus, Denmark: Akademisk Forlag, 1975. While this collection perpetuates Wain's label as an "Angry Young Man," it offers an insightful reading of Wain's novels, particularly *Hurry on Down.*

Walzer, Michael. "John Wain: The Hero in Limbo." *Perspective* 10 (Summer/Autumn, 1958): 137-145. In his consideration of Wain's first three novels, Walzer maintains that Wain develops a new kind of picaresque hero.

James Curry Robison
(Revised by *Jerry Bradley*)

ALICE WALKER

Born: Eatonton, Georgia; February 9, 1944

Principal short fiction

In Love and Trouble: Stories of Black Women, 1973; *You Can't Keep a Good Woman Down*, 1981.

Other literary forms

Alice Walker is known for her achievements in both prose and poetry; in addition to her short-story collections, she has published several novels, volumes of poetry, collections of essays, and children's books. Her novels *The Third Life of Grange Copeland* (1970), *Meridian* (1976), *The Color Purple* (1982), and *The Temple of My Familiar* (1989) examine the struggles of African Americans, especially African-American women, against destruction by a racist society. Her poetry is collected in *Once: Poems* (1968), *Five Poems* (1972), *Revolutionary Petunias and Other Poems* (1973), *Goodnight, Willie Lee, I'll See You in the Morning: Poems* (1979), *Horses Make a Landscape Look More Beautiful* (1984), and *Her Blue Body Everything We Know: Earthling Poems, 1965-1990* (1991). *In Search of Our Mothers' Gardens: Womanist Prose* (1983) is a collection of essays important to an understanding of Walker's purposes and methods as well as the writers influential on her fiction. A later collection of nonfiction prose is *Living by the Word: Selected Writings, 1973-1987* (1988). Walker also wrote *Langston Hughes: American Poet* (1974) and *To Hell with Dying* (1988) for children. The anthology she edited entitled *I Love Myself When I Am Laughing . . . and Then Again When I Am Looking Mean and Impressive: A Zora Neale Hurston Reader* (1979) did much to revive interest in the fiction of Zora Neale Hurston, the writer she considers one of the major influences on her fiction.

Achievements

From the beginning of her career, Walker has been an award-winning writer. Her first published essay, "The Civil Rights Movement: What Good Was It?" won first prize in *The American Scholar's* annual essay contest in 1967. Her first novel was written on a fellowship at the MacDowell Colony in New Hampshire. *Revolutionary Petunias and Other Poems* was nominated for a National Book Award and won the Lillian Smith Award of the Southern Regional Council in 1973. *In Love and Trouble* won the Richard and Hinda Rosenthal Award from the American Institute of Arts and Letters in 1974. *The Color Purple*, which remained on *The New York Times* list of best-sellers for more than twenty-five weeks, was nominated for the National Book Critics Circle Award and won both an American Book Award and the Pulitzer Prize for Fiction. Walker's many honors include a National Endowment for the Arts grant in 1969, a Radcliffe Institute Fellowship in 1971-1973, and a Guggenheim Fellowship in 1978. She has been praised for her ability to get inside the minds of passive, inarticulate characters, to combine cruelty and compassion, the weight of oppression and the buoyancy of affirmation so that they are deeply felt and keenly understood at once. Unfavorable reviews of Walker's work usually complain that she always makes the men villains and the women heroes. Walker herself confirms her "womanist" bias. Despite some demurs about a feminist slant, the response to *The Color Purple* was overwhelmingly positive, and there is increasing critical attention being paid to her work. Walker is an inspired writer who continually dares to confront the worst and celebrate the best in the African-American experience.

Biography

Alice Malsenior Walker was born in Eatonton, Georgia, to sharecropper parents on February 9, 1944. She attended Spelman College in Atlanta on scholarship, transferring to Sarah Lawrence in New York, from which she was graduated in 1965. While working in the Civil Rights movement in Mississippi in the summer of 1966, she met Melvyn Rosenman Levanthal, an attorney, whom she married in 1967. After residing for seven years in Jackson, Mississippi, the couple returned to the East in 1974, where Walker served as a contributing editor for *Ms.* magazine. The two were divorced in 1976, sharing joint custody of a daughter, Rebecca. Walker moved to California in 1978, where she continued to write and remained politically active.

Analysis

The heroism of black women in the face of turmoil of all kinds rings from both volumes of Alice Walker's short stories like the refrain of a protest song. *In Love and Trouble* reveals the extremes of cruelty and violence to which poor black women are often subjected in their personal relationships, while the struggles in *You Can't Keep a Good Woman Down* reflect the social upheavals of the 1970's.

Such subjects and themes lend themselves to a kind of narrative that is filled with tension. The words "love" and "trouble," for example, in the title of the first collection, identify a connection that is both unexpected and inevitable. Each of the thirteen stories in this collection is a vivid confirmation that every kind of love known to woman brings its own kind of suffering. Walker is adept at pairing such elements so as to create pronounced, and revealing, contrasts or intense conflicts. One such pair that appears in many of these short stories is a stylistic one and easy to see: the poetry and prose that alternate on the page. Another unusual combination at work throughout the short fiction may be called the lyrical and the sociological. Like the protest song, Walker's stories make a plea for justice more memorable by giving it a poetic form. She breathes rhythmic, eloquent language into the most brutish and banal abuses.

These two elements—similarity of subject matter and the balance of highly charged contraries—produce a certain unity within each volume. Yet beyond this common ground, the stories have been arranged so as to convey a progression of interconnected pieces whose circumstances and themes repeat, alternate, and overlap rather like a musical composition. The first three stories of *In Love and Trouble*, for example, are all about married love; the next two are about love between parent and child; then come three stories in which black-white conflict is central; the fourth group concerns religious expression; and the last three stories focus on initiation. Other themes emerge and run through this five-set sequence, linking individual motifs and strengthening the whole. Jealousy is one of those motifs, as is the drive for self-respect, black folkways, and flowers, in particular the rose and the black-eyed Susan.

The four stories to be discussed suggest the breadth of Walker's imagination and narrative skills. "Roselily" is a good place to begin, being the first story of *In Love and Trouble* and striking an anticipatory note of foreboding. "The Child Who Favored Daughter" is an equally representative selection, this time of the horrific destruction of the black woman. The third selection, "The Revenge of Hannah Kemhuff," is as cool and clear as "The Child Who Favored Daughter" is dark and fevered. The narrator recounts a tale of voodoo justice, specifically crediting Zora Neale Hurston, author of *Mules and Men* (1935). The last story of this collection, "To Hell with Dying," is an affirmative treatment of so many of the themes Walker has previously developed more darkly.

"Roselily" takes place on a front porch surrounded by a crowd of black folk, in sight of Highway 61 in Mississippi during the time it takes to perform a wedding ceremony. As the preacher intones the formal words, the bride's mind wanders among the people closest to her there—the bridegroom, the preacher, her parents, sisters, and children. His religion is different from hers, and she knows that he disapproves of this gathering. She speculates uneasily about their future life together in Chicago, where she will wear a veil and sit on the woman's side of his church and have more babies. She is the mother of four children already but has never been married. He is giving her security, but he intends, she realizes, to remake her into the image he wants. Even the love he gives her causes her great sadness, as it makes her aware of how unloved she was before. At last, the ceremony over, they stand in the yard, greeting well-wishers, he completely alien, she overcome with anxiety. She squeezes his hand for reassurance but receives no answering signal from him.

The ambivalence felt by the bride in this magnetic mood piece is intensified by poetic and fairy tale elements. First, there are the ceremonial resonances of the words between the paragraphs of narrative, stately and solemn like a slow drumbeat. As these phrases alternate with Roselily's thoughts, a tension develops. At the words *"Dearly Beloved,"* a daydream of images begins to flow, herself a small girl in her mother's fancy dress, struggling through "a bowl of quicksand soup"; the words *"we are gathered here"* suggest to her cotton waiting, ready to be weighed, a Mississippi rural countriness she knows the bridegroom finds repugnant; *"in the sight of God"* creates in her mind the image of God as a little black boy tugging at the preacher's coattail. Gradually, a sense of foreboding builds. At the words *"to join this man and this woman"* she imagines "ropes, chains, handcuffs, his religion." The bridegroom is her rescuer, like Prince Charming, and is ready to become her Pygmalion. Like Sleeping Beauty, Roselily is only dimly aware of exchanging one form of confinement, of enchantment, for another. At the end of the ceremony, she awakes to his passionate kiss and a terrible sense of being *wrong.*

While "Roselily" is a subtle story of a quiet inner life, "The Child Who Favored Daughter" records the circumstances of a shocking assault. It begins, also, on a front porch. A father waits with a shotgun on a hot afternoon for his daughter to walk from the school bus through the front yard. He is holding in his hand a letter written by her to her white lover. Realizing what her father knows, the girl comes slowly down the dusty lane, pausing to study the black-eyed Susans. As his daughter approaches, the father is reminded of his sister, "Daughter," who also had a white lover. His intense love for his sister had turned to bitterness because she gave herself to a man by whom he felt enslaved; his bitterness poisoned all of his relationships with women thereafter. He confronts the girl on the porch with the words "White man's slut!" then beats her with a stable harness and leaves her in the shed behind the house. The next morning, failing to make her deny the letter and struggling to suppress his "unnamable desire," he slashes off her breasts. As the story ends, he sits in a stupor on the front porch.

This story of perverted parental love and warring passions is about the destructive power of jealousy and denial. Its evil spell emanates from the father's unrepented and unacknowledged desire to possess his sister. He is haunted by her when he looks at his own daughter. Once again, a strongly lyrical style heightens the dominant tone, in this case, horror. Short lines of verse, like snatches of song, are interspersed with the narrative, contrasting sharply in their suggestion of pure feeling with the tightly restrained prose. The daughter's motif associates her with the attraction of natural beauty: *"Fire of earth/ Lure of flower smells/ The sun."* The father's theme sounds his particular resignation and doom: *"Memories of years/ Unknowable women—/ sisters/ spouses/ illusions of soul/."* The resulting trancelike confrontation seems inevitable, the two moving through a pattern they do not control, do not understand.

In "The Revenge of Hannah Kemhuff," a woman who has lost husband, children, and self-respect, all because a charity worker denied her food stamps, comes to the seer, Tante Rosie, for peace of mind. Tante Rosie assures the troubled woman that the combined powers of the Man-God and the Great Mother of Us All will destroy her enemy. Tante Rosie's apprentice, who narrates the story, teaches Mrs. Kemhuff the curse-prayer printed in Zora Neale Hurston's *Mules and Men.* Then she sets about to collect the necessary ingredients for the conjure: Sarah Sadler Holley's feces, water, nail parings. Her task seems to become almost impossible when her mentor tells her that these items must be gained directly from the victim herself. Nevertheless, with a plan in mind, the young woman approaches Mrs. Holley, tells her that she is learning the profession from Tante Rosie, and then asks her to prove that she, as she claims, does not believe in "rootworking." It is only a short while until Mrs. Kemhuff dies, followed a few months later by Mrs. Holley, who had, after the visit of the apprentice, taken to her bedroom, eating her nails, saving her fallen hair, and collecting her excrement in plastic bags and barrels.

This is the first story in the collection in which the black community comes into conflict with the white. It is a conflict of religious traditions and a strong statement in recognition of something profound in African folkways. Mrs. Holley failed Mrs. Kemhuff years before in the greatest of Christian virtues, that of charity. Mrs. Kemhuff, though now reconciled with her church, cannot find peace and seeks the even greater power of ancient conjure to restore her pride. Like other African-American writers who have handled this subject, Walker first acknowledges that voodoo is widely discounted as sheer superstition, but then her story argues away all rational objections. Mrs. Holley does not die as the result of hocus-pocus but because of her own radical belief, a belief in spite of herself. There is something else about this story that is different from those at the beginning of the collection. Instead of a dreamy or hypnotic action, there are alert characters speaking and thinking purposefully, clearly. This is one strand of many evolving patterns that emerge as the stories are read in sequence.

"To Hell with Dying" is the last story in the collection and a strong one. A more mellow love-and-trouble story than most preceding it, it features a male character who is not the villain of the piece. Mr. Sweet Little is a melancholy man whom the narrator has loved from childhood, when her father would bring the children to Mr. Sweet's bedside to rouse him from his depression with a shout: "To hell with dying! These children want Mr. Sweet!" Because the children were so successful in "revivaling" Mr. Sweet with their kisses and tickling and cajoling ways, they were not to learn for some time what death really meant. Years pass. Summoned from her doctoral studies in Massachusetts, the twenty-four-year-old narrator rushes to Mr. Sweet's bedside, where she cannot quite believe that she will not succeed. She does induce him to open his eyes, smile, and trace her hairline with his finger as he once did. Still, however, he dies. His legacy to her is the steel guitar on which he played away his blues all those years: that and her realization that he was her first love.

It is useful to recognize this story as an initiation story, like the two that precede it, "The Flowers" and "We Drink the Wine in France." Initiation stories usually involve, among other things, an unpleasant brush with reality, a new reality. A child, adolescent, or young adult faces an unfamiliar challenge and, if successful, emerges at a new level of maturity or increased status. Always, however, something is lost, something must be given up. As a very small girl, the narrator remembers, she did not understand quite what was going on during their visits to the neighbor's shack. When she was somewhat older, she felt the weight of responsibility for the dying man's survival. At last, after she has lost her old friend, she is happy, realizing how important they were to each other. She has successfully negotiated her initiation into the mysteries of love and death, as, in truth, she had already done, to the best of her ability, at those earlier stages.

This often-reprinted story is a culmination of the struggle between Death and Love for the lives of the girls and women, really for all the blacks of *In Love and Trouble*, one which well represents Walker's talent and demonstrates her vision of blacks supporting and affirming one another in community.

If *In Love and Trouble* is Walker's tribute to the down-and-out black woman, then

You Can't Keep a Good Woman Down is her salute to black women who are pushing ahead, those who have crossed some barriers and are in some sense champions. There are black women who are songwriters, artists, writers, students in exclusive Eastern schools; they are having abortions, teaching their men the meaning of pornography, coming to terms with the death of a father, on one hand, or with the meaning of black men raping white women, on the other. Always, they are caught up short by the notions of whites. In other words, all the political, sexual, racial, countercultural issues of the 1970's are in these stories, developed from what Walker calls the "womanist" point of view.

This set of stories, then, is somewhat more explicitly sociological than the first and somewhat less lyrical, and it is also more apparently autobiographical, but in a special sense. Walker herself is a champion, so her life is a natural, even an inescapable, source of material. Walker-the-artist plays with Walker-the-college-student and Walker-the-idealistic-teacher, as well as with some of the other roles she sees herself as having occupied during that decade of social upheaval. Once a writer's experience has become transformed within a fictive world, it becomes next to impossible to think of the story's events as either simply autobiography or simply invention. The distinction has been deliberately blurred. It is because Walker wants to unite her public and private worlds, her politics and her art, life as lived and life as imagined, that, instead of poetry, these stories are interspersed with autobiographical parallels, journal entries, letters, and other expressions of her personality.

There are three stories that deserve special attention, "Nineteen Fifty-five," "Fame," and "Source." To begin with, they serve as checkpoints for the collection's development, from the essentially simple and familiar to the increasingly complex and strange, from 1955 to 1980. Furthermore, these stories are independently memorable.

The opening story, "Nineteen Fifty-five," is presented from the perspective of a middle-aged blues singer, Gracie Mae Still, whose signature song, recorded by a young white man named Traynor, brings him fame and fortune. Gracie Mae records her impressions of Traynor in a journal, beginning with their first meeting in 1955 and continuing until his death in 1977. Over the years, the rock-and-roll star (obviously meant to suggest Elvis Presley) stays in touch with the matronly musician, buying her lavish gifts—a white Cadillac, a mink coat, a house—and quizzing her on the real meaning of her song. From the army, he writes to tell her that her song is very much in demand, and that everyone asks him what he thinks it means, really. As time goes by and his life disappoints him, he turns to the song, as if it were a touchstone that could give his life meaning. He even arranges an appearance for himself and Gracie Mae on the Johnny Carson show, with some half-developed notion of showing his fans what the real thing is and how he aspires to it. If he is searching for a shared experience of something true and moving with his audience, however, he is to be disappointed again. His fans applaud only briefly, out of politeness, for the originator of the song, the one who really gives it life, then squeal wildly for his imitation, without any recognition of what he wanted them to understand. That is the last time the two musicians see each other.

In part, this story is about the contribution that black music made to the spirit of the times and how strangely whites transformed it. The white rock-and-roll singer, who seems as much in a daze as some of the women of *In Love and Trouble*, senses something superior in the original blues version, but he misplaces its value, looking for some meaning to life that can be rolled up in the nutshell of a lyric. In contrast to the bemused Traynor, Gracie Mae is a down-to-earth champion, and her dialect looks forward to Walker's masterful handling of dialect in *The Color Purple*. She repeatedly gives Traynor simple and sensible advice when he turns to her for help, and she has her own answer to the mystery of his emptiness: "Really, I think, some peoples advance *so* slowly."

The champion of "Fame" is Andrea Clement White, and the events take place on one day, when she is being honored, when she is being confronted by her own fame. She is speaking to a television interviewer as the story begins. The old woman tells the young interviewer that in order to look at the world freshly and creatively, an artist simply cannot be famous. When reminded by the young woman that she herself is famous, Andrea Clement White is somewhat at a loss. As the interview continues its predictable way, the novelist explaining once again that she writes about people, not their color, she uneasily asks herself why she does not "*feel*" famous," why she feels as though she has not accomplished what she set out to do.

The highlight of the day is to be a luncheon in her honor, at which her former colleagues, the president, and specially invited dignitaries, as well as the generally detested former dean, will all applaud her life accomplishments (while raising money). All the while, the lady of the hour keeps a bitingly humorous commentary running in her mind. Her former students in attendance are "numbskulls," the professors, "mediocre." Out loud, she comments that the president is a bore. No matter how outrageous her behavior, she is forgiven because of her stature; when she eats her Rock Cornish hen with her hands, the entire assembly of five hundred follows suit. At last, however, the spleen and anxious bravado give way to something out of reach of the taint of fame: a child singing an anonymous slave song. Recalled to her dignity, the honored guest is able to face her moment in the limelight stoically.

In this comic story of the aggravations and annoyances that beset the publicly recognized artist, Walker imagines herself as an aging novelist who does not suffer fools gladly. She puts the artist's inner world on paper so that something of her gift for storytelling and her habits of mind become visible. The stress of the occasion and being brought into forced contact with her former president and dean trigger her aggressive imagination, and her innate narrative gift takes over. She visualizes using her heavy award as a weapon against the repulsive, kissing dean, hearing him squeal, and briefly feels gleeful. The story, however, is something more than simply a comic portrait of the artist's foibles. When Andrea Clement White questions herself about her own sense of fame, admits her own doubts, she is searching for something certain, as Traynor is searching in "Nineteen Fifty-five," though not so blindly. Like him, she is called out of the mundane by a meaningful song.

The last story of *You Can't Keep a Good Woman Down* is "Source," and in it Walker brings the social conscience of an antipoverty worker in Mississippi into relationship with the expanding consciousness of the alternative life-style as practiced on the West Coast. This is the story of two friends, Irene and Anastasia, who had attended college together in New York. When funding for Irene's adult-education project was cut, she traveled to San Francisco for a change of scene, to be met by Anastasia, who was living on welfare with some friends named Calm, Peace, and their baby, Bliss, all under the guidance of a swami named Source. The two young women were unable to find any common ground, Irene believing in collective action and Anastasia believing that people choose to suffer and that nothing can be changed. After walking out on a meeting with Source, Irene was asked to leave. Years later, the two meet again in Alaska, where Irene is lecturing to educators. Anastasia is now living with an Indian and passing for white. This time, the two women talk more directly, of color, of Anastasia's panic when she is alone, of her never being accepted as a black because of her pale skin. Irene is brought to face her own part in this intolerance and to confess that her reliance on government funding was every bit as insecure as had been Anastasia's reliance on Source. Their friendship restored and deepened, the two women embrace.

The title of this story suggests a theme that runs throughout the entire collection, the search for a center, a source of strength, meaning, or truth. This source is very important to the pioneer, but it can be a false lure. When Irene recognizes that she and Anastasia were both reaching out for something on which to depend, she states what might be taken as the guiding principle for the champion: "*any* direction that is away from ourselves is the wrong direction." This final portrait of a good woman who cannot be kept down is a distinctively personal one. It is women not distracted by external influences, true to themselves, and able to open themselves to one another, who will triumph.

Walker's short fiction adds a new image to the pantheon of American folk heroes: the twentieth century black woman, in whatever walk of life, however crushed or blocked, still persevering. Even those who seem the most unaware, the most poorly equipped for the struggle, are persevering, because, in their integrity, they cannot do otherwise. The better equipped know themselves to be advocates. They shoulder their dedication seriously and cheerfully. They are the fortunate ones; they understand that what they do has meaning.

Other major works

NOVELS: *The Third Life of Grange Copeland*, 1970; *Meridian*, 1976; *The Color Purple*, 1982; *The Temple of My Familiar*, 1989.

POETRY: *Once: Poems*, 1968; *Five Poems*, 1972; *Revolutionary Petunias and Other Poems*, 1973; *Goodnight, Willie Lee, I'll See You in the Morning: Poems*, 1979; *Horses Make a Landscape Look More Beautiful*, 1984; *Her Blue Body Everything We Know: Earthling Poems, 1965-1990*, 1991.

NONFICTION: *I Love Myself When I Am Laughing . . . and Then Again When I Am*

Looking Mean and Impressive: A Zora Neale Hurston Reader, 1979 (edited); *In Search of Our Mothers' Gardens: Womanist Prose,* 1983; *Living by the Word: Selected Writings, 1973-1987,* 1988.

CHILDREN'S BOOKS: *Langston Hughes: American Poet,* 1974; *To Hell with Dying,* 1988.

Bibliography

Awkward, Michael. *Inspiriting Influences: Tradition, Revision, and Afro-American Women's Novels.* New York: Columbia University Press, 1989. Though dense, Awkward's book may be useful in placing Walker within the context of her African-American literary heritage and in providing some possibilities for interpreting *The Color Purple* and for understanding the connections between Zora Neale Hurston, Jean Toomer, and Walker. The book is laden with critical jargon but is nevertheless important in placing Walker in context historically, thematically, and politically. Awkward emphasizes the creative spirit of African-American females and their search for self in a nonpatriarchal community as themes of Walker's fiction. Endnotes may lead researchers to other useful materials on Walker's fiction as well as on works by and on other African-American women.

Bloom, Harold, ed. *Alice Walker.* New York: Chelsea House, 1989. An important collection of critical essays examining the fiction, poetry, and essays of Walker from a variety of perspectives. The fourteen essays, including Bloom's brief introduction, are arranged chronologically. Contains useful discussions of the first three novels, brief analyses of individual short stories, poems, and essays, and assessments of Walker's social and political views in connection with her works and other African-American female authors. A chronology of Walker's life and a bibliography may be of assistance to the beginner.

Butler-Evans, Elliott. *Race, Gender, and Desire: Narrative Strategies in the Fiction of Toni Cade Bambara, Toni Morrison, and Alice Walker.* Philadelphia: Temple University Press, 1989. Focusing on the connections between gender, race, and desire, and their relationship to the narrative strategies in the fiction of these three contemporary writers, Butler-Evans argues that Walker's works are "structured by a complex ideological position" oscillating between "her identity as 'Black feminist' or 'woman-of-color' and a generalized feminist position in which race is subordinated." Useful discussions of Walker's first three novels are included. Although no attention is given to short fiction per se, the student may receive assistance with understanding Walker's "womanist" position in all her works. Includes somewhat lengthy endnotes and a bibliography.

Davis, Thadious M. "Alice Walker's Celebration of Self in Southern Generations." *Southern Quarterly* 21 (1983): 39-53. Reprint. *Women Writers of the Contemporary South.* Edited by Peggy Whitman Prenshaw. Jackson: University Press of Mississippi, 1984. An early but still useful general introduction to the works and themes of Walker, emphasizing particularly her concern for a sense of identity/self and her folk heritage. Davis discusses most significant works briefly, points out the sense of outrage at injustice in Walker's fiction, including several short stories, and also makes frequent references to her essays.

Mills, Sara, Lynne Pearce, Sue Spaull, and Elaine Millard. *Feminist Readings, Feminists Reading.* Charlottesville: University Press of Virginia, 1989. Analyzes Walker as a feminist writer from a feminist perspective. The book devotes the discussion of Walker mostly to *The Color Purple*, which is interpreted as an example of "authentic realism" designed for a female audience and as part of a female tradition beginning in the nineteenth century. More important, Walker is a part of the "self-conscious women's" revisionary tradition that has been evident since the early 1980's. Contains endnotes and a bibliography, as well as a glossary of terms related to feminist literary criticism and to literary theory in general.

Pryse, Marjorie, and Hortense J. Spillers, eds. *Conjuring: Black Women, Fiction, and Literary Tradition.* Bloomington: Indiana University Press, 1985. This useful book contains brief analyses of several Walker short stories as well as her first three novels; most of the discussion of Walker is, however, devoted to *The Color Purple*. Tracing the roots of Walker's works to folk tradition, this study, a collection of essays on various African-American female authors, emphasizes the influence of Zora Neale Hurston as well. Although there is not an essay devoted entirely to Walker, the book would be of some help in understanding Walker's literary tradition and heritage.

Wade-Gayles, Gloria. "Black, Southern, Womanist: The Genius of Alice Walker." In *Southern Women Writers: The New Generation*, edited by Tonette Bond Inge. Tuscaloosa: University of Alabama Press, 1990. An excellent, thorough introduction to the life and literary career of Walker. Placing emphasis on Walker's voice as a black, Southern woman throughout her works and arguing that Walker's commitment is to the spiritual wholeness of her people, Wade-Gayles examines several essays that are important to an understanding of her fiction and beliefs, her first three novels, both collections of short stories, and her collections of poetry. Supplemented by a bibliography of Walker's works, endnotes, and a useful secondary bibliography.

Rebecca R. Butler
(Revised by *D. Dean Shackelford*)

ROBERT WALSER

Born: Biel, Switzerland; April 15, 1878
Died: Herisau, Switzerland; December 25, 1956

Principal short fiction

Fritz Kochers Aufsätze, 1904; *Aufsätze*, 1913; *Geschichten*, 1914; *Kleine Dichtungen*, 1914; *Der Spaziergang*, 1917 (*The Walk and Other Stories*, 1957); *Prosastücke*, 1917; *Kleine Prosa*, 1917; *Poetenleben*, 1917; *Seeland*, 1919; *Die Rose*, 1925; *Selected Stories*, 1982 (foreword by Susan Sontag); *Aus dem Bleistiftgebiet: Mikragramme aus den Jahren 1924-1925*, 1985; *Masquerade and Other Stories*, 1990.

Other literary forms

Robert Walser's reputation as a prose miniaturist long obscured his achievement as a novelist. He published three novels, *Geschwister Tanner* (1907; the Tanner siblings), *Der Gehülfe* (1908; the assistant), and *Jakob von Gunten* (1909; English translation, 1969). The latter is generally acknowledged to be the most impressive work. *Der "Räuber"-Roman* (1972; the "bandit" novel), a boldly personal, experimental work, was published posthumously. His most important dramatic works were published in the volume *Komödie: Theatralisches* (1919; comedy: theatrical writings). He also wrote poetry, the merit of which has been the subject of some controversy.

Achievements

In the early decades of the twentieth century, critics praised the psychological complexity and stylistic finesse of Walser's stories and essays. The novelist Robert Musil even asserted that Franz Kafka's first book, *Betrachtung* (1913; *Meditation*, 1940) was a "special case of the Walser type." Walser's fiction appeared both in avant-garde reviews and in newspaper *feuilletons*. By the 1920's, however, his increasingly experimental prose had begun to alienate the editors and newspapers on whom he depended for a living. After he ceased writing in 1933, his work fell into oblivion.

Critics in Germany and Switzerland rediscovered Walser in the 1960's. The edition of collected works by Jochen Greven, which began appearing in 1966, gathered together for the first time all the short fiction that had appeared in scattered newspapers and reviews. Readers could at last appreciate the range and versatility of his prose. Walser is now widely regarded as one of the most significant writers in twentieth century German literature. Although English translations by Christopher Middleton appeared as early as 1957, what brought Walser's work to the attention of English-speaking readers was the publication in 1982 of the *Selected Stories*, with a foreword by Susan Sontag.

One of Walser's greatest gifts as a writer was his ability, as Christian Morgenstern put it, to "see the world as a continuous wonder." He made no attempt to separate perceptions that are "significant" from those that are "trivial." While some readers

find this rejection of conventional discriminations frustrating, others find its hetero-
doxy refreshing. In a brief but now classic essay of 1929, Walter Benjamin evoked the
enigma of Walser's seemingly artless art: "While we are used to seeing the mysteries of style emerge out of more or less fully developed and purposeful works of art,
here we are faced with language running wild in a manner that is totally uninten-
tional, or at least seems so, and yet that we find attractive and compelling. A letting
go, moreover, that ranges through all forms from the graceful to the bitter."

Biography

Robert Otto Walser was born in Biel, Switzerland, on April 15, 1878. His father,
Adolf Walser, a bookbinder by trade, was, by all accounts, a convivial individual, if
a rather lackluster businessman. His mother, whose maiden name was Elisa Marti,
was socially ambitious but psychically labile. She died in 1894, when Robert was
sixteen.

Walser spent his active years as a writer in four cities: Zurich (1896-1905), Berlin
(1905-1913), then his native Biel (1913-1921), and, finally, Bern (1921-1929). His work
falls into four phases, which coincide with the periods he spent in those cities. Frequently switching both jobs and addresses, he lived on what he himself described as
"the periphery of bourgeois existences." He sold much of his short fiction to newspapers and reviews, some of which he later published in book form. He supplemented this meager income mostly through menial clerical jobs. While in Berlin, he
attended a school for servants. For a brief period he was employed as a butler at
Dambrau Castle in Upper Silesia.

The years in Berlin were crucial for his artistic development. Through his brother
Karl, a painter and illustrator, he came into contact with leading intellectual figures.
Yet, although cosmopolitan Berlin left its mark on his increasingly sophisticated
prose, he never lost the outsider's contempt for the established order. His relations
with the writers Hugo von Hofmannsthal and Frank Wedekind and the industrialist
and politician Walter Rathenau were stormy.

Walser's three Berlin novels attracted some favorable critical attention but relatively few readers. He could not interest publishers in further novels, and some
manuscripts were lost. After his return to Biel in 1913, he turned his back on the
novel and continued writing *feuilleton* essays and short stories. During his lifetime
he wrote more than thirteen hundred individual pieces of short prose. In 1921 he
moved to Bern, claiming that he wished to make his prose more cosmopolitan in outlook. His style became increasingly experimental, and editors began to reject his
submissions. In the mid-1920's his anxiety about writing literally paralyzed his hand,
leading him to invent what he called his "pencil method" of composition. In a tiny
script, he wrote texts now known as microgrammes. A selection of hitherto unpublished microgrammes, which had been deciphered painstakingly by scholars in Zurich, was published in 1985 under the title *Aus dem Bleistiftgebiet* (from the pencil
territory).

By the late 1920's, Walser was leading the life of a recluse and hearing persecuting voices from which he could find no escape. On January 25, 1929, he was admitted to the Waldau asylum near Bern. At first, he appears to have reached almost thankfully for the new role of inmate, which he was to play diligently, mending sacks and refusing special concessions, for the remaining twenty-seven years of his life. Yet, at times, he longed to be set free. In 1933, in apparent protest against his transfer from Waldau to the asylum at Herisau, in the canton of Appenzell-Ausserrhoden, he gave up writing altogether. He died at the age of seventy-eight on Christmas Day, 1956.

Analysis

Robert Walser's early reputation as a miniaturist was misleading. His essays and stories actually form the nucleus of a larger work, which he once described as a "sliced-up or torn-apart novel of myself." The main protagonist in this autobiographical "novel" is not so much Walser as his poetic self. This self adopts a wide variety of roles, such as that of the servant, the artist, and the child. Yet Walser never identifies for long with these fictional alter egos. His stance toward them is ironic, haughty, or nonchalant. Having adopted them with the flick of a pen, he can discard them just as swiftly. More crucial than their individual identities is their unmistakable voice, which remained remarkably constant throughout his career. By turns effusive and reticent, self-effacing and self-inflating, long-winded and laconic, solitary and convivial, this voice determines the cadences of his prose.

Throughout his career, Walser struggled to reconcile his modernist practice with his conservative ideals. His literary values were firmly rooted in Swiss literary tradition. Among Walser's idols was the civic-minded nineteenth century novelist Gottfried Keller, who is renowned for his lyrical realism. Walser's own prose, however, is closer to the self-conscious experimentation of modernists such as Virginia Woolf.

While not a major achievement, his first book, *Fritz Kochers Aufsätze* (Fritz Kocher's essays), is a characteristic product of the Zurich phase. Walser adopted the persona of a schoolboy writing compositions on hackneyed themes such as friendship and nature. These neo-Romantic effusions are tongue-in-cheek, but tiresome nevertheless. Walser's stylistic dexterity only becomes apparent when he lets the schoolboy mask slip. Alternating with the purple prose of Fritz Kocher are stretches of sophisticated and self-conscious writing, which poke fun not only at the convention of schoolboy essays but also at language itself.

The tone becomes more urgent in the final piece in the collection "Der Wald" (the forest). Kocher intimates that he is driven into the forest by unspecified woes, but this oblique confession ends abruptly. Kocher claims that he must be careful not to divulge too much about himself. Here he is clearly speaking on behalf of Walser himself, the Walser who does not want readers to recognize the self lurking behind his numerous personas. This attitude is stated unequivocally in "Das Kind" ("The Child"): "Nobody has the right to treat me as if he knew me."

It has been said of Kafka's stories that they are alienated fairy tales. This is true also of Walser's. His two Zurich fairy tales in free verse are indispensable for an understanding of his short prose. In *Aschenbrödel* (1901; *Cinderella*, 1985) and *Schnee-*

wittchen (1901; *Snowwhite*, 1985), which Benjamin called "one of the most profound compositions in recent literature," Walser's heroines rebel against the script of the Grimm Brothers by refusing to allow themselves to be rescued. They owe their creativity to the sisters and stepmother who torment them. Without that hostility, they would be lost. Happiness and reciprocated love would destroy what they most prize in themselves. Thus, they chase away the Prince Charmings.

There are examples in the short prose both of this bleak vision and of a radiant counterpoint. In "Seltsame Stadt" ("A Strange City"), for example, Walser conjures up a Utopian society. The inhabitants of this singular city are dolls, relatives, perhaps, of the graceful puppets that Heinrich von Kleist describes in his essay "Über das Marionettentheater" ("The Marionette Theater"). They revere life and treasure the senses and can thus dispense with preachers and artists. Surfacing here is the conviction that in a truly civilized society the professional artist would be super-fluous. The narrator dwells in a rather fetishistic manner on the shoes and trousers of the women. These obsessions recur in the short prose, most flagrantly, perhaps, in "Hose" ("Trousers"), which is less about women's emancipation than about Wal-ser's trousers fetish.

The story "Oskar" is uncharacteristically forthright. Written in Biel but reflecting on the Zurich years, it describes the origins of Walser's stylization of himself as a self-denying hermit. Oskar discovers within himself a need for solitude. He is not content to satisfy this need, and he feels compelled to make life harsher by denying himself such creature comforts as a warm room in winter. His shaping of this idio-syncratic persona is partly involuntary, partly willed. The rationale for his seemingly masochistic behavior is aesthetic. He expects the solitude to sharpen his appetite for life. As Oskar's isolation intensifies, however, the narrator intimates the human cost of his wayward odyssey.

In Berlin, Walser retained the pose of the naïve provincial, but his prose became increasingly sophisticated. The theater stimulated his imagination, and he wrote frequently for the influential review *Die Schaubühne*. Although he was ostensibly commenting on the plays of Wedekind, Gerhart Hauptmann, and others, his real subject was the self-impersonation that he himself practiced in the medium of prose. Ideally, he wanted his fiction to enact an appealing version not only of himself but also of life itself. He was, however, fully aware that this quest for life in art raises tortuous epistemological questions. Even as early as 1902, in the dramatic sketch *Die Knaben* (1902; the boys), an actor is chided for confusing life with appearances and "the body with its reflexes."

In "Beantwortung einer Anfrage" ("Response to a Request"), Walser illustrates graphically the exploitation of the self on which his art is based. The narrator offers advice to an actor who has asked him for a sketch that he can perform. Instead of giving the actor a script, the narrator advises him to use his body as his material. Carefully choreographed gestures will enable him to manipulate the audience's re-sponse. If physical pain is to horrify the spectator, then it must be elegantly enacted. The uncharacteristically violent self-immolation at the end of the story anticipates the lurid effects of the later expressionists. More important, however, the execution of this sketch mirrors the workings of Walser's prose. It, too, manipulates images of the self, relying for its effects on emotional dissonance and stylistic incongruity.

In Biel, Walser regressed stylistically. He did not always distance himself successfully from the neo-Romantic clichés that once again invaded his prose. In "Die Einfahrt" (the entrance), for example, the description of his return to the fatherland aboard a train full of noble workers is downright mawkish. Nature affords him a screen onto which he can all too easily project the fulfillment of secret desires. In "Der Wald" (the wood), the forest becomes the setting for an illusionary erotic encounter. This sketch could be contrasted with the less self-indulgent treatment of the same motif in *Fritz Kochers Aufsätze.*

The Walk and Other Stories is an exceptional chronicle of the Biel years. Walser is more candid than elsewhere about the darker emotions underlying his surface exuberance. The title "The Walk" evokes both a physical activity and a philosophy of life, as "the Way" evokes Christianity and Taoism. This hero is as self-evasive as his fictional cousins of this period, but he, at least, reflects about the gaunt figure of Tomzack, a personification of the dark forces within him. Walser subjects his neo-Romantic motifs to probing scrutiny. It is fear that drives the stroller into the center of a fairy-tale forest. The prose reflects upon this evasion even as it narrates it.

Walser was at his most innovative formally during the years in Bern. In moving to that city in 1921, he openly rejected the pastoral idylls that mar the Biel prose. His aim was to reflect the internal workings of human consciousness. While the artist figure remains prominent, the landscape through which he now strolls is that of his own mind. Some readers find this "aimless ambling" (Walser) as infuriating as others find it intriguing. One early example of the former type of response was provided by a critic who attacked Walser for misrepresenting the nineteenth century playwright Georg Büchner in "Ein Dramatiker" (a dramatist). Walser responded by describing the offending text as "an imaginary, small, short, thin, slim, nervous, healthy, cheeky, timid story," composed in the manner of "carpet weaving, of a game with words, of something mosaic-like" in the hope that readers would detect "the novella-likeness of his apparent essay."

Eine Ohrfeige und Sonstiges (1925; *A Slap in the Face et cetera*, 1985) is one of the most provocative texts of the Bern years. It is hard to assign it to any one genre. Walser showers the reader with an assortment of diary-like entries, anecdotes, aphorisms, fragmentary stories and miniature fairy tales. The opening paragraph forces the reader to plunge immediately into a narrative that juxtaposes events as if they were elements in a collage. Elsewhere in his final collection, *Die Rose* (the rose), Walser suggests that this freewheeling method of composition allows him to play on "the instrument of his fancies."

The opening lines of *A Slap in the Face et cetera* represent clipped renderings of actual impressions prompted by a brief visit to Biel. Instead of developing the initial allusions to a schoolteacher and a sergeant, however, the narrator flits into the tiny auditorium of a theater, which immediately suggests its opposite, a giant railway station he has recently observed. He teases the reader by withholding key information, such as the name of the playwright, who turns out to be Oscar Wilde. Walser perceives an affinity between his fate and that of the Irishman. Later, in the middle of a meditation on the vagaries of the literary marketplace, he invokes the eighteenth century poet Friedrich Hölderlin, who suffered a mental breakdown and spent the last thirty-six years of his life in seclusion.

Walser strews fragmentary fictions amid diary-like entries of this kind. One of these miniature stories is a grotesque fairy tale about a mother, Lady Hypocrite, and her son, "little trouserlegs." Walser is playing here on the register of unacknowledged childhood traumas. Lurking beneath such fairytale figures as the passionately wicked mother is an autobiographical substratum that he banishes from the surface of his prose. Instead, he finds refuge in his own playfulness, indulging in whimsical allusions to high culture and reveling in his own power to mold the fairy tale any way he chooses. He clings to this high-wire exuberance, which cannot, however, entirely distract the attention of the reader from the abyss below.

These fragmentary fictions often reveal as much as they conceal. In a final fiction, introduced by a banner headline, Walser develops the motif of the romantic triangle toward an ingenious anticlimax. His heroes often have a weakness for Platonic relationships in which they can indulge their fantasies without fear of losing them to a paltry reality. In this fragment, the narrator's totally imaginary infatuation with a married woman, whom he has never met, suggests the fragility of the threads linking an isolated dreamer—the narrator and behind him, of course, Walser himself— to the world of others.

Skepticism about the epistemological status of fiction had been a feature of Walser's prose ever since the Zurich years, but the debate within him about his poetic principles intensified in the mid-1920's. The incomprehension that greeted the verbal playfulness of the Bern prose affected him deeply. He edged slowly toward silence. In *A Slap in the Face et cetera*, he could still transmute his skepticism about fiction into verbal high jinks, but by the late 1920's his tone had changed. In "Brief an einen Besteller von Novellen" ("Letter to a Commissioner of Novellas"), he explains somewhat defensively why he cannot deliver works that conform to the traditional genre. In mock-bureaucratic language, he argues that traditional novellas can no longer do justice to contemporary life, which has turned into "something tentative, cautiously groping." In "Für die Katz" ("For Zilch") he wryly conceded the pointlessness of his literary productivity. In 1933, he renounced literature for good.

Other major works

NOVELS: *Geschwister Tanner*, 1907; *Der Gehülfe*, 1908; *Jakob von Gunten*, 1909 (English translation, 1969); *Der "Räuber"-Roman*, 1972.

PLAYS: *Aschenbrödel*, 1901 (fairy-tale play; *Cinderella*, 1985); *Schneewittchen*, 1901 (fairy-tale play; *Snowwhite*, 1985); *Die Knaben*, 1902 (sketch); *Komödie: Theatralisches*, 1919.

POETRY: *Gedichte*, 1909; *Unbekannte Gedichte*, 1958.

MISCELLANEOUS: *Eine Ohrfeige und Sonstiges*, 1925 (*A Slap in the Face Et Cetera*, 1985); *Das Gesamtwerk*, 1966-1975 (13 volumes); *Robert Walser Rediscovered: Stories, Fairy-Tale Plays, and Critical Responses*, 1985.

Bibliography

Avery, George. *Inquiry and Testament: A Study of the Novels and Short Prose of Robert Walser.* Philadelphia: University of Pennsylvania Press, 1968. This introduction to Walser is aimed at both the general reader and the student of German literature. Deals with the themes, the style, and the structure of the Swiss writer's fiction in the context of European literary developments of the early twentieth century.

Hamburger, Michael. "Explorers: Musil, Robert Walser, Kafka." In *A Proliferation of Prophets: Essays on German Writers from Nietzsche to Brecht.* Manchester, England: Carcanet Press, 1983. Views "freedom and ambivalence" as hallmarks of Walser's art, claiming that he combines the freedom of the essay and the poem with the art of prose fiction.

Harman, Mark, ed. *Robert Walser Rediscovered: Stories, Fairy-Tale Plays, and Critical Responses.* Hanover, N.H.: University Press of New England, 1985. Along with translations, some previously published, are commentaries by major critics, contemporary and modern. Followed by a chronology, notes, a select bibliography, and an index of Walser's works. Essential reading.

_____. "Stream of Consciousness and the Boundaries of Self-Conscious Fiction: The Works of Robert Walser." *Comparative Criticism* 6 (1984): 119-134. Views the fairy tales, short prose, and novels of Walser as parts of an "autobiographical construct." In spite of their confessional aspects, Walser's works are products of craftsmanship and reflection.

Sontag, Susan. Foreword to *Selected Stories*, by Robert Walser. Translated by Christopher Middleton, et al. Manchester, England: Carcanet New Press, 1982. Views Walser as a "miniaturist" in short prose and comments on the "refusal of power" and compassionate despair of his work. See also Christopher Middleton's "Postscript," pp. 191-194.

Mark Harman
(Revised by *Anna M. Wittmann*)

WANG ANYI

Born: Shanghai, China; 1954

Principal short fiction

Liu shi, 1982 (novella; *Lapse of Time*, 1988); *Leng tu*, 1982 (novella); *Xiao bao zhuang*, 1985 (novella; *Baotown*, 1989); *Huang shan zhi lian*, 1986 (novella; *Love on a Barren Mountain*, 1991); *Xiao cheng zhi lian*, 1986 (novella; *Love in a Small Town*, 1988); *Jin xiu gu zhi lian*, 1987 (novella); *Lapse of Time*, 1988.

Other literary forms

In addition to her short fiction, Wang Anyi published a travelogue entitled *Mu nü tong you mei li jian* (mother and daughter traveling together in America), in 1986. Addressed to a Chinese audience, this book is essentially derived from notes and observations written during the author's tour of the United States. The author's mother, Ru Zhi'juan, is an accomplished writer herself.

Achievements

Wang first started publishing in November, 1976; in less than a decade, she had already been recognized as a prolific writer of substantial achievement. Her short story "Ben ci lie che zhong dian zhan" ("Destination") was chosen for the Chinese National Award for Short Stories in 1982, and her novella *Lapse of Time* was the winner of the National Award for Short Novels in 1983. In 1985, the novella *Baotown* was the topic of a seminar hosted by the Writers' Association of Shanghai shortly after its publication. The Three Loves Trilogy, written in 1986, has attracted attention as a controversial work because of its depiction of illicit or extramarital love affairs—a sensitive issue that, in China, is considered to be a "forbidden territory."

Biography

Wang Anyi was born in Shanghai in 1954. Her mother, Ru Zhi'juan, is an accomplished writer whose career began in 1947. Thanks to her cultured family background, Wang was exposed to music, art, and literature as a child. She finished her junior high school education in 1969, the third year of the Cultural Revolution, a period during which a cataclysmal chaos extended all over China.

In 1970, like many other teenagers across the Chinese nation, Wang was sent to a rural area in the province of Anhwei to join a production brigade as a "young intellectual" (high school graduate) to be "re-educated by the poor and lower-middle peasants." In 1972, however, she managed to find a position in the orchestral troupe of the Xuzhou City Commission for Literature and Arts in the province of Kiangsu; it was during this period that she started writing. In 1978, as the political climate began to change for the better, Wang was transferred back to Shanghai, where she started working in the editorial department of *Childhood* magazine. In 1980, she enrolled in the Fifth Annual Writers' Workshop hosted by the Writers' Association of China. Upon graduation at the end of the year, Wang returned to her editorial work and emerged rapidly as an important writer.

Analysis

Wang Anyi's career coincides with an important historical juncture in contemporary Chinese literature. Prior to the death of Mao Tse-tung and the fall of the Gang of Four in 1976, Chinese writers were required to play a subservient role and serve the immediate interests of politics. After the introduction of the economic reform in 1978, however, a relatively ameliorated environment allowed writers to pursue authentic and diversified means of expression with a certain amount of liberty. Wang is one of the young writers who seized such an opportunity. Although she once regarded herself as independent of literary movements, she admits that she has benefited from trends such as the "Literature of Wound," the "Literature of Transvaluation," the "Literature in Search of Roots," and the "Quest for Urban Awareness." These tendencies are evident in her works, but the style is peculiarly her own, and in the end, they also culminate in a uniquely lyrical form of humanistic expression.

An example representative of Wang's short stories is "And the Rain Patters On," which is reminiscent of the "Literature of Wound," a groundbreaking literary trend that has as its theme the injuries, injustices, sufferings, and aftermaths of the Cultural Revolution. In this story, meticulously crafted from lyrical flashbacks, symbols, and motifs, Wenwen, a woman sent to the countryside as an "educated youth," returns to Shanghai and finds herself to be a spinster and out of place in a world being transformed by modernity. Unable to catch up with the latest fashions, she finds romance to be elusive. While her family has been trying to arrange for her to meet and date a marriageable man (Xiao Yan), she dreamily yearns for a relationship that would somehow be different. One rainy night, after missing the last bus home, she is given a ride on a bike by a man about whom she feels ambivalent. The man is simply an ordinary good samaritan who happened to pass by, but Wenwen is touched by his casual remark about the beauty of street lamps in the rain and by his account about his having been saved by another good samaritan. She begins to hope and even trust that she will run into this stranger again. Claiming that she has eventually found a boyfriend, Wenwen rejects Xiao Yan, though to the chagrin of her family it is clear that she is simply daydreaming. Toward the end of the story, the narrator asserts that there are many pleasures in life, and dreaming is one of them; one has to insist on believing that dreams will come true, or else life would be unbearable. Encouraging and disturbing at the same time, this message exemplifies the tensions between ideality and reality, and the conflicts between the inner life and the outside world.

"And the Rain Patters On" also typifies Wang Anyi's persistent efforts in juxtaposing idealistic yearnings and realistic pressures, combining these opposites into a new humanism through lyrical expression and psychological representation. Such efforts can be found in most of her short stories in *Lapse of Time*—for example, in "Destination." In this award-winning piece, because of the mundane pressures of life in Shanghai, Chen Xin is confronted with his family's suggestion that he arrange to marry any woman who has a room to offer as dowry. Realizing, however, that "ahead of him there would be another ten, twenty, and thirty years" and that "he must give his future some serious thought," Chen Xin refuses to compromise and is embroiled in a familial conflict, which is left unresolved in the story. In spite of this conflict, however, the story contains an important touch of humanism as the family, fearing that he may commit suicide, comes searching for him after he has disappeared into the streets for the entire night after a quarrel. Finally, Chen Xin is described as being reconciled to the thought that he will be in search of his true destination—a paradox typical of Wang Anyi's fiction in that her protagonists are deprived materialistically and yet remain spiritually unvanquished.

Whether consciously or otherwise, in many of her stories Wang's new humanism focuses on the pervasive phenomenon of alienation under the socialist regime, though in an existential manner she decides that her protagonists are capable of rising or staying above the mire. For example, in one of her most triumphant stories, "The Base of the Wall," A'nian (son of a working-class family)—chooses to befriend and assist Duxing (daughter of a supposedly antireactionary family from the other side of the broken wall) after he has had a glimpse, through a diary that he has stolen, into the inner life of the sensitive, intelligent, and ostracized "class enemy" whom he and the other kids used to abuse. By eliminating the bigotry from the children of his own neighborhood and by bringing children from both sides of the wall closer to one another, A'nian has dismantled the barrier arbitrarily set up to pit one part of humanity against another.

All the above themes—tensions between ideality and reality, conflicts between the inner life and the outside world, the paradox between spirituality and materiality, the triumph of humanism over alienation under socialism—are explored to fuller extents in *Lapse of Time*. The novella is a series of sketches chronicling the awakening, growth, and transformation of a housewife during the Cultural Revolution. Duanli, a college graduate, is married to Wenyao, the son of a Shanghai businessman. At the beginning of the Cultural Revolution, the properties of the family are seized by the Red Guards. Wenyao is a superfluous man incapable of meeting the new challenges of life; his brother, Wenguang, for fear of being implicated, distances himself from his father. The responsibility of caring for the family of nine falls on the shoulders of Duanli, who finds it difficult to cope with poverty. No longer a "bourgeois lady of the house," she learns the meaning of life anew, starting from the basics of survival. Gradually, Duanli has in effect become the "guardian" of the household. Upon restitution and the return of the family properties after the Cultural Revolution, fortune again seems to smile on the family, and everyone feels complacent and justified in demanding a better life to make up for the losses of the fateful decade. Duanli, who has become a practical person, feels the same and quits working, but after two years of tiresome and unauthentic social life, she is troubled by the loss of her sense of vitality previously gained from the fateful decade. In the end, she decides to resume her job at the factory, not only to fight boredom but also to continue with her search for the meaning of life and to prevent life from lapsing into oblivion. Full of details about quotidian struggles and the sordid nature of life in contemporary China, the novella most likely will pluck at the heartstrings of millions of readers who, having emerged from a decade of hardships, find themselves entrenched in a whole series of struggles not only to achieve a better economic life but also to establish a significance for themselves.

Whereas *Lapse of Time* enlarges on urban consciousness as a condition for the definition of humanity in an alienated society, *Baotown* is an attempt to explore the historical, cultural, and symbolic dimensions of humanity in a rustic and remote corner of rural China. The legend of King Yu of Xia (c. 21-16 B.C.E.), the tamer of the great flood and the founder of the first dynasty in Chinese history, is invoked, somewhat ironically, in the preface in order to situate Baotown in a mythical and historical context. A folk ballad on numbers, which contains quasi-nonsensical cliché references to random events in Chinese history, recurs throughout the story as a leitmotif. The nonlinear plot is constructed intricately around an odd assortment of two dozen characters, four of whom are responsible for the major event in the history of Baotown. The first of these is Picked-Up. Having been reared by his "aunt," an unmarried woman who claims that she picked him up as a baby from the street, he runs away and settles in Baotown to cohabit with, and slave for, a widow, but he is despised by the community. The second is Bao Fifth Grandfather, an old man who has become an "end-of-the-liner" upon the death of his grandson and only descendant. He is befriended by Dregs, the third character and the youngest son of Bao Yanshan. This little boy in the end loses his life for the sake of Bao Fifth Grandfather during a flood, but his body is salvaged by Picked-Up. The fourth character is Bao Renwen, a young man whose aspiration to be a writer is fulfilled when he provides a written account about the accident for broadcast on radio. Unknowingly, he not only immortalizes Dregs but also helps to create a sense of importance for Bao Yanshan and to dignify Picked-Up. Written with a mixed sense of humor, irony, satire, sympathy, and lament, *Baotown* is a dazzling work thanks to its technical experimentation and its penetration into the human psyche as it is shaped by the historical and cultural conditions of China. The mythmaking process occurring in both the preface and the conclusion of the novella is especially thought-provoking.

Just as *Baotown* was still arousing much enthusiasm among its readers, Wang moved on to transcend herself even further, in 1986, by turning out the controversial Three Loves Trilogy. The three novellas share the common theme of unorthodox love, but each work has its unique focus. In *Love on a Barren Mountain*, which deals with extramarital love and sex, Wang focuses on the intensity of an obsessive relationship between a talented but superfluous man and a seductive woman of questionable reputation. They can each be described as married to the right person of their choice, until their fatal encounter tells each of them that the other could have been a better match. It is a poignant tragedy of desire which ends in the lovers' suicide, though death itself does not seem to constitute a real resolution. The omniscient narrator is careful not to take a judgmental stand, as if to suggest that love of such intensity is beyond any ordinary sense of right and wrong or good and evil.

The second piece in the trilogy, *Love in a Small Town*, deals with the strange relationship between two dancers of a sleazy troupe. Both performers have been deformed as a result of improper training, the woman being larger and the man smaller in size than normal. Their relationship is full of sadomasochistic contradictions: they both hate and crave each other so intensely that if they are not trying to beat each other's brains out, they are burning with desire for each other. They are condemned to a relationship that amounts to mutual punishment and destruction through either sexual contact or physical combat. Such a consuming affair drags both parties deeper and deeper into a quagmire. Eventually, actually contemplating suicide, the woman, who has been evading the man for a long period, decides to satiate her desire for the last time as if she were to die in a battle. Miraculously, this last union makes the woman pregnant and gives her the courage to live for herself and her twins as an unmarried mother and an outcast, whereas the man sinks so low that he becomes a good-for-nothing gambler and alcoholic. The solution to the contradictions in the story is therefore polarized between the rise above and the fall below the line that sets humanity apart from bestiality. In this stunning story, which reads like a parable if not a pathological case study, it seems that the author is raising the question of what to do with the inherent deformity or deficiency of human nature itself.

The third piece of the trilogy, *Jin xiu gu zhi lian* (love in embroidered brocade valley), differs sharply from the first and the second in that here the focus is on an extramarital relationship that boils down to phantasmagoria. In the story, an editor takes part in a conference held in the Lushan Mountains, a scenic tourist resort. With household chores behind her, she is distanced from her contempt-breeding husband, who has become all too familiar. Surrounded by men of talents, she feels that she has fallen in love with a writer who she thinks is also in love with her. Although the romantic scenery intimates that the romance is real, nothing actually has transpired. Returning to live her life of daily routines, for a while she hopes that the "romance" will materialize even if it entails a terrible scandal, but finally she is reconciled to the thought that it would suffice only to have a wonderful impression of the valley. This dreamy story is a subtle exploration of the distinctive nature of feminine desire and sexual difference in the context of married life in contemporary China. At issue is not whether the woman and her husband love each other, but rather how love itself can stay uncontaminated by the practical concerns of everyday life and survive the wear and tear of familiarity.

The three stories of the trilogy are independent of one another but also interrelated. They constitute a progression toward the resolution of the question of love, sex, and marriage on psychological rather than moral grounds. In these stories, every single character has gone on trial; although in the end no one really triumphs, readers begin to sense that the author's examination of the characters' innermost thoughts, feelings, desires, and secrets, however perverse, has sharpened and deepened their understanding of humanity itself. As none of the characters is given a name, the trilogy seems to be inviting readers to witness the introspections of the characters themselves and, in the process, start an introspection of the anonymous man and woman within the readers' own psyche.

Having grown up privileged and yet given opportunities to experience and sympathize with the conditions of the deprived in both urban and rural China during a tumultuous age, Wang is a dynamic and conscientious writer equipped with a wide variety of technical resources, including lyricism, cinematic flashes, and psychological realism. Assessing her own career, she stated in "To Face Myself" that the overall theme that she has been attempting to formulate, after much rational deliberation, is that humankind's greatest enemy is itself. According to this proposition, Wang believes that a human being has to struggle against not only the world outside but also, more important, the self within. Furthermore, she observes that such a struggle is by definition a solitary and lifelong campaign, but in the sense that it is experienced by all human beings on different battlefronts, it is also a collective endeavor that can be shared. The short stories and novellas analyzed above certainly bear out her characterization of the human struggle. Her preoccupation with such a struggle offers a unique humanistic vision perfectly adapted to the social, political, historical, and cultural conditions of contemporary Chinese literature.

Other major works

NONFICTION: *Mu nü tong you mei li jian*, 1986.

Bibliography

Hung, Eva. Introduction to *Love in a Small Town*. Hong Kong: Chinese University of Hong Kong, 1988. Contains an overview of Wang Anyi's life and career up to 1987, focusing on Wang's views on women and the authorities' condemnation of the sexuality in the Three Loves Trilogy.

_____. Introduction to *Love on a Barren Mountain*. Hong Kong: Chinese University of Hong Kong, 1991. An informed discussion and analysis of the backgrounds, issues, themes, and techniques of the three novellas in the Three Loves Trilogy both individually and as a progression. Argues that Wang Anyi has adopted a woman-centered attitude in her treatment of relationships between men and women.

Kinkley, Jeffrey. Preface to *Lapse of Time*. San Francisco: China Books & Periodicals, 1988. An introductory overview of Wang Anyi's short fiction translated for collection in *Lapse of Time*. Focusing on the humanism by which Wang's works are informed, Kinkley provides brief but useful analyses of their historical background and social contexts, as well as the author's motivations, preoccupations, themes, techniques, and style.

Li Ziyun. Preface to *Best Chinese Stories, 1949-1989*. Beijing: Chinese Literature Press, 1989. An extremely useful analysis of the development of short fiction as an engaging art form in the postliberation era. Major trends, along with representative authors and works, are identified and discussed in the context of the political movements in contemporary China.

Wang, Anyi. "Biographical Note—My Wall." in *Lapse of Time*. San Francisco: China Books & Periodicals, 1988. The author identifies the wall separating the neighborhood of the deprived from the neighborhood of the privileged (she grew up in the latter) as the spiritual source of her art. Wang explains how, because of the symbolic impact of the wall, she can be likened to an acrobat walking a tightrope both in her life and in her fiction.

Balance Chow

SYLVIA TOWNSEND WARNER

Born: Harrow, Great Britain; December 6, 1893
Died: Maiden Newton, Great Britain; May 1, 1978

Principal short fiction

Some World Far from Ours, and Stay Corydon, Thou Swain, 1929; *Elinor Barley*, 1930; *Moral Ending and Other Stories*, 1931; *The Salutation*, 1932; *More Joy in Heaven, and Other Stories*, 1935; *The Cat's Cradle Book*, 1940; *A Garland of Straw and Other Stories*, 1943; *The Museum of Cheats*, 1947; *Winter in the Air, and Other Stories*, 1955; *A Spirit Rises*, 1962; *A Stranger with a Bag, and Other Stories*, 1966 (U.S. edition, *Swans on an Autumn River: Stories*, 1966); *The Innocent and the Guilty: Stories*, 1971; *Kingdoms of Elfin*, 1977; *Scenes of Childhood*, 1981; *One Thing Leading to Another: And Other Stories*, 1984; *Selected Stories of Sylvia Townsend Warner*, 1988.

Other literary forms

In addition to the short stories for which Sylvia Townsend Warner is best known, she wrote seven novels: *Lolly Willowes: Or, The Loving Huntsman* (1926), *Mr. Fortune's Maggot* (1927), *The True Heart* (1929), *Summer Will Show* (1936), *After the Death of Don Juan* (1938), *The Corner That Held Them* (1948), and *The Flint Anchor* (1954). She also wrote several collections of poetry, which were published as *Collected Poems* (1982), a biography, a travel guidebook, and a volume of literary criticism, and she translated two books from French into English.

Achievements

In 1926, Warner's first novel, *Lolly Willowes*, was the first Book-of-the-Month Club selection; her second novel, *Mr. Fortune's Maggot*, was a selection of the newly formed Literary Guild. Her later novels did not attain the same popularity, but her short stories, 144 of which were published in *The New Yorker* over a period of four decades, gained for her a wide readership.

In 1967, she became a Fellow of the Royal Society of Literature (she wryly commented that it was the first public acknowledgment she had received since she was expelled from kindergarten) and in 1972, an honorary member of the American Academy of Arts and Letters. Her short story "The Love Match" was awarded the Prix Menton for 1968.

No full-length critical assessment of Warner's achievement as novelist, short-story writer, and poet has been produced. John Updike noted in a favorable review that her "half century of brilliantly varied and superbly self-possessed literary production never won for her the flaming place in the heavens of reputation that she deserved." As far as her achievement in the short story is concerned, however, she certainly ranks alongside H. E. Bates and V. S. Pritchett, her two British contemporaries, whose work most resembles her own.

Biography

Sylvia Townsend Warner was born in Harrow, Middlesex, on December 6, 1893. She was educated mostly at home (her father was a schoolmaster), having been considered a disruptive influence in kindergarten. Her early talent was for music, and in 1914 she was set to travel to Vienna to study under Arnold Schönberg, but the outbreak of World War I prevented it. In 1916, after the death of her father, she moved to London and was a member of the editorial committee which compiled the ten-volume *Tudor Church Music* (1922-1929). Her first publication was a collection of poetry, *The Espalier*, in 1925, a time when she thought of herself primarily as a poet. In the 1920's, she met the novelist T. F. Powys, who proved to be influential on her early poetry and fiction. In 1930, Warner moved to the country and lived with her friend Valentine Ackland in a Dorset village. During the 1930's, she and Ackland became involved in left-wing politics, joining the Communist Party and serving with the Red Cross in Barcelona during the Spanish Civil War. In subsequent years, Warner lived the quiet life of an English gentlewoman in rural Dorset, managing to sustain her literary output up to her final years. She died in 1978.

Analysis

One of the notable features of Sylvia Townsend Warner's short stories is her elegant, precise, epigrammatic, and witty prose. These qualities are particularly noticeable when she focuses on what she knows best: the niceties of English middle- and upper-class life as they reveal themselves in day-to-day domestic and social routines, and the sudden disruption of those routines. As in the novels of her British contemporary, Barbara Pym, her detached and humorous observance of the oddities of humanity is one of the chief pleasures to be gained from her stories. She has a sharp but sympathetic eye for eccentricity of all kinds, and her stories cover a wide range of situations and points of view.

Perhaps because of the variety of her fiction, it would be misleading to pinpoint specific themes or leading ideas. Warner's stories do not reveal a consistent or dominant mood or atmosphere. She does not espouse a philosophy or champion a cause. Her subject matter is the infinite variety of human nature: its follies, regrets, hopes, deceits, compromises, its small defeats and victories, the tidy chaos of the average human life. The stories frequently develop out of an apparently insignificant event or chance encounter or an incident or memory from the protagonist's past, which resurfaces to affect the present. A sudden rift is produced in the otherwise smooth fabric of daily life, and often an ironic twist at the end will reveal a new dimension to a relationship or to the inner life of the protagonist.

Warner is a traditionalist. She does not experiment with modern techniques (her chief technical device is the flashback); her stories succeed through strong characterization and plotting. There is an old-fashioned quality about her and her fictional world. Almost all of her stories are set in England, with a carefully evoked spirit of place (perhaps this accounts in part for her success in *The New Yorker*, since she usually portrays a timeless, civilized England that popular American culture has tended to idealize).

Warner has a Thomas Hardy-like awareness of the ironies of fate (Hardy was a major influence on her early poetry) and of the tricks that time plays. Many of her stories (for example, "The Sea Is Always the Same," "Johnnie Brewer," and "A Second Visit") center on the protagonist's return, after a gap of many years, to a former home or place of memories. In *"Hee-Haw!"* from *Winter in the Air, and Other Stories*, Mrs. Vincent returns to the village in Cornwall, where for three years, thirty years previously, she had lived turbulently with her first husband, Ludovick, a young artist who was later to gain eminence. The first sound she hears on her return is the unchanging, regular sound of the foghorn from the lightship (*Hee Haw! Hee Haw!*), which seems to span the thirty years of her absence, giving a sense of permanence and familiarity to the external environment. What of her internal environment? She is introduced to an old man in the hotel bar, who needs little prompting to recall the famous artist. His recollections, however, shock her. He tells her that Ludovick and his wife (or girlfriend, he did not know which) were the happiest couple he had ever seen, and he relates several incidents in which they were playing and laughing together. Mrs. Vincent, however, knowing how stormy her relationship with Ludovick was, assumes without question that the old man must be referring to another woman. In a wave of jealousy, she realizes that she has discovered, thirty years after the event, her husband's infidelity. She is left to her anger and her melancholy; an old wound has been reopened in a way that she would not have imagined possible.

The strength of *"Hee-Haw!"* is in the contrast between the ease with which the reader guesses the truth (although the truth is never overtly established) and the inability of Mrs. Vincent to recognize that her relationship with Ludovick might have looked quite different from the outside. It is at once a poignant tale of reminiscence and a reminder of the subjectivity of the experience of life. Appearances are not what they seem, and memory is only shifting sand.

"Winter in the Air" also focuses on a return. A middle-aged woman, Barbara, returns to live in London after a twelve-year absence, following the breakup of her marriage. The story consists of a series of flashbacks to the final stages of her marriage two months previously, interspersed with Barbara's thoughts as she arranges the furniture in her new apartment. The reader is given a minimum of clues regarding the reasons for the divorce, and the chief interest of this otherwise slight, although typical story, lies in the fact that nine-tenths of its emotional force lies below the surface. Deep emotions surface only momentarily.

What Barbara really feels, though, is contained in the half-remembered snatches of a quotation from William Shakespeare's *The Winter's Tale* (1623) which flash into her mind: the dignified, despairing speech of Hermione, the wronged wife, whose chief comfort in life, the favor of her husband, has gone, though she does not know how or why it went. As Barbara sits down to write to Willie, she knows that in real life one does not say such things, and all she is prepared to commit to paper is a platitude about her new charwoman; this, however, is as unsatisfactory to her as confessing her true feelings and she tears up the letter and throws it away. Neither truth nor platitude can be uttered, and the deeper emotional terrain of her life must remain as silent as the silence which she notices enveloping her new apartment. Silence will hide secrets and heal pain, and life will go on. The story finishes with Barbara projecting herself into the mundane thoughts of the charwoman about the weather: winter is in the air. This final thought has a slightly ominous connotation; whether it hints at Barbara's future loneliness, old age, or simply the demise of emotional honesty and communication, Warner rightly leaves it to the reader to decide.

Swans on an Autumn River contains what is often regarded as Warner's finest story, "A Love Match." It centers on a quiet conservative couple, Justin Tizard and his elder sister Celia. Justin returns on leave after the Battle of the Somme in 1916, in which Celia's fiancé has been killed. He stays at her apartment in London, but during his sleep he relives the terrible scenes of battle, raving incoherently. Celia, sleepless, listens in horror in the adjoining room. The following day, as they stroll casually around London, an old woman mistakes them for man and wife. The incident is one of several foreshadowings of what is to come. Two nights later, Celia is again awakened by Justin's ravings. She goes to his side to comfort him, and the combination of her compassion and his distress drives them into the physical expression of love.

Afterward, they feel no regret, and as the years go by they find happiness together. They possess an intuitive insight into each other's feelings, feel no need to impress each other, and are not particularly concerned with each other's likes and dislikes. Their common childhood memories act as a bond between them. They also become practiced at shielding their true relationship from their neighbors in Hallowby, the English village to which they move in 1923, and soon become one of the most respectable of couples.

Their lives are upset in the 1930's when Celia, who has become bored with local society and has developed a reputation for supporting unusual causes, receives a series of anonymous letters which claim that her secret is common knowledge in the village. The letters turn out to be only idle gossip from one of Justin's disappointed female admirers, and he soon puts a stop to them. Nothing has changed, and the secret remains intact.

The final outcome is carefully developed to produce the maximum effect. During World War II, Hallowby is bombed. Rescue workers entering a bombed house find a bedroom floor deep in rubble. Slates from the roof have fallen on the bed, crushing the two bodies that lay there. One of the villagers at the scene offers the opinion that Justin went into Celia's bedroom to comfort her. Others agree, and the coroner accepts this hypothesis as truth.

Warner's comment that the story's success was a victory for "incest and sanity" was only partly tongue in cheek. Rarely has incest been so sympathetically portrayed. Warner places subtle emphasis on the ease with which the lovers communicate and the depth of their love. The very criminality of their liaison adds to its preciousness for them. The ambiguity of the conclusion is also important. It is not made explicit whether the villagers genuinely believe their own explanation, whether they simply cannot comprehend the implications of what they see, or whether they guess the truth but, out of common human decency, desire to shield the lovers from shame. The open-endedness of this conclusion reflects the necessary mixture of emotions which the story has raised and left unresolved. The image of the two lovers in death, locked together in the tenderness of their illegal union and surrounded by the debris of their ruined house, remains vividly in the reader's mind.

"Swans on an Autumn River" also culminates in a strong visual image, which juxtaposes opposites to suggest the unattainable nature of an ideal. Norman Repton, an engineer in his late sixties, visits Ireland for the first time on a business trip. It is a country for which he has always felt a romantic longing, fueled by the poetry of William Butler Yeats. The country does not meet his expectations, however, and he · soon discovers that he is an alien in an unfamiliar land.

Repton is attracted to the river, which is one of two central symbols in the story. It is as if the river has power to compensate him for his old age, his weak physical condition, and the dissatisfaction with life that he feels. At night, he leaves the curtain of his room undrawn, so he can see the river, which also casts its lightly dancing reflection on the ceiling. In spite of this, he is aware of neither, being alternately sunk heavily in sleep or at the mercy of his bladder and digestion. His low vitality is a strong contrast to everything that the flowing river and its reflection suggests. In its ease, serenity, and sparkling movement, it represents another realm of being, but it is a realm which is forever closed to him, however much he longs for it.

This theme is restated and developed by another powerful symbol in the climax of the story. When he wakes in the morning, he sees a gathering of swans on the river. He looks at them enraptured, as if they were his own treasure. He grabs some bread and rushes out of the hotel, by which time eighteen swans have collected. The swans come flocking toward him as he excitedly tosses them the bread. He notes how skillfully they swim "without check or collision" (unlike his own troubled and unsatisfactory life). When the feeding is interrupted by a swarm of gulls competing for the bread, Repton strikes at one of them and becomes so angry that he loses all thought of where he is. He only succeeds in making a fool of himself, falling down and hitting his head on the pavement. To two passersby, he is nothing more than a corpulent old Englishman behaving eccentrically, and the story ends with a policeman arranging for an ambulance to take him away.

The poetry of Yeats may well have been in Warner's mind when she wrote this story. The swans resemble those in "The Wild Swans at Coole" which "drift on the still water,/ Mysterious, beautiful." In their effortlessness, they seem to belong to a realm of eternity, and they are contrasted in the story with the frequent emphasis on the limitations and restrictions of ordinary bodily life. Repton himself calls to mind the lines from Yeats's "Sailing to Byzantium": "An aged man is but a paltry thing,/ A tattered coat upon a stick, unless/ Soul clap its hands and sing. . . ." Repton cannot clap his hands and sing, however, and he cannot be gathered into the "artifice of eternity" which the swans on the river symbolize. "Swans on an Autumn River" thus becomes a tragic story of the disparity between the infinity of human desire and the finite realities within which it must operate.

The Innocent and the Guilty is the only one of Warner's collections to be organized under a specific theme. She had confessed to an "obsessive" concern with this theme, but the title is wholly ironic ("Perhaps one day, I shall . . . write a story where the innocent are charming and the guilty nauseating"). The ironic purpose is clear from "Truth in the Cup," in which a group of self-righteous villagers, celebrating in the local hotel on a stormy night, lament the moral decay of the young. Like sinful man in Genesis, however, they become victims of a catastrophic flood. It is also clear in "The Quality of Mercy," in which a drunken young woman and the local toughs who help her home are more virtuous than the "respectable" sister who greets them with abuse and recrimination.

The distinctions between innocence and guilt become blurred in "But at the Stroke of Midnight," one of Warner's most ambitious stories. It is a mysterious tale, with a hint of the supernatural, and it centers on the motif of rebirth. The protagonist is Lucy Ridpath, an undistinguished middle-aged woman who escapes from her dull marriage to seek a new life. Adopting the name Aurelia, she goes through a number of adventures in London and becomes like "a nova—a new appearance in the firmament, the explosion of an aging star." She has a powerful effect on everyone she meets. A clergyman sees her as a tranquil, spiritual woman; others find themselves curiously attracted to her and do her unexpected favors.

Leaving London to stay at a guesthouse, she adopts a stray cat and calls it Lucy. (Cats appear with somewhat alarming frequency in Warner's fiction.) She moves to a country cottage and successfully tries her hand at being a landscape artist. It seems that her rebirth is accomplished. The title, however, with its Cinderella connotations, suggests that it will not last. So it turns out. One cold wet night, Lucy returns late, mortally injured, and the moment the cat dies, Aurelia realizes that she is no longer Aurelia but Lucy Ridpath once more. When morning breaks, she goes outside to bury the cat, but she finds herself immersed in floodwater. Walking toward the road, she has a half-conscious desire to drown, and as she wades deeper in the water, she falls and is swept away by the current.

This curious but stimulating story, a mixture of realism and fantasy, is one of Warner's very few attempts to deal with an archetypal theme. It does not entirely succeed. The ending is abrupt and the reason for Lucy's death is unexplained. The cat, it seems, mysteriously embodies her former self, to which she must return when the cat dies. It is quite possible that Warner intended such a supernatural implication. In one of her early stories, "Early One Morning," from the collection *The Salutation*, an old woman dies and her soul immediately passes into one of the local greyhounds. Perhaps the tragedy of "But at the Stroke of Midnight" is that having once known rebirth, Lucy cannot lapse back into a former state. Caught between two selves, the old and the new, she can be neither.

In "Oxenhope," Warner returns to a favorite theme, the effects of the passing of time, as experienced by a protagonist who returns to former haunts. As the story develops, it becomes a subtle meditation on the presence of mortality and the longing for immortality.

William, a man in his sixties, returns to the village where he had stayed for a month when he was seventeen. As he drives through, he recognizes everything in the landscape. He thinks about the old shepherd he had known, with his prodigious memory that seemingly would never die, and he wants to know all the changes that the unchanging valley has seen. As he reminisces, the narrative passes freely between present event and past remembrance; past and present seem to merge. He finds the gravestone of the woman who had befriended him and cleans it so that the name stands out, just as he had done with the other family gravestones so many years previously. He notices, however, that the most recent name is the least visible, as if the woman had not expected to be remembered.

Fully aware of the imprint of mortality, he decides that the past is irrecoverable and that there is no purpose in staying. Then comes the ironic twist in the tale, so characteristic of Warner. He meets a local boy, who talks to him about local legends. One story is of a man who "set fire" to the loch and sent flames leaping up around his boat. William immediately realizes that the man was him—out in a rowing boat he had taken a match to bubbles of marsh gas as they rose to the surface of the water, and the fire had been the result. He leaves the village satisfied, with no need even of a backward glace, realizing that he is lodged in the collective memory of the locality, which lends him a kind of immortality. The subtlety of the observed paradox and its implications reveal Warner's fiction at its best. Human life remains embedded in the past even when the past has seemed to vanish or to be vanishing, and yet the knowledge of this fact paradoxically frees the present from the past's stifling grip.

Two more collections are worthy of comment. *Kingdoms of Elfin* is a collection of fantasies about fairy kingdoms. The product of Warner's final creative years, these stories display considerable ingenuity (and Warner clearly relishes the telling of them), but few rank with her best work. The fantasy setting does not supply the moral bearings necessary in order to feel and respond fully to the odd adventures of the fairy protagonists. Warner invents her own fairy lore with considerable aplomb, but the kingdoms she describes are not mythical or otherworldly. On the contrary, they tend to parallel human institutions, particularly the hierarchical structure of medieval or Renaissance society. In consequence, much of the pleasure to be gained from them is in the occasional acid comment about the superstitions of religion, or in the gentle mocking of the social pretenses and snobbery and the political plotting and maneuvering that bedevil both human and fairy worlds.

Scenes of Childhood is a posthumous collection of Warner's reminiscences about her upbringing in Edwardian England, a time "when there was a Tzar in Russia, and scarcely an automobile or a divorced person in Mayfair." Impressionistic sketches rather than fully developed stories, they display her epigrammatic style to best advantage. Extracting much harmless fun from the eccentricities of upper-middle-class

English life, she parades an assortment of odd characters ranging from her parents to great aunts, nannies, retired majors, French teachers, and a butler whose smile was so ghastly that he had to be got rid of (he revenged himself by joining the fire brigade and ruining the Warner's kitchen while putting out a minor fire).

At their best, Sylvia Townsend Warner's short stories constitute a quiet exploration of the oddities and ironies of the human condition, as it unfolds itself in time, fate, and circumstances. She is an acute observer, but she is careful not to judge. Her humor, always tart, is never malicious. She is a realist, and few of her stories end in unqualified optimism. She is aware of the pain of loss and the mockery that time makes of human ideals. She notes the human capacity for self-deceit but also the ability to make peace with limitations. Rarely faltering in the smoothness of her controlled, elegant, economical prose, she is a craftswoman whose finely wrought stories entertain and delight.

Other major works

NOVELS: *Lolly Willowes: Or, The Loving Huntsman*, 1926; *Mr. Fortune's Maggot*, 1927; *The True Heart*, 1929; *Summer Will Show*, 1936; *After the Death of Don Juan*, 1938; *The Corner That Held Them*, 1948; *The Flint Anchor*, 1954.

POETRY: *The Espalier*, 1925; *Time Importuned*, 1928; *Opus 7*, 1931; *Whether a Dove or a Seagull: Poems*, 1933; *Boxwood*, 1957; *Twelve Poems*, 1980; *Collected Poems*, 1982.

NONFICTION: *Jane Austen*, 1951; *T. H. White: A Biography*, 1967; *Letters*, 1982.

Bibliography

Ackland, Valentine. *For Sylvia: An Honest Account*. New York: W. W. Norton, 1985. A brief but poignant autobiography by Warner's lover, detailing the years with Warner and the painful separation caused by Ackland's struggle with alcoholism. Bea Howe's lengthy foreword discusses her firsthand understanding of the influence of Ackland on Warner's personal and professional life.

Brothers, Barbara. "Through the 'Pantry Window': Sylvia Townsend Warner and the Spanish Civil War." In *Rewriting the Good Fight: Critical Essays on the Literature of the Spanish Civil War*, edited by Frieda S. Brown et al. East Lansing: Michigan State University Press, 1989. Places Warner in the context of her contemporaries regarding the period of the Spanish Civil War. Bibliography.

Harmon, Claire. *Sylvia Townsend Warner: A Biography*. London: Chatto & Windus, 1989. An even and thorough biography with illustrations, a bibliography, and an index. Deals openly and prominently with the relationship between Valentine Ackland and Warner. Gives a biographical and historical context of Warner's work but with little critical detail.

Maxwell, William, ed. Introduction to *Letters: Sylvia Townsend Warner*. New York: Viking, 1982. The novelist and editor for *The New Yorker* and Warner's longtime personal friend shows great admiration for Warner's work. Maxwell notes her historical astuteness, her "ironic detachment," and her graceful formalism of language. Maxwell also considers the letters in the light of their being a writer's "left-over energy" and written without the inhibition of editorial or critical judgment. Includes a brief biographical sketch.

Strachan, W. J. "Sylvia Townsend Warner: A Memoir." *London Magazine* 19, no. 8 (November, 1979): 41-50. An overview of Warner's fiction, with a close look at the elements of fantasy and realism. *Kingdoms of Elfin* and *Lolly Willowes*, for example, seem incongruent given Warner's activity during World War I, but such realistic works as *The Flint Anchor* demonstrate her earthy, pragmatic quality. Even her most fantastic works reveal reason "firmly in control."

Updike, John. "Jake and Olly Opt Out." *The New Yorker* 55 (August 20, 1979): 97-102. In this comparative review of Kingsley Amis' *Jake's Thing* (1978) and Warner's *Lolly Willowes*, Updike looks at the role of nature in Warner's work and discerns a subtle strain of feminism. He argues that, unlike Amis and other former poets-turned-novelists, Warner's poetic style retains elements of "magic and music" and that her talent merits a much greater recognition than she has received.

West, Anthony. "The World We Live in and the World of Dreams." Review of *The Flint Anchor*. *The New Yorker* 30 (October 9, 1954): 175-178. West discusses Warner's clarity of thought and expression, her graceful style, and the psychological insight into family relationships. Particularly impressive is Warner's deft presentation of a large and historically significant theme in the subtle form of family anecdotes and gossip.

Bryan Aubrey
(Revised by *Lou Thompson*)

ROBERT PENN WARREN

Born: Guthrie, Kentucky; April 24, 1905
Died: Stratton, Vermont; September 15, 1989

Principal short fiction

Blackberry Winter, 1946; *The Circus in the Attic and Other Stories*, 1947.

Other literary forms

In addition to his short fiction, Robert Penn Warren published ten novels, several volumes of poetry, a play, a biography, two collections of critical essays, three historical essays, three influential textbooks, several children's books, two studies of race relations in America, one memoir, and several book-length treatises on literature. He won a host of distinguished awards, including three Pulitzer prizes, two for poetry and one for fiction. Three of his novels have been filmed, and one of them, *All the King's Men* (1946), has been presented in operatic form.

Achievements

Honored as a major American poet and novelist, Warren displayed uncommon versatility in significant contributions to almost every literary genre. His work has been translated worldwide, and his short stories are widely anthologized. While he is best known for his novel *All the King's Men*, which won the Pulitzer Prize, he was most prolific as a poet whose awards included two Pulitzer Prizes and an appointment as America's first poet laureate.

The subject of Warren's fiction, and much of his poetry, is Southern rural life in the late nineteenth and early twentieth centuries. He reveals a rootedness in his subject and its values, a concern for moral issues, and a gift for dialogue and environmental detail that lends distinctiveness to his work. His short stories, for example, are set down in rich, vigorous style, and they delineate the flow of time, the influence of past on present, and the painful necessity of self-knowledge.

Biography

Robert Penn Warren was educated at Guthrie High School and was graduated from Vanderbilt University in Nashville, Tennessee (B.A., 1925), where he was associated with the Fugitive Group of poets; he did graduate work at the University of California (M.A., 1927), Yale University, and Oxford, and as a Rhodes scholar (D.Litt., 1930). In 1930, he contributed an essay, *I'll Take My Stand*, to the Agrarian symposium. Between 1935 and 1942, he was an editor of the *Southern Review* and was influential in the articulation and practice of the New Criticism. After an active career as a professor of English at a number of American colleges and universities, he retired from Yale in 1973. His first marriage to Emma Brescia in 1930 ended in divorce in 1950. He and his second wife, the writer Eleanor Clark, herself a National Book Award winner, had one son and one daughter.

Warren won the Pulitzer Prize for Fiction in 1947, the Pulitzer Prize for Poetry in 1958 and 1979, and the National Book Award in 1958. From 1944 to 1945, he was the second occupant of the Chair of Poetry at the Library of Congress. In 1952 he was elected to the American Philosophical Society; in 1959 to the American Academy of Arts and Letters; and in 1972 to the American Academy of Arts and Sciences. In 1967, he received the Bollingen Prize in Poetry, and in 1970 the National Medal for Literature and the Van Wyck Brooks Award. In 1974, he was chosen to deliver the third Annual Jefferson Lecture in the Humanities. In 1975 he received the Emerson-Thoreau Award of the American Academy of Arts and Sciences; the next year the Copernicus Award from the Academy of American Poets; and in 1977 the Harriet Monroe Prize for Poetry. Other awards included the Shelley Memorial Prize and the Presidential Medal of Freedom. In 1986, Warren achieved the unique distinction of becoming the first poet laureate (by act of Congress) of the United States. Warren's life spanned almost the whole twentieth century. After producing a rich final harvest of work from the mid-1970's to the mid-1980's, he died in 1989 at age eighty-four at his summer residence in Vermont. He left to posterity a canon of outstanding creative effort.

Analysis

Many of Robert Penn Warren's stories feature an adult protagonist's introspective, guilty recollections of imperishable childhood events, of things done or left undone or simply witnessed with childish innocence. Thus "Blackberry Winter" (the literal reference is to an unseasonable, late spring cold snap) opens with a nine-year-old boy's unbroken, secure world, a small community permeated with the presence and warmth of protective loved ones. A vaguely sinister city-clothed stranger happens by and is given a job burying drowned chicks and poults by the boy's mother. Later the boy watches with his father and neighboring farmers as a dead cow, the yoke still around her neck, bobs down a flooding creek past fields of ruined tobacco plants. Then the boy finds a somehow shocking heap of litter washed out from under the house of his father's black help. Dellie, who lives there, is sick in bed with "woman-mizry," and after calling him to her side, gives her son little Jebb a sudden, "awful" slap. Big Jebb predicts that the cold snap will go on and on and that everything and everyone will die, because the Lord is tired of sinful people.

Later on, when the boy's father explains that he cannot afford to hire any help now but offers the stranger fifty cents for a half day's work, the stranger curses the farm and leaves, followed by the curious boy, whom he also curses. "You don't stop following me and I cut yore throat, you little son-of-a-bitch." "But I did follow him," the narrator tells us, "all the years." At the end of the story all the sureties of the boy's world have been threatened, and in the epilogue we learn that the farm was soon lost, his parents died, and little Jebb has gone to prison. The narrator has learned that the essence of time is the passing away of things and people; he has been exposed to natural and moral evil.

"When the Light Gets Green" (the reference is to a peculiar, ominous shade of greenish light just before a storm) recalls "Blackberry Winter" in its setting, characterization, and theme, as well as in its retrospective point of view. The story's first two sentences display the technique: "My grandfather had a long white beard and sat under the cedar tree. The beard, as a matter of fact, was not very long and not very white, only gray, but when I was a child. . . ." Grandfather Barden had served as a Confederate cavalry captain in the Civil War; he had been a hero, but now he is old and thin and his blue jeans hang off his shrunken hips and backside. During a bad hailstorm in the summer of 1914 which threatens his son-in-law's tobacco crop, the old man has a stroke and collapses, and later upstairs in his room waits to die—unloved, as he believes. His is the necessarily uncomprehending and hopeless fight that love and pride put up against time and change. His grandson, who visits him but cannot speak, suffers the guilt of having tried and failed both to feel and to communicate the impossible love the old man needed.

Mr. Barden, as we learn in the epilogue, lived until 1918, by which time other catastrophes had intervened—the farm sold, his son-in-law fighting in France, where he would soon be killed, his daughter working in a store. "I got the letter about my grandfather, who died of the flu," the story concludes, "but I thought about four years back, and it didn't matter much." The now adult narrator is puzzled and shamed by his failure and betrayal of his grandfather. In the dual perspective of the story Warren infuses a self-condemnatory ambivalence toward the old man which gives to the narrative the quality of expiation.

"Prime Leaf," Warren's first published story, derives from the Kentucky tobacco wars of the first decade of the twentieth century, in which tobacco farmers organized in an attempt to secure higher prices from the tobacco buyers. The focus of the story is upon contention within the Hardin family, most directly between Old Man Hardin and Big Thomas, his son, but also involving Thomas' wife and young son. Old Man Hardin leaves the farmers' association rather than support the use of force against those members who object to the association's price fixing. Big Thomas, whom he had originally convinced to join the association, refuses to resign immediately. Their reconciliation occurs only after Big Thomas wounds one of a party of barn-burning night riders raiding the Hardins' property. Big Thomas decides that he will wait at home for the sheriff, but his father urges him to ride into town to justice, and on the way Big Thomas is ambushed and killed. The opposition of father and son is a contest between idea and fact, between idealism and pragmatism. Old Man Hardin is a kind and morally upright man but is also notably detached, remote, and unyielding. To his idealism is opposed his son's stubborn practicality, born of hard experience.

In delineating the conflict of the two men, with its tragic and ironic outcome, Warren did not espouse the beliefs of either, but focused on the incompleteness of each. Old Man Hardin, embodying the rocklike integrity of the gentleman-farmer tradition, places an unwise reliance on what he still—despite much evidence to the contrary—takes to be the due processes of law. He cannot save his son and is in a way responsible for his death. Big Thomas, firing at the night riders until his rifle jams, before yielding to his father, does not resolve in acceptable fashion the problem of ends and means.

"The Circus in the Attic" is a long and crowded tale about the meaning—or apparent meaninglessness—of history. It features, appropriately enough, a would-be local historian, Bolton Lovehart, a frail, frustrated man of aristocratic antecedents, whose deepest desire is simply to be free and himself. The only child of a weak father and an almost cannibalistically possessive mother, Bolton as a boy makes several doomed gestures of resistance. To his mother's subsequent horror, he participates in a riverbank baptismal ceremony; later he runs off with a carnival but is immediately retrieved. During his first year at college his now widowed mother has a heart attack; such at least is her story, although she will not allow a specialist to examine her and treats her son's suggestion as treason. In any event, Bolton does not return to college and life closes in on him. He begins to see a young woman, but, realizing that Bolton's mother has the stronger hold, she deliberately seduces and then abandons him.

Establishing the context of local history back to the first white settlers, Warren provided a series of vivid and ironic vignettes, one of which distinguishes between the official, heroic, United Daughters of the Confederacy version of the Civil War battle of Bardsville and the half-comic, half-sordid truth of the unremarkable little affair. One of the heroes, Cash Perkins, full of liquor, climbed on the wrong horse, a particularly mean one, and was carried, helpless and roaring, directly into Yankee rifle range. The truth of the other memorialized hero, Seth Sykes, was somewhat more involved. He cared nothing for Secession, said so publicly, and lost a stomp-and-gouge fight over it. Then he said he hoped the Yankees would come, which they soon did, to take his corn, for which they offered him a note. He would have none of it; he had offered them meat but not his corn. He resisted and was killed. Of the official, patriotic versions of these two deaths, Warren wrote, ". . . people always believe what truth they have to believe to go on being the way they are."

Bolton Lovehart's major resource and consolation is the painstaking creation of a tiny circus—complete with animals and clowns and trapeze artists and a lion tamer—which he carves in the attic office where he is supposedly composing his study of local history. Upon his mother's death (finally, she does have a heart attack), it appears that he may at last enter into a life of his own. Shortly before World War II, Bolton marries, finds a hero in his braggart stepson, a posthumous Medal of Honor winner, and becomes for a time in his reflected energy and glory a current affairs expert and historian of sorts. His wife, however, who has been unfaithful to him, is killed in an automobile crash, his stepson is taken from him, and at last he returns to the creation of those small, inanimate, innocent, wooden objects whose world alone he cherishes, controls, and understands. Bolton Lovehart's is less a fully human life than a kind of pathetic facsimile. His study of Bardsville's past—and by extension, humans' study of history—seems to assert that historical causation and "truth" are unknowable, that all humans are equally unimportant, and that all people are trapped in their own dark compulsions.

Warren is commonly identified as a Southern writer and associated with such other premier representatives of that area as William Faulkner and Eudora Welty. So long as "Southern" is not equated with "regionalist" in the limiting sense of that term, the description is accurate if not very illuminating. In another sense, however, as is apparent in his short fiction, Warren was a provincial, at least insofar as he retained an attachment to and an awareness of generally humanistic values—moral, social, and theological—often regarded as a vital part of the region's heritage. Thus the frequently noticeable tension between stylistic understatement (apparent in passages quoted earlier) and thematic intensity characteristic of the stories seems a reflection of a pull between the old humanistic conception of human wholeness and a naturalistic belief in the fragmented and unintegrated nature of human experience.

Warren published his last short story, "The Circus in the Attic," in 1947; thereafter he published as stories fourteen prepublication excerpts from his novels. Although in his nearly twenty years as a short-story writer Warren produced some fine work, both the author and a good many of his readers have found his achievement in short fiction less satisfying than that in other genres, notably poetry and the novel.

Explanations for his limited success in and satisfaction with short fiction might start with the fact that when he wrote many of the stories collected in *The Circus in the Attic and Other Stories*, he was a beginner, at least in fiction. It is also the case, as Warren conceded, that he wrote for the quick buck, which did not come. Most of the stories did not represent major efforts; as Arthur Miller has said of his own short stories, they were what came easier. Finally, and most importantly, the form itself seems to have inhibited Warren's natural talents and inclinations.

In writing stories in the 1930's and 1940's, Warren appears to have backed into what was for him an unhappy compromise; stories were neither long enough nor short enough, offered neither the satisfying extensive scope of the novel nor the demanding intensive concision of the poem. Short stories might occasionally serve as sketches for novels ("Prime Leaf," discussed earlier, is the prototype of Warren's first published novel, *Night Rider*, 1939), but Warren found that the overlap between the short story and the poem was bad for him, that stories consumed material that would otherwise have become poems. Thus he said, "Short stories are out for me."

Despite such demurrers, however, Warren's achievement in the short story is that of a major talent. Warren's ear never failed him; the voices from the past and of the present always ring true. No one writing in his day had a better ear—one could almost say recollection, if one did not know Warren's age—for the voices of late nineteenth and early twentieth century America. His eyes were open to both the panorama and to the smallest evocative detail: from the trapper looking across the mountains to the West to the cracked and broken shoe of a tramp. He was intensely alive to the natural world. This is not to say simply that the natural backgrounds of the stories are vividly realized and accurately observed, although Warren was here the equal of Ernest Hemingway or Faulkner, but that such observation and realization provide the bases for those effects characteristic of his stories, for the evocation of atmosphere, for tonal modulation, and for symbolic representation.

Other major works

NOVELS: *Night Rider*, 1939; *At Heaven's Gate*, 1943; *All the King's Men*, 1946; *World Enough and Time*, 1950; *Band of Angels*, 1955; *The Cave*, 1959; *Wilderness*, 1961; *Flood*, 1964; *Meet Me in the Green Glen*, 1971; *A Place to Come To*, 1977.

PLAY: *Proud Flesh*, 1947.

POETRY: *Thirty-six Poems*, 1935; *Eleven Poems on the Same Theme*, 1942; *Selected Poems 1923-1943*, 1944; *Brother to Dragons: A Tale in Verse and Voices*, 1953; *Promises: Poems 1954-1956*, 1957; *You, Emperors, and Others: Poems 1957-1960*, 1960; *Selected Poems: New and Old, 1923-1966*, 1966; *Incarnations: Poems 1966-1968*, 1968; *Audubon: A Vision*, 1969; *Or Else—Poem/Poems 1968-1974*, 1974; *Selected Poems, 1923-1975*, 1976; *Now and Then: Poems 1976-1978*, 1978; *Brother to Dragons: A New Version*, 1979; *Being Here: Poetry 1977-1980*, 1980; *Ballad of a Sweet Dream of Peace*, 1980 (will Bill Komodore); *Rumor Verified: Poems 1979-1980*, 1981; *Chief Joseph of the Nez Percé*, 1983; *New and Selected Poems, 1923-1985*, 1985.

NONFICTION: *John Brown: The Making of a Martyr*, 1929; *An Approach to Literature: A Collection of Prose and Verse with Analysis and Discussions*, 1936 (with Cleanth Brooks and John Thibaut Purser); *Understanding Poetry: An Anthology for College Students*, 1938, 1950, 1960 (with Cleanth Brooks); *Understanding Fiction*, 1943, 1959 (with Cleanth Brooks); *Modern Rhetoric*, 1949 (with Brooks; better known as *Fundamentals of Good Writing: A Handbook of Modern Rhetoric*); *Segregation: The Inner Conflict of the South*, 1956; *Selected Essays*, 1958; *The Legacy of the Civil War: Meditations on the Centennial*, 1961; *Who Speaks for the Negro?*, 1965; *Faulkner: A Collection of Critical Essays*, 1966; *Randall Jarrell, 1914-1965*, 1967 (with Robert Lowell and Peter Taylor); *American Literature: The Makers and the Making*, 1974 (with R. W. B. Lewis); *Democracy and Poetry*, 1975; *Portrait of a Father*, 1988; *New and Selected Essays*, 1989.

Bibliography

Bohner, Charles. *Robert Penn Warren*. 1962. Rev. ed. Boston: Twayne, 1981. This lucid survey encompasses details of Warren's literary career and an analysis of his major themes. Also provides a study of the development of his art as evidenced in his novels and short fiction, his poetry (through *Being Here: Poetry 1977-1980*), and his major essays. The survey also includes a detailed chronology and a valuable select bibliography.

Clark, William Bedford, ed.. *Critical Essays on Robert Penn Warren*. Boston: G. K. Hall, 1981. A comprehensive collection of criticism by leading literary scholars of Warren's major work as novelist, poet, biographer, and essayist. Among the contributors are Harold Bloom, Malcolm Cowley, Carlos Baker, John Crowe Ransom, and Randall Jarrell. The collection includes a valuable 1969 interview with Warren by Richard Sale.

Guttenberg, Barnett. *Web of Being: The Novels of Robert Penn Warren*. Nashville: Vanderbilt University Press, 1975. Guttenberg examines nine novels of Warren from *Night Rider* through *Meet Me in the Green Glen* with emphasis on the existential element. He advances the premise that through all the novels the individual struggles to attain the true being of selfhood through self-awareness.

Justus, James H. *The Achievement of Robert Penn Warren.* Baton Rouge: Louisiana State University Press, 1981. A cogent study of Warren's work from the premise that the latter largely derives from the cultural circumstances of time and place in his career. The book is divided into four sections dealing, respectively, with Warren's themes, poetry, nonfiction prose, and novels.

Nakadate, Neil. *Robert Penn Warren: A Reference Guide.* Boston: G. K. Hall, 1977. This helpfully annotated reference guide to significant scholarship on Warren and his work encompasses writings by Warren from 1929 to 1977, and about him from 1925 to 1975. A checklist of doctoral dissertations and master's theses on Warren is also included.

Strandberg, Victor. *The Poetic Vision of Robert Penn Warren.* Lexington: University Press of Kentucky, 1977. A thorough and lively discussion of Warren's poetry offering elucidation of major poems and an examination of the development of the poet's three major themes: "Poems of passage, the undiscovered self, and mysticism." The study supersedes Strandberg's *A Colder Fire* (1965).

Watkins, Floyd C., John T. Hiers, and Mary Louise Weaks, eds. *Talking with Robert Penn Warren.* Athens: University of Georgia Press, 1990. A collection of twenty-four interviews, extending from 1953 to 1985, in which Warren talks about his work with characteristic honesty, openness, folksiness, and wit from the joint perspective of writer, interpreter, and critic. The group of interviewers includes Ralph Ellison, Marshall Walker, Bill Moyers, Edwin Harold Newman, Floyd C. Watkins, and Eleanor Clark.

Allen Shepherd
(Revised by *Christian H. Moe*)

JEROME WEIDMAN

Born: New York, New York; April 4, 1913

Principal short fiction

The Horse That Could Whistle 'Dixie,' 1939; *The Captain's Tiger,* 1947; *My Father Sits in the Dark,* 1961; *Nine Stories,* 1963; *The Death of Dickie Draper, and Nine Other Stories,* 1965.

Other literary forms

Jerome Weidman's published works include plays, essays, travelogues, more than twenty novels, autobiographical sketches, one autobiographical volume, and numerous short-story collections and uncollected short stories. He is probably best known for his dramatic scripts, including the musicals *Fiorello!* (produced in 1959, published in 1960) and *Tenderloin* (produced in 1960, published in 1961), done in collaboration with George Abbot, and a musical version of his first novel, *I Can Get It for You Wholesale* (1937), produced and published in 1962.

Achievements

As a fiction writer, Weidman is known best for his unpleasant, sometimes brutal, portrayal of Jewish characters in novels such as *I Can Get It for You Wholesale* and *What's in It for Me?* (1938), and in short stories such as "The Kinnehórrah," "Chutzbah," and "The Horse That Could Whistle 'Dixie.'" He portrays characters more sensitively in his novels *Fourth Street East: A Novel of the Way It Was* (1971) and *The Enemy Camp* (1958) and in his stories "My Father Sits in the Dark" and "Movable Feast." Many of the settings in his novels and short stories are drawn from the areas in which he grew up—New York's Lower East Side and the Bronx, and many of the activities his characters pursue are drawn from his own experiences as a child growing up in the slums and from his experiences as an office boy, an accountant, a law student, and a writer. Weidman won a Pulitzer Prize in 1960 for his collaboration on *Fiorello!*

Biography

Educated in stints at City College, New York, 1931-1933; Washington Square College, 1933-1934; and New York University Law School, 1934-1937, Jerome Weidman married Elizabeth Ann Payne and has three children. He was cowinner of the Pulitzer Prize in drama and winner of the New York Drama Critics Circle Award and the Antoinette Perry ("Tony") Award, all for *Fiorello!* in 1960. He is a member of the Authors Guild and Dramatists Guild of Authors League of America of which he served as president from 1969 to 1974, and the Writers Guild of America West. Settling in the San Francisco area in the early 1990's, Weidman's work on a second autobiographical volume and short stories and sketches are also drawn from his Lower East Side childhood and his young adulthood living in the Bronx.

Analysis

While Jerome Weidman's novels, *I Can Get It for You Wholesale* and *What's in It for Me?*, are often neglected because of his brutally realistic treatment of unsavory Jewish characters, his short stories are frequently humorous, good-natured jabs at not only the Jewish community but also the world as a whole. His early stories, particularly those in *The Horse That Could Whistle 'Dixie,'* are remarkably well constructed and display the work of a writer who has a clear conception of what he portrays. His later work, often marred by hasty writing and commercialism, retains the same sense of humor, but often lapses into the maudlin and into fits of bathos. Such flaws should be no surprise in the stories of a man who freely admits that his primary aim in writing is to make money.

Weidman draws extensively on his life as a child and young man trying to survive in the slums of New York, first on Fourth Street East and later in the Bronx. In fact, he claims that all of his short stories, even those with female protagonists, are more or less autobiographical. The people of Weidman's stories are almost universally playing the game of life, and Weidman's stories reflect the gamesmanship of their situations. The puzzles to be pieced together and the games to be played by Weidman's characters are the puzzles and games that all people have played at one time or another and, as such, Weidman's stories become something of a mirror of life. The mirror is faceted and reflects many pieces of a whole, however, and it is making those pieces reflect a steady image that is the challenge for the reader and for the characters alike.

It is the task, set for himself, of the youngster in "My Father Sits in the Dark" to "figure out" why his father, night after night, sits quietly alone in his darkened house. None of the pieces the young man sorts out seems to fit. The family is poor, but his father would not worry about money. He would not worry about the family's health, either. None of the conventional answers fits. It is not until the young man confronts his father in the dark kitchen of the house that the pieces seem to fit. His father is an immigrant. His home in Austria did not have electricity, which made him familiar with the dark, so dark now provides for him a comfortable, nostalgic feeling. When the son asks the father why he sits in the dark, his father replies that it helps him think. When asked what he thinks about, he replies, "Nothing." The implication is that the old man does not have to have a more rational reason to sit in the dark and that the son, with his rationalized, fabricated understanding of the situation, has come to an incomplete understanding, but an understanding nevertheless. The fact that Weidman is playing the conflicts of modern society against the idyllic Old World is evident, but he does not belabor the point; he only reveals the exultant son going back to bed after he finally accepts his father's explanation for sitting in the dark. The outcome makes both happy, but there is no real resolution for the reader.

The same sort of puzzle appears in "Three-Two Pitch." Harry Powell is a bright young graduate on a three-month internship with the office of the best public relations specialist in New York. Powell, from Cleveland, is considered a "hick," but he takes his father's advice to ingratiate himself with the secretary of the office in order to succeed. His succcess is such that he is prepared to marry the secretary before the action begins. D. J., Powell's employer, has a yearly commitment to have lunch with his Cleveland high school teacher, Doc Hapfel, but this year, after making the arrangements, he gets "tied up" and tells Harry to meet Hapfel and begin without him. In the course of the lunch, during which Doc becomes drunker and drunker, a series of calls from D. J.'s office (from the secretary Powell is thinking of marrying) relate that D. J. will be later and later, and after every call, Doc seems to know, intuitively, what has been said—as if he were going through a familiar ritual. When Doc finally collapses and Powell is forced to cope with the situation, he begins to put the pieces together. The lunch happens every year; D. J. always sends his intern to lunch with Doc; D. J. is always tied up; he will always come later. Doc finally admits he has not seen D. J. for years, and when Powell discovers, fortuitously, that D. J. has not been in town all day, but is in Detroit, he realizes that he has been duped and used to pacify the expectations of an old man.

Weidman stresses the conflict between "hick" Cleveland and sophisticated New York, but the principal theme is the puzzle which Powell must put together. The pieces are the secretary, D. J., Doc Hapfel, and Harry Powell himself. Before Harry can solve the puzzle, he must assimilate all of the pieces and come to an understanding of the situation and of himself. When he does solve the puzzle, the solution is devastating. He understands he has no place in New York, that he has been used, and that his self-esteem has blinded him to all of these realities. Only by returning to Cleveland and entering law school, as his father counseled him to do at the start of the story, can Powell provide a definitive, if somewhat unsatisfactory, solution to the whole puzzle.

"I Knew What I Was Doing," presents life as more of a game than a puzzle, but the same unsavory undertone attaches itself to the outcome. Throughout the story, Myra, a fashion model, plays one potential escort against another until she works herself up from a mere stock clerk to a wealthy clothing buyer. By portraying her game of enticement and entrapment, Weidman shows her as a cold, calculating woman who succeeds at the game because she knows the rules so well. The irony of her role is that her chumps, the men in her life, fall so predictably within the rules of the game. One of them, however, nearly upsets the game plan when he falls in love with Myra and proposes marriage almost simultaneously with her conquest of the rich clothing buyer. She retains her composure, however, and tells this, the most ensnared chump, to "paste it [a marriage license] in your hat." Weidman's characters in this story are little more than pawns being played by the queen. Weidman is not particularly interested in character here, but rather in the progress of the match. The story is, perhaps, the epitome of Weidman's depiction of gameplaying.

At the other end of the spectrum is "The Horse That Could Whistle 'Dixie.'"

Rather than flat, featureless characters, Weidman gives us a thoroughly reprehensible father playing the age-old game of growing up with his unwilling son. After watching many children ride the ponies at the zoo pony ride and sneering fatuously at those who only ride in the horse cart and not astride the beasts, the father drags the son to the ponies and forces him to ride. Despite the child's tearful entreaties and the sensible suggestions of the attendant, who can see that the child is terrified, the father forces the child to ride not once, but four times. At the end, the child is a "whipped, silent mass of tear-stained quivering fright" who has finally satisfied his father's sense of propriety. Here the game has no winner, no ending, and no understanding. The son does not understand the father's motives, the father does not understand the son's reluctance, and the crowd watching the events does not want to understand. This is the most undesirable of Weidman's games, in which a person is forced to play by someone else's rules.

From the gentle "My Father Sits in the Dark," to the savage "The Horse That Could Whistle 'Dixie,'" Weidman portrays, fabricates, and manipulates the games people play and the puzzles that they are. If readers are to understand the games and puzzles, they must abandon credulity and prepare themselves for the inconsistencies that the gamesmaster builds into the game.

Other major works

NOVELS: *I Can Get It for You Wholesale*, 1937; *What's in It for Me?*, 1938; *I'll Never Go There Anymore*, 1941; *The Lights Around the Shore*, 1943; *Too Early to Tell*, 1946; *The Price Is Right*, 1949; *The Hand of the Hunter*, 1951; *Give Me Your Love*, 1952; *The Third Angel*, 1953; *Your Daughter Iris*, 1955; *The Enemy Camp*, 1958; *Before You Go*, 1960; *The Sound of Bow Bells*, 1962; *Word of Mouth*, 1964; *Other People's Money*, 1967; *The Center of the Action*, 1969; *Fourth Street East: A Novel of the Way It Was*, 1971; *Last Respects*, 1972; *Tiffany Street*, 1974; *The Temple*, 1975.

PLAYS: *Fiorello!*, 1959; *Tenderloin*, 1960; *I Can Get It for You Wholesale*, 1962; *Cool Off!*, 1964; *Pousse-Café*, 1966; *Ivory Tower*, 1968 (with James Yaffe); *The Mother Lover*, 1969; *Asterisk! A Comedy of Terrors*, 1969.

NONFICTION: *Letter of Credit*, 1940; *Traveler's Cheque*, 1954; *Back Talk*, 1963; *Praying for Rain*, 1986.

Bibliography

Bannon, Barbara A. "Authors and Editors." *Publishers Weekly* 196 (July 28, 1969): 13-15. Uses the publication of Weidman's *The Center of the Action* as a starting point for a treatment of his literary career. The article discusses aspects of the relationship between Weidman's fiction and his life. Accompanied by a photograph of Weidman.

Barkham, John. "The Author." *Saturday Review* 45 (July 28, 1962): 38-39. This interview, concerning Weidman's fiction and theater work, accompanies a review of Weidman's novel *The Sound of Bow Bells.* Barkham's essay examines some of

Weidman's ideas about the way stories should be written and treats Weidman's daily schedule as a writer. A photograph of Weidman accompanies the review.

Liptzin, Sol. *The Jew in American Literature.* New York: Bloch, 1966. This volume discusses Weidman in the context of American literature. Liptzin briefly compares Weidman to Budd Schulberg in connection with their treatment of "the Jewish go-getter" and of "unpleasant Jewish money-grubbers."

Sherman, Bernard. *The Invention of the Jew: Jewish-American Education Novels, 1916-1964.* New York: Yoseloff, 1969. Treats Weidman's *I Can Get It for You Wholesale* as a rogue-hero novel. Sherman places the work in a tradition beginning with *The Rise of David Levinsky* by Abraham Cahan and running through *Haunch, Paunch, and Jowl* by Samuel Ornitz and *What Makes Sammy Run* (1941) by Budd Schulberg.

Weidman, Jerome. "PW Interviews: Jerome Weidman." Interview by Lisa See. *Publishers Weekly* 230 (September 12, 1986): 72-73. Uses the publication of Weidman's autobiographical volume, *Praying for Rain,* as a point of departure for surveying his literary career. Also treats some of Weidman's ideas about composition. Includes a photograph of Weidman.

Clarence O. Johnson
(Revised by *Richard Tuerk*)

DENTON WELCH

Born: Shanghai, China; March 29, 1915
Died: Crouch, Kent, England; December 30, 1948

Principal short fiction

Brave and Cruel, 1948; *A Last Sheaf*, 1951; *The Stories of Denton Welch*, 1985.

Other literary forms

Besides his short-story collections, Denton Welch published several novels, an unfinished novel, journals, and uncollected poems. Both the unfinished novel and the short-story collections were published after his death.

Achievements

Welch's fiction has been favorably compared to that of Jean Cocteau, Marcel Proust, André Gide, Christopher Isherwood, and Truman Capote. Few writers began their career with the kind of precocious brilliance and searing honesty that characterized the early works of Welch. Dead at age thirty-three after thirteen years of debilitating pain resulting from a bicycle accident in 1935, Welch had been known primarily as a painter until he began writing only six years before his death. His first work garnered high critical praise from a number of respected and established British literary figures, such as Edith Sitwell, Sir Herbert Read, and Cyril Connolly, to name but a few. His direct narrative manner, sexual openness, and dazzling prose style contrasted greatly with the highly realistic war fiction that was being produced throughout the 1940's. Much of his short fiction documents the fall from innocence to experience that oversensitive young boys undergo when they lose a parent or a friend through death or misunderstanding. A number of his later stories are also superb portraits of the initial stirrings of artistic impulse and demonstrate how creative adolescents learn to trust their imaginations and begin to become artists. An authentically original voice, Welch writes in a style that appears completely nonderivative. Few writers have dramatized so precisely the agony of adolescence, a phase he labeled as "sordid and fearful."

Biography

Denton Welch was born in Shanghai, China, into a family of wealth and privilege. His father was a prosperous rubber merchant, and his American-born mother a devoted Christian Scientist. He spent much of his youth traveling back and forth between Asia and Europe in the company of his mother, to whom he was inordinately devoted because of his father's absence. To his great disappointment, he was enrolled in one of England's finest boarding schools, Repton, which his two older brothers attended. The typical life-style of an English boys' school brought traumatic change in the young boy's life, especially in the wake of the casual days spent with his mother traveling throughout the world. He so detested Repton that he ran away, preferring to visit well-known cathedrals at Salisbury and Exeter. He finally found satisfaction at the Goldsmith School of Art in London, where he was able to develop his considerable talent as a painter and where he enjoyed the relaxed and open atmosphere of an art school.

Two experiences profoundly altered Welch's relatively secure and happy life: the first was the death of his beloved mother when he was eleven years old, and the second, at age twenty, was a catastrophic bicycle accident that left him a permanent invalid and contributed to his early death at the age of thirty-three. The last thirteen years of his life were spent in great pain and discomfort but were, ironically, his most artistically productive years.

From his early published writings, Welch found great and encouraging praise from Sitwell, who called him "a born writer." Renowned literary editors such as Connolly and Read found his work fresh and completely original. In an age that rarely allowed mention of sexual matters, Welch's candor about his homosexuality disturbed a number of England's conservative literary intelligentsia. More disturbing to them, however, was the originality of his writing style and its apparent artlessness and absence of any discernible literary influences.

Analysis

Denton Welch's early stories deal with the recurrent theme of the loss of an innocent vision of the world. There is usually a fall of some kind in which an innocent young boy learns some devastating information that alters, or will soon alter, the way he feels about his life thereafter. One of Welch's finest stories, "The Coffin on the Hill," documents an eight-year-old boy's first serious confrontation with mortality. The story concerns an Easter voyage of a family on a boat up a river in China. The story is told through the eyes of the eight-year-old as he experiences the mysteries of the Orient. The ship is, obviously, a symbol of an ark floating on the river of life, and life on the ship is Edenic. Welch is an unashamedly symbolic writer.

The cooks on the ship playfully tease the young boy with stories about drowned people in the river who, if he fell into the water, would pull him down to the bottom. His response is to return to his cabin, assume the fetal position, and hug his strange doll, which he has named "Lymph Est." The family then visits an ancient Chinese graveyard, where the boy sees, while off on his own, an open grave with a rotting corpse in it. He is so stunned by the sight that he returns to his family but is unable to separate the lesson of death from the fear and the sure knowledge that even his dear mother will someday become mere dust and ashes. Though he is only eight, his sensitive nature already has begun to torment him: "For I knew that she would come to it at last; and that knowledge was unbearable." His last act is to throw his favorite doll into the river as a sign of his growing maturity but also as a kind of propitiatory sacrifice that might somehow appease the gods of necessity and fate.

"At Sea" can be viewed as a further development of the same themes found in "The Coffin on the Hill." Again, there is a sea journey of a young boy, Robert, with his mother, but in this story the boy is pathologically attached to her to such an extent that their relationship becomes the major focus of the story. There is no father in the story at all. There is, however, a male character named Mr. Barron, who expresses some interest in Robert's mother and asks her to dance at a party. Robert's Oedipal jealousy so enrages him that he wets himself and publicly humiliates himself and his embarrassed mother. The reader discovers that his mother is showing signs of some eventual illness that seems fatal and, as in "The Coffin on the Hill," the youthful protagonist is forced to face the inevitable death of his mother.

Welch introduces a princess and her little dog, who tries repeatedly to break his leash and gain freedom, characters presenting fairly obvious mirror images of Robert chained to his mother's love. Some critics see Mr. Barron's name as a pun on Charon, the mythical guide and personification of death, who is leading Robert's beloved mother in a dance of death. The title of the story also foreshadows the plight of the boy after his mother's death, when he will surely be "at sea" or alone and lost. One of the strange rituals that the boy practices is writing elaborate letters in spite of the fact that he can neither read nor write, so that the reader sees him as someone who also cannot "read" or interpret the signs or portents of the catastrophe of his mother's impending death. The narrative ends with a highly emotional loss of innocence as the boy realizes that his mother is ill. As he views her in a semiconscious state, he says: "He wanted to sing something so consummate and wonderful that his mother would turn over and smile and be happy forever; but he knew that she was dying and that she could not save herself." It is fairly clear that both of these extremely well-crafted stories are, if not blatantly autobiographical, at least fictive expressions of the deep and abiding loss that Welch experienced during his mother's lingering illness and eventual death when he was eleven years old. His mother was a strict Christian Scientist and refused medication throughout her fatal illness, a fact that embittered Denton Welch against the beliefs and practices of that religion. Indeed, he quotes hymns and some of Mary Baker Eddy's writings at the conclusion of "At Sea." Not only does this story and several of his novels record young children's loss of innocence, but also it particularly records the disappearance of the core of his emotional being, the love of his mother.

"When I Was Thirteen" is, unquestionably, one of his most accomplished stories; it certainly is his most famous and most frequently anthologized one. The reader sees only the beginning of a fall from innocence to knowledge. The major character experiences a violent beating from his brother after spending a day and night with an older lad named Archer. He has absolutely no understanding of the names his brother is calling him: "Bastard, Devil, Harlot, Sod!"—except "Devil."

The story details a holiday trip that the unnamed narrator and his older brother, William, a student at Oxford, spend in Switzerland. William prefers the company of his fellow Oxford students and virtually abandons his young brother, who rather enjoys his solitude. Shortly after his brother leaves for an extended ski trip, the thirteen-year-old meets the handsome, charming, and friendly Archer, who is the same age as William. The younger boy is flattered by the attention of the attractive

Archer, and they spend time together eating, skiing, and drinking. The younger boy is exhilarated by the contact and states quite honestly: "I had never enjoyed myself quite so much before. I thought him the most wonderful companion, not a bit intimidating, in spite of being rather a hero . . . and thought that, apart from my mother, who was dead, I had never liked anyone so much as I liked Archer." They get somewhat drunk together, bathe in the same water, and give each other body rubs. Nothing overtly sexual takes place, and though the language describing their contact is highly sensual, even sexual, innocence prevails. Indeed, the evening ends with Archer singing "Silent Night" in German and: "I began to cry in the moonlight with Archer singing my favorite song; and my brother far away up in the mountain."

Though the boy sleeps at Archer's that night, he awakens with a hangover the next morning and goes back to his hotel just as his brother, William, returns from his ski trip. Once William hears about the boy's escapades, he assumes that Archer has sexually seduced his brother and proceeds to beat his innocent brother, plunging his head in a basin of ice water and phallically plunging his fingers down his brother's throat forcing him to vomit. Welch has so brilliantly constructed the story that the reader, not the boy, experiences the fall from innocence to knowledge, anticipating the boy's fall when he discovers what those words mean in the future. What the thirteen-year-old will find out is that what he experienced as genuine love, affection, and care from Archer is labeled, by the world, as sodomy and prostitution. Welch also cleverly uses the name "Archer" as a possible mythic echo of Cupid whose arrows cause people to fall in love.

Welch has further indicted types such as William and his friends who hate and fear Archer but do not know why. Robert Phillips, the most reliable critic on Welch, theorizes that William may be projecting his own fear of his homosexual feelings toward Archer. This fear, in turn, causes him to read homosexual undertones in perfectly innocent relationships. Archer is probably homosexual, but he is also rich, independent, and comfortable in his sexuality. It could also simply be that William's violent response to his brother's friendship is jealousy. The story is so rich in its construction that Welch enables the reader to interpret it in many equally valid ways. This story is one of his first to document various steps in a young boy's rite of passage from childhood to the more manly ceremonies of smoking and drinking with an older male whom he admires and wants to imitate.

"The Judas Tree" is another story that is thematically related to "The Coffin on the Hill" and "At Sea" insofar as all three show how young people perceive the pain and loneliness of old age and begin to feel within themselves foreshadowings of their own dwindling powers. Specifically, this story concerns a young art student who is pursued by Mr. Clinton, a retired schoolmaster. They meet on the street of an English town as the older man offers to let the younger man sniff the bouquet of hyacinths, narcissus, and daffodils that he is carrying. The figure of Mr. Clinton carries echoes of Oscar Wilde, who frequently carried flowers, and the ominous pervert from James Joyce's "An Encounter," who persisted in trying to engage a boy in sexual conversation. There is also a suggestion of the strangers that the closeted

Aschenbach from Thomas Mann's "Death in Venice" kept encountering on his trip south.

The obviously lonely retired schoolmaster begs the art student to paint for him a picture of Judas actually hanging on the tree where he committed suicide, since of all the pictures that he has collected of Judas, none portrays him actually in the throes of death. He also proposes that he give the young man voice lessons as payment for the picture. The young man promises to paint the picture but then decides that there is something deeply disturbing in their relationship and tells the man that he has no time. The desperate older man immediately rejects the art student's friendship, treating him as one who has "betrayed" his promise, a Judas figure, and the story concludes on a despairing note as the art student declares: "How old and mad and undesirable he must be feeling!" The reader is left with the distinct impression that he is also describing himself in his inevitable later years.

Welch's next story, "The Trout Stream," could certainly be considered a novella, since it is divided into three major sections and runs to about twenty-six pages. In this well-constructed piece, a young boy sets out on another voyage of discovery with his sensitive and beautiful mother. This time it is a land voyage to an Edenic setting of an English manor presided over by Mr. Mellon. It is also a story of the fall of a great house, a genre that was particularly popular in British and American fiction throughout the nineteenth century.

The central character, Mr. Mellon, is the lord of his manor but is also paralyzed from the waist down and must be confined to a wheelchair. The large house is strangely sterile and lifeless, and the young narrator keeps finding artifacts such as a beautifully carved ivory piece of a beggar covered with rats, an object that symbolizes the servant class that surrounds Mr. Mellon and attends to his needs. The name Mellon is also used to suggest the American family of the same name known for their fabulous wealth. The young boy becomes friendly with the housekeeper, Mrs. Slade, and her daughter, Phyllis. An unattractive, blunt girl, Phyllis takes the young boy on a tour of the grounds to show him the artificial trout stream that Mellon has built. The trout, like the characters in the story, are controlled and trapped by Mellon's pervasive power and wealth. The story concludes with Mellon building a more impressive estate, which is even more sterile than the first. Part 3 shows the narrator, now a young man, returning to the ruins of the estate after Mrs. Slade has drowned herself in the trout stream because Mellon rejected her, and after Phyllis has run away with the handsome chauffeur, Bob. All Mellon's effort to create his own little human "trout stream" or regenerated Eden has failed, and he is left lonely and helpless at the story's conclusion. Welch's novella has become another parable of the ravages of time even on the rich and powerful.

"Brave and Cruel," the title story of Welch's first short-story collection, is one of his most compelling creations. The major characters are both artists of a sort. David, the narrator, is a painter, but Micki Beaumont is a con artist par excellence. Micki Beaumont claims to be a returning hero after World War II and entertains the local crowd with fascinating tales of his bravery as a fighter pilot. Everyone believes him because of his charm and good looks. He asks the quiet Katherine Warde to marry him, and she accepts. The major theme of the story is appearance versus reality, or how normal people see what they want to see even though the artist, David, suspects Micki's stories from the beginning. As the story unfolds, the community discovers that Micki's real name is Potts, not Beaumont—that is, a little pot rather than a "beautiful mountain" (the literal translation of the French *beau mont*). Though everyone knows that Micki is a charming con artist, the Warde family, strangely enough, stays in contact with him throughout his embarrassing arrest and disgrace. The snobbish David sees him years later on a bus, dressed in expensive clothes and seemingly prosperous. "Brave and Cruel" is certainly one of Welch's best constructed stories and also discusses on a very sophisticated level how people need their fictions, even though they know them to be fictions, to vivify their banal lives. The necessity of art and illusion becomes, in this story, one of Welch's most serious themes.

Many critics consider the short story "The Fire in the Wood" to be his finest work. Again, the main character, Mary, a virgin, is an artist who cannot seem to find a subject that engenders enthusiasm or "fire" in her imagination. Her name obviously evokes the Blessed Virgin but also suggests "sea," or the primordial repository of archetypes that artists use for inspiration. The plot also shows strong affinities with a number of D. H. Lawrence's tales in which dried-up artist types meet sexually charged primitive innocents whose naturalness and physical energy revitalize their artistic powers. *Lady Chatterley's Lover* (1928) is the prototype of such stories. Mary, the artist, meets Jim, the woodsman or Adam figure, in an artificial woods that a wealthy man had designed to surround his proposed mansion but died before it could be completed. Like the trout stream in the story of the same name, the "wood" becomes a man-made, regenerated Eden in which Mary tempts the innocent Jim into an adulterous affair. Jim, however, has saved Mary not only by becoming her lover but also, more important, by becoming a model for her reawakened artistic energies. At the story's conclusion, reality intrudes as Mary discovers that what appeared to be innocent and noble is merely another sordid tale of madness, greed, and retribution. The important "fall" in the tale is Mary's coming into reality and leaving her adolescent dreamworld. The fall then is a *felix culpa*, or "happy fall," because Mary may now be able to ground her imagination in reality rather than fantasy.

Two stories in Denton Welch's second collection stand out as exceptionally well wrought: "The Hateful Word" and "The Diamond Badge." "The Hateful Word" bears a strong resemblance to "The Fire in the Wood": both stories use a female narrator, or what several critics call an Albertine voice—that is, the female voice through which Proust speaks in much of his fiction even though the speaker in the actual story is a male. Both Proust and Welch used this device as a method of covering their homosexuality. An aging woman offers a gardening job to a young German prisoner named Harry Diedz. Her name, Flora Pinkston, symbolizes her passionate (pink) nature and her desire that Harry "till" her garden. Her first name means "flower." The obvious Freudian overtones are difficult to overlook. The plot is also very Laurentian insofar as it describes a frustrated but passionate woman married to a dull lawyer who has not been able to satisfy her sexual needs. The young, handsome German gardener is paid to come each day and revive her neglected garden. Flora momentarily loses control of herself and passionately kisses the sensuous but polite young man. Though embarrassed by her pass, he tries, nevertheless, to explain that he feels toward her the way he feels toward his mother. He states: "You are like mother to me—my English mother." The word "mother"—the hateful word—devastates Flora and simultaneously awakens her to the harsh reality of her middle years, ushering away any residual illusions of appealing to young males.

The final story in *A Last Sheaf* is one of Welch's most sophisticated psychological tales, involving issues of control and manipulation. Susan Innes writes to the author of a book that she has just finished reading and succeeds in getting an invitation to visit him. She does not know that the author, Andrew Clifton, is terribly deformed and is taken care of by a young, handsome man named Tom Parkinson. Obviously, Clifton loves Parkinson very deeply. Susan is shocked by Clifton's deformity, a fact that changes her whole attitude toward him. She stays the night but experiences a nightmare during which Tom Parkinson comes into her room to comfort her. She is very attracted to Tom and decides to "accidentally" leave a beautiful diamond pin or badge behind to ensure further contact and, perhaps, another invitation. Finally, after months of silent waiting, she reads a new story by Andrew Clifton called "The Diamond Badge" and realizes that the story is really about her attempt to manipulate both Andrew and Tom. Shortly after reading the story, she receives her diamond badge back without a comment. Andrew had not even sent it registered mail. Susan's attempt to control the lives of these two men merely exposed her selfish and mean-spirited attitude toward both of them.

The majority of the stories in Welch's collection *Brave and Cruel* deal with the crises of childhood and adolescence and particularly with falls from a childish innocence into the painful knowledge of emerging adulthood. The second collection, *A Last Sheaf*, concerns the specific difficulties that young artists experience when they first attempt to practice their creative talents. In both collections, the protagonists are overly sensitive, introspective, and isolated. They feel profoundly separated from the normal world and suffer terribly from that alienation. As time passes, they experience increased desperation and take dangerous and, sometimes, self-destructive steps to alleviate their emptiness.

Other major works

NOVELS: *Maiden Voyage*, 1943; *In Youth Is Pleasure*, 1944; *A Voice Through a Cloud*, 1950 (unfinished novel).

POETRY: *Dumb Instrument: Poems and Fragments*, 1976.

NONFICTION: *I Left My Grandfather's House*, 1958; *The Journals of Denton Welch*, 1984.

Bibliography

De-la-Noy, Michael. *Denton Welch: The Making of a Writer.* New York: Viking, 1984. This standard biography uses much material never before published. The biographer uses many of Welch's letters, letters to Welch from his friends, and materials from personal recollections of those who knew him.

Gooch, Brad. "Gossip, Lies, and Wishes." *The Nation* 240 (June 8, 1985): 711-713. Gooch praises Welch for his ability to make even the smallest objects into mementos by the precision of his writing. Though Welch seems haunted by death and time, he is never morbid and can, at times, be flippant about tombs and graveyards.

Hollinghurst, Alan. "Diminished Pictures." *The Times Literary Supplement*, no. 4264 (December 21, 1984): 1479-1480. Hollinghurst finds Welch's aestheticism anything but precious. It helped him focus his attention on art objects during times of great physical and mental pain. He wrote to save himself and to enrich his life.

Phillips, Robert. *Denton Welch.* New York: Twayne, 1974. The only book-length critical treatment of all Welch's work. Phillips' interpretations are thorough, though he tends to find Freudian and Jungian patterns most helpful. He also intelligently points out some of the affinities that Welch shared with D. H. Lawrence and James Joyce.

Updike, John. "A Short Life." In *Picked-Up Pieces.* New York: Alfred A. Knopf, 1975. Updike calls Welch an authentic existential writer insofar as his agony enabled him to create a world particle by particle. He sees Welch's autobiographical account of his terrible accident as "a proclamation of our terrible fragility."

Patrick Meanor

EUDORA WELTY

Born: Jackson, Mississippi; April 13, 1909

Principal short fiction

A Curtain of Green and Other Stories, 1941; *The Wide Net and Other Stories,* 1943; *The Golden Apples,* 1949; *The Bride of the Innisfallen and Other Stories,* 1955; *The Collected Stories of Eudora Welty,* 1980.

Other literary forms

In addition to her many short stories, Eudora Welty has published novels, essays, reviews, an autobiography, a fantasy story for children, and a volume of photographs of Mississippi during the Depression, *One Time, One Place: Mississippi in the Depression, A Snapshot Album* (1971), taken during her stint as photographer and writer for the Works Progress Administration.

Achievements

Welty possesses a distinctive voice in Southern, and indeed in American, fiction. Her vibrant, compelling evocation of the Mississippi landscape, which is her most common setting, has led to comparisons between her work and that of other eminent Southern writers such as William Faulkner, Carson McCullers, and Flannery O'Connor. Welty's graceful, lyrical fiction, however, lacks the pessimism that characterizes much of established Southern writing, and though her settings are distinctly Southern, her themes are universal and do not focus on uniquely Southern issues.

The honors and awards that Welty has amassed throughout her long career are so many as to defy complete listing in a short space. Among her major achievements are four O. Henry Awards for her short stories (first prizes in 1942, 1943, and 1968, and a second prize in 1941), two Guggenheim Fellowships (1942, 1949), honorary lectureships at Smith College (1952) and the University of Cambridge (1955), election to the National Institute of Arts and Letters (1952) and to the American Academy of Arts and Letters (1971), honorary LL.D. degrees from the University of Wisconsin (1954) and Smith College (1956), a term as Honorary Consultant to the Library of Congress (1958-1961), the William Dean Howells Medal of the American Academy of Arts and Letters for *The Ponder Heart* (1954), the Gold Medal for Fiction of the National Institute of Arts and Letters (1972), the Pulitzer Prize in fiction (awarded in 1973 for her 1972 novel *The Optimist's Daughter*), the National Medal of Literature and Medal of Freedom (1981), the National Medal of Arts (1986), and the naming of the Jackson Public Library in her honor (1986).

Biography

Eudora Welty was born on April 13, 1909, in Jackson, Mississippi. In the Welty household, reading was a favorite pastime, and Welty recalls in her autobiography, *One Writer's Beginnings* (1984), both being read to often as a young child and becoming a voracious reader herself. Her recollections of her early life are of a loving and protective family and of a close, gossip-prone community in which she developed her lifelong habit of watching, listening to, and observing closely everything around her. Her progressive and understanding parents encouraged her in her education, and in 1925, she enrolled at the Mississippi State College for Women. After two years there, she transferred to the University of Wisconsin and was graduated with a B.A. in English in 1929.

Welty subsequently studied advertising at the Columbia University Business School; her father had recommended to her that if she planned to be a writer, she would be well advised to have another skill to which she could turn in case of need. During the Depression, however, she had little success finding employment in the field of advertising. She returned to Mississippi and spent the next several years working variously as a writer for radio and as a society editor. In 1933, she began working for the Works Progress Administration, traveling throughout Mississippi, taking photographs, interviewing people, and writing newspaper articles. She later credited this experience with providing her with much material for her short stories as well as sharpening her habit of observation. During these working years, she wrote short stories and occasionally traveled to New York in an effort to interest publishers in her work, with little success. Her first short story, "Death of a Traveling Salesman," was published in 1936 by a "little" magazine called *Manuscript*. Her ability as a writer soon attracted the attention of Robert Penn Warren and Cleanth Brooks, editors of *The Southern Review*, and over the next years her writing appeared in that magazine as well as in *The New Yorker*, *The Atlantic Monthly*, and *The Sewanee Review*.

Her first collection of short stories, *A Curtain of Green and Other Stories*, appeared in 1941, with a preface by Katherine Anne Porter. Welty's reputation as an important Southern writer was established with this first volume, and, at the urging of her editor and friend John Woodburn, who encouraged her to write a longer work of fiction, she followed it with her fabular novel *The Robber Bridegroom* in 1942. Thenceforth, she continued with a fairly steady output of fiction, and with each successive publication, her stature as a major American writer grew. Although fiction is her primary field, she has written many essays and critical reviews and has dabbled in the theater. In addition to stage adaptations of *The Robber Bridegroom* and *The Ponder Heart*, she has collaborated on a musical (never produced) entitled *What Year Is This?* and has written several short theatrical sketches. In 1984, her autobiography, *One Writer's Beginnings*, appeared and quickly became a best-seller.

Welty has spent most of her life living in, observing, and writing about Jackson and the Mississippi Delta country. Her frequent visits to New York, and her travels in France, Italy, Ireland, and England (where she participated in a conference on American studies at the University of Cambridge in 1955) have provided her with material for those few stories that are set outside her native Mississippi. From time to time, she has lectured or taught but in general has preferred the quiet and privacy of her lifelong home of Jackson.

Analysis

Although some dominant themes and characteristics appear regularly in Eudora Welty's fiction, her work resists categorization. The majority of her stories are set in her beloved Mississippi Delta country, of which she paints a vivid and detailed picture, but she is equally comfortable evoking such diverse scenes as a Northern city or a transatlantic ocean liner. Thematically, she concerns herself both with the importance of family and community relations and, paradoxically, with the strange solitariness of human experience. Elements of myth and symbol often appear in her work, but she uses them in shadowy, inexplicit ways. Perhaps the only constant in Welty's fiction is her unerring keenness of observation, both of physical landscape and in characterization, and her ability to create convincing psychological portraits of an immensely varied cast of characters.

One of her earliest stories, "Death of a Traveling Salesman," tells of a commercial traveler who loses his way in the hill country of Mississippi and accidentally drives his car into a ravine. At the nearest farm dwelling, the salesman finds a simple, taciturn couple who assist him with his car and give him a meal and a place to stay for the night. The unspoken warmth in the relationship of the couple is contrasted with the salesman's loneliness, and he repeatedly worries that they can hear the loud pounding of his heart, physically weakened from a recent illness and metaphorically empty of love. When he leaves their house in the morning, his heart pounds loudest of all as he carries his bags to his car; frantically he tries to stifle the sound and dies, his heart unheard by anyone but himself.

Another relatively early story, "A Worn Path," recounts an ancient black woman's long and perilous journey on foot from her remote rural home to the nearest town. The frail old woman, called Phoenix, travels slowly and painfully through a sometimes hostile landscape, described in rich and abundant detail. She overcomes numerous obstacles with determination and good humor. Into the vivid, realistic description of the landscape and journey, Welty interweaves characteristically lyrical passages describing Phoenix's fatigue-induced hallucinations and confused imaginings. When Phoenix reaches the town, she goes to the doctor's office, and it is revealed that the purpose of her journey is to obtain medicine for her chronically ill grandson. A poignant scene at the story's close confirms the reader's suspicion of Phoenix's extreme poverty and suggests the likelihood that her beloved grandson will not live long; old Phoenix's dignity and courage in the face of such hardship, however, raise the story from pathos to a tribute to her resilience and strength of will. Like her mythical namesake, Phoenix triumphs over the forces that seek to destroy her.

"Why I Live at the P.O." is a richly comic tale of family discord and personal alienation, told in the first person in idiomatic, naturalistic language that captures the sounds and patterns of a distinctive Southern speech. It is one of the earliest examples of Welty's often-used narrative technique, what she calls the "monologue that takes possession of the speaker." The story recounts how Sister, the intelligent and ironic narrator, comes to fall out with her family over incidents arising from her younger sister Stella-Rondo's sudden reappearance in their small Southern town, minus her husband and with a two-year-old "adopted" child in tow. Welty's flair for comedy of situation is revealed as a series of bizarrely farcical episodes unfolds. Through the irritable Stella-Rondo's manipulative misrepresentations of fact and Sister's own indifference to causing offense, Sister earns the ire of her opinionated and influential grandfather Papa-Daddy, her gullible, partisan mother, and her short-tempered Uncle Rondo. Sister responds by removing all of her possessions from communal use in the home and taking up residence in the local post office, where she is postmistress. Inability to communicate is a recurrent theme in Welty's short fiction; in this case, it is treated with a controlled hilarity that is chiefly comic but that nevertheless reveals the pain of a family's disunity. This story is one of the best examples of Welty's gift for comic characterization, her gentle mockery of human foibles, and her ear for Southern idiom and expression.

Although Welty disliked having the term "gothic" applied to her fiction, "Keela, the Outcast Indian Maiden" has a grotesque quality that characterizes much of Southern gothic writing. Steve, a former circus sideshow barker, has enlisted the help of Max in finding a small, clubfooted black man who used to be exhibited in the sideshow as "Keela, the Outcast Indian Maiden." As a sideshow freak, he was forced to behave savagely and eat live chickens. Max has brought Steve to the home of Little Lee Roy, who is indeed the man Steve seeks.

As Little Lee Roy looks on, Steve tells Max the disgusting details of the sideshow act and explains how Little Lee Roy was ill-treated by the circus until a kind spectator rescued the victim from his degrading existence. Although he persistently refers to Little Lee Roy as "it" and, unlike Max, refuses to address Little Lee Roy directly, Steve expresses guilt and regret over his role in Little Lee Roy's exploitation. There are subtle resonances of the South's troubled legacy in the way the obviously culpable Steve tries to diminish his role in this ugly episode of oppression by pleading ignorance. He claims that he never knew that the sideshow freak was a normal man and not the savage beast that he was displayed as being in the circus. The simple-minded Little Lee Roy, however, reacts to these reminders of his bizarre past with uncomprehending glee; he seems to have forgotten the pain and unpleasantness of his life with the circus and remembers it only as a colorful adventure. Steve cannot expiate his guilt; he has nothing to offer Little Lee Roy to compensate him for his brutal treatment. He says awkwardly to Max, "Well, I was goin' to give him some money or somethin', I guess, if I ever found him, only now I ain't got any." After the white men's departure, Little Lee Roy's children return, but they hush him when he tries to tell them about the visitors who came to talk to him about "de old times when I use to be wid de circus." The ugly incidents have left no scar on their simple victim; rather, it is the victimizer who suffers an inescapable burden of guilt and shame.

"The Wide Net" is a fabular tale of the mysteries of human relationships and the potency of the natural world. Young William Wallace returns home from a night on the town to find a note from his pregnant wife saying that she has gone to drown herself in the river. William Wallace assembles a motley collection of men and boys to help him drag the river. The river's power as a symbol is apparent in the meaning that it holds for the many characters: to youngsters Grady and Brucie it is the grave of their drowned father; to the rough, carefree Malones, it is a fertile source of life, teeming with catfish to eat, eels to "rassle," and alligators to hunt; to the philosophical and somewhat bombastic Doc, it signifies that "the outside world is full of endurance." It is also, the river-draggers discover, the home of the primeval "king of the snakes."

Throughout the story, Welty deliberately obscures the nature of William Wallace's relationship with his wife, the history behind her threat, and even whether William Wallace truly believes his wife has jumped in the river. Characteristically, Welty relies on subtle hints and expert manipulation of tone rather than on open exposition to suggest to her readers the underpinnings of the events that she describes. This deliberate vagueness surrounding the facts of the young couple's quarrel lends the story the quality of a fable or folktale. The young lover must undergo the test of dragging the great river, confronting the king of snakes, and experiencing a kind of baptism, both in the river and in the cleansing thunderstorm that drenches the searchers, before he is worthy of regaining his wife's love. Like a fable, the story has an almost impossibly simple and happy ending. William Wallace returns from the river to find his welcoming wife waiting calmly at home. They have a brief, affectionate mock quarrel that does not specifically address the incident at all, and they retire hand in hand, leaving the reader to ponder the mystery of their bond.

"Livvie" has a lyrical, fabular quality similar to that of "The Wide Net." Livvie is a young black woman who lives with her elderly husband, Solomon, on a remote farm far up the old Natchez Trace. The strict old husband is fiercely protective of his young bride and does not allow her to venture from the yard or to talk with—or even see—other people. The inexperienced Livvie, however, is content in Solomon's comfortable house, and she takes loving care of him when his great age finally renders him bedridden. One day, a white woman comes to her door, selling cosmetics. Livvie is enchanted with the colors and scents of the cosmetics but is firm in her insistence that she has no money to buy them. When the saleswoman leaves, Livvie goes into the bedroom to gaze on her ancient, sleeping husband. Desire for wider experience and a more fulfilling life has been awakened in her, and as her husband sleeps, she disobeys his strictest command and wanders off down the Natchez Trace. There, she comes upon a handsome, opulently dressed young man named Cash, whom she leads back to Solomon's house. When Solomon awakes and sees them, he is reproachful but resigned to her need for a younger man, asking God to forgive him for taking such a young girl away from other young people. Cash steals from the room, and as Livvie gazes on the frail, wasted body of Solomon, he dies. In a trancelike shock, Livvie drops Solomon's sterile, ticking watch; after momentary hesitation, she goes outside to join Cash in the bright light of springtime.

"Livvie" is almost like a fairy tale in its use of simple, universal devices. The beautiful young bride, the miserly old man who imprisons her, the strange caller who brings temptation, and the handsome youth who rescues the heroine are all familiar, timeless characters. Welty broadens the references of her story to include elements of myth and religion. Young Cash, emerging from the deep forest dressed in a bright green coat and green-plumed hat, could be the Green Man of folklore, a symbol of springtime regeneration and fertility. In contrasting youth with age and old with new, Welty subtly employs biblical references. Old Solomon thinks rather than feels but falls short of his Old Testament namesake in wisdom. Youthful Cash, redolent of spring, tells Livvie that he is "ready for Easter," the reference ostensibly being to his new finery but suggesting new life rising to vanquish death. The vague, dreamy impressionism of "Livvie," which relies on image and action rather than dialogue to tell the story (except in the scenes featuring the saleswoman), adds to this folktalelike quality.

In "A Still Moment," Welty uses historical characters to tell a mystically imaginative tale. Lorenzo Dow, the New England preacher, James Murrell, the outlaw, and John James Audubon, the naturalist and painter, were real people whom Welty places in a fictional situation. Dow rides with an inspired determination to his evening's destination, a camp meeting where he looks forward to a wholesale saving of souls. With single-minded passion, he visualizes souls and demons crowding before him in the dusky landscape. Dow's spiritual intensity is both compared and contrasted to the outlook of the outlaw Murrell, who shadows Dow along the Natchez Trace. Murrell considers his outlawry in a profoundly philosophical light, seeing each murder as a kind of ceremonial drawing out and solving of the unique "mystery" of each victim's being. Audubon, like Dow and Murrell, has a strange and driving intensity that sets him apart from other men. His passion is the natural world; by meticulously observing and recording it, he believes that he can move from his knowledge to an understanding of all things, including his own being.

The three men are brought together by chance in a clearing, each unaware of the others' identities. As they pause, a solitary white heron alights near them in the marsh. As the three men stare in wonder at the snowy creature, Welty identifies for the reader the strange similarity of these outwardly diverse men: "What each of them had wanted was simply *all*. To save all souls, to destroy all men, to see and record all life that filled this world." The simple and beautiful sight of the heron, however, causes these desires to ebb in each of them; they are transfixed and cleansed of desire. Welty uses the heron as a symbol of the purity and beauty of the natural world, which acts as a catalyst for her characters' self-discovery. Oddly, it is Audubon, the lover of nature, who breaks the spell. He reaches for his gun and shoots the bird, to add to his scientific collection. The magic of the moment is gone, and the lifeless body of the bird becomes a mere sum of its parts, a dull, insensate mass of feathers and flesh. Audubon, his prize collected, continues on his way, and the horrified Dow hurries away toward his camp meeting, comforted by the vivid memory of the bird's strange beauty. The dangerous Murrell experiences an epiphanic moment of self-realization; the incident has reminded him poignantly of all men's separateness and innocence, a thought that reconfirms in him his desire to waylay and destroy. It is only through a brief but intense moment of shared feeling and experience that the men can recognize their essential loneliness. As in "The Wide Net" and "Livvie," the most important communication must be done without words.

"Moon Lake" is from the collection *The Golden Apples*, the stories of which are nearly all set in or around the mythical community of Morgana, Mississippi, and feature a single, though extensive, cast of characters. Thematically, it shares with "A Still Moment" the sense of the paradoxical oneness and interconnectedness of the human condition. The story describes a sequence of events at a camp for girls at the lake of the story's title. The characteristically lushly detailed landscape is both beautiful and dangerous, a place where poisonous snakes may lurk in the blackberry brambles and where the lake is a site for adventure but also a brown-watered, bug-filled morass with thick mud and cypress roots that grasp at one's feet. The story highlights the simultaneous attraction and repulsion of human connection. Antipathies abound among the group assembled at the lake: the lake's Boy Scout lifeguard, Loch, feels contempt for the crowd of young girls; the Morgana girls look down on the orphan girls as ragged thieves; rivalry and distrust crops up among individual girls. The sensitive Nina yearns for connection and freedom from connection at the same time; she envies the lonely independence of the orphans and wishes to be able to change from one persona to another at will, but at the same time she is drawn to Easter, the "leader" of the orphans, for her very qualities of separateness and disdain for friendship.

Nina and her friend Jinny Love follow Easter to a remote part of the lake in an unsuccessful attempt to cultivate her friendship, and when they return to where the others are swimming, Easter falls from the diving platform and nearly drowns. The near-drowning becomes a physical acting out of the story's theme, the fascinating and inescapable but frightening necessity of human connection. Without another's help, Easter would have died alone under the murky water, but Loch's lengthy efforts to resuscitate the apparently lifeless form of Easter disgust the other girls. The quasi-sexual rhythm of the resuscitation is made even more disturbing to the girls by its violence: Loch pummels Easter with his fists, and blood streams from her mud-smeared mouth as he flails away astride her. The distressing physical contact contrasts with the lack of any emotional connection during this scene. One orphan, a companion of Easter, speculates that if Easter dies she gets her winter coat, and gradually the other girls grow bored of the spectacle and resent the interruption of their afternoon swim. Jinny Love's mother, appearing unexpectedly at the camp, is more concerned with the lewdness that she imputes to Loch's rhythmic motions than with Easter's condition and she barks at him, "Loch Morrison, get off that table and shame on you." Nina is the most keenly aware of the symbolic significance of the incident and of the peril of connection; she reflects that "Easter had come among them and had held herself untouchable and intact. Of course, for one little touch could smirch her, make her fall so far, so deep."

Another story from *The Golden Apples* is "The Whole World Knows," which features the adult Jinny Love Stark, whom readers have met as a child in "Moon Lake," and Ran McLain, who appears briefly in "Moon Lake" and other stories in this collection. The story addresses the inescapable net of personal and community relations and the potentially stifling and limiting nature of small-town life. Welty uses a monologue form similar to the one in "Why I Live at the P.O.," but in this story, told by Ran, the tone is lamenting and confessional rather than comically outraged.

Ran and Jinny are married but have separated, ostensibly over Jinny's infidelity. They both remain in the claustrophobically small town of Morgana, living in the same street and meeting occasionally in the town's bank, where Ran works alongside Jinny's lover, Woody Spights. On the surface, the story centers on Ran's developing relationship with a Maideen Sumrall, a foolish, chattering young country girl with whom he has taken up as a way of revenging himself on his wayward wife. The true focus, however, is on the causes of the deterioration of Ran's marriage to the lively, enthusiastic Jinny, revealed obliquely through other events in the story. The reasons for Jinny's initial infidelity are only hinted at; her irrepressibly joyous and wondering outlook is contrasted with Ran's heavy and brooding nature, indicating a fundamental incompatibility. Ran's careless and selfish use of Maideen, to whom he is attracted because she seems a young and "uncontaminated" version of Jinny, suggests a dark side to his nature that may be at the root of their estrangement. There is a vague suggestion, never clearly stated, that Ran may have been unfaithful to Jinny first. The merry, carefree Jinny baffles and infuriates Ran, and he fantasizes about violently murdering both Jinny and her lover, Woody. His true victim, however, is Maideen, the vulnerable opposite of the unflappable, independent Jinny. After Ran roughly consummates his shabby affair with the semi-willing Maideen, he wakes to find her sobbing like a child beside him. Readers learn in another story that Maideen eventually commits suicide. The story ends inconclusively, with neither Ran nor Jinny able or even entirely willing to escape from their shared past, the constricted community of Morgana being their all-knowing "whole world" of the story's title. As in "Moon Lake," true connection is a paradox, at once impossible, inescapable, desirable, and destructive.

"Where Is the Voice Coming From?" was originally published in *The New Yorker*, and it remained uncollected until the appearance of the complete *The Collected Stories of Eudora Welty* in 1980. In it, Welty uses a fictional voice to express her views on the Civil Rights struggle in the South. The story, written in 1963 in response to the murder of Medgar Evers in Welty's hometown of Jackson, is told as a monologue by a Southern white man whose ignorance and hate for African Americans is depicted as chillingly mundane. He tells how, enraged by black activism in the South, he determines to shoot a local Civil Rights leader. He drives to the man's home late on an unbearably hot summer night, waits calmly in hiding until the man appears, and then shoots him in cold blood. The callous self-righteousness of the killer and his unreasoning hate are frighteningly depicted when he mocks the body of his victim, saying "Roland? There was only one way left for me to be ahead of you and stay ahead of you, by Dad, and I just taken it. . . . We ain't never now, never going to be equals and you know why? One of us is dead. What about that, Roland?" His justification for the murder is simple: "I done what I done for my own pure-D satisfaction." His only regret is that he cannot claim the credit for the killing.

Welty scatters subtle symbols throughout the story. The extremely hot weather, which torments the killer, reflects the social climate as the Civil Rights conflict reaches a kind of boiling point. To the killer, the street feels as hot under his feet as the barrel of his gun. Light and dark contrast in more than just the black and white skins of the characters: the stealthy killer arrives in a darkness that will cloak his crime and he finds light shining forth from the home of his prey, whose mission is to enlighten. When the killer shoots his victim, he sees that "something darker than him, like the wings of a bird, spread on his back and pulled him down."

Unlike most of Welty's fiction, "Where Is the Voice Coming From?" clearly espouses a particular viewpoint, and the reader is left with no doubt about the writer's intention in telling the story. The story, however, embodies the qualities that typify Welty's fiction: the focus on the interconnections of human society; the full, sharp characterization achieved in a minimum of space; the detailed description of the physical landscape that powerfully evokes a sense of place; the ear for speech and idiom; and the subtle, floating symbolism that insinuates rather than announces its meaning.

Other major works

NOVELS: *The Robber Bridegroom*, 1942; *Delta Wedding*, 1946; *The Ponder Heart*, 1954; *Losing Battles*, 1970; *The Optimist's Daughter*, 1972.

NONFICTION: *Place in Fiction*, 1957; *Three Papers on Fiction*, 1962; *One Time, One Place: Mississippi in the Depression, A Snapshot Album*, 1971; *The Eye of the Story: Selected Essays and Reviews*, 1978; *One Writer's Beginnings*, 1984.

CHILDREN'S LITERATURE: *The Shoe Bird*, 1964.

Bibliography

Appel, Alfred, Jr. *A Season of Dreams: The Fiction of Eudora Welty.* Baton Rouge: Louisiana State University Press, 1965. This broad survey of Welty's work examines individual works as well as more general themes and concerns in Welty's fiction, through *The Bride of the Innisfallen and Other Stories.* Chapters on comedy, elements of the gothic and grotesque, and Welty's form and technique contribute to the value of this solid, if somewhat dated, study.

Evans, Elizabeth. *Eudora Welty.* New York: Frederick Ungar, 1981. This accessible survey discusses both Welty's fiction and her essays and reviews. The brief literary biography of Welty in the opening chapter is useful and offers interesting information on Welty's relationship with her publishers and editors in the early part of her long literary career.

Prenshaw, Peggy Whitman, ed. *Conversations with Eudora Welty.* Jackson: University Press of Mississippi, 1984. A collection of interviews with Welty spanning the years 1942-1982. Welty talks frankly and revealingly with interviewers such as William F. Buckley, Jr., and Alice Walker about her fiction and her life, addressing such topics as her methods of writing, her Southern background, her love of reading, and her admiration for the works of writers such as William Faulkner, Elizabeth Bowen, and Katherine Anne Porter.

Vande Kieft, Ruth M. *Eudora Welty.* 1962. Rev. ed. Boston: Twayne, 1987. This comprehensive examination of Welty's fiction offers detailed explications of many of Welty's works as well as chapters on particular aspects of her writing, such as elements of comedy and Welty's deliberate desire to "mystify" her readers.

Westling, Louise. *Sacred Groves and Ravaged Gardens: The Fiction of Eudora Welty, Carson McCullers, and Flannery O'Connor.* Athens: University of Georgia Press, 1985. Westling examines Welty's fiction, along with the work of other eminent female Southern writers, as part of a tradition of Southern women's writing. Westling brings a feminist perspective to bear on such aspects of Southern women's writing as myth, sexuality, and the symbolic power of place. Welty's fiction is analyzed as a feminine celebration of a matriarchal society in which women can find freedom and fulfillment outside the social strictures of traditional Southern life.

Catherine Swanson

GLENWAY WESCOTT

Born: Kewaskum, Wisconsin; April 11, 1901
Died: Rosemont, New Jersey; February 22, 1987

Principal short fiction

Like a Lover, 1926; *Good-bye, Wisconsin,* 1928; *The Babe's Bed,* 1930; *The Pilgrim Hawk: A Love Story,* 1940.

Other literary forms

Glenway Wescott honed his writing skills early in his career by writing poetry: *The Bitterns* (1920) and *Natives of Rock* (1925). He went on to write three novels, *The Apple of the Eye* (1924), *The Grandmothers* (1927), and *Apartment in Athens* (1945), and two volumes of essays, *Fear and Trembling* (1932) and *Images of Truth* (1962). Additional works include a hagiography entitled *A Calendar of Saints for Unbelievers* (1932) and a nonfiction volume, *The Best of All Possible Worlds: Journals, Letters, and Remembrances, 1914-1937* (1975).

Achievements

Of all the expatriated Americans who were living in Europe during the 1920's, Wescott is most notable for the pursuit of his theme. Regardless of whether Wescott was writing about his native Wisconsin or Europe, he always returned to his theme of returning home. In a sense, Wescott's single novella, three novels, and numerous short stories can be viewed as a journey in search of the source of the creative self.

Because Wescott stopped writing fiction at the age of forty-four, some critics have classified him as a writer who had the qualities needed for great achievement but who failed to live up to the promise of his early works. Although Wescott's body of work is relatively small, his technical achievements were significant. Not only was he a master of the carefully turned aphorism, but also he invented the technique of the participating narrator. Wescott may not be a major American writer, but he still ranks as one of the most distinctive prose stylists in twentieth century American fiction.

Biography

Glenway Wescott's life is made up of two diametrically opposed phases. He was born on a farm in Kewaskum, Wisconsin, on April 11, 1901. Glenway was very close to his mother, who nurtured his interests in music, acting, and literature. He soon, however, proved to be a great disappointment to his father, Bruce Peters Wescott, because he hated the drudgery of farm work. When Glenway was thirteen, his relationship with his father became openly hostile as the result of a minor incident, and he was shunted from relative to relative. During his last two years at Waukesha High School, Glenway lived with his father's brother, a preacher named William Samuel

Wescott. His uncle's vast library opened an entirely new world for the young man, which he continued to explore in the literary society to which he belonged in high school.

By the time Wescott was sixteen, his experiences were no longer like those of other boys who had grown up on Wisconsin farms. After graduating from high school in 1917, Wescott went to Chicago. While he was living with the wealthy mother of his uncle's wife, Wescott attended the University of Chicago. His new experiences, like his previous ones on the farm in Wisconsin, were later to serve as material for his fiction. Wescott had no interest in a literary career when he first entered the university, but his distaste for required courses led him to enroll in several literature courses during his first semester. His enthusiasm for literature soon led to his involvement in the university's newly formed Poetry Club. Through the imagistic poetry that he wrote as a college student, Wescott learned how to solidify an intense moment and to etch it into the consciousness with sharp imagery.

In 1918, Wescott went to New Mexico to recover from a failed homosexual relationship that had driven him to attempt suicide. Between 1918 and 1920, he began writing poetry based on his New Mexico experiences and published it in a volume entitled *The Bitterns*. Harriet Monroe was so impressed with Wescott's work that she hired him to work for *Poetry* in 1921. It was also in 1921 that Wescott published his first short story, "Bad Han," which launched his career as a prose writer. Wescott's developing style was influenced by writers whom he met while working for the magazine, including Edwin Arlington Robinson.

It was during the summer of 1921 that Wescott traveled to Europe with his friend Monroe Wheeler. During the next eleven years, Wescott produced the fiction that established him as a midwestern prodigy. He became financially solvent following the publication in Europe of two novels, *The Apple of the Eye* and *The Grandmothers*, and a collection of short stories, *Good-bye, Wisconsin*. He was less successful with his two departures from fiction, *Fear and Trembling* and *A Calendar of Saints for Unbelievers*, both written in 1932.

Convinced that Europe had become a "rat trap" for him, Wescott returned to the United States in 1933 and settled in New York. While he was growing accustomed to living in the United States again, Wescott produced no fiction at all until 1940. In many ways, World War II shocked him into writing again. *The Pilgrim Hawk: A Love Story*, which continued to be his most popular work, changed the minds of those critics who believed that he had "written himself out." In 1945, he wrote *Apartment in Athens* in an attempt to convince his publisher that he was still a "valuable property."

Despite the success of *Apartment in Athens*, Wescott produced no more works of fiction, even though he did begin several projects. In 1962, a collection of essays entitled *Images of Truth* established him as one of the most influential critics in the United States, because he was writing to the cultivated general reader, not to the most sophisticated and highbrow critics. Wescott's profiles of six writers whom he admired offered a memorable insight into how his own fiction-writer's mind perceived the world. Although this, his final work, did not totally satisfy his faithful coterie of admirers, who had looked forward to the kind of a large complex novel that they believed he had the ability to write, it eloquently confirmed his faith in the literary life. It was a fitting end to the career of this melancholy yet tantalizing literary figure.

Analysis

Glenway Wescott's short fiction employs many of the same themes and techniques that he used in his first two novels. The two major themes continue to be the self and love. A technical innovation that he first used in *The Grandmothers*, the participating narrator, also appears in his short fiction. His use of symbols is also similar to what he had done in his first two novels. The bird remained his favorite symbol and was usually placed at the center of the story. Except for *The Babe's Bed*, the short stories that appear after *Good-bye, Wisconsin* are inferior in quality and demonstrate how Wescott lost his enthusiasm for a literary form once he had mastered it. The next short form with which he experimented, the novella, perfected certain techniques of prose fiction that he used with mixed results in his short stories.

Wescott shaped a number of his early experiences into short stories in which he employed impressionistic techniques instead of the mere transcription of events. To a certain extent, the ten short stories and title essay in *Good-bye, Wisconsin* illustrate reasons why Wescott could not stay in Wisconsin. They cannot, however, be dismissed simply as regional stories in that the universal truths of which they speak could be found anywhere.

Several of the stories that deal, in one way or another, with the search for the self illustrate the ways in which rural Wisconsin impedes that search. "The Sailor" goes beyond being a regional story in the way that it also includes the theme of love. Terrie, who is another of Wescott's expatriates, has joined the navy to escape the depressing surroundings of rural Wisconsin. After spending some time in France, he recounts his adventures there to his brother, Riley. By the time Terrie has finished his narration, he has revealed that he has been severely traumatized by a failed love affair that he had with a French prostitute named Zizi. Riley, however, sees the stories as nothing more than tales of whiskey and women. Sensing Riley's lack of understanding, Terrie is filled with a thirst that cannot be quenched at home. Emotions such as the ones that Terrie encountered in Europe are foreign to Wisconsin.

Wisconsin serves primarily as the setting for a transition from innocence to experience in "In a Thicket." Lilly is a fifteen-year-old girl who lives with her senile grandfather in a house surrounded by a thicket. After hearing about a black convict who escaped the night before from a nearby prison, she stays up all night waiting for him to appear. When she finally sees him at the door, she stands transfixed until he walks away. The three-inch gash that she finds in the screen door the next morning symbolizes the figurative loss of her virginity. The sexual side of her nature has been awakened by the intruder, and she emerges from the thicket of her childhood into the world of the senses.

Like "In a Thicket," "The Whistling Swan" takes place in Wisconsin, but it focuses instead on the theme of love. Like Terrie in "The Sailor," the protagonist of "The Whistling Swan," Hubert Redd, is an expatriot. He is, however, closer to Wescott himself in that he is an artist, a composer, and a sophisticate who is aware of both the advantages and drawbacks of living in Europe and the United States. He returns to his hometown in Wisconsin after his wealthy patrons withdraw their support on the grounds that he is immoral and untalented. The love that he feels for his childhood sweetheart complicates his life because it conflicts with his desire to return to Europe and resume his artistic pursuits. Redd's inner conflict is resolved when he impulsively shoots a swan and simultaneously kills that part of himself that draws him to Paris. The intentional ambiguity of the ending poses the possibility that he is sobbing, not because he has killed the swan, but because he has destroyed the creative impulse that made him unhappy in Wisconsin.

"A Guilty Woman" traces a woman's progression from a type of love that enslaves to the type that liberates. Evelyn Crowe is a forty-five-year-old ex-convict who served six years in prison for murdering her lover, Bill Fisher. Fisher had been initially attracted to her because he relished the challenge of corrupting and abandoning an "old maid." Upon her release from prison, she is taken in by her friend Martha Colvin to live on her farm in Wisconsin. While living there, Evelyn is attracted to Martha's bachelor friend, Dr. John Bolton. She resists the romantic impulse that is building up inside her until she realizes that the passionless life to which she had returned was a form of pride. No longer content to be a self-sufficient spinster, she finally allows herself to fall in love. Wescott finds a kind of courage in Evelyn's flexibility, which he believed was discouraged by small-town America.

The short story that merited the most critical acclaim was "Like a Lover." Like Lilly in "In a Thicket," Alice Murray is an isolated girl who is mesmerized by a man, in this case, an older man named Hurst. Despite her mother's protests, she marries him. The assortment of whips and clubs that her husband keeps in the house, however, terrifies her and drives her back to her mother's house. She remains in isolation for seven years until she learns that Hurst is to marry Mrs. Clayburn, a widow. Even though Mrs. Clayburn believes Alice's words of warning, she admits that she is unable to break the spell that he holds over her. For two months following Mrs. Clayburn's marriage, Alice is tormented by ominous nightmares that foretell the woman's murder. The story concludes with the appearance of Alice's friend, Mary Clifford, riding frantically from the Hurst farm, waving her arms. Shocked by what she knows has happened to the new Mrs. Hurst, Alice faints and falls backward on the porch. Ostensibly, "Like a Lover" exploits the same kind of scandalous material that Wescott used in "A Guilty Woman." The godlike power that the men in both stories have over women, however, illustrates Wescott's belief, discussed in depth two years later in *A Calendar of Saints for Unbelievers*, that the love for God is similar to the love for a man or a woman in that both forms of affection render a person completely helpless.

The Babe's Bed, which is a thirty-five-page short story published as a book in

Paris, is, in a sense, a postscript to the introductory essay in *Good-bye, Wisconsin*. Both were written after Wescott returned to Wisconsin for a short visit and concern an expatriated American who compares the Midwest to Europe. In both works, Wisconsin and the United States in general are found to retard the development of the self.

The story is told from the limited point of view of a nameless bachelor who returns home. As in other stories by Wescott, dramatic tension is created through the narrator's conflicting impulses. The bachelor becomes so lost in fantasies involving his sister's baby that he becomes detached from reality. He begins by imagining that the baby is his and then convinces himself that his married sister is his mother. The climax occurs at the dinner table when the baby screams at being placed in the harness that serves as its bed. The baby's bed, which is the story's central symbol, bears a close resemblance to the mental web that has ensnared the bachelor. Before he attacks everyone at the table, he realizes that he has been living in a fantasy world and directs his anger toward himself before he can do any real harm to his loved ones.

With the publication of *The Pilgrim Hawk: A Love Story*, Wescott created what many critics have referred to as a genuine short masterpiece. The novella differs from most of Wescott's previous fiction in that it concerns expatriated Americans living in France instead of rural midwestern Americans. The story is retold in 1940 by the protagonist, Alwyn Tower, who interrupts his first-person narrative to comment on such matters as love, marriage, religion, alcoholism, and individual and artistic freedom. The events that he recalls took place during one day in May of 1928 or 1929 in France at the house of Alexandra Henry, a great friend of Tower. The story focuses on the arrival of Madeleine and Larry Cullen, a rich, handsome couple from Ireland who arrive unexpectedly with their chauffeur, Ricketts, and Madeleine Cullen's falcon, Lucy. For the most part, the action of the novella takes the form of a conversation among the four main characters.

As the Cullens chat about money and neighbors, it becomes clear that the hawk symbolizes the Cullens' relationship and the Cullens themselves. Madeleine resembles the feathered predator in the way she uses her charms to capture and hold her prey, Larry, who is too weak to escape the hold that she has on him. Both she and her husband, however, are hawklike in that they are prisoners of their own appetites. Although the hawk is consistent with the bird symbolism in Wescott's other stories and novels, it differs in the way it revolves, taking on different meanings in different situations.

Tower continues to attach symbolic meanings to the hawk until it comes to stand for himself and Alexandra as well. Eventually, he builds a tower of symbolic meanings that blinds him to the "petty" facts that constitute reality. The process continues until Cullen, in a drunken stupor, attempts to kill someone; Madeleine, who reports the event just before she and her husband leave for Paris, never makes it clear whether Larry tried to kill himself or Ricketts in a fit of jealous rage. This violent turn of events shocks Tower back to reality, enabling him to descend from the symbolic tower that he has constructed. He recognizes that the "whisper of the devil" is the fear that he has attached the wrong meanings to things in order to make life more meaningful.

Other major works

NOVELS: *The Apple of the Eye*, 1924; *The Grandmothers*, 1927; *Apartment in Athens*, 1945.

POETRY: *The Bitterns*, 1920; *Natives of Rock*, 1925.

NONFICTION: *Elizabeth Madox Roberts: A Personal Note*, 1930; *Fear and Trembling*, 1932; *A Calendar of Saints for Unbelievers*, 1932; *Images of Truth*, 1962; *The Best of All Possible Worlds: Journals, Letters, and Remembrances, 1914-1937*, 1975.

MISCELLANEOUS: *The Maugham Reader*, 1950 (edited); *Short Novels of Colette*, 1951 (edited); *Twelve Fables of Aesop, Newly Narrated*, 1954.

Bibliography

Hoffman, Frederick J. *The Twenties*. New York: Viking, 1968. The six-page discussion of Wescott's career examines the midwestern elements in his work. Although it could serve as an introduction to Wescott's fiction, the section is somewhat limited in scope.

Johnson, Ira. *Glenway Wescott: The Paradox of Voice*. Port Washington, N.Y.: Kennikat Press, 1971. Johnson has written what is by far the most incisive look into Wescott's career. The book explicates and criticizes each of Wescott's works in detail. He also demonstrates how each work reflects Wescott's development as a writer. The book does not, however, provide sufficient insight into Wescott's early life to qualify as a biographical study.

Kahn, Sy Myron. *Glenway Wescott: A Critical and Biographical Study*. Ann Arbor, Mich.: University Microfilms, 1957. Much of the biographical information that is included in Kahn's dissertation cannot be found anywhere else. By showing how Wescott's experiences influenced each of his major works, Kahn has made an indispensable contribution to Wescott scholarship.

Rosco, Jerry. "An American Treasure: Glenway Wescott's *The Pilgrim Hawk*." *The Literary Review* 15 (Winter, 1988): 133-142. Rosco's analysis of Wescott's famous novella is taken from information provided by Wescott himself during his last interview. Wescott's personal reflections regarding how he wrote the story and how he was influenced by W. Sommerset Maugham are particularly revealing.

Rueckert, William H. *Glenway Wescott*. New York: Twayne: 1965. In this work, which is the first book-length appraisal of Wescott, Rueckert attempts to revise Wescott's reputation as a man of letters who produced only one minor masterpiece. Although Rueckert's analysis is perceptive, he does not examine each work in enough depth to support his premise that Wescott is a major artist who deserves more attention.

Zabel, Morton Dawen. *Craft and Character: Texts, Method, and Vocation*. New York: Viking, 1957. In chapter 2, Zabel tries to demonstrate how *The Pilgrim Hawk* stands in relation to other twentieth century fables. Like Wescott himself, though, Zabel concentrates more on the style than on the substance of Wescott's work.

Alan Brown

JESSAMYN WEST

Born: North Vernon, Indiana; July 18, 1902
Died: Napa, California; February 23, 1984

Principal short fiction

The Friendly Persuasion, 1945; *Cress Delahanty*, 1953; *Love, Death, and the Ladies' Drill Team*, 1955; *Except for Me and Thee: A Companion to the Friendly Persuasion*, 1969; *Crimson Ramblers of the World, Farewell*, 1970; *The Story of a Story and Three Stories*, 1982; *Collected Stories of Jessamyn West*, 1986.

Other literary forms

Best known for her first collection of short stories, *The Friendly Persuasion*, Jessamyn West also published eight novels during her long literary career, including *Leafy Rivers* (1967), set on the frontier in nineteenth century Ohio, and *South of the Angels* (1960), set, like many of her short stories, in Southern California. West also published an opera libretto based on the life of John James Audubon, *A Mirror for the Sky* (1948), and a collection of poems, *The Secret Look: Poems* (1974). Among her screenplays was that for the film *Friendly Persuasion* (1956), written in collaboration. Her autobiographical writings include an account of the production of that film, *To See the Dream* (1957); *Hide and Seek: A Continuing Journey* (1973), the story of her early life; *The Woman Said Yes: Encounters with Life and Death—Memoirs* (1976), dealing with her illness with tuberculosis and her sister's sickness and suicide; and *Double Discovery: A Journey* (1980), a travel diary. She edited *The Quaker Reader* in 1962.

Achievements

Ever since the publication of her first book, West has had a large and loyal following. Critics praise her craftsmanship: her clear prose, her vivid realization of the natural setting, her historical accuracy, her effective creation of characters who are complex human beings beneath their seemingly simple surface. Her accomplishments have been recognized by the Indiana Authors' Day Award in 1957, the Thormod Monsen Award in 1958, and the Janet Kafka Prize in 1976, as well as by the awarding of honorary doctorates both in her native Midwest and in her longtime home, California. West's works are divided between the Midwestern frontier of her family's past and the new frontier of twentieth century Southern California. The fact that her fiction is authentically regional does not limit her appeal, however, for her themes transcend local color, dealing as they do with survival as a moral and loving being in a difficult and dangerous world.

Biography

Jessamyn West was born in North Vernon, Indiana, on July 18, 1902. After moving with her parents to California, she completed her education at Fullerton High School, at Whittier College, where she received a B.A. in English in 1923, and at the University of California, Berkeley. Although she had published short stories based on her family's Quaker past, she did not collect them in a book until 1945, thus publishing her first book at the age of forty-three. Later, she taught at numerous universities and at Breadloaf. Her last book, *The State of Stony Lonesome* (1984), was completed shortly before her death, on February 23, 1984, at her longtime home in Napa, California.

Analysis

Jessamyn West's short stories fall into two categories: those which treat various episodes in the lives of a single family and are gathered in a single volume, and those which more conventionally are quite separate in plot and character, gathered in the customary collections. The books *The Friendly Persuasion, Except for Me and Thee: A Companion to the Friendly Persuasion*, and *Cress Delahanty* fall into the first category. Although some critics have called them novels, the sketches of which each volume is composed are obviously separate. The fact that an acknowledgment preceding *The Friendly Persuasion* refers to "stories in this book" which had been published in various magazines makes West's own assumptions clear. In the introduction to *Collected Stories of Jessamyn West*, Julian Muller calls those earlier volumes "novels," while admitting that the chapters could stand alone, and thus he omits those sketches from his collection. A complete analysis of West's short fiction, however, must include the consideration of those works on an individual basis, even though a study of her long fiction might also include them.

The *Collected Stories of Jessamyn West* included all the stories from two previous volumes, *Love, Death, and the Ladies' Drill Team* and *Crimson Ramblers of the World, Farewell*, along with eight additional stories which Jessamyn West wished to have included. According to the editor, those stories which were omitted, West believed, needed revision.

The focus in all West's work is a basic tension in human life. On the one hand, humans yearn to be free of restraints; on the other hand, they desire to love and to please the beloved, thus voluntarily to accept limitations on their individuality. The beloved is not only their human partner: the term also suggests divinity, speaking to the spirit directly, in the Quaker tradition. Although social or religious groups may presume to judge the conduct of West's characters, the final judgment must be their own, guided by their separate and sacred consciences. According to the editor of the *Collected Stories of Jessamyn West*, West's first published story was "99.6." Set in a tuberculosis sanatorium, the story reflects West's own experience. The protagonist, Marianne Kent, desperately watches her temperature, hoping for the change which would signal some improvement in her health. Aware of her own feverish condition, the consumption which is truly consuming her, she wishes that the nurse would help her with an illusion, with the suggestion that perhaps the heat she feels comes from warmer weather outside, not from her own fever. Although the obvious antagonists

are Marianne Kent and her disease, at the conclusion of the brief story the protagonist turns to God, pleading with Him for some sign of hope, for some reduction
from 99.6. Thus, the real struggle is a spiritual one. Mrs. Kent must accept what
divinity permits.

In *The Friendly Persuasion* stories, set in the nineteenth century among the Indiana Quakers of the Ohio River Valley, conscience is always a consideration. The
Irish Quaker Jess Birdwell, a devout man but one who has a mind of his own, is
married to Eliza Cope Birdwell, a stricter Quaker—in fact, a Quaker minister, who
must consider the community's judgment of her as well as God's. "Music on the
Muscatatuck" illustrates the stresses on the relationship between Jess and Eliza,
which result from their differences in temperament and convictions. After describing the natural beauty of the Birdwell farm, the comfort and plenty of their pretty
home, the goodness of Eliza as a wife, and Jess's own prosperity, West sets the
problem: Jess likes music; as a Quaker, he is supposed to have nothing to do with it.

Jess's temptation comes when, like Eve in the Garden, he is separated from his
mate. On a business trip to Philadelphia, he meets an organ salesman; already seduced by his own love of music, he stops by the store. The result is inevitable: he
orders an organ.

When Jess returns home, he cannot find the words to tell Eliza, who follows the
Quaker teachings about music, what he has done. Unfortunately, when the organ
arrives, Eliza makes a miscalculation about Jess's male pride: she commands him to
choose between the organ and her. Jess moves the organ in the house, and Eliza is
left in the snow, pondering her next course of action. Fortunately, Eliza knows the
difference between her domain and that of the Lord. She compromises, and the
organ goes in the attic. All goes well until a church committee comes to call just
when the Birdwell's daughter Mattie has slipped up to the attic to play on the organ.
Surely God inspires Jess Birdwell in this crucial situation, for he prays and continues
praying until the music stops. The committee concludes that angels have provided
the accompaniment; Jess suspects that the Lord, who has kept him praying for so
long, has made His statement. Just as Eliza is about to announce her triumph, however, the music once again comes from the attic, and Jess again responds.

The story is typical of West. The human beings involved live close to their natural
setting; they are ordinary people, neither rich nor poor. Although they may disagree
with one another and although they often have much to learn, they are usually basi-
cally good, and at the end of the story, some resolution of their conflict with one
another and with their spiritual scruples is suggested. The tone is also typical. Perhaps one reason for West's popularity is that, in an age when many writers do not
seem to like their own characters, and for good reason, she is honestly fond of hers.
As a result, she laughs at their foibles and follies, their deficiencies in wisdom, and
their mistakes in judgment without negating the fact of their basic goodness.

One of the endearing qualities of the Birdwell family is that, despite their strict
religious convictions, they accept differences within the family; each member is expected, above all, to follow his or her own conscience. In the Civil War story "The

Battle of Finney's Ford," what was supposed to be a fight against Morgan's raiders proves to be no fight at all, because Morgan's raiders change their route. In the meantime, however, the Birdwell boys must decide whether to fight. One of them, Joshua, says that he is willing to kill, if necessary; the other, Labe, will not join the town's defenders. Ironically, at the end of the story, Josh says that the reason he must fight is that he so dislikes fighting, while Labe admits that he must not fight because he truly enjoys fighting. Thus the real "The Battle of Finney's Ford" has been a battle of conscience for the boys and, for the parents, a struggle to let them make their own decisions. The slightness of the external plot, typical of many of West's stories, does not reduce the magnitude of the internal action. For Jess, Eliza, Josh, and Labe, there is a major spiritual battle; as usual, the element of love is present in the resolution of the conflict.

Although *Cress Delahanty* is set in twentieth century California rather than nineteenth century Indiana, and although it lacks the specific Quaker religious background, the importance of the natural setting, the basic goodness of the characters, and the emphasis on spiritual problems are similar to the stories in *The Friendly Persuasion*. For example, "Fifteen: Spring" deals with Cress's selfish encounter with death, just as in the previous volume "The Meeting House" had followed Jess Birdwell through a similar crisis. In "Fifteen: Spring," Cress has developed a schoolgirl crush on a dying man, the father of sons her age. In her egotism, she wishes to be important to him, even to die in his place, if necessary, but after a visit to his home, after realizing that God is in charge, not Cress, she learns that she is not of major importance to her beloved, nor is her love of any help to him. Ironically, the final consolation comes from his wife, who recalls her own lost youth and, from her own tragic situation, finds pity for foolish Cress.

Many of West's stories deal wth young people who are being initiated into life. In *Love, Death, and the Ladies' Drill Team*, "A Time of Learning" describes the encounter of nineteen-year-old Emmett Maguire, a talented sign- and housepainter, with his first love, Ivy Lish. Emmett loves the seemingly perfect girl with all of his heart. When he paints her picture, it is an act of total commitment. Unfortunately, Emmett must learn that the beloved is not always worthy of the emotion she inspires. As other men know, Ivy is consistently unfaithful. When Emmett learns that she has given his painting to another lover, his immediate impulse is toward revenge: he will paint her on the barn, as ugly as she has proved herself to be, for all to see. Then comes his spiritual crisis. Somehow, he finds, he cannot paint ugliness, or perhaps he cannot hate. When he paints a larger-than-life picture of her on the barn, he finally forgets about her in the joy of realizing that he is indeed a good painter. Thus, finally, his love of art is more important than her betrayal of him, and his wish to love defeats his temptation to hate.

West clearly believes, however, that it is not only the young who must learn about life. One of the optimistic elements in her stories is the suggestion that life is learning itself. Because most of her major characters are willing to expand their consciousnesses, anxious to revise their judgments, they are appealing. Thus, in *Except for Me and Thee: A Companion to the Friendly Persuasion*, the Quaker preacher Eliza Birdwell, a stubborn woman with a strict conscience, must deal with the issue of fugitive slaves. In the long story "Neighbors," Eliza must not only decide whether to obey the law, as her religion dictates, by turning over the fugitive slaves who seek refuge with her, or to hide them and defy the law of her country; she must also come to terms with Jess's involvement in running slaves to freedom, at the risk of his life and his liberty. The decision is not easy, but in changing her mind about the law and in acquiescing to the demands of Jess's conscience, Eliza herself grows spiritually.

Not all of West's stories have so hopeful a conclusion. In "The Condemned Librarian," from *Crimson Ramblers of the World, Farewell*, an embittered teacher, who believes that she has not been able to realize her dreams, consults a woman doctor who, against all odds, has risen from being a high school librarian to her present profession. Perversely, the teacher refuses to reveal her symptoms to the doctor, and, despite all of her efforts, the doctor fails to diagnose tuberculosis. As a result, the teacher nearly dies, but to her delight, the doctor must abandon her practice and go back to being a high school librarian. The title "The Condemned Librarian" makes it clear that hatred has, in this situation, had a great triumph, but ironically, the person most trapped is the bitter teacher, who must live with the knowledge that she herself is condemned. Although she feels happy thinking of the doctor's misery, she admits that the old magic is gone from her teaching. Clearly, by her spite she has corroded her own soul.

Other stories of that collection, however, end with understanding and reconciliation. For example, "Live Life Deeply" begins with the disappearance of fourteen-year-old Elspeth Courtney, who has turned up at the maternity ward of the local hospital. Her distraught father, pursuing her, discovers that she had been on Reservoir Hill early that morning, contemplating suicide because, as she confided to the troubled man she met there, a teacher she admired had made fun of her for a composition entitled "Live Life Deeply." The stranger had been worrying about his wife's cesarean section, while Ellie had been worrying about her humiliation. When the baby is born, the stranger's problem is solved. Then, the new father solves Ellie's problem by pointing out that she wants to live life fully and that her pain is as much a part of a full life as the excitement and joy of the birth. Convinced, Ellie begins to plan her next composition, which will deal with her experiences in the maternity ward. Now that she understands that pain and joy are both a part of life and that both are necessary to make life interesting, she can move ahead, accepting even her setbacks.

In all of Jessamyn West's stories, whether the setting is the past or the present, Indiana or California, an individual, young or old, has the opportunity to grow spiritually. If, like the teacher in "The Condemned Librarian," one chooses to hate instead of to love or if one refuses to permit freedom of conscience to others, one's life will be miserable. Many ordinary people, however, live lives as meaningful and as exciting as those of Jess Birdwell, Cress Delahanty, and Elspeth Courtney. In her carefully crafted accounts of everyday life, Jessamyn West has revealed the drama of spiritual conflict in these later centuries as compellingly as did the productions of *Everyman* in medieval times.

Other major works

NOVELS: *The Witch Diggers*, 1951; *Little Men*, in *Star Short Novels*, 1954; *South of the Angels*, 1960; *A Matter of Time*, 1966; *Leafy Rivers*, 1967; *The Massacre at Fall Creek*, 1975; *The Life I Really Lived*, 1979; *The State of Stony Lonesome*, 1984.

PLAY: *A Mirror for the Sky*, 1948 (libretto).

SCREENPLAY: *Friendly Persuasion*, 1956.

POETRY: *The Secret Look: Poems*, 1974.

NONFICTION: *To See the Dream*, 1957; *Love Is Not What You Think*, 1959; *Hide and Seek: A Continuing Journey*, 1973 (autobiography); *The Woman Said Yes: Encounters with Life and Death—Memoirs*, 1976; *Double Discovery: A Journey*, 1980.

ANTHOLOGY: *The Quaker Reader*, 1962.

Bibliography

Prescott, P. S. "The Massacre at Fall Creek." *Newsweek*, April 14, 1975, 86. According to Prescott, the ingredients in a "good old-fashioned novel" combine suspense, violence, and villainy with sentiment. *The Massacre at Fall Creek* is a concrete example of this genre. Jessamyn West's expertise, according to Prescott, extends not only to the "good old-fashioned novel" but to other literary forms as well.

Shivers, Alfred S. *Jessamyn West*. New York: Twayne, 1972. This biography of Jessamyn West probes the religious influences of her Quaker beliefs on her literary endeavors, thus providing an essential clue to her character and personality. Shivers incorporates his literary criticism of her works to 1972.

Welty, Eudora. "A Search: Maddening and Infectious." *The New York Times Book Review*, January 14, 1951, 5. Welty discusses the characterizations and plot of *The Witch Diggers*, which she embeds in the metaphor of a game of charades. She states that both contain elements of the known and the unknown bound into a solvable puzzle so that this game is a clever metaphor for *The Witch Diggers*.

West, Jessamyn. *Double Discovery: A Journey*. New York: Harcourt Brace Jovanovich, 1980. West's own memoir incorporates her youthful letters and journals from her first trip abroad with her later rediscovery of that long-lost youthful self. This autobiography gives readers a glimpse of a woman's description of the development of her adult self.

_____. *The Woman Said Yes: Encounters with Life and Death*. New York: Harcourt Brace Jovanovich, 1980. West's account of her experiences as a survivor of tuberculosis is intermingled with an account of her mother's life. This amalgamation of two lives lets interested readers delve into another facet of West's intellectual and artistic development.

Yalom, Marilyn, and Margo B. Davis, eds. *Women Writers of the West Coast: Speaking of Their Lives and Careers*. Santa Barbara, Calif.: Capra Press, 1983. Jennifer

Chapman's chapter discusses the role of religion—in this case, Quakerism—in West's life and work.

Rosemary M. Canfield Reisman
(Revised by *Maxine S. Theodoulou*)

EDITH WHARTON

Born: New York, New York; January 24, 1862
Died: St. Brice sous Forêt, France; August 11, 1937

Principal short fiction

The Greater Inclination, 1899; *Crucial Instances,* 1901; *The Descent of Man,* 1904; *The Hermit and the Wild Woman,* 1908; *Tales of Men and Ghosts,* 1910; *Xingu and Other Stories,* 1916; *Here and Beyond,* 1926; *Certain People,* 1930; *Human Nature,* 1933; *The World Over,* 1936; *Ghosts,* 1937; *The Collected Short Stories of Edith Wharton,* 1968.

Other literary forms

Edith Wharton's prolific career includes the publication of novels, novellas, short stories, poetry, travel books, criticism, works on landscaping and interior decoration, a translation, an autobiography, and wartime pamphlets and journalism. Her novel *The Age of Innocence* (1920) was awarded the Pulitzer Prize in 1921. Several of her works have been adapted for the stage, including *The Age of Innocence* and the novels *Ethan Frome* (1911), *The House of Mirth* (1905), and *The Old Maid* (1924). The dramatization of *The Old Maid* was awarded the Pulitzer Prize for drama in 1935. Films based on Edith Wharton's works include *The House of Mirth, The Glimpses of the Moon* (1922), and *The Old Maid.*

Achievements

Wharton's talent in affording her reader an elegant, well-constructed glance at upper-class New York and European society won for her high esteem from the earliest years of her career. The novel *The House of Mirth* was her first best-seller and, along with *Ethan Frome* and *The Age of Innocence,* is considered to be one of her finest works. During World War I, Wharton served the Allied cause in Europe by organizing relief efforts and caring for Belgian orphans, work for which she was inducted into the French Legion of Honor in 1916 and the Order of Leopold (Belgium) in 1919. In the United States, the 1920's would see Wharton's literary career flower. In 1921, she became the first woman to receive the Pulitzer Prize, awarded to her for *The Age of Innocence*; in 1923, she also became the first female recipient of an honorary degree of doctor of letters from Yale University; in 1927, she was nominated for the Nobel Prize in Literature; in 1928, her novel *The Children* was the Book-of-the-Month Club selection for September. By 1930, Wharton was one of the most highly regarded American authors of the time and was elected to the American Academy of Arts and Letters. After Wharton's death in 1937, her fiction was not as widely read by the general public as it was during her lifetime. Feminist literary scholars, however, have reexamined Wharton's works for their unmistakable portrayal of women's lives in the early 1900's.

Biography

Edith Newbold Jones was born into the highest level of society. Like most girls of her generation and social class, she was educated at home. At the age of twenty-three she married a wealthy young man, Edward Wharton; they had no children. Wharton divided her time between writing and her duties as a society hostess. Her husband, emotionally unstable, suffered several nervous breakdowns, and in 1913, they were divorced. Wharton spent a great deal of time in Europe; after 1912 she returned to America only once, to accept the honorary degree of Doctor of Letters from Yale University in 1923. During World War I, Wharton was very active in war work in France for which she was made a Chevalier of the Legion of Honor in 1916. Realizing that after her death her friends would suppress much of her real personality in their accounts of her life, and wanting the truth to be told, Wharton willed her private papers to Yale University, with instructions that they were not to be published until 1968. These papers revealed a totally unexpected side of Wharton's character: passionate, impulsive, and vulnerable. This new view of the author has had a marked effect on more recent interpretations of her work.

Analysis

Because many of Edith Wharton's characters and themes resemble those of Henry James, her work has sometimes been regarded as a derivative of his. Each of these authors wrote a number of stories regarding such themes as the fate of the individual who challenges the standards of society, the effect of commercial success on an artist, the impact of European civilization on an American mentality, and the confrontation of a public personality with his own private self. Further, both James and Wharton used ghost stories to present, in allegorical terms, internal experiences which would be difficult to dramatize in a purely realistic way. Wharton knew James and admired him as a friend and as a writer, and some of her early short stories— those in *The Greater Inclination* and *Crucial Instances*, for example—do resemble James's work. As she matured, however, Wharton developed an artistic viewpoint and a style which were distinctly her own. Her approach to the themes which she shared with James was much more direct than his: she took a more sweeping view of the action of a story and omitted the myriad details, qualifications, and explanations which characterize James's work.

It is not surprising that Wharton and James developed a number of parallel interests. Both writers moved in the same rather limited social circle and were exposed to the same values and to the same types of people. Not all their perceptions, however, were identical since Wharton's viewpoint was influenced by the limitations she experienced as a woman. She was therefore especially sensitive to such subtle forms of victimization as the narrowness of a woman's horizons in her society, which not only denied women the opportunity to develop their full potential but also burdened men with disproportionate responsibilities. This theme, which underlies some of her best novels—*The House of Mirth* is a good example—also appears in a number of her short stories, such as "The Rembrandt."

The narrator of "The Rembrandt" is a museum curator whose cousin, Eleanor Copt, frequently undertakes acts of charity toward the unfortunate. These acts of charity, however, often take the form of persuading someone else to bear the brunt of the inconvenience and expense. As "The Rembrandt" opens, Eleanor persuades her cousin to accompany her to a rented room occupied by an elderly lady, the once-wealthy Mrs. Fontage. This widowed lady, who has suffered a number of financial misfortunes, has been reduced from living in palatial homes to now living in a dingy room. Even this small room soon will be too expensive for her unless she can sell the one art treasure she still possesses: an unsigned Rembrandt. The supposed Rembrandt, purchased under highly romantic circumstances during the Fontages' honeymoon in Europe, turns out to be valueless. The curator, however, is moved by the dignity and grace with which Mrs. Fontage faces her situation, and he cannot bring himself to tell her that the painting is worthless. He values it at a thousand dollars, reasoning that he himself cannot be expected to raise that much money. When he realizes that his cousin and Mrs. Fontage expect him to purchase the painting on behalf of the museum, he temporizes.

Meanwhile, Eleanor interests an admirer of hers, Mr. Jefferson Rose, in the painting. Although he cannot really spare the money, Rose decides to buy the painting as an act of charity and as an investment. Even after the curator confesses his lie to Rose, the young man is determined to relieve Mrs. Fontage's misery. The curator, reasoning that it is better to defraud an institution than an individual, purchases the painting for the museum. The only museum official who might question his decision is abroad, and the curator stores the painting in the museum cellar and forgets it. When the official, Crozier, returns, he asks the curator whether he really considers the painting valuable. The curator confesses what he has done and offers to buy the painting from the museum. Crozier then informs the curator that the members of the museum committee have already purchased the painting privately, and beg leave to present it to the curator in recognition of his kindness to Mrs. Fontage.

Despite its flaws in structure and its somewhat romantic view of the business world, "The Rembrandt" shows Wharton's concern with the relationship between helpless individuals and the society which produced them. Her portrait of Mrs. Fontage is especially revealing—she is a woman of dignity and breeding, whose pride and training sustain her in very difficult circumstances. That very breeding, however, cripples Mrs. Fontage because of the narrowness which accompanies it. She is entirely ignorant of the practical side of life, and, in the absence of a husband or some other head of the family, she is seriously handicapped in dealing with business matters. Furthermore, although she is intelligent and in good health, she is absolutely incapable of contributing to her own support. In this very early story, Wharton applauds the gentlemen who live up to the responsibility of caring for such women. Later, Wharton will censure the men and the women whose unthinking conformity to social stereotypes has deprived women like Mrs. Fontage of the ability to care for themselves and has placed a double burden on the men.

As Wharton matured, her interest in victimization moved from the external world of society to the internal world of the individual mind. She recognized the fact that adjustment to life sometimes entails a compromise with one's private self which constitutes a betrayal. One of her most striking portrayals of that theme is in "The Eyes." This tale employs the framework of a ghost story to dramatize an internal experience. The story's aging protagonist, Andrew Culwin, has never become part of life, or allowed an involvement with another human being to threaten his absolute egotism. One evening, as his friends amuse themselves by telling tales of psychic events they have witnessed, Culwin offers to tell a story of his own. He explains that as a young man he once flirted with his naïve young cousin Alice, who responded with a seriousness which alarmed him. He immediately announced a trip to Europe; but, moved by the grace with which she accepted her disappointment, Culwin proposed to her and was accepted. He went to bed that evening feeling his self-centered bachelorhood giving way to a sense of righteousness and peace. Culwin awakened in the middle of the night, however, and saw in front of him a hideous pair of eyes. The eyes, which were sunken and old, had pouches of shriveled flesh beneath them and red-lined lids above them, and one of the lids drooped more than the other. These eyes remained in the room all night, and in the morning Culwin fled, without explanation, to a friend's house. There he slept undisturbed and made plans to return to Alice a few days later. Thereupon the eyes returned, and Culwin fled to Europe. He realized that he did not really want to marry Alice, and he devoted himself to a self-centered enjoyment of Europe.

After two years, a handsome young man arrived in Rome with a letter of introduction to Culwin from Alice. This young man, Gilbert Noyes, had been sent abroad by his family to test himself as a writer. Culwin knew that Noyes's writing was worthless, but he temporized in order to keep the handsome youth with him. He also pitied Noyes because of the dull clerk's job which waited for him at home. Finally, Culwin told Noyes that his work had merit, intending to support the young man himself if necessary. That night, the eyes reappeared; and Culwin felt, along with his revulsion, a disquieting sense of identity with the eyes, as if he would some day come to understand all about them. After a month, Culwin cruelly dismissed Noyes, who went home to his clerkship; Culwin took to drink and turned up years later in Hong Kong, fat and unshaven. The eyes then disappeared and never returned.

Culwin's listeners, of course, perceive what the reader perceives: the eyes which mock Culwin's rare attempts to transform his self-centered existence into a life of involvement with someone else are in fact his own eyes, looking at him from the future and mocking him with what he would become. The eyes also represent Culwin's lesser self, which would in time take over his entire personality. Even in his youth, this lesser self overshadows Culwin's more humane impulses with second thoughts of the effect these impulses are likely to have on his comfort and security. The story ends as Culwin, surprised by his friends' reaction to his story, catches sight of himself in a mirror, and realizes the truth.

Wharton's twin themes of social and self-victimization are joined most effectively in a later story which many readers consider her best: "After Holbein." The title refers to a series of woodcuts by Hans Holbein the Younger, entitled "The Dance of Death." They show the figure of death, represented by a skeleton, insinuating himself into the lives of various unsuspecting people. One of these engravings, entitled "Noblewoman," features a richly dressed man and woman following the figure of death.

The story begins with a description of an elderly gentleman, Anson Warley, who has been one of the most popular members of New York society for more than thirty years. In the first three pages of the story, the reader learns that Warley fought, long ago, a battle between his public image and his private self; and the private self lost. Warley gradually stopped staying at home to read or meditate and found less and less time to talk quietly with intellectual friends or scholars. He became a purely public figure, a frequenter of hot, noisy, crowded rooms. His intellect gave itself entirely to the production of drawing-room witticisms, many of them barbed with sarcasm. On the evening that the story takes place, Warley finds himself reminded of one of these sallies of his. Some years earlier, Warley, who had been dodging the persistent invitations of a pompous and rather boring society hostess, finally told his circle of friends that the next time he received a card saying "Mrs. Jasper requests the pleasure," he would reply, "Mr. Warley declines the boredom." The remark was appreciated at the time by the friends who heard it; but in his old age Warley finds himself hoping that Mrs. Jasper never suffered the pain of hearing about it.

At this point in the story, Wharton shifts the scene to a mansion on Fifth Avenue, where a senile old woman prepares herself for an imaginary dinner party. She wears a grotesque purple wig, and broad-toed orthopedic shoes under an ancient purple gown. She also insists on wearing her diamonds to what she believes will be another triumph of her skill as a hostess. This woman is the same Mrs. Jasper whom Warley has been avoiding for years. She is now in the care of an unsympathetic young nurse and three elderly servants. Periodically, the four employees go through the charade of preparing the house and Mrs. Jasper for the dinner parties which she imagines still take place there.

While Mrs. Jasper is being dressed for her illusory dinner party, Anson Warley is preparing to attend a real one. Despite his valet's protests concerning his health, Warley not only refuses to stay at home but also insists on walking up Fifth Avenue in the freezing winter night. Gradually he becomes confused and forgets his destination. Then he sees before him Mrs. Jasper's mansion, lighted for a dinner party, and in his confusion, he imagines he is to dine there. He arrives just as Mrs. Jasper's footman is reading aloud the list of guests whom Mrs. Jasper thinks she has invited.

When dinner is announced, Warley and Mrs. Jasper walk arm in arm, at a stately processional gait, to the table. The footman has set the table with heavy blue and white servants' dishes, and he has stuffed newspapers instead of orchids into the priceless Rose Dubarry porcelain dishes. He serves a plain meal and inexpensive wine in the empty dining room. Lost in the illusion, however, Warley and Mrs. Jasper imagine that they are consuming a gourmet meal at a luxuriously appointed table in the presence of a crowd of glittering guests. They go through a ritual of gestures and conversation which does indeed resemble the *danse macabre* for which the story is named. Finally, Mrs. Jasper leaves the table exhausted and makes her way upstairs to her uncomprehending and chuckling nurse. Warley, equally exhausted and equally convinced that he has attended a brilliant dinner party, steps out into the night and drops dead.

"After Holbein" is a powerful story primarily because of the contrasts it establishes. In the foreground are the wasted lives of Warley and Mrs. Jasper, each of whom has long given up all hope of originality or self-realization for the sake of being part of a nameless, gilded mass. The unsympathetic nurse, who teases Mrs. Jasper into tears, acts not from cruelty but from her inability to comprehend, in her own hopeful youth, the tragedy of Mrs. Jasper's situation. This nurse is contrasted with Mrs. Jasper's elderly maid, Lavinia, who conceals her own failing health out of loyalty to her mistress, and who is moved to tears by Mrs. Jasper's plight. Even the essential horror of the story is intensified by the contrasting formality and restraint of its language and by the tight structuring which gives the plot the same momentum of inevitability as the movements of a formal dance.

Warley and Mrs. Jasper have been betrayed from within and from without. They have traded their private selves for public masks, and have spent their lives among others who have made the same bargain. Lavinia's recollections suggest to the reader that Mrs. Jasper subordinated her role as mother to her role as hostess; and her children, reared in that same world, have left her to the care of servants. Her friends are dead or bedridden, or they have forgotten her. She exists now, in a sense, as she has always existed: as a grotesque figure in a world of illusion.

Warley, too, has come to think of himself only in terms of his social reputation—he will not accept the reality of his age and infirmity. Thus, as he drags one leg during his icy walk along Fifth Avenue, he pictures a club smoking room in which one of his acquaintances will say, "Warley? Why, I saw him sprinting up Fifth Avenue the other night like a two-year-old; that night it was four or five below." Warley has convinced himself that whatever is said in club smoking rooms by men in good society is real. None of the acquaintances, however, to whom he has given his life is with him when he takes that final step; and it would not have mattered if anyone had been there. Warley is inevitably and irrevocably alone at last.

Wharton's eleven volumes of short stories, spanning thirty-nine years, record her growth in thought and in style. They offer the entertainment of seeing inside an exclusive social circle which was in many respects unique and which no longer exists as Wharton knew it. Some of Wharton's stories are trivial and some are repetitive; but her best stories depict, in the inhabitants of that exclusive social world, experiences and sensations which are universal.

Other major works

NOVELS: *The Touchstone*, 1900; *The Valley of Decision*, 1902; *Sanctuary*, 1903; *The House of Mirth*, 1905; *The Fruit of the Tree*, 1907; *Madame de Treymes*, 1907; *Ethan Frome*, 1911; *The Reef*, 1912; *The Custom of the Country*, 1913; *Summer*, 1917;

The Marne, 1918; *The Age of Innocence*, 1920; *The Glimpses of the Moon*, 1922; *A Son at the Front*, 1923; *Old New York*, 1924 (4 volumes; includes *False Dawn*, *The Old Maid*, *The Spark*, and *New Year's Day*); *The Mother's Recompense*, 1925; *Twilight Sleep*, 1927; *The Children*, 1928; *Hudson River Bracketed*, 1929; *The Gods Arrive*, 1932; *The Buccaneers*, 1938.

POETRY: *Verses*, 1878; *Artemis to Actæon*, 1909; *Twelve Poems*, 1926.

NONFICTION: *The Decoration of Houses*, 1897 (with Ogden Codman, Jr.); *Italian Villas and Their Gardens*, 1904; *Italian Backgrounds*, 1905; *A Motor-Flight Through France*, 1908; *Fighting France from Dunkerque to Belfort*, 1915; *French Ways and Their Meaning*, 1919; *In Morocco*, 1920; *The Writing of Fiction*, 1925; *A Backward Glance*, 1934; *The Letters of Edith Wharton*, 1988.

Bibliography

Auchinloss, Louis. *Edith Wharton: A Woman in Her Time*. New York: Viking Press, 1971. An entertaining biography with excellent photographs of Wharton and her life and time. Offers a limited literary analysis of Wharton's fiction.

Bloom, Harold, ed. *Edith Wharton*. New York: Chelsea House, 1986. This volume offers a representative selection of the body of criticism on the fiction of Edith Wharton. Several essays present a feminist analysis of her work.

Lewis, R. W. B. *Edith Wharton: A Biography*. New York: Harper & Row, 1975. The definitive biography on Wharton. Uses the previously inaccessible papers of the Yale Collection to provide a meticulous portrait of the author.

McDowell, Margaret B. *Edith Wharton*. Boston: Twayne, 1975. A perceptive biography and analysis of Wharton's body of writings. Chapter 6 discusses her most important short fiction.

Nevius, Blake. *Edith Wharton: A Study of Her Fiction*. Berkeley: University of California Press, 1961. Examines two recurrent themes in Wharton's fiction: the tension that arises between an individual's public and private selves, and the desire for individual freedom and the need to assume social responsibility.

Walton, Geoffrey. *Edith Wharton: A Critical Interpretation*. Rutherford, N.J.: Fairleigh Dickinson University Press, 1970. A thorough discussion of Wharton's writings. The detailed criticism offers a fresh perspective. Provides limited biographical treatment.

Wolff, Cynthia Griffin. *A Feast of Words: The Triumph of Edith Wharton*. New York: Oxford University Press, 1977. This insightful study analyzes Wharton's life and psychological development as reflected in her major works.

Joan DelFattore
(Revised by *Mary F. Yudin*)

JOHN EDGAR WIDEMAN

Born: Washington, D.C.; June 14, 1941

Principal short fiction

Damballah, 1981; *Fever: Twelve Stories*, 1989.

Other literary forms

John Edgar Wideman's career began officially in 1967 with the appearance of his first novel, *A Glance Away*. After this first publication, he has repeatedly returned to the novelistic form in works such as *Hurry Home* (1970); *The Lynchers* (1973); *Hiding Place* (1981), intended as the middle volume of what is called the Homewood Trilogy; *Sent for You Yesterday* (1983), the final volume in the Homewood Trilogy; *Reuben* (1989); and *Philadelphia Fire* (1990). In addition, Wideman has written a work of autobiographical nonfiction entitled *Brothers and Keepers* (1984), in which he compares his own life to that of a troubled younger brother serving a lifetime jail sentence. Wideman has also written regularly on African-American topics for *The New York Times Book Review* and has published scholarly work on African-American predecessors such as Charles Waddell Chesnutt and W. E. B. Du Bois.

Achievements

Wideman has distinguished himself both as a strong contemporary voice within the African-American literary tradition and as a serious scholar examining the legacy of his predecessors in that tradition. His early fictional technique reflects his aesthetic debt to Anglo-American narrative experimentation ranging from the originators of the English novel in the eighteenth century to the great modernists of the twentieth century; racial concerns, while evident, did not predominate in his first works. With the 1980's, however, Wideman deliberately began exploring African-American literary forms in accordance with his growing desire to reengage his own racial identity and reach out more directly to an African-American readership. Accordingly, he published the three works that constitute the Homewood Trilogy as trade paperbacks rather than in initial hard cover, so as to increase their accessibility. The trilogy's third volume, *Sent for You Yesterday*, received the PEN/Faulkner Award for Fiction for its innovative fusion of subject matter and novelistic technique. The traumatic experience of a brother's crime and punishment, which was an important source for the 1983 novel, also prompted the nonfictional *Brothers and Keepers*, in which Wideman's quest for forms adequate to the polyphonic character of the African-American experience takes on great personal urgency; the autobiography was nominated for the National Book Critics Circle Award.

Biography

John Edgar Wideman was the first of five children born to Bette French and Edgar

Wideman. His youth was spent in the African-American community of Homewood, within the city of Pittsburgh, Pennsylvania, and his fiction draws heavily upon the experiences of his family across a century of Homewood history. As a youth, Wideman demonstrated the same blend of athletic and academic ambition that often distinguishes his fictional characters and dramatizes their divided allegiances. Upon graduation as Peabody High School valedictorian, Wideman received a Benjamin Franklin scholarship to the University of Pennsylvania and subsequently played for its basketball team, hoping someday to be drafted by the National Basketball Association. Selected for the Philadelphia Big Five Basketball Hall of Fame and tapped for Phi Beta Kappa, Wideman also won a Rhodes Scholarship; upon completion of his B.A. at the University of Pennsylvania in 1963, he attended the University of Oxford, where, in 1966, he earned a B.Phil. as a Thouron Fellow. Having been an active writer since his undergraduate years, Wideman secured a Kent Fellowship from the University of Iowa's Writers' Workship in 1966. His first novel, *A Glance Away*, appeared in 1967, winning for him immediate attention as a significant new voice in contemporary American letters.

Alongside his creative endeavors, Wideman has steadily pursued an academic career. In 1966, he accepted a teaching position at the University of Pennsylvania, where he later headed the Afro-American Studies program from 1971 to 1973 and rose to the rank of professor of English; he was also assistant basketball coach from 1968 to 1972. Academic appointments brought him to Howard University, the University of Wyoming at Laramie, and the University of Massachusetts at Amherst. The National Endowment for the Humanities in 1975 named him a Young Humanist Fellow; in 1976, the U.S. State Department selected him for a lecture tour of Europe and the Near East. That same year, he held a Phi Beta Kappa lectureship. Wideman married Judith Ann Goldman in 1965, and they have three children: Daniel, Jacob, and Jamila. The family tragedy of his youngest brother, Rob, who was convicted in 1978 for armed robbery and murder, was grimly reiterated in 1988, when Wideman's son Jacob received a life sentence for the 1986 murder in Arizona of a teenage traveling companion.

In speaking about the formative influences upon his writing, Wideman asserts that his creative inclinations underwent a transformation upon his arrival as a new faculty member at the University of Pennsylvania, where students of color assumed him to be as well versed in the African-American literary legacy as he was in the Anglo-American tradition. His responsiveness to their concerns prompted him not only to create the university's African-American Studies Program but also to recover the cultural identity that he had self-consciously minimized in pursuit of the dominant culture's standards of academic excellence. His subsequent writing, fiction and nonfiction alike, repeatedly sounds the autobiographical theme of "coming home," and Wideman not only dissects the obstacles that thwart such return but also espouses the belief that art can at least make possible a temporary reconciliation between past and present. By paralleling his own multigenerational family history and the community history of Homewood, Wideman fuses personal and collective memory to create a mythology of the human condition at once particular and universal.

Analysis

John Edgar Wideman's avowed artistic end is the creation of characters whose rich inner lives testify to a "sense of themselves as spiritual beings" that challenges the deterministic simplicities often dominant in literary depictions of the African-American sensibility. Like Richard Wright, Ralph Ellison, and James Baldwin before him, Wideman insistently links naturalistic detail to an existential quest for meaning and integrity that is complicated by the peculiar difficulties of sustaining one's humanity under the degradations of racism. While the material consequences of racist injustice are ever-present in his stories, Wideman makes clear that his most pressing concern is the threat posed to the souls of its victims. In turn, he suggests that the renewal of contemporary African-American society, increasingly ravaged by hopelessness and self-destructiveness, lies in a self-conscious recovery of, and healing through, the cultural identity he so rigorously documents in his evocation of Homewood. Thus in Wideman's fiction the struggle of individual souls in an absurd and dehumanizing world does not unfold in a completely existentialist void; his characters move within a community whose past vitality derived from history, traditions, language, and relationships linking generations back beyond the darkness of slavery. The imaginative architecture that unifies the Homewood Trilogy employs interpenetrating plot lines, family trees, and community legends to make clear that Wideman's real subject is the communal survival once made possible by the heroic decency against great odds of its citizens.

Damballah, the collection of twelve short stories that begins the trilogy, announces Wideman's intentions aesthetically as well as thematically. The fuguelike polyphony of voices achieved by bringing together separate narratives drawn from a wide spectrum of Homewood personalities and historical moments captures not only the community's diversity but also the power of oral culture in all of its forms—speech, music, storytelling—to nourish and sustain it in the midst of unrelenting racial hostility. In "The Chinaman," a narrative "I" identified elsewhere as John (and quite evidently an autobiographical presence) explains that the funeral of his maternal grandmother, Freeda, had reconnected him with old family legends that he had years earlier set aside as unworthy of serious literary treatment. Listening months later to his own mother describe Freeda's death and thereby complete a story he had been unable to finish alone, he concludes, "the shape of the story is the shape of my mother's voice." Wideman's narrator repeatedly explains that this text is a collaborative project in which narratives culled from the collective memory of his family are woven together through the mediating agency of his own consciousness to reveal a design that affirms the faith in human possibility now leaching away in the ruins that were once Homewood.

Wideman's preoccupation with the crisis of black men in modern America—a crisis vividly depicted in his own estrangement from his origins and his brother

Rob's criminality and imprisonment—explains the placement of his maternal grandfather, John French, at the center of these stories. French's defiant courage, loyalty, quick wit, tough-minded devotion to his family, and acute survival instincts make him a model of masculine virtue for a new generation desperately in need of his example. He stands in seemingly obvious contrast to his equally talented but blighted grandson Tommy Lawson, the narrator's drug-addicted brother, whose crimes destroy his future and who is the counterbalancing focus of the last third of the collection. Yet, French lives on in Tommy's rebellious energy and probing mind, making the youth's current circumstances all the more tragic.

Wideman also records the voices of the strong women who have sustained the community throughout the crises surrounding their men and whose emotional anguish reflects the complex emotional dynamic between black men and women in Wideman's fiction. Freeda Hollinger French, the text's matriarch, proves herself capable of swift, violent intervention to safeguard her child or her husband in "Lizabeth: The Caterpillar Story." Lizabeth French Lawson actually gives birth to the narrator in "Daddy Garbage" within a story line juxtaposed to the grim discovery of another infant's frozen corpse and the moral imperative of the two old men who find it and insist upon a decent burial: as the future is denied to one child and extended to another, one perceives a subtle echo of the divergent paths Lizabeth's own sons will pursue in later years.

Wideman's sensitivity to the orality of African-American culture leads him to seek linguistic approximations for the music and talk-story patterns at the heart of African-American imaginative expression. His prose resonates with the jazz rhythms of African-American vernacular and often quotes directly from the musical yoking of human misery and triumph in what is called the blues. In "The Songs of Reba Love Jackson," a successful Gospel singer admits that her artistry expresses emotional nuances beyond the power of language alone: "Couldn't speak about some things. She could only sing them. Put her stories in the songs she had heard all her life so the songs became her stories." In the closing piece of the volume, "The Beginning of Homewood," the narrator creates a wall of sound from the voices he has unloosed in the preceding stories; writing to his brother Tommy in prison, he acknowledges that his real task as a writer has been to hear and synthesize those women's testimonials to the community's history of defeat and transcendence:

> The chorus wailing and then Reba Love Jackson soloing. I heard May singing and heard Mother Bess telling what she remembers and what she had heard about Sybela Owens. I was thinking the way Aunt May talks. . . . [H]er stories exist because of their parts and each part is a story worth telling . . . the voice seeks to recover everything, that the voice proclaims *nothing is lost*, that the listener is not passive but lives like everything else within the story.

Wideman's most immediate purpose here is to tell the story of the slave woman Sybela Owens who, together with her white master/lover, fled the south, settled on Bruston Hill, the symbolic navel of Homewood, and began the family line that has produced his own family. By embedding Sybela's story of physical and spiritual redemption within a meditation on his brother's grim circumstances, the narrator conveys the continued urgency of such issues for African Americans; he also engages in the metafictional self-reflexiveness that characterizes his generation of American writers as he muses over the act of writing and its problematic relationship to lived events. Wideman has even bigger aims with Sybela, however, for his imaginative energy also transforms her into a mythic female progenitor who becomes a thematic counterpart to the African slave Orion ("Ryan") introduced in the first (and title) story, "Damballah." Like Sybela, Orion resists the degradation of his circumstances, so much so that his unyielding integrity leads to his execution by enraged whites who accuse him of sexual crimes. Before his death, however, he inspires an American-born slave boy with the mysterious power of his native religious beliefs, having taught him to chant to Damballah, the "good serpent of the sky" and a paternal deity whose wisdom and benign oversight make of the cosmos one transcendent family. Despite Wideman's sophisticated postmodernist affinity for refracting illusions of "reality" through multiple conflicting subjectivities, he seeks, finally, an integrative vision in which the mythic and historical coalesce to offer the hope of spiritual renewal.

While *Damballah* draws its cumulative power from its unifying narrative sensibility and its consistent focus upon the citizens past and present of Homewood, *Fever: Twelve Stories* demonstrates a much looser internal logic grounded in thematic rather than storytelling interlacings. Once again, Wideman uses the short story to escape the constraints of novelistic continuity and reconfigure—this time through unrelated voices—motifs that literally assume international proportions. His most striking theme correlates the historical catastrophes of American slavery, the Holocaust, and modern international terrorism, thereby suggesting a common pattern of scapegoating and racist antagonism that transcends the experience of any single group of victims.

"The Statue of Liberty" and "Valaida," for example, both demonstrate how episodes of interracial miscommunication and self-indulgent fantasizing about the imaginary "Other" continually compromise the possibility of real human engagement. Moreover, in the latter story, a Jewish Holocaust survivor relates to his black maid a story of the jazz performer whose actions in a wartime concentration camp saved his life; her droll response resists the intended empathy he has attempted to build between them: "Always thought it was just you people over there doing those terrible things to each other." In "Hostages," an Israeli expatriate and daughter of Auschwitz survivors reflects on her first marriage to an Israeli Arab and her current marriage to a wealthy businessman who offers a prime target for Moslem terrorists; finally she sees herself as a hostage to the comfortable but isolated life she leads and meditates on the Talmudic lesson of the Lamed-Vov, or "God's hostages," predestined "sponges drawing mankind's suffering into themselves."

"Fever," the volume's title story—and its most accomplished—depicts the 1793 yellow fever epidemic in Philadelphia, a crisis attributed to African slaves brought up North from the Caribbean but in fact a result of the internally bred corruption of the swamp-ridden city. A metaphor for the pervasive racial contagions of this iron-ically dubbed "City of Brotherly Love," the fever levels all distinctions of race, gender, and class even as it triggers responses affirming them. The story's protago-nist, Richard Allen, is a minister exhausting himself in Christian service to dying whites and blacks alike. Eventually confronted by the angry monologue of an in-fected Jewish merchant unimpressed by his humanity, he too is told of the Lamed-Vov, the implication being that Allen has been arbitrarily selected "to suffer the reality humankind cannot bear," enduring an unimaginable and unrelieved burden of "earth, grief and misery." A nihilistic voice in the text, Abraham deconstructs Al-len's faith and further magnifies the din of conflicting perspectives—past and pres-ent, conciliatory and confrontational—that make the story the touchstone of the volume's exploration of compassion as a limited but essential response to incompre-hensible suffering, be its origins cosmic or human—or both.

Elsewhere, Wideman contrasts vision versus blindness ("Doc's Story" and "When It's Time to Go") to illustrate very different positionings by African Americans within the racially charged dominant culture through which they try to move. Wide-man's attunement to the musical textures of African-American culture again asserts itself, as does his interest in the drama of the individual alienated from his root culture by his ambitions. "Surfiction" offers an exercise in postmodern pastiche that is both a self-conscious parody of the imaginative stasis to which contemporary critical and aesthetic practice can lead and a serious study of the ways in which human determination to communicate across the void poignantly subverts even the most sophisticated intellectual distancing devices. Finally, then, the reader of this volume is left musing on the cultural incompatibilities institutionalized by ideolo-gies of difference—racial, gender, ethnic, nationalistic—and the heroic folly of the Richard Allens of the world who resist them against all odds.

Other major works

NOVELS: *A Glance Away*, 1967; *Hurry Home*, 1970; *The Lynchers*, 1973; *Hiding Place*, 1981; *Sent for You Yesterday*, 1983; *Reuben*, 1989; *Philadelphia Fire*, 1990.
NONFICTION: *Brothers and Keepers*, 1984.

Bibliography

Bell, Bernard W. *The Afro-American Novel and Its Tradition*. Amherst: University of Massachusetts Press, 1987. Bell provides a short but incisive overview of Wide-man's evolving concerns as an African American as well as a postmodernist inno-vator. He also notes Wideman's evocative uses of history as an imaginative para-digm and identifies as his major theme "the conflict between [his protagonists'] ascribed and achieved identities as black men."
Bennion, John. "The Shape of Memory in John Edgar Wideman's *Sent for You Yesterday*." *Black American Literature Forum* 20 (1985): 143-150. While the sole analytic emphasis of this essay is the novel that closes the Homewood Trilogy, it nevertheless offers a useful introduction to major themes in Wideman's fiction.

Berben, Jacqueline. "Beyond Discourse: The Unspoken Versus Words in the Fiction of John Edgar Wideman." *Callaloo* 8 (1985): 525-534. Although this essay is primarily a study of the novel *Hiding Place*, the second volume in the Homewood Trilogy, Berben also discusses the mythic character of Homewood as it unfolds in *Damballah*. Berben's argument that Wideman regularly evaluates his characters according to their ability to deal with truth and break free from self-delusion offers useful insight into all Wideman's writing.

Coleman, James W. *Blackness and Modernism: The Literary Career of John Edgar Wideman*. Jackson: University Press of Mississippi, 1990. Coleman regards the personal pattern of Wideman's alienation from and return to Homewood as reiterated in his aesthetic movement "from an uncritical acceptance of the forms and themes of mainstream modernism . . . to a black voicing of modernism and postmodernism that is consistent with Afro-American perspectives. . . ." The book deals with all Wideman's work through 1989, includes a later interview with him, and appends a brief bibliography of critical sources.

O'Brien, John, ed. Interview in *Interviews with Black Writers*. New York: Liveright, 1973. In this early interview, Wideman sets forth his interest in aesthetic experimentation at the expense of fictional realism, his penchant for fabulation, and the relationship between his racial subjects and his artistic choices in rendering them.

Samuels, Wilfred D. "Going Home: A Conversation with John Edgar Wideman." *Callaloo* 6 (1983): 40-59. Samuels asks Wideman to discuss his movement from a Eurocentric literary aesthetic to one grounded in African-American culture, language, and art forms. Central to that shift has been his imaginative "return to Homewood" and his increasing preoccupation with the emotional complexity of growing up black and male in the United States.

Barbara Seidman

MARIANNE WIGGINS

Born: Lancaster, Pennsylvania; November 8, 1947

Principal short fiction

Herself in Love and Other Stories, 1987; *Learning Urdu*, 1990; *Bet They'll Miss Us When We're Gone*, 1991.

Other literary forms

During Marianne Wiggins' career, she has produced several novels: *Babe* (1975), *Went South* (1980), *Separate Checks* (1984), and *John Dollar* (1989).

Achievements

Wiggins' works have produced considerable critical comment and recognition. In 1989, she received fiction grants from both the National Endowment for the Arts and the Whiting Foundation. Also, because of a two-year period spent in hiding from Islamic fundamentalists, Wiggins' career was briefly thrown off course; she has since resumed public appearances in support of her work.

Biography

Marianne Wiggins was born November 8, 1947, in Lancaster, Pennsylvania, the daughter of John Wiggins (a grocer and a preacher who also tried farming) and Mary Klonis. Probably because she was born in the Amish region of Pennsylvania, Wiggins has always had a fascination with "utopian" communities. She considered her father the classic American "lost father"; an unsuccessful grocer and a farmer who lost his land, he eventually committed suicide. He was a stern and religious man who attended the church founded by his father. Wiggins' mother, rather paradoxically, was an exotic Greek woman whose family had emigrated to Virginia.

For the first years of Wiggins' life, she was reared as a fundamentalist Christian. Then, at age nine, she was baptized into the Greek Orthodox church. Often ill as a child—she had hepatitis and later had a kidney removed—Wiggins spent much of her time reading. She first married at age seventeen, to Brian Porzak, a film distributor, on June 6, 1965, and they had one child, Lara. Wiggins and Porzak were divorced in 1970, after which Wiggins had a brief career as a stockbroker, trying to support her daughter as a single parent.

On January 23, 1988, Wiggins married Salman Rushdie, a well-known author living in England. Their life together was thrown into disarray, however, with the publication of Rushdie's *The Satanic Verses*, in 1988. With the ensuing uproar that this novel produced in the Islamic world and the subsequent death sentence issued by the Ayatollah Ruhollah Khomeini in Iran, Wiggins and Rushdie had to leave their London home and go into hiding, at times separately. This enforced exile undermined their relationship, and in 1991, Wiggins came out of hiding and acknowledged that the marriage had failed. That same year, her short-fiction collection *Bet They'll Miss Us When We're Gone*, which contains some of her most autobiographical work, was published.

Analysis

Marianne Wiggins' work focuses largely on the decisions that women face—and make—throughout their lives. Her writing is based on the belief that "it's the role of writers to touch the nerve that otherwise, untouched, lulls [people] to complacency." She has stated that she writes about what she fears, a tenet that she believes is the underlying provocation in the role of the writer.

If that is true, then perhaps one of Wiggins' greatest fears is that of going mad. In "Kafkas," the mental condition of a young woman with a doctorate (presumably in philosophy) deteriorates noticeably while searching for a man by the last name of Kafka who will discuss philosophy with her. She goes about her search by calling information in major cities throughout the United States and asking for all the listings of male Kafkas. She then calls each one, looking for her soul mate, explaining that she is searching for a husband who can give her the name Fran Kafka.

When her sister, Dina, discovers (by way of a seven-hundred-dollar telephone bill) what Fran is doing, she confronts Fran. It becomes clear at this point, however, that regardless of whether this project started off as a mere amusement, it has become very serious indeed. When Dina tells Fran that she must leave, Fran replies that she cannot, "They'll kill me, Dina. Can't you hear them? There are Indians out there."

Similarly, an undercurrent of violence and madness runs through "Green Park," in which a woman takes back her married lover (who had left her for his wife) only to plan a way of avenging her previous hurts. The power of the story lies in the chilling way in which the main character never lets on to her lover the pain and rage that she is feeling.

As her lover carefully shaves her legs, the main character thinks to herself about what it would be like if he cut her. The reader is held in thrall waiting for the slip that will lead to the "red ribbon, a bright racine vine in the water, a shimmering curtain, her blood, unfurling itself like a shoot, turning the water not crimson or brilliant, but soft pink and pearly and rose." His comment that he "gardened like hell to forget" her leads to her thought that there is "an instant when she might have said that he's cut her."

"Among the Impressionists" also speaks about lost love, although it is love of a much more fleeting, imaginary kind. Lucy is an elderly woman who fantasizes during her daily trip to the National Gallery (the story is set in London) that she meets a different artist (and sometimes more than one) each day. One day, it is Edgar Degas; another, it is Camille Pissarro. To each artist whom she meets, Lucy tells him—or her, for Lucy often meets Mary Cassatt—that she is meeting her lover.

Lucy's rendezvous, however, is nothing more than a pathetic re-creation of a one-time meeting with a young man whom she dismissed rather abruptly, being too shy to converse with him. Her missed chance has left her, fifty years later, worn down by "haunting regrets." As a love story, "Among the Impressionists" is extremely tragic: a life wasted on a memory. Wiggins finishes the story with Lucy's description to Édouard Manet of what she and her lover do each day when they meet:

> We look at each other. We stare and we stare until the edges of the things around us start to grow invisible. . . . Until the world itself begins to grow invisible, until the only thing we see is what exists between two lovers.

With this fantasy, Lucy has been able to insulate herself from the disappointments of her life, unlike the character Fran, in "Kafkas," who is becoming separated from reality in a much more painful way. Fran stares at her sister, although she is "looking less at Dina than at the *distance* that the walls define, the way they seem to form a ring around their voices."

In the collection *Bet They'll Miss Us When We're Gone*, each story ends with the date and place that it was written, many of them chronicling the travels and travails of Wiggins' life in exile with Rushdie. These stories are very autobiographical, despite Wiggins' assertion in a 1990 interview that she could not write about their life in hiding for personal and safety reasons.

"Croeso i Gymru" begins with a forceful announcement, the first part of which reads, "We were on the lam in Wales." This sentence perhaps most succinctly sums up Wiggins' feelings from this period (though using different words, she has stated similar ideas during interviews). In addition, when her first-person main character says, "I depend on books for meaning. I depend on them for definition," the reader can believe that the key to Wiggins' emotional survival during this time was, in fact, being able to read and to continue writing.

The strain of the time that Wiggins spent in hiding comes through best in "Croeso i Gymru." There was the worry that people will recognize who she is, for she was allowed to go out (although presumably Rushdie was not). She occupied her time learning Welsh, reading the local, very rural newspapers, and walking among the meadows, inhabited only by sheep and British military personnel out playing war games as Harrier jump jets swoop by overhead. Most of all, however, she and her protectors sit and "wait for one aged psychopath to die."

Probably the most obviously autobiographical of the *Bet They'll Miss Us When We're Gone* stories, "Grocer's Daughter," was written long before the troubles of 1989, in Martha's Vineyard, in May of 1979. Yet, perhaps it was this rough period that caused Wiggins to remember earlier hurts and hardships. The story describes Wiggins' father, John, a man whom "life defeated." Wiggins describes him as a man who told her "strange, portenting things: if I ate too much bread, I'd get dandruff." She goes on to flesh out his description with the statement, "He read *Reader's Digest*, *Coronet*, and *Pageant* and didn't believe in evolution."

Yet, this piece is not all humorous anecdotes; Wiggins' motive in writing was also to achieve a healing in herself, for she says,

There were times I didn't like him. He left abruptly. He left me much unfinished business. . . . I'd like to turn to him today and say, "I love you: too late: I'm sorry: you did the best you could: you were my father: I learned from you: you were an honest man.

Wiggins' writing is at its strongest with these heartfelt remembrances and regrets, for it speaks to the universal feelings that many adult children have upon their parents' death. The dedication page for *Bet They'll Miss Us When We're Gone* reads only "remembering my father," but it is this motivation that gives the warmth that infuses the best of Wiggins' work.

Other major works

NOVELS: *Babe*, 1975; *Went South*, 1980; *Separate Checks*, 1984; *John Dollar*, 1989.

Bibliography

Field, Michele. "Marianne Wiggins." *Publishers Weekly* 235 (February 7, 1989): 57-58. Written just prior to the uproar over *The Satanic Verses*, this article supplies many biographical details, many of which help to give a background for interpreting Wiggins' work. The article also provides a synopsis of Wiggins' writing career as well as what has motivated her "explicit and frightening" writing.

James, Caryn. "Marianne Wiggins and Life on the Run." *The New York Times*, April 9, 1991, C13. This brief article is partly a discussion of *Bet They'll Miss Us When We're Gone* and partly a commentary on the reasons why Wiggins believed that it was necessary, ultimately, to leave Rushdie. It discusses Wiggins' feelings while in hiding and how the experience affected her writing, especially by increasing and intensifying its autobiographical nature.

_____. "Wiggins: Author, Feminist, and Wife of Rushdie." *The New York Times*, April 4, 1990, C17, C21. This article gives biographical details and talks about Wiggins' life in London, her marriage to Salman Rushdie, and her writings in *Herself in Love and Other Stories*. Written early in Wiggins' exile, it reveals much of Wiggins' character and personality. Most notable about her frame of mind at that time was her determination to stand by Rushdie and not to be cowed by anyone.

Phillips, Andrew. "A Life in Hiding." *Maclean's* 102 (August 21, 1989): 30. This article is most useful for a brief but clear picture of the events that forced Wiggins and Rushdie into hiding. It also discusses, however, the disruption to Wiggins' life and career, notably that as she seemed poised on the brink of success, she was forced to withdraw from the limelight and it notes the repercussions that this withdrawal had on her career.

Jo-Ellen Lipman Boon

JOY WILLIAMS

Born: Chelmsford, Massachusetts; February 11, 1944

Principal short fiction
Taking Care: Short Stories, 1982; *Escapes: Stories*, 1990.

Other literary forms
Although Joy Williams is known mainly for her short fiction, she is also the author of three novels—*State of Grace* (1973), *The Changeling* (1978), and *Breaking and Entering* (1988)—and a book of nonfiction, *Florida Keys: A History and Guide* (1986).

Achievements
Williams has established herself as one of the preeminent practitioners of the short-story form in the United States. Along with Raymond Carver, Richard Ford, and a handful of other writers, she has perfected a style and content that accurately render life in late twentieth century America. It is not a pretty picture she paints: in Williams' stories, characters cannot communicate, couples cannot connect, and children are being abandoned or reared by others.

Williams has been the recipient of numerous awards in her career, including a Guggenheim Fellowship in 1974. Her stories regularly appear in the leading U.S. literary journals—*Esquire, The New Yorker, Grand Street*—and many have been collected in the annual *Best American Short Stories* or *Prize Stories: The O. Henry Awards* collections and in other prime anthologies of contemporary American fiction.

Biography
Born in 1944, Joy Williams grew up in the small Maine town of Cape Elizabeth, where both her father and her grandfather were Congregational ministers. She holds degrees from Marietta College, in Ohio, and from the University of Iowa. Married to Rust Hills, the writer and fiction editor at *Esquire*, she has one daughter, Caitlin. She has taught in the writing programs at several leading U.S. universities (including the University of California at Irvine and the University of Arizona) and splits her time between homes in Arizona and Florida.

Analysis
Joy Williams is a short-story writer with a dark vision encased in a clean prose style. While a few of her stories have an experimental, almost surrealistic form, and often a wry, ironic tone, the bulk fall into what can be called the realist mode, minimalist division: Williams deals with American family life in the last third of the twentieth century, focusing on troubles, handicaps, and incompletions. She interests

readers in these subjects without divulging all the information that they might or-dinarily want or need about the characters and their situations. What further dis-tinguishes her stories is a prose style that is clean but highly metaphorical, for the images and motifs of the stories often carry the meaning more deeply than the ac-tion or exposition.

Hers is not a reassuring portrait of contemporary American life. The families are often dysfunctional, physically as well as psychologically: parents abandon children, by leaving or by dying, and children wander in life without guidance. Alcohol is a cause of the unhappiness as well as its hoped-for cure. In nearly all her stories, love is being sought but is rarely found, and nearly as rarely expressed. Characters seem unable to ask the questions that might free them from their unhappiness; the best they can hope for is an escape to some other state, physical or emotional. Disabil-ities, addictions, dead animals, arguments in restaurants, and car accidents abound in Williams' stories.

Williams' first collection, *Taking Care*, contains stories published in the 1970's and early 1980's in *The New Yorker, Partisan Review, The Paris Review, Esquire, Ms.*, and other leading vehicles of contemporary American fiction. These stories show a firmness and subtlety that have marked Williams' style over her entire career (although there was probably more range here than in her second collection). The themes that would mark that career are clearly established in this first collection. While many of the stories are riveting in their subject matter, they leave readers with a sense of hollowness and futility. There are few resolutions in Williams, even early in her career, but there are the tensions, violence, and disconnections that mark most of her stories.

In the title story, for example—a story that closes the collection and has since been widely anthologized—"Jones, the preacher" is "taking care" of two genera-tions: a wife dying of leukemia and a six-month-old baby girl whom his daughter has left him to care for before fleeing to Mexico. Jones baptizes his granddaughter and then brings his wife back from the hospital; in the last line of the story, "Together they enter the shining rooms"—rooms made "shining" by Jones's love and care. This epiphanic ending, however, cannot erase all the abandonment and death. Jones is surely "taking care" of more than his required load in this life, and there is a heaviness, a spiritual sadness, that is expressed appropriately in Williams' flat, terse prose style.

Other stories in *Taking Care* have similar themes and forms. In "Traveling to Pridesup," three sisters in their eighties and nineties, "in a big house in the middle of Florida," find a baby abandoned in a feed bag on their mailbox. In the journey in their old Mercedes to find someone to help, Lavinia gets them lost, drives hundreds of miles in circles, and finally crashes. In a tragicomic mix reminiscent of Flannery O'Connor, the story ends with a painful revelation, "the recognition that her life and her long, angry journey through it, had been wasteful and deceptive and unneces-sary."

In "Winter Chemistry," two students spy on their teacher every night and inadvertently kill him when they are caught. "Shepherd" concerns a young woman who cannot get over the death of her German shepherd and who will probably lose her boyfriend because of it. (" 'We are all asleep and dreaming, you know,' " he tells her in a speech that might apply to characters in other stories in *Taking Care*. " 'If we could ever actually comprehend our true position, we would not be able to bear it, we would have to find a way out.' ") In "The Farm," alcohol, infidelities, and the accidental killing of a hitchhiker will destroy the central couple. "Breakfast," too, has many of the stock Williams ingredients: parents who abandon their children, a half-blind dog, and characters who are both alcoholic and lacking direction.

Possibly the only difference in *Taking Care* from Williams' later fiction is that there appears to be more humor in these early stories, and more effort by Williams to perfect a wry, ironic style. ("The Yard Boy," for example, is a surreal caricature of a kind of New Age spiritual character.) Yet the other landmarks are there as well: the style is often flat and cryptic, events and incidents seem to have more a symbolic than a representational quality, and people pass by one another without touching or talking. There is little love in these stories (even in those that are supposedly love stories), but often a violence beneath the surface that is constantly threatening to bubble up and destroy the characters or kill their animals (as in "Preparation for a Collie" or "Woods"). People rarely have names; rather, they are "the woman," "her lover," "the child." Williams writes easily about children, but hers are children who are wandering in an adult world without supervision or love (as in "Train" or "The Excursion.") Williams works here in the great American tradition of Sherwood Anderson's *Winesburg, Ohio* (1919), in which characters become what Anderson called "grotesques." Williams writes of grotesques as well, of bizarre characters who are lost or losing or obsessive, and whom nothing, apparently, will save.

These elements can be found throughout the title story of Williams' second collection, *Escapes*. The narrator, a young girl, describes the time when her alcoholic mother (abandoned by the father) took her to see a magician. The mother, drunk, wanders onstage and has to be removed. Layers of escape, both literal and metaphorical, characterize this story: the father's abandonment of his dysfunctional family; the magician's illusions ("Houdini was more than a magician, he was an escape artist"); the mother's addiction to alcohol; and the daughter's dreams of escaping her lot: "I got out of this situation," Lizzie writes in the last line of the story, "but it took me years."

Williams' later short fiction is unique not only for this bleak view of human nature, in which people are shown trapped and searching for some inexpressible transcendence, but for a prose style that is both less and more than it appears: less because, like other minimalists whom Williams resembles (such as Raymond Carver and Ann Beattie), she draws only the outlines of the action and leaves the characters' backgrounds to the reader's imagination, and more because Williams manipulates metaphors and motifs in such a way that they carry a heavy weight of meaning in her stories. In "Escapes," for example, the old magician's illusion of sawing a woman in half becomes the vehicle for the story's theme: the alcoholic mother tells her daughter that she witnessed that trick performed by Houdini when she was a child. She wanted to be that lady, "sawed in half, and then made whole again!" Her subsequent intrusion into the show by walking onstage is her attempt to escape by realizing that dream, "to go and come back," but the dream is impossible to realize, and therefore self-destructive. The usher escorts mother and daughter out of the theater, assuring the drunken woman that she can "pull [herself] through." She will not, however, succeed in reconstructing herself and her life, and in the end, the reader suspects, the daughter will escape only by abandoning the mother.

The stories in *Escapes* thus seem to work at cross-purposes: while the prose style is clean and uncluttered, the motifs and metaphors lead readers to meanings beneath the surface, to a depth that is full of horror and despair. In the second story, "Rot" (first reprinted in the O. Henry Prize collection of 1988), these concerns and formal characteristics continue. Dwight persuades his wife, who is twenty-five years younger than he is, to allow him to park the vintage Thunderbird he has just bought in their living room. The car is full of rot and rust—a symbol, readers may suspect, of the couple's marriage. The reader learns little about these characters, what they do or where they are headed; instead, symbolism replaces information: the rusting car was found in a parking lot with its owner dead inside it; now Dwight sits in the car in the living room and looks dead.

The other stories in *Escapes* take a similar approach: "The Skater," which was chosen to appear in the 1985 collection *Best American Short Stories*, presents a family, parents and a daughter, on a tour of East Coast prep schools. It slowly becomes apparent that the sickness at the heart of this family is the memory of the daughter—like the skater of the title who glides in and out of the story at several points—who died the previous year; the parents simply want Molly to be away from the sadness of their home.

The young woman in "Lulu" puts an old couple to bed after all three have gotten drunk one morning; she then attempts to drive off with their boa constrictor, apparently searching for love (she wonders, "Why has love eluded me"). In "Health," a twelve-year-old girl is undergoing ultraviolet treatments to help her recover from tuberculosis but is surprised by a man who walks in during one of her tanning sessions, as she lies naked on the couch. The grandmother of "The Blue Men" tries, in part through use of alcohol, to assuage her grief over her dead son, who was executed for murdering a police officer. "The Last Generation," the collection's closing story, depicts a father, numbing his pain over his wife's death through drink and work and neglecting his own children.

Williams' bleak vision is mitigated only by the sureness of her prose and the symbolic poetry of her language. "Bromeliads," in which a young mother abandons her new baby to her parents, becomes the central metaphor of the story's meaning. As the young woman explains, bromeliads are "thick glossy plants with extraordinary flowers. . . . They live on nothing. Just the air and the wind"—a perfect description of the mother herself. In "White," a couple has moved from Florida to Connecticut to escape the memory of their two babies, who have died. They cannot, however, escape their grief, even in alcohol and evasion. At a party they throw for a departing Episcopal priest, the husband describes a letter that the couple has recently received from the woman's father; after the greeting, the letter contains nothing, "just a page, blank as the day is long." The letter becomes a symbol for the missed communication, the things that are not said and that may in fact be inexpressible, abandonment and death among them.

In the end, readers are left with the bleakness of Williams' stories—despite a minimalist style and a use of metaphor that almost negates that vision. Nevertheless, Williams remains one of the more highly regarded short-fiction writers in modern-day America, often anthologized and the recipient of numerous awards. Along with Raymond Carver, Ann Beattie, Richard Ford, and a handful of other contemporaries, she continues to produce works that are read by university students and the general public alike, and younger writers emulate her polished style.

Other major works

NOVELS: *State of Grace*, 1973; *The Changeling*, 1978; *Breaking and Entering*, 1988.
NONFICTION: *Florida Keys: A History and Guide*, 1986.

Bibliography

Hills, Rust. Review of *State of Grace*. *Esquire* 80 (July, 1973): 26, 28. Hills recognizes that Williams has a problem with structure but praises her language: ". . . open the novel to virtually any page and you'll instantly see it—a kind of strange phosphorescent style describing disquieting, dark and funny goings-on. Sentences are brilliant, gorgeous, surprising. . . ."

Kirkus Reviews. Review of *Escapes*. 57 (November 15, 1989): 1633. This anonymous reviewer recognizes that "Williams' weird, seemingly anesthetized, protagonists are usually in flight: from inexorable fate, from the oppressive past, from reality itself."

Kornblatt, Joyce. "Madness, Murder, and the Surrender of Hope." Review of *Taking Care*. *The Washington Post Book World*, March 21, 1982, 4. Noting her similarity to Flannery O'Connor and Joyce Carol Oates, the reviewer here sees the redemptive qualities of Williams' work, for in the "fragile gestures" of these stories, "we glimpse, merely glimpse, an order of being that eschews randomness, that ascribes value, that insists on love in the face of destructiveness."

Malinowski, Sharon. "Joy Williams." In *Contemporary Authors*, edited by Deborah A. Straub. Vol. 22. Detroit: Gale Research, 1988. A good summary of Williams' career, including long passages from reviews of her novels and her short-story collections through 1982. "In Williams's fiction, the ordinary events of daily life are susceptible to bizarre turns of horror and individuals are lost in their private selves, unable to comprehend the forces which shape their lives. Although Williams occasionally alleviates her bleak vision with humor, a sense of hopelessness and despair remains central to her work."

Williams, Joy. "Joy Williams." Interview by Molly McQuade. *Publishers Weekly*

237 (January 26, 1990): 400-401. This brief but wide-ranging interview allows Williams to talk about her career and her sense of her own writing; words, for example, are intended "to affect the reader in unexpected, mysterious, subterranean ways. The literal surface has to be *very* literal—smooth and exact—yet what makes it strange is what's teeming underneath. Stories should be something other than they appear to be. . . . They should make you uncomfortable."

David Peck

TENNESSEE WILLIAMS
Thomas Lanier Williams

Born: Columbus, Mississippi; March 26, 1911
Died: New York, New York; February 25, 1983

Principal short fiction

One Arm and Other Stories, 1948; *Hard Candy: A Book of Stories*, 1954; *The Knightly Quest: A Novella and Four Short Stories*, 1967; *Eight Mortal Ladies Possessed: A Book of Stories*, 1974; *Collected Stories*, 1985.

Other literary forms

In addition to his three dozen collected and uncollected stories, Tennessee Williams wrote two novels, a book of memoirs, a collection of essays, two volumes of poetry, numerous short plays, a screenplay, and more than twenty full-length dramas. Among the most important of his plays are *The Glass Menagerie* (1944), *A Streetcar Named Desire* (1947), *Cat on a Hot Tin Roof* (1955), and *The Night of the Iguana* (1961).

Achievements

Williams' most obvious achievements in literature lie in the field of drama, where he is considered by many to be America's greatest playwright, a standing supported by two Pulitzer Prizes, a Commonwealth Award, a Medal of Freedom (presented by President Jimmy Carter), and an election in 1952 to a lifetime membership in the National Institute of Arts and Letters. Williams himself, however, felt that his short fiction contained some of his best writing. Indeed, besides stories appearing in his own collections, Williams published stories in many of America's most prestigious magazines, including *The New Yorker* and *Esquire*, and many have been selected for various anthologies, including three in Martha Foley's *Best American Short Stories* annual anthologies. Williams' short stories and plays alike dramatize the plight of the "fugitive," the sensitive soul punished by a harsh, uncaring world; in the stories, however, readers find specific and frequent voice given to a theme and subject only hinted at in Williams' drama, at least until his later, less memorable, plays: the plight of the homosexual in a bigoted society.

Biography

Descended on his mother's side from a Southern minister and on his father's from Tennessee politicians, Thomas Lanier (Tennessee) Williams moved with his family from Mississippi to St. Louis shortly after World War I. He attended the University of Missouri and Washington University, finally graduating from the University of Iowa. After odd jobs in the warehouse of a shoe factory, ushering at a movie house, and even a stint screenwriting in Hollywood, he turned full-time writer in the early 1940's, encouraged by grants from the Group Theatre and Rockefeller Foundation.

Despite purchasing a home in Key West, Florida, in 1950, Williams spent most of the remainder of his life living for short periods in a variety of locales in Europe, the United States, and Mexico. His two Pulitzer Prizes early in his career, plus four Drama Critics Circle awards, solidified Williams' reputation as a playwright; the quality of his writing declined, however, after the early 1960's, in great part as a result of drug dependency. He died, alone, in a New York City hotel room in 1983.

Analysis

Although during his lifetime Tennessee Williams was commonly held to be without peer among America's—many would say the world's—playwrights, he began his career writing short fiction, with a story entitled "The Vengeance of Nitocris" in *Weird Tales* in 1928. As late as 1944, when his first theatrical success was in rehearsal, George Jean Nathan reportedly observed that Williams "didn't know how to write drama, that he was really just a short story writer who didn't understand the theatre." Today, however, in proportion to the worldwide audience familiar with Williams' dramas, only a handful know more than a story or two, usually from among the ones later transformed into stage plays. Seven of Williams' full-length dramas, in fact, had their genesis in the fiction: *The Glass Menagerie* in "Portrait of a Girl in Glass"; *Summer and Smoke* (1947) in "The Yellow Bird"; *Cat on a Hot Tin Roof* in "Three Players of a Summer Game"; *The Night of the Iguana* and *Kingdom of Earth* (1968) in stories of the same names; *The Milk Train Doesn't Stop Here Anymore* (1963) in "Man Bring This Up Road"; and *Vieux Carré* (1977) in "The Angel in the Alcove" and "Grand."

The play *The Night of the Iguana* is sufficiently different from its progenitor to indicate how Williams rethought his material in adapting it to another medium. Both works portray a spinsterish artist, Miss Jelkes; but while Hannah in the play has fought for and achieved inner peace, Edith's harsher name in the story belies her edginess, neurosis, and lack of "interior poise." Having channeled her own "morbid energy" into painting, she discerns in the contrasting "splash of scarlet on snow . . . a flag of her own unsettled components" warring within her. When a servant at the Costa Verde hotel tethers an iguana to the veranda, Edith recoils hysterically from such brutality against "one of God's creatures," taking its suffering as proof of a grotesque "universe . . . designed by the Marquis de Sade." This picture of cosmic indifference, even malevolence, occurs in a handful of Williams' stories, most notably in "The Malediction," in which the lonely Lucio exists in a meaningless universe verging on the absurd, ruled by a God "Who felt that something was wrong but could not correct it, a man Who sensed the blundering sleep-walk of time and hostilities of chance" and "had been driven to drink." Edith finds God personified in a violent storm "like a giant bird lunging up and down on its terrestrial quarry, a bird with immense white wings and beak of godlike fury."

Her fellow guests at the hotel are two homosexual writers. Squeamish and yet attracted by the forbidden nature of their relationship, Edith insinuates herself into their company only to become the object of a desperate attack on her "demon of virginity" by the older of the two. Although she has earlier hinted that she always answers, with understanding, cries for help from a fellow sufferer, she ferociously fends off his pathetic advances, metaphorically associated with the predatory "bird of blind white fury." Afterward, however, once the younger man has mercifully cut loose the iguana, Edith feels her own "rope of loneliness had also been severed," and—instead of drawing back in "revulsion" from "the spot of dampness" left on her belly by the older writer's semen—exclaims "Ah, life," evidently having reached through this epiphanic moment a new acceptance and integration of her sexuality. Yet, unlike Hannah, whose compassionate response to Shannon in the play is for him a saving grace and who can affirm, along with Williams, that "Nothing human disgusts me unless it's unkind, violent," Edith's inability to answer unselfishly the older man's need—the cardinal sin in Williams—may have permanently maimed him by destroying his self-respect.

Williams does not always capitalize fully on his gift for writing dialogue in his stories. For all its interest in light of the later play, the pace of "The Night of the Iguana" is curiously desultory and enervated, which might not have been true if the story had been written from Edith's point of view. Williams does indeed prove adept at handling first-person narration in several autobiographical tales, whose content seems hardly distinguishable at times from the sections of the *Memoirs* (1975). He can, however, become annoyingly self-conscious when, in authorial intrusions analogous to the nonrepresentational techniques that deliberately destroy the illusion of reality in his dramas, he breaks the narrative line in a dozen or so stories to interject comments about himself as writer manipulating his materials, sometimes apologizing for his awkwardness in handling the short-story form, or for playing too freely with chronology or radically shifting tone. At times these stories provide some notion of Williams' aesthetic theories and practice, as when, in "Three Players of a Summer Game," for example, he discusses the method by which the artist orders experience by a process that distorts and "yet . . . may be closer than a literal history could be to the hidden truth of it." These "metafictional" asides might indicate his conception of character portrayal. On that point—while without qualms at employing clinical details when necessary—Williams insists, in "Hard Candy," on the need for "indirection" and restraint rather than "a head-on violence that would disgust and destroy" if he is to remain nonjudgmental and respect the "mystery" at the heart of character.

An almost identical comment occurs in "The Resemblance Between a Violin Case and a Coffin," part of a small group of *rites de passage* stories in the Williams canon. The story centers on a love triangle of sorts as the young narrator faces the destruction of the "magical intimacy" with his pianist sister as she enters adolescence—that "dangerous passage" between the "wild country of childhood" and the "uniform world of adults"—and turns her attentions towards a fellow musician, Richard Miles. It is as if she has deserted the narrator and "carried a lamp into another room [he] could not enter." He resents the "radiant" Richard, but also feels a frightening prepubescent physical attraction for the older boy. Like many of Williams' adult neurotics whose libidinous desires rebel against their Puritan repressions, the narrator longs to touch Richard's skin, yet recoils in shame and guilt from the boy's offer of his hand as if it were somehow "impure." Seeing Richard play the violin, however, provides an epiphany as the narrator "learns the will of life to transcend the single body" and perceives the connection between Eros and Thanatos. For the narrator equates the act of playing the phallic violin with "making love," and the violin case to "a little black coffin made for a child or doll." He mourns the loss of youth and innocence and the birth of the knowledge of sin and death.

Tom, the authorial voice in *The Glass Menagerie*, confesses to "a poet's weakness for symbols," and one of Williams' own hallmarks has always been an extensive use of visual stage symbolism—"the natural speech of drama." As he remarks in one of his essays, it can "say a thing more directly and simply and beautifully than it could be said in words"; he employs symbols extensively, however, in only a handful of stories, although he does rely heavily on figurative language. In the earlier stories the imagery is ordinarily controlled and striking, as, for example, in this line (reminiscent of Karl Shapiro's "cancer, simple as a flower, blooms") describing the doctor's tumor from "Three Players of a Summer Game": "An awful flower grew in his brain like a fierce geranium that shattered its pot." In the more recent tales, however, Williams' diction frequently becomes overwrought and demonstrates some lack of control, falling into what he criticizes elsewhere in the same essay as "a parade of images for the sake of images."

If the mood of "The Resemblance Between a Violin Case and a Coffin" is tender and elegiac, the tone of a much later *rite de passage* story, "Completed," is chilling, but no less haunting and memorable. Miss Rosemary McCord, a student at Mary, Help a Christian School, is a withdrawn debutante subjected by her unsympathetic mother to a pathetic and bizarre coming-out dance. The onset of menstruation has been late in coming for Rosemary, and when it finally does arrive, she is pitifully unprepared for it. Ironically, the fullness of physical development in Rosemary coincides with a death wish; her only "purpose in life is to complete it quick." Her one understanding relative, the reclusive Aunt Ella, deliberately retreats from the external world through morphine; the drug brings her comforting apparitions of the Virgin Mary and tears of peace. Rosemary goes to live with her, aware that she has been taken captive and yet willingly submissive, ready to be calmed through drugs and her own reassuring visions of the Virgin. Her life—apparently the latest of several variations on that of Williams' own sister—is over before it began. Perhaps it is, however, only in such a sheltered, illusory life that this fragile, sensitive girl can exist.

The other "passage" that threads through Williams' stories is that from life to death, obsessed as he is with what he terms "a truly awful sense of impermanence," with the debilitating effects of time on both physical beauty and one's creative powers, and the sheer tenacity necessary if one is to endure at least spiritually undefeated. In "Sabbatha and Solitude," the aging poetess (undoubtedly semi-autobiographical) finds that the process of composition is a trial not unlike the Crucifixion that results only in "a bunch of old repeats," while in the picaresque "Two on a Party," the blond and balding queen and hack screenwriter exist at the mercy of that "worst of all enemies . . . the fork-tailed, cloven-hoofed, pitchfork-bearing devil of Time."

"Completed" is one of Williams' few later stories—"Happy August the Tenth" is another—that can stand alongside some of his earliest as a fully successful work. Just as there was a noticeable diminution in the power of his later dramas compared with the ones from *The Glass Menagerie* through *The Night of the Iguana*, so, too, each successive volume of short fiction was less impressive than its predecessor. As Williams' vision of the universe darkened and became more private, the once elegiac tone acquired a certain stridency and sharp edge; and as Williams developed a tough, self-protective shell of laughter as a defense against his detractors, some of the dark humor—what he once called the "jokes of the condemned"—became directed towards the pathetic grotesques who increasingly peopled his works, whereas once there was only compassion.

Thus, two of the most representative stories, "One Arm" and "Desire and the Black Masseur," neither of which, significantly, has ever been dramatized, appeared in his first collection. Unquestionably the most macabre of all his tales is "Desire and the Black Masseur," which details the fantastic, almost surreal sadomasochistic relationship between the insecure, sexually repressed Anthony Burns and an unnamed black masseur at a men's bath. Burns, whose name blends that of a Christian saint with the suggestion of consummation by fire—here metaphoric—suffers from an overly acute awareness of his own insignificance, as well as of his separateness and lack of completeness as a human being. Williams views the latter as an inescapable fact of the human condition and proposes three means available to compensate for it: art, violent action, or surrendering oneself to brutal treatment at the hands of others. Burns chooses the third path, submitting himself as if in a dream, finding at the punishing hands of the masseur first pain, then orgasmic pleasure, and ultimately death. Although the masseur thus secures a release from his pent-up hatred of his white oppressors, this tale should not be construed as a social comment reflecting Williams' attitude toward black/white relations, hardly even peripherally a concern in his work, despite his being a Southern writer. Blacks figure importantly in only two other stories. In the ribald "Miss Coynte of Greene," the title character's long-frustrated female eroticism erupts into nymphomania, her pleasure intensified by the dark skin of her sexual partners. In "Mama's Old Stucco House," Williams' gentlest foray into the black/white terrain, the failed artist Jimmy Krenning is cared for physically and emotionally after his own mother's death by the black girl Brinda and her Mama, the latter having always functioned as his surrogate mother.

That "Desire and the Black Masseur" is to be read on levels other than the literal appears clear when Williams places its climax at the end of the Lenten Season. The death and devouring of Burns becomes a ritual of expiation, a kind of black mass and perversion of the sacrifice on Calvary, even accomplished in biblical phraseology. Indeed, counterpointed with it is a church service during which a self-proclaimed fundamentalist preacher exhorts his congregation to a frenzy of repentance. What Williams has written, then, is not only a psychological study of man's subconscious desires and an allegory of the division between innocence and evil within all men, but also a parable exposing how excessive emphasis on guilt and the need for punishment at the hands of a vengeful God have destroyed the essential New Testament message of love and forgiveness. So Burns's strange rite of atonement stands as a forceful indictment of a Puritanism that creates a dark god of hate as a reflection of one's own obsession with evil, which is one of the recurrent emphases in almost all of Williams' important dramas, especially *Suddenly Last Summer* (1958) and *The Night of the Iguana.*

Something of the obverse, the possibility for transcending one's knowledge of evil and isolation, occurs in "One Arm," the quintessential—and perhaps the finest—Williams story, in which can be discerned nearly all the central motifs that adumbrate not only his fiction but also his plays. Oliver Winemiller, a former light heavyweight champion who in an accident two years earlier lost an arm, is one of Williams' "fugitive kind," a lonely misfit, cool, impassive, now tasting, like Brick in *Cat on a Hot Tin Roof,* "the charm of the defeated." Since all he possessed was his "Apollo-like beauty," after his physical mutilation he undergoes a psychological and emotional change; feeling that he has lost "the center of his being," he is filled with self-loathing and disgust. He enters on a series of self-destructive sexual encounters, finally committing a murder for which he is sentenced to die.

While in confinement awaiting execution, he receives letters from all over the country from his male lovers, confessing that he had aroused deep feelings in them, that he had effected a "communion" with them that would have been, if he had only recognized it, a means of "personal integration" and "salvation." If it was not until very late in his dramas that Williams openly treated homosexuality with sympathy, in his stories his nonapologetic and compassionate attitude existed from the very first. Oliver's epiphany, that he had been loved, liberates him from his self-imposed insularity; ironically, however, this rebirth makes his approaching death harder to accept. On the eve of his execution, he recognizes that the Lutheran minister who visits him has used religion as an escape from facing his own sexuality, and he desperately hopes that by forcing the minister to come to terms with himself and his "feelings" he can thereby somehow repay his debt to all those who had earlier responded to him with kindness. The minister, however, recognizing a forbidden side of himself and still suffering guilt over his adolescent sexual awakening during a dream of a golden panther, which Oliver reminds him of, refuses to give Oliver a massage and rushes from his cell. Oliver goes to his execution with dignity, gripping the love letters tightly between his thighs as a protection from aloneness.

The doctors performing the autopsy see in Oliver's body the "nobility" and purity of an "antique sculpture." Yet Williams reminds his readers in the closing line that "death has never been much in the way of completion." Although the work of art is immutable, it is not alive as only the emotionally responsive person can be, for the true artist in Williams is the person who goes out unselfishly to answer the cry for help of others, and the real work of art is the bond of communion that is formed by that response. Thus "One Arm" incorporates virtually all of Williams' major attitudes, including his somewhat sentimental valuation of the lost and lonely; his romantic glorification of physical beauty and worship of sexuality as a means of transcending aloneness; his castigation of Puritan repression and guilt that render one selfish and judgmental; and his Hawthornian abhorrence of the underdeveloped heart that prevents one from breaking out of the shell of the ego to respond with infinite compassion to all God's misbegotten creatures.

Although Williams' stories, with their frequent rhetorical excesses, their sometimes awkward narrative strategies, and their abrupt shifts in tone, technically do not often approach the purity of form of Oliver's statue, they do, nevertheless—as all good fiction must—surprise the reader with their revelations of the human heart and demand that the reader abandon a simplistic perspective and see the varieties of human experience. What in the hands of other writers might seem a too specialized vision, frequently becomes in Williams' work affectingly human and humane.

Other major works

NOVELS: *The Roman Spring of Mrs. Stone*, 1950; *Moise and the World of Reason*, 1975.

PLAYS: *Battle of Angels*, 1940; *This Property Is Condemned*, 1941 (one act); *The Lady of Larkspur Lotion*, 1942 (one act); *The Glass Menagerie*, 1944; *Twenty-seven Wagons Full of Cotton*, 1945 (one act); *You Touched Me*, 1945 (with Donald Windham); *Summer and Smoke*, 1947; *A Streetcar Named Desire*, 1947; *American Blues*, 1948 (collection); *Five Short Plays*, 1948; *The Long Stay Cut Short: Or, The Unsatisfactory Supper*, 1948 (one act); *I Rise in Flame, Cried the Phoenix*, 1951 (one act); *The Rose Tattoo*, 1951; *Camino Real*, 1953; *Cat on a Hot Tin Roof*, 1955; *Orpheus Descending*, 1957 (revision of *Battle of Angels*); *Suddenly Last Summer*, 1958; *The Enemy: Time*, 1959; *Sweet Bird of Youth*, 1959 (based on *The Enemy: Time*); *Period of Adjustment*, 1959; *The Night of the Iguana*, 1961; *The Milk Train Doesn't Stop Here Anymore*, 1963 (revised); *The Eccentrities of a Nightingale*, 1964 (revision of *Summer and Smoke*); *Slapstick Tragedy: The Mutilated and the Gnädiges Fräulein*, 1966 (one act); *The Two-Character Play*, 1967; *The Seven Descents of Myrtle*, 1968 (as *Kingdom of Earth*); *In the Bar of a Tokyo Hotel*, 1969; *Confessional*, 1970; *Dragon Country*, 1970 (collection); *The Theatre of Tennessee Williams*, 1971-1981 (7 volumes); *Small Craft Warnings*, 1972 (revision of *Confessional*); *Out Cry*, 1973 (revision of *The Two-Character Play*); *Vieux Carré*, 1977; *A Lovely Sunday for Creve Coeur*, 1979; *Clothes for a Summer Hotel*, 1980; *A House Not Meant to Stand*, 1981.

SCREENPLAYS: *The Glass Menagerie*, 1950 (with Peter Berneis); *A Streetcar Named Desire*, 1951 (with Oscar Saul); *The Rose Tattoo*, 1955 (with Hal Kanter); *Baby Doll*, 1956; *The Fugitive Kind*, 1960 (with Meade Roberts, based on *Orpheus Descending*); *Suddenly Last Summer*, 1960 (with Gore Vidal); *Stopped Rocking and Other Screenplays*, 1984.

POETRY: *In the Winter of Cities*, 1956; *Androgyne, Mon Amour*, 1977.

NONFICTION: *Memoirs*, 1975; *Where I Love: Selected Essays*, 1978.

Bibliography

Falk, Signi Lenea. *Tennessee Williams*. 2d ed. Boston: Twayne, 1978. Though devoting most of her attention to Williams' plays, Falk addresses many of the short stories. Falk's discussions of "One Arm," "Desire and the Black Masseur," and "Portrait of a Girl in Glass" are especially interesting. Contains a useful, though dated, bibliography.

Gunn, Drewey Wayne. *Tennessee Williams: A Bibliography*. Metuchen, N.J.: Scarecrow Press, 1980. Gunn's work is the most thorough bibliography of Williams studies available.

Spoto, Gary. *The Kindness of Strangers: The Life of Tennessee Williams*. Boston: Little, Brown, 1985. Spoto's study is the closest to a definitive biography of Williams. Provides, however, only passing mention of the short stories. A brief bibliography follows the text.

Tharpe, Jac, ed. *Tennessee Williams: A Tribute*. Jackson: University Press of Mississippi, 1977. A collection of fifty-three essays on various aspects of Williams' art. Many note Williams' short fiction in passing, and four are fully (or in the main) devoted to the short fiction. Contains a bibliography.

Vannatta, Dennis. *Tennessee Williams: A Study of the Short Fiction*. Boston: Twayne, 1988. The only book-length study of Williams' short fiction. Contains a selection of essays concerning Williams' short fiction by various scholars and a selection of Williams' own letters, essays, and reviews.

Thomas P. Adler
(Revised by *Dennis Vannatta*)

WILLIAM CARLOS WILLIAMS

Born: Rutherford, New Jersey; September 17, 1883
Died: Rutherford, New Jersey; March 4, 1963

Principal short fiction

The Knife of the Times and Other Stories, 1932; *Life Along the Passaic River*, 1938; *Make Light of It: Collected Stories*, 1950; *The Farmers' Daughters: The Collected Stories of William Carlos Williams*, 1961; *The Doctor Stories*, 1984.

Other literary forms

Best known as a poet, William Carlos Williams nevertheless wrote in a variety of literary forms (some of them defying categorization) including poetry, novels, short stories, prose poetry, essays, autobiography, and plays. *Paterson*, his extended poem published in four separate volumes (1946-1951), with a fifth volume serving as a commentary (1958), is his most famous and enduring work.

Achievements

Williams was one of the major figures of literary modernism whose peers included Ezra Pound and Wallace Stevens. Highly influenced by the visual arts and the imagist movement, Williams' work was marked by a rejection of metaphysics, characterized by his famous dictum: "No ideas/ But in things." Williams' objective approach to literature is reflected in the coarse realism of his short stories. His prose shares the basic principles of his poetic theory: use of an American idiom, adherence to a locale, communication through specifics, and belief in organic form. The pastiche effects of Williams' poetry and prose had a profound influence on the next generation of American literary modernists, particularly the so-called Objectivist School, which included Louis Zukofsky, George Oppen, Carl Rakosi, and Charles Reznikoff. Williams received numerous awards, including the Dial Award in 1926, the National Book Award in 1950, the Bollingen Award in 1953, and, posthumously, the Pulitzer Prize in Poetry in 1963.

Biography

After attending public schools in New Jersey, spending time in Europe, and then finishing high school in New York, William Carlos Williams enrolled in the University of Pennsylvania's Medical School in 1902. While completing his M.D. there, he met Ezra Pound, Hilda Doolittle, and the painter Charles Demuth. In 1910, he began work as a general practitioner in Rutherford, New Jersey; in addition to this practice, from 1925 on he became a pediatrician at Passaic General Hospital. Williams held these positions until several strokes forced him to retire in 1951. His medical and literary careers always coexisted. In 1909, he had his first volume, *Poems*, privately published. As his reputation grew, he traveled to Europe several times and encountered such writers as James Joyce, Gertrude Stein, and Ford Madox Ford. He married Florence Herman in 1912, and they had two sons. Williams died on March 4, 1963, in his beloved Rutherford.

Analysis

M. L. Rosenthal claims that William Carlos Williams' short stories "are often vital evocations of ordinary American reality—its toughness, squalor, pathos, intensities." As such, this short fiction tends to exhibit distinctive characteristics. First, its style is the American idiom, with heavy reliance on dialogue and speech rhythm. Second, Williams inevitably writes of his own locale and stresses the Depression's dramatic effect on ordinary working people. Third, as he shows in his poem "A Sort of a Song," there should be "No ideas/ But in things"; in other words, details should suggest underlying ideas, not vice versa. Fourth, Williams himself is often present, but as a doctor, never as a poet; thus biography and autobiography constitute important plot elements. Last, the author allows plot to develop organically, which affects length (the tales range from one to thirty pages) and structure (the stories may appear diffuse or highly compressed).

Williams published two main short-story anthologies: *The Knife of the Times and Other Stories* and *Life Along the Passaic River*. In 1950, he collected these and other stories into a single volume called *Make Light of It*; then, in 1961, this was superseded by his complete collected stories entitled *The Farmers' Daughters*. Although these stories may indicate progressive technical sophistication or experimentation, they all treat "the plight of the poor" (as Williams says on several occasions) or the physician's frequently ambiguous role of healing the sick within an infected society.

On the choice of title for his first short-story anthology, Williams observes "The times—that was the knife that was killing them" (the poor). A typical story is "Old Doc Rivers," which provides a full background on one rural general practitioner. It also contains a strong autobiographical element because the narrator is a younger doctor (apparently Williams). An enormously complex picture emerges of Doc Rivers: efficient, conscientious, humane, yet simultaneously crude, cruel, and addicted to drugs and alcohol. The story builds this portrait by piling up specifics about the physician's personal and professional lives and interweaving case studies among the young doctor-narrator's comments. The narrator is astonished by Rivers' psychological sharpness, intuition for the correct diagnosis, and ability to inspire blind faith in his patients. As with many Williams tales, the reader's moral response is ambiguous, for when sober, Rivers is not a good doctor, yet when drunk or doped, he is at least as good as anyone else. The plot follows a roughly chronological structure which charts Rivers' gradual mental and physical decline. This story's particular strengths are its narrator voice, concrete details, re-creation of dialogue, and exploration of the doctor-patient relationship.

Williams further considers the physician-patient relationship in "Jean Beicke" and "A Face of Stone," representative of his second short fiction collection. Told by a pediatrician-narrator (but this time an established, not a beginning, doctor), "Jean

Beicke" is set in a children's ward during the Depression and recounts the story of a "scrawny, misshapen, worthless piece of humanity." Although Jean is desperately ill, she wins the hearts of the physicians and nurses by her sheer resilience: "As sick as she was," the narrator marvels, "she took her grub right on time every three hours, a big eight ounce bottle of milk and digested it perfectly." Yet little Jean's symptoms puzzle the medics, and despite initial improvement, she finally dies. Up to this point, doctors and readers alike have been ignorant of her previous history, but when her mother and aunt visit the dying infant, it is learned that she is the third child of a woman whose husband deserted her. As her aunt says, "It's better off dead—never was any good anyway." After the autopsy, the doctors discover they have completely misdiagnosed Jean. The storyteller ends the tale like this:

> I called the ear man and he came down at once. A clear miss, he said. I think if we'd gone in there earlier, we'd have saved her.
> For what? said I. Vote the straight Communist ticket. Would it make us any dumber? said the ear man.

Williams thought "Jean Beicke" was "the best short story I ever wrote." One reason is its involved narrator, whose sophisticated social conscience (why cure these Depression babies only to return them to a sick society?) contrasts with the nurses' instinctive (but perhaps naïve) humanitarianism. The story's careful structure takes us from external details—Jean's misshapen body, tiny face, and pale blue eyes—to internal ones—in the postmortem—and so suggests that beneath society's superficial ills lie fundamental, perhaps incurable, troubles. Once again, Williams shows his skill for catching the speech patterns of ordinary Americans, especially in the monologue of Jean's aunt. Finally, the author's main achievement is to individualize yet not sentimentalize Jean and to dramatize her life-and-death struggle so that it matters to him—and to the reader.

In "A Face of Stone," the doctor-narrator becomes the main character. A harried family doctor, he finds himself at the end of a busy morning confronted by a young Jewish couple. The husband, one of "the presuming poor," insists that he examine their baby, while the wife maintains an expressionless, stony face. As the doctor approaches the baby boy, his mother clutches him closer and is extremely reluctant to relinquish him. Frustrated and tired, the doctor is brusque and patronizing. When he eventually looks at the child, he discovers that it is quite healthy. During the winter, the people request a house call, but he refuses to go; then, in the spring, they return and still protest that the child is unwell. Conquering his annoyance at their persistence, the family doctor checks the boy and says that he simply needs to be fed regularly and weaned.

Now the physician expects the consultation to finish, but the young Jew asks him to examine his wife. The doctor is by this time exhausted and furious; however, he starts to check this passive, poverty-stricken, physically unattractive woman. Then, almost accidentally, he discovers she is a Polish Jew who has lost her whole family. Immediately, he forgets her ugliness, grasps her intense anxiety for her baby, and realizes the strong bond between wife and husband: ". . . suddenly I understood his half shameful love for the woman and at the same time the extent of her reliance on him. I was touched." The woman smiles for the first time when the doctor prescribes painkillers for her varicose veins and she senses that she can trust him.

This story effectively dramatizes the shifting reactions between patients and doctors as they try to establish a viable relationship. Often, a physician may exploit his position of power (as this one does at the beginning) and forget that his clients are human. If he does, he turns into Doc Rivers at his worst. The best relationship occurs when both parties move beyond stereotypes to view each other as individuals. Because the doctor narrates the tale, the reader follows his process of discovery, so when he stops stereotyping the couple, the reader does too. Williams once again successfully uses dialogue to convey character interaction. Also, as in "Jean Beicke," he reveals people through detail (such as the woman's ripped dress, bow legs, and high-heeled, worn-out shoes).

Williams composed few notable short stories after *Life Along the Passaic River,* mainly because he diverted his energies into longer projects (novels, plays, and *Paterson*). From the early 1940's to the mid-1950's, however, he worked on a long short story which he eventually called "The Farmers' Daughters" (and whose title he used for his collected short fiction). The title characters are Helen and Margaret, two Southern women who have been (and continue to be) betrayed by their men. Their similar background and experience form the basis of an enduring, unshakable friendship that terminates only with Margaret's death. Technically, this is one of Williams' best stories: it unfolds quickly in a "paragraph technique" as the narrator—once more a doctor—re-creates the women's conversations and letters, then links them chronologically with his own comments. The teller refers to himself in the third person, so that most of the time the story progresses through dialogue. This extract, in which Margaret and the doctor chat, illustrates the strength of using direct, idiomatic speech:

> What's your favorite flower, Margaret?
> Why?
> I just want to know.
> What's yours?
> No. Come on—don't be so quick on the trigger so early in the evening. I think I can guess.
> Petunias! (emphasizing the second syllable.) God knows I've seen enough of them. No.
> Red roses. Those are really what I love.

Unlike Williams' previous stories, "The Farmers' Daughters" relies on complex character depiction and development rather than on plot or theme.

Most short-story writers merely write, but Williams left behind theoretical as well as practical evidence of his interest in the genre. *A Beginning on the Short Story (Notes)* (1950) outlines his basic tenets: truthfulness, unsentimentality, and simplicity. "The finest short stories," he states, "are those that raise . . . one particular man or woman, from that Gehenna, the newspapers, where at last all men are equal, to

the distinction of being an individual." From the herd of humanity, Williams succeeds in individualizing Doc Rivers, little Jean Beicke, the Jewish couple, Margaret,
Helen, and all his various doctor-narrators.

Other major works

NOVELS: *The Great American Novel*, 1923; *A Voyage to Pagany*, 1928; *White Mule*,
1937; *In the Money*, 1940; *The Build-Up*, 1952.

PLAYS: *A Dream of Love*, 1948; *Many Loves and Other Plays*, 1961.

POETRY: *Poems*, 1909; *The Tempers*, 1913; *Al Que Quiere!*, 1917; *Kora in Hell:
Improvisations*, 1920; *Sour Grapes*, 1921; *Spring and All*, 1923; *Last Nights of Paris*,
1929 (translation with Elena Williams); *Collected Poems, 1921-1931*, 1934; *An Early
Martyr and Other Poems*, 1935; *Adam & Eve & the City*, 1936; *The Complete Collected Poems of William Carlos Williams, 1906-1938*, 1938; *The Broken Span*, 1941;
The Wedge, 1944; *Paterson*, 1946-1958; *The Clouds*, 1948; *Selected Poems*, 1949; *Collected Later Poems*, 1950, 1963; *Collected Earlier Poems*, 1951; *The Desert Music
and Other Poems*, 1954; *A Dog and the Fever*, 1954 (translation with Elena Williams); *Journey to Love*, 1955; *Pictures from Brueghel*, 1962; *Selected Poems*, 1985;
The Collected Poems of William Carlos Williams: Volume I, 1909-1939, 1986; *The
Collected Poems of William Carlos Williams: Volume II, 1939-1962*, 1988.

NONFICTION: *In the American Grain*, 1925; *A Novelette and Other Prose*, 1932; *A
Beginning on the Short Story (Notes)*, 1950; *The Autobiography of William Carlos
Williams*, 1951; *Selected Essays of William Carlos Williams*, 1954; *The Selected Letters of William Carlos Williams*, 1957; *I Wanted to Write a Poem: The Autobiography
of the Works of a Poet*, 1958; *The Embodiment of Knowledge*, 1974; *A Recognizable
Image*, 1978; *William Carlos Williams, John Sanford: A Correspondence*, 1984; *William Carlos Williams and James Laughlin: Selected Letters*, 1989.

Bibliography

Gish, Robert. *William Carlos Williams: A Study of the Short Fiction*. Boston: Twayne,
    1989. A very fine single volume study of Williams' substantial contributions to the
    short story and the essay.
Kenner, Hugh. *A Homemade World: The American Modernist Writers*. New York:
    Alfred A. Knopf, 1975. A useful introduction to Williams and his work. Estab-
    lishes the author's significance within the milieu of his fellow modernist writers.
Paul, Sherman. *The Music of Survival: A Biography of a Poem by William Carlos
    Williams*. Urbana: University of Illinois Press, 1968. One of the best introductory
    monographs on Williams' poem "The Desert Music." This volume is useful be-
    cause it lucidly examines Williams' poetic methods, which were also utilized in
    his prose.
Sayre, Henry M. *The Visual Text of William Carlos Williams*. Urbana: University of
    Illinois Press, 1983. Sayre ably demonstrates the influence that modernist painters
    and photographers had on Williams' poetry and prose, and he examines the visual
    effects of the graphic presentation of Williams' poetry on the printed page.

Vendler, Helen, ed. *Voices and Visions: The Poet in America*. New York: Random House, 1987. A well-written introduction to the American literary modernists. Includes a substantial chapter on Williams. This book is tied to the Public Broadcasting Service television series of the same name.

Kathryn Zabelle Derounian
(Revised by *William E. Grim*)

LARRY WOIWODE

Born: Carrington, North Dakota; October 30, 1941

Principal short fiction
The Neumiller Stories, 1989.

Other literary forms
For the most part, Larry Woiwode is a writer of fiction, primarily the novel; his several novels, which have received critical acclaim, are, however, closely related to his short stories in style, setting, and characters. He has also written a book of poetry and was included in a book containing the work of five North Dakota poets.

Achievements
Woiwode has used his life and his North Dakota and Illinois childhood to create a series of fictional autobiographical works, both in short stories and in novels, rooted in a narrowly circumscribed region peopled by a family that spans several generations. Like his Southern counterparts William Faulkner and Flannery O'Connor, he is a regionalist whose depiction of his characters' values, religion, and family transcends the immediate and topical because his themes—memory, death, guilt, identity—are universal. Even when his characters leave the Midwest, they take those values with them, and the clash of those values with more urban ones, those of New York in his novel *Poppa John* (1981), provide some of Woiwode's best fiction. That fiction is expressed in a style that encompasses shifting points of view, the inclusion of non-"literary" materials such as diaries, letters, lists, and prose that creates a sense of a prose photograph, an image caught in time.

Biography
Larry Woiwode was born on October 30, 1941, in Carrington, North Dakota, and grew up in nearby Sykestown, a small, predominantly German American town. His father, Everett Woiwode, taught high school English, and when Woiwode was ten, his father moved the family to Manito, Illinois. For reasons that Woiwode has not explained, he spent much of his childhood away from his family, although his frequent letters home reflect his concern for family. In high school, he wrote poems that appeared regularly in a local newspaper, and while attending the University of Illinois at Urbana-Champaign (1959-1964), he continued his writing, was published often, won some writing prizes, and gained an associate degree in rhetoric. After leaving college, he worked briefly in Florida with a theatrical company, before moving to New York, where, after some Off-Broadway acting, he began his professional writing career.

According to Woiwode, William Maxwell, an editor for *The New Yorker*, was responsible for shifting his writing from what he calls "postmodernism" to a concern for an authentic voice, one rooted in his past. At Maxwell's urging, he became a free-lance writer and was soon publishing stories and poems in such journals as *The Atlantic Monthly, The New Yorker,* and *Harper's.* Four of those stories formed the nucleus of *What I'm Going to Do, I Think* (1969), his first novel and the winner of the William Faulkner Award for best first novel of the year. He was subsequently awarded a Guggenheim Fellowship (1971, 1972) and spent 1973 and 1974 as writer-in-residence at the University of Wisconsin. *Beyond the Bedroom Wall: A Family Album* (1975), his second novel, features narrative shifts, unconventional, nonliterary material, and many Neumiller characters. It, too, received critical acclaim.

Before he continued the Neumiller saga in *Born Brothers* (1988), he wrote two other books: *Even Tide* (1977), a collection of poems, and *Poppa John,* an atypical Woiwode novel about the plight of an elderly out-of-work actor in soap operas. Both works reflect Woiwode's deepening religious faith. Woiwode, reared as a Roman Catholic, and his wife joined the Orthodox Presbyterian church in 1977, and his writing has continued to focus on religious issues and to employ Christian symbols, allusions, and myths. *Born Brothers,* in fact, is a conscious reworking of the Jacob and Esau story with an overlay of the Cain and Abel tale.

After deciding that New York was not the place for family life, Woiwode and his family lived, by his admission, in about ten states before settling on a ranch in North Dakota, which he has described as a "state of mind, as fictional as real" for him. After buying the ranch, however, Woiwode found it financially necessary to turn to teaching, and he took a position teaching English and creative writing at the State University of New York at Binghamton, finding time to write during the summers, when he returns to the ranch.

Analysis

Larry Woiwode's short fiction has appeared in a number of magazines, most notably *The New Yorker,* where he received the encouragement and guidance of William Maxwell, whose support Woiwode acknowledges in the preface to his *The Neumiller Stories.* After the stories' publication, many of them were revised and included in *Beyond the Bedroom Wall: A Family Album,* a long, multigenerational novel that resembles an "album," or scrapbook, because it contains lists, diaries, and descriptions of photographs, the last a recurrent motif in his fiction. The sprawling nature of his novel accommodated the Neumiller stories, which required varying degrees of editing, a process that had to be repeated when ten of the stories were reworked again for their appearance in *The Neumiller Stories.* For example, the revisions to "The Suitor" were so substantial that Woiwode believed that it was appearing "for the first time." The other three stories in the collection were written in the 1980's and so had no "novelistic" life prior to their publication.

Although *The Neumiller Stories* is divided into three parts representing three phases of Woiwode's literary career (1964-1967, 1968-1972, and 1982-1989), the stories are more than a random sampling of his short fiction. The collection seems unified in character, setting, and theme, and while the stories do not progress sequentially from the first North Dakota Neumillers to the last, there is novel-like development with flashbacks, and the last three stories focus on the latest Neumillers. Moreover, the collection begins and ends with a male attempting to deal with the death of Alpha Neumiller, who serves as the center of the collection of stories—the date of her death becomes the point from which the time and setting of each story is measured and located.

"Deathless Lovers," the first story, occurs within a year of Alpha's death and concerns a brief conversation between an unnamed boy, probably Jerome, and his grandmother. Unlike the rest of the stories, it is written in the present tense, a literary device Woiwode used in his early stories but soon abandoned because of its limits. In this six-page story, the shortest in the collection, the present tense is workable and appropriate because it suggests the temporary suspension of time, the sense of the snapshot, the moment not to be forgotten. Even though the boy is with his maternal grandmother, his thoughts are of his mother; it is, ironically, his grandmother's "youth and grace" that "enable him to forget she is not his mother," who resembles the grandmother but who also was sick and weak before her traumatic death.

Half the story concerns the turbulent relationship between the grandmother and grandfather, which the boy accurately perceives as love because of the "so, so" she croons to her invalid husband. Her love for the boy is not stated but is reflected in her "so, so" assurance to the boy as she takes him in her arms. The smell of her dress is "a smell he will remember in its layers of detail . . . whenever he loves a woman, fears that he'll lose her, and his love becomes so smothering and possessive that she runs from him." The grandmother is the mother, who in turn becomes all women he loves and fears losing, and that fear is encapsulated in his memory as a moment, a smell that will recur throughout his life. In Woiwode's fiction, characters cannot escape such moments and memories, which shape their actions.

A nine-year-old serves as the first-person narrator of "Beyond the Bedroom Wall," which concerns his perception of the events surrounding Alpha's death. One of Woiwode's literary strengths is his ability to capture a child's thoughts, apprehensions, and sense of isolation. In this story, Jerome's physical isolation in his windowless bedroom mirrors his isolation from the adult world. The "wall" is both physical and emotional. After dreaming about being unable to follow his mother, Jerome wakes to find a "wall" on the wrong side of his bed: "If there was a wall where I was convinced there was none, I couldn't imagine what waited for me in that emptiness where the wall should be." Jerome senses the "emptiness" is his mother's death, which has yet to happen but which will always stay with him.

In both "The Visitation" and "Pheasants," memory is associated, metaphorically and literally, with the photograph. Through a metaphorical photograph, the visit by Jerome's uncles becomes a "visitation" as Conrad, Elling, and Alpha become spirits: "As if he were viewing a photograph that had been snapped of them at that moment, and began receding into his mind . . . retreating like spirits he had taken by surprise." In "Pheasants," Alpha's memory of "her mother's favorite photograph of her, taken when she was a child of five or six" is juxtaposed with her current situation as hopes are juxtaposed to reality. What might have been, symbolized by the attractive neighbor, differs from what is and makes her "capable of doing, serious harm to her sons," the physical manifestations of her constricted situation.

"The Beginning of Grief," which ends the first part of Woiwode's book, also uses optical imagery to describe the diminished world in which Martin, Alpha's husband, lives after her death: "imprisoned within the sphere of his eye. The size of his world now." Alpha, "at the periphery of every thought," lives on in the gestures and "averted eyes" of their children, who also attempt, with varying degrees of success, to cope with their mother's death. In this story, Woiwode shifts the focus from Jerome to Charles, the second son, whose bad behavior is caused by Alpha's death. Martin, who seems unaware that he, too, is affected by his wife's death, loses control and kicks Charles, but the two are eventually reconciled—not verbally, for both are incapable of expressing their feelings in words, but physically, through reaching out to each other.

The second five stories, written between 1968 and 1972, are more varied, though family history links them together. "The Suitor" recounts Martin's proposal to Alpha in 1939; "Pneumonia," interesting because of a dramatic shift in point of view, concerns their son Charles's narrow escape from death. While "The Old Halvorson Place" is also about Martin, Alpha, and their family, it seems more ambitious in its treatment of history, incorporating not only the Neumiller saga but also a history of the house, which Alpha realizes is not really theirs. As in "Beyond the Bedroom Wall," the house seems alive, throbbing with memories that impinge on the lives and actions of the children. From the start, the attic, which contains the Halvorson remnants, including a rolltop desk, a Victrola, and family photographs, is off limits to the children, who nevertheless play there, thereby tampering "with the heart of the house." Jerome becomes so fascinated with a 1901 photograph of a girl named Lydia that she "had Jerome in her possession." While the rest of the house "was becoming Alpha's," the "heart" of the house is not hers; when Father James Russell, whose family had also lived at the "Halvorson Place," appears to tell her about his family's life there, Alpha is defeated: "now the Russells, as well as the Halvorsons, would always occupy a part of their house."

The past also lives on in "Marie," a story told from the perspective of Martin and Alpha's older daughter, who has unconsciously assumed her dead mother's role. Her borrowed identity is threatened by Laura, a widow Martin will soon marry. As she reviews the family situation at the Christmas holidays, Marie turns to the favorite photograph of her mother and prays, "Oh, Mom, come back, come back." She looks at the family album but finds that the "pattern had been lost." Marie wants to preserve the status quo, to keep things the way they are, and to preserve her identity: "I was just starting to find out where I belong in this family." At the end of the story, Marie has so thoroughly identified with her mother that her father's impending marriage is a rejection of her mother and, more significantly, of her.

"Burial," the last of the second five stories, is both a beginning and an end, for it is a flashback containing information about the first North Dakota Neumiller, Otto, and also an account of how Charles, Otto's son, not only buries his father but also comes to terms with the past and closes a "chapter" of his life. An exhausted and hung-over Charles returns to North Dakota to bury his father and make arrangements for his aunt Augustina. After he arrives, he must confront not only his father's dead body, which he prepares for burial (he even makes his father's coffin), but also the legacy that his father left: a community mistakenly convinced that Otto "owes" them money. In his father's house, he meets his father's "presence": "It was the height of his father. The presence turned a new side in Charles's direction." Only by obeying his father's wishes for burial can the Hamlet-like Charles exorcise his father's ghost and be free.

The last three of *The Neumiller Stories*, written between 1982 and 1989, do form the basis for another of the Neumiller novels. All three involve Charles, Martin, Martin's wife Katherine, Alpha's son, and their life in New York City. Like Fitzgerald protagonists, they are Westerners in a corrupt East, where they are "disenfranchised," alienated from others, one another, and themselves. "Firstborn," narrated through Charles's consciousness, depicts him as an egocentric young man who feels trapped into marriage, guilty of the death of his newborn son, and only after the birth of his fourth child "freed into forgiveness" and able to "begin again to see." Charles's forgiveness comes only after his prayer, "Good God, forgive me," and reflects the Christian influence on Woiwode's writing.

"A Brief Fall," which alludes to Katherine's affair, concerns her second pregnancy, but the story is told from her perspective, and the portrait of Charles reveals him as an insecure person using sex to counterbalance the loss of youth that he experiences. When she meets Robert Kennedy, Katherine sees "a picture of the shattering end of his brother, the President, which seemed the end of youth, and of Charles." At the end of the story, however, a waiting Katherine looks in the mirror, another "frame" like the artist's "frame" that incorporates art and perhaps reality, and sees "a new and untraceable geography of weighty beauty."

This upbeat ending is followed by "She," the last of the stories. In it, the first-person narrator is a writer (the link between Woiwode and "Charles" runs throughout the three stories) who tells a story within the story itself. Using Estrelaria, an Indian from Guatemala, he returns again to his mother's death: "These incidents began to interconnect . . . because of my mother," and "most of the incidents were concerned with her, or with the continuing aftereffects of her death." At the end of the story, the narrator reflects on the emotional and geographical identification between land, mother, and (the last words of the book) "my wife." Thus, it is the mother's "legacy" that enables Charles to persevere, that allows the writer "Charles" to structure experience, and that provides Woiwode with a center for his multigenerational fictional world.

Other major works

NOVELS: *What I'm Going to Do, I Think*, 1969; *Beyond the Bedroom Wall: A Fam-*

ily Album, 1975; *Poppa John*, 1981; *Born Brothers*, 1988; *Indian Affairs*, 1991.

POETRY: *Poetry North: Five North Dakota Poets*, 1970 (with Richard Lyons, Thomas McGrath, John R. Milton, and Antony Oldknow); *Even Tide*, 1977.

Bibliography

Current Biography Yearbook, 1989, edited by Charles Moritz. New York: H. W. Wilson, 1989. The essay on Woiwode traces his life and literary work and reviews critical responses to his novels. For the most part, the novels are discussed in terms of their autobiographical content, especially of the characters, including those who most resemble Woiwode himself. Although it does not contain much criticism about Woiwode's work, this essay is particularly helpful, since it identifies and evaluates the available secondary sources. Bibliography.

Flower, Dean. Review of *The Neumiller Stories*. *The Hudson Review* 43 (Summer, 1990): 311. Flower's extensive and perceptive review of Woiwode's stories examines the early stories, their alterations in novel form, and their "un-gathering," revising, and "unrevising" in *The Neumiller Stories*. For Flower, the stories form a "superb family chronicle," with the three new stories adding new layers to the Neumiller characters. Of particular interest is Flower's comment on the way Woiwode "expands the frame" at the end of the story and leaves his readers with an image that resembles a snapshot, a moment caught in time.

Siconolfi, Michael T. Review of *The Neumiller Stories*. *America* 163 (December 1, 1990): 434-435. In this lengthy, informative review, Siconolfi discusses the reworkings of stories as they become parts of novels and then resurface as the short stories in this collection. He maintains that while Woiwode's stories can stand on their own, they also are interrelated "like distant branches of a family tree," an apt comparison since the stories are rooted in family. While Siconolfi mentions several of the stories, he focuses on Woiwode's gift at working the "nurturing, eternal feminine" and on the novelist's acknowledging of his grandmother's influence.

Tallent, Elizabeth. Review of *The Neumiller Stories*. "Before the Bedroom Wall." *The New York Times Book Review*, December 17, 1989, 17. Tallent points out that ten of the thirteen stories had appeared before, once in journals and once in revised form, in Woiwode's *Beyond the Bedroom Wall: A Family Album*. In their latest form, the stories seem, to Tallent, to lack some of the immediacy and detail they had in the novel. Her review is of special interest because she notes that Alpha Neumiller's death in childbirth is the pivotal event in the collection and that the collection begins and ends with a boy's, then a man's, projection of Alpha's persona onto another female character.

Woiwode, Larry. "An Interview with Larry Woiwode." *Christianity and Literature* 29 (Winter, 1979): 11-18. Woiwode discusses the autobiographical nature of his work, the Jacob/Esau biblical framework of *Born Brothers*, the "mechanics of memory," his religious rebirth, the influence of William Maxwell, and his future writing plans. This frank, informative interview contains a considerable amount of biographical information, most of which is applied to Woiwode's writing, and some perceptive comments about the Christian themes of *Born Brothers*.

_____. Interview by Michele Field. *Publishers Weekly* 234 (August 5, 1988): 67-68. This interview, conducted in London, where Woiwode was staying with his family while teaching college students, concerns Woiwode's roots in North Dakota, his resemblance to Charles (the writer/brother in *Born Brothers*), biographical details, the eccentric style of *Beyond the Bedroom Wall*, and his future writing plans, which involve a biography of Leo Tolstoy and a "campus" novel. One of the most interesting topics Woiwode discusses is the way that he "overlaps" some of the "elements," reworks the characters and events, and adds to the fictional world he is creating.

Thomas L. Erskine

THOMAS WOLFE

Born: Asheville, North Carolina; October 3, 1900
Died: Baltimore, Maryland; September 15, 1938

Principal short fiction

From Death to Morning, 1935; *The Hills Beyond*, 1941; *The Complete Short Stories of Thomas Wolfe*, 1987.

Other literary forms

While some novelists are failed poets, a tradition that began with Cervantes in the early seventeenth century, Thomas Wolfe was a failed playwright. None of his plays was accepted for commercial production. Wolfe is most famous (his fame in the 1930's was international) for his early novels. His first editor unfortunately persuaded him to stay away from the novella or short novel form, and the editor of his posthumous novels essentially pieced them together out of shorter pieces that Wolfe saw as short novels, not as parts of a rambling, protean novel. Hugh Holman's collection of Wolfe's short novels and Richard Kennedy's study of his last editor's stewardship are beginning to establish Wolfe's very real talent for the shorter forms.

The best-known of Wolfe's novels are *Look Homeward, Angel* (1929) and *You Can't Go Home Again* (1940). Wolfe's notebooks are also very informative, not only to scholars but also to young writers interested in the processes through which a writer refines experience (and Wolfe was more able to do this than his first wave of admirers would admit). It is particularly fascinating to see how the "real" incident that inspired one of the scenes in "Death the Proud Brother" became transformed into that scene.

Achievements

It can be argued that Wolfe did not write short stories at all and that his "stories" were only fragments torn from the single great body of his life's work. Even Francis E. Skipp, the editor of *The Complete Short Stories of Thomas Wolfe*, acknowledges that Wolfe or his editors cut and shaped these fragments into discrete units to suit monetary or publishing needs as opportunities presented themselves. Since Wolfe seldom if ever seriously applied himself to writing individual stories rather than pieces belonging to the grand epic of his own self-expression, it is unfair to hold him rigorously to the standards of the modern story.

Wolfe's reputation was at one time enormous both at home and abroad. He has often been the writer that young writers read; age and artistic maturity, however, usually dampen that youthful enthusiasm. Although many critics praised his work, a reaction against Wolfe set in even during his lifetime. Among his detractors was Bernard De Voto who, in a 1936 essay called "Genius Is Not Enough," attacked Wolfe, citing his first two novels as books full of "long, whirling discharges of words, unabsorbed in the novel, unrelated to the proper business of fiction, badly if not altogether unacceptably written. . . . " The controversy continues. Wolfe's real strength, formerly obscured by the hands of his editors, may indeed lie in the novella or short-novel form. Whatever the critical opinion, Wolfe will always have supporters. William Faulkner said, "My admiration for Wolfe is that . . . he was willing to throw away style, coherence, all the rules of preciseness, to try to put all the experience of the human heart on the head of a pin. . . . "

Biography

Thomas Clayton Wolfe was the youngest child of Julia Elizabeth Westall and William Oliver Wolfe, a Pennsylvania mason and stonecutter who went South to find work. One of Wolfe's brothers, Benjamin Harrison Wolfe, died at age eighteen, as does the brother in *Look Homeward, Angel*. Although Wolfe's mother did run a tourist home, The Old Kentucky Home, it is important to remember that his family was very prosperous; one scholar estimates that they were financially in the upper two percent of the town's population. Although this fact does not mean that an affluent adolescent cannot suffer the torments of the damned, it nevertheless somewhat negates the concept of Thomas Wolfe as the poor, suffering, and morbidly sensitive child, which was fashioned by the early members of his literary cult. The Wolfes were German, an unusual ethnic origin in that part of Carolina, where most of the people were Scotch-Irish or English, and they lived in the western, mountain end of North Carolina, which had more in common with East Tennessee, Appalachian Ohio, and mountain Pennsylvania than with eastern North Carolina, the Tidewater of Virginia, or even northern Mississippi (the setting of Faulkner's stories). Both ethnic background and geographic environment are reflected strongly in Wolfe's works.

Wolfe was enrolled at the University of North Carolina at Chapel Hill; at that time it was the university's only campus and was restricted to males during his first two years. He majored in the classics and in English literature, and he began his writing career as a playwright with the Carolina Playmakers. By college age, Wolfe had achieved his full growth (he was six feet, six inches tall and later, as a slightly older man, weighed two hundred and fifty pounds) and in appearance was a man of epic proportions as well as epic ambitions. Wolfe went to Harvard University in 1920 to study under George Pierce Baker at the drama workshop; he left Harvard in 1923, after earning an M.A. in English and writing *Welcome to Our City*, later performed in 1947, and *The Mountains* (1970), about a family feud.

From 1924 to 1930 he led a rather unhappy existence as an English instructor at New York University, a private university on Washington Square. He was not able to find a producer for *Welcome to Our City* or *Mannerhouse* (1948), a play about the Civil War. In 1925, he met Aline Bernstein, and their stormy relationship became the most important one in his short life. Aline Frankau Bernstein was almost twenty years older than Wolfe. When she was still nineteen, she had married a broker, Theodore Bernstein, and became interested in making sets and costumes for her friends in Neighborhood Playhouse when it was founded in 1915, soon becoming the first woman member of United Scenic Artists. As her biographer says, "without intending to, she rather took the color out of those men at hand." In 1925, she met Wolfe; a relationship developed which Wolfe described as "the met halves of the broken talisman." In 1926, he went to Europe with Aline and began *Look Homeward, Angel*, with some assistance, both literary and financial, from her. In 1928, after another trip abroad with Aline and a breakup with her, he finished *Look Homeward, Angel*, and Scribner's showed interest in the manuscript. The editor who found Wolfe's gigantic manuscript and who greatly helped him during his early career was Maxwell Perkins. With Perkins' constant help, Wolfe published *Look Homeward, Angel*, which sold fifteen thousand copies and earned for Wolfe about six thousand dollars. Although Wolfe, at this point in his career, wanted to publish two shorter novels, one of which had already been partly set in type, Perkins gave Wolfe what modern scholars conclude was "unfortunate" advice and leadership; he advised him to work on yet another big novel. Upon Perkins' advice, he concentrated on *Of Time and the River* (1935); three years after its publication he died of tuberculosis of the brain, a rare condition that had not immediately been diagnosed. Although he had been working in his last years toward shorter and more controlled stories which used different viewpoint techniques, when he died, Edward C. Aswell at Harper's gave the public what they wanted: he created the "old" Wolfe by piecing together two more gigantic novels. There is no doubt that Wolfe needed editing and that he placed himself at the mercy of those who edited his works, and the massive amount of material written prior to his death became the basis from which Aswell would create *The Web and the Rock* (1939) and *You Can't Go Home Again* (1940).

Analysis

Some of Thomas Wolfe's short stories were printed in *The Hills Beyond*, a posthumous volume compiled by Edward C. Aswell after he had published Wolfe's two "novels" of his own creation. The tough-minded old Confederate general of the story "The Dead World Relived" mourns a South ten times as full of frauds after the Civil War as before it; the story is unforgettable and furnishes a much-needed corrective to the myth that Southerners in the American literary renaissance of the 1920's and 1930's could hardly wait to start writing about the old Colonels. "A Kinsman of His Blood" is a short, concise, and moving story in its subtly achieved pathos and its nostalgia for what life and history are, rather than for what we might want them to be, and is probably the best story in the collection. The action takes place entirely in the foreground, and the story is really that of Arthur Pentland, also known from the beginning of the story as Arthur Penn. The viewpoint through which the reader sees Arthur is that of the ubiquitous Eugene Gant; the third character in the story is Eugene's uncle, Bascom Pentland, who appears in *Of Time and the River*. It could be the tale of any three men related to each other; Arthur is the son of Bascom and the only one "who ever visited his father's house; the rest were studiously absent, saw their father only at Christmas or Thanksgiving." Even so, the relation between Bascom and Arthur is "savage and hostile."

Arthur is a huge, obese, dirty, disheveled, grubby, distraught man who has trouble speaking clearly and coherently. The reader is told nothing of the history of his problems, or of Eugene's background, and knows only that the conflict is stark, ugly, and dramatic. Some of Arthur's behavior is clearly sociopathic. His table manners are not only embarrassing, but even offensive. On one occasion, he tells an anecdote about a Harvard man who climbed into a cage with a gorilla; although the man knew fourteen languages, the gorilla killed him. Arthur's summation of the incident is as frightening as anything in European fiction which tries to depict the mindless, anarchic malevolence of the crazy or the revolutionary.

Arthur decides that his grammar school teacher really loves him; even though the woman ignores his protestations of love, then tries to silence him with rudeness, he persists. He refuses to believe his mother when she tells him the woman does not really care for him, and he storms out "like a creature whipped with furies." Finally, he goes to California to see the woman. Arthur is a pitiful, subnormal, obviously seriously disturbed creature, but frightening in his obesity, his filth, his animal-like inability to understand human beings. The story ends with Eugene, out walking in the rain through the South Boston slums, spotting Arthur as he shuffles along, a bundle of old newspapers under one arm. Eugene, a nice man, is glad to see him and offers to shake his hand. Arthur denies twice that he is Arthur Pentland, then says he is Arthur Penn and screams out in terror, begging Eugene to leave him alone. There is no sentimentality here; this is tragedy, however small and prosaic.

The only collection of short fiction Wolfe prepared himself and saw through publication was *From Death to Morning*; it contains the stories "No Door" and "Death the Proud Brother."

"No Door" is about a writer and his short acquaintance with "well-kept people who have never been alone in all their life," in this case a man who lives in a penthouse near the East River furnished with several sculptures by Jacob Epstein, rare books and first editions, and a view of Manhattan which displays its "terrific frontal sweep and curtain of starflung towers, now sown with the diamond pollen of a million lights." The writer is told by these people how marvelous it is to live alone with creatures of the slums. Their remarks trigger recollections of the lower depths of stinking, overcrowded, working-class Brooklyn. The writer hangs around, partly amused, partly chagrined, partly in awe of the rich man and his mistress, thinking that *they* may be the ones who will open the door to the life of glamour and ease for which he, as a poor writer, yearns. Even as he hopes, however, he knows it is useless: these creatures are foreign to him. He tells of the agony and senselessness and brutality and sordidness of his existence, and the man and his mistress condescendingly and patronizingly wish his lot were theirs. Finally, at the end of the evening, he returns to Brooklyn and hears two old people discussing the death of a priest, and the story ends on a note of desperation and impotent fury.

The effect of the story depends on the consciousness of the narrator, here appearing in the first person although the reader sees him through the second person, an almost unheard-of viewpoint in English. Wolfe makes his points subtly, the length is a rather modest one for him, his satirical eye is sharp, and the rhetoric meshes with the inner turmoil lying just beneath the surface of conversation. If Wolfe had written more stories like this he might have been one of the giants of the American short story.

"Death the Proud Brother" is a very long, almost unstructured, 22,000-word novella which attempts to present as a unified narrative several unrelated incidents of death and loneliness. Wolfe said of this story, "It represents *important* work to me." The story's thematic unity arises from the narrator's successful unifying of all the incidents within his own consciousness, drawing the world to him, exercising implicit rights of selection, unlike the third-person, omniscient narrators of Wolfe's last novels. This story is a masterpiece in its conjunction of viewpoint and material. Only this viewpoint could master this material, and only disjointed, logically discrete material such as the story presents requires a first-person viewpoint.

There is no plot, but there is some structure. Wolfe describes three violent deaths. The fourth death is that of an old bum on a bench, and it occurs quietly, imperceptibly, anonymously—he is a "cipher." His death, which takes up the bulk of the novella, furnishes Wolfe with a chance to study America. If it is true that everybody talks about America but nobody can find it, then Wolfe came closest in this last movement of the novella, which was his favorite. The story is typically Wolfean in many ways; by the passion and the wise guile of his rhetoric, Wolfe becomes so thoroughly a part of the writing that he, too, becomes a cipher—the transparent narrator. It surely is no accident that the death which moves the narrator so profoundly is the death of an urban Everyman. This is the kind of story, perhaps even the story itself, that caused Faulkner to say that Wolfe had tried to put all of life on the head of a pin.

Other major works

NOVELS: *Look Homeward, Angel*, 1929; *Of Time and the River*, 1935; *The Web and the Rock*, 1939; *You Can't Go Home Again*, 1940; *The Short Novels of Thomas Wolfe*, 1961.

PLAYS: *Welcome to Our City*, 1947 (published only in German as *Willkommen in Altamont*, 1962); *Mannerhouse*, 1948; *The Mountains*, 1970.

POETRY: *The Face of a Nation: Poetical Passages from the Writings of Thomas Wolfe*, 1939; *A Stone, a Leaf, a Door: Poems by Thomas Wolfe*, 1945.

NONFICTION: *The Story of a Novel*, 1936; *Thomas Wolfe's Letters to His Mother*, 1943; *The Portable Thomas Wolfe*, 1946; *The Letters of Thomas Wolfe*, 1956; *The Notebooks of Thomas Wolfe*, 1970; *The Thomas Wolfe Reader*, 1982; *The Autobiography of an American Novelist: Thomas Wolfe*, 1983; *Beyond Love and Loyalty: The Letters of Thomas Wolfe and Elizabeth Nowell*, 1983; *My Other Loneliness: Letters of Thomas Wolfe and Aline Bernstein*, 1983.

Bibliography

Donald, David Herbert. *Look Homeward: A Life of Thomas Wolfe*. Boston: Little, Brown, 1987. Donald's painstakingly thorough examination of the huge volume of Wolfe's papers, including the published and unpublished manuscripts, and of Wolfe criticism has produced a work that, in its scope, depth, and readability, makes it the essential biography, replacing such earlier works as Elizabeth Nowell's *Thomas Wolfe: A Biography* (1960) and Andrew Turnbull's *Thomas Wolfe* (1968). A distinguished historian, Donald is on less solid ground when he ventures into the more literary concerns of interpretation and criticism. The questions surrounding the roles of Wolfe's editors and the legitimacy of the published texts are explored if not resolved. Contains exhaustive notes but no formal bibliography.

Field, Leslie A., ed. *Thomas Wolfe: Three Decades of Criticism.* New York: New York University Press, 1968. This collection contains landmark essays by many of the most important critics in the field of Wolfe criticism; revealed are the central issues and the range of critical response provoked by Wolfe's work from its first publication through the mid-1960's.

_____. *Thomas Wolfe and His Editors.* Norman: University of Oklahoma Press, 1987. Examines the parts played by Wolfe's editors, with special attention to the work of Edward C. Aswell. Wolfe's posthumous publications are traced from Wolfe's early drafts and original outlines to the published versions.

Idol, John Lane, Jr. *A Thomas Wolfe Companion.* New York: Greenwood Press, 1987. An expression of the resurgence of interest in Wolfe by an unabashed devotee, this handy book is a potpourri of Wolfeana with glossaries of characters and places, genealogical charts of Wolfe's fictional families, a descriptive and "analytic" bibliography of primary works, and an annotated bibliography of secondary materials. Also contains information on the various collections of Wolfe material, The Thomas Wolfe Society, The Thomas Wolfe Review, and even times and prices of tours of the holy sites.

McElderry, Bruce R. *Thomas Wolfe.* New York: Twayne, 1964. An excellent basic introduction to Wolfe's life and work, McElderry's study provides lucid analysis well supported by standard critical opinion, including a chapter on the shorter fiction. Contains a useful chronology and annotated select bibliographies of primary and secondary sources.

Phillipson, John S., ed. *Critical Essays on Thomas Wolfe.* Boston: G. K. Hall, 1985. Contains twenty-three essays, most formerly published, written between 1970 and the early 1980's. Arranged by genre, the book contains seven essays on Wolfe's short fiction.

John Carr
(Revised by *Douglas Rollins*)

TOBIAS WOLFF

Born: Birmingham, Alabama; June 19, 1945

Principal short fiction
In the Garden of the North American Martyrs, 1981; *Back in the World*, 1985.

Other literary forms
Besides short stories, Tobias Wolff has published a novella, *The Barracks Thief* (1984), and a memoir, *This Boy's Life* (1989). He also edited an anthology, *Matters of Life and Death: New American Stories* (1983).

Achievements
Wolff is an outstanding contemporary craftsman of the American short story. Working slowly, sometimes taking months and countless drafts, he polishes each story into an entertaining, gemlike work that reads with deceptive ease. He has said, in interviews, that he needs time to get to know his characters but that the finished story no longer holds any surprises for him. For the reader, the result is full of surprises, insights, humor, and other line-by-line rewards, particularly in character portrayal and style. The influences on his work—his friend Raymond Carver and earlier masters such as Guy de Maupassant, Anton Chekhov, Sherwood Anderson, Ernest Hemingway, and Flannery O'Connor—indicate the company Wolff intends to keep.

The quality of his work has earned for Wolff much critical respect and numerous literary prizes. He received a Wallace Stegner Fellowship in 1975-1976 to study creative writing at Stanford University, and even before he published his first book, he won a National Endowment for the Arts Fellowship (1978), a Mary Roberts Rinehart grant (1979), and an Arizona Council on the Arts and Humanities Fellowship (1980). He has also won several O. Henry short story prizes (1980, 1981, and 1985), a Guggenheim Fellowship (1982), and a second National Endowment for the Arts Fellowship (1985). Wolff's *In the Garden of the North American Martyrs* received the St. Lawrence Award for Fiction (1982), and his *The Barracks Thief* took the PEN/Faulkner Award for Fiction (1985).

Wolff's talents and working methods seem to be focused on the shorter fictional forms. He first wrote *The Barracks Thief* as a novel, but after he finished the paring and polishing, it turned out to be a novella. Although his memoir, *This Boy's Life*, is novel-length, it is also rather picaresque, consisting of a collection of loosely tied together stories.

Biography
Readers are lucky to have two prime sources dealing with Tobias Wolff's parents and Wolff's early life: Wolff's own memoir, *This Boy's Life*, and a recollection of his

father entitled *The Duke of Deception: Memories of My Father* (1979), written by Wolff's older brother, the novelist Geoffrey Wolff. Together, the two memoirs portray a remarkable family, though Rosemary Loftus Wolff, Wolff's mother, wryly observed that, if she had known so much was going to be told, she might have watched herself more closely.

The one who bore watching, however, was Wolff's inventive father, a genial Gatsby-like figure who, in pursuit of the good life, forged checks, credentials, and his own identity. He began as Arthur Samuels Wolff, a Jewish doctor's son and boarding-school expellee, but later emerged as Arthur Saunders Wolff, an Episcopalian and Yale University graduate. A still later reincarnation was as Saunders Ansell-Wolff III. On the basis of forged credentials, he became an aeronautical engineer and rose to occupy an executive suite. During his time, however, he also occupied a number of jail cells. Still, he showed remarkable creativity in his fabrications, so perhaps it is not surprising that both his sons became writers of fiction. Family life with him was something of a roller coaster, exciting but with many ups and downs. Eventually, this instability led to the family's breakup in 1951: twelve-year-old Geoffrey remained with the father, while the mother took five-year-old Tobias, who had been born June 19, 1945, in Birmingham, Alabama, one of several locations where the family had chased the American Dream. Henceforth reared separately, sometimes a country apart, the two boys were not reunited until Geoffrey's final year at Princeton University.

Meanwhile, Tobias and his mother lived first in Florida, then in Utah, and finally in the Pacific Northwest, where his mother remarried. The stays in Utah and the Pacific Northwest are recounted in *This Boy's Life*, which covers Wolff's life from the age of ten until he left for Hill School in Pottstown, Pennsylvania (where he faked his references to be accepted). He attended Hill School for a time but did not graduate and instead ended up joining the military. From 1964 to 1968, Wolff served in the United States Army Special Forces and toured Vietnam as an adviser to a South Vietnamese unit. After this service, deterred by the antiwar movement in the United States, he traveled to England, where he prepped to enter the University of Oxford and then enrolled. He received a B.A., with first class honors, from the University of Oxford in 1972.

Returning to the United States, he worked first as a reporter for *The Washington Post*, then at various restaurant jobs in California, and finally entered the Stanford University creative writing program. He received an M.A. from Stanford in 1978. While at Stanford, he met and became friends with other writers, including Raymond Carver, and taught for a period of time. While pursuing his own writing, Wolff has taught creative writing at Goddard College, Arizona State University, and Syracuse University. In 1975, he married Catherine Dolores Spohn, a teacher and social worker; they have two sons, Michael and Patrick.

Analysis

No overriding theme, message, or agenda seems to unite Tobias Wolff's work—

only his interest in people, their quirks, their unpredictability, their strivings and failings, and their predicaments as human beings. Despite their dishonesty and dope-taking, most of his characters fall within the range of a very shaky middle-class respectability or what passes for it in contemporary America. Although most of them do not hope for much, many still have troubles separating their fantasies from reality. Despite their dried-up souls, vague remnants of Judeo-Christian morality still rattle around inside their rib cages, haunting them with the specter of moral choice (Wolff himself is a Catholic). It is perhaps emblematic that a considerable amount of action in his stories occurs inside automobiles hurtling across the land-scape (except when they break down or fly off the road).

Wolff himself has called his stories autobiographical (just as his memoir is some-what fictionalized), but this seems true only in a broad sense. Wolff goes on to say that many of his characters reflect aspects of himself and that he sometimes makes use of actual events. According to Wolff, "The Liar" mirrors himself as a kid: the story is about a boy who reacts to his father's death by becoming a pathological liar. A story that appears to make use of an actual event is "The Missing Person," about a priest who, to impress his drinking buddy, fabricates a story about killing a man with his bare hands. Before he knows it, the buddy has spread the news to the nuns. Wolff related a similar story about himself in an *Esquire* article ("Raymond Carver Had His Cake and Ate It Too," September, 1989), recalling his friend Carver after Carver's death from cancer. In a tale-swapping competition with Carver, known for his bouts with alcohol, Wolff bested his friend by fabricating a story about being addicted to heroin; aghast, Carver repeated the story, and people began regarding Wolff with pity and sorrow.

A truly autobiographical story titled "Our Story Begins" (a double or triple en-tendre) probably gives a more typical view of Wolff's sources of inspiration: un-canny powers of observation and a good ear. In this story, Charlie, an aspiring writer who barely supports himself by working as a busboy in a San Francisco restaurant, is discouraged and about ready to quit. On his way home through one of those notorious San Francisco fogs, however, he stops at a coffeehouse. There he over-hears a conversation between a woman, her husband, and another man. The man tells a story about a Filipino taxi driver's fantastic love obsession with a local woman, and the trio talking turn out to be a love triangle themselves. Charlie soaks it all in with his cappuccino, then, newly inspired by these riches, heads home through the fog. Wolff brings these three stories in one to a close with a patented ending: a Chinese woman carrying a live lobster rushes past, and a foghorn in the bay is likewise an omen that "at any moment anything might be revealed."

Wolff's patented ending is an updated open version of O. Henry's surprise ending, which wrapped things up with a plot twist. Wolff's endings are usually accomplished with a modulation of style, a sudden opening out into revelation, humor, irony, symbolism, and/or lyricism. Such an ending is illustrated by "Next Door," the first story of *In the Garden of the North American Martyrs*. A quiet couple are scan-dalized by the goings-on next door, where everybody screams and fights and the husband and wife make love standing up against the refrigerator. To drown out these raucous neighbors, the couple turn up their television volume, go to bed, and watch the film *El Dorado.* Lying next to his wife, the husband becomes sexually aroused, but she is unresponsive. The seemingly uneventful story ends when the husband suddenly images how he would rewrite the movie—an ambiguous ending that suggests both his desire for some of the lusty, disorderly life next door (and in the movie) and the quiet, passionless fate that he is probably doomed to endure.

The next story, "Hunters in the Snow," perhaps Wolff's best, is much more eventful and has an unforgettable ending. The story is set in the wintry fields of the Northwest, where three deer hunters, supposedly old buddies, rib and carp and play practical jokes on one another. The ringleader, Kenny, who is driving his old truck, is unmerciful to Frank and especially Tub. Tub, however, wreaks a terrible revenge when one of Kenny's practical jokes backfires and, through a misunderstanding, Tub shoots him, inflicting a gruesome gut wound. Frank and Tub throw Kenny into the back of the pickup truck and head off over unfamiliar country roads for the hospital fifty miles away. After a while, Frank and Tub become cold from the snow blowing through a hole in the windshield and stop at a tavern for a beer, where they strike up a sympathetic conversation with each other. Leaving the directions to the hospital on the table, they hit the road again. A little further on, Frank and Tub have to stop at the next tavern for another beer and, this time, a warm meal. Self-absorbed, they continue their discoveries that they have much in common and become real pals. Meanwhile, Kenny is cooling in the back of the truck, and the story ends when they get under way again:

> As the truck twisted through the gentle hills the star went back and forth between Kenny's boots, staying always in his sight. "I'm going to the hospital," Kenny said. But he was wrong. They had taken a different turn a long way back.

The title story, "In the Garden of the North American Martyrs," shows that academics can be just as cruel as hunters (or, in this case, the old Iroquois). The story's protagonist is Mary, a mousy historian who has a terrible teaching job at a college in the rainy Northwest. She is invited by her friend Louise—who is a member of the history faculty of a posh college in upstate New York, Iroquois country—to interview for a job opening there. When Mary arrives on campus, she finds that she has been cruelly exploited: the interview is only a setup to fulfill a college requirement that a woman be interviewed for every job opening. As the story ends, Mary changes the topic of her demonstration lecture and—before horrified faculty and students assembled in the college's modernized version of the longhouse—delivers a grisly account of how the Iroquois "took scalps and practiced cannibalism and slavery" and "tortured their captives."

Two other memorable stories in Wolff's first collection explore the bittersweet possibilities of relationships that never come to fruition. In "Passenger," the strictly behaved protagonist, Glen, is conned into giving a ride to the aging flower child

Bonnie and her dog Sunshine. They become a working unit in the car, like an informal but close-knit family, and the reader sees that they are good for each other but realizes that the relationship probably would not last much longer than the day's journey; the probability is symbolized by a hair-raising incident along the way, when the dog leaps on the driver, Glen, causing the car to go spinning down the wet highway out of control. In "Poaching," a real family gets together again, briefly: a divorced woman visits her former husband and their small son. It is clear that husband and wife should reunite for their own good and the good of the child, but neither will make the first move—even though they sleep together in the same bed. The state of their relationship is symbolized by an old beaver who tries to build his lodge in a pond on the property and is quickly shot.

The stories in *Back in the World*, Wolff's second collection, are not quite as finished as the ones in his first but include several worth noting. The title is a phrase used by American soldiers in Vietnam to refer to home. Ironically, from Wolff's stories it appears that "back in the world" is also a crazy battle zone. Besides "The Missing Person" and "Our Story Begins," other stories that stand out are "Coming Attractions," "Desert Breakdown, 1968," and "The Rich Brother."

"Coming Attractions," the collection's first story, showcases a precocious teenage girl who is every parent's nightmare. She shoplifts and makes random anonymous phone calls late at night: for example, she calls and wakes an unfortunately named Mr. Love, sixty-one years old, and gets him excited about winning a big contest. First, however, he has to answer the question: "Here's the question, Mr. Love. I lie and steal and sleep around. What do you think about that?" Still, she reveals another side of herself at the end, when she dives to the bottom of an ice-cold swimming pool in the middle of the night and fishes out an abandoned bike for her little brother.

The two other stories feature cars. In "Desert Breakdown, 1968," the car of a young family fresh back from Germany—a former American soldier, his pregnant German wife, and their first child—breaks down at an isolated service station in the Mojave desert. The locals do not lift a hand to help, except for a woman who runs the station, and the husband is tempted to abandon his young family there. The story demonstrates that men cannot be depended on, but women are quite capable of taking care of themselves: the German wife beats up one of the local cowboys, and the station operator goes out and shoots rabbits for dinner. In "The Rich Brother," the collection's last story, the life-styles of two brothers clash. The rich brother drives to a distant religious commune to rescue his young brother, but on the way home, they quarrel and the rich brother abandons the young one along the roadside. As the story ends, however, the rich brother is having second thoughts, afraid to get home and face the questions of his wife: "Where is he? Where is your brother?"

These last lines sound like the text for a sermon (indeed, straight out of Genesis), though Wolff rarely sermonizes. If he comments at all, he usually comments indirectly, through symbolism or his patented ending. Above all, Wolff is a lover of good stories and is content to tell them and let them stand on their own.

Other major works

NOVEL: *The Barracks Thief*, 1984.
NONFICTION: *This Boy's Life*, 1989.
ANTHOLOGY: *Matters of Life and Death: New American Stories*, 1983.

Bibliography

Peters, Joanne M., and Jean W. Ross. "Tobias Wolff (Jonathan Ansell)." In *Contemporary Authors*, edited by Hal May. Vol. 117. Detroit: Gale Research, 1986. Peters gives a brief overview of Wolff's work, but more important is the interview by Ross. In the interview, Wolff talks about his reasons for writing short stories, the writers who have influenced him, his working methods and sources of inspiration, his own reading, and his teaching of creative writing.

Prose, Francine. "The Brothers Wolff." *The New York Times Magazine.* February 5, 1989, 22. Prose's fine article, which is also collected in *The New York Times Biographical Service* (February, 1989), introduces the writing of the Wolff brothers, Geoffrey and Tobias. Traces how they grew up apart but became inseparable, even bearing striking resemblances to each other. The article also provides background on their parents, particularly their father.

Wolff, Tobias. "A Forgotten Master: Rescuing the Works of Paul Bowles." *Esquire* 103 (May, 1986): 221-223. Wolff's article not only helps rescue a forgotten master but also provides an index of what Wolff values in writing. He praises Bowles for the mythic quality of his stories, the clarity of his language, his ability to shift moods at will, and his ability to depict a wide range of international characters. He feels that Bowles's pessimism might have contributed to his lack of popularity.

_____. *This Boy's Life: A Memoir.* New York: Atlantic Monthly Press, 1989. Wolff's memoir, besides being interesting reading in itself, gives useful background on his residence in Utah and the Pacific Northwest, his school pals, his relationship with his mother and stepfather, and his activities. The memoir covers the period from his tenth birthday to his late teenage years.

Harold Branam